SECURITY AND PRIVACY IN DYNAMIC ENVIRONMENTS

IFIP – The International Federation for Information Processing

IFIP was founded in 1960 under the auspices of UNESCO, following the First World Computer Congress held in Paris the previous year. An umbrella organization for societies working in information processing, IFIP's aim is two-fold: to support information processing within its member countries and to encourage technology transfer to developing nations. As its mission statement clearly states,

> IFIP's mission is to be the leading, truly international, apolitical organization which encourages and assists in the development, exploitation and application of information technology for the benefit of all people.

IFIP is a non-profitmaking organization, run almost solely by 2500 volunteers. It operates through a number of technical committees, which organize events and publications. IFIP's events range from an international congress to local seminars, but the most important are:

- The IFIP World Computer Congress, held every second year;
- Open conferences;
- Working conferences.

The flagship event is the IFIP World Computer Congress, at which both invited and contributed papers are presented. Contributed papers are rigorously refereed and the rejection rate is high.

As with the Congress, participation in the open conferences is open to all and papers may be invited or submitted. Again, submitted papers are stringently refereed.

The working conferences are structured differently. They are usually run by a working group and attendance is small and by invitation only. Their purpose is to create an atmosphere conducive to innovation and development. Refereeing is less rigorous and papers are subjected to extensive group discussion.

Publications arising from IFIP events vary. The papers presented at the IFIP World Computer Congress and at open conferences are published as conference proceedings, while the results of the working conferences are often published as collections of selected and edited papers.

Any national society whose primary activity is in information may apply to become a full member of IFIP, although full membership is restricted to one society per country. Full members are entitled to vote at the annual General Assembly, National societies preferring a less committed involvement may apply for associate or corresponding membership. Associate members enjoy the same benefits as full members, but without voting rights. Corresponding members are not represented in IFIP bodies. Affiliated membership is open to non-national societies, and individual and honorary membership schemes are also offered.

SECURITY AND PRIVACY IN DYNAMIC ENVIRONMENTS

Proceedings of the IFIP TC-11 21st International Information Security Conference (SEC 2006), 22-24 May 2006, Karlstad, Sweden.

Edited by

Simone Fischer-Hübner
Karlstad University, Sweden

Kai Rannenberg
Goethe University, Frankfurt, Germany

Louise Yngström
Stockholm University/Royal Institute of Technology, Sweden

Stefan Lindskog
Karlstad University, Sweden

 Springer

Security and Privacy in Dynamic Environments
Edited by S.Fischer-Hübner, K. Rannenberg, L. Yngström, and S. Lindskog

    p.   cm. (IFIP International Federation for Information Processing, a Springer Series in Computer Science)

ISSN: 1571-5736 / 1861-2288 (Internet)

                                        eISBN: 10: 0-387-33406-8
ISBN 978-1-4419-4127-5   eISBN: 978-0-387-33406-6

9 8 7 6 5 4 3 2 1
springeronline.com

Foreword

This book contains the Proceedings of the 21st IFIP TC-11 International Information Security Conference (IFIP/SEC 2006) on "Security and Privacy in Dynamic Environments" held in May 22–24 2006 in Karlstad, Sweden. The first IFIP/SEC conference was arranged in May 1983 in Stockholm, Sweden, one year before TC-11 was founded, with the active participation of the Swedish IT Security Community. The IFIP/SEC conferences have since then become the flagship events of TC-11. We are very pleased that we succeeded with our bid to after 23 years hold the IFIP/SEC conference again in Sweden.

The IT environment now includes novel, dynamic approaches such as mobility, wearability, ubiquity, ad hoc use, mind/body orientation, and business/market orientation. This modern environment challenges the whole information security research community to focus on interdisciplinary and holistic approaches whilst retaining the benefit of previous research efforts. Papers offering research contributions focusing on dynamic environments in addition to other aspects of computer security and privacy were solicited for submission to IFIP/SEC 2006. We received 141 submissions which were all reviewed by at least three members of the international program committee. At a one-day program committee meeting, the submitted papers were discussed, and 35 papers were selected for presentation at the conference, which means an acceptance rate of 24.8%. A special emphasis of IFIP/SEC 2006 is on Privacy and Privacy Enhancing Technologies, which is addressed by 9 of the 35 accepted papers. Further topics addressed include security in mobile and ad hoc networks, access control for dynamic environments, new forms of attacks, security awareness, intrusion detection and network forensics.

These Proceedings also include the papers of the following two workshops that are associated with SEC 2006: the workshop on "Security Culture" organized by IFIP Working Group 11.1/11.8 as well as the I-NetSec'06 workshop on "Privacy and Anonymity Issues in Networked and Distributed Systems" organized by IFIP Working Group 11.4. Both workshops were organized autonomously by the respective IFIP Working Groups. They had their own call for papers, program committees, and selection processes with acceptance rates of papers similar to the one of the main IFIP/SEC 2006 conference.

IFIP/SEC 2006 is organized in cooperation with Karlstad University, SIG Security, and Dataföreningen i Sverige. We would like to thank Microsoft AB, Karlstads kommun, SAAB AB, and TietoEnator, who are sponsoring IFIP/SEC 2006. Furthermore, we gratefully thank all authors, members of the program committees, and additional reviewers for their contributions to the scientific quality of this conference and the two workshops. Last but not least, we owe thanks to the organizing committee, and especially to its chair Dr. Albin Zuccato, for all the efforts and dedication in preparing this conference.

February 2006

Simone Fischer-Hübner (Conference General Chair)
Kai Rannenberg and Louise Yngström (Program Committee Co-Chairs)
Stefan Lindskog (Publication Chair)

Organization

IFIP/SEC 2006 is organized by IFIP TC-11 (Technical Committee on Security & Protection in Information Processing Systems) in cooperation with Karlstad University, SIG Security, and Dataföreningen i Sverige.

Conference Chairs

Conference General Chair
Simone Fischer-Hübner, Karlstad University, Sweden

Program Committee Co-Chairs
Kai Rannenberg, Goethe University Frankfurt, Germany
Louise Yngström, Stockholm University/Royal Institute of Technology, Sweden

Organizing Committee Chair
Albin Zuccato, Karlstad University, Sweden

Publication Chair
Stefan Lindskog, Karlstad University, Sweden

Sponsorship Chair
Christer Magnusson, Stockholm University/Royal Institute of Technology, Sweden

Program Committee

Helen Armstrong, Curtin University, Australia
Tuomas Aura, Microsoft Research, UK
Richard Baskerville, Georgia State University, USA
Rolf Blom, Ericsson Research, Sweden
Reinhard Botha, Nelson Mandela Metropolitan University, South Africa
Caspar Bowden, Microsoft EMEA Technology Office, UK
Bill Caelli, Queensland University of Technology, Australia
Jan Camenisch, IBM Zurich Research Laboratory, Switzerland
Bruce Christianson, University of Hertfordshire, UK
Roger Clarke, Xamax Consultancy, Australia
Richard Clayton, University of Cambridge, UK
Frédéric Cuppens, ENST Bretagne, France
Mads Dam, Royal Institute of Technology, Sweden
Bart De Decker, Katholieke Universiteit Leuven, Belgium
Yves Deswarte, LAAS-CNRS, France

Daniel J. Ragsdale, United States Military Academy, USA
Indrajit Ray, Colorado State University, USA
Hanne Riis Nielson, Technical University of Denmark, Denmark
Pierangela Samarati, Universita' di Milano, Italy
David Sands, Chalmers University of Technology, Sweden
Ryoichi Sasaki, Tokyo Denki University, Japan
Ingrid Schaumüller-Bichl, ITSB Linz, Austria
Matthias Schunter, IBM Zurich Research Laboratory, Switzerland
Anne Karen Seip, Kredittilsynet (FSA), Norway
Andrei Serjantov, The Free Haven Project, UK
Nahid Shahmehri, Linköping University, Sweden
Leon Strous, De Nederlandsche Bank, The Netherlands
Masato Terada, Hitachi Ltd., Japan
Stephanie Teufel, University of Fribourg, Switzerland
Teemupekka Virtanen, Helsinki University of Technology, Finland
Basie von Solms, University of Johannesburg, South Africa
Rossouw von Solms, Nelson Mandela Metropolitan University, South Africa
Jozef Vyskoc, VaF, Slovak Republic
Matthew Warren, Deakin University, Australia
Tatjana Welzer, University of Maribor, Slovenia
Gunnar Wenngren, Swedish Defence Research Agency (FOI), Sweden
Felix Wu, University of California, USA
Hiroshi Yoshiura, The University of Electro-Communications, Japan
Albin Zuccato, Karlstad University, Sweden

Additional Reviewers

Eric Alata
Magnus Almgren
Fabien Autrel
Jabiri Kuwe Bakari
Theodore Balopoulos
Zinaida Benenson
Nafeesa Bohra
Philippe Bulens
Sudip Chakraborty
Sebastian Clauß
Stefano Crosta
Sabrina De Capitani di Vimercati
Ivan Dedinski
Liesje Demuynck
Wolfgang Dobmeier
Stelios Dritsas
Claudiu Duma

Anas Abou El Kalam
Ludwig Fuchs
Joaquin Garcia
Stelios Georgiou
Steven Gevers
Almut Herzog
Amine Houyou
Martin Johns
George Kambourakis
Ioanna Kantzavelou
Guenter Karjoth
Maria Karyda
Stefan Koepsell
Jan Kolter
Markus Kuhn
Tobias Kölsch
Patrick Lambrix

Ulf Larson
Jens-Ove Lauf
Soo Bum Lee
Dimitris Lekkas
Tina Lindgren
Henning Makholm
Martin Meints
Patrick S. Merten
Pietro Michiardi
Ilya Mironov
Jose A. Montenegro
Björn Muschall
Gregory Neven
Flemming Nielson
Svetla Nikova
Thomas Nowey
Jens Oberender
Andriy Panchenko
Lexi Pimenidis
Klaus Ploessl
Nayot Poolsappasit
Torsten Priebe
Thomas Probst

Henrich C. Pöhls
Rodrigo Roman
Christoffer Rosenkilde Nielsen
Rene Rydhof Hansen
Christian Schläger
Daniel Schreckling
Jan Seedorf
Sandra Steinbrecher
Martin Steinert
Gelareh Taban
Marianthi Theoharidou
Kerry-Lynn Thomson
Terkel Tolstrup
Bill Tsoumas
Johan van Niekerk
Robert N. Watson
Rolf Wendolsky
Kristof Verslype
Andreas Westfeld
Yu Yu
Ye Zhang
Melek Önen

Organizing Committee

Christer Andersson, Karlstad University, Sweden
Johan Eklund, Karlstad University, Sweden
Leonardo A. Martucci, Karlstad University, Sweden

Main Sponsor

Microsoft AB

Sponsors

Karlstads kommun
SAAB AB
TietoEnator

IFIP WG 11.1/11.8 Security Culture Workshop

Workshop Chairs
Steven Furnell, University of Plymouth, UK (Chair WG 11.1)

Daniel J. Ragsdale, United States Military Academy, USA (Chair WG 11.8)

Program Committee
Helen Armstrong, Curtin University, Australia
Matthew Bishop, University of California at Davis, USA
Jeimy Cano, Universidad de los Andes, Bogotá, Colombia
Ronald Dodge, United States Military Academy, USA
Paul Dowland, University of Plymouth, UK
Lynette Drevin, Potchefstroom University, South Africa
Jean-Noel Ezingeard, Henley Management College, UK
Steven Furnell, University of Plymouth, UK
Lynn Futcher, Nelson Mandela Metropolitan University, South Africa
Dimitris Gritzalis, Athens University of Economics & Business, Greece
Jorma Kajava, University of Lapland, Finland
Sokratis Katsikas, University of the Aegean, Greece
Phillip Lock, University of South Australia, Australia
Natalia Miloslavskaya, Moscow Engineering Physics Institute, Russia
Ahmed Patel, Centre for Network Planning (CPN), Aalborg University, Denmark
Guenther Pernul, University of Regensburg, Germany
Reijo Savola, VTT Technical Research Centre of Finland, Finland
Jill Slay, University of South Australia, Australia
Stephanie Teufel, University of Fribourg, Switzerland
Alexander Tolstoy, Moscow Engineering Physics Institute, Russia
Rossouw von Solms, Nelson Mandela Metropolitan University, South Africa
Louise Yngström, Stockholm University/Royal Institute of Technology, Sweden

IFIP WG 11.4 I-NetSec'06 Workshop

Program Committee Chair
Bart De Decker, Katholieke Universiteit Leuven, Belgium

Program Committee
Yves Deswarte, LAAS-CNRS, France
Hannes Federrath, University of Regensburg, Germany
Simone Fischer-Hübner, Karlstad University, Sweden
Keith Martin, Royal Holloway, University of London, UK
Refik Molva, Institut Eurecom, France
Andreas Pfitzmann, Dresden University of Technology, Germany
Kai Rannenberg, Goethe University Frankfurt, Germany
Pierangela Samarati, Universita' di Milano, Italy
Vitaly Shmatikov, SRI International, USA

Table of Contents

Attacks, Vulnerability Analysis, and Tools

Access Control and Authentication I

Security Protocols

Intrusion Detection

IFIP WG 11.1/11.8 Security Culture Workshop

IFIP WG 11.4 I-NetSec'06 Workshop

Improving Availability of Emergency Health Information without Sacrificing Patient Privacy

Inger Anne Tøndel

SINTEF ICT, Trondheim, Norway
Inger.A.Tondel@sintef.no

Abstract. To give proper medical treatment, it is important to have access to updated health information on patients. In emergency situations where the treatment is not planned in advance, vital information will seldom be readily available. Smart cards can improve this, but one has to make sure that patient privacy is not sacrificed to improve availability. This paper discusses possible security solutions for an emergency health card, and evaluates to what extent we can assure availability and privacy at the same time.

1 Introduction

Availability of health information and efficient communication between physicians are main concerns within health care. Many cases of medical malpractice could have been avoided if relevant patient information had been available at the right place at the right time. Although medical information has found its ways into electronic patient records (EPRs), these EPRs will often not be available for health personnel not having a pre-established relationship with the patient. The vision of a Universal Patient Record [5, 8] recognizes that patients typically are treated by different types of health personnel in several healthcare organisations. Information on patients is therefore fragmented among different geographical locations, resulting in a need for better communication of all types of patient information [8].

Availability of health information is important in day to day treatment of patients [9], but the main challenges arise in emergency situations where the physicians have no prior relationship with the patient. Several technologies can be used for improving availability of health information in emergency situations, thereby improving patient treatment. One alternative is smart cards [11], which are in many ways ideal for providing emergency information; they are easy to carry and fit well in a wallet. In addition, information is available also in situations where network connections cannot be obtained [1, 6]. The main alternative is the use of centralized servers where such emergency information can be stored [5], but with such a solution, availability of network connections is required. Another alternative to smart cards is ordinary paper cards. This is an easy solution, but provides insufficient security.

Health information is sensitive information, and when handling such information patient privacy needs to be a main concern. Ideally, improving availability of information for legitimate users should not result in laxer security against other parties. This is not a major challenge in systems where the legitimate users are well defined. In

Please use the following format when citing this chapter:

Author(s) [insert Last name, First-name initial(s)], 2006, in IFIP International Federation for Information Processing, Volume 201, Security and Privacy in Dynamic Environments, eds. Fischer-Hubner, S., Rannenberg, K., Yngstrom, L., Lindskog, S., (Boston: Springer), pp. [insert page numbers].

emergency treatment situations, however, the legitimate user cannot be known in advance. One does not know when and where the emergency health information will be needed. The picture becomes even more complicated if one considers using the emergency health card internationally.

There exists many types of smart card use within health care today, e.g. to improve authentication and to hold information on patients as well as health personnel. In this paper, the focus will be on an emergency health card [13], and on how to achieve privacy while not reducing availability of information. Other issues regarding the emergency health card will not be addressed. For health information, legislation puts strict requirements on the protection needed. Knowledge of legislation is therefore important to be able to state what level of protection is adequate. Legislation is however not further discussed in this paper. This is mainly due to the complexity of national and international legislation within this area.

The paper starts with looking at smart cards within health care in general. Then the emergency health card is described in more detail, and the privacy issues of this card discussed. Different possible privacy enhancing technologies are described and the adequacy of the different solutions and possible combinations of solutions are discussed.

2   The Use of Smart Cards within Health Care

Smart cards have found their way into health care systems of different countries. Several types of health cards have been developed, storing different types of information related to patients. An electronic health card for people with diabetes in Germany is described in [3]. [15] describes an e-prescription system where patient smart cards play an important part. [7] describes the first phase of the national health insurance smart card project in Taiwan, and [10] describes health card initiatives in Malaysia. These are just examples. [7] refers to health card projects in Belgium, France and Slovenia, among others.

Most health cards today focus on special patient groups and day to day communication, rather than emergency functionality [2]. This is reflected in the security solutions. An example is the smart card used for e-prescription as described in [15] and the health card solution described in [6] where access to health information is controlled by a PIN provided by the patient. As will be discussed in this paper, this is a solution that can cause problems in emergency situations where the patient may be in shock or even unconscious. However, work has also been done to improve emergency care. The US Armed Forces have developed Personal Information Carriers (PICs) that can store medical records of soldiers [4, 14]. In wartime the independence of communication links is a main advantage, but as [4] states, there are disadvantages with the PIC approach; it is a challenge to provide access to appropriate personnel while denying access to the enemy. Solutions to this problem are however not further described.

An example of a civilian project that focuses on emergencies is FieldCare [12]. But, as opposed to the emergency health card discussed in this paper, FieldCare focuses on communication between cooperating personnel after an emergency has taken place. No information on the health status of patients before the emergency is available. There has also been done little work on security in this project. Another initiative is the Pocket

Doctor System proposed in [14]. This initiative recognizes the importance of knowledge of prior medical history when initiating treatment in emergency situations. A solution is presented where the patient carries a smart card, PDA or similar mobile device that is able to communicate via a wireless interface, and thereby can be easily detected. In the Pocket Doctor System there has been done some work on security, ensuring encryption of the wireless link. In addition patients are able to restrict access to some types of information on the device using passwords. This is a solution that will be considered also in this work, despite the limitations of passwords when it comes to emergency situations, as argued above.

For an emergency health card to be successful, interoperability and wide deployment is of high importance. One approach is to create a reference architecture for smart card based health card applications, as described in [2]. Within the proposed reference architecture it is possible to encrypt and sign information. How such mechanisms can be used in the emergency health card application will be discussed in this paper. Another approach is taken in [1], that describes a web-enabled framework for smart card application. This solution takes into account that smart cards comes with local processing capabilities, and lets the smart cards carry their own record management applet. This ensures that medical information stored on a smart card from hospital A is readable by hospital B. The framework includes a security component that supports authentication and a hierarchical approach to access control, providing different access rights to different types of health professions. However, no details are provided regarding how the access rights of health personnel at a (for the card) unknown organisation is determined.

3   The Emergency Health Card

The emergency health card is not a real application, but an abstract entity that can be used as a basis for discussing privacy vs. availability because of its strict requirements in both respects. The intended use of the application is illustrated in Figure 3. The card will not hold the full medical record of patients, only the core medical information needed in emergency situations. The general health information stored on the card is provided by a physician having knowledge of the patient's health condition. However, the users of the information are mainly health personnel with no previous relationship with the patient. It is possible to write information on the card related to the type of emergency treatment given. This way the patient's primary physician can be updated on the situation at a later stage. Four main types of users have been defined, as described in Table 1.

4   Privacy Issues

Health information is sensitive, and several parties could benefit from getting access to this type of information. Such parties can be insurance companies, possible future employers, journalists (if you are a celebrity) or neighbours and other people you know. With a card solution, you will to some extent be responsible for keeping the health card safe yourself. But since it often will be hard to protect oneself from dedicated robbers, some additional protection is beneficial.

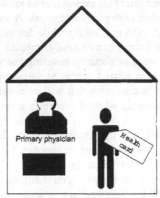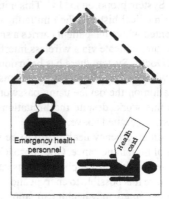

1. The primary physician provides the patient with an emergency health card containing important health information relevant if the patient need emergency health treatment

2. The patient needs some medical treatment, and this treatment is provided by a physician with no previous relationship with the patient. The physician therefore uses the card of the patient to get important information on blood type, allergies, drugs used, etc. to be able to decide on the right treatment. After the treatment has taken place, the physician writes information on the treatment on the card so that this information is available to other physicians at a later stage.

3. The patient shows the emergency health card to his primary physician after having received treatment from another physician. The primary physician thereby gets to know what treatment has been given and may use this information to further follow up the patient

Fig. 1. Illustration of the use of the emergency card application.

Table 1. Description of the different types of users.

User	Description	Access requirements
Card owner	The person that owns the card. Information on the card is related to this person. The owner physically holds the card and is responsible for bringing the card along at all times.	Does not need any access to the information or functionality of the card.
Primary physician	This is the physician chosen by the card owner to be his/her primary physician. This doctor has a special responsibility for the card owner.	Should have access to all information and functionality of the card.
Emergency health personnel	Physicians or other types of health personnel not having a relationship with the card owner. Due to the situation, this person needs information on the card owner to provide proper treatment.	Should have access to emergency health information, and should have access to write information on the emergency treatment given.
Administrative Clerk	A person working at a medical office, responsible for administrative tasks.	Needs access to identification information.

Protection of health information is also important for other reasons. It is in every patient's interest that health information is correct. Erroneous information may result in wrong medical treatment. Erroneous information may also make it hard to prove that medical malpractice has taken place. One may come across unethical doctors that would hide any traces of medical malpractice, or that would like to take opportunities to obtain power over patients. These doctors will have access to the information and functionality of the health card.

5   Possible Solutions

Since protection of the patients' privacy is important, controlling who gets access to the information on the card is a main concern. In addition non-repudiation and integrity are considered important to assure the information on the health card is indeed correct. In the following, different possible solutions to achieve privacy and non-repudiation are discussed.

5.1   Access Control

Enforcing access control will result in some groups not getting access to information. This is the intention of doing access control in the first place, that no one should get access to the information unless they are authorized to get access. However, one must be careful not to shut out legitimate users at the same time. This is especially important in a solution in which a main goal is to enhance availability of information in emergency situations. You will not have time to wait to get access, if you are a legitimate user. If a patient has to choose between correct treatment and increased privacy, chances are high that correct treatment is considered most important. This must be taken into account when considering access restricting solutions.

In this paper, all types of access restricting technologies are considered as access control solutions. This means that authentication solutions and encryption are considered together with more pure access control solutions that come into play after authentication has taken place. Authentication of health personnel in general is however considered out of scope.

Centralized Solutions One possibility is to rely on a central server to enforce access control. This server could, after successful authentication of users, grant access on a per card basis, or to all cards based on knowledge of profession or position of the user. Access could for instance be granted by making the correct encryption key or access token available for the user.

Choosing such a centralized solution results in reduced availability, since access to the card can only be achieved when a network connection and the central server are available. One could also argue that by choosing such a solution, the importance and advantages of the smart card is reduced, since one could fetch the emergency health information on the same server.

An alternative centralized solution is to control access to the card by controlling who gets access to an application needed to use the functionality of the card. Doctors would then need to authenticate to be able to download the application. The application should be downloaded before an emergency situation takes place, and would only be valid for a limited period. With such a solution, one will not be dependent on network connections to get access to information after the downloading is complete. However, the solution has its drawbacks. Doctors will be required to use time to download and reinstall applications. This task may be seen by doctors as unnecessary, and thereby reduce user-friendliness of the health card system. It may also be hard to control that applications are not distributed to unauthorized users. In addition, this solution has some look and feel of security by obscurity, which seldom inspires confidence.

Another drawback of the application-centred approach is that with this solution it is not possible to give different type of access to primary physicians and emergency health personnel.

Patient Oriented Solutions It is possible to let the patient control access to the card. In this setting this means both providing the physical card to the health personnel, and open the card by providing a PIN or a fingerprint or some other authentication token. In many ways this is an easy and good approach; however one still has to solve what to do if the patient is unconscious or so badly hurt that he/she is not able to make access control decisions. Authentication based on PIN codes will be useless in such situations. Biometrics should work, but doctors may find it uncomfortable stealing for instance fingerprints to get access to information. Another problem with this method is the difficulty of remembering PIN codes that are not often used. Biometrics does not have this problem, but may suffer from false negatives. It is also a more expensive solution. Another consideration is whether it is appropriate to make access control decisions the responsibility of patients maybe being in an awkward situation, possibly psychically unstable.

Card Oriented Solutions One option is to put the main focus on the card, and let the card keep an overview of who has access to what information. This will work well for controlling access to functionality only meant for primary physicians, but the approach fails when it comes to emergency health personnel and administrative clerks. There is no way the card can be able to know in advance the identity of all relevant users of this kind. Having a password or an encryption key known by all users is a possibility, but not very secure. A secret known by all possible users will probably not be a secret for long.

An example of information that only needs to be available to the primary physician is information on emergency treatment given by other physicians. The primary physician is also the only one that should be able to change or delete emergency health information on the card. Access to this information and functionality can be controlled by encrypting the information with the public key of the primary physician, and by knowledge of passwords or other types of secrets.

5.2 Non-Repudiation and Integrity

Using signatures is the common way of stating who is responsible for the information, both in the electronic and paper based world. Signatures are also a natural choice for achieving non-repudiation of information in this case. Every physician that writes information to the card would then need to sign the information with his or her private key. For other doctors to be able to check the signature later, the certificate of the doctor should be available to all subsequent readers of the information.

Using signatures requires that a PKI is in place. It would also be beneficial to include the relevant certificates on the card, since that would result in the certificates always being available. This may however not be possible due to limited storage capacity on smart cards. Availability of certificates is not as important as availability of emergency health information. It is however worth noting that it will not necessarily be a need for storing many certificates on the card. The primary physician of the card holder will be the one responsible for the information on the card. This physician will probably have written most of the information. In addition physicians providing emergency treatment may write information to the card, but this information will not be present on the card forever, only until it has been read by the primary physician.

5.3 Some Notes about Logging

Logging is a much used mechanism to be able to trace behaviour of users in systems. With the mechanisms discussed up till now, it is possible to trace who has written what information, and that the information has not been altered, but it will not be possible to see who has accessed the information. For health information, access history is of relevance, because privacy is so important. Logs may be used to be able to trace any access to information on the card, but also comes with some challenges. A smart card will not have enough storage to be able to store logs above a very limited size. An alternative is to store the logs on a central server, resulting in the need for available network connections for the mechanism to work. With such an approach, anyone wanting to hide their traces could just disconnect from the network.

One should mark that with normal usage the logs will probably not get that big, if they are transferred to some computer system at the next visit with the primary physician. Storing logs on the card may therefore be rational, since full logs may be taken as a sign of misuse.

6 Discussion

Based on the descriptions of the main alternative security enhancing solutions, it seems that only non-repudiation and integrity can be achieved in a fairly straightforward manner. Privacy is much harder to achieve. No alternative seems to fit perfect for the job, as can be seen in the summary of the solutions in Table 2.

6.1 Possible Combinations of Solutions

None of the privacy enhancing solutions seem to be able to do the job entirely, but combinations of the alternatives may still provide useful solutions. If considering the centralized access control server, this centralized solution can be combined with the patient-centred approach. The centralized access control system could be used if this

Table 2. Comparision of privacy enhancing colutions.

Solution	Drawbacks
Centralized access control server	May reduce availability. High costs due to high availability requirements. May have scaling problems if using the card on international basis.
Centralized application control	Security by obscurity. May be hard to limit availability of the application. May reduce user-friendliness. Cannot distinguish the different user groups.
Patient oriented solution	Patients may be unconscious, or in other ways incapable of making access control decisions. May reduce user-friendliness for both physicians and patients.
Card oriented solutions	Will only work for controlling access for primary physicians.

one is available. If not, the patient may provide access as an alternative. With this combination, the dependence on the availability of the central server is reduced. The dependence on the patient's choices and condition is also reduced; however the problem with unethical doctors and others tricking patients into giving access to information is still relevant. On the other hand, one may ask if this is a real problem since patients may be tricked into revealing the same information verbally without having a card.

The centralized access control server can also be combined with the centralized application control solution. As in the above case, such a solution would use the access control server if available, and grant access based on the availability of an application if not, possibly with reduced access rights. As for the above combination this reduces the problems encountered by the centralized access control server. However, the uncertainty of relying on the presence of an application to prove access rights still applies.

The centralized application control approach can also be combined with the patient-centred or the card-centred approaches. If the patient-centred approach is chosen for combination, health personnel having access to the application may be allowed to access information on the card, but the patient decides the amount of information available. This may be done by providing pin codes to the physician. The patient may now be more certain the doctor is really allowed to access health cards in general. However, the main disadvantages of the patient oriented approach still apply. Combining the centralized application approach with the card-centred solution may be more successful. In this case, primary physicians can access information on the card by using the card-centred approach, while emergency doctors are given access to emergency functionality by virtue of having the application available. This way the main disadvantages of all involved approaches are reduced. One is now able to distinguish between primary physicians and emergency health personnel, and to protect emergency information in general.

As the reader surely has noticed, a few alternatives have been left out in the above discussion. This is due to a judgment of the relevance of the combinations:

- Combining a centralized server with a card-centred approach does not reduce any problems related to emergency operation which is the main problem with availability of the centralized approach.
- Combining a patient-centred and a card-centred solution is not much better than a patient-centred solution since the family doctor of the patient is well known by the patient and not part of the problem when it comes to a patient's access rights enforcement.

One may however combine three or more alternatives. One example of such a solution is to combine one of the centralized solutions with both the card-centred and patient-centred approaches. In such a solution the card will hold information on who is the primary physician, the application or the central access server will hold information on the profession and position of the user, and the card owner will be able to provide access in case the other access control mechanisms fail. But relying on the user to remember passwords that will probably never be used may be optimistic. Biometrics should therefore be used in such a setting.

6.2   Different Protection Requirements for Different Types of Information

An issue that has not been discussed up till now is what type of information will be needed on such a card. Without trying to make a full description of the content, examples of information that can be relevant are name, identification information (for instance photographs) and information on next of kin, religion, blood type, allergies, medications and diagnosis. In addition the card may contain information on emergency treatment given.

The different types of information mentioned above will probably have different needs for protection. Name, identification information and blood type are examples of information that probably could have been printed on the outside of the card without reducing privacy in a great extent. Information on medication and diagnosis may on the other hand be very sensitive.

It is possible to create systems that specify the protection needs of information. Defining protection needs may be the responsibility of the user that writes the information to the card, or it may be specified by the system beforehand, and it may be done at different levels of detail. Because of user-friendliness aspects, it may be advantageous to make the specification of security needs beforehand, and specify the needed security level rather than the actual mechanisms to use, but other solutions are possible.

Assigning security levels to all information on the card makes it possible to give higher protection to the most sensitive information. If combining different access control solutions, one may say that some solutions provide more security than others, and let the type of access control conducted influence the type of information that becomes available to a user. Note however, that it is not only sensitivity that should be considered when assigning security levels to information. The importance of having this information available in an emergency situation is also of high importance.

6.3   What Level of Privacy is "Good Enough"?

The answer to this question will depend on who you're asking. One may say that it should be sufficiently hard to get access to sensitive personal information, but then again, what is "sufficiently hard"? With this emergency health card, the owner of the card will have some responsibility regarding keeping the card safe. How much more is really needed? Is it enough that health personnel need to have a specific application to read the card, or do we need one complex centralized solution that for instance is able to respond to challenges made by the card and provide the answer to the user after he/she has been properly authenticated?

In this emergency health card application, the primary physician shall have access to all functionality and all information on the card. It should therefore be very hard for intruders to get access to functionality only intended for the primary physician. This can be solved with the card-centred approach. Other types of health personnel will have more limited access, though they will probably need access to all or most of the emergency health information. If not, this information need not be put on the card in the first place. Some of this information may be very sensitive, but very important to provide high quality emergency care.

It is hard to provide access only to health personnel involved in patient treatment, since one does not know beforehand who these will be. Maybe part of the access control therefore should lie in the decision on what information to include on the card. This could be a decision made by the primary physician and the patient together. Technically, we can make it harder for intruders to get access to this information, for instance by encoding the information in proprietary ways so that only the correct application can easily read it, or by requiring a valid finger print from the patient; but it will never be foolproof. Dedicated intruders may still be able to get hold of information. However, if we do our job well, it will probably be easier to get to the information by other means.

6.4   How Much is Privacy Worth compared to Cost and User-Friendliness?

Some of the privacy enhancing solutions discussed will reduce user-friendliness or increase implementation costs. Therefore some judgment is needed regarding whether or not the increased privacy is really worth the effort.

Centralized access control servers may prove to be a costly solution, especially because of the strict availability requirements. The costs may be even higher if considering using the card internationally. Biometrics may also be costly to implement, because of all the extra equipment needed.

Reduced user-friendliness will be experienced by the centralized application control solution, since health personnel would need to download the application themselves, especially if this need to be repeated often because of limited validity periods of applications (to increase security). The patient-centred approach also may reduce user-friendliness, both for patients and health personnel. Using passwords that need to be remembered by the patient is particularly hopeless, since these probably will not be remembered in the first place, and will not be available anyway if the patient is unconscious, in shock or similar.

7 Conclusion

The strict availability requirements, and the fact that the users cannot be predicted beforehand, seem to make it impossible to guarantee full patient privacy. However, by being careful with what information to put on such a card, and by combining different solutions, it seems to be possible to achieve adequate protection of information in most cases. More work needs to be done regarding what level of protection is actually needed, and compare this to the cost of solutions, both when it comes to user-friendliness and development and equipment costs. Maybe we will find that we can easily make a solution that will be good enough for most people, while celebrities may feel that they do not get adequate protection. They may compensate for this by physically protecting the card better. However, here again the conflict between availability and privacy comes into play.

Acknowledgments

This paper is based on work done in my Masters thesis at the Norwegian University of Science and Technology (NTNU). I would like to thank Professor Svein J. Knapskog at NTNU and my supervisors Ståle Walderhaug, Per Håkon Meland and Lillian Røstad at SINTEF ICT for helpful feedback during this research.

References

1. Alvin T.S. Chan, Jiannong Cao, Henry Chan, and Gilbert Young. A Web-Enabled Framework for Smart Card Application in Health Services. *Communications of the ACM*, 44(9):77–82, 2001.
2. A. Georgoula, A. Giakoumaki, and D. Koutsouris. A Multi-layered Architecture for the Development of Smart Card-based Healthcare Applications. In *Proceedings of the 25th Annual International Conference of the IEEE Engineering in Medicine and Biology Society*, volume 2, pages 1378–1381, 2003.
3. G. Gogou, A. Mavromatis, and N. Maglaveras. DIABCARD CCMIS - A Portable and Scalable CPR for Diabetes Care. *IEEE Transactions on Biomedical Engineering*, 49(12):1412–1219, 2002.
4. Dean S. Hartley. Simulating without data. In *Proceedings of the 2002 Winter Simulation Conference*, pages 975–980, 2002.
5. Jagib S. Hooda, Erdogan Dogdu, and Raj Sunderraman. Health Level-7 Compliant Clinical Patient Records System. In *Proceedings of the 2004 ACM symposium on Applied computing*, pages 259–263, 2004.
6. Geylani Kardaas and E. Turhan Tunali. Design and implementation of a smart card based healthcare information system. *Computer methods and programs in biomedicine*, 81:66–78, 2006.
7. Chien-Tsai Liu, Pei-Tun Yang, Yu-Ting Yeh, and Bin-Long Wang. The impacts of smart cards on hospital information systems - An investigation of the first phase of the national health insurance smart card project in Taiwan. *International Journal of Medical Informatics*, 75:173–181, 2006.
8. Michael R. McGuire. *Automation of the Patient Medical Record: Steps Toward a Universal Patient Record*. http://www.uprforum.com/, 2001.

9. Per Håkon Meland, Lillian Røstad, and Inger Anne Tøndel. How to mediate between health information security and patient safety. In *Proceedings of PSAM 8*, 2006. To appear.

10. Jay Mohan and Raja Razali Raja Yaacob. The Malaysian Telehealth Flagship Application: a national approach to health data protection and utilisation and consumer rights. *International Journal of Medical Informatics*, 73:217–227, 2004.

11. Katherine M. Shelfer and J. Drew Procaccino. Smart Card Evolution. *Communications of the ACM*, 45(7):83–88, 2002.

12. I. Svagård, J. Gorman, and B. Haugset. How mobile IT-support and patient tags can improve information flow and patient tracking in prehospital medicine. *Akuttjournalen*, 13(2):120–124, 2005.

13. Inger Anne Tøndel. Personal data carriers. Master's thesis, Norwegian University of Science and Technology, Department of Telematics, 2004.

14. D. K. Vawdrey, E. S. Hall, C. D. Knutson, and J. K. Archibald. A Self-Adapting Healthcare Information Infrastructure Using Mobile Computing Devices. In *5th International Workshop on Enterprise Networking and Computing in Healthcare Industry (Healthcom 2003)*, pages 91–97, 2003.

15. Yanjiang Yang, Xiaoxi Han, Feng Bao, and Robert H. Deng. A Smart-Card-Enabled Privacy Preserving E-Prescription System. In *IEEE Transactions on Information Technology in Biomedicine*, volume 8, pages 47–58, 2004.

Ensuring Privacy for Buyer-Seller E-Commerce[1]

George Yee, Larry Korba, and Ronggong Song

Institute for Information Technology
National Research Council Canada
1200 Montreal Road, Building M-50, Ottawa, ON, Canada K1A 0R6
{George.Yee, Larry.Korba, Ronggong.Song}@nrc-cnrc.gc.ca
http://www.iit-iti.nrc-cnrc.gc.ca

Abstract. The growth of the Internet has been accompanied by the growth of e-services (e.g. e-commerce, e-health). This proliferation of e-services and the increasing regulatory and legal requirements for personal privacy have fueled the need to protect the personal privacy of e-service users. Existing approaches for privacy protection such as the use of pseudonym technology, and personal privacy policies along with appropriate compliance mechanisms are predicated on the e-service provider having possession and control over the user's personal data. In this paper, we propose a new approach for protecting personal privacy in buyer-seller e-commerce: keeping possession and control over the buyer's personally identifiable information in the hands of the buyer as much as possible, with the help of a smart card and a trusted authority. Our approach can also be characterized as distributing personally identifiable information only on a "need to know" basis.

1 Introduction

This work presents a new approach for protecting personal privacy in buyer-seller e-commerce. The approach is based on keeping possession and control over the buyer's personally identifiable information in the hands of the buyer as much as possible.

The motivation for this approach comes from the fact that once buyer personal information is in the hands of a seller, it becomes very difficult to ensure that the seller will respect the buyer's privacy preferences. In addition, it is a hard problem to guarantee that a seller will not circumvent any kind of private data access control that might be in place. We were therefore led to the following proposition: let the buyer, as much as possible, not transfer his/her personally identifiable data to the seller but instead keep it in his/her possession and retain control over it.

Our proposed approach employs selective disclosure of the buyer's information and a smart card, in conjunction with the buyer's personal privacy policy, to keep *control* of the buyer's personally identifiable data in the hands of the buyer as much as possible, rather than in the hands of the seller.

We use the term "bse-service" to mean "buyer-seller e-service", a service that consists of the purchase of goods by a buyer from a seller across the Internet (e.g.

---

[1] NRC Paper Number: NRC 48461

Please use the following format when citing this chapter:
Author(s) [insert Last name, First-name initial(s)], 2006, in IFIP International Federation for Information Processing, Volume 201, Security and Privacy in Dynamic Environments, eds. Fischer-Hubner, S., Rannenberg, K., Yngstrom, L., Lindskog, S., (Boston: Springer), pp. [insert page numbers].

Amazon.com). Goods may be physical (e.g. computers) or informational (e.g. stock quotes). The service is performed by application software (service processes) that is owned by the seller. The seller has a privacy policy that spells out what buyer personal information is needed for its service and how the personal information will be handled. The buyer has a personal privacy policy that defines what personal information he/she is willing to disclose and how that information is to be handled by the seller.

In the literature, elemental components of our proposal exist, but not, as far as we can tell, assembled into the approach presented here. For example, Clarke [7] wrote about smart cards (he actually was complaining that their use destroys privacy), anonymity, and the use of pseudonyms and trusted third parties. Laudon [8] suggested that individuals could sell their private information in an information market, and thus maintain control over their private information (the maintaining control part is similar to what we propose here but the means for doing so is completely different). However, Laudon's proposal is flawed in that it does not discuss the potential abuse of private information in a market setting (e.g. theft).

Smart cards have been around for over 3 decades and have been applied across many domains including e-commerce [1, 2]. Their computational, memory, and security features make them ideal for portable data applications requiring security [2].

Figure 1 (adapted from [9]) gives an example of buyer/seller privacy policies for an online pharmacy. *Policy Use* indicates the type of online service for which the policy will be used. *Valid* holds the time period during which the policy is valid. The required fields (e.g. collector, what) of these policies are derived from Canadian privacy legislation [9]. This legislation is a good source for deriving privacy policies since it is representative of privacy legislation in many countries. These are minimum privacy policies in the sense that the fields *collector, what, purposes, retention time,* and *disclose-to* form the minimum set of fields required to satisfy the legislation for any one information item. Each set of such fields is termed a *privacy rule* describing a particular information item. Privacy policies need to be machine-readable and may be expressed using a XML-based language such as APPEL [3].

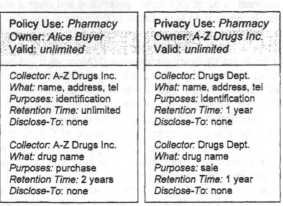

Fig. 1. Example buyer (left) and seller (right) privacy policies.

Note that all information that the buyer discloses to a seller is considered personal information and described in the buyer's personal privacy policy. Some of this information is personally identifiable information (PII), i.e. the information can identify the buyer. For example, "name", "address", and "telephone number" are PII. There may be other information described in a personal privacy policy that is not personally identifiable information (non-PII), i.e. the information by itself cannot identify the buyer. For example, the selection of Aspirin as a medication at an online pharmacy cannot normally identify the buyer.

Section 2 presents our approach for using selective disclosure and smart cards to protect consumer personal information. Section 2 also gives an example of applying our approach. Section 3 presents our conclusions and plans for future research.

2 Using Selective Disclosure and Smart Cards to Protect Privacy

Our goal is to protect a buyer's privacy according to his/her personal privacy policy. This policy can be violated by the seller (or other potential attackers) who would normally be in possession and control of the buyer's submitted personal information. Our answer to privacy protection is simple: *remove the buyer's PII from the possession and control of the seller.* We accomplish this by having the buyer's personal information in a smart card, called a *privacy controller*, owned by the buyer and in his/her possession. The personal information in the privacy controller can only be entered and accessed by the buyer. Using the privacy controller, the buyer is able to selectively disclose (explained below) his/her PII only when necessary, not to the primary service provider (i.e. the seller), but to trusted support providers that support the primary provider with business services that do require the user's PII. Further, the privacy controller smart card will process the buyer's PII according to his/her privacy policy. The buyer is anonymous to the seller at all times.

We require that the primary service can do without the buyer's PII. For this to be true, the primary service must be decomposable into components that do and do not need the user's PII. For example, bse-services can be decomposed into three components, namely order entry and processing, order delivery, and order payment, in which only order delivery and order payment may need the user's PII. In fact, for informational services, the network delivery of information may even do without the user's PII (i.e. allow him/her to be anonymous), through the use of anonymous communications (e.g. using a MIX network such as JAP [10]). Thus, the primary service provider or seller does not need the buyer's PII but makes use of support services that do need the PII, namely shipping (for physical goods) and payment services from other providers. Paypal [6] is an example of a payment service provider.

We further require the services of a trusted authority (a Certificate Authority with an extended role) to program the smart card to act as a privacy controller, to keep the true identity of the user should there be a need to recover it (e.g. in legal proceedings), and to distribute the smart card. Figure 2 illustrates our approach.

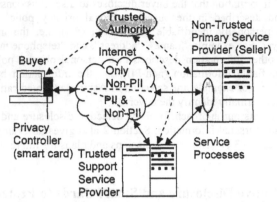

Fig. 2. Using selective disclosure and smart card to protect buyer privacy.

Our approach is really applying the need-to-know principle to bse-services, distributing PII only where appropriate. A bse-service is decomposed into a *primary service* that does not require PII and *support services* that do require PII but are trusted to maintain the anonymity of the buyer. The user's privacy controller discloses PII only to the support services that require the buyer's PII.

2.1 Selective Disclosure and Resultant Privacy Policy Transformations

The redirection of PII from the primary service provider to support service providers necessitates the controller updating the privacy rules in the buyer's policy. Thus, if the online pharmacy for Figure 1 uses a trusted shipper, Global Shipping Inc., the first rule in the consumer policy (see Figure 1) would be transformed to:

> *Collector:* Global Shipping Inc.
> *What:* name, address, tel
> *Purposes:* shipping
> *Retention Time:* unlimited
> *Disclose-To:* none

The controller knows the destination of the re-direction from information provided by the primary service provider. The corresponding rules in the privacy policy of the primary service provider would already reflect such destinations, since it is set up to make use of support providers. In this way, the buyer has only to deal with the primary service provider in his/her privacy policy.

2.2 Privacy Controller and Service Process Requirements

The privacy controller processes each privacy rule component in the buyer's privacy policy as follows:

a) *Collector*: Confirm that the collector named by the service processes is the collector specified in the buyer's policy.
b) *What*: Confirm that the information item requested by the service processes is as specified in the buyer's policy.
c) *Purposes*: Confirm that the purposes for which the information will be used are as specified in the buyer's policy.
d) *Retention Time*: Destroy the buyer's personal information at the end of its retention time.
e) *Disclose-To*: Confirm that the receiving party in the case of a disclosure request is the party specified in the buyer's privacy policy.

The service processes must cooperate with the privacy controller where necessary in order to carry out the above requirements (e.g. provide the seller's privacy policy to the privacy controller).

These requirements dictate the functionality of the privacy controller and the primary service processes (PSP). The privacy controller, in acting to ensure compliance with the buyer's privacy policy, runs in two phases as described below. In phase 1, the controller essentially transforms the buyer's policy for PII redirections and compares policies. In phase 2, the controller enforces the buyer's privacy policy. Phase 2 can only be reached if phase 1 is successful (if phase 1 is unsuccessful, the buyer and seller can enter into negotiation [5] failing which the buyer can choose another seller).

Privacy Controller Processing for Buyer Privacy Policy Compliance. In phase 1 (see Figure 3),
- Establish a connection to the seller and download the seller's privacy policy and support service provider information.
- Transform the buyer's privacy policy for PII redirections, as described above.
- Verify that the privacy rules in the seller's privacy policy matches the privacy rules in the buyer's privacy policy (comparing privacy policies for a match is outside the scope of this paper but see [4]). If this verification fails, inform the buyer and terminate (or negotiate privacy policies as indicated above). Otherwise, proceed to phase 2.

In phase 2,
- Prompt buyer for each information item (II) and accept only II of the types specified in the buyer's privacy policy.
- Store buyer's II in its personal information store.
- Destroy the buyer's II if the retention time is up.
- Disclose only non-PII to the PSP as described above.
- Accept requests from the PSP to disclose the buyer's II (PII and non-PII) to support service providers as allowed by the buyer's privacy policy, passing along the II's retention time. These support providers are not allowed to further disclose the buyer's PII. Note: the typical buyer would normally not be receiving disclosures. In this work, only providers receive disclosures, e.g. a trusted shipping company receiving an address disclosure for shipping purposes.

Service Processing. The PSP executes during the controller's phase 2 processing, as follows:

- Perform normal processing for the service that is offered by the seller, including requesting non-PII from the privacy controller needed for service processing.
- If needed, request the controller to disclose information to trusted support providers.

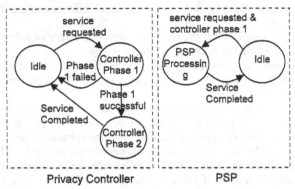

Privacy Controller   PSP

Fig. 3. High-level state machines for privacy controller and PSP.

2.3 Role of the Trusted Authority and Additional Operational Details

The trusted authority is a certificate authority with an extended role, called an extended CA or "eCA" for short. Prior to the commencement of any bse-service, the eCA works to familiarize sellers and buyers with its services. Sellers can "subscribe" to the eCA and arrange their service processes to work with the privacy controller smart card (e.g. conform to smart card interfacing requirements). The smart card is remotely programmed by the eCA to be used as the privacy controller and to work with the sellers that have subscribed to the eCA (e.g. download seller's privacy policy, upload buyer's information). The programming automatically allows the smart card to be used with new sellers that may subscribe to the eCA later. The eCA distributes these smart cards to service users through local electronics outlets (e.g. Best Buy). When purchased at a local electronics outlet, the smart card only has the ability to automatically connect to the eCA (in addition to normal smart card functions). The eCA also selects and confirms a number of support providers as trusted parties for business services such as shipping and payment. Further, the eCA issues digital certificates to all sellers for use in authenticating themselves.

A buyer who wants to buy from sellers that subscribe to the eCA registers with the eCA's web site through a secure channel. After paying the eCA an appropriate fee using a secure credit card transaction, the buyer receives from the eCA a number of different pseudonyms and a digital certificate (for authentication purposes) that identifies the buyer using the pseudonyms (one pseudonym for each seller the buyer wants to use). In processing the buyer's credit card, the eCA also checks the buyer's name, address information, and credit history with the credit card company.

To use a bse-service, the buyer connects the smart card to a USB port on his/her computer. The buyer is automatically connected to the eCA's website after mutual authentication (using digital certificates) through a secure channel. The eCA then remotely programs the smart card for use as a privacy controller, instructing the controller to use the buyer's pseudonyms for identification purposes with bse-service providers (one pseudonym with each provider) (note: this is done only if the smart card has not been programmed previously). The buyer is then allowed to select which seller to use. After the buyer selects the seller, the website prompts the buyer to enter a privacy policy to be used with the selected seller if this is the buyer's first use of the seller. Note that the website is better equipped with appropriate graphical interfaces than the smart card for the buyer to enter a privacy policy. The entered policy or a previously entered policy (they are stored on the eCA's website) is then automatically downloaded to the smart card. At this point, the controller automatically begins phase 1 processing. A pop-up window appears indicating an anonymous connection to the bse-service with successful 2-way authentication through a secure channel and with the seller's privacy policy downloaded (controller phase 1 processing). The privacy controller then transforms the buyer's policy for PII redirections and compares the buyer's privacy policy (previously entered) with the provider's privacy policy for compatibility. If this is successful, the privacy controller initiates phase 2 processing. Otherwise, the privacy controller initiates a privacy policy negotiation session with the seller that takes place via the privacy controller. If this negotiation is successful, the privacy controller can begin phase 2. If neither the original phase 1 nor the negotiation is successful, the buy must choose a different seller. Once the controller starts phase 2, the seller's service processes are initiated. The latter then requests non-PII from the controller and requests it to send information disclosures (possibly sending PII to trusted parties (e.g. address for shipping)) as the service requires. Service output is sent back to the user via the controller-service processes channel.

It follows from the above that the eCA can link the user's pseudonym with the user. This is allowed on purpose, so that when necessary the seller can request the true identity of the buyer. For example, this may be necessary in a medical emergency where an e-pharmacy seller needs to contact the buyer, or where there is a dispute involving the buyer, and the buyer's real name is needed for legal proceedings.

2.4 Security Measures

Based on the above operating scenarios, the vulnerability areas include: a) storage of personal data, b) distribution of the smart card through local electronic outlets, c) sending data disclosures, d) communication between the privacy controller and the service processes, and between the buyer and the eCA's web site, e) disclosure of non-PII to the service processes, i.e. although the data is non-PII, could their combinations collected over time compromise the anonymity of the buyer? f) traceable communications over the Internet, g) dishonest parties masquerading as trusted parties, h) Trojan horse programs in the buyer's computer, and i) the buyer loses his/her smart card, either by accident or theft.

We discuss our security measures for each vulnerability area in turn as follows:
a) Storage of personal data: the data is secured on the smart card (processor-enabled) using symmetric encryption (e.g. 3DES). The key for the encryption algorithm can be generated (e.g. using a SHA-2 hash function) by the smart card from the user's password for accessing the card. Further, the smart card incorporates a locking mechanism that locks out any attacker who tries to access

the card by trying to guess the password – the locking mechanism can lock the user out, for example, after 5 tries. Thus, the attacker first of all cannot access the card because he/she does not know the password. Even if the attacker uses some special technology to get at the data, he/she cannot read it since it is encrypted. Finally, the attacker cannot decrypt the data because he/she again does not know the password, used to generate the encryption key. To protect the password from Trojan horses, the password mechanism and storage is physically isolated from the area of the smart card that can connect to the Internet.

b) Distribution of the smart card through local electronic outlets: the risk is that an attacker could modify the card before it is sold to i) connect to a fake website controlled by the attacker, or ii) introduce malware into the card that would later play havoc with any programming; possibility i) is defeated by required mutual authentication between the user and the eCA; possibility ii) can be defeated using built-in card self sanity checks together with malware detection software run on the card by the eCA prior to remote programming.

c) Sending / receiving data disclosures: the privacy controller establishes a secure channel (SSL or secure VPN) to the receiving party for use in data conveyance; the sending controller authenticates the receiving party using the receiving party's digital certificate before any data is sent. Receiving parties are pre-screened by the eCA, who issues them digital certificates for authentication purposes.

d) Communication between privacy controller and service processes: the controller establishes a secure channel (SSL or secure VPN) to the service processes to be used for communication purposes. The controller authenticates the service processes using their digital certificates issued to them by the eCA. Similarly, the service processes authenticates the controller using the digital certificate issued to the buyer by the eCA. This same secure procedure is used for communication between the user and the eCA's website.

e) Disclosure of non-PII leads to compromising anonymity: we believe that this risk is minimal for bse-services. Identity discovery from non-PII depends on the size of the buyer population, the method of selective disclosure, and the amount of non-PII data in circulation pertaining to the individual. This risk can be minimized if the buyer population is the whole Internet community. However, some bse-services operate only regionally so this may not apply. Next, this risk may be further minimized by employing more effective methods for selective disclosure. Finally, bse-services require minimal non-PII, resulting in minimal non-PII data in circulation for any one individual, thereby further reducing this risk.

f) Traceable communications over the Internet: the controller not only establishes a secure channel for communication with the service processes but establishes it using a MIX network (e.g. JAP [10]). By so doing, the seller would find it very difficult to trace the identity of the buyer using the buyer's Internet connection.

g) Dishonest parties masquerading as trusted parties: first, the reputation of the eCA is established (as for a regular CA); for example, the eCA could be subjected to inspection audits and other forms of testing to ensure that processes and responsibilities carried out are trustworthy. After the eCA is established to be trustworthy, it has the responsibility to make sure that all trusted support providers are indeed trustworthy, perhaps by using a similar series of inspections and testing as was done for it.

h) Trojan horse programs running in the buyer's computer could modify the buyer's privacy policy or redirect the buyer's PII disclosures to the attacker. However, this data is only in transit to/from the smart card and would be encrypted. Further, the user can regularly run diagnosis software that identifies and deletes the offending programs.

i) If the buyer loses his/her smart card either by accident or theft, the person who finds the smart card or the person who stole it could masquerade as the original owner and incur services at that owner's expense or could somehow gain access to the original owner's PII. To reduce the risk of this happening, as mentioned in a), the smart card requires a password for access and has a locking mechanism that locks out the attacker after a fixed number of attempts (e.g. 5) to try and guess the password. If the legitimate buyer were to forget this password, the eCA could reset it through a secure connection to the eCA's website.

2.5 Security Vulnerability Analysis

We affirm the security of our approach by analyzing some possible attacks to see if they have any chance of success.

- *Substitution attack* – the attacker replaces the privacy controller with a version that appears to function normally but allow the covert capture of the user's PII. *Chance of success: very low – since the smart card requires a password and has a locking mechanism as described in Section 2.4(a).*

- *Modification attack* – the attacker modifies the privacy controller in order to obtain copies of the user's PII. This includes malicious attempts to read the PII from the store of the privacy controller. *Chance of success: very low – the data is encrypted and the key is produced from the card access password as the seed. Attempts at guessing the password are limited by the smartcard's locking mechanism.*

- *Man-in-the-middle attack* – the attacker makes copies of the user's PII disclosures on their way to the recipients (e.g. trusted shipping company). *Chance of success: low – the PII is sent using a secure channel. Similar answer (i.e. use of a secure channel) for such an attack on the communication between the buyer and the eCA's web site.*

- *Support provider spoofing attack* – the attacker pretends to be the legitimate recipient of a disclosure involving PII and captures the buyer's PII. *Chance of success: very low – the fake recipient would fail authentication by the sending controller.*

- *eCA spoofing attack, including web site phishing* – the attacker pretends to be the eCA and programs the buyer's smart card to steal the buyer's PII for the attacker. *Chance of success: very low – the fake eCA would fail authentication.*

- Privacy policy attack – the attacker modifies the user's and provider's privacy policies to possibly direct PII disclosures to self (if allowed by the PSP) or to extend the retention time hoping that more time will allow a modification attack to succeed. Chance of success: very low – the privacy policies are encrypted while on route to the privacy controller. Further, both policies are securely stored at all their locations. See also Section 2.4(h).

- Inferred identity attack on the PSP – the attacker captures a user's non-PII by compromising the PSP; the attacker accumulates this data over a long period of time in the hope that by analyzing the data, some pattern will emerge that will identify the user. Chance of success: low – already discussed above in Section 2.4(e).
- Inferred identity attack on the SSP – the attacker captures a user's PII by compromising the SSP. Chance of success: low – depends on how well the SSP is protected from attack – since the provider is trusted, the eCA would have made sure that all appropriate safeguards were in place.
- Seller collusion attack to identify a buyer by linking pseudonyms – Chance of success: very low – a buyer's privacy controller automatically uses a different pseudonym with each seller.
- Support provider insider attack – the support provider becomes untrustworthy and compromises the user's anonymity. Chance of success: low – as mentioned in Section 2.4(g), the eCA has the responsibility to ensure that the support provider is trustworthy, not only at one time but all the time, perhaps by subjecting the support provider to regular and spontaneous inspection audits and testing.

The above brief analysis shows that our security measures are not fool proof against attacks, but probably provide enough of a deterrent to discourage most attacks.

2.6 Application Example

Consider an online pharmacy, E-Drugs, Inc. (fictitious name), that has subscribed to use the privacy protection services of Privacy Watch, Inc. (fictitious name), the eCA that has implemented our approach.

1. Alice, wishing to anonymously fill an electronic prescription, discovers by browsing PW's website that E-Drugs is available as a PW-subscribed seller.
2. (Omit this step if Alice has purchased from a PW seller before.) Alice registers with PW and is assigned a number of pseudonyms to be used as identification with sellers, e.g. a seller only knows Alice as "Patient21". She also receives a digital certificate from PW to be used for authentication purposes. Alice purchases a PW-issued smartcard from a local electronics outlet.
3. Alice connects her smart card to the USB port on her computer. After successful mutual authentication, she is connected to PW's web site via a secure channel.
4. (Omit this step if Alice has purchased from a PW seller before.) PW remotely programs Alice's smart card to be used as her privacy controller.
5. PW requests Alice to select a seller. After she selects E-Drugs, and enters her personal privacy policy on PW's web site (only if not previously entered for this seller), the privacy controller downloads Alice's privacy policy to the smart card. The controller is then connected to the service processes at E-Drugs automatically and anonymously through a secure channel and mix network. After successful mutual authentication, the controller downloads E-Drugs' privacy policy. After successfully transforming Alice's policy for PII redirections and

verifying that her privacy policy is compatible with E-Drugs' privacy policy, the privacy controller requests Alice's electronic prescription, shipping address, and credit card number.

6. Alice enters the requested information (disk location for the prescription) on her computer with the privacy controller making sure that the information corresponds with her privacy policy. The information is securely stored in the privacy controller. Upon request from E-Drugs' service processes, and after checking again with Alice's privacy policy, the controller discloses to the service processes details about the prescription (including the digital signature of the prescribing physician) but withholds Alice's name, address, and credit card number. Upon request from E-Drug's service processes, the controller sets up a secure channel to a trusted payment center (support provider) and authenticates the payment center before disclosing to the center Alice's credit card number. The trusted payment center maintains the patient's anonymity to the outside world by keeping the pseudonym-patient link secret (as do all trusted support providers). The trusted payment center was designated as trusted by PW beforehand and issued a digital certificate for authentication purposes. Similarly, the controller discloses Alice's name and address to a trusted shipping center that also keeps the pseudonym-patient link secret. Both the trusted payment center and the trusted shipping center use the pseudonym-patient link to link the order to the patient. If the patient tried a re-use attack to fill the prescription more than once, this would be detected by both these support providers through the pseudonym-patient link.

7. Alice receives her order the next day from the trusted shipping center.

3 Conclusions and Future Research

We have presented a novel approach to protect the privacy of buyers in buyer-seller e-commerce based on keeping control of the PII in the hands of the buyer, trusted support service providers, and an eCA acting as a trusted authority. In this approach, we chose to use a smart card for its portability, secure storage capability, and the fact that it needs to be connected to the Internet only for the duration of a service, reducing the risk of an Internet originated attack. Our approach may be characterized as distributing PII on a "need to know" basis and as a generalization of the use of trusted support providers such as Paypal [6] to protect privacy.

We believe our approach is very usable. The process of registering with the eCA is similar to the current way of registering with websites for a service or membership. The user only has to get the smart card once and can use it with all existing and new sellers that subscribe to the eCA. The user only has to plug the smart card in a USB port on his/her computer to begin the process of connecting to a service. Further, smart card use has been growing at a high rate, in part because the way they are used is similar to how millions of people use magstripe cards to access their bank accounts.

Some other advantages of our approach is that it is straightforward, employs existing technology, and would be fairly easy to set up. Another advantage is that the privacy controller automatically discloses private information according to the user's privacy policy. The extra costs of setup and operation for our approach could be recovered from increased sales due to buyers feeling more comfortable that their privacy is protected.

A possible issue with our approach is that the use of a single eCA is a point of vulnerability and represents a monopoly situation. A possible resolution might be the use of several eCAs where each eCA has its provider or seller following. The buyer can then choose which eCA he/she would like to use based on the providers or sellers available at each respective eCA web site.

In terms of how security is weakened or strengthened, the use of an eCA is probably comparable to the use of a CA for PKI (Public Key Infrastructure).

As part of future research, we would like to address any issues with our approach and develop improved algorithms for selective disclosure to reduce the risk of patterns in disclosed non-PII that can identify the user.

References

1. Shelfer, K.M., Procaccino, J.D.: Smart Card Evolution. Communications of the ACM, Vol. 45, No. 7 (2002) 84
2. Carr, M.R.: Smart card technology with case studies. Proceedings, 36th Annual International Carnahan Conference on Security Technology (2002) 158-159
3. W3C: A P3P Preference Exchange Language 1.0 (APPEL 1.0). Accessed April 22, 2004 at: http://www.w3.org/TR/P3P-preferences/
4. Yee, G., Korba, L.: Comparing and Matching Privacy Policies Using Community Consensus. Proceedings, 16th IRMA International Conference, San Diego, California (2005)
5. Yee, G., Korba, L.: Bilateral E-services Negotiation Under Uncertainty. Proceedings, The 2003 International Symposium on Applications and the Internet (SAINT2003), Orlando, Florida (2003)
6. Paypal. Accessed June 20, 2005 at: https://www.paypal.com/
7. Clarke, R.: Identification, Anonymity and Pseudonymity in Consumer Transactions: A Vital Systems Design and Public Policy Issue. Accessed October 3, 2005 at: http://www.anu.edu.au/people/Roger.Clarke/DV/AnonPsPol.html
8. Laudon, K.C.: Markets and Privacy. Communications of the ACM, Vol. 39, No. 9 (1996)
9. Yee, G., Korba, L.: Semi-Automatic Derivation and Use of Personal Privacy Policies in E-Business. International Journal of E-Business Research, Vol. 1, No. 1, 54-69. Idea Group Publishing (2005)
10. JAP. Accessed June 20, 2005 at: http://anon.inf.tu-dresden.de/desc/desc_anon_en.html

A General Certification Framework with Applications to Privacy-Enhancing Certificate Infrastructures

Jan Camenisch, Dieter Sommer, and Roger Zimmermann

IBM Research, Zurich Research Lab
Säumerstrasse 4, CH-8803 Rüschlikon, Switzerland
{jca, dso, zim}@zurich.ibm.com

Abstract. Interactions in electronic media require mutual trust to be established, preferably through the release of certified information. Disclosing certificates for provisioning the required information often leads to the disclosure of additional information not required for the purpose of the interaction. For instance, ordinary certificates unnecessarily reveal their binary representation.
We propose a certificate-based framework comprising protocol definitions and abstract interface specifications for controlled, that is well-specified, release of data. This includes controlled release during the certification of data and controlled release of certified data. The protocols are based on proofs of knowledge of certificates and relations over the attributes, ensuring that no side information but only the specified data are revealed. Furthermore, the protocols allow one to release certified data in plain or encrypted form and to prove general expressions over the data items. Our framework can be seen as a generalization of anonymous credential systems, group signature, traceable signature, and e-cash schemes. The framework encompasses a specification language that allows one to precisely specify what data to release and how to release them in the protocols. We outline how our framework can be implemented cryptographically. The key application of our framework is the user-controlled release of attributes. Leveraging ideas of public key infrastructures, a privacy PKI (pPKI) can be built on top of the framework. We consider our framework a central building block to achieve privacy on the Internet.

1 Introduction

In today's interactions in electronic media users are frequently required to release personally identifying information (PII). A basic principle fostered by consumer protection agencies and privacy advocates is the idea of data minimization stating that the amount of data being provided should be minimal for a given purpose. Another principle is that users should be in control of their data.

The digital world makes it easy for organizations to build extensive profiles of users based on the data they obtain in interactions. It also provides new ways of protecting the privacy of users by employing cryptography to limit the amount of data being released in an interaction following the data minization principle.

Today's infrastructures within electronic media have often not been designed to take privacy into consideration. Scalable privacy support within such infrastructures

Please use the following format when citing this chapter:

Author(s) [insert Last name, First-name initial(s)], 2006, in IFIP International Federation for Information Processing, Volume 201, Security and Privacy in Dynamic Environments, eds. Fischer-Hubner, S., Rannenberg, K., Yngstrom, L., Lindskog, S., (Boston: Springer), pp. [insert page numbers].

requires the availability of a privacy architecture which allows for integrating privacy principles into the infrastructures. Research efforts involving privacy architecures are currently ongoing, for example, within the European PRIME project [28]. A privacy architecture includes privacy-enhancing authorization mechanisms allowing decisions to be based on a requester's (certified) attributes rather than on her identity, and languages for requesting general (certified) statements from a party. It is likely that such privacy architectures will emerge within the next few years.

In this paper, we define a general framework for data minimization allowing for precise specifications of what certified data to release to whom in a transaction and sketch the required cryptographic mechanisms. The full paper [13] gives an application of the framework to build a privacy-enhanced PKI (pPKI).

Our framework allows a party to obtain certificates while the issuer does not necessarily learn all data items being certified, but the issuer knows—through a proof performed by the party—that the party has a certificate from a particular issuer on such a data item. It furthermore allows the party to prove properties over certified data without revealing any other information, even not the certificate itself. The proofs encompass proofs of polynomial relations over certified data items and the computation of commitments and encryptions of polynomials over certified data items. The proofs allow for logical conjunction and disjunction operators over predicates on data items, encryptions, and commitments. The framework includes protocol descriptions with API definitions for obtaining certificates and proving knowledge and properties of certificates while being able to control precisely what data to release and to whom. We present a specification language for specifying this release of data.

Related Work. The research area our framework is positioned in was pioneered by Chaum who defined the concepts of credential systems, see for example [16], group signature schemes [19], and electronic cash systems [17]. Our framework can be seen as a generalization of these systems, as well as anonymous attestation schemes [5], traceable signature schemes [25] and identity escrow schemes [26]. Indeed, our framework can be instantiated to obtain a generalized anonymous credential system, a group signature scheme, traceable signature scheme, or an e-cash scheme. The pseudonym system of Brands [4] also provides efficient techniques for proving relations among committed values, but his overall construction falls short of supporting multi-show unlinkability thus restricting its applicability.

A cryptographic framework for releasing certified data has been proposed by Bangerter et al. [1]. The framework provides an initial step towards a general framework as put forth in our paper. The basic idea of using signature protocols for obtaining and proving signatures remains the same, but our approach is more general with respect to several aspects. It provides much more powerful proof capabilities like the proof of disjunctions, more general predicates and more functionality with respect to verifiable encryption. Moreover, our framework is more concrete in that we provide a specification language and concrete protocol interfaces close to an API-level making it ready for implementations and integration into privacy architectures and infrastructures. The high level of abstraction of our specification language allows for an easy integration into privacy architectures. The implementation of our framework is readily employable for pseudonymous authentication.

Paper Outline. We first present our generalized framework for controlled data release in Section 2 including an interface specification for the protocols and the definition of a specification language and semantics for data release. Section 3 outlines the cryptographic instantiation of our framework. Section 4 concludes our work.

2 A General Certification Framework Supporting Controlled Release of Data

We define a general framework for the controlled release of certified data and controlled release of data for certification. Controlled release of certified data means that the releasing party can specify which information on data items of certificates to release and to whom. Controlled release of data for certification means that the issuer of a certificate learns only a specified subset of the data items being certified and for the remaining items only knows that particular parties have certified them for the certificate receiver.

Controlled release of certified data encompasses the release of (partial) information on the data items of certificates or polynomials over data items, either in clear or encrypted form. This involves computation of commitments and encryptions of certified data items or of multivariate polynomials.

Encryptions that contain a value that provably fulfills a multivariate polynomial relation between certified data items of multiple certificates, other commitments, and encryptions have a wide field of applications, such as conditional show of data, or escrow of values that provably fulfill some relation with respect to certified data items.

Our framework is based on Bangerter et al.'s framework [1], but offers more evolved functionality, in particular with respect to general proofs of conjunctions and disjunctions of predicates and a concrete specification language for specifying what information to release.

2.1 Cryptographic Building Blocks

The basic cryptographic building blocks of our framework are special signature schemes, commitment schemes, encryption schemes, and zero-knowledge proofs of knowledge.

Commitment Schemes. A *commitment scheme* allows a party to commit to a tuple $(x_1, \ldots, x_u)$ of (secret) values to another party. A commitment does not reveal any (computational) information on the tuple to the other party (hiding property) and prevents the committing party to change the values being committed to at a later stage (binding property). Either one of the properties can be information theoretic, but not both at the same time.

The *Commit* operation requires a public key PK and a type specifier. In many schemes a random group element r is created and returned as part of o_i.

$$(c_i, o_i) := Commit(x_{i,1}, \ldots, x_{i,l}, PK) \tag{1}$$

The object c_i contains the information to be sent to the other party, namely the cryptographic commitment, and the public key. The object o_i contains $x_1, \ldots, x_u$ and randomness r and is retained by the committing party. If the commitment is used in a later proof, o_i provides the secret information knowledge of which is proved and c_i provides the corresponding information for the verifying party.

Signature Schemes and Protocols. In our framework we make use of *signature protocols* for obtaining and proving knowledge of signatures on tuples of messages. Each message can either be known to the signer, he can know a commitment of it or have no information on it. Obtaining a signature is a protocol between the receiver of the signature and the issuer where the issuer learns only a subset of the messages to be signed. Proving knowledge of a signature on a tuple of messages is a protocol between a prover and a verifier where information on the messages m_i is revealed selectively, i.e., allowing for proving relations on commitments to the messages m_i. Theoretically, such protocols can be obtained for any signature scheme, but these constructions would not be practical due to the required computational effort.

Two signature schemes with practical protocols, the SRSA-CL scheme [7] and the BL-CL scheme [8] are schemes that we use within our framework. These schemes allow proofs to be performed on the messages m_i being signed. The schemes particularly allow that a signature be issued on messages that are not known to the issuer, but to which the issuer only knows a commitment. These schemes fit ideally into our framework as they allow the efficient discrete logarithm-based proofs of knowledge and relations between discrete logarithms of different certificates, commitments, and encryptions. For reasons of generality, schemes like RSA [29] fit into the framework as well, but without any of the privacy benefits of the above schemes.

Verifiable Encryption. Our framework makes use of *encryption schemes* to encrypt values within the protocol for proving knowledge of certificates. The encryption gets a tuple of messages $(m_1, \ldots, m_k)$, a label L, and a public key PKE as input and outputs the encryption of the tuple.

The decryption algorithm requires a ciphertext, a label L, and a decryption key SKE as input and outputs a tuple of messages $(m_1, \ldots, m_k)$. The label L must be the same one as used for the encryption, it encodes a condition under which decryption may be performed and is cryptographically bound to the ciphertext. The key SKE is private to a party trustworthy for a particular application. The party performs a decryption only in case the condition that is presented is fulfilled.

Within the certificate proof protocol properties over the messages m_i of an encryption that has been computed can be proved, in particular polynomial relations to data items of certificates, commitments, and other encryptions.

The verifiable encryption schemes of Camenisch and Damgård [6] and of Camenisch and Shoup [11] are applicable to our framework. The latter are particularly suitable as they integrate smoothly into the discrete logarithm-based zero-knowledge proof protocols.

Zero-knowledge Proofs of Knowledge. In a *zero-knowledge proof* of knowledge a prover convinces a verifier that she knows a witness w such that a predicate P is fulfilled without releasing any further information on w. We employ *zero-knowledge proofs* for obtaining signatures and for proving knowledge of signatures. Within proof protocols, zero-knowledge proofs are used for proving knowledge of certificates, and proving relations between data items of certificates, commitments, and encryptions.

Concepts. A *certificate* on a tuple $(d_1, \ldots, d_k)$ of data items is a tuple $(d_1, \ldots, d_k, \sigma)$, where σ is a signature on the data items. A certificate is obtained via an instance of the CertificateIssuance protocol. Knowledge of a certificate can be proved via the CertificateProof protocol. A certificate as defined in our framework allows one to treat data items individually in case the advanced signature protocols are being employed.

A *certificate image* or *image* is the result of a proof protocol involving one or multiple certificates. An image contains the assertion over the certificates that has been proved. We note that the image does—if our advanced signature protocols are used—not contain the signature of the issuer, but a transcript of a proof of knowledge of the signature performed by the owner. A proof can be made non-interactive by applying the Fiat-Shamir heuristics. This allows for a message to be signed. The signer is identified only by the properties being shown by the proof.

During the issuing protocol of a certificate, the signature on the data items is computed by the issuer without all data items being known to the issuer in clear and sent to the receiver. The proof protocol of a certificate proves to the verifier the prover's knowledge of a signature on data items while selectively revealing them or proving statements about them, and making commitments and encryptions of polynomials over data items. Multi-show unlinkability follows immediately from the fact the a certificate is not disclosed, but knowledge of it is proved using the appropriate cryptographic mechanisms.

We note that for the protocols defined below, certificates, commitments, and encryptions are defined on tuples of data items rather than on single items.

2.2 Certificate Issuance Protocol

The issuance of a certificate is a protocol CertificateIssuance between a receiver and an issuer. The outcome for the receiver is a certificate for the data items $d_1, \ldots, d_k$ of which the issuer only learns a subset. A proof involving the certificate can later be done with respect to the issuer's public key for signature verification, PKS_I.

A data item to be signed can either be known to the issuer in plaintext form, be known as a commitment to the data item, the data item can be jointly randomly generated, or it can be unknown to the issuer, i.e., known to the receiver only.

Known data items are used for all items that are contributed by the issuer or that the issuer has to know from a policy point of view. Committed data items are useful for the case where the receiver has proved before that the committed value is a particular data item appearing in another certificate and where this data item is to be included into the new certificate without the issuer learning it. An example for this is when the name and other personal data from a passport certificate should be included into the certificate to be issued. Jointly randomly generated data items are useful for limited-show certificates such as e-coins. Data items unknown to the issuer can be used to realize e-coins, as well.

During the execution of the protocol, the data items to be jointly randomly generated are computed and the issuer computes a value being (almost) a signature on the data items $d_1, \ldots, d_k$ and sends it to the receiver. The receiver obtains the final signature by tweaking the received signature by an easy computation with a value generated earlier in the protocol.

Protocol Interface Specification. The protocol CertificateIssuance for issuing a certificate is a protocol between a receiver and an issuer. Common input is presented to both parties and each party additionally receives private input. Both parties obtain commitments as output, the receiver in addition gets opening information to the commitments and the newly issued certificate as output. The certificate the receiver obtains is comprised of a tuple $(d_1, \ldots, d_k, \sigma)$ of data items d_i and the signature σ on the data items. The way the signature has been obtained for each individual data item is not reflected in the certificate.

Let $d_1, \ldots, d_k$ be the data items on which to obtain a certificate. Some of the items may be unknown as of the start of the protocol. Let $D = \{1, \ldots, k\}$ be the set of indices for the data items. Let the sets D_{known}, $D_{\mathrm{committed}}$, D_{random}, and D_{unknown} partition D. Thus, $D = D_{\mathrm{known}} \cup D_{\mathrm{committed}} \cup D_{\mathrm{random}} \cup D_{\mathrm{unknown}}$ and the subsets are mutually disjoint. A data item d_i with $i \in D_{\mathrm{known}}$ is known to both parties, a data item d_i with $i \in D_{\mathrm{committed}}$ is known by the receiver only, the issuer has a commitment thereof. A d_i with $i \in D_{\mathrm{random}}$ is generated within the protocol, and a d_i with $i \in D_{\mathrm{unknown}}$ is known by the receiver, the issuer has no data regarding it. The interface of the protocol is specified as follows:

CertificateIssuance

Common input	$\{d_i : i \in D_{\mathrm{known}}\}, \{c_i : i \in D_{\mathrm{committed}} \cup D_{\mathrm{random}}\}, PKS_I, \chi$
Receiver private input	$\{o_i : i \in D_{\mathrm{committed}} \cup D_{\mathrm{random}}\}, \{d_i : i \in D_{\mathrm{unknown}}\}$
Issuer private input	SKS_I
Receiver output	$\{c_i, o_i : i \in D_{\mathrm{random}}\}, cert$
Issuer output	$\{c_i : i \in D_{\mathrm{random}}\}$

The commitments and openings $\{c_i, o_i : i \in D_{\mathrm{random}}\}$ are uninstantiated when presented as protocol input and are generated during the protocol execution. The o_is contain the randomly generated data items for retrieval by the receiver and the c_is the corresponding commitments.

Any commitment c_i contains—regardless of its instantiation state—information on the commitment public key, the algorithm, and the number of values in the tuple it will be a commitment of. After the protocol execution, the previously uninstantiated commitments and corresponding openings have been generated and the commitments can be retrieved by both parties, the opening information, however, on the receiver side only.

Issuance Specification Language. The issue specification χ passed in both party's inputs is expressed using a simple language specifying for each data item how it is contributed to the protocol and what information the issuer learns about it. This is defined by a triple for each data item: The first element is the index of the data item being specified where $cert[i]$ refers to d_i of the certificate, the second element is a specifier of the issuance mode for the item being either of known, committed, random, or unknown. The last element is—depending on the second element—either a reference d_i to a data item of the input, an index $c_i[j]$ to an instantiated commitment, an index to an uninstantiated commitment, or a reference d_i to a data item depending on whether the second element specifies known, commitment, random, or unknown, respectively.

$$\chi = \{(cert[1], \mathrm{known}, d_1), (cert[2], \mathrm{committed}, c_1[1]), \\ (cert[3], \mathrm{random}, c_2[1]), (cert[4], \mathrm{unknown}, d_2)\} \tag{2}$$

The specification in Example (2) is for issuing a certificate on $(d_1, \ldots, d_4)$ where $D_{known} = \{1\}$, $D_{committed} = \{2\}$, $D_{random} = \{3\}$, and $D_{unknown} = \{4\}$. After successful protocol execution, $o_3[1]$ contains the randomly generated data item d_3 and $c_3[1]$ contains a commitment of d_3.

2.3   Certificate Proof protocol

The protocol CertificateProof is a protocol between a prover and a verifier that allows the prover to prove to the verifier knowledge of valid certificates and general statements over the data items of multiple certificates, commitments, and encryptions. It further allows one to compute commitments and encryptions specified through multivariate polynomials over data items, encryptions, and commitments.

The underlying key principle is that certificates are not sent, but statements regarding them are proved using zero-knowledge proofs of knowledge such that no more information than what is specified is revealed. From the applied cryptographic mechanisms it follows immediately that multiple proofs over the same certificate are mutually unlinkable and unlinkable to the CertificateIssuance protocol instance it was issued in.

Protocol Interface Specification. The common inputs to the prover and verifier are the public keys for signature verification $PKS_{I_1}, \ldots, PKS_{I_k}$, (possibly uninstantiated) commitments $c_1, \ldots, c_u$, and (possibly uninstantiated) encryptions $e_1, \ldots, e_v$. Let the sets $\hat{C} \subseteq C = \{1 \ldots, u\}$ and $\hat{E} \subseteq E = \{1, \ldots, v\}$ contain the indices of uninstantiated commitments and uninstantiated encryptions, respectively. The prover additionally gets as input a list of certificates $cert_1, \ldots, cert_k$ having been obtained from issuers $I_1, \ldots, I_k$, (uninstantiated) opening information $o_1, \ldots, o_u$ corresponding to the commitments, and a prover-side proof specification ξ_P. The verifier gets a verifier-side proof specification ξ_V as input.

The verifier's output are the commitments $\{c_i : i \in \hat{C}\}$ and encryptions $\{e_i : i \in \hat{E}\}$ having been computed during the protocol execution and a certificate image Π containing the statement conveyed through the proof together with the proof transcript. The prover's output are the commitments and openings $\{c_i, o_i : i \in \hat{C}\}$ and the encryptions and corresponding plaintexts $\{e_i, p_i : i \in \hat{E}\}$.

CertificateProof	
Common input	$PKS_{I_1}, \ldots, PKS_{I_k}, c_1, \ldots, c_u, e_1, \ldots, e_v$
Prover private input	$cert_1, \ldots, cert_k, o_1, \ldots, o_u, p_1, \ldots, p_v, \xi_P$
Verifier private input	ξ_V
Prover output	$\{c_i, o_i : i \in \hat{C}\}, \{e_i, p_i : i \in \hat{E}\}$
Verifier output	$\{c_i : i \in \hat{C}\}, \{e_i : i \in \hat{E}\}, \Pi$

Commitments. The set $C = \{1, \ldots, u\}$ defines the indices i of the commitments and openings: $\{c_i, o_i : i \in C\}$. The subset of the commitments and corresponding openings $\{c_i, o_i : i \in \hat{C} \subseteq C\}$ are uninstantiated, i.e., the commitment contains only information on the commitment public key and further parameters, but not yet a cryptographic commitment and the openings contain not yet the opening information for the commitments. The objects $\{c_i, o_i : i \in C \setminus \hat{C}\}$ are instantiated commitments and openings.

Uninstantiated commitments in the proof protocol allow one to create commitments during the protocol execution that can later be used to issue a signature on the value being committed to or to use it within other proofs. An application example for this is if an organization issues a certificate that shall contain the user's identity from another certificate. To achieve this, the other certificate is first proved and the identity data item is being committed to. Then the new certificate is issued using that commitment and other data items.

Encryptions. Analogously, the set $E = \{1, \ldots, v\}$ defines the indices for the encryptions e_i and corresponding plaintexts p_i. The subset $\hat{E} \subseteq E$ defines again the set of uninstantiated encryptions and plaintexts. An uninstantiated encryption contains an algorithm identifier, a label L, and an encryption public key PKE_T of a party T, and the number of elements in the plaintext tuple of the encryption. The label L defines a condition under which party T will perform a decryption. The same label that has been used for encryption and a private key SKE_T known to T has to be passed to the decryption algorithm in order for the algorithm to decrypt correctly. Considering these properties, the encryptions realize a conditional show of the underlying values under condition L.

Uninstantiated encryptions will be computed during the protocol execution. After the protocol has terminated, the encryptions and corresponding plaintexts can be retrieved, plaintexts only by the prover.

Proof Specification. The proof specification defines what statement to prove over the list of certificates, commitments, and encryptions, thereby also defining what values to commit to and what values to encrypt. The proof specification ξ_P for the prover and ξ_V for the verifier are very similar, the only difference being that the prover's specification in addition contains a language element to specify what parts of a disjunction to prove. The specification language will be further elaborated on below.

Specification Language. A proof specification ξ_P or ξ_V is a logical formula in propositional logics without negation over a class of predicates defined below.

Variables. The predicates in a formula refer to variables to reference data items, certificates, committed values, and encrypted values of the input. We stress that a variable always references the secret input of the prover and is used for expressing a statement over this secret input. Secret input are certificates, commitment opening information, and plaintexts to encryptions. The verifier only has corresponding data objects that do not allow to infer the secrets. Such objects are commitments or encryptions.

Referenced commitments and encryptions and their corresponding opening and plaintext objects can be either uninstantiated or instantiated. Data items are references to the (secret) data items of certificates expressed with variables of the form $cert_i[j]$ where i is the index of the certificate the data item is contained in and j is the index within the data items of the certificate. This notation allows to have multiple certificates of the same type, e.g. bank statements being used. A variable $c_i[j]$ refers to the j-th value of the tuple of values committed to with commitment i. A variable $e_i[j]$ refers to the j-th plaintext value corresponding to the tuple of values being the plaintext for the i-th encrypted tuple. If a c or e refers to an uninstantiated instance, restrictions are imposed on the usage of the variable.

Predicates. A predicate is composed of either a term or a comparison operator and two terms as arguments. A term is either an atom or an expression. An atom is either a variable or a constant. An expression is either an arithmetic operator applied to expressions, or an atom. Parantheses can be used to override standard precedence.

Multivariate polynomial arithmetic relations are defined over an interval in $\mathbb{Z}$, e.g. $[-2^{256} + 1; 2^{256} - 1]$, with operators being "+" and "·". The exponentiation operator is expressed as usual.[1] The usual semantics applies for all operators over the integers. The relational operator in a predicate can be any of $=$, $\neq$, $>$, $<$, $\geq$, or $\leq$ with their usual semantics in the integers. All results of expressions must be within the integer interval defined through the system parameters.

$$cert_1 \qquad (3)$$

$$cert_1[1] \qquad (4)$$

$$cert_1[1] \geq c_1[2] \tag{5}$$

$$10 \cdot cert_1[1] + 20 \cdot cert_2[1]^4 = enc_1[1] + 40 \tag{6}$$

Example (3) expresses knowledge of the signature of certificate $cert_1$. Example (3) is equivalent to Example (4). Example (4) states knowledge of a signature of the data item d_1 of $cert_1$ without any further statement. It implies knowledge of the certificate. In Example (5) a greater-than-or-equal relation is stated between the data item d_1 in $cert_1$ and the second element of the tuple committed to with c_1. Example (6) states a more general polynomial relation.

Specification Formula. The specification formula is a formula in propositional logics without negation and with predicates as defined above. Thus the logical operators are the conjunction ($\wedge$) and disjunction ($\vee$) operators. The usual precedence and semantics of the operators applies. Parantheses can be applied in their usual semantics for changing precedence. It is conceivable that an XML-based corresponding prefix notation instead of the infix notation used here be used in practice due to easier processing.

We introduce the $\langle \rangle$ language element to allow a prover to specify what predicates of a formula to fulfill with secrets provided as input. This is required as a logical formula can allow that multiple different clauses in its disjunctive normal form (DNF) be fulfillable by the certificates provided as input, for example both predicates in the formula $cert_1[1] = 10 \vee cert_1[2] = 20$ can be fulfilled with one certificate $cert_1$ with appropriate data items. One pair of $\langle \rangle$ elements can span multiple $\wedge$-connected predicates. When constructing the DNF of a formula, the $\langle \rangle$-annotation propagates to the DNF representation with the predicates it spans. It is important for the semantics of instantiation of commitments and encryptions that in exactly one clause of the DNF all predicates have a $\langle \rangle$ annotation. The $\langle \rangle$ notation is, of course, only applied to the prover's specification. The remainder of the proof specification is equal for the prover and verifier in the protocol.

$$\langle cert_1[1] > 21 \rangle \vee cert_2[1] \tag{7}$$

Example (7) specifies that the certified data item $cert_1[1]$ is greater than 21 or that the prover knows a signature on data item $cert_2[1]$. It evaluates to true if either of the predicates is fulfilled. The $\langle \rangle$ notation defines that the prover provides $cert_1$ as input.

---

[1] Processing of exponents requires additional runtime linear in the length of an efficiently computable addition chain for the exponent.

Uninstantiated Variables. Instantiated variables (encryptions and commitments) are instantiated through the presented certificates, commitments, and encryptions. Uninstantiated commitments are instantiated as a first step in the protocol and uninstantiated encryptions are computed. Both are specified by the ⟨ ⟩-annotated predicates they appear in when considering the DNF of the formula. Predicates annotated with ⟨ ⟩ must be consistent to each other in defining variables' values. Predicates not within ⟨ ⟩ can make different statements about the variables. When a commitment or encryption is not defined by ⟨ ⟩ predicates, it is initialized with a random value. After the instantiation phase all committed and encrypted values are fixed.

The actual instantiation of the variable and its underlying commitment or encryption is governed by the prover by the ⟨ ⟩ language element. Thus one can think of it being correctly instantiated when referring to it in predicates.

$$c_1[1] = cert_1[1] + cert_2[1]^2 \tag{8}$$

$$cert_1[1] + cert_1[2] = cert_1[3] + c_1[1] \tag{9}$$

$$(cert_1[1] > 10 \wedge e_1[1] = cert_1[1]) \vee \langle(cert_1[1] \leqslant 10 \wedge e_1[1] = cert_1[2])\rangle \tag{10}$$

$$\langle(cert_1[1] = 10)\rangle \vee (cert_1[1] = 20 \wedge e_1[1] = cert_1[2]) \tag{11}$$

The uninstantiated variable $c_1[1]$ gets assigned $cert_1[1] + cert_2[1]^2$ in example (8). In example (9), the uninstantiated variable $c_1[1]$ gets assigned $cert_1[1] + cert_1[2] - cert_1[3]$. In Example (10) above, $e_1[1]$ is instantiated with $cert_1[2]$. In Example (11) $e_1[1]$ is instantiated with a random number.

Semantics of the Specification. The semantics of propositional logics without negation, like that of the logical operators, and of the defined class of predicates translates directly into the semantics of a specification formula. The semantics of the variables is defined by using the set of the prover's certificates and the provided encryptions and commitments as the universe to interpret the formula.

The entailment semantics (formal semantics) of a specification formula is that of propositional logics without negation with the class of predicates as defined. This formal semantics is, for example, required for automated reasoning over a valid proof specification. An application of this is computing an access decision.

Certificate Images. Depending on the way the proof is performed cryptographically, the certificate image can be either convincing to third parties or does not contain any information on whether the proof was actually executed. We denote the further a *transferable image* and the latter a *non-transferable* image. The transferable image is based on a non-interactive proof of knowledge [23] and has much the same properties as a conventional certificate, i.e., it is a statement about its owner endorsed by an issuing party. In fact, a transferable image can be endorsed by multiple parties in case certificates of different issuers were involved in the proof. This concept of a certificate containing conjunctions and disjunctions of predicates over data items of different issuers is a new concept. It is interesting to note that this certificate is created within a proof protocol which did not involve any issuers and nevertheless is a statement endorsed by all these issuers. Thus, a transferable certificate image of a certificate in our framework much resembles the classical idea of a certificate. Additionally, a message can be signed with a transferable image, the signer being identified through the proved statement only. This allows new applications of certifying, for example, public keys.

Example for Using our Framework. When considering current directions of legislation towards preventing unconditional anonymity, use cases based on conditional anonymity become increasingly important. Consider, for example, a service provider being required to provide—under well-defined conditions such as a court order—an identity-equivalent item of the service requester for each transaction. Assume existence of a US authority and a European Union authority each providing a public key for encryption. Consider furthermore that users have electronic passport certificates issued either by the US or the European Union. Let the certificate $cert_1$ in the example be a US passport, $cert_2$ a European Union passport. Assume a user has only a US passport. Let the data item $d_1[1]$ be the passport number in the passports which, if known to the respective authority, easily allows to find the associated holder.

$$\langle(e_1[1] = cert_1[1] \wedge e_1[2] = 1 \wedge e_2[2] = 0)\rangle\vee$$
$$(e_2[1] = cert_2[1] \wedge e_2[2] = 1 \wedge e_1[2] = 0) \quad (12)$$

Example 12 states either of the following: *i)* The prover has a United States passport and its serial number is encrypted in $e_1[1]$, the constant 1 is encrypted in $e_1[2]$ indicating that e_1 is the encryption containing a valid passport number. For encryption the public key of the US authority and an appropriate L_{US} (both provided in the input) is used. Additionally, a 0 is encrypted in $e_2[2]$ indicating that e_2 contains no passport number. For the latter, the EU public key and EU condition L_{EU} is used. No statement is made regarding $e_2[1]$. *ii)* The user has a European Union passport and this passport's serial number's encryption is $e_2[1]$ and the constant 1 is encrypted in $e_2[2]$ indicating that e_2 contains the user's passport number. This is done using the encryption key of the EU agency and a condition L_{EU}. A 0 is encrypted under the US key and condition in $e_1[2]$. No statement is made regarding $e_1[1]$.

   By using this proof of a disjunction, no information on which passport the user has is conveyed. Only in the rare case when the encryptions have to be decrypted by the respective government agency under the defined condition, will it also be clear what country the user is a citizen of.

3   Cryptographic implementation

In the common parameters model we build upon several known protocols for proving statements about discrete logarithms, such as (1) proof of knowledge of a discrete logarithm modulo a prime [30] or a composite [24, 22], (2) proof of knowledge of equality of representation modulo two (possibly different) prime [18] or composite [10] moduli, (3) proof that a commitment opens to the product of two other committed values [9, 14, 3], (4) proof that a committed value lies in a given integer interval [15, 9, 2], and also (5) proof of the disjunction or conjunction of any two of the previous [20].

   That is, we can use these protocol to efficiently prove the statements we defined among messages that are (1) committed using the Pedersen [27] or Damgard-Fujisaki commitment schemes [22], (2) encrypted using the Camenisch-Shoup encryption scheme, or (3) signed using the Camenisch-Lysyanskaya signature schemes [7, 8] without revealing the messages themselves. For obtaining concurrent zero-knowledge proofs, Damgård's construction [21] is applied. Non-interactive zero-knowledge proofs are obtained by using the Fiat-Shamir heuristic [23]. The latter in addition allows one to create a group signature scheme of the protocol for proving certificates. The detailed protocol specifications are to appear in a research report [12].

4   Conclusion

We defined a general certificate framework for obtaining certificates and (partially) releasing certified data either in plain or encrypted form. In particular, our framework is a step to realize proactive privacy. The framework includes cryptographic primitives for realizing the functionality, definition of protocol interfaces for the CertificateIssuance and CertificateProof protocols, and a powerful specification language with using semantics of propositional logics that allows a prover to precisely specify what data to release in a transaction. We briefly outline our implementation efforts. In the full paper [13] we explain how to apply our framework to define privacy extensions to the current Internet certificate infrastructure. Our contributions can pave the way to deploying long-needed privacy technology within communication networks such as the Internet.

Acknowledgements
Part of the work reported in this paper is supported by the European Commission by the IST Project PRIME. The PRIME project receives research funding from the European Community's Sixth Framework Programme and the Swiss Federal Office for Education and Science.

References

1. Bangerter, E., Camenisch, J., and Lysyanskaya, A. A cryptographic framework for the controlled release of certified data. In *Twelfth International Workshop on Security Protocols 2004* (2004), LNCS, Springer Verlag.
2. Boudot, F. Efficient proofs that a committed number lies in an interval. In *EUROCRYPT 2000*, vol. 1807 of *LNCS*, Springer Verlag, pp. 431–444.
3. Brands, S. Rapid demonstration of linear relations connected by boolean operators. In *EUROCRYPT '97* (1997), vol. 1233 of *LNCS*, Springer Verlag, pp. 318–333.
4. Brands, S. *Rethinking Public Key Infrastructure and Digital Certificates— Building in Privacy*. PhD thesis, Eindhoven Institute of Technology, Eindhoven, The Netherlands, 1999.
5. Brickell, E., Camenisch, J., and Chen, L. Direct anonymous attestation. In *ACM CCS '04*, ACM Press, pp. 132–145.
6. Camenisch, J., and Damgård, I. Verifiable encryption, group encryption, and their applications to group signatures and signature sharing schemes. In *ASIACRYPT 2000*, vol. 1976 of *LNCS*, Springer Verlag, pp. 331–345.
7. Camenisch, J., and Lysyanskaya, A. A signature scheme with efficient protocols. In *Third Conference on Security in Communication Networks* (2002), vol. 2576 of *LNCS*, Springer Verlag, pp. 274–295.
8. Camenisch, J., and Lysyanskaya, A. Signature schemes and anonymous credentials from bilinear maps. In *CRYPTO 2004*, Springer Verlag.

9. Camenisch, J., and Michels, M. Proving in zero-knowledge that a number n is the product of two safe primes. In *EUROCRYPT '99*, vol. 1592 of *LNCS*, Springer Verlag, pp. 107–122.
10. Camenisch, J., and Michels, M. Separability and efficiency for generic group signature schemes. In *CRYPTO '99* (1999), vol. 1666 of *LNCS*, Springer Verlag, pp. 413–430.
11. Camenisch, J., and Shoup, V. Practical verifiable encryption and decryption of discrete logarithms. In *CRYPTO 2003*, LNCS.
12. Camenisch, J., and Sommer, D. Tech. Rep. Research Report RZ 3646, IBM Zurich Research Laboratory, 2006.
13. Camenisch, J., Sommer, D., and Zimmermann, R. A general certification framework with applications to privacy-enhancing certificate infrastructures. Tech. Rep. 3629, IBM Zurich Research Laboratory, November 2005.
14. Camenisch, J. L. *Group Signature Schemes and Payment Systems Based on the Discrete Logarithm Problem*. PhD thesis, ETH Zürich, 1998. Diss. ETH No. 12520, Hartung Gorre Verlag, Konstanz.
15. Chan, A., Frankel, Y., and Tsiounis, Y. Easy come – easy go divisible cash. In *EUROCRYPT '98* (1998), vol. 1403 of *LNCS*, Springer Verlag, pp. 561–575.
16. Chaum, D. Untraceable electronic mail, return addresses, and digital pseudonyms. *Communications of the ACM 24*, 2 (Feb. 1981), 84–88.
17. Chaum, D. Blind signature systems. In *CRYPTO '83*, Plenum Press, p. 153.
18. Chaum, D., and Pedersen, T. P. Wallet databases with observers. In *CRYPTO '92*, vol. 740 of *LNCS*, Springer-Verlag, pp. 89–105.
19. Chaum, D., and van Heyst, E. Group signatures. In *EUROCRYPT '91* (1991), vol. 547 of *LNCS*, Springer-Verlag, pp. 257–265.
20. Cramer, R., Damgård, I., and Schoenmakers, B. Proofs of partial knowledge and simplified design of witness hiding protocols. In *CRYPTO '94* (1994), vol. 839 of *LNCS*, Springer Verlag, pp. 174–187.
21. Damgård, I. Efficient concurrent zero-knowledge in the auxiliary string model. In *EUROCRYPT 2000*, vol. 1807 of *LNCS*, Springer Verlag, pp. 431–444.
22. Damgård, I., and Fujisaki, E. An integer commitment scheme based on groups with hidden order. In *ASIACRYPT 2002*, vol. 2501 of *LNCS*, Springer.
23. Fiat, A., and Shamir, A. How to prove yourself: Practical solutions to identification and signature problems. In *CRYPTO '86*, vol. 263 of *LNCS*, Springer Verlag, pp. 186–194.
24. Fujisaki, E., and Okamoto, T. Statistical zero knowledge protocols to prove modular polynomial relations. In *CRYPTO '97*, vol. 1294 of *LNCS*, Springer Verlag, pp. 16–30.
25. Kiayias, A., Tsiounis, Y., and Yung, M. Traceable signatures. In *EUROCRYPT*, vol. 3027 of *LNCS*, Springer, pp. 571–589.
26. Kilian, J., and Petrank, E. Identity escrow. Theory of Cryptography Library, Record Nr. 97-11, http://theory.lcs.mit.edu/~tcryptol, Aug. 1997.
27. Pedersen, T. P. Non-interactive and information-theoretic secure verifiable secret sharing. In *CRYPTO '91*, vol. 576 of *LNCS*, Springer Verlag, pp. 129–140.
28. PRIME project. www.prime-project.eu.org.
29. Rivest, R., Shamir, A., and Adleman, L. A method for obtaining digital signatures and public-key cryptosystems. *Communications of the ACM 21*, 2 (Feb. 1978), 120–126.
30. Schnorr, C. P. Efficient signature generation for smart cards. *Journal of Cryptology 4*, 3 (1991), 239–252.

Authenticated Query Flooding in Sensor Networks

Zinaida Benenson[1], Felix C. Freiling[2], Ernest Hammerschmidt[1]
Stefan Lucks[2], and Lexi Pimenidis[1]

[1] Department of Computer Science, RWTH Aachen University, Germany
{zina,ernest,lexi}@i4.informatik.rwth-aachen.de
[2] Department of Computer Science, University of Mannheim, Germany
{freiling, lucks}@uni-mannheim.de

Abstract. We propose a novel mechanism for authentication of queries in a sensor network in case these queries are flooded. In our protocol, the base station appends an authenticator to every query, such that each sensor can verify with certain probability that the query is sent by the base station. Implicit cooperation between sensor nodes during the flooding process ensures that legitimate queries propagate quickly in the network, whereas the propagation of illegitimate queries is limited to only a small part of the network.

1 Introduction

Wireless sensor networks consist of a large amount of sensor nodes, which are small low-cost wireless computing devices equipped with different sensors. They measure and collect environmental data. Access to these data is organized via a special gateway, called base station, which sends queries into the sensor network and gives the required sensor data to the users.

According to some paradigms for organizing sensor networks, such as Directed Diffusion [11] and TinyDB [14], the base station floods the sensor network with the query, as identifiers and locations of sensor nodes which are able to answer a particular query are not known to the base station beforehand. An example of such a query is "which sensor nodes measure temperature above θ grad?".

As data gathered by the sensor network may be valuable or critical, it should be protected from the unauthorized access. In particular, only the base station should be allowed to send queries. In this work, we consider how the base station can authenticate its queries, such that only legitimate queries are answered by the sensor nodes.

Our idea is based on the fact that in general, before the query reaches the nodes which are able to answer it, it has to be flooded through some significant part of the network. Thus, if some mechanism allows the sensor nodes to verify the legitimacy of the query probabilistically, illegitimate queries will be dropped before they get deeply into the network and reach their target nodes.

We developed a probabilistic protocol which restricts propagation of fake queries to a logarithmic part of the network. Some sensor nodes in our protocol may fail to recognize a fake query. This does not matter much, however, as long as their number is "very small". We think, logarithmic part of the network qualifies for the term "very small", considering that sensor networks may consist of thousands and hundred thousands of nodes.

Please use the following format when citing this chapter:
Author(s) [insert Last name, First-name initial(s)], 2006, in IFIP International Federation for Information Processing, Volume 201, Security and Privacy in Dynamic Environments, eds. Fischer-Hubner, S., Rannenberg, K., Yngstrom, L., Lindskog, S., (Boston: Springer), pp. [insert page numbers].

Roadmap We review related work in Section 2. We define Authenticated Query Flooding (AQF) in Section 3, and present our basic protocol AQF-pass, accompanied by theoretical analysis and simulation results, in Section 4. In Section 5, we discuss possible improvements to the basic protocol, and overview our ongoing and future work.

2   Related Work

One possibility for an entity to authenticate its messages to multiple receivers is *authenticated multicast* (or *broadcast*). The receivers can verify the origin of the message using some attached authentication information, called *authenticator*. However, no receiver can generate the authenticator, and therefore, cannot impersonate the sender.

Some approaches to authenticated broadcast in sensor networks exist in the literature. In SPINS [18], authenticated streaming multicast μTESLA is realized using one-way hash chains, time synchronization, and symmetric keys shared by the base station with each sensor in the network. μTESLA is a very efficient protocol. Its security depends on the security of the underlying time synchronization mechanism. However, devising a protocol which globally synchronizes time in a large sensor network seems to be a difficult problem [7].

Relatively inexpensive digital signatures can also be used for authenticated flooding (see, e.g., [20]), assuming that each sensor node is preloaded with the public key of some certification authority. However, these signatures are still very expensive considering the limited resources of sensor nodes.

Our protocol uses only symmetric cryptography. The protocol is based on the ingenious protocol by Canetti et al. [3], but it has a much better performance, as our protocol relies on the implicit cooperation between the sensor nodes which occurs when the authenticated query is flooded into the network.

3   System Model

Sensor Network Architecture Sensor network is spread over a large geographic area and consists of homogeneous sensor nodes which are similar to Telos sensor nodes [16] in construction and performance. They may have 8 or 16 bit microcontroller, with the amount of RAM varying between 2 kB and 10 kB and flash memory ranging from 48 kB to 128 kB. The speed of radio communications is in the order of 100 kbps.

There is also a base station in the network which is a laptop class device. The base station is trusted by sensor nodes. It can flood queries into the sensor network. The queries sent by a base station are called *legitimate queries*.

Adversary Model The adversary is an illegitimate entity interested in the data produced by the sensor network. The goal of the adversary is to post *arbitrary* queries to the sensor network, just like the base station can do. The queries sent by the adversary are called *illegitimate* (or *fake*) *queries*.

The adversary can capture some sensor nodes. Capturing means gaining information from a sensor node through direct physical access. In this case, we assume that the adversary knows the cryptographic keys of the captured nodes. As discovered in [1], node capturing requires non-negligible amount of time and resources. Therefore, we assume that the adversary can capture only a small amount of sensor nodes, in order of tens, but certainly not of hundreds.

Definition of Authenticated Query Flooding Let WSN be a sensor network. After receiving a query, each sensor node *decides* whether the query comes from the base station. If its decision is positive, we say that the sensor *accepts* the query. Consider an arbitrary query q. The WSN design satisfies *authenticated query flooding (AQF)* if it satisfies the following properties:

- (Safety) If a sensor s in WSN accepts the query q as a legitimate query, then q is a legitimate query, e.g., q was originated by the base station.
- (Liveness) Any legitimate query q will be received by all sensors in WSN.

4 Basic Authenticated Query Flooding: AQF-pass

We now describe our basic protocol for authenticated query flooding, called AQF-pass. This protocol uses the *pass* strategy which is explained below in the protocol description. In a nutshell, if the sensor cannot decide whether the query is legitimate or not, it *passes* it to its neighbors. In Section 5 we discuss other possible strategies for this case.

4.1 Preliminaries

ID-Based Key Predistribution Random key predistribution for sensor networks originates from [6]. The idea is that each sensor node is preloaded with randomly chosen k keys, called *key ring*, from the key pool of size l. The values of l and k can be chosen such that any two nodes have at least one common key with a given probability. However, here we do not care about the probability that two neighboring sensors share a key, because in our scheme, key predistribution is used not for secure and authenticated communication between the neighboring sensor nodes, but for authenticated flooding.

ID-based key predistribution was introduced in [22]. The keys in the key pool are numbered from 1 to l. Each sensor s with a unique identifier id_s is first assigned k distinct integers between 1 and l by applying a pseudorandom number generator $PRG()$ with the seed id_s. Then the sensor s is preloaded with the keys whose identifiers are these k numbers from the sequence of pseudorandom numbers $PRG(id_s)$.

This method of choosing key rings enables to characterize sets of key identifiers very efficiently, as only the corresponding short seed needs to be known. This helps to save energy in a sensor network if the set of key identifiers needs to be transmitted over the air, as radio communication is very expensive in terms of energy. In this case, only the seed x is transmitted. Then, any sensor can determine if it knows some keys from a set of key identifiers KID_x characterized by the seed x. It computes $PRG(x) = KID_x$ and compares its own key identifiers to the key identifiers from KID_x.

1-bit MACs In our protocol, we use message authentication codes (MACs) with 1-bit output. The idea of using MACs with single bit output originates from [3]. We view a 1-bit MAC under a given key as a random function, i.e., we require the following:

- A single 1-bit MAC (under an unknown random key) cannot be feasibly guessed with any probability significantly exceeding $\frac{1}{2}$.
- Similarly, an m-bit string of m 1-bit MACs under m independent random keys cannot be guessed with probability significantly more than $\frac{1}{2^m}$.

4.2 AQF-pass: Protocol Description

We assume that an ID-based key predistribution scheme is deployed in the sensor network. The protocol description follows.

Base station The base station first computes the query q and a hash from the query $x = h(q)$ using a hash function $h()$. Then it generates m key identifiers for the underlying ID-based key predistribution scheme: $KID_x = PRG(x) = (kid_1, \ldots, kid_m)$. We denote the corresponding key sequence $K_x = (k_{kid_1}, \ldots, k_{kid_m})$.

Then the base station computes m 1-bit MACs on $h(q)$ using keys from K_x. We call these m 1-bit MACs *authenticator* for q, denoted as $macs(q)$.

The base station floods the query q into the sensor network, accompanied by the authenticator for the query.

Sensor nodes Upon receiving the query q with the authenticator $macs(q)$, each sensor s first computes $x = h(q)$ and the sequence of key identifiers $KID_x = PRG(x)$. It compares the key identifiers from KID_x to its own key identifiers in order to find out if s knows some keys from K_x.

If s knows some keys, it verifies the corresponding 1-bit MACs from $macs(q)$. If any of them does not verify correctly, then the sensor drops the query. If all verifiable MACs are correct, the sensor forwards the query to his neighbors according to the underlying flooding mechanism.

If the sensor is not able to verify any MACs (i.e., the sensor does not know any keys from K_x), than the sensor forwards the query to his neighbors according to the underlying flooding mechanism. We say that the sensor *passes* the non-verifiable query. This action gives the name to the algorithm AQF-pass.

4.3 AQF-pass: Analysis

The query of a legitimate user will be flooded into the sensor network without any obstacles. However, a query forged by an adversary will only be able to reach a limited part of the network, as some sensor nodes will discard the query. In the following, we analytically determine how many 1-bit MACs should be appended to a query in order to limit the propagation of a fake query to a logarithmically small part of the network.

The variables used in the analysis are summarized in Table 1.

Table 1. Variables used in the analysis of AQF-pass.

meaning of the variable	variable	typical values
number of nodes in the sensor network	n	1000 – 10000
number of keys in the key pool	l	10000 - 100000
number of keys in the key ring of a node	k	50 - 250
node density (average number of neighbors of a node)	d	5 - 50
number of captured senor nodes	$\tilde{n}$	≤ 30
number of captured keys	$\tilde{b}$	Formula 1
number of keys in the authenticator which the adversary knows	$E_{\tilde{b}}$	Formula 2
number of right bits in the fake authenticator	B	Formula 3
probability that the message will be forwarded	p_f	Formula 4
size of the authenticator	m	100 - 500 bits

Propagation Probability of a Fake Query Using a common model for cryptographic hash functions [2], it is infeasible to first choose some x and then search for an appropriate value q with $h(q) = x$, or to fix *any* properties for the desired x and then search for a query q with satisfying $h(q)$. For different queries q, the adversary always receives independent random values $x = h(q)$.

Therefore, we assume that the adversary uses the following strategy: It computes the seed $x = h(q)$ for its query q, computes the appropriate sequence of key identifiers KID_x using $PRG(x)$, and hopes that it knows enough keys with identifiers from KID_x in order to be able to construct a fake query.

In the following, we compute the probability of a fake query generated as above to successfully propagate through the sensor network assuming that the adversary captured $\tilde{n}$ sensor nodes and guessed the bits of authenticator which it could not compute.

If $\tilde{n}$ sensor nodes are compromised, then the adversary knows in average $\tilde{b}$ keys:

$$\tilde{b} = l(1 - (1 - \frac{k}{l})^{\tilde{n}}) \tag{1}$$

Formula 1 assumes that the keys are distributed according to a uniform probability distribution. Given that the adversary knows $\tilde{b}$ keys out of l, we can compute the average number of bits in a MAC of length m that will be correct due to the adversary's partial knowledge of the key space l:

$$E_{\tilde{b}} = m\frac{\tilde{b}}{l} \tag{2}$$

Since the attacker knows nothing about the other keys in the authenticator, it has to guess the other bits. There it will have the probability of 50% to guess the correct value. This lets us compute the total number of correct bits in the faked authenticator:

$$B = E_{\tilde{b}} + \frac{m - E_{\tilde{b}}}{2} = \frac{m(\tilde{b} + l)}{2l} \tag{3}$$

We can finally compute the probability p_f that a sensor accepts the query with the fake authenticator:

$$p_f = \left(\frac{l - k}{l} + \frac{k}{l} \frac{B}{m} \right)^m \tag{4}$$

The expression in the parentheses gives the probability that one bit of the authenticator passed the test by a particular sensor node. The first summand expresses the probability that the sensor node does not share any keys with the claimed set of key identifiers $PRG(x)$. The second summand shows the probability that either the adversary could compute the appropriate bit or guessed it.

Limiting the Propagation of Fake Queries The last section calculated the probability each single sensors forwards the faked query. It is yet open, however, how the network as a total behaves, namely, whether the query reaches a significant number of nodes, or is stopped from doing so.

To calculate the parameters that have to be set in order to stop a fake query from reaching a critical mass of nodes, we make use of the theory by Erdös and Rényi [5] which is also used in [10]: a random (n, p)-graph[3] becomes disconnected if $pn < 1$, i.e., if the average number of outgoing connections from a node is fewer than 1. In this case the largest connected component is of the size $\Theta(\log(n))$.

In our sensor network, each sensor has d neighbors on average, and each neighbor forwards the query with probability p_f. Then, we have a (d, p_f)-graph for query dissemination and therefore, we have to adjust the parameters that we can control, such that:

$$p_f d < 1 \tag{5}$$

From Formulas 4 and 5 it follows:

$$\frac{1}{d} > p_f \tag{6}$$

$$\Leftrightarrow \frac{1}{d} > \left(\frac{l - k}{l} + \frac{k(\tilde{b} + l)}{2l^2} \right)^m \tag{7}$$

$$\Leftrightarrow m > \frac{\log d}{-\log \left(1 - \frac{k(l - \tilde{b})}{2l^2} \right)} \tag{8}$$

We have variable parameters $d, l, k, \tilde{n}$ (or $\tilde{b}$ instead of $\tilde{n}$) for the length of the authenticator m. The administrators of the network control parameters d, l, k and m, while the adversary controls $\tilde{n}$, and therefore, also $\tilde{b}$.

---

[3] A random (n, p)-graph has n nodes, and the connection between any two nodes exists with probability p.

The next task is to find suitable ranges for d, l, k and m, such that the adversary is unable to send fake queries for reasonable ranges of $\tilde{n}$. We did so analytically, as well as in a simulation (see Section 4.4).

Reasonably, the more nodes the attacker has compromised, i.e., the more keys it has, the more difficult it gets to keep the attacker from broadcasting illegitimate queries. Also dense networks are harder to protect, due to the high connectivity of query propagation in these networks, as our approach stops an illegitimate query only if the average connectivity of query propagation drops below 1 (Formula 5).

The results of the analytical evaluation using Formula 8 are presented on Figure 1. We considered $n = 1000$ nodes, key pool size $l = 10,000$, node density $d \in \{7, 15\}$ and key ring size $k \in \{75, 150\}$.

Firstly, we comment on the choice of the node density parameter. If the node density is too high, then the capacity of wireless networks decreases. On the other hand, if the network density is too low, the network may become disconnected. Node density required to ensure connectivity can be estimated as $\Theta(\log n)$ [21], but the exact number of neighbors remains an open problem. For networks of moderate size, 6 to 8 neighbors may be considered [17]. Thus, we chose density 15, at which the network should certainly be connected, and density 7 which seems to be a border case.

Figure 1 shows that in the range of tens of compromised nodes, the needed authenticator size increases reasonably slow. The best results are reached for the small node density 7 and the large key ring size 150. In this case, if the adversary captured around 10 sensor nodes, authenticator size around 300 bits suffices to thwart propagation of fake queries.

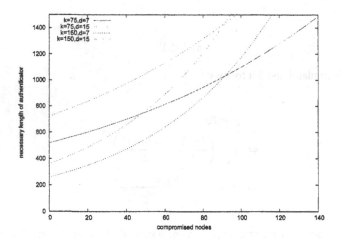

Fig. 1. Necessary authenticator size, depending on node density, key ring size, and the number of compromised nodes. The size of key pool is $l = 10000$.

4.4   Simulation Results

We simulated AQF-pass using Shawn [13], a discrete event simulator for large wireless sensor networks. We used a key pool of $l = 10,000$ keys and varied node density $d \in \{7,15\}$ and key ring size $k \in \{75,150\}$. In each simulation run, 1000 nodes were randomly and uniformly placed such that the given node density d was satisfied. The source of the query (base station or the adversary) was also placed randomly in the sensor field. The query was sent, accompanied by the authenticator of size m. We looked into the number of nodes reached by an illegitimate query for $m = 50, 100, 150, \ldots, 500$ assuming that the adversary captured $\tilde{n} = 0, 1, 2, 4, 16, 32, 64, 128$ nodes. For each combination of parameters, 50 protocol runs on different network topologies were performed. Due to space limit, we only present the most significant results here.

At node density 15 and key ring size 75 all the networks were fully connected, that is, legitimate queries always reached all of nodes. However, also illegitimate queries reached a significant part of the network even if no nodes were captured, until the authenticator size reached the unacceptable 500 bits. This confirms our analytical results showing that in this case, authenticator size of around 700 bits are needed.

Formula 8 indicates that the size of the authenticator decreases with the decreasing node density and increasing key ring size. In Figure 2, results for node density 7 and key ring size 150 are presented. With node density 7, the network may already become disconnected. However, the number of sensors which are disconnected from the network in this case was negligible.

With this parameters, authenticator size of 200 bit already suffices for tens of captured nodes as considered in our adversary model. Analytical results suggest authenticator of around 300 bits here.

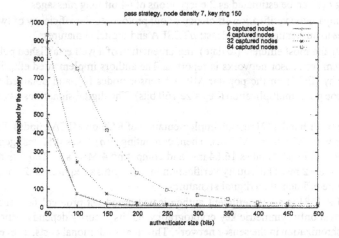

Fig. 2. Number of nodes reached by the fake query depending on authenticator size, with node density 7 and key ring size 150.

4.5 Estimated Verification Efficiency

Although we have not implemented AQF-pass yet, we roughly estimate its running time here.

We assume key pool size $l = 10,000$, and key ring size $k = 150$. Therefore, the size of a key identifier is 14 bits, we take 16 bits for convenience of computation. As our analysis and simulations suggest authenticator size m of 200-300 bits, we assume $m = 256$ for convenience. The verification of the query q consists of computing its hash value $h(q)$, generating 256 key identifiers using $PRG(h(q))$, and finally, computing some MACs on $h(q)$. On average, a sensor node would know $\frac{m \cdot k}{l}$ keys from the authenticator. Thus, the sensor node needs to generate $256 \cdot 16 = 4096$ pseudorandom bits, and to compute $\lceil \frac{256 \cdot 150}{10,000} \rceil = 4$ MACs on average.

We assume that both the $PRG()$ and the MAC are implemented using a single block cipher with the block size B as a primitive. As in the following we want to compare the efficiency of AQF-pass to existing implementations of other authenticated broadcast protocols, we assume that this cipher is RC5 [19] with $B = 64$.

Pseudorandom numbers can be generated using the block cipher in counter (CTR) mode [15]. Then, generating N pseudorandom bits corresponds to encrypting N bits.

For the MAC computation, we use the CBC-MAC [15], and then take the first bit of its output for the 1-bit MAC. Time to compute CBC-MAC on N bits can be estimated as encrypting B bits $\lceil \frac{N}{B} \rceil$ times. With block size 64, and the output of the hash function 160 bits, computing the CBC-MAC on $h(q)$ can be estimated as 3 encryptions of 64 bit long messages.

At present, the cryptanalysis of hash functions is a very fast developing research area. Therefore, it is difficult to choose a "right" hash function to use. We assume that we use SHA-1 [15]. We very roughly estimate its computation time as time to compute a MAC on 128 bits (the hash function should be more efficient than the MAC). Thus, computing $h(q)$ an be estimated as 2 encryptions of 64 bit long messages.

We compare the verification efficiency of our protocol to the efficiency of two other approaches to authenticated broadcast: μTESLA and digital signatures.

In [8,9], the most efficient (to date) implementation of a well established public key cryptosystem for sensor networks is reported. The authors implemented elliptic curve cryptography (ECC) on the popular MICA2 sensor nodes [4], and obtained time of 0.81s for one point multiplication (key size 160 bits). The digital signatures have length of 320 bits.

On the other hand, [12] reports implementation of RC5 on MICA2 nodes. Encrypting 64 bits with RC5 takes 0.26 ms. Then, computing $h(q)$ takes 0.52 ms, generating 4096 pseudorandom bits takes 16.64 ms, and computing 4 MACs on 160 bits requires $4 \cdot 3 \cdot 0.26 = 3.12$ ms. Thus, query verification in AQF-pass requires 20.28 ms, which is much more efficient than digital signatures.

μTESLA [18] is a very efficient authenticated broadcast protocol for sensor networks. It uses only symmetric key cryptography, but its security depends critically on clock synchronization in the sensor network. This incurs additional costs, as even loose clock synchronization in a network with 1000 nodes is a non-trivial task. Verification of μTESLA broadcast messages takes at most 17.8 ms.

μTESLA also uses RC5 as a building block. Encryption of 64 bits in CTR mode takes 0.55 ms, and computing CBC-MAC on 64 bits takes 0.64 ms. Thus, using the same hardware, AQF-pass would take 44.16 ms, which is 2.5 times slower than μTESLA. On the other hand, our AQF-pass does not require clock synchronization, which may be worth the performance decrease.

5 Discussion and Future Work

Strategies for propagation of non-verifiable queries In the protocol AQF-pass, if the node cannot verify the query, it passes the query to all its neighbors. This is only one of possible strategies. Another obvious strategy is AQF-stop, where the node drops the non-verifiable query. In this case, the legitimate queries also can be dropped, so care should be taken about their propagation probability as well. We analyzed and simulated this approach, and found out that it does not bring significant improvements. When the authenticator size is too small, legitimate queries do not propagate well, as too many nodes cannot verify the queries and drop them. With the growth of the authenticator size, however, the event *stop* (meaning "a sensor cannot verify the query") gets so rare, that the performance of AQF-stop gets very similar to that of AQF-pass. Nevertheless, the *stop* strategy seems to be promising, as it decreases the number of sent messages in the network, and therefore, saves energy. Thus, we are looking at how to increase the probability of the drops. We now explore the following strategy: if the sensor could only verify h bits of the authenticator, it drops the query with probability $\frac{1}{2^h}$.

Flooding strategies The protocol AQF-pass works efficiently for sparse sensor networks. The reason it gets worse with denser networks lies in the fact that if each sensor node has a lot of neighbors, each forwarding event increases the probability of a query to get trough the network. And as the adversary always can guess at least half of the bits in the authenticator, even queries with completely guessed authenticator propagate successfully. To thwart this disadvantage, we plan to use more sophisticated flooding mechanisms, such as gossiping.

Preventing a sophisticated attack While the proposed protocol has its merits, there is a weakness in the protocol that has to be taken into account. If an attacker is able to send a query q with different authenticator $macs(q)$, it might gain a broader access to the network in case the attacker can observe parts of the network. The attack works as follows: if the attacker has no knowledge about a single bit in $macs(q)$, it sends one message with the bit set, and one with the bit cleared. It can then guess from the number of nodes accepting the message, whether the bit should be set or not. This can be repeated for all bits that are unknown to the attacker, until the message either reaches a sufficient number of sensors, or the attacker knows how to set all bits correctly.

To thwart this attack, it has to be avoided that a message q can be sent with different $macs(q)$. The first proposal to counter the attack is that each sensor stores the number of invalid requests it received from its neighbors. Further messages from a neighbor are only forwarded if the number of invalid queries from it is below a certain threshold, or according to some probability distribution that depends on this number, e.g. exponentially decreasing probability. This scales quite well, since the amount of data stored is independent from the number of relayed messages, does not need a timestamp, and is equal to the number of a node's neighbors. This counter technique isolates compromised sensors, such that they are unable to send future requests.

Verification efficiency Finally, efficiency of the authenticator verification remains to be determined exactly. We are now working on design of an efficient 1-bit MAC scheme, and plan to implement the query verification on the real sensor nodes.

References

1. Alexander Becher, Zinaida Benenson, and Maximilian Dornseif. Tampering with motes: Real-world physical attacks on wireless sensor networks. In *3rd International Conference on Security in Pervasive Computing (SPC)*, April 2006.
2. M. Bellare and P. Rogaway. Random oracles are practical: A paradigm for designing efficient protocols. In *ACM Conference on Computer and Communications Security*, pages 62–73, 1993.
3. Ran Canetti, Juan Garay, Gene Itkis, Daniele Micciancio, Moni Naor, and Benny Pinkas. Multicast security: A taxonomy and some efficient constructions. In *Proc. IEEE INFO-COM'99*, volume 2, pages 708–716, New York, NY, March 1999. IEEE.
4. Crossbow, Inc. MICA2 data sheet. Available at http://www.xbow.com/Products/Product_pdf_files/Wireless_pdf/MICA2_Datasheet.pdf.
5. P. Erdös and A. Rényi. On the evolution of random graphs. *Publ. Math. Inst. Hungar. Acad. Sci.*, pages 17–61, 1960.
6. Laurent Eschenauer and Virgil D. Gligor. A key-management scheme for distributed sensor networks. In *Proceedings of the 9th ACM Conference on Computer and Communications Security*, pages 41–47. ACM Press, 2002.
7. Saurabh Ganeriwal, Srdjan Capkun, Chih-Chieh Han, and Mani B. Srivastava. Secure time synchronization service for sensor networks. In *WiSe '05: Proceedings of the 4th ACM workshop on Wireless security*, pages 97–106, New York, NY, USA, 2005. ACM Press.
8. Vipul Gupta, Matthew Millard, Stephen Fung, Yu Zhu, Nils Gura, Hans Eberle, and Sheueling Chang Shantz. Sizzle: A standards-based end-to-end security architecture for the embedded internet. In *Third IEEE International Conference on Pervasive Computing and Communication (PerCom 2005)*, Kauai, March 2005.
9. Nils Gura, Arun Patel, Arvinderpal Wander, Hans Eberle, and Sheueling Chang Shantz. Comparing elliptic curve cryptography and rsa on 8-bit CPUs. In *Cryptographic Hardware and Embedded Systems (CHES); 6th International Workshop*, pages 119–132, August 2004.
10. Joengmin Hwang and Yongdae Kim. Revisiting random key pre-distribution schemes for wireless sensor networks. In *SASN '04: Proceedings of the 2nd ACM workshop on Security of ad hoc and sensor networks*, pages 43–52. ACM Press, 2004.
11. Chalermek Intanagonwiwat, Ramesh Govindan, Deborah Estrin, John Heidemann, and Fabio Silva. Directed Diffusion for wireless sensor networking. *IEEE/ACM Trans. Netw.*, 11(1):2–16, 2003.
12. Chris Karlof, Naveen Sastry, and David Wagner. TinySec: A link layer security architecture for wireless sensor networks. In *Second ACM Conference on Embedded Networked Sensor Systems (SensSys 2004)*, November 2004.

13. A. Kröller, D. Pfisterer, C. Buschmann, S. P. Fekete, and S. Fischer. Shawn: A new approach to simulating wireless sensor networks. In *Design, Analysis, and Simulation of Distributed Systems, SpringSim 2005*, April 2005.

14. Samuel Madden, Michael J. Franklin, Joseph M. Hellerstein, and Wei Hong. The design of an acquisitional query processor for sensor networks. In *SIGMOD '03: Proceedings of the 2003 ACM SIGMOD International Conference on Management of Data*, pages 491–502, New York, NY, USA, 2003. ACM Press.

15. Alfred J. Menezes, Paul C. Van Oorschot, and Scott A. Vanstone. *Handbook of Applied Cryptography*. CRC Press, Boca Raton, FL, 1997.

16. moteiv Corp. Telos revision B datasheet. Available at http://www.moteiv.com/products/docs/telos-revb-datasheet.pdf.

17. J. Ni and S. Chandler. Connectivity properties of a random radio network. *IEE Communications*, 141:389–296, August 1994.

18. Adrian Perrig, Robert Szewczyk, J. D. Tygar, Victor Wen, and David E. Culler. SPINS: security protocols for sensor networks. *Wireless Networks*, 8(5):521–534, 2002.

19. Ronald L. Rivest. The RC5 encryption algorithm. In *Fast Software Encryption*, pages 86–96, 1994.

20. Stefaan Seys and Bart Preneel. Efficient cooperative signatures: A novel authentication scheme for sensor networks. In *2nd International Conference on Security in Pervasive Computing*, number 3450 in LNCS, pages 86 – 100, April 2005.

21. Feng Xue and P. R. Kumar. The number of neighbors needed for connectivity of wireless networks. *Wirel. Netw.*, 10(2):169–181, 2004.

22. Sencun Zhu, Shouhuai Xu, Sanjeev Setia, and Sushil Jajodia. Establishing pair-wise keys for secure communication in ad hoc networks: A probabilistic approach. In *IEEE International Conference on Network Protocols*, November 2003.

Identity Based Message Authentication for Dynamic Networks

Pietro Michiardi and Refik Molva

Institut Eurecom
2229, route des Cretes BP 193, 06904 Sophia-Antipolis, France
{pietro.michiardi, refik.molva}@eurecom.fr

Abstract. This paper presents a message authentication scheme built on top of an original construct that combines a simple form of identity based cryptography with an iterated version of RSA. Our scheme blends the features of identity based cryptography and stream authentication while at the same time offering security comparable to that of the basic RSA cryptosystem. As opposed to other authentication schemes available in the literature, our solution does not rely on any public key infrastructure and, like any identity based cryptosystems, it does not require public key certificates. A basic security analysis, performance evaluation and storage requirements of our scheme are also provided in the paper. Furthermore, we explore a challenging application of our scheme: a scalable and lightweight key distribution service that offers authentication services to an infrastructure-less ad hoc network and that can be coupled with existing secure routing solutions.

1 Introduction

In this paper we propose a message authentication scheme (that we call IB-MAC) built on top of an original construct that combines a simple form of identity based cryptography[1] with an iterated version of RSA. In our solution, users are able to locally generate a chain of authentication material that we call *authentication tickets* using as seed the secret information (that we call a *master authentication ticket*) delivered by a key distribution center (KDC). By removing the reliance on a public key infrastructure, our scheme is particularly suitable for networks with multiple dynamic sources whereas other authentication schemes available in the literature suffer from the limitations imposed by certificate management requirements. We also describe an interesting application of our scheme: IB-MAC can be used as a basis to provide a lightweight key distribution mechanism for peer authentication in infrastructure-less ad hoc networks. In the proposed solution there is no need for a network infrastructure and the security bootstrap phase is lightweight: the key distribution center is involved neither in networking operations nor in any further security operations beyond the bootstrap phase. The remainder of the paper is organized as follows: we present the IB-MAC authentication scheme and focus on the technique used to generate the authentication material. A basic assessment of the security properties of our scheme is provided. We then focus on the performance analysis of the IB-MAC scheme both in terms of computational and

---

[1] In the remainder of the paper ID-based and identity based have the same meaning.

Please use the following format when citing this chapter:

Author(s) [insert Last name, First-name initial(s)], 2006, in IFIP International Federation for Information Processing, Volume 201, Security and Privacy in Dynamic Environments, eds. Fischer-Hubner, S., Rannenberg, K., Yngstrom, L., Lindskog, S., (Boston: Springer), pp. [insert page numbers].

message overhead and storage requirements. Finally, we describe an application of the IB-MAC scheme for key-distribution and message authentication in ad hoc networks.

2   The IB-MAC scheme

In our solution, users contact a key distribution center (KDC) and receive a secret called the *master authentication ticket* M which is tightly bound to the users' identity (ID). M is used as a seed to generate a *chain of authentication tickets* by iterative RSA encryption over the secret M. IB-MAC authentication tickets are then proposed as symmetric keying material for a message authentication protocol designed for *loosely time-synchronized users*. As opposed to similar stream authentication schemes available in the literature [9, 10], our solution does not rely on any public key infrastructure and, like any ID-based cryptosystem, it does not require public key certificates for system users.

We now describe the basic stages of the IB-MAC scheme.

2.1   KDC setup

The idea behind our identity based scheme is the use of a single common RSA key pair for all users within a system. The public key is assumed to be publicly known while the private key is held by the KDC. The proposed cryptosystem uses computations in Z_n, where n is the product of two distinct odd primes p and q. For such an integer n, note that $\phi(n) = (p-1)(q-1)$. The formal description of the KDC bootstrap phase is as follows.

Key-distribution Center (KDC) setup:

1. KDC generates: two large random odd primes p and q
2. KDC computes: $n = p \cdot q \rightarrow$ RSA-like modulus (common to all users)
3. KDC selects: **small** $e \in Z_{\phi(n)}^*$, $k \in$ N $\rightarrow$ Public values e and k (common to all users)
4. KDC computes: $d = e^{-k} \bmod \phi(n) \rightarrow$ Master Secret Key

The KDC uses the RSA modulus to generate a master secret key d that corresponds to a public exponent e^k: this operation is equivalent to the legacy RSA key-pair generation.

We stress that our scheme is not exposed to the well known common modulus attack whereby anyone, based on one's knowledge of a single key-pair, can simply factor the modulus and compute other users' private keys. In the present context, the secret key d is only known to the KDC and kept secret from the users of the system. Our scheme relies on a single keypair of which the private key is only known by the KDC. Further discussion on the common modulus attack is presented in section 3.

Master secret key generation As explained in section 2.1 the secret key used by the KDC to generate master authentication tickets is of the form: $d = e^{-k} \bmod \phi(n)$. Since the secret key d is generated only once during the system initialization and used to process all user requests, the KDC can afford to run a complex algorithm to generate

d. However, an efficient way for calculating d can be derived based on the following observation: $d = e^{-k} \bmod \phi(n) = \left(e^{-1}\right)^k \bmod \phi(n)$. The inverse of the public exponent e can be easily calculated, and then it is sufficient to apply the square and multiply algorithm to compute the exponentiation.

2.2 Sender setup

In order to produce authenticated packets, the sender needs to contact the KDC that is in charge of issuing a master authentication ticket.

Distribution of Master Authentication Ticket:

Sender $\rightarrow$ **KDC** : ID

KDC generates: $H(ID) = C$

KDC $\rightarrow$ **Sender** : $M = C^d \bmod n$ *(securely)*

Upon verification of the sender identity ID, the KDC generates and **securely** distributes to the sender the following master authentication ticket: $M = \left(H(ID)\right)^d \bmod n$, where the function $H()$ is a one-way collision resistant function, applied to the user identity ID. M can be thought of as the KDC's digital signature over the user's identity ID[2].

Sender setup:

1. Retrieve the public values n, e, k
2. Contact KDC to obtain the master authentication ticket M
3. Generate k time-dependent authentication tickets T_k

Next, the sender divides the time into uniform intervals of duration τ_{int}. Time interval 1 starts at time τ_1, time interval 2 at time $\tau_2 = \tau_1 + \tau_{int}$, etc. The sender computes authentication tickets T_i by iterative exponentiation of the master authentication ticket M using the public exponent e as shown below. Each authentication ticket is then assigned to a time interval starting with time interval τ_1 and ticket T_k, continuing with time interval τ_2 and ticket T_{k-1} and so on. The one-way authentication ticket chain is used in the reverse order of generation, so any value of a time interval can be used to derive values of previous time intervals. The sender uses the length k of the one-way chain as obtained from the KDC: this length limits the maximum transmission duration before a new one-way authentication ticket chain must be created. Note that in this paper we assume that chains are sufficiently long for the duration of communication. It is part of our future work to find an additional mechanism that would allow any user to self-generate a new authentication ticket chain without the need to contact the KDC [3].

Ticket generation (Sender): Generation: $\uparrow$ and Releasing: $\downarrow$ order

---

[2] Note however that the public exponent used for the digital signature does not correspond to the one adopted by a legacy RSA signature.

[3] In general, the need for such an additional scheme would depend on the particular scenario in which our scheme is applied. Indeed one could think of applications in which secure message authentication would be offered only to users that payed for a pre-defined amount of authentication tickets. In this case, our scheme should be extended in order to the number k of authentication tickets delivered to the users by the KDC, while at the same time preserving the basic properties of the original scheme. This is another interesting future research direction.

$$T_k = M^{e^k} \bmod n$$
$$T_{k-1} = M^{e^{k-1}} \bmod n$$

...

$$T_{k-i} = M^{e^{k-i}} \bmod n, \text{ with } i \leq k$$

...

$$T_1 = M^e \bmod n$$

2.3 Transmission of authenticated messages

Message authentication requires a source of asymmetry, such that the receivers can only verify the authentication information, but not generate valid authentication information. In our scheme we adopt the key idea behind the TESLA scheme [9] that suggest to use time as a source of asymmetry. This can be done if we assume loose time synchronized between senders and receivers: up to some time synchronization error Δ, all parties agree on the current time[4].

Subsequently to the setup phase, the sender assigns each authentication ticket sequentially to the selected time intervals (one ticket per time interval). Note that using the one-way chain of authentication tickets in reverse order of generation renders computationally infeasible for an attacker to forge authentication tickets. Furthermore, any values of a time interval can be used to derive values of previous time intervals. The sender generates a message authentication code (MAC) and attaches it to each packet. The MAC is computed over the contents of the packet that needs to be transmitted. For each packet, the sender determines the time interval and uses the corresponding value from the one-way chain of authentication tickets as a cryptographic key to compute the MAC (see [3] for details). Along with the packet, the sender also sends the authentication ticket it used to generate the MAC in the previous time interval and its unique identifier (ID). Upon receipt of a packet, the receiver verifies the authentication ticket contained in the packet and uses it to check the correctness of the MAC of the buffered packet that corresponds to the time interval of the authentication ticket. If the MAC is correct, the receiver accepts the packet. Every time a sender transmits a message, it appends a MAC to the message, using the authentication ticket corresponding to the current time interval as the key to compute the MAC. The authentication ticket for time interval τ_i remains secret until it is revealed in the packet corresponding to time interval τ_{i+1}. Figure 1 depicts the time intervals and some sample packets transmitted by the sender along time. Formally, a generic packet sent at time interval τ_i is of the form:
$P_i = \{m_i, MAC_{T_{k-i}}(m_i), T_{k-(i-1)}, ID_{SENDER}\}$ where:

- m_i is the message,
- $MAC_{T_{k-i}}(m_i)$ is the MAC generated with T_{k-i},
- $T_{k-i} = M^{e^{k-i}} \bmod n$ is the ticket for time interval τ_i,
- $T_{k-(i-1)} = M^{e^{k-i-1}} \bmod n$ is the disclosed ticket for time interval τ_{i-1},
- ID_{SENDER} is the unique identifier of the sender.

---

[4] The interested reader should refer to TESLA [9] for a thorough discussion on time synchronization issues.

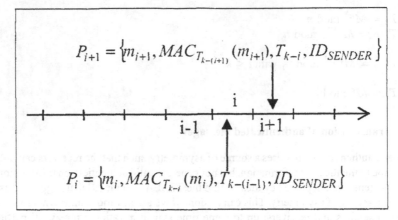

Fig. 1. Sending authenticated messages.

2.4 Verification of message authentication information at the receiver

Upon reception of packet P_{i+1} the receiver extracts the authentication ticket T_{k-i} that can be used to authenticate the previously received packet P_i. The receiver has to verify that the authentication ticket T_{k-i} corresponds to the identity ID_{SENDER} specified in the packet P_i. To that effect, the receiver only has to perform i exponentiations with e that is a small exponent[5]:

$$(T_{k-i})^{e^i} = \left(M^{e^{k-i}}\right)^{e^i} = \left(\left(C^d\right)^{e^{k-i}}\right)^{e^i} = \left(\left(C^{e^{-k}}\right)^{e^{k-i}}\right)^{e^i} = H(ID_{SENDER})$$

(1)

If $H(ID_{SENDER})$ obtained in expression (1) equals the hash function applied to the ID_{SENDER} specified in the packet P_i, then the authentication ticket is valid and it can be used as a key to verify the MAC for packet P_i.

When a sender discloses an authentication ticket, all parties potentially have access to that ticket and can create a bogus packet and forge a MAC. Therefore, as packets arrive, the receiver must also verify that their MACs are based on safe keys, i.e. a key that is only known by the sender, by checking that the time interval the sender could be in (in the example above, τ_{i+1}) is greater than the time interval corresponding to the disclosed authentication ticket (in the example above, τ_i). Receivers must discard any packet that is not safe, because it may have been forged.

3 Basic security analysis

In this section we propose a basic security analysis of the IB-MAC scheme by assuming that an attacker (internal or external) trying to break the cryptosystem is actually

---

[5] We omitted the $\mod n$ notation for sake of simplicity.

trying to determine the secret master key safely guarded by the key distribution center (KDC) by using disclosed authentication tickets collected over time or by performing a known-plaintext attack. Further, we consider an attacker who tries to gather a valid authentication ticket by submitting bogus identity information to the KDC or to generate valid authentication tickets from past authentication tickets. The reader should note that it is out of the scope of this section to provide a *formal* proof of the security of our scheme.

3.1 Common modulus attack

To avoid generating a different $n = p \cdot q$ modulus for each user, one could envision to fix n once and for all. A trusted central authority could provide user i with a unique pair $< e_i, d_i >$ from which user i would form a public key $< n, e_i >$ and a secret key $< n, d_i >$. At first glance, a scheme using a common modulus may seem to work: a ciphertext $C = M^{e_A} \bmod n$ intended for Alice cannot be decrypted by Bob, since Bob does not possess d_A. However the resulting system is insecure: Bob can use his own exponents $< e_B, d_B >$ to factor the modulus n. Once n is factored Bob can recover Alice's private key d_A from her public key e_A. The demonstration of how Bob can find the factorization of the common modulus n can be found in [4]. In the IB-MAC system proposed in this paper the common modulus attack is prevented. By analyzing the KDC setup phase and the sender setup phase, it is possible to observe that as compared to the typical common modulus attack scenario described above, no secret keying material is delivered to the users. The modulus n is used to generate a key d that is securely kept by the KDC. d is used to encrypt the hashed identity of a user requesting for a master authentication ticket M, unlike with the common modulus attack, and the secret M provided to each user is not a private key but the result of an encryption with the private key d. Thus, the attack detailed in [4] can not be perpetrated against the IB-MAC system.

3.2 Impersonation through blinding

Suppose now that an attacker wishes to impersonate a party known under the identity ID by gaining access to the master ticket M for identity ID. The attacker knows that M is computed by encrypting the hashed identity $C = H(ID)$. Now, the attacker randomly chooses g and computes $C^* = g^{e^k} C$. Subsequently, the attacker receives the following ticket from the KDC: $M^* = (C^*)^d \bmod n$. Based on the definition of C^* we have: $M^* = (g^{e^k} C)^d \bmod n = g^{e^k \cdot d} C^d \bmod n = g \cdot M$. Thus M can be retrieved using $M = \frac{M^*}{g}$. A simple observation however shows the infeasibility of this attack: finding a bogus identifier ID^* such as $H(ID^*) = g^e C = g^e H(ID)$ requires inverting the one-way hash function $H()$, which is computationally infeasible. As a rule, the study of the impersonation attack suggests to perform the initial authentication of users applying for a master authentication ticket by requesting the full identifier ID of the user rather than a hashed value of the identifier.

3.3   Forging authentication tickets

Suppose now that an attacker wishes to forge an authentication ticket using a previously revealed authentication ticket. Suppose that a legitimate sender discloses the authentication ticket: $T_k = M_{ID}^{e^k} \bmod n$, where M_{ID} is the master authentication ticket for the identifier ID. It is straightforward to show that finding M_{ID} is as hard as breaking the RSA cryptosystem. However, we want to show that also forging the authentication ticket T_{k-1} by an attacker holding T_k is as hard as breaking the RSA system. Since

$$T_{k-1} = M_{ID_{SENDER}}^{e^{k-1}} \bmod n = \left(M_{ID_{SENDER}}^{e^k} \right)^{e^{-1}} \bmod n \text{ , in order to derive } T_{k-1}$$

from T_k, the attacker would have to solve the following equation: $T'_{k-1} = \sqrt[e]{T_k} \bmod n$, which is again equivalent to breaking the RSA system. On the other hand, suppose an attacker with identity ID^* holds the master authentication ticket $M^* = (C^*)^d \bmod n$. The attacker also knows $C = H(ID)$, where ID indicates the identity of a legitimate user. Let $x = \frac{C^*}{C}$. Now[6],

$$T_{k-1} = M_{ID}^{e^{k-1}} = \left(C^d \right)^{e^{k-1}} = \left(\left(\frac{C^*}{x} \right)^d \right)^{e^{k-1}} = \left(\frac{M^*}{x^d} \right)^{e^{k-1}}$$

but it is evident that the attacker cannot generate the value x^d that is needed to forge the authentication ticket T_{k-1}. Indeed: $\left(x^d \right)^{e^{k-1}} = x^{de^{k-1}} = x^{e^{-1}} = \sqrt[e]{x}$ where $d \cdot e^k = 1 \bmod \phi(n)$. Solving the e-th root of x modulo n is as hard as breaking the RSA system.

4   Performance evaluation

In this section we discuss the performance of the IB-MAC scheme in terms of computational overhead, message overhead and storage requirements. We use as a reference the TESLA scheme as it is the natural basis of IB-MAC. At first glance TESLA outperforms IB-MAC for the three aforementioned performance metrics. However, if we focus on an alternative performance metric that we call **bootstrap overhead**, that measure the number of messages exchanged by *all* entities when a new entity joins the group, IB-MAC shows better performances as compared to TESLA. The bootstrap cost is particularly interesting for some applications, as we will discuss in section 5.

4.1   Computational overhead

We assume the authentication ticket generation phase (as well as the TESLA key chain generation) to be executed *off-line*. In IB-MAC each ticket verification operation is equivalent to a **modular exponentiation** with exponent e (see equation 1), which is considered to be a costly operation. Ticket verification costs could be deemed prohibitive for using IB-MAC in wireless sensor networks: recent studies propose, however, the use of public-key cryptography for this type of networks [5, 6]. Conversely, a TESLA verifier only bears the cost of a **hash function execution**.

---

[6] We omitted the $\bmod n$ notation for sake of simplicity

We performed some tests to assess the time needed for a verifier with limited computational power, such as mobile terminal, to verify IB-MAC authentication tickets. We studied the cost of IB-MAC ticket generation/verification for identities derived from IP addresses using a modified version of OpenSSL [1], cross-compiled for an IPAQ 38xx series with a 400Mhz X-Scale/Arm processor and Linux operating system. The choice of the hardware platform that we used for our tests is motivated by a potential application of the IB-MAC scheme that we present in section 5. Results are presented in table 1, where we assumed $k = 10000$. Note that the ticket generation time column refers to the time required by a user for the generation of k authentication tickets, expressed in seconds.

Table 1. Performance of IB-MAC ticket generation/verification.

RSA key length	Ticket generation time [s]	Ticket verification [ticket/s]
512 bits	6.82	1465.8
1024 bits	19.06	524.75
2048 bits	63.57	157.3

4.2   Message overhead

We now focus on the overhead imposed by IB-MAC for every transmitted message. Referring to figure 1, the sender needs to build a packet including the current message, the MAC of the current message and the authentication ticket used as a key for the MAC of the previous message. Each authentication ticket adds an overhead equivalent to the key size used to generate the master authentication ticket from which subsequent authentication tickets are derived. Assuming for example a key length of 512bit, each packet generated by the sender will suffer from a **64 bytes** overhead. In TESLA the message overhead depends on the hash function used to generate the TESLA keys, and can be assumed to be equivalent to 160bit, that is **20 bytes**. TESLA saves more than 30% bandwidth as compared to IB-MAC.

4.3   Storage requirements

Storage requirements can be a potential issue that has to be taken into account when designing an authentication scheme for devices with limited storage capacity. Based on a reference implementation of RSA available in the OpenSSL package, the block size of a cipher text (i.e. an authentication ticket) is equal to the key length. Using a key length of 512-bit, the authentication ticket is 512-bit long. Thus, space requirements for every mobile (sender) node to store authentication tickets is equal to: $k \cdot$ key length , where k is the number of elements of the hash chain, i.e. the total number of authentication ticket that need to be generated, as imposed by the system parameter k. In TESLA, the sender entity has to store an hash chain of k elements, each element being of size 160bit. Again, storage requirements are less demanding than for the IB-MAC scheme.

However, it should be noted that in TESLA the verifier entity stores the public key certificate of every other sender entity in the system ($N - 1$, where N is the number of entities in the group), which can be in the order of thousands of bytes [1] per certificate (depending on the key size used to sign the certificate, the length of the certificate chain, etc). This requirement is **necessary** to verify the authenticity of the root element of the hash chain used by a potential sender.

4.4 Bootstrap overhead

Bootstrapping security associations between entities represents a recurrent cost in terms of message exchange that could reduce the effectiveness of an authentication scheme such as TESLA, especially in dynamic environments in which new entities **frequently** join and leave a group. Let us consider a group of N entities that share a security association, i.e. every entity is in possession of the public key certificate of every other entity. A new member joining the group have to send her public key certificate (used to authenticate the root element of the TESLA hash chain) to every existing group member, while at the same time she should expect to receive the public key certificate of every existing member. This translates in a message exchange cost that goes as $O(N^2)$: TESLA does not scale well when the group size is large. In IB-MAC, the bootstrapping overhead is reduced to zero. IB-MAC tickets are self-authenticating since the verifier only need to know the public exponent e used by the group to verify the authenticity of a packet, as explained in section 2.4. When group joins and leave are expected to be frequent, IB-MAC represents a scalable and effective tool to bootstrap security associations with a minimum overhead.

Table 2 summarizes the different performance metrics we considered in this section. For the sake of simplicity some details have been omitted: the reader should refer to the corresponding sections to have details of overhead evaluation.

Table 2. Performance comparison of IB-MAC and TESLA.

Overhead	TESLA	IB-MAC
Computation (at verifier)	1 hash function	1 modular exp.
Message	20 bytes + (N-1) certificates	64 bytes
Storage	$k \cdot 20$ bytes	$k \cdot 64$ bytes
Bootstrap	$O(N^2)$ messages	0

5   IB-MAC for message authentication in mobile ad hoc networks (MANET)

A challenging requirement for message authentication is raised in the context of mobile ad hoc networking. As a motivating example, a variety of secure routing solutions for ad hoc networks have been proposed in the literature (see for example, [2] chapter 12).

In spite of the large number of solutions, ad hoc routing does not seem to raise any new security requirement with respect to routing in classical networks, apart from key management problems that have been often left aside by current solutions available in the literature. Key management approaches try to answer the hard question of how to establish security associations with no a-priori knowledge, no a-priori trust and lack of infrastructure. Several original key management schemes based on advanced crypto-graphic constructs have been suggested in the literature (see [2] for a literature survey) but they all fall short in meeting the ultimate goal of building a keying infrastructure "from scratch" since they all involve a complex (and often unrealistic) key set-up phase.

In this section we describe a key distribution mechanism based on the IB-MAC scheme that offers authentication services to an infrastructure-less ad hoc network. The main features of our solution range from relaxed networking infrastructure require-ments to a scalable and lightweight security bootstrap phase with respect to network dynamics. The IB-MAC scheme can be coupled, for example, with the ARIADNE [7] secure routing protocol. Due to space limitation we suggest the reader to refer to [8] for a detailed description of a variation of ARIADNE based on IB-MAC.

Figure 2 shows a typical scenario in which one (or more) KDC offers both naming and authentication services.

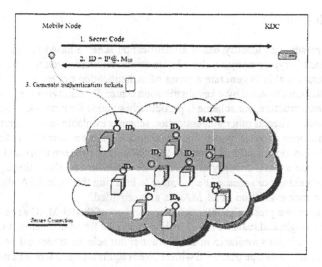

Fig. 2. Application of IB-MAC for naming and key management in open ad hoc networks.

During the bootstrap phase, a mobile node (for example node N_{ID_9}) that needs authentication services contacts the closest KDC and provides initial authentication in-formation. This initial authentication information can take the form of a secret code printed on a **prepaid card** that is delivered by a (automatic) teller, or a secret code printed on tickets delivered at the entrance of confined areas like shopping malls, airports, conference sites.

By providing the initial authentication information to the KDC, the mobile node **securely** receives a unique identifier (that in our case is represented by an IP address for the ad hoc network) and a master authentication ticket M_{ID}. Using IP addresses as node identities allows exploiting existing addressing mechanisms to provide network-wide known and unique node identifiers. However, one might consider the scenario in which nodes' IP addresses might constantly change due for example to hand overs between different ad hoc networks. Moreover, self-organized addressing schemes might be preferable to the addressing scheme proposed in this section. In these situations, an additional overhead for node re-authentication and for the generation of new authentication tickets have to be taken into account. We will address these issues in our future research, were we also plan to use cross-layer information (e.g. pseudonyms used in peer-to-peer applications) to provide a suitable naming service. The IB-MAC system is robust against impersonation through spoofing, as explained in section 3: furthermore, by introducing a monetary overhead prior to the obtention of a master authentication ticket, we make bogus authentication ticket generation an expensive operation. For the purpose of this paper we assume that authentication ticket chains are sufficiently long for the whole duration of the communication in the ad hoc network.

6 Conclusion

This paper presents an identity based authentication scheme based on a simple form of identity based cryptography combined with stream authentication techniques. In our solution, users are able to generate a chain of authentication tickets using as seed the secret information delivered by a key distribution center. By removing the reliance on a public key infrastructure, our scheme is particularly suitable for networks with multiple dynamic sources whereas other authentication schemes available in the literature suffer from the limitations imposed by certificate management requirements. In addition, there is no need for any organizational structure among users or between users and the KDC. We also provide a basic security analysis of our scheme and show through various attacks that breaking our scheme is equivalent to breaking the basic RSA algorithm. A basic performance evaluation of IB-MAC is also provided.

Furthermore, we present an interesting application of the IB-MAC scheme in providing a lightweight and scalable key distribution service for ad hoc networks. As compared to other solutions available in the literature, our scheme trades-off an increased computational and message overhead with relaxed requirements in terms of networking infrastructure while offering a security bootstrap phase that does not entail a burdensome credential exchange between all nodes due to network dynamics.

References

1. Openssl, available from http://www.openssl.org.
2. S. Basagni, M. Conti, S. Giordano, and I. Stojmenovic. *Mobile ad hoc networking*. IEEE Press, Wiley and Sons, US, 2004.

3. M. Bellare, R. Canetti, and H. Krawczyk. Keying hash functions for message authentication. *Lecture Notes in Computer Science*, 1109, 1996.
4. Dan Boneh. Twenty years of attacks on the RSA cryptosystem. *Notices of the American Mathematical Society (AMS)*, 46(2):203–213, 1999.
5. G. Gaubatz, J-P. Kaps, and B. Sunar. Public-key cryptography in sensor networks- revisited. In *Proceedings of 1st European Workshop on Security in Ad-Hoc and Sensor Networks (ESAS)*, Heidelberg, Germany, August 2004.
6. V. Gligor, G. Tsudik, and D. Wagner. Security in ad-hoc and sensor networks. *Panel session in IEEE Symposium on Security and Privacy*, May 2005.
7. Yih-Chun Hu, Adrian Perrig, and David B. Johnson. Ariadne: A secure on-demand routing protocol for ad hoc networks. In *Proceedings of the Eighth Annual International Conference on Mobile Computing and Networking* (MobiCom), September 2002.
8. P. Michiardi and R. Molva. Identiy based message authentication for dynamic networks. Research Report RR-pending, Institut Eurecom, 2005.
9. A. Perrig, R. Canetti, D. Tygar, and D. Song. The tesla broadcast authentication protocol. In *RSA Cryptobytes*, volume 5, 2002.
10. A. Perrig, R. Canetti, J. D. Tygar, and D. X. Song. Efficient authentication and signing of multicast streams over lossy channels. In *IEEE Symposium on Security and Privacy*, pages 56–73, 2000.

Providing Authentication and Access Control in Vehicular Network Environment

Hasnaa Moustafa[1], Gilles Bourdon[1], and Yvon Gourhant[2]

France Telecom R&D
38-40 rue de General Leclerc, 92794 Issy Les Moulineaux, France[1]
2 avenue Pierre Marzin, F-22307 Lannion, France[2]
{hassnaa.moustafa, gilles.bourdon, yvon.gourhant}@francetelecom.com

Abstract In this paper we make use of the recent advances in 802.11 technologies and the new perspectives for ad hoc networks to provide a novel architecture for Inter-Vehicular communication on highways. This architecture provides authentication and access control for mobile clients on highways and ensures network transparency to mobile clients in their vehicles. We propose an integrated solution considering the service provider as the core entity for all authentication and access control operations. We develop an AAA (Authentication, Authorization, and Accounting) mechanism to authenticate mobile clients with respect to service providers authorizing them to services' access, and ensuring a confidential data transfer between each communicating parties. Our mechanism adapts 802.11i standard to the vehicular environment setting up secure links, in layer 2, that guarantee confidential data transfer. To achieve a reliable transfer, we propose a routing approach based on the Optimized Link State Routing (OLSR) protocol that is expected to provide a reliable routing infrastructure in such a hybrid scalable wireless environment. Also, we present a simple and appropriate scheme for assigning IP addresses to mobile clients. Finally, we give a brief analysis and discuss the advantages and limitations of the proposed architecture.

1 Introduction

Due to the great advances in wireless technologies over the last years, ad hoc networks are reaching a stage where they can support the mixing of different services in order to provide an infrastructure useful for the mobile users. The 62nd IETF meeting described three scenarios for these networks: ad hoc networks as standalone networks that are not connected to any external network, ad hoc networks at the edge of an infrastructure network, which are standalone networks connected to the Internet via one or more Internet gateways, and ad hoc networks as intermittent networks that may be standalone for most of the time but temporarily connected to an infrastructure network e.g. mobile users in cars or trains.

Currently, Inter-Vehicle Communication Systems (IVCS) are attracting considerable attention from the research community as well as the automotive industry [1]. The new ad hoc networks trend and the recent advances in wireless technology, allow several possible vehicular network architectures. Three alternatives

Please use the following format when citing this chapter:

Author(s) [insert Last name, First-name initial(s)], 2006, in IFIP International Federation for Information Processing, Volume 201, Security and Privacy in Dynamic Environments, eds. Fischer-Hubner, S., Rannenberg, K., Yngstrom, L., Lindskog, S., (Boston: Springer), pp. [insert page numbers].

include [2]: a pure wireless vehicle-to-vehicle ad hoc network (V2V), a wired backbone with wireless last hops, or a hybrid architecture using V2V communications that does not rely on a fixed infrastructure, but can exploit it for improving performance and functionality when it is available.

An important research and development aspect in vehicular networks concerns the usage of standardized transmission systems like 802.11 in ad hoc mode, the development of protocols and security mechanisms for trusted ad hoc communications, with geographical addressing and reliable routing. Several ad hoc network functionalities and integration strategies are required for services' delivery to users in vehicular networks. Essential features like information routing, security, authentication, authorization and charging should be considered. The routing of information should be reliable and scalable, minimising resources' consumption and delay. The security mechanisms must guarantee that only authorized users can access the ad hoc network resources and services offered by the provider. Also, eavesdropping as well as modification of the transmitted data must be prevented.

In this paper, we propose a novel architecture intended for vehicular networks on highways and present some potential services that aim at assisting drivers as well as passengers. An authentication, authorization and accounting (AAA) scheme is developed for convenient and secure communication between mobile users, authorizing only subscribed users to access the services offered by the provider. Our proposed architecture introduces the concept of ad hoc networking for mobile users' communication. In this context, we propose an approach that adapts Optimized Link State Routing (OLSR) protocol [3] to the vehicular environment aiming to provide reliable data transfer. Also, we give a preliminary solution for the lack of IP addressing within the vehicular environment. The remainder of this paper is organized as follows. Section 2 reviews the relevant literature and contributions, highlighting the motivation to our architecture. The proposed architecture is described in Section 3. In Section 4, we give a brief analysis. Finally, we conclude the paper with Section 5.

2   Literature Review and Related Contributions

Significant parts of the research work in vehicular communication have been supported by the German federal Ministry of Education and Research (BMBF) within the *FleetNet-Internet on the road* project [4] and the *Network on Wheels: NoW* project [5]. The basic goal of these projects is to develop a platform for inter-vehicle and vehicle-to-roadside communication allowing Internet access, based on wireless multi-hop communication. In fact, a close cooperation between the European Car-2-Car Communication Consortium (C2C CC) [6] and the NoW project is being established in order to promote the project results towards European standardization. The *InternetCar* project [7] in Japan is working to develop and deploy a system that provides the Internet connectivity to automobiles, and the EU DAIDALOS project [8] addresses the main aspects of integrating heterogeneous networks technologies including ad hoc networks.

Several approaches employ broadcast to provide intelligent transportation system (ITS) services in vehicular environments, including traffic monitoring, congestion avoidance and safety messages' transfer. A driver assistant is proposed in [9] exploiting upstream traffic information with the assumption that traffic information is sensed by each individual vehicle and analyzed with other vehicles information, and then it is broadcasted. A location-based broadcast communication protocol is proposed in [10], using the information concerning nearby vehicles, aiming to provide highway safety message transfer. Also, a safety-oriented model is designed in [11] based on the concept of ad hoc peer-to-peer (P2P) networking to support the exchange of safety-related data on highways. As an alternative to broadcast dependent approaches, a mobility-centric data dissemination algorithm intended for vehicular networks is presented in [2] exploiting the broadcast nature of wireless transmission but combining opportunistic and geographical forwarding, and a new efficient IEEE 802.11 based multihop broadcast protocol is proposed in [12] that is designed to address the broadcast storm and reliability problems.

In the context of hybrid ad hoc networks applications, ad hoc networks integration in vehicular communication is highly expected. Thus, some ad hoc routing propositions are suggested as solutions for data dissemination on highways. The approach presented in [13] multicast messages among highly mobile hosts in ad hoc networks, with the assumption that the source is stationary and the receivers move at high speeds, mostly towards the source. An extension to this approach is proposed in [14], which considers source and receivers sets that change dynamically based on the content of the transmitted information and the mobility of the receivers and the source. This model introduces sensors to generate the required information, and then pass it to a central node in each region.

From our investigation to the relevant contributions, we noticed that they mostly tackle the problem from an application view and are assumption based. Several propositions focus on providing ITS services in vehicular environment that is especially useful on highways. These propositions provide solutions in terms of message dissemination among mobile clients that are mostly broadcast dependent, and ad hoc routing has emerged as one of the solutions to provide safety and/or traffic situation messages' transfer. Recently, Internet connectivity becomes one of the target services due to the great advances in 802.11 technologies. This approach is highly promoted by many large projects working towards providing Internet connectivity to mobile users in their vehicles, which led to the emergence of new design trends by automotive industry for future cars. In this paper, we focus on vehicular communication on highways addressing one of the promising applications of hybrid ad hoc networks. We follow a realistic approach, considering the benefit of both mobile clients on highways and service providers. We propose a novel architecture providing an integrated solution that achieves: services provision ranging from ITS to Internet connectivity, constructing a virtual infrastructure for vehicular communication, mobile clients' authentication, confidentiality in data transfer and reliability in routing the information.

3   The Proposed Architecture

We start by defining the services offered by the service provider, and then we propose an appropriate architecture design considering vehicular-to- vehicular and vehicular-to-road communication in order to achieve the offered services. We develop an AAA scheme based on 802.11i [15] for authenticating mobile clients with respect to the service provider at the entry points of highways , authorizing them to access the offered services according to their subscription. This scheme also assures the confidentiality and the integrity in data transfer between each two parties. For information routing, we benefit from the ad hoc networks that are randomly constructed between mobile clients, proposing an approach that adapts OLSR to the vehicular communication environment as well as a suitable and simple mechanism to provide mobile clients with the required IP addresses achieving appropriate routing.

3.1 Architecture Design Overview

The general objective of this architecture is to support communication and data transfer between mobile clients (moving vehicles) as well as mobile clients' access to some offered services on highways. These services include (vehicular network access enabling inter-vehicles communication and data transfer, safety and traffic condition messages' transfer, speed limit reminder messages, and mobile clients' Internet access) and they are provided by the network operator, the ISP (Internet Service Provider) or the WISP (Wireless Internet Service Provider). We propose two possible business models that are discussed in Section 3.2. The proposed architecture is not limited to these defined services and is quite general to support services' extension. It combines a fixed network infrastructure and a virtual infrastructure constituted by mobile ad hoc networks comprising three core entities as shown in Figure 1: a) Access network, which is the fixed network infrastructure and forms the back-end of the architecture. b) Wireless mobile ad hoc networks, constructed by the moving vehicles and form the architecture front-end. c) 802.11 WLAN infrastructure in the form of access points (APs), providing a limited wireless infrastructure and is connected to the backbone access network infrastructure, and thus forming the interface between the architecture front and back ends. These APs are installed on highways entry points and are scattered at gas stations and rest houses areas along the highways.

The APs have three important roles: they are considered as Area Border Routers (ABRs) for mobile clients, linking them to the access network. They play a role in routing the information among mobile clients and constructing the virtual routing infrastructure, this is discussed in Section 3.4. Furthermore, they play an important role in authenticating mobile clients at the entry points at the beginning; this is detailed in Section 3.3. Ad hoc network chains are constructed among mobile clients; these chains may be separated or temporally linked. We define an ad hoc network chain as a group of geographical dynamic clusters, continuously reconfiguring among mobile nodes. Each cluster is composed of mobile nodes having the same proximity, the same movement direction, and the same average speed. We assume that there is a fixed cluster that always exists in the coverage area of each AP, which can be considered as a geographical virtual cluster.

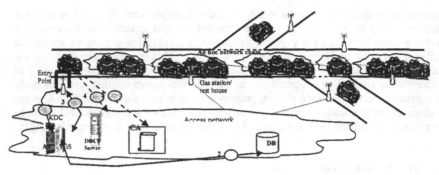

Fig. 1. Architecture design.

3.2 Business Model

We assume two possible business models, each of which is associated to the clients' Internet subscription or telephone subscription (fix or mobile telephone): *pure package* (pay before use), where the billing is monthly fixed whether the client will use the services or not. *On-use package* (use before pay) in which the billing is associated to the network access authorization (discussed in Section 3.3), which is obtained at the entry points of highways.

3.3 The Authentication, Authorization, and Accounting (AAA) Mechanism

We propose a solution that uses the mobile users' service providers as the core entity for all AAA processes [16], adapting the 802.11i standard to ad hoc networking environment. This allows each two communicating parties to properly authenticate and encrypt the data transfer between themselves. To provide a stronger encryption mechanism, we assume that 802.11i employs the Advanced Encryption Standard (AES) promoted by the WPA2 [17] for 802.11 devices. The Business model in Section 3.2, discusses the mobile clients billing process. The developed authentication and authorization processes are presented in this section. In our approach, we treat three issues: a) client/service provider mutual authentication at the entry point, b) client/client authentication and secure communication, c) AP/client authentication and secure data transfer. A successful client/service provider mutual authentication authorizes each client to access the required services during his voyage. The client/client and AP/client mutual authentication are carried out between each two nodes sharing the same proximity, which are authenticated and authorized by the service provider at the entry point. This allows links to be setup in layer 2 among authenticated and authorized nodes. Although 802.11i considers the RADIUS server as the default authentication server (AS) employing it in conjunction with Extensible Authentication Protocol (EAP) [18], RADIUS does not outfit our previously discussed issues as it does not provide authorization for special services but rather provides authorization for channel access. Accordingly, we apply a Kerberos authentication model [19] authenticating clients at the entry point and authorizing them to services' access.

In Kerberos model, every service requires some credentials for the client in the form of a ticket. There are two types of tickets: *Ticket Granting Ticket* (TGT) and *Ticket Granting Service* (TGS). The TGT allows the client to obtain service tickets (TGSs), while the TGS is the ticket that grants the clients the services' access. So the client must first obtain a TGT, then requests a TGS for each service that he needs. A Kerberos server contains a Key Distribution Center (KDC), which encompasses two parts: an authentication service part that plays the role of an AS and grants the TGT after each successful authentication, and a TGS part for granting TGS tickets for each authenticated client having a valid TGT. To apply Kerberos authentication model in our architecture, each client at the entry point authenticates via the AS in the Kerberos KDC and obtains a TGT. The TGT indicates mutual authentication between the client and the service provider. Then, the client uses the obtained TGT to request a TGS for each service he needs. We assume that two services are requested at the entry point: 1) a network access service, by which each authenticated client is assigned an IP address. 2) a public key certificate service, by which each authenticated client obtains a certificate that he uses later for authentication and secure communication with other clients.

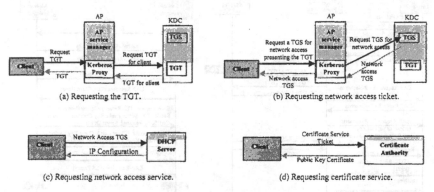

(a) Requesting the TGT.

(b) Requesting network access ticket.

(c) Requesting network access service.

(d) Requesting certificate service.

Fig. 2. Kerberos authentication model.

Figure 2, describes the message flow for applying the Kerberos model. Since 802.11i requires the client to initially authenticate to an AP in order to gain access to the network, via employing IEEE/802.1x, we introduce the notion of Kerberos proxy [20]. The AP at the entry point is a Kerberos proxy and at the same time plays the role of the authenticator that authenticates each client after consulting the Kerberos AS. Then, it provides the client with network access through TGS grants. Figure 2(a) shows the process of client's authentication, obtaining the TGT from the AS. In Figure 2(b), the client presents the TGT and requests a TGS for network access (any other service can be requested). Figure 2(c), shows the client IP configuration through communicating a DHCP server and presenting the network access TGS (the process of IP configuration is detailed in Section 3.5). In Figure 2(d), the client obtains the public key certificate, presenting the corresponding TGS that is assumed to be obtained in a similar way to Figure 2(b). Figure 3, illustrates the authentication messages' exchange, where we employ EAP-Kerberos [20, 21] since the AS is not directly accessible to the client. The client exchanges the authentication messages with the AP (Kerberos proxy) using EAP, and the AP consults the AS through a Kerberos request to authenticate the client. Then the AP sends a TGS request to the TGS center, granting the client the requested services' tickets. To this end, mutual authentication with the service provider and services' authorization are achieved for each client. As no actual data transfer takes place at this phase, we are restricted to mutual authentication and services' authorization and do not involve the 802.11i encryption key generation phase. As seen in Figure 3, the AS generates a session key after obtaining a password proof for the client. This session key is contained in the TGT and is received by both the client and the AP, providing also mutual authentication between them. Then, each client is granted a network access and a public key certificate TGSs, through which he respectively obtains an IP configuration and a certificate that, is used afterwards for setting up links in layer 2 with other vehicles during the voyage. EAPoL protocol (EAP over LAN), which is defined as a part of the 802.1X specification, runs between the client and the authenticator encapsulating EAP-Kerberos. The corresponding messages exchange is shown in Figure 3.

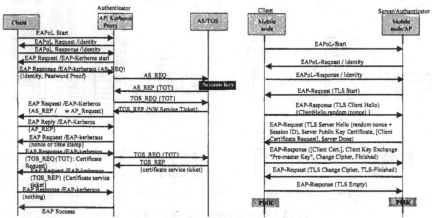

Fig. 3. EAP-Kerberos messages exchange.   **Fig. 4.** EAP-TLS messages exchange.

The second step is to setup secure links in layer 2 between each two communicating parties that are authenticated. In this case, we employ 802.11i in an ad hoc mode, without introducing an AS. Authentication is completely carried out by each two communicating nodes, making use of the previously obtained certificates. Firstly, we employ EAP-TLS [22] between each nodes pair that fall in the same proximity, and wants to communicate. A *public key client-server* approach is used, where each authenticating pair acts as a client-server pair using the obtained certificates at the initial Kerberos authentication and service-granting phase. This saves the overhead of certificates' generation during authentication. We assume that the client does not send the TLS *certificate verification* signal as it has already a certificate signed by the CA. Figure 4, illustrates the corresponding messages' exchange. The client generates a pre-master key, when it receives the server certificate. This is in the form of a 48 bytes random number encrypted with the server public key, then decrypted by the server using the server private key. The client and server use a *Hash {Pre-master key, Server nonce, Client nonce}* to generate a Pairwise Master Key (PMK), providing mutual authentication between the client-server pair. We assume that TLS session resumption [23] may take place if each client is capable of storing a copy of the PMK, thus minimizing layer 2 delays with clients' mobility. Secondly, to obtain an increased security on each authenticated link, we introduce the 802.11i encryption phase via employing the 4-way Handshake between the client and the server. In this case EAPoL-Key messages are used in the messages' exchange, which are intended to allow secret key information exchange. Firstly, PMK is used to generate a Pairwise Temporal Key (PTK) for encrypting unicast data transfer on the link. Then, a Group Temporal Key (GTK) is generated for encrypting broadcast and multicast data transfer on the link. Thereby, all upcoming data transfer on the authenticated link will be encrypted using the generated keys ensuring communication privacy and secure data transfer. We follow the WPA2 proposed key exchange message [24], reducing latency and overhead.

3.4 Routing

To provide appropriate routing infrastructure among the authenticated links in layer 2, an appropriate ad hoc routing protocol is required to be employed at layer 3. We tend to apply a proactive routing approach to ensure the continuous existence of a routing infrastructure among vehicles, proposing a solution that remediates the proactive approach overhead. This solution uses the OLSR protocol and adapts it to the vehicular environment. OLSR protocol is chosen as it is a proactive protocol that minimizes the control packets flooding and is suitable for large and dense networks when communicating over a large subset of nodes. Moreover, OLSR auxiliary functions support communication with external networks. This is useful in providing Internet connectivity service in our architecture.

Adapting OLSR to the Proposed Architecture: we extend OLSR to include the notion of *Local Scope (LS)*. We define the LS as the logical subnet constructed among each group of nodes sharing the same geographical area. Each LS is dynamic and continuously re-configurable. The former is due to the nodes' mobility changing their geographical area, and the latter is due to the nodes membership change (joining or leaving different LSs) according to their connectivity. An Ad hoc chain is formed by a group of connected LSs that may be temporally linked to an AP through one LS of the chain. The whole vehicle-vehicle network is the collection of ad hoc chains that may be temporally connected or separated. The classical OLSR protocol executes in each LS *"Intra LS routing"*, where each LS member node stores in its routing table routes to all possible destinations in its LS. While routing between different LSs *"Inter LS routing"* takes place through *gateway nodes*, which we define as the border nodes at each LS.

LS Construction and Intra LS Routing: each LS is constructed by a *root node* that may be fix or mobile (AP or client), using the ad hoc IP flooding protocol presented in [25]. A new multicast group is specified for flooding, given the name "ALL_IPv4_MANET_NODES". Each root node floods an *LS-construct* packet with a multicast address associated to the group, and a pre-defined maximum hop count

(*TTL*) to limit the flooding radius to the local geographical scope. The maximum hop value is selected in terms of the desired LS size and the density of vehicles on highways. The *LS-construct* packet has a unique identifier (*LS-ID*), identifying the LS that is being constructed. Each node receiving the packet, if it is not already a member in other LS, stores a copy of the *LS-ID* and becomes an LS member. The reception redundancy is detected and each node receives each flooded packet only once. This phase takes place in a periodic manner for continuous LS construction and maintenance, allowing *LS-ID* soft state storage at each LS member. A node elects it self as a root node following the *first declaration win* (FDW) rule, used in passive clustering construction in ad hoc networks [26], where the node that sends the *LS-construct* packet first becomes the root node. We add the condition that this node should be granted the network access at the entry point and it does not receive any *LS-construct* packets for a timeout period. Using the LS mechanism, OLSR provides routing within a limited geographical scope. All transmitted OLSR packets by each node carry the corresponding *LS-ID* as well as the node's type (gateway, non gateway), and are only received by the same LS member nodes. This introduces fewer overheads in transmission size and routing tables' storage and maintenance, allowing scalability of the protocol's operation among numerous nodes that may constitute the vehicular network.

Inter LS Routing: *gateway nodes* in each LS are last nodes receiving the *LS-construct* packet during the LS construction. They are nodes that have neighbors in its range belonging to different LSs, we call these neighbors *Inter LS neighbors*. Gateway nodes are responsible for Inter LS routing through proactively maintaining routing paths, in their routing tables, to their one hop Inter LS neighbors. A root node having only Inter neighbors in its one hop neighbor table understands that it is separated from its LS and accepts the first *LS-Construct* packet coming from another root node. Thus it joins the announced LS.

Data Structures: a new record (*node-info*) is created at each node, storing the node's type (gateway, no gateway) with respect to its LS as well as the *LS-ID*. Otherwise, no additional data structure is needed compared to OLSR as we assume that each node announces its type in all transmitted control packets during the Intra LS routing. Thus, all member nodes of each LS are aware of their gateway nodes and store the type of each destination in their routing tables. Section 4, gives the required implementation consideration.

Data Transfer: we distinguish between two types of data transfer: regular transfer, including inter-vehicles communication for routing data between defined pair(s) as well as Internet access. And emergency transfer, including safety and traffic condition messages' dissemination. In regular transfer, the adapted-OLSR routing protocol proceeds employing classical OLSR for Intra LS routing and using gateway nodes for Inter LS routing. A node that does not find a route for the destination in its Intra LS routing table, transfers the data packet to its gateway nodes that forward it to their Inter LS neighbors, until the destination is localized. We assume that reception redundancy is detected and discarded. In emergency transfer, data is locally disseminated within the LS. In this case, routing switches to flooding to the previously defined multicast group, following the same approach of *LS-construct* packet propagation. If dissemination extension (including more than LS) is desired, gateway nodes are employed to forward the packets to their Inter LS neighbors.

Connection to Access Network: We assume that APs are equipped with multiple interfaces, including non OLSR interfaces connected to the access network. Each AP is then charged with injecting routing information of this external network to the OLSR VANET nodes, via employing the OLSR *Host and Network Association (HNA)* message. The HNA messages periodically inject external networks information to ad hoc network nodes, including the external network address and the net mask. We thus assume that each AP along the highway periodically diffuses this message in its virtual fixed cluster. Each mobile vehicle falling in this cluster (i.e. member nodes of a given LS that fall in this cluster) will receive this diffused access network information and creates/updates its association set repository with the recent access network information as well as the corresponding AP. Consequently, each node requesting an Internet connectivity service utilizes this stored information.

3.5 IP Addressing

Mobile clients construct dynamic ad hoc network chains during their continuous movements, at the same time the problem of IP address configuration is not yet resolved in such a dynamic environment devoid of any fixed infrastructure or centralized administration. As a simple solution, we make use of the existing infrastructure at the entry points of highways in order to provide each mobile client with an IP configuration. Our solution is based on using a Dynamic Host Configuration Protocol (DHCP) server with IPv4, considering the following assumptions: a) after the authentication of each mobile client (obtaining TGT ticket), it requests a network access TGS. b) a DHCP server exists at the entry point of each highway, using the dynamic allocation mechanism [27], where each client having a network access TGS can directly communicate with the DHCP server and achieve the IP configuration service. c) each address assigned by the DHCP server to the client has a fixed *lease* decided by the server, and the client is not allowed to require *lease* extension. d) IP address release is carried out by the server, when an IP address *lease* is expired the server gets back the IP address and reallocates it to another client. Thus, *DHCPRELEASE* message is not used. Although this proposed scheme provides a simple solution, it partially solves the clients' IP configuration problem as it limits the size of services' access (this is discussed in Section 5).

4 Brief Analysis

In our AAA scheme, Kerberos authentication combines authentication and services' authorization embedding clients' credentials in tickets. We succeed in authenticating clients through contacting the AS only once, minimizing the load on the AS and reducing the delay imposed by layer 2. Applying 802.11i in ad hoc mode ensures continuous authentication for communication parties and secure links setup. This employs EAP-TLS, avoiding the shared secret weakness of the PSK authentication proposed by the standard for ad hoc mode. Moreover, TLS session resumption possibility allows a fast roam back between authenticated clients and reduces disconnection latency. In our routing approach, introducing local scopes is expected to reduce routing overhead caused by high nodal density while involving only one extra control packet. OLSR support for sleep mode and external networks helps respectively in saving equipments' batteries and providing a partial solution for Internet connectivity.

5 Conclusion and Limitations

In this paper we propose a new architecture for vehicular communication and diverse services' access on highways, integrating ad hoc networking with 802.11 technologies. Our architecture is extensible to any services, it does not require any changes in the 802.11i standard, and it does not involve new wireless technologies develop a novel AAA mechanism independent of layer 3 routing protocol and particularly suitable for vehicular environment. To the best of our knowledge, ours is among the primary schemes integrating 802.11i security in an ad hoc environment and introducing Kerberos model and EAP-Kerberos in 802.11i WLAN environment. We make use of the ad hoc networks construction among mobile clients to achieve reliable information dissemination, via proposing a mechanism that adapts OLSR to the scalable vehicular environment. This scheme benefits from OLSR proactive approach in the sense of providing continuous routing infrastructure while proposing a remedy for its limited scalability due to the continuous propagation of routing messages among all nodes. For realistic routing environment, we present a simple IP configuration scheme based on DHCP and IPv4. The limitation of this architecture is the lack of continuous Internet connectivity among mobile clients as they change their IP domain. Also, this architecture does not support IPv6. A next step is to integrate micro/macro mobility management along the vehicular network and between vehicular networks in different highway branches. We also intend to provide an IPv6 support, based on the existing OLSR IPv6 solutions.

6 References

1. Hartenstein H. et al.: Position-Aware Ad Hoc Wireless Networks for Inter-vehicle Communications: The Fleetnet Project, ACM symposium on Mobile Ad Hoc Networking and Computing, MobiHoc, 2001
2. Wu J. et al.: MDDV: A Mobility-Centric Data Dissemination Algorithm for Vehicular Networks, first ACM VANET Workshop, Philadelphia, PA, USA, 2004
3. Clausen T. and Jacquet P.: Optimized Link State Routing Protocol (OLSR), RFC 3626, October 2003.
4. The FleetNet Project http://www.Fleetnet.de/
5. The Network on Wheels Project http://www.informatik.unimannheim.de/pi4/lib/projects/NoW
6. The Car 2 Car Communication Consortium http://www.car-2-car.org
7. The InternetCAR Project http://www.sfc.wide.ad.jp/InternetCAR/
8. The EU Project DAIDALOS http://www.ist-daidalos.org
9. Wischhof L. et al.: Adaptive Broadcast for Travel and Traffic Information Distribution Based on Inter-Vehicle Communication, IEEE IV'2003, 2003
10. Xu Q. et al.: Design and Analysis of Highway Safety Communication Protocol in 5.9 GHz Dedicated Short Range Communication Spectrum, IEEE VTC'03, 2003

11. Chisalita I. and Shahmehri N.: A Peer-to-Peer Approach to Vehicular Communication for the Support of Traffic Safety Applications, 5th IEEE Intelligent Transportation System Conference (ITS), 2002
12. Korkmaz G. et al.: Urban Multi-Hop Broadcast Protocol for Inter-Vehicle Communication Systems, first ACM VANET Workshop, Philadelphia, PA, USA, 2004
13. Briesemeister L., and Homel G.: Role-Based Multicast in Highly Mobile but Sparsely Connected Ad Hoc Networks, in IEEE/ACM Workshop on Mobile Ad Hoc Networking and Computing (MobiHOC), 2000
14. Zhou H. and Singh S.: Content based multicast (CBM) in ad hoc networks, in IEEE/ACM Workshop on Mobile Ad Hoc Networking and Computing (MobiHOC), 2000
15. IEEE Std. 802.11i: Medium Access Control Security Enhancements July 2004
16. Moustafa H., Bourdon G., Gourhant Y.: AAA in vehicular communication on highways with ad hoc networking support: a proposed architecture, proceeding of the VANET ACM workshop in conjunction with MobiCom 2005, Germany, September 2005
17. WiFi Alliance http://www.wi-fi.org/OpenSection/protected_access.asp
18. Aboba B. and Calhoun P., RADIUS (Remote Authentication Dial In User Service) Support For Extensible Authentication protocol (EAP), RFC 3579, September 2003
19. Kohl J. and Neuman B. C.: The Kerberos Network Authentication Service (Version 5), RFC 1510, September 1993
20. Trostle J. et al.: Initial and Pass Through Authentication Using Kerberos V5 and the GSS-API (IAKERB), IETF Internet Draft, draft-ietf-cat-iakerb-09.txt, October 2002
21. N/A: EAP-Kerberos, IETF Internet Draft, draft-someoneeapkerberos-00.txt, February 2005
22. Aboba B., Simon D.: PPP EAP TLS Authentication Protocol, RFC 2716, October 1999
23. Salowey J. et al.: TLS Session Resumption without Server-Side State, IETF Internet Draft, draft-salowey-tls-ticket-02.txt, February 2005
24. AiroSpace : White Paper http://www.airospace.com/technolog/technote_auth_enc_wlan.php
25. Perkins C., Belding-Royer E. M., Das S.: IP Flooding in Ad hoc mobile Networks, IETF Internet Draft, draft-ietf-manet-bcast-02.txt, November 2001
26. Gerla M., Kwon T. J., and Pei G.: On Demand Routing in Large Ad hoc Wireless Networks with Passive Clustering, IEEE WCNC 2000, September 2000
27. Droms R.: Dynamic Host Configuration Protocol, RFC 2131, March 1997

A Framework for Web Services Trust

Marijke Coetzee and Jan Eloff

Information and Computer Security Architectures (ICSA) Research Group
Department of Computer Science, University of Pretoria, Pretoria, South Africa
marijke@acm.org, eloff@cs.up.ac.za

Abstract. Today, organisations that seek a competitive advantage are adopting virtual infrastructures that share and manage computing resources. The trend is toward implementing collaborating applications supported by web services technology. In order to enable secure interoperation between participants of these environments, trust is an important requirement to address. Current solutions to trust between web components are limited, as they are usually established via cryptographic mechanisms, in the presence of trusted third parties. To accommodate the dynamic and fluid nature of web services environments, a framework for trust assessment and computation is presented. The trust framework is characterised by information and reasoning. It has mechanisms that allow web services entities to manage trust autonomously, by activating a trust level and trust types by means of a rule-based fuzzy cognitive map.

1 Introduction

With the globalisation of the world economy, more and more organisations are realising the need to move to open standards in order to collaborate with business partners. Web Services technology represents a response to the need for a flexible and efficient business collaboration environment. It provides a technical infrastructure to ensure that applications from different organisations can interoperate. Application-to-application interactions automatically perform operations that previously required human interventions, such as searching and buying goods at a pre-determined price, coordinating flight reservations and streamlining invoicing and shipping processes.

Web services are Extensible Markup Language (XML) applications mapped to programs, objects, databases or comprehensive business functions [21]. Web services standards define the format of message that are exchanged, and specify the interface to which the message is sent. The web services architecture is based upon the interactions between three roles [10]: a web services provider that hosts a web service and its operations, a web services broker that makes web services publicly accessible, and a web services requestor that integrates web services operations with its application environment.

The decision to allow cross-domain application integration is critically dependent on whether a business partner can be trusted. In order to establish trust between web services, the Web Services Trust Language or WS-Trust [12] was published. WS-Trust relies on mechanisms such as cryptography, trusted third parties and key

Please use the following format when citing this chapter:

Author(s) [insert Last name, First-name initial(s)], 2006, in IFIP International Federation for Information Processing, Volume 201, Security and Privacy in Dynamic Environments, eds. Fischer-Hubner, S., Rannenberg, K., Yngstrom, L., Lindskog, S., (Boston: Springer), pp. [insert page numbers].

management schemes. The resulting trust that is established is of a limited nature, as it does not take into account evidence and previous experiences. Trust management solutions [4, 23] enable cross-domain movement of entities, represented by credentials. The required trust relationships are not easy to establish as they may have to be negotiated, are complex and time-consuming to implement, and are manually configured by administrators.

To address trust requirements for cross-domain application integration, this paper presents a framework for web services trust. The framework gives a web service the ability to determine the trustworthiness of others at execution time, instead of determining such trustworthiness manually or by means of cryptographic PKI frameworks. The framework makes explicit the role of security mechanisms and controls in trust assessment, and identifies additional elements such as competence, over which trust can be formed.

The remainder of this paper is structured as follows: Section 2 gives an example. Section 3 presents a brief background to characteristics of social trust. Section 4 describes these characteristics as they may be applied to web services, and introduces a definition for trust management. Section 5 describes the framework for web services trust. The framework is characterised by automated assessment of information and trust inference. A rule-based Fuzzy Cognitive Map is used to infer a trust level. Section 6 describes a prototype implementation. Section 7 concludes the paper.

2 Motivating example

This example considers eBooks, a web services provider that provides a retail service to sell academic books, and eLoans, a web services requestor. eLoans provides study loans to students. To more effectively manage a student loan, eLoans enables students to purchase books by integrating operations of eBooks at its portal. When eBooks interacts with eLoans, it exposes itself to risk.

When establishing new business relationships with web services requestors, eBooks needs to determine their trustworthiness. A number of checks can be made such as the verification of the identity of eLoans, the country that eLoans is located in, as this may ensure legal protection in the face of misconduct, the credit record of eLoans, contracts and agreements that are in place to provide protection, the existence of insurance against loss, and encryption algorithms used when sensitive information is sent across a network. eBooks has little means to determine the trustworthiness of eLoans other than with time-consuming and expensive processes that quickly become outdated.

To be able to support the instant application integration provided by web services technology, mechanisms are required to dynamically assess the trustworthiness of eLoans. In order to address an automated approach to trust assessment, the next section introduces characteristics of trust to be considered in the framework for web services trust.

3 Trust

Trust between web services requires characteristics of human and organisational behaviour, as decisions need to be made in unfamiliar environments when complete information is not available. From a large body of work on trust [2, 3, 8, 13, 15, 19, 20, 22], the following characteristics of trust are highlighted for the purposes of this research:

1. *Trust is used to reduce complexity when decisions are made.* In work by Luhman [19], trust is seen as a mechanism used to perceive the complexity of future interactions that may lead to unfavourable outcomes. A trustor has no other choice, than to make a decision to trust, based on limited information known about the other party.

2. *Trust is formed from different types of trust.* The decomposition of trust is reported in literature. Marsh [20] identifies types over which trust is formed such as competence. Chervany and McKnight [8] defined a high-level typology of trust that identifies the situational decision to trust, dispositional trust, trusting beliefs and system trust. Castelfranchi and Falcone [7] identify honesty and competence as some of their belief components. A model of inter-organisational trust identifies competence, predicatability and goodwill as components of trust between organisations [22].

3. *The basis of trust is intuitive reasoning over information.* Humans continually assess each other as they collect information through experiences, observations, and recommendations from others [2]. Assumptions are soon made in relationships such as: "it is very likely that Sue is trustworthy". It is not possible for humans to exactly determine Sue's trustworthiness by stating "the probability that Sue is trustworthy is 8". If, because of previous experiences, the general trusting disposition of Jill is to be very distrustful, her trust in the system and in others is lowered.

Trust for eBooks is next investigated, to determine its synergy with mentioned characteristics of human trust.

4 Trust for eBooks

Research on trust formation between applications has had its origins in trust management systems [4, 23]. Trust management [4] makes use of mechanisms such as identities, certificates, signatures and keys to establish trust relationships across domains. Grandison [16] later extended the definition of trust management to: *"the activity of collecting, encoding, analysing and presenting evidence relating to competence, honesty, security or dependability with the purpose of making assessments and decisions regarding trust relationships for Internet applications."* Evidence could include credentials such as certificates for proof of identity or qualifications, risk assessments, usage experience or recommendations. This definition highlights the fact that trust is not only formed over the verification of a digital identity, but also over other categories of information. A drawback of this work is that initial trust values are not computed, but are assigned by an administrator after information and evidence is processed.

In order to enable eBooks to determine the trustworthiness of its web services requestors dynamically, this research aims to extend the definition of trust management to an automated process of trust assessment that includes above-mentioned characteristics of trust as follows:

1. Trust is used to reduce complexity when decisions are made. eBooks makes a decision to trust eLoans, after an evaluation of possibly limited information it has on characteristics of eLoans.

2. Trust is formed from different types of trust. Inspired by the way humans trust, this research maintains that trust between eBooks and eLoans can be formed by three types of trust as follows:

- An assessment of the properties of the *internal environment* of eBooks to establish its self-confidence and its general disposition to its web services requestors.
- An assessment of the properties of the *external environment* or institution within which the trust relation between eBooks and eLoans exists. This increases trust to reflect moderate levels.
- An assessment of the properties of eLoans. Trust evolves and can grow over time to a high level that reflects goodwill.

3. The basis of trust is intuitive reasoning over information. It is not possible to directly portray the intuitive manner in which humans trust. eBooks can exhibit a form of intuitiveness if it can make inferences from incomplete information and can react in unfamiliar situations. This can be achieved if trust information can be identified for the three mentioned trust types. For eBooks, an intuitive trust decision is replaced with a formal process of trust assessment and mathematical reasoning. Trust concepts are numerically formed from information that is arranged together due to similarity. This enables eBooks to follow humanistic reasoning as trust concepts are defined to be fuzzy of nature. eBooks can include tolerance for imprecision, uncertainty and partial truth in its reasoning, similar to the way that humans do.

Based on the above characteristics, the following definition for trust management and of a trust concept is proposed:

Definition - Trust management: *The automated assessment of information and evidence, relating to the properties of the internal environment, the properties of the external environment, and the properties of the other party, with the purpose of establishing trust concepts from which a trust level can be inferred.*

Definition – Trust concept: *A trust concept is a fuzzified category of information or evidence that is populated with a value between 0 and 1.*

5.   Framework for web services trust

The framework for web services trust is characterised by a phased approach where trust evolves over time. The automation of trust assessment and formation is supported by the web services architecture as follows:

- *Publish trust information:* Web services providers and requestors needs to inform others how it will behave in order to establish a trust relationship with them, and what it may expect from them.

- *Discover trust information:* Information is gathered by locating and inspecting XML policies, references, and certificates.
- *Trust formation:* XML policies and other information are analysed and evaluated. The result of this phase is a basic level of trust.
- *Trust evolution:* Web services monitor all further SOAP [5] interactions in order to evaluate the trust held towards others. If all transactions are processed smoothly, trust evolves so that future interactions may be granted access to more sensitive resources or risky transactions.

Common sources of information that can be used to form trust are: metadata such as WS-Policy [6] or WSLA (Web Service Level Agreements) [11] documents that is required by complex web services; references and recommendations that are formatted in XML and added to SOAP headers; and experiences that can be recorded by inspecting SOAP messages. The gathering of trust information has been described in a preceding paper by the authors [9].

Fifteen trust concepts are identified for trust formation in the next section, of which some are only named, and others are discussed. Trust concepts such as compliance to agreements, level of vulnerabilities, implemented security mechanisms and predictability represent a realistic view of a web services requestor such as eLoans, and the stability of the environment in which web services operations of eBooks are to be used. Trust concepts embody the beliefs of eBooks to provide a basis over which trust can be inferred. The strength of trust is thus a function of the assessment of information [7].

Trust concepts are interrelated, with feedback links that propagate influences to trust types. Axelrod's work on Cognitive Maps introduced a way to represent such processes [1]. When information is assessed to form trust concepts, numerical data is uncertain, and the formulation of a mathematical model is difficult. Efforts to address this problem should rather rely on natural language statement in the absence of formal models. Fuzzy Cognitive Maps (FCM), as introduced by Kosko [18] is used by this research to address the trust assessment process. This research is inspired by the work of Castelfranchi and Falcone [7], that have shown how humanistic forms of trust can intuitively be mimicked by a FCM. This paper extends their work to application-to-application interactions. The next section describes the approach to trust calculation.

5.1   A proposal for web services trust calculation

In order to enable a web service to form trust relationships with others, a trust manager is proposed. The trust manager, shown in Figure 1, is accommodated in the web services architecture, before any web services interaction takes place. The trust manager is knowledgeable about the requirements of the web service, the standards that are used and the threshold of trust that is required. When requests are sent to a web service, accompanied by references and recommendations, its trust manager will intercept the request in order to verify the validity of information with independent third parties. The trust manager records experiences by inspecting SOAP messages. It also mediates all trust-related interactions with partners and strangers, while it intelligently processes all information that it sources, or that is presented to it.

A FCM, shown in Figure 1, is associated with each web services entity such as eLoans. A web services entity infers a trust level for others according to the structure of the FCM. The FCM enables a web services entity to make intuitive decisions based on observations and experiences. Nodes of a Fuzzy Cognitive Map represent trust concepts that are used to describe main behavioural characteristics of the system. An Interface component intercepts SOAP messages, applies rules to analyse and categorise information, and stores information in a database. The Trust Inference component populates nodes of the FCM with values in the fuzzy interval range [0, 1] after information is fuzzified. Finally, a trust level is inferred. Trust levels are defined as the set {*ignorance, low, moderate, good, high*}, where *ignorance* ⊆ *low* ⊆ *moderate* ⊆ *good* ⊆ *high*.

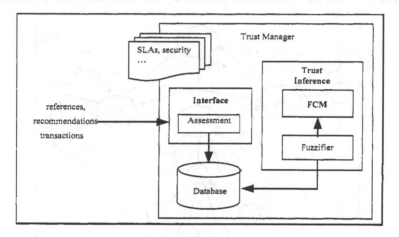

Fig. 1. Web services architecture for trust.

5.2   Trust inference

Fuzzy Cognitive Maps [17] are dynamical systems that relate fuzzy sets and rules. They are fuzzy graph structures that consist of nodes and weighted arcs, which store information. A Fuzzy Cognitive Map can represent the trust-forming process of eBooks in a symbolic manner, similar to the way in which humans cognitively manipulate trust concepts. A Fuzzy Cognitive Map consisting of n concepts is represented by a $1 \times n$ state vector A, which gathers the values of the n concepts; and by an $n \times n$ edge matrix E, with elements e_{ij}. The activation level A_i, for each concept C_i, is calculated by the following rule [18].

$$A_i = f\left(\sum_{j=1}^{n} A_j \, e_{ij} \right)$$

The value of e_{ij} indicates how strongly concept C_i influences C_j. A_i represents the level of activation of a node. A discrete time simulation is performed by iteratively applying a summation and threshold process to state vector A. A_i is the activation level of concept C_i at time t+1 and A_j is the activation of concept C_j at time t. f is a threshold function that transforms the summation into the interval [0,1]. Next, the FCM of eBooks is described.

5.3   eBooks FCM

The design of the FCM for web services trust is shown in Figure 2. It depicts 4 labeled nodes that represent the three trust types as described below. The remaining 15 nodes represent trust concepts that are populated with fuzzy values. To commence with the discussion on the design of the FCM, the three types of trust and their interrelationships are first discussed. Trust concepts are discussed in next paragraphs.

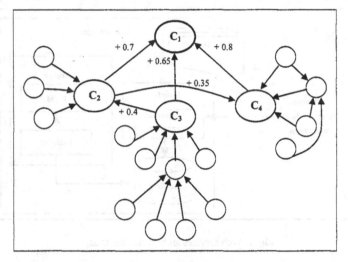

Fig. 2. FCM for trust between eBooks and eLoans.

The concepts representing each node are: C_1 - the trust level that eBooks infers for eLoans, C_2 – the trust in the internal environment of eBooks, C_3 – the trust in the external environment between eBooks and eLoans, and C_4 –the trust that eBooks has in eLoans.

The FCM models the interactions between the three types of trust that form the level of trust that eBooks holds towards eLoans. Input from experts is used to determine causal influences on trust [18]. Each arc is drawn and weighted through intuition and may be modified through experimentation. Causal relationships between concepts are represented by signed and weighted arcs. The arcs of the graph represent the impact that one concept has on another and vary in the interval [-1, +1]. For instance, a value +0.8 for the trust in eLoans (C_4) increase the trust (C_1) by 80%.

– The trust in the internal environment of eBooks (C_2) and the trust in the external environment between eBooks and eLoans (C_3) have a moderate to strong influence on trust as their weights are set to +.7 and +.65 respectively.

- The trust that eBooks has in eLoans (C_4) has a strong influence on trust, as the weight is set to +0.8.
- The trust in the internal environment of eBooks (C_2) has a causal effect on the trust that eBooks has in eLoans (C_4). If eBooks is very sure about the risk of an endeavour and has expertise in dealing with that risk, eBooks can increase its belief in eLoans to reflect its self-confidence.
- The trust in the external environment that exists between eBooks and eLoans (C_3) has a causal effect on the trust in the internal environment of eBooks (C_2). If eBooks is transacting with eLoans in a familiar environment, eBooks is bound to feel very sure of itself, even though it may have vulnerabilities in its environment to consider.

The activation of a trust level (C_1) by trust concepts is implemented by a fuzzy rule. Fuzzy rules map input concepts to an output concept [14]. For this discussion, it is assumed that eBooks requires a high level of trust with eLoans. This is implemented with the following rule in the FCM:

If   *the trust in the internal environment* is **sufficient** and
        the trust in the external environment is **good** and
        the trust in eLoans is **high**
then
        the trust level is **high**

The fuzzy rule specifies that all trust concepts must be at a high level for the trust in eLoans to be "high". In order to activate "high" trust, thresholds are set to activate trust concepts. Trust assessment and fuzzification of information sources qualify trust concepts to be at a "high" level. If so, the value of a trust assessment category is set to 1 (otherwise 0). For instance, if information gathered and processed increments the trust assessment of the external environment (C_3) to more than 0.7, it is within the "good" range, and is activated to 1 in order to influence the trust level. In a similar manner, if the trust assessment of requestor Y (C_4) is more than 0.8 and the trust assessment of the internal environment (C_2) is more than 0.75, they are in the "high" range, and are activated to 1. These activation thresholds are defined intuitively.

To activate a trust level (C_1), an activation threshold is set for each trust level. This threshold specifies the minimum strength to which the incoming relationship degrees must be aggregated in order to achieve "high" trust. Trust is "high" if all trust concepts are activated as they become "high". If a web service requires other levels of trust such as "low" or "moderate", thresholds for trust concepts trust types are implemented accordingly. The population of nodes representing the trust types of the FCM is next given.

5.4   Population of trust concepts

The focus of this research is to aim towards an automated process of trust assessment and inference. As the trust in the other party (C_4) is most representative of this aim, it is discussed in the next paragraph. Trust in the internal environment (C_2) and trust in the external environment (C_3) are partly populated by administrator intervention and their automation is the focus of future research. Trust concepts over which they are inferred are briefly described as background to the discussion that follows.

Trust in the internal environment (C_2) is populated after risk assessments have been conducted. Three nodes, show in Figure 3, represent the vulnerabilities in the systems of eBooks, the confidence of eBooks, and the complexity of the systems of eBooks. Trust in the external environment (C_3) is formed by nodes representing legislation that may exist, assurances, compliance, and security mechanisms that are inferred from identity mechanisms used, supported integrity algorithms, supported confidentiality algorithms, and adherence to best practice. These two trust types form a basic level of trust based on risk evaluations, security mechanisms and guarantees, over which trust in eLoans can evolve.

The discussion now focuses on the third trust type, the trust in the other party, eLoans (C_4). For the purpose of activating trust (C_1) with the fuzzy rule, it is assumed that the trust in the internal environment is *sufficient*, and the trust in the external environment is *good*. For trust in eLoans to be *high*, the trust in the properties of eLoans needs to be *high*.

5.4.1 Trust in eLoans

As eBooks interacts with eLoans, it gains information about characteristics of eLoans, organised according to its compliance to agreements, competence and predictability. Over time, the establishment of these characteristics leads to a measure of goodwill. The trust eLoans (C_4) is inferred from related trust concepts as depicted in Figure 3. The concepts representing each node are: C_{16} – the compliance of eLoans to agreements, C_{17} – the competence of eLoans, C_{18} – the predictability of eLoans and C_{19} – the goodwill developed towards eLoans. A high-level description of the population of each of node with a fuzzy value in the range $[0,1]$ is now given.

C_{16} – eLoans compliance to agreements
Compliance to agreements is the belief that eLoans is honest in its interactions with eBooks. To ensure quality of service, a web services requestor and provider jointly defines a machine-readable service level agreement (SLA) as a part of a service contract that can be monitored by one or both parties. Such agreements are defined in XML-based policies with either WS-Policy or WSLA, and are monitored. The compliance of web services requestors to agreements can be determined by inspecting a large variety of parameters. For this discussion, eBooks monitors the following two parameters:

- The SLA may state that no more than 10 transactions are allowed per minute. If this restriction is exceeded, a record is written to a database to indicate the level transgression by using a factor between 1 and 10, where 10 represents the worst case.
- Security requirements may be stated in WS-policy documents. If eLoans does not adhere to these requirements, it can be recorded to a database as an improper event. Records are written to the database according to a predefined set of rules. Records are aggregated to a value between 0 and 1 to indicate the level of compliance. For instance, if a value of .45 is derived, the level of compliance to agreements is *not sufficient*. A value of .8 means that the level of compliance to agreements is *good*. The causal relationship reflects the fact that if eLoans complies with agreements, the trust in it increases by .5.

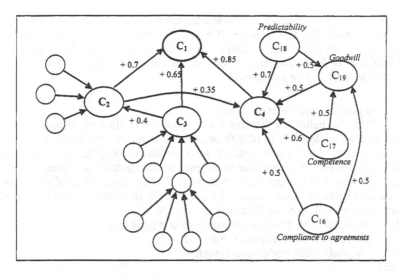

Fig. 3. Activation of trust in eLoans.

C_{17} – The competence of eLoans
Competence is the belief that eLoans has the ability or necessary skills to perform a task. The competence of eLoans can be determined by evaluating recommendations and references that are submitted. Certificates state competence levels such as credit ratings, audit information, endorsements, ISO 9000 certification, privacy seals, or Better Business Bureau statements. Recommendations from other entities are also used to determine competence. Recommendations are only accepted from entities that are identified by a public key. The trust in the public key, determined by trust computation where possible, determines the weight assigned to a recommendation.

Recommendations, references and other statements are evaluated and a value between 0 and 1 is derived to populate node C_{17}. For instance, if a value of .3 is derived, the competence of eLoans is *low*. A value of .8 means that the level of competence is *high*. The causal relationship reflects the fact that if eLoans is competent, the trust in it increases by .6.

C_{18} – The predictability of eLoans
Predictability is the belief that the actions of eLoans is consistent, so that a forecast can be made about how eLoans will behave in a given situation. This can be achieved by inspecting SOAP messages that are sent and received, and by recording for instance, the number of messages, the number of messages in error, the value of transactions, date of transaction fulfillments, and the validity of message details. The focus of this monitoring is to determine a score for each interaction from when a transaction is initiated, until it is fulfilled. If, for instance, an invalid credit card is submitted, the level of transgression is recorded by taking into account the value of the transaction.

The score for each interaction is evaluated and a value between 0 and 1 is derived to populate node C_{18}. For instance, if a value between .5 and .65 is derived, the predictability of eLoans is *moderate*. A value of .8 means that the level of predictability is *high*. The causal relationship reflects the fact that if eLoans is predictable, the trust in it increases by .7.

C_{19} – The goodwill held towards eLoans
Goodwill is the belief that eLoans cares about the welfare of eBooks. It is not established by an assessment of information, but is rather established over time as eBooks realises the benefits gained from increased cooperation with eLoans. Thresholds are set for compliance to agreements, competence and predictability to computationally infer goodwill. The activation of the level of goodwill (C_{19}) by related trust concepts is implemented by a fuzzy rule. In order to have a high level of goodwill towards eLoans, the following rule is used:

If   *the compliance of eLoans to agreements is* **good** and
      the competence of eLoans is **high** and
      the predictability of eLoans is **high**
then
      the goodwill towards eLoans is **high**

Causal relationships reflect the fact that as eLoans complies with agreements, is found to be competent, and predictable, goodwill increases in each case by .5.

6 Prototype

A prototype of limited scope was implemented to illustrate the viability of the trust assessment framework. Trust in the internal and external environment currently populated by administrator intervention, and its automation is the focus of future research. The prototype was developed in the .NET platform. It consists out of the Interface component, a database, and the Trust Inference component.

The interface component is implemented as a SOAP extension, and intercepts all SOAP requests. Requests are inspected to determine the nature of the information that it carries. Information is categorised according to predefined rules, and stored in a database. Information is time-stamped to ensure that out-dated information can be discarded. The database consists out of a variety of tables where different types of information are stored. All tables relate to the identity of a web service requestor.

Next, the trust inference component interrogates tables from the database, and fuzzifies information to populate nodes of the Fuzzy Cognitive Map with values between 0 and 1. The FCM is finally invoked. It infers a trust level over all trust types and trust components. Values for trust types and final trust are time-stamped and stored in a table in the database for future references by for instance, an authorisation component.

7 Conclusion

Experimentation shows that the FCM performs well. A gradual increase in trust is evident as trust concepts are populated. Small changes in trust concepts do not affect the level of trust. The approach to trust is highly intuitive and is based on incomplete information. The FCM enables eBooks to identity reliable business partners with whom it can foster stronger and more meaningful relationships, as eLoans can only achieve a high level of trust if it consistently behaves well. An important contribution made by this research is that trust is composed from different trust types. In some situations, it may be important to interact with parties with whom no familiarity exists, but in the knowledge that the trust in the environment is high.

Even though trust is built by exchanging digital credentials, trust is not built iteratively as in automated trust negotiation (ATN) systems [24]. A trust level is calculated, that reflects a history of interactions and other characteristics of a web services entity and its environment. In a similar vein to this work, trust is computed in the SECURE project [25] over information and evidence. In SECURE, the structure of information is not made explicit, and the approach to trust calculation is not intuitive.

This research is a first step towards an automated trust formation process for web services. It is unique in that trust types and trust concepts are identified for web services environments that are practical to implement. The structure of the FCM can be considered as the main contribution of the paper. It is illustrated that much of the required information is available in machine-readable format, and can thus automatically be gathered and assessed. The causal relationships and fuzzy rules are still the focus of much experimentation. It is important to note that an individualised FCM can reflect the personal considerations of a web service, such as confidence, steadiness, or knowledge of vulnerabilities, by the manner in which causal weights are assigned.

n important focus of further research is identifying problems with the input and output of the FCM, and the assigning of the weights of the causal links. This may be helped by computational training methods, but there is no certainty that the single best set of causal links will be found.

Acknowledgement

The financial assistance of the Department of Labour (DoL), the National Research Foundation (NRF) in South Africa under Grant Number 2054024, Telkom and the IST through THRIP towards the current research is hereby acknowledged.

References

1. Axelrod, R., Framework for a General Theory of Cognition. Berkeley: Institute of International Studies, (1972).

2. Abdul-Rahman A., A framework for desentralised trust reasoning, PHD thesis. Department of Computer Science, University of London, (2004).
3. Barber B., Logic and Limits of Trust. New Jersey: Rutgers University Press, (1983).
4. Blaze M., Feigenbaum J., Ioannidis J., & Keromytis A., "The KeyNote Trust-management System, version 2," IETF, RFC 2704, September, (1999).
5. Box D., Ehnebuske D., Kakivaya G., Layman A., Mendelsohn N., Nielsen H.F, Thatte S. & Winer D., (2000), Simple Object Access Protocol (SOAP) 1.1, http://www.w3.org/TR/SOAP/, May (2000).
6. Box D., Web Services Policy Framework (WS-Policy), http://www.ibm.com/developerworks/library/ws-policy/index.html, (2003).
7. Castelfranchi C, Falcone R., Pezzulo G., A Fuzzy Approach to a Belief-Based Trust Computation., in Trust, reputation and security theory and practice, Bologna, Italy, July,Lecture notes in Computer Science, Vol 2631, (2002).
8. Chervany N.L. & Mgknight D.H., The meanings of trust. Technical Report 94-04, Carlson School of Management, University of Minnesota, (1996).
9. Coetzee M. & Eloff JHP, Autonomous trust for Web Services, INC 2005 (The 5th International Network Conference), 5 – 7 July, Samos, Greece, (2005) Also available at http://csweb.rau.ac.za/staff/marijke/marijke_coetzee.htm.
10. Coyle F.P., XML, Web services and the data revolution, Addison-Wesley, (2002).
11. Dan A., Davis D., Kearney R., King R., Keller A., Kuebler D., Ludwig H., Polan, M. Spreitzer, and Youssef A., Web Services on demand: WSLA-driven Automated M. Management, IBM Systems Journal, Special Issue on Utility Computing, Volume 43, Number 1, pages 136-158, IBM Corporation, March, (2004).
12. Della-Libera G. et al., Web Services Trust Language (WS-Trust), http://www.ibm.com/developerworks/library/ws-trust/index.html, (2003).
13. Deutsch M., Cooperation and Trust: Some theoretical notes, in Nebraska Symposium on Motivation, M.R. Jones (ed.) Nebraska University Press, (1962).
14. Eloff J.H.P. & Smith E., Cognitive fuzzy modeling for enhanced risk assessment in a health care institution, IEEE Intelligent systems and their applications, Vol 14, no 2, pp 2-8, (2000).
15. Gambetta D., Can we trust Trust?, Chapter 13, pp. 213-237. Basil Blackwell. Reprinted in electronic edition from Department of Sociology, University of Oxford (1988).
16. Grandison T.W.A., Trust Management for Internet Applications, PhD Thesis, Imperial College of Science, Technology and Medicine, University of London, Department of Computing, (2003).
17. Kosko B., Fuzzy Cognitive Maps, International Journal of Man-Machine Studies, Vol 24, pp 65-75, (1986).
18. Kosko B., Fuzzy Engineering, Prentice Hall, Upper Saddle River, New Jersey, (1997).
19. Luhman N., Trust and Power. Wiley, (1979).
20. Marsh S., Formalising Trust as a Computational Concept, PhD Thesis, University of Stirling, UK, (1994).
21. Newcomer E. Understanding Web Services, Addison-Wesley, USA. (2002).
22. Ratnasingam P.P., Interorganizational trust in Business to Business e-commerce, PhD thesis, Erasmus University Rotterdam, (2001).
23. Rivest R. & Lampson B., "SDSI - A Simple Distributed Security Infrastructure," October (1996).
24. Winslett M. An Introduction to Trust Negotiation. Nixon & Terzis (eds), In Proceedings of the First International Conference, iTrust Heraklion, Crete, Greece, May 28-30, Springer. (2002).
25. SECURE, Bacon J., Belokosztolszki A., Dimmock N., Eyers D., Moody K., Using Trust and Risk in Role-Based Access Control Policies, Proceedings of Symposium on Access Control Models and Technologies SACMAT04, (2004).

Trust: An Element of Information Security

Stephen Flowerday and Rossouw von Solms

The Centre for Information Security Studies, P. O. Box 77000, Nelson Mandela
Metropolitan University, Port Elizabeth, 6031, South Africa
sflowerday@telkomsa.net, rossouw.vonsolms@nmmu.ac.za

Abstract. Information security is no longer restricted to technical issues but
incorporates all facets of securing systems that produce the company's
information. Some of the most important information systems are those that
produce the financial data and information. Besides securing the technical
aspects of these systems, one needs to consider the human aspects of those that
may 'corrupt' this information for personal gain. Opportunistic behaviour has
added to the recent corporate scandals such as Enron, WorldCom, and
Parmalat. However, trust and controls help curtail opportunistic behaviour,
therefore, confidence in information security management can be achieved.
Trust and security-based mechanisms are classified as safeguard protective
measures and together allow the stakeholders to have confidence in the
company's published financial statements. This paper discusses the concept of
trust and predictability as an element of information security and of restoring
stakeholder confidence. It also argues that assurances build trust and that
controls safeguard trust.

1 Introduction

Trust and controls help curtail opportunistic behaviour, therefore confidence in
information security management can be achieved. Besides the technical aspect of
information security and IT that should be implemented using best practices, one
needs trust to help curb 'cheating' and dishonesty. This paper focuses on the
information found within the financial statements of a company. Stakeholder,
especially investor, confidence needs to be restored in the board of directors in the
domain of financial reporting. The avalanche of corporate governance scandals such
as Enron, WorldCom, Tyco, and Parmalat has caused many to be suspicious of the
information found within financial statements.

It has been necessary to draw from the work in other research disciplines to extend
the study of trust and risk to this domain. This fragile, yet important concept, *trust*,
greases the wheels of industry. Trust allows the various users of information, found
within information systems, confidence when making decisions.

An important aspect of corporate governance is the management of risk.
Companies today use a system of controls in their efforts to manage their risk. Often
these controls focus on the company's various financial processes and systems. The
reason for this is that these important processes and systems are often the target of
security breaches. It has therefore become imperative that the security for these

Please use the following format when citing this chapter:

Author(s) [insert Last name, First-name initial(s)], 2006, in IFIP International Federation for Information
Processing, Volume 201, Security and Privacy in Dynamic Environments, eds. Fischer-Hubner, S., Rannenberg,
K., Yngstrom, L., Lindskog, S., (Boston: Springer), pp. [insert page numbers].

systems is comprehensive. Both opportunistic behaviour, which involves a human element, and the conventional technical IT security threats, need to be addressed.

It is stressed that [1], *"security is not a separable element of trust"*. This statement collaborates that both trust and security-based mechanisms are classified as safeguard protective measures [2]. Together these provide technological, organisational and relationship benefits to the various company stakeholders.

This paper introduces the concept of trust and uncertainty reduction followed by what constitutes trustworthiness. Self-centred opportunism, 'cheating' and dishonesty are classified as unfavourable behaviour, consequently behaviour is addressed using game theory to illustrate possible outcomes. The very close relationship that trust and risk have, is discussed with assurances being emphasised as an element to help build trust. Finally, a trust strategy is emphasised as a way to avoid unfavourable behaviour and to build and safeguard the concept of trust.

2   The Theory of Trust

Trust should not be left in the domain of philosophers, sociologists, and psychologist but also needs to be addressed by all attempting good governance. Can there be any doubt that fairness, accountability, responsibility, and transparency [3] are facets that contribute to the building and safeguarding of trust? Trust is not something that simply happens. It is fragile and not easily measured or identified [4].

2.1   Uncertainty Reduction Theory and Trust

In general, trust is defined as a psychological state comprising the intention to accept vulnerability, based upon positive expectations of the intentions or behaviour of another [5]. Trust also refers to the notion of the degree one risks: this risk is predicated on the belief that the other party is beneficent and dependable [6]. The notion of trust is that it involves the willingness of a trustee [7] *(the recipient of trust or the party to be trusted, i.e. board of directors)* who will perform a particular action important to the trustor *(the party that trusts the target party or the trusting party, i.e. investors)*.

If no uncertainty exists between the two parties, it indicates that no risk or threat is found in future interaction between the parties [8]. Noting that we do not live in a perfect world and we don't have perfect competition it is therefore impossible to have absolute uncertainty free interaction *(in other words, a degree of uncertainty always exists)*. One needs to make an effort to reduce uncertainty and to increase predictability about how the other party will act. Both the board of directors and the various company stakeholders should consider this.

It is emphasised that through communication and the exchange of information about each party, a decrease in uncertainty occurs [9]. According to Berger [10] uncertainty about the other party is the *"(in)ability to predict and explain actions"*. Thus the basic premise of Uncertainty Reduction Theory, if one applies the principles to the various company stakeholders, is that it attempts to reduce uncertainty and to increase predictability about each party's behaviour. This confirms that uncertainty can only be reduced by the information shared and a knowledge as to the condition of this information, which will affect the (un)certainty level [10].

Without a certain degree of predictability, a party has no basic assumption of how the other party will or will not utilise their trusting behaviour [8]. When one party is able to predict a degree of the other party's future actions this leads to a decrease in one's perceived vulnerability *(risk is perceived to be reduced)*. Therefore uncertainty reduction is a necessary condition for the development of trust. One's predictability about the other should be increased, thus reducing uncertainty via communicating (producing financial statements for the various stakeholders) with the other party. As a result: when more uncertainty is reduced, perceived predictability should be increased and vulnerability will be minimised (based upon prior experience). This highlights the paramount importance that the information found within the company financial statements has its integrity intact. If not, a trust problem will occur.

2.2   Trustworthiness

Fig. 1 is a proposed model of trust of one party for another which highlights the elements of trustworthiness [7]. This model illustrates that the level of trust and the level of perceived risk in a situation will lead to risk-taking in a relationship. It also touches on a trustor's propensity, which is said to be influenced by how much trust one has for a trustee prior to information on that particular party being available. Propensity will differ in a party's inherent willingness to trust others [7].

In this model, the three elements that help to create and define a trustworthy party are discussed. These elements are: *Integrity, Benevolence,* and *Ability*. This perception of trust can be applied to corporate governance in the following way:

- Integrity-based trust refers to whether the directors are honest and fair and not *'fudging the numbers'*. Some scholars in their research have used the words *reliability* or *predictability* in place of integrity [2, 11].
- Benevolence-based trust implies that the directors would be loyal, keep the best interests of the various company stakeholders at heart, and not seek to be self-serving and opportunistic. Some scholars have used the words *goodwill* or *openness* in place of benevolence [2, 11].
- Ability-based trust relates to the director's *skill level*, for example, their technical competence and understanding of information systems and security. Some researchers favour the word *competence* rather than *ability*, however, little difference is found in the meanings of these words [2, 11, 12].

Perceived trustworthiness requires honesty and integrity. These are attributes that a party needs to demonstrate so that when opportunities to *'cheat'* arise, they will be turned down. As stated [7], *"... if the trustee had something to gain by lying, he or she would be seen as less trustworthy"*. In addition, the more perceived benevolence and integrity found in a party, the more likely it will be to predict a favourable future outcome for a relationship with that party [13].

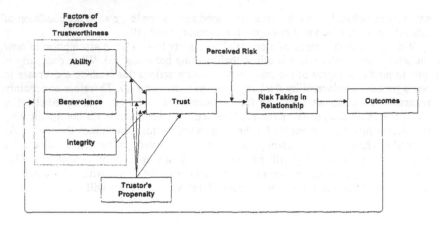

Fig. 1. Proposed Model of Trust [7].

2.3   Trust, Behaviour and Game Theory

Perceived risk and trust affect behaviour and this varies at different stages of a relationship [14]. Risk is dominant in the early stages and trust, in long-term relationships. One needs to consider the *cause and effect* relationship between *trust and risk,* which have an effect on *behaviour*. This view of trust is important because in order to build trust, the perceived risks by the various company stakeholders, especially investors, need to be catered for to avoid unfavourable behaviour.

Gefen et al. [14], from their research, found that the risk perception is more than a mere *"moderating influence"* affecting behaviour. They claim that the perceived risk *"mediates"* the affect trust has on behaviour. This, again, highlights the importance of information security in reducing the *'threats'* (both human and technical) that financial information systems are exposed to.

Economists and mathematicians have used game theory in their study of trust since 1944 [15]. These formal trust models consider how *'players'* discover trust and can quantify how trust or mistrust can occur [16, 17]. This paper discusses the principles of two games and the mathematical route will not be pursued.

Game theory involves the behaviour of rational decision makers *(players)*, whose decisions affect each other. These players could be the company investors and managers, or any of the company stakeholders that may have conflicting interests. As emphasised [17, 18], an essential element of game theory involves the amount of information known about each other by the various players. The information the various players have will determine their behaviour. Also to be noted are the *'rules'* of the game (codes, regulations, policies, etc. that the company needs to comply to).

A classic example of game theory is known as the Prisoner's Dilemma. There are two prisoners in separate cells, faced with the dilemma of whether or not to be police informants. Without further communication, the two players need to trust each other to have integrity and to be benevolent. The following are possible outcomes.

If neither become informants and defect, the police have insufficient or only circumstantial evidence to convict them and therefore both players receive light sentences. If trust is lacking and both turn and become informants for the police, through their defection, both players receive heavy sentences. If one player defects and becomes a police informant, that player is set free and the player that did not defect is convicted and receives a very heavy sentence due to the testimony of the player that defected. The dilemma of the scenario highlights the issue of trusting the other player without continuous communication. Applied to a corporate governance setting the 'communication' could be affected by both the *accuracy* (fraud) and *reliability* (confidentiality, integrity and availability) of the information found within the company financial statements.

As observed [19], if the police were to tell the prisoners (players) that the interrogation is ongoing and without a foreseeable end, a pattern emerges and cooperation can become stable. This is the discovery of trust as the players learn to trust each other over time and the perceived risk element is reduced. If one applies this model of trust to corporate governance it can be assumed that, over time, trust will be established between the various stakeholders, including the CEO, the board of directors and investors.

Axelrod [20] suggests that, with time, a pattern of cooperative behaviour develops trust as in game theory. However, one could trust the director's ability (technical and information security capabilities) but not the integrity of the person behind the systems that may act opportunistically. This highlights that trust is more specific than *'I trust the board of directors'*. One should clarify what it is that I trust the board of directors to do.

To explain this concept another way an everyday example will be used. Note that trust is not transitive and is rather domain specific [21]. Example: one might entrust their colleague with $100 loan, but not entrust the same resource to that colleague's friend whom you do not know. Trust therefore weakens as it goes through intermediaries. Furthermore, to re-emphasise a related aspect, one might trust their colleague by loaning them $100 but not allow them access to your bank account to withdraw the $100 themselves. The second example highlights the domain specificity of trust. One does not blindly trust, but one trusts a party in a specific area or domain.

To continue with the prisoner's dilemma, the interests of the players are generally in conflict. If one chooses the high-risk option and the other chooses the low, the former receives a maximised positive outcome and the latter a maximised negative outcome. There are cases of opportunistic behaviour, such as the directors of the over-valued telecommunications companies who cashed in and sold their shares totalling more than US$6 billion in the year 2000, yet they touted the sector's growth potential just as it was about to collapse [22]. The investors chose the high risk option and remained committed while many directors 'defected' choosing the low risk option and short term financial gains.

Kydd [23] stresses a different point of the Prisoner's Dilemma by pointing out that, strictly speaking, there is no uncertainty about motivations, or behaviour and the dominant strategy would be to defect. As a result, uncertainty is smuggled in through the back door. He emphasises that *"...trust is fundamentally concerned with this kind of uncertainty"*. Kydd's research discusses trust and mistrust, and, claims that there is no uncertainty in the prisoner's dilemma about whether the other side prefers to sustain the relationship. He questions whether future payoffs are valued highly enough to make sustained cooperation worthwhile, or whether they are not and the parties will defect. He states that trust is therefore perfect or nonexistent. To model trust in the prisoner's dilemma one must introduce some uncertainty, either about preferences or about how much the parties value future interactions [23]. Applying Kydd's argument to the various company stakeholders illustrates that there needs to be a *win win* situation for all. The information one party has, needs to be had by the other parties as well. Conflicts of interest need to be avoided so that the benefits of opportunistic behaviour are minimised.

Another game theory game, the *Stag Hunt*, is less well known than the Prisoner's Dilemma, however, its probably more suited to this paper. Moreover, the Stag Hunt game is also known as the *Assurance Game*. Assurance being core to building trust highlights the importance of this game. An important focus is, if one-side thinks the other will cooperate, they also prefer to cooperate. This means that players with the Assurance Game preferences are trustworthy. Kydd states: *"They prefer to reciprocate cooperation rather than exploit it"*. This denotes that it makes sense to reciprocate whatever one expects the other side to do, trust or suspicion.

The Stag Hunt (assurance game) is about two hunters who can either jointly hunt a stag (an adult deer/buck, a rather large meal) or individually hunt a rabbit (tasty, but substantially less filling). Hunting a stag is quite challenging and requires mutual cooperation. If either hunts a stag alone, the chance of success is minimal. Hunting a stag is most beneficial for the group however, requires a great deal of trust among its members. Each player benefits most if both hunt stag. Thus, hunting a stag both players trust their counter-player to do the same. Conversely, a player hunting rabbit lacks trust in the counter-player. Deciding not to risk the worst possible outcome (not getting the stag) is to decide not to trust the other player. On the other hand, *"if trust exists then risk can be taken"* [16].

Cooperation is possible between trustworthy parties who know each other to be trustworthy. This can be likened to the CEO, the board of directors, and the investors. They need independent and objective assurances that the other party is trustworthy. In the Prisoner's Dilemma, cooperation can be sustainable only if the players care enough about future payoffs because they will fear that attempts to exploit the other party will be met with retaliation [24]. In the Assurance Game (Stag Hunt) the level of trust one party has for the other party is the probability that it assesses the other party as trustworthy [23].

Kydd adds that the minimum trust threshold will depend on the party's own tolerance for the risk of exploitation by the other side. To consider the situation of the CEO, board of directors and the investors, cooperation needs to be the overwhelming option to avoid cheating and mistrust. This leads back to the elements of the trustworthiness model proposed by Mayer et al. [7] that integrity, benevolence and ability are required. The best option is clearly the hunting of the stag together, as it maximises the return on effort and becomes a win win situation. Applied to a corporate setting it illustrates the need for positive cooperation and trust between the various stakeholders and the avoidance of conflicts of interest.

The development of positive uncertainty reduction should be the basis for engaging in cooperative behaviour. When a positive piece of information about the company is presented (financial statements with assurances), the uncertainty will be reduced, as a result, the chance of engaging in cooperative behaviour will be increased. In contrast, where higher uncertainty levels exist between parties, or a piece of information negatively confirms predictions, then the competitive course of action will more likely to be engaged. In a cooperative situation, both participants feel that they are perceived as benevolent. Therefore they can willingly place themselves in vulnerable positions. Under this condition, the various parties are likely to establish or perceive a relationship of mutual trust. This again highlights the point that the stakeholders need assurances to trust the information found within the financial statements (validation by auditors). This emphasises the importance of information security and that it should safeguard the *accuracy* (fraud) and *reliability* (confidentiality, integrity and availability) of information.

3 Risk, Security and Assurances

It is vital that positive predictability needs to occur for trust to increase between the various parties (stakeholders). Therefore one should ensure that through various security mechanisms, the information found within the financial statements is correct. The knowledge, via independent and objective assurances, that information security is adequate and the risks contained assist in building confidence.

3.1 The Dark-Side of Trust: Risk

Queen Elizabeth 1st in her address to Parliament in 1586 concluded with: *"In trust I have found treason"* [25]. At what stage of a relationship is one relying on trust to the point that one is overly exposed to risk? In perfect competition, Humphrey and Schmitz [26] contend, *"risk is ruled out by the assumptions of perfect information and candid rationality"*. However, they emphasise that in today's world the issue of trust exists because transactions involve risk, as we do not have perfect competition.

Noorderhaven [27] observes that in context of a transaction relationship, if adequate security safeguards are in place for a transaction to go ahead, then it is not a trust transaction. However, if the actual information security safeguards and controls in place are less than adequate, a trust-based relationship is assumed as the existence of trust is inferred.

To expand on this, risk is present in a situation where the possible damage may be greater than the possible return [28]. Therefore, as stated [5], *"risk creates opportunity for trust"*. This is in harmony with Gefen et al. [14] and game theory [18, 20] that postulate that trust can *grow* and *evolve* over time.

It highlights the premise that trust can decrease uncertainty about the future and is a requirement for continuing relationships where parties have opportunities to act opportunistically [29]. This is in agreement with the theory that trust affects the trustor's risk taking behaviour [7]. To summarise, if the level of trust surpasses the perceived risk, one would engage in the relationship. Nevertheless be cautious, as trust is the positive view of risk exposure as *"trust is risk"* [30].

3.2   Trust and Security

Camp [1] is an advocate that both *"technical competence"* and *"good intent"* are required to ensure security. She further emphasises that: efforts at securing systems should involve not only attention to networks, protocols, machines and policies, but also a thorough understanding of how social agents (individuals and parties) participate in, and contribute to trust. One can lose sight of the fact that conventional security technology, if implemented perfectly, still does not equate to trust [19].

Although it may be desirable, 100% security is not feasible and it is commonly accepted that not all risk can be eliminated [31]. This residual or inherent control risk is based on the notion that additional investments in controls or safeguards will not eliminate this type of risk. This means that the various company stakeholders are forced into a trust-based relationship.

It is widely accepted that reduced risk and increased trust are both likely to increase the likelihood of engaging in transactions [14]. DeMaio [32] champions that one should try to build business environments based on each party's willingness and ability to continuously demonstrate to the other's satisfaction that all dealings are honest, open, and that the 'rules' are followed. DeMaio states, *"e-Trust is all about mutual assurance."*

3.3   Mutual Assurance and Confidence

Mutual assurances help to build confidence between the various company stakeholders in a similar manner as with the hunters in the Stag Hunt/Assurance game. In the same manner, VeriSign can provide confidence that an active key-holder has signed a document and it can be assumed that the document is untainted because of VeriSign's independence. Therefore, it follows that auditors verify a company's financial statements (validation) and provide assurances. The only difference is that VeriSign and the Stag Hunt game provides the assurance in real-time, something the auditing profession needs to address.

Mutual assurance should exist between stakeholders, reassuring each other that the risks are mitigated to an acceptable level and that the degree of (un)certainty is appropriate. The adage of *"trust but verify"* should exist as the various stakeholders demonstrate to each other, via objective and independent audits, that the agreed upon best practices are maintained.

The confidence that the various company stakeholders have in their relationship is determined by two factors: one being the level of trust and the other the perception of how adequate or inadequate the controls are that govern the conditions of the arrangement [33]. To achieve a favourable relationship between the stakeholders, one has to find the right *balance* between trust and control.

Fig. 2 illustrates how trust and controls work together in securing a transaction or a business process. Triangle A, B, D is the *Control* area and triangle A, D, C is the *Trust* area. The line E, F is a hypothetical positioning of the company's Risk Appetite. The area of the rectangle A, B, D, C is the business process area or transaction area. When one views the Risk Appetite line (E to F) one will note that the white area is protected by controls and the dark area is the 'risk' exposure or the area protected by trust. Depending on how much the parties *'trust'* each other will affect the positioning of the Risk Appetite line.

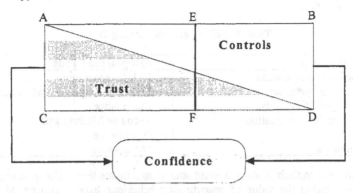

Fig. 2. The Relationship between Trust, Controls and Confidence.

However, to summarise: absolute trust and absolute control are two opposing extremities of approach for attaining confidence (personal communication, Todd, August 2005). The solution is somewhere in the middle ground between trust and control. There are those that argue the company should position itself on the trust side in an effort to reduce costs [34, 35]. However, practicalities and realism are *forces* that pull the solutions into the control end of the spectrum.

4 A Trust Strategy

Strategy, by its nature, concerns itself with the future. Companies today operate in an uncertain world where the markets have become increasingly more competitive. The Turnbull Report [36] emphasises that taking risks is what companies do. It is the justification for profit and therefore the identification and assessing of risks is required so that the risks are appropriately managed.

A company should craft a strategy considering their relationship with their various stakeholders. An important aspect of this strategy is managing the uncertainty of future events i.e. managing and containing the risks to an acceptable level. The board of directors should consciously attempt to *build* and *safeguard* trust between them and their investors.

Todd [35] researched trust in the technical arena, specifically focusing on e-commerce. He divided trust into two domains and had subsections in each domain. Todd based his research on Gerck's work [37]. Gerck appears to have originally divided trust into these two domains, *establishing* and *ensuring* trust. Additionally, Gerck focused on trust and risk refinement as a means of reducing uncertainty.

For the purpose and focus of this paper, the domains have been renamed to *Building* and *Safeguarding* trust and the subsections have been modified accordingly. From the study of the concept of trust it appears that one builds trust over time and then one needs to safeguard trust due to its fragile nature. The following are points (Table 1) which must be taken into account when one considers building and/or safeguarding trust.

Table 1. Building and Safeguarding Trust.

Building Trust	Safeguarding Trust
Benevolence/Openness	Risk Management
Ability/Competence	Security Safeguards and Controls
Integrity/Predictability	Compliance
Constant Communication	Recourse Mechanisms
Ethics	Governance
Assurances	'Assurances'

A company, in their strategy, should attempt to mitigate their risks to an acceptable level by reducing the value of opportunistic behaviour from occurring. Moreover, information security audits should be preformed to assure that the technical side of security is adequate as security helps to safeguard trust. Additionally, assurances help to establish trust in the level of confidence placed in the information. The assurances establish a more accurate level of trust *(the truth)* as to the condition of security safeguards and controls. To refer back to the Stag Hunt/Assurance Game, it is the assurances provided by one hunter to the other that keep them *'confident'* that both parties are committed to the hunt. If not, insecurities 'creep' in and alternatively a hunter may decide to hunt a rabbit and the Stag Hunt collapses. Establishing trust sets a level of confidence.

5 Conclusion

Trust and information sharing between the various company stakeholders has taken place since formal commerce began. The information's integrity is of utmost importance, especially the information found within financial statements. This information needs to be trusted. However, the various stakeholders have their own goals and motivations in addition to the shared goals. Conflicts of interest arise and each party is vulnerable. Each also needs to trust the other to have integrity, benevolence, and ability. Companies should have a trust strategy to guide them in building and safeguarding trust, with independent and objective assurances being part of this strategy.

To have a positive outcome, trust needs to increase and uncertainty needs to be reduced to an acceptable level. This could be through assurances provided by auditors *validating* the *reliability* and *accuracy* of the information (the auditors report on the system of internal controls and the accuracy of the financial statements) or through evolving relationships (as discussed in game theory). *To avoid unfavourable behaviour, uncertainty needs to be contained and the level of trust needs to surpass the perceived risks.* This will ensure that a relationship will flourish. Within a competitive society, the various company stakeholders cannot enter into partnerships with blind trust, believing that everyone will do the right thing [38].

The development of cooperative behaviour and mutual trust should be a goal of all company stakeholders. One cannot escape that trust and controls affect confidence and is the acceptance of a degree of insecurity (as shown in Fig. 2). In conclusion, both *"technical competence"* and *"good intent"* are required to ensure security [1]. Therefore, *confidence in information security management requires trust and trust requires information security to help safeguard it.*

Acknowledgement

The financial assistance of the National Research Foundation (NRF) towards this research is hereby acknowledged. Opinions expressed and conclusions arrived at, are those of the authors and are not necessarily to be attributed to the NRF.

References

1. Camp, L.J.: Designing for Trust. In: Falcone, R., Barber, S., Korba, L., Singh, M., (eds.): Trust, Reputation, and Security: Theories and Practice. Springer-Verlag; Berlin Heidelberg New York (2002) 15-29.
2. Ratnasingham, P., Kumar, K.: Trading Partner Trust in Electronic Commerce Participation. (2000) http://portal.acm.org/citation.cfm?id=3598.
3. King II Report: King Report on Corporate Governance for South Africa. Institute of Directors in Southern Africa (2002) 17-19.
4. Handfield, R.B., Nichols Jr., E.L.: Supply Chain Redesign: Transforming Supply Chains into Integrated Value Systems. Financial Times Prentice Hall, New Jersey (2002).
5. Rousseau, D.M., Sitkin, S.B., Burt, R.S., Camerer, C.: Not So Different After All: A Cross-Discipline View of Trust. Academy of Management Review. Vol. 23(3) (1998) 391-404.
6. Johnson-George, C., Swap, W.C.: Measurement of Specific Interpersonal Trust: Construction and validation of a scale to assess trust in a specific other. Journal of Personality and Social Psychology. Vol. 43(6) (1982) 1306-1317.
7. Mayer, R.C., Davis, J.H., Schoorman, F.D.: An Integrative Model of Organizational Trust. Academy of Management Review. Vol. 20(3) (1995) 709-734.
8. Pearce, W.B.: Trust in interpersonal communication. Speech Monographs. Vol. 41(3) (1974) 236-244.
9. Berger, C.R., Calabrese, R.J.: Some Explorations in Initial Interaction and Beyond: Toward a developmental theory of interpersonal communication. Human Communication Research. Vol. 1 (1975) 99-112.
10. Berger, C.R.: Communicating Under Uncertainty. In Roloff, M., Miller, G. (eds.): Interpersonal Processes: New directions in communication research. Sage, Newbury Park USA (1987) 39-62.
11. Mishra, A.K.: Organizational Responses To Crisis: The centrality of trust. In Kramer, R.M., Tyler, T.R., (eds.): Trust in organizations: Frontiers of theory and research. Sage, California (1996) 261-287.
12. Abrams, L.C., Cross, R., Lesser, E., Levin, D.Z.: Nurturing Interpersonal Trust in Knowledge-sharing Networks. Academy of Management. Vol. 17(4) (2003) 64–77.
13. Larzelere, R.E., Huston, T.L.: The Dyadic Trust Scale: Toward understanding interpersonal trust in close relationships. Journal of Marriage and the Family. Vol. 42 (1980) 595-604.

14. Gefen, D., Rao, V.S., Tractinsky, N.: The Conceptualization of Trust, Risk and Their Relationship in Electronic Commerce: The Need for Clarification. IEEE Computer Society (2002) http://csdl.computer.org/comp/proceedings/hicss/2003/1874/07/187470192b.pdf.
15. Von Neumann, J., Morgenstern, O.: Theory of Games and Economic Behaviour. Princeton University Press, Princeton USA (1953).
16. Kimbrough, S.O.: Foraging for Trust: Exploring Rationality and the Stag Hunt Game. (2005) http://opim.wharton.upenn.edu/~sok/sokpapers/2005/itrust-2005-final.pdf.
17. Murphy, P.: Game Theory Models for Organizational/Public Conflict. Canadian Journal of Communication. Vol. 16(2) (1991) http://info.wlu.ca/~wwwpress/jrls/cjc/BackIssues/16.2/murphy.html.
18. Hayes, F.: Is Game Theory Useful for the Analysis and Understanding of Decision Making in Economics? (2005) http://www.maths.tcd.ie/local/JUNK/ econrev/ser/html/game. html.
19. Khare, R., Rifkin, A.: Weaving a Web of Trust. (1998) http://www.w3j.com/7/s3. rifkin.wrap.html
20. Axelrod, R.: The Complexity of Cooperation: Agent-Based Models of Competition and Collaboration. Princeton University Press, New Jersey (1997)
21. Zand, D.E.: Trust and Managerial Problem Solving. Administrative Science Quarterly. Vol. 17(2) (1972) 229-239.
22. Clarke, T.: Theories of Corporate Governance: The Philosophical Foundations of Corporate Governance. Routledge UK (2004) 11.
23. Kydd, A. H.: Trust and Mistrust in International Relations. Princeton University Press, Princeton USA (2005) 7-12.
24. Axelrod, R.: The Evolution of Cooperation. Basic Books, New York (1984).
25. Partington, A. (ed.): The Oxford Dictionary of Quotations, 4th ed. University Press, New York Oxford (1996).
26. Humphrey, J. Schmitz, H.: Trust and Inter Firm Relations in Developing and Transition Economies. Journal of Development Studies. Vol. 34(4) (1998) 33-61.
27. Noorderhaven, N.G.: Opportunism and Trust in Transaction Cost Economies. In: Groenewegen, J., (ed.): Transaction Cost Economics and Beyond. Kluwer Academic, Boston (1996) 105-128.
28. Luhmann, N.: Familiarity, Confidence, Trust: Problems and Alternatives. In: Gambetta, D.G., (ed.): Trust: Making and Breaking Cooperative Relations. Basil Blackwell, New York (1988) 94-107.
29. Limerick, D., Cunnington, B.: Managing the new organization: A Blueprint for Networks and Strategic Alliances. Jossey-Bass, San Francisco (1993).
30. Camp, L.J.: Trust and Risk in Internet Commerce. The MIT Press, England (2000).
31. Greenstein, M., Vasarhelyi, M.: Electronic Commerce: Security, Risk, Management and Control, 2nd ed. McGraw-Hill, New York (2002).
32. DeMaio, H.B.: B2B and Beyond: New Business Models Built on Trust. John Wiley & Sons, USA (2001).
33. Cox, R., Marriott, I.: Trust and Control: The Key to Optimal Outsourcing Relationships. Gartner database (2003).
34. Fukuyama, F.: Trust: the Social Virtues and the Creation of Prosperity. Free Press USA (1996) 27.
35. Todd, A.: The Challenge of Online Trust: For online and offline business. (2005) http://www.trustenablement.com/trust_enablement. htm#RiskManagement.
36. Turbull Report. Internal Control: Guidance for Directors on the Combined Code. The Institute of Chartered Accountants in England & Wales (1999/2005).
37. Gerck, E.: End-To-End IT Security. (2002) http://www.nma.com/papers/e2e-security.htm.
38. Bavoso, P.: Is Mistrust Holding Back Supply-Chain Efforts? Optimize, and InformationWeek (2002) http://www.optimizemag.com/printer/014/ pr_squareoff_yes.html.

Security-by-Ontology: A Knowledge-Centric Approach

Bill Tsoumas, Panagiotis Papagiannakopoulos, Stelios Dritsas, Dimitris Gritzalis

Information Security and Critical Infrastructure Protection Research Group
Dept. of Informatics, Athens University of Economics and Business
76 Patission Ave., Athens GR-10434, Greece
{bts, papajohn, sdritsas, dgrit}@aueb.gr

Abstract. We present a security ontology (SO), which can be used as a basis of security management of an arbitrary information system. This SO provides capabilities, such as modeling of risk assessment knowledge, abstraction of security requirements, reusable security knowledge interoperability, aggregation and reasoning. The SO is based on the exploitation of security-related knowledge, derived from diverse sources. We demonstrate that the establishment of such a framework is feasible and, furthermore, that a SO can support critical security activities of an expert, e.g. security requirements identification, as well as selection of certain countermeasures. We also present and discuss an implementation of a specific SO. The implementation is accompanied by results regarding how a SO can be built and populated with security information.

1 Introduction

The introduction of new technologies in conjunction with the dynamic character of Information Systems (IS) brings in attention several categories of information security risks, while in the same time underpins the importance of sound security management. Traditionally, the security controls requirements come up as a result of an IS Risk Assessment (RA) review, given the thorough intervention of security expert. This is an effort-consuming intervention, which has not yet been properly assisted by automated processes, especially in large and complex organizations, which are heavily IS-dependent. In such organizations "a security program in order to be successfully incorporated must be multi-dimensional...these include physical elements, people as well as computers and software" [1].

Our objective is to provide a management framework in order to support the IS security management, as defined with the PDCA cycle (Plan-Do-Check-Act) introduced in [2]. Our work is not directly related with RA approaches per se; nevertheless, it supports the security management process with the use of RA results providing automated support. The creation of such a framework was based in the research direction depicted in [3], that is a) the process in specifying safeguards, b) taking under consideration the nature of the organization's flexibility and c) the creation of adaptive safeguards. We propose a structured approach, in order to support the process leading from informal, high-level statements found in policy and RA documents, to deployable technical countermeasures. The outcome of this process

Please use the following format when citing this chapter:
Author(s) [insert Last name, First-name initial(s)], 2006, in IFIP International Federation for Information Processing, Volume 201, Security and Privacy in Dynamic Environments, eds. Fischer-Hubner, S., Rannenberg, K., Yngstrom, L., Lindskog, S., (Boston: Springer), pp. [insert page numbers].

will be a knowledge-based, ontology-centric security management system, eventually bridging the IS risk assessment and the organizational security policies gap with security management solutions. In order to achieve this, it is important to separate the *IS security needs* into two distinct parts: (a) security requirements (*"Controls"*, or the *"What"* part), and (b) their actual implementation in a technical level (*"Technical Countermeasures"* - TC, or the *"How"* part).

We define our basic security knowledge container as a Security Ontology (SO). A SO formulates the basic concepts from the RA process, and in the same time extends the legacy DMTF CIM schema [4] with ontological support. We populate the SO with security information from various sources, ranging from infrastructure-related information to lexical analysis of the high-level statements; the latter stem from RA (security controls) using information extraction (IE) techniques. Wherever the requirements are deemed inadequate, a standards-based, security-best-practices database[1] (ready-to-use controls – refer to section 4) is used in order to fill the gaps.

In the sequel, the terms "Control" and "Countermeasure" will refer to the same concept, considered from a different view; the former is used in the Ontology part (security requirement - "What"), while the latter in the TC database part (technical implementation - "How"). Although in this work we focus on the RA domain, our approach can be applied equally to all domains of IS security management.

The paper is organized as follows; in section 2 we report on related work. In section 3 we define our SO, whereas in section 4 we focus on the attributes of security controls. We present our ontology-centered security management framework in section 5; we setup our case study and present practical results on control attributes extraction in section 6; finally, we conclude with further research in section 7.

2   Related work

Although the need for a SO has been recognized by the research community [5],[6], only partial attention has been drawn for a common solution. The legacy DMTF approach (i.e. the root of our SO), lacks: (a) the security management aspect, (b) the centralized management of security management information, and (c) the domain knowledge perspective. The modelling of CIM with OWL has been proposed by Clemente et al. in [7]. Work in [6] deal mainly with access control issues; standards discussed include XML Signatures and integration with SAML [8] and XACML [9]. Research on KAON [10] focuses mostly on the managing infrastructure of generic ontologies and metadata, whereas in [11] authors present a policy ontology based on deontic logic, elaborating on delegation of actions. The CIM-Ponder mapping is discussed in [12][13], while Raskin et al. presented an ontology-driven approach to information security [14]. With respect to Semantic Web languages, the design of the KAoS [15] policy ontology suggests the use of a description logic inference engine to analyze policy rules and the Rei [11] policy ontology uses F-Logic to compute the policy restrictions and constraints. The policy analysis mechanism in the e-Wallet system [16] exploits the XSLT and JESS technologies, and the SOUPA [17] policy language is similar to Rei but the specific policy ontology has limited support for

---

[1] The details of this database and its detailed structure, is out of scope of this paper.

meta-policy reasoning. Most of these approaches are related with specific aspects of security and specific application domains, while our approach is suitable for every IS. Furthermore, all aforementioned approaches lack the security standards support, which we use for modeling the security requirements.

3   A BS7799-based Security Ontology for RA

The kernel of our approach is the formulation of an adequate container of the IS security requirements. This container has to fulfill the following high-level attributes: (a) the containment of IS security requirements in such a way, that it is possible to combine them and draw conclusions, (b) the linkage to a global information management framework, and (c) the adherence to globally accepted information security management standards. At a later stage, these security requirements can be used for querying repositories of TC to formulate the proper *Actions* to mitigate the risks.

We model our security knowledge container across the Common Information Model (CIM) [3], a conceptual information model developed by Distributed Management Task Force (DMTF) and ontologies (*"an explicit specification of a conceptualization"* [18]), which have been widely used as an effective means to support knowledge sharing and reuse. Thus, we combine the engineering view of CIM with the knowledge representation world of ontologies.

Extending the modelling of CIM with OWL (Clemente et al. [7]) into the security management domain, we define a generic Security Ontology (SO)[2], as *"an ontology that elaborates on the security aspects of a system"*. The SO is formulated as a CIM *Extension Schema* enriched with ontological semantics, modelling the security management information stemming from the RA process (*"What"* part of security needs); in addition, SO is linked with the legacy CIM concepts in order to access the already modelled IS information. While there is no standard method for ontology development [19], we followed the collaborative approach for ontology design [20], building an ontology by a group of people improving the ontology in every iterative round, following the 3-phase approach of [21]:

1. *Phase 1: SO conceptual modelling* is done by using the overall framework in [20] and the security standards ISO/IEC 17799 [22], BS 7799 Part 2 [1], AS/NZS 4360 [23] and the CRAMM Method [24], for extracting the necessary security concepts and their underlying relations;
2. *Phase 2: Linking with CIM as an Extension Schema* is done by introducing the *SecurityManagedElement* concept which inherits from CIM_ManagedElement, populated with certain attributes from [22], [1],[23],[24] and is the sub-root for all security-related sub-ontologies;
3. *Phase 3: Implementing the SO in OWL* is done by using Protégé and its' embedded OWL plugin [25]. The resulting SO is depicted partially in Fig. 1.

---

[2] In the sequel, the terms "Security Ontology" and "Ontology" will be used interchangeably and refer to the RA sub-ontology.

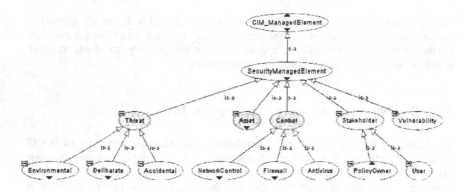

Fig. 1. Security Ontology for Risk Assessment.

The SO concepts have been populated with axioms and relevant semantic constraints, resulting to more than 150 SO concepts, with more than 400 properties. Figure 2 depicts the defined restrictions from the Control concept related to *Asset* protection.

```
Class(Control complete restriction(Protects allValuesFrom(Asset)))

SubClassOf(Control restriction(AcquisitionCost cardinality(1)))
SubClassOf(Control restriction(Subject minCardinality(1)))
SubClassOf(Control SecurityManagedElement)
SubClassOf(Control restriction(LevelOfAssurance minCardinality(1)))
SubClassOf(Control restriction(Effectiveness minCardinality(1)))
SubClassOf(Control restriction(OperationalCost cardinality(1)))
```

Fig. 2. User-defined restrictions for the Control concept.

4 IS asset control semantics

In the case of any risk management methodology, every IS asset is associated with certain threats, which can be then mitigated in an acceptable level by applying specific security controls. Thus, our first task is to define the basic attributes and properties to adequately define a control (depicted in Table 1).

Table 1. Control definition.

Control Structure	
Control Identifier	Unique identifier
Target *	The IS asset that this control is going to be applied (IP address, operating system, open ports & services, etc.)
Subject *	The entity that is going to apply the control to the Target
Control Group *	Categorizes the control in a group
Control Subgroup *	Categorizes the control in a subgroup (further)
Action *	Action(s) to be taken for the control to be applied
Constraints [] *	Time, place, and subject constrains
Type	[Managerial	Procedural	Technical]
SecurityAttributes2Preserve	[Confidentiality	Integrity	Availability	Non-Repudiation]

Control Structure		
Type Of Control	[Protective | Detective | Corrective]	
Risk Mitigation Factor	[High | Medium | Low]	
Control Purpose	[Security | Audit]	

In our SO, every Asset is associated with a set of Threats and every Threat is mitigated by a set of Controls. Thus, every Asset contains this information in the form of a *Threats-Controls[]* array, with each row representing a single threat for the specific asset, along with an array of controls that mitigate the specific threat. This two-dimensional array is shown in Fig. 3; at the ontology implementation level, we dynamically create a series of individuals, which are linked with the respective threats. The attributes *Control Group* and *Control Subgroup* follow the related CRAMM taxonomy for Controls [24]. Using mainly RA information sources, we try to give values in each Control attributes facilitating the binding of each control with appropriate and specific TC by narrowing the search space in the database of collected TC, using the Control attributes as query parameters. We also implement a layered control refinement at the TC database side, resulting in a set of concrete technical actions, which have to be followed in order to implement the initial control. We use the JESS tool [26] providing for different rules in each distinct refinement layer.

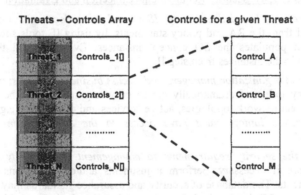

Fig. 3. Decomposition of Threats-Controls array for a given Asset.

5 Framework description

In this section, we extend the generic architecture for IS security management, based on an ontology-centric approach defined in [19]. The aim is to associate the security requirements ("What"), stemming from the security knowledge sources, with the appropriate actions ("How"), and eventually deploy them to the IS.

To accomplish these tasks, four main phases are proposed: (a) Building of SO, in order to simulate the underlying IS, (b) Security Requirements Collection and Evaluation, capturing the IS security requirements ("What") from high-level policy statements into appropriate instances of the SO concepts, (c) Security Actions Definition, matching every security requirement with the appropriate technical security controls ("How"), eventually producing a set of Actions for every IS device instance, and (d) Security Actions Deployment and Monitoring, which can be accomplished by piping the necessary data to a policy-based management platform, such as Ponder [26]. Our approach is modular enough, in such a way that enhancements in any given component(s) can be applied with a minimal overhead to the architecture.

The necessary steps, in order to establish the proposed IS security management framework, are briefly presented at Fig. 4 (the numbers in this figure denote the sequence of main actions in each phase).

Phase A (Step 1): Building of Security Ontology

I.   *Get IS asset infrastructure data*; vital data concerning the IS Assets (for example, network topology, technologies used, servers, wireless access points, services and active ports) are located through the use of scanning tools such as Nmap [28];

II.   *Generate ontology concepts' instances from infrastructure data*; ontology instances are generated and populated with data (step I) via Protégé API calls [25].

Phase B (Steps 2, 3, 4): Security Requirements Collection and Evaluation

III. *Extract security knowledge from the IS RA and policy documents*; information is extracted from the RA and policy statements, by using IE tools such as GATE [29], and populates the SO concept instances. Eventually fill the gaps (if possible) in the instances from step II.

IV.   *Justify with organization managers and discuss business decisions*; management input may influence dramatically the security requirements of the IS, since it might affect network topologies, active services and open ports (e.g. *"salesmen with wireless laptops must have access to the Sales system during the weekend"*).

V.   *Present the security requirements to management and security experts for evaluation*; if necessary, perform adjustments and/or corrections to security requirements. The database of security and assurance standards may be used for enriching the SO, in case the information gathered so far is deemed insufficient.

Phase C (Step 5): Security Actions Definition

VI.   *Associate the security requirements ("What") with technical security countermeasures ("How")*; using the information from steps I-V, a matching algorithm performs the linking of security requirements (from the SO) with deployable TCs (from the Database of TCs), customized for the concept instance under question. TC refinement is performed, resulting to a set of N tuples of the form $(IS\ Asset_i,\ Action_1...Action_{m_i})$, where N is the number of IS Assets identified in the RA and m the number of Actions realizing the security requirements of the specific IS Asset$_i$.

VII. *Transform the actions identified into a Ponder-compatible input;* conversion of the Actions specified in step VI into a form that can be piped into Ponder rules or a similar framework through an appropriate interface.

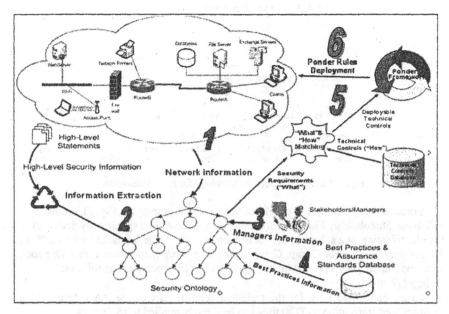

Fig. 4. Ontology-based IS Security Management framework.

Phase D (Step 6): Security Actions Deployment and Monitoring

VIII. *Deploy the Ponder rules over the IS infrastructure;* employ Ponder management framework in order to apply the set of *Actions* over the IS devices.

IX. *Iterate from step I in a timely basis;* stay current with the IS and policy changes.

6 Case-study: Control attributes acquisition

In this section, we present a case study focused on the implementation of the first three steps (i.e. I-III), as part of a RA exercise. We utilize security knowledge from: (a) network-level data referring to the IS infrastructure, and (b) high-level control statements from RA, in order to identify the control requirements.

Having defined and implemented our model SO, the next steps are: (a) to create the relevant ontology concept instances for IS assets, and (b) to populate each Threats-- Controls[] array with the control characteristics (defined in section 4).

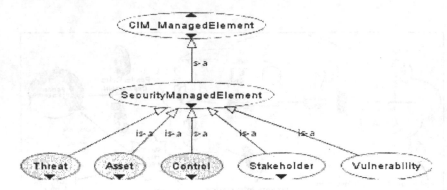

Fig. 5. Case Study: Security Ontology for Risk Assessment.

In order to keep it simple, a cut-down SO version is employed (Fig. 5), consisting of *Threat, Stakeholder, Vulnerability, Control*, and *Asset*. We specifically deal with the identification of a subset of the control attributes at Table 1 (marked with an "*"): *Target, Subject, Control Group, Control Subgroup, Action*, and *Constraints*. Our conventions and heuristics related to the input data and IE process are as follows:

Input Data
- We are concerned only for the technical controls part of the RA output, which (after their translation to TCs) they can be directly applied to IS devices
- Network information is considered to be accurate and precise
IE process
- If the *Target* cannot be identified, Target defaults to *Information* as a resource
- If the *Subject* cannot be identified, Subject defaults to a predefined group of users (e.g. administrators or network operators).
- We rely on syntactic patterns of the control description, such as
  - <Noun> <to> <Verb> <Something>
  - <Verb> <Something> <Preposition> <Something>
  - <Verb> <Something> <to> <Something> <Preposition><Something>
  - <Verb> <Something> <to> <Something> <List of Prepositions> <Something>, where the word "Between" exists in the <List of Prepositions>

6.1 Testbed IS description

Our test network is depicted in Fig. 6. Following the methodology outlined in section 5, we used an Nmap scanner/parser [28] to isolate the necessary information for creating the relevant IS asset instances in our ontology - i.e. four SO instances are going to be created, one for the router *Alcatel Speed Touch*, one for the *3COM* router and two for the laptops.

The next step is to fill each instance with the retrieved information (e.g. OS, its version, open ports, etc.), using the Protégé OWL Java API [25]. Finally, we feed the control statements (from RA output, Table 2Table 2), to our IE program.

We implemented the IE in Java using the GATE API [29] and JAPE [30], annotating the IE results on the analyzed texts. Apart from the pattern recognition, a number of heuristic rules operate on these annotations as well. Finally, *Target Scope* is also provided – i.e. it is specified whether the specific control applies *only* to the IS asset under question, or to *a set of IS assets (Scope of Control Application)*.

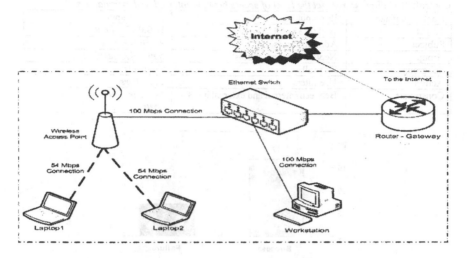

Fig. 6. Case-Study: Network Topology.

Table 2. Control statements from RA output.

ID	Control from Risk Assessment output
1	Use asymmetric algorithms for signatures
2	Use filters to restrict the level of access between internal and external hosts
3	Use filters to control which systems are permitted connections with the Internet
4	Passwords to be at least 6 characters long

6.2 Results and discussion

In order to evaluate our approach, we compared the results of our method with security experts' opinion, using the human expertise as a benchmark. The results from the proposed method are summarized in Fig. 7, with a success detection ratio of up to 71% in comparison with security experts' output. The criteria for success or failure were the ability of the IE to identify correctly the network elements in the text and further classify them in the correct Control Group/SubGroup categories of [24].

As a more detailed example, we focus on the control No 2 (see Table 2) which is related with the router depicted at Fig. 6. In Table 3, we compare the results from the automated extraction (2nd column), against the experts-derived output (3rd column).

Table 3. Automated Control attributes extraction - comparison with expert output.

Control: *"Use filters to restrict the level of access between internal and external hosts"*

Control attribute	IE output	Expert output
Target	10.0.0.138, All_Assets[3]	10.0.0.138, *Routers*
Subject	Administrators	*Administrators*
Group	NetworkAccessControls	*NetworkAccessControls*
Subgroup	Firewalls	*Firewalls*
Action	Use filters	*Use filters*
Constraints	Between internal and external hosts	*Between internal and external hosts*

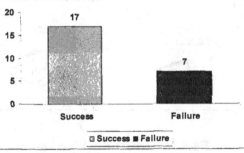

Fig. 7. Automated information acquisition results.

Our IE approach is based on pattern recognition of high-level control statements. Such a method could provide satisfying results, as long as it can be combined with implicit knowledge. Our method was successful into recognizing the network elements and categorizing the controls into the correct *Control Group/Subgroup*, facilitating more accurate identification of *Actions* during the TCs database querying.

This new approach towards the formal representation of security requirements can effectively support security expert's work in an automated way. The modular nature of the framework makes it flexible and tolerant to any changes to both network topology and high-level statements.

On the other hand, our approach can be improved in terms of IE process accuracy, to support more effectively the Control Scope feature (e.g. the IE program identified incorrectly the scope of the control as "All_Assets", i.e., applicable to every IS asset), as well as the identification of constraints (apart from isolation of text describing the possible constraint). *Implicit security knowledge* must be taken into account, e.g. in the control presented above, this control should not be applied to all assets (as stated by the IE output), but only to network assets that are connected to the Internet (i.e. routers).

---

[3] An example of the *Control Scope* feature, locating (falsely) "All_Assets" as the control scope.

7 Conclusions and further research

In this work we proposed a centralized framework for security knowledge acquisition and management, using a knowledge-centric approach gathering security information from a variety of sources, separating security requirements from their technical implementations. Furthermore, we defined and implemented a standards-based knowledge container (Security Ontology), which: (a) models the Risk Assessment domain and extends the CIM model with ontological semantics; (b) abstracts the security management requirements of a CIM-based domain from the actual implementation, therefore reducing the complexity of controls management; (c) defines a structure for the abstraction of security control attributes; (d) can be used for reusable knowledge interoperability, aggregation and reasoning, using security knowledge from diverse and (already modeled) sources. Finally, we demonstrated the feasibility of security information extraction from RA statements, using IE techniques.

Regarding future work, we envisage the enhancement of heuristic rules so as to produce more concrete and accurate results, as well as the development of a standards-based, best-practices database with implicit security knowledge, in order to support the information extraction and decision making process; further work on countermeasures refinement is necessary, while the evaluation of the results will be assisted by the further enrichment of the ontology with more semantic rules.

References

[1]   National Research Council: Computers At Risk: Safe Computing in The Information Age, System Security Study Committee/ Nat.ional Academy Press, Washington (1991).
[2]   British Standard 7799, Part 2 (1999), Information Technology - Specification for Information Security Management System, BSI.
[3]   Baskerville, R.: Research Notes: Research Directions in Information Systems Security, International Journal of Information Management, 14 (5), 385-387, 1994
[4]   DMTF CIM Policy Model v. 2.9, available at http://www.dmtf.org
[5]   Donner, M.: Toward a Security Ontology, IEEE Security and Privacy, Vol. 1-3, (2003).
[6]   Denker, G.: Access Control and Data Integrity for DAML+OIL and DAML-S, SRI International, USA (2002).
[7]   Clemente, F., et. al: Representing Security Policies, in Web Information Systems, in Proc. of the Policy Management for the Web Workshop (WWW 2005), Japan (2005).
[8]   OASIS Security Service TC, SAML, available at http://www.oasis-open.org.
[9]   XACML Specification v. 1.1, available at http://www.oasis-open.org.
[10] Bozsak, E., Ehrig, M., Handschub, S., Hotho, J.: KAON – Towards a Large Scale Semantic Web, in Proc. of the 3rd EC-WEB Conference, Bauknecht, K., et al. (Eds.), France (2002).
[11] Kagal, L. et al.: A policy language for a pervasive computing environment, 4th IEEE International Workshop on Policies for Distributed Systems and Networks, Italy (2003).
[12] Lymberopoulos, L., Lupu, E., Sloman, M.: Ponder Policy Implementation and Validation in a CIM and Differentiated Services Framework, in Proc. of the 9th IEEE/IFIP Network Operations and Management Symposium, Seoul, South Korea (2004).
[13] Alcantara, O., Sloman, M.: QoS policy specification - A mapping from Ponder to the IETF, Dept. of Computing, Imperial College, United Kingdom.

[14] Raskin, V. et al.: Ontology in Information Security: A Useful Theoretical Foundation and Methodological Tool, in Proc. of the New Security Paradigms Workshop, V. Raskin, et al. Eds. USA (2001).

[15] Uszok, A. et al.: KAoS: A Policy and Domain Services Framework for Grid Computing and Semantic Web Services, 2nd Intl. Conference on Trust Management, UK (2004).

[16] Gandon, L., Sadeh, N.: Semantic web technologies to reconcile privacy and context awareness, Web Semantics Journal, Vol. 1, No. 3 (2004).

[17] Chen, H. et al.: SOUPA: Standard ontology for ubiquitous and pervasive applications, in Proc. of the 1st International Conference on Mobile and Ubiquitous Systems: Networking and Services, USA (2004).

[18] Gruber T.: Toward principles for the design of ontologies used for knowledge sharing, in Formal Ontology in Conceptual Analysis and Knowledge Representation. Kluwer Academic Publishers (1993).

[19] Noy N., McGuiness D., "Ontology Development 101: A Guide to Creating Your First Ontology", Stanford Knowledge Systems Laboratory Technical Report KSL-01-05 and Stanford Medical Informatics Technical Report SMI-2001-0880, March 2001.

[20] Holsapple C., Joshi K., "A collaborative approach to ontology design", Comm. of the ACM, 45(2):42-47, 2002.

[21] Tsoumas, V., Dritsas, S., Gritzalis, D.: An Ontology-Based Approach to Information Systems Security Management, in 3rd Intl. Conference on Mathematical Models, Methods and Architectures for Computer Network Security (MMM-2005), Russia (2005).

[22] ISO/IEC 17799, Information technology - Code of practice for information security management, ISO (2000).

[23] Australian/New Zealand Standard for Risk Management 4360 (1999).

[24] United Kingdom Central Computer and Telecommunication Agency. CCTA Risk Analysis and Management Method: User Manual, v. 3.0, UK CCTA (1996).

[25] Protégé Ontology Development Environment, at http://protege.stanford.edu/

[26] Ernest Friedman-Hill, "JESS – The Rule Engine for the Java Platform", Sandia National Laboratories, http://herzberg.ca.sandia.gov/jess/index.shtml (Nov. 2005)

[27] Damianou, N. et al.: The Ponder Policy Specification Language, in Proc. of the Policies for Distributed Systems and Networks Workshop, Lecture Notes in Computer Science, Vol. 1995. Springer-Verlag, (2001) 18-39.

[28] Nmap scanner, available at http://www.insecure.org/nmap

[29] Cunningham, H. et al.: GATE: A Framework and Graphical Development Environment for Robust NLP Tools and Applications, in Proc. of the 40th meeting of the Association for Computational Linguistics (ACL'02), USA (2002).

[30] Cunningham, H., Maynard, D., Tablan, V.: JAPE: a Java Annotation Patterns Engine, (2nd edition), Dept. of Computer Science, Univ. of Sheffield, United Kingdom (2000).

A Methodology for Designing Controlled Anonymous Applications

Vincent Naessens[1] and Bart De Decker[2]

[1] K.U.Leuven Campus Kortrijk, Department of Computer Science,
E. Sabbelaan 53, 8500 Kortrijk, Belgium
Vincent.Naessens@kuleuven-kortrijk.be
[2] K.U.Leuven, Department of Computer Science,
Celestijnenlaan 200A, 3001 Heverlee, Belgium
Bart.DeDecker@cs.kuleuven.be

Abstract. Many anonymous applications offer unconditional anonymity to their users. However, this can provoke abusive behavior. Dissatisfied users will drop out or liability issues may even force the system to suspend or cease its services. Therefore, controlling abuse is as important as protecting the anonymity of legitimate users. However, designing such applications is no sinecure. This paper presents a methodology for designing controlled anonymous environments. The methodology generates a conceptual model that compromises between privacy requirements and control requirements. The conceptual model allows to derive performance and trust properties and easily maps to control mechanisms.

1 Introduction

Many existing privacy-enhancing applications (anonymous mail systems, anonymous publication services, etc) offer unconditional anonymity to their users. As unconditional anonymity can provoke abusive behavior (spam mail, publishing copyrighted or criminal contents, etc) and as new application domains are explored (anonymous payments, anonymous auctions, etc), anonymity control becomes an extremely important issue. However, designing controlled anonymous applications is no sinecure because of several reasons:

- *Opposite requirements.* A reasonable trade-off must be found between the interests of the users (which mainly have privacy requirements) and the interests of the system administrators and law enforcement (which mainly have control requirements).
- *Complexity of building blocks.* Anonymous credentials [2, 3] are used as building block for anonymity control. However, enhancing an application with anonymous credentials while preserving the anonymity requirements is no sinecure. Some models achieve an acceptable level of control but do not comply with the anonymity requirements. Others do not succeed to capture all control requirements.

This paper presents a methodology that eases the design of controlled anonymous applications. The advantages of the methodology are fourfold. First, the methodology allows designers to express anonymity requirements and control requirements at a high

Please use the following format when citing this chapter:

Author(s) [insert Last name, First-name initial(s)], 2006, in IFIP International Federation for Information Processing, Volume 201, Security and Privacy in Dynamic Environments, eds. Fischer-Hubner, S., Rannenberg, K., Yngstrom, L., Lindskog, S., (Boston: Springer), pp. [insert page numbers].

level. Second, the methodology generates a conceptual model from which anonymity/-trust/performance properties can be derived. Third, the methodology provides alternative design decisions that partially avoid conflicts between requirements and proposes reasonable conflict resolution strategies. Fourth, the conceptual model can easily be mapped to control mechanisms.

The paper is organized as follows: section 2 describes some terminology; an overview of the methodology is given in section 3. Section 4 evaluates the methodology. Section 5 discusses related work. We conclude in section 6 with a summary of the major achievements.

2   Basic terminology

This section defines the basic terminology that is used in the rest of this paper, namely actions, environmental attributes and rights.

An *action* is a sequence of interactions between two subjects: a user and a service provider[3]. The set of actions in a particular system is $\mathcal{A} = \{A_1, ..., A_k\}$. Actions are either anonymous or identifiable. An action is identifiable if any publicly known unique environmental attribute of the sender is revealed when the action is performed. Otherwise, it is anonymous.

An *environmental attribute* is a user's attribute whose lifetime extends to multiple actions. $\mathcal{E} = \{\varepsilon_1, ..., \varepsilon_l\}$ defines the set of environmental attributes. Access to certain services can depend on the value of these attributes. Some environmental attributes (such as a mailbox address) are *unique* and others (such as age) aren't. A special type of environmental attribute is defined, namely *ID*. *ID* refers to any publicly known unique environmental attribute (such as SSN, driver's license number, etc) of an individual.

A *right* is a token that is required to perform an action. Each right r_x belongs to a type R_i. $\mathcal{R} = \{R_1, ..., R_m\}$ defines the set of right types. We assume the following properties of rights[4]. First, the values of a set of environmental attributes can be stored in a right. Users retrieve new rights when performing certain actions successfully. Thereafter, the user can prove the ownership of that right. In addition, the subject may choose to prove any attribute (or property of these attributes). Hence, rights are used to fulfil access control conditions. We further assume that two or more proofs of the same right cannot be linked unless the value of a unique environmental attribute is proven. Moreover, a proof can be deanonymizable. If so, the proof can be linked to the right itself by a designated external entity if a condition is fulfilled.

3   Design methodology

First, the requirements are classified according to four categories: privacy requirements, control requirements, performance requirements and trust requirements. Next, a sam-

---

[3] Pfitzmann [11] distinguishes between senders and recipients. PRIME [1] distinguishes between users and data controllers. Hence, the terminology depends on the specific setting in which the concepts are used.

[4] Rights are introduced at the conceptual design phase to enforce control requirements. At the implementation phase, rights are mapped to anonymous credentials.

ple application is introduced on which the design steps will be applied. The conceptual design phase is discussed in the third subsection. Thereafter, we focus on how conflicts between design decisions and requirements can be avoided/resolved. Finally, the conceptual model is transformed using high-level credential primitives.

3.1 Requirements

Privacy requirements Privacy requirements are typically defined in terms unlinkabilities between two items. $Unlinkable(x, y)$ expresses that the two items x and y may not be linked. In our methodology, x and y are either actions or environmental attributes. However, unlinkability requirements between application data can easily be transformed to unlinkability requirements between actions. Assume that $d_i \in appl\_data(a_i)$ and $d_j \in appl\_data(a_j)$, then $Unlinkable(d_i, d_j)$ can be transformed to $Unlinkable(a_i, a_j)$. Pfitzmann [11] distinguishes between anonymity and unlinkability. However, each anonymity requirement can easily be transformed to an unlinkability requirement as follows: $Anonymous(a_i) \Leftrightarrow Unlinkable(a_i, ID)$. Although coarse-grained parameters reduce the maximal amount of unlinkability requirements, many expressions are still possible. The maximal amount of unlinkability requirements of an application with 8 actions and 7 environmental attributes is $(8 + 7)^2 = 225$. To reduce the amount of anonymity requirements that have to be expressed explicitly, unlinkability requirements are split according to three categories: high priority requirements should be preserved in all circumstances; moderate priority requirements should be preserved as long as the user abides the rules; low priority requirements are not expressed explicitly. However, the methodology aims to preserve unlinkabilities as much as possible.

Control requirements In controlled environments, access to certain services is restricted. The *access requirements* are split according to three categories. First, order/multiplicity constraints restrict the order of actions and the number of times actions may be performed. Second, service providers may enforce users to authenticate. Authentication can either be identifiable or attribute-based. In the latter case, the user must reveal the value (or properties) of environmental attributes.

Unfortunately, access policies cannot prevent all types of abusive behavior. *Control measures* are defined to discourage such behavior. However, control measures are performed only if some type of abusive behavior is detected: $fulfils(a_i, cond) \rightarrow measure$. The methodology supports three types of control measures. First, the system may demand to reveal the identity of the user (i.e, accountability). Second, it must be possible to revoke permissions of the subject. Third, the system may need to link attributes from the same user.

Performance requirements Modelling anonymity/control requirements may decrease the performance of the system. First, proofs/initializations of rights increase the *processing time* per action. Second, service providers have to *store evidence* to enable control measures. Moreover, the system may be more attractive if rights are stored on smart cards. However, the storage capacity of smart cards is limited. Therefore, the stakeholders can define an upper bound for the amount of proofs/initializations per action, the maximal amount of rights in the system and the maximal amount of evidence that has to be stored.

Trust requirements Trust requirements are also defined from two viewpoints. Users fundamentally mistrust system entities. They expect them to collaborate with each other and to combine their knowledge. Consequently, at least one trusted external entity should be required to reveal certain links between items. On the other hand, the system needs to rely on entities to make evidence available when performing a control measure.

3.2 Description of the application

The design steps that are introduced in the next sections are applied to a sample application, namely an integrated student environment. Users (i.e, students) register at the registration desk R. Users must reveal uniquely identifying information when registering. After registration, they can create a mailbox and activate an e-learning environment. The mail servers and the e-learning environment are administered by M and E respectively. An *address* is assigned to each mailbox. Students can only retrieve mail from their own mailbox.

Students have to prove the *discipline* for which they subscribed to activate the e-learning environment successfully. After successful activation, students can perform certain actions (such as viewing announcements, consulting schedules, etc) within the e-learning environment under a pseudonym identifier *pid*. They can also submit complaints anonymously. Moreover, they can register for the courses within their discipline after which they can take self-tests about the course and participate in course discussions on chat boards under a *nym*. Each course is administered by the teacher T.

Users must be held accountable for sending abusive mail and for submitting offensive messages to chat boards. Further, system should take measures to discourage spam. In addition, one high priority unlinkability requirement and three moderate priority unlinkability requirements are expressed:

UR_1^h: $Unlinkable(pid,ID)$
UR_1^m: $Unlinkable(address,ID)$
UR_2^m: $Unlinkable(send,address)$
UR_3^m: $Unlinkable(nym,ID)$

3.3 Conceptual design phase

The conceptual design phase consists of three steps and uses multiple graph-based formalisms. In the initial design step, *multiplicity/order constraints* are modelled and represented in a Flow Graph. Next, the Flow Graph is transformed to a Petri Net representation which is further enhanced with *access constraints*. Finally, *control measures* are modelled. In addition, a linkability graph is used to evaluate the anonymity/trust properties. As multiple formalisms are used, the semantics of each attribute within a formalism and a set of rules to transform a model within one formalism to a model within another formalism must be defined. For a detailed description of the transformation rules, we refer to [9].

Flow Graph In the initial design step, *multiplicity/order constraints* are represented graphically by a Flow Graph $FG = \{A, E\}$. Each vertex represents one action $A_i \in \mathcal{A}$. Each directed edge $e = [A_i, A_j]$ defines that action A_i must precede action A_j. Moreover, a multiplicity is assigned to each edge. The multiplicity (with $multiplicity(e) \in \mathbb{N} \cup \infty$) denotes the number of times action A_j may be performed after action A_i. The order dependencies in the student application are represented in figure 1. Note that the service provider is assigned to each action.

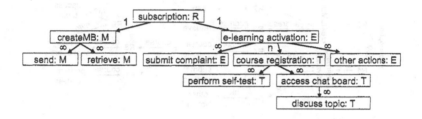

Fig. 1. Flow Graph.

Petri Net The Flow Graph is transformed to a Petri Net. A Petri Net is a four-tuple $(\mathcal{A}, \mathcal{R}, \mathcal{P}, \mathcal{I})$. Each transition corresponds to an action $A \in \mathcal{A}$; each place $R \in \mathcal{R}$ defines a container of rights of the same type; each token within a place R defines a right $r_i \in R$. each input arc $[R, A] \in \mathcal{P}$ defines that the user must spend a right $r \in R$ to perform action A; each output arc $[R, A] \in \mathcal{I}$ corresponds to a right $r \in R$ that is retrieved when action $A \in \mathcal{A}$ is performed successfully. A *natural number* is assigned to each input arc and each output arc. This number defines the number of rights that are spent and retrieved respectively. The default value is 1.

Each node in the Flow Graph maps to a transition in the Petri Net. The transformation of an edge in the Flow Graph depends on its multiplicity. A bidirectional arc between a place and a transition denotes that the number of valid tokens in the place is not changed when the transition has fired (see figure 2). Semantically, a bidirectional arc defines that the user must prove the ownership of a right; a unidirectional input arc defines a right that is spent.

After transformation, the Petri Net is enhanced with *access constraints*. First, each *input arc* is labelled with a set of (properties of) environmental attributes that a user must prove to perform a certain action. For instance, the user must prove the discipline *disc* for which he subscribed when activating the e-learning environment. Similarly, the user must prove that the *course* for which he wants to take a self-test forms part of his curriculum. Second, each *output arc* is labelled with a set of attributes that are initialized. Note that each attribute must be initialized before it is used in proofs. Figure 2 represents the Petri Net that is derived from the

Flow Graph enhanced with constraints on environmental attributes. Several *performance properties* can be derived from the Petri Net. The number of input and output arcs connected to an action define the number of proofs and initializations respectively. As each token is mapped to a credential (see section 3.5), the maximal number of tokens is linear to the amount of storage space for users. The latter property can be derived by running Petri Net simulations. For other properties that can be derived from Petri Nets, see [8]. Among others, *liveness* shows how often actions can be performed, *persistence* investigates if enabled actions remain enabled after performing other actions, etc.

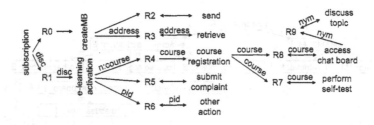

Fig. 2. Petri Net.

Linkability graph A linkability graph $LG_c = \{U, L\}$ is used to analyze the (un)linkability properties in the system. Each unit $u \in U$ is either an action, a right or unique environmental attribute. The set of entities to which the unit is revealed are assigned to each node. Each $l \in L$ defines a direct link between two units. Two properties [5] are assigned to each direct link, namely a set of additional entities (typically external/trusted entities) that are required to link both units and the conditions that must be fulfilled to link them.

A set of rules is defined to generate the LG_c from the Petri Net. The full lines in figure 3 denote the direct links [6] that can be derived from the Petri Net. Moreover, a set of queries are defined on LG_c. For instance, all paths between two given units that can be linked by any given subset of entities can be queried.

Modelling control measures In the next design step, control measures are modelled. To perform a control measure successfully, the system must be able to link the illicit action $action_{illicit}$ to another $unit_{target}$. To reveal the identity of a subject, the illicit

---

[5] Moreover, a cardinality ratio can be assigned to each link. It returns the maximal number of unit instances to which a given unit instance can be linked.

[6] For simplicity, the set of entities to which each unit is revealed is omitted in fig. 3.

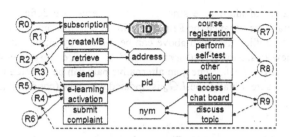

Fig. 3. Linkability graph.

action must be linked to any publicly identifying information *ID*. To deny a user to access a certain service, the illicit action must be linked to a right that is required to access the service. Frequently, units cannot be linked directly. The set of control measures that are possible in the current model can be derived from LG_c. For that purpose, LG_c is extended with conditional links that can be enforced using the following property that is defined on rights in section 2: *a deanonymizable proof can be linked to the right itself by a designated external entity if a condition is fulfilled.* Hence, if a subject sends an offensive message to a chat board, that unacceptable action can be linked conditionally to *R9*. As *R9* is retrieved when accessing the chat board, *access_chat_board* can be linked conditionally to *R8*, etc. The dotted lines in figure 3 denote the conditional links that can be enforced to take a countermeasure if some type of abuse occurs in action *discuss_topic*. A right that is linked (in)directly to the illicit action in the extended linkability graph can be revoked. Similarly, the identity of a subject can be revealed if the illicit action can be linked to *ID*. Hence, the designer can get an overview of all possible control measures given a particular abuse.

Thereafter, the designer marks the desired control measures. All paths between the illicit action and the identity or the right that must be revoked can automatically be derived from the extended linkability graph. For instance, the following path can be used to reveal the identity of the subject after he has sent an offensive message (dead threat, blackmail, etc) to the chat board:

$$P_{sel} = [\ discuss\_topic, R9, access\_chat\_board, R8, course\_registration, R4,$$
$$elearning\_activation, R1, subscription, ID]$$

If multiple paths exist to enforce a control measure, one path is selected. The selection strategy can depend on multiple factors: the path length (which is related to the amount of evidence that is stored), the trust level of each involved entity and the number of entities that are relied on, etc.

However, certain paths may also conflict with different types of requirements. As $Unlinkable(pid, ID)$ is a high priority requirement, selecting the path P_{sel} to enforce the accountability measure is unacceptable (see figure 3). A selected path may also clash with trust requirements if at least one entity that has to deliver evidence is not trusted by the system. Finally, the amount of evidence that is stored by selecting a path may be unacceptable.

Therefore, a set of alternative strategies (or patterns) are defined to avoid conflicts[7]. These strategies enhance the Petri Net with new transitions, places and/or arcs. For instance, the conflict discussed above can be avoided by introducing a new place $R10$ and three new arcs, namely $[subscription, R10]$, $[R10, course\_registration]$ and $[course\_registration, R10]$. Hence, an alternative path can be selected to enforce the accountability measure. Finally, the LG_c is updated with new (conditional) links based on the selected path.

3.4 Conflict avoidance versus conflict resolution

Multiple alternatives exist to model control measures. Hence, conflicts between control requirements and anonymity/trust requirements can partially be *avoided*. However, some conflicts cannot be resolved by simply applying another strategy. As new arcs may be introduced, the set of proofs per action may increase which may imply conflicts with performance requirements. If so, it might be possible to avoid conflicts by revising the control measures that were modelled before (i.e, the methodology can be enhanced with automatic backtracking). This means that acceptable alternatives for previous control measures are tried if no acceptable solution is available for the current control measure.

If the backtracking algorithm fails too, a strategy must be defined to *resolve* conflicts. Abandoning the current control measure is reasonable if the priority of the control measure is low.

Another strategy is to weaken/remove other requirements. For instance, the maximal acceptable amount of proofs may be increased for one or multiple actions. Similarly, certain unlinkability requirements can be omitted prior to rerunning the backtracking algorithm.

A more advanced strategy is to provide the designer (and/or stakeholders) with a set of alternatives. Although the backtracking algorithm fails to return an alternative without conflicts, it may successfully return models for which the number of conflicts and/or for which the sum of the priorities of the conflicting requirements is lower than a predefined number.

3.5 Implementation phase

Anonymous credentials are used as building blocks to realize the model. Idemix [3] is an anonymous credential system that helps to realize anonymous yet accountable transactions. In this section, some rules of thumb are summarized to generate credential primitives. We refer to [9] for a detailed overview of the realization of the conceptual model.

Each right $R \in \mathcal{R}$ corresponds to a credential type. Input/output arcs are transformed to credential show/credential issue protocols. Credential shows sometimes result in a transcript that can be deanonymized by a third party if a particular condition is fulfilled. Deanonymization reveals the nym on which the credential was issued. Moreover, application data can be signed during a credential show.

---

[7] [9] gives an overview of alternative strategies.

In addition, the paths that are assigned to control measures are mapped to chains of evidence. Each element in a chain defines an atomic piece of evidence at the implementation level that is required to perform the control measure.

3.6   Evaluation of the student environment

The optimized Petri Net for sample application is depicted in figure 4. A subset of properties that can be derived automatically from the models are summarized below.

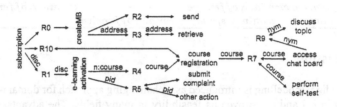

Fig. 4. Optimized Petri Net model.

Performance properties The maximum number of tokens (i.e, credentials) in $\mathcal{R}_x$={R0, R1, R2, R3, R5, R10} is 4. The maximum number of tokens in $\mathcal{R}_y$={R4, R7} is n (with n defines the number of courses). The space that is required to store one credential is slightly overestimated to 4 kB. Hence, all tokens that are required to go through activations, to use the mail services and use a subset of services within the e-learning environment (i.e, $\mathcal{R}_x$) can be stored on a smart card with 32 kB of rewritable memory. All services can be accessed from a smart card with 64 kB of rewritable memory assuming that the number of courses $n \leq 12$. Moreover, the processing time per action remains acceptable: only one proof is required for each type of action that can be performed unlimited.

Control measures The entities that are required to perform a control measure can automatically be derived from the linkability graph and is listed below. We used a single trusted deanonymizer D to reveal certain conditional links. However, trust can be distributed over a set of entities. The evidence that must be stored by each individual entity is omitted for simplicity.

	R	M	E	T	D
$(discuss\_topic, offensive) \rightarrow reveal(ID)$	✓			✓	✓
$(send, criminal) \rightarrow reveal(ID)$	✓	✓			✓
$(send, spam) \rightarrow denyPermission(send)$		✓			✓

Anonymity properties The entities that are required to link two given units and the conditions that must be fulfilled to link them can also be queried on the linkability graph. Among others, $AR_1^h : Unlinkable(pid,ID)$ is preserved unconditionally. The table below returns the link conditions between environmental attributes/actions that are used in UR_1^m, UR_2^m and UR_3^m (see section 3.2). For instance, criminal/spam mails can be linked to the users' mailbox address. However, only criminal mails (illegal contents, blackmail, etc) can be linked to the identity of the initiator.

	ID	address	nym	send
ID	–	$crimin.$	$offensive$	$crimin.$
address	$crimin.$	–	$crimin. \wedge offensive$	$crimin. \vee spam$
nym	$offensive$	$crimin. \wedge offensive$	–	$crimin. \wedge offensive$
send	$crimin.$	$crimin. \vee spam$	$crimin. \wedge offensive$	–

4 Discussion

Multi-paradigm modelling is introduced as a challenging approach for domain-specific modelling in [6] and has proven its feasibility in many fields. The advantage of using multiple formalisms in the design process of controlled anonymous applications is twofold. First, vertical multi-modelling (FG versus Petri Net) allows to model at different levels of abstraction. Second, horizontal multi-modelling (Petri Net versus LG_c) allows to derive models that allow for analysis and evaluation. Moreover, $Atom3$ [5] provided a powerful tool to define formalisms and generate models within the predefined formalism.

The methodology allows to define multiple types of access requirements and control measures. Moreover, it provides powerful evaluation mechanisms and alternatives. Therefore, it may certainly ease the design other applications with interactions between users and service providers such as business and e-government environments. However, future research is needed to extend the methodology to environments (such as P2P systems) with dynamic access policies and variable service providers. In this paper, only a subset of the methodology is presented. First, the actions that are defined in the sample application are static blocks. However, or-splits/or-joins constructs [8] allow to assign conditions on initializers/proofs. For instance, a right to retrieve a driver's license is only granted if the subject passed the practical exam successfully. Second, all environmental attributes in the sample application are constants. However, the methodology also allows to enhance the application with environmental variables. Mutators are assigned to output arcs. They specify how the value of these variables is updated. For instance, the amount of available disk space decreases/increases if the subject stores/removes files, the reputation level of a participant in an auction system may change after each transaction, etc.

5 Related work

The methodology is complementary with existing design/evaluation tools. K. Irwin and T. Yu [7] introduce a formal framework that reasons about the acceptability of attribute based access control policies with respect to identifiability and information sensitivity. The identifiability is the property of how specifically an attacker can narrow down the identity of a user given the properties that he has disclosed. The sensitivity represents the impact of revealing information. Additional parameters can be considered to decide about the acceptability of a certain access policy such as asymmetric attributes, cross-attribute predicates, benefit analysis, etc. However, these parameters are often difficult to quantify.

E. Van Herreweghen [13] shows how various service providers' behavior can be made verifiable and how trust of users and service providers in the correct operation of other service providers could be minimized by defining appropriate liabilities and punishments in service providers' certificates. The liabilities specify the obligations towards service providers to reveal information depending on business agreements and contracts.

A. Pashalidis and C. Mitchell [10] consider timing attacks that may be launched by colluding organizations who wish to link actions from the same subject and propose solutions to tackle those attacks.

Graph-based models [4, 14] already exist for anonymity/unlinkability analysis. However, there are some important differences. First, existing models do not consider conditional links. Although omitting this feature is feasible to analyze anonymity properties in unconditional anonymous applications, evaluating conditional links becomes extremely important in controlled anonymous applications. Second, the current models analyze the anonymity properties towards one single entity (i.e, attacker/profiler). Our approach is more flexible as multiple entities are considered. On the contrary, some models support probabilistic links. Note that additional rules can be defined to add probabilistic links to LG_c. However, estimating reliable probabilities is often very complex and depends on many factors: the setting in which the system is used (i.e, the number of participants, etc), the semantics of application data (i.e, the message contents, etc), etc. Hence, those models are more appropriate for profiling purposes whereas LG_c is a useful tool to analyze unlinkability properties at the design stage of controlled anonymous applications.

6 Conclusion

In this paper, we presented a methodology for designing applications with two opposite types of requirements: privacy and control requirements. Using multiple models allows to evaluate anonymity properties, trust properties and performance properties. Several alternatives are defined at each design step that partially avoid conflicts between requirements. Moreover, fair conflict resolution strategies are defined. The final model foresees an easy mapping to control mechanisms. The paper also discusses how the methodology can be combined with other tools to improve certain properties. However, future research is required to apply the methodology to settings with dynamic access control policies and variable service providers.

References

1. E. Bangerter, J. Camenisch, and A. Lysyanskaya. A Cryptographic Framework for the Controlled Release Of Certified Data. In *Twelfth International Workshop on Security Protocols*, 2004.
2. S. Brands. Rethinking Public Key Infrastructure and Digital Certificates Building in Privacy. PhD thesis, Eindhoven Institute of Technology, 1999.
3. Jan Camenisch, Els Van Herreweghen. Design and Implementation of the Idemix Anonymous Credential System. Research Report RZ 3419, IBM Research Division, June 2002. Also appeared in *ACM Computer and Communication Security*, 2002.
4. D. Cvrcek and V. Matyas. On the role of contextual information for privacy attacks and classification. In *Privacy and Security Aspects of Data Mining workshop*, IEEE ICDM, Brighton, UK, 1 November 2004.
5. J. de Lara, H. Vangheluwe, and M. Alfonseca. Meta-modelling and graph grammars for multi-paradigm modelling in AToM3. In *Software and Systems Modeling (SoSyM)*, 3(3): pages 194–209, August 2004.
6. J. de Lara and H. Vangheluwe. Model-Based Development: Meta-Modelling, Transformation and Verification. The Idea Group Inc., 2005. http://www.cs.mcgill.ca/ hv/publications/04.OOmanagement.pdf
7. K. Irwin and T. Yu. An identifiability-based access control model for privacy protection in open systems. In *The Electronic Society archive Proceedings of the 2004 ACM workshop on Privacy in the electronic society*. Washington DC, p. 43–51.
8. T. Murata. Petri Nets: Properties, Analysis amd Applications. In *Proceedings of the IEEE*, Vol 77(4). pp.: 541–579.
9. V. Naessens and B. De Decker. Design patterns for modelling controlled anonymous applications. DistriNet Report, Dept. of Computer Science, K.U.Leuven, 2005.
10. A. Pashalidis and C. J. Mitchell. Limits to anonymity when using credentials. In *Proceedings of the 12th International Workshop on Security Protocols*, Cambridge, UK, Springer-Verlag LNCS, April 2004.
11. A. Pfitzmann and M. Kohntopp. Anonymity, unobservability and pseudonymity: a proposal for terminology. In *Designing Privacy Enhancing Technologies: Proceedings of the International Workshop on the Design Issues in Anonymity and Observability*, LNCS 2009, pages 1–9. Springer-Verlag, 2000.
12. W.B. Teeuw, H. van den Berg. On the Quality of Conceptual Models. In *Proceedings of the ER'97 Workshop on Behavioral Models and Design Transformations: Issues and Opportunities in Conceptual Modeling*.
13. E. Van Herreweghen. A Risk Driven Approach to Designing Privacy Enhanced Secure Applications. In *Proceedings of the 19th IFIP International Information Security Conference(SEC2004) - Embedded Workshop Privacy and Anonymity in Networked and Distributed Systems (I-NetSec'04)*, August 2004.
14. A. Zugenmaier, M. Kreutzer, and G. Muller. The Freiburg Privacy Diamond: An attacker model for a mobile computing environment. In *Kommunikation in Verteilten Systemen (KiVS) '03*, Leipzig, 2003.

Design Options for Privacy-Respecting Reputation Systems within Centralised Internet Communities

Sandra Steinbrecher

Technische Universität Dresden, Fakultät Informatik
D-01062 Dresden, Germany
steinbrecher@acm.org

Abstract. Reputation systems play an important role in Internet communities like eBay. They allow members of the community to estimate other members' behaviour before an interaction. Unfortunately the design of current reputation systems allows to generate user profiles including all contexts the user has been involved in. A more privacy-enhancing design of reputation systems is needed while keeping the trust provided to the members by the use of reputations. We will present design options for such a system and analyse the privacy it provides with common information-theoretic models. The analysis of our reputation system also allows to analyse similar aspects of privacy in other systems, especially privacy-enhancing identity management.

1 Introduction

With the growth of the Internet more and more people spend a lot of their spare time in so-called Internet communities instead with friends or relatives at their domicile. Most of these virtual friends they have neither met in the past nor will meet them in the future. The spectrum of Internet communities reaches from mailing lists, newsgroups and discussion forums to role-playing and electronic marketplaces. Most of these communities are implemented in a centralised way. There is a community provider which offers the technical system where the community members meet. The members typically want to specify the security requirements - especially confidentiality and integrity of information and actions - such a system should fulfill. But even more than on the systems they have the requirements on the other (usually initially unknown) members they are interacting with.

Example 1 (Self help forums). Someone seeking advice might get technical integrity of other users' answers, but if they give him false advice, technical integrity is meaningless for his problem. Someone who wants his question within the community to be kept confidential from others than legitimated readers might get this guaranteed by the system, but this is insufficient if legitimate readers distribute this information manually.

The measures to reach confidentiality and integrity within a technical system are well-known: By adding digital signatures integrity of digital information or actions can be guaranteed. This needs appropriate public-key infrastructures. But by signatures people only get evidences for others' misbehaviour. Every dispute between individuals has

Author(s) [insert Last name, First-name initial(s)], 2006, in IFIP International Federation for Information Processing, Volume 201, Security and Privacy in Dynamic Environments, eds. Fischer-Hübner, S., Rannenberg, K., Yngström, L., Lindskog, S., (Boston: Springer), pp. [insert page numbers].

to be solved outside the Internet community in a legal process based on national and international law. Confidentiality of digital information can be reached by using encryption. Confidentiality of actions needs appropriate anonymity systems e.g., anonymity on the IP level can be reached by Web mixes [1] or Tor [9], both more or less based on Chaum's Mixes [3].

But beneath these technical measures members of Internet communities need trust in each other that other members do not make technical measures (if applied or even more than not applied) obsolete by their misbehaviour.

When becoming a member of an Internet community an individual develops a new partial digital (or virtual) identity within this community. He starts with a new pseudonym and has to gain a reputation for this pseudonym within the community depending on his (mis)behaviour and its valuation by other members, especially how trustworthy he has been.

Reputation systems can collect the experiences members made with interactors in a technically efficient way. These experiences may help other members to estimate the future behaviour of interactors they have no personal experience with. But it does not prevent any member from making bad experiences with interactors because e.g., reputation usually is context-dependent and subjective. Although 'social attacks' (e.g., members may lie about others' behaviour [6] or members may suddenly change their behaviour) are possible, a usually large number of reputations and an honest majority of members will hopefully reach that dissatisfied members are the exception. For the case that two members are dissatisfied with an interaction, technical measures (like e.g. digital signatures under agreements made) could still give them the possibility to reach legal enforceability of the other's behaviour. So reputation systems do not make other technical security measures obsolete, but hopefully reduce the cases where expensive legal enforceability might become necessary. Note the social and legal aspect of Internet communities cannot be discussed in further detail here.

A very-popular example of Internet communities are marketplace communities whose security was studied in [20].

Example 2 (Marketplace communities). The members of a marketplace community are allowed to sell and buy arbitrary items within the community. One of the greatest providers is eBay (http://www.ebay.com/). After an item within the community has been sold the respecting seller and buyer have to exchange item purchased and money. This is usually done by bank transfer and conventional mail. Many of these exchanges are successful, but unfortunately some are not. Although the money lost might be little and fraud seems to occur only rarely (for instance an eBay representative indicates [25] that 'Fewer than 0.01 percent of all listings on eBay result in a confirmed case of fraud'), the nuisance perceived by the customer is high, and can hamper the further development of marketplace communities. Reputation systems were introduced to most providers' service to collect the experience sellers and buyers made. They are used as a cheap alternative and unfortunately not as an additional option to expensive public-key measures and infrastructures. After every exchange the respective members may give comments or/and marks to each other that are added to the members' public reputation (usually together with the annotator and the exchange considered as context information).

Reputation systems as data bases for community members' experiences with each other should be protected by means of technical data protection to ensure users' right of informational self-determination [15]. Beneath the members' legitimate interest in informing themselves about future interactors, numerous data collectors will be desirous to get access to such large data bases which contain information who interacted at which time with whom in which context. Unfortunately reputation systems currently in use in electronic marketplace communities [14] allow to generate interest and behaviour profiles of pseudonyms (e.g. time and frequency of participation, valuation of and interest in specific items). If the pseudonym becomes related to a real name, as it typically does for trading partners, the profile becomes related to this real name as well.

In [6] an electronic marketplace community with an alternative unidirectional reputation system (where buyers rate sellers) is outlined: Only the provider of the marketplace is able to link identities of members to their pseudonyms in transactions and reputations received in them, but it only publishes estimated reputations of members not their true identities. But this linkability and control of reputations by the provider is not desirable in all scenarios (e.g. if the provider might be corrupted by an attacker). In this paper we try to outline more privacy-respecting but also centralised alternatives of a reputation system that allows bidirectional reputation.

But before going into details of our reputation system we need to give an overview of common models, terms, and measurement methods common in privacy-enhancing technologies in section 2.

Based on this in section 3 we present a model of a centralised Internet community with design options for a privacy-respecting reputation system.

The analysis of the anonymity/unlinkability provided by our privacy-enhancing reputation system follows in section 4. Additionally in contrast to previous approaches our system tries to keep the level of trust provided to the members by the use of reputations at the same level than in not privacy-respecting approaches.

2   Privacy-Enhancing Technologies and Their Measurement

Privacy-enhancing technologies on the IP and application layer try to minimize the data necessary for applications, especially they try to provide confidentiality of circumstances of an action. In this section we give a short overview of privacy-enhancing technologies, privacy-enhancing and -respecting application design and the measurement of anonymity and unlinkability these technologies or applications reach.

2.1   Anonymity

Anonymity of a subject means it is 'not identifiable within a set of subjects, the anonymity set.' [13]. In typical examples a subject's anonymity usually is related to an action. Then the anonymity set is formed by all actors who might have executed the action. For Internet communities the anonymity set is a subset of the community. But the size of the anonymity set is not sufficient to measure a user's anonymity, the 'anonymity is the stronger, the larger the respective anonymity set is and the more evenly distributed' the action's execution 'of the subjects within that set is.', I.e., not only the size of the respective anonymity set determines the anonymity of a certain subject but also how likely a subject of the anonymity set might have executed the action.

There exist several approaches how to describe and measure anonymity. We skip approaches based on formal languages and logics (e.g., [22, 17, 16, 19, 11] because they do not include probabilism that we assume to be necessary for an analysis of anonymity in Internet Communities and only present approaches based on information theory that allow to assign probability distributions to anonymity sets. Then the optimal situation (where every subject in the anonymity set might have executed the action with the same probability) can be compared with the situation where the subjects might be assigned different probabilities because of additional information. In the following we present the information theoretic model from [7, 18] shortly and in a slightly extended version [21] where anonymity regarding arbitrary actions is considered:

Let A be a non-empty set of actions of arbitrary size and $U = \{u_1, \ldots, u_n\}$ be a set of subjects (the anonymity set regarding a specific action $a \in A$) of size n. Given an action a every subject $u_i \in U$ with $i \in \{1, \ldots, n\}$ executes a with the a priori probability $\frac{1}{n}$ and with the a posteriori probability $p_i = P_a(X = u_i) > 0$ (with X random variable) for a possible attacker's view on the system. Naturally $\sum_{i=1}^{n} p_i = 1$. Then there exist two possibilities to describe the global anonymity a system provides for action a:

- Serjantov and Danezis [18] define the a posteriori entropy to be the **effective size of the anonymity probability distribution** $(p_1, \ldots, p_n)$:

$$H(X) = -\sum_{i=1}^{n} p_i \log_2(p_i). \tag{1}$$

- Diaz et al. [7] use the normalised information of what the attacker has learnt ($\max(H(X)) - H(X)$) with $\max(H(X)) = \log_2(n)$ and define the **global degree of anonymity** a system provides as

$$d(U) := 1 - \frac{max(H(X)) - H(X)}{max(H(X))} = \frac{H(X)}{max(H(X))}. \tag{2}$$

The normalisation has the effect that only the probability distribution not the size of the anonymity set is measured in the degree of anonymity. Both degree and size of an anonymity set have to be given to describe the anonymity a system provides.

Users typically are not only interested in the global anonymity a system provides in the average case but in the local anonymity a specific individual $u \in U$ might reach in the worst case. A similar anonymity measure for this case can be defined, but because we want to study the global anonymity in an Internet community we omit this approach here and refer to [23] for details.

2.2 Unlinkability

In an extension to anonymity of a person the unlinkability of his actions can be measured in a similar way. Unlinkability of two items (e.g., actions) within a system means that 'within the system (comprising these and possibly other items), from the attackers perspective, these items of interest are no more and no less related after his observation than they are related concerning his a-priori knowledge '[13].

Unlinkability of items within one set (e.g. actions that might be executed by the same user) can be measured as following [21]: Let $A = \{a_1, \ldots, a_n\}$ be the set of items within a given system. For someone with full knowledge of the system some items of this set are related while others are not. The notion of 'is related' should form an equivalence relation $\sim_{r(A)}$ on the set A. By this relation A is split in l ($1 \leq l \leq n$) equivalence classes $A_1, \ldots, A_l$ with $\forall i, j \in \{1, \ldots, l\}$, $i \neq j$: $A_i \cap A_j = \emptyset$ and $A_1 \cup \ldots \cup A_l = A$. Then items are related to each other iff they belong to the same equivalence class.

An attacker on unlinkability of items within one set knows A but a priori should not know the structure of $\sim_{r(A)}$.

For a random variable X let $P(a_i \sim_{r(A)} a_j) := P(X = (a_i \sim_{r(A)} a_j))$ denote the attacker's a posteriori probability that given two items $a_i, a_j \in A$, X takes the value $(a_i \sim_{r(A)} a_j)$ (or a_i and a_j are related). And $P(a_i \not\sim_{r(A)} a_j)$ denotes the analog probability that a_i and a_j are not related.

The degree of (i, j)-unlinkability $d(i, j)$ describing the unlinkability of two items $a_i, a_j \in A$ a system provides is

$$d(i, j) := H(i, j) := H(X)$$
$$= -P(a_i \sim_{r(A)} a_j) \cdot \log_2(P(a_i \sim_{r(A)} a_j))$$
$$-P(a_i \not\sim_{r(A)} a_j) \cdot \log_2(P(a_i \not\sim_{r(A)} a_j)).$$

Both anonymity measurement and unlinkability measurement will be needed to describe the privacy our reputation system could provide.

2.3 Privacy-enhancing identity management

Within an Internet community a user develops one or several partial digital (or virtual) identities within this community, 'each represents the person in a specific context or role. [...] A pseudonym can be used as an identifier for a partial identity.' [13].

Identity management systems try to help users to manage the various partial identities they might have for specific applications like Internet communities. User-controlled privacy-enhancing identity management [4] gives the possibility of pseudonymous interaction on the Internet that tries to satisfy the security requirements of all parties involved. Typically the user-server scenario is considered. A user can protect against unauthorised access to personal information while by the use of credentials issued by identity providers the server can be sure pseudonymous users are reliable and can be made accountable for misbehaviour. E.g., the use of an identity management system is applicable to the scenario of classical e-commerce on the Internet as sketched in [5]. But it also could be applied to more general scenarios like Internet communities with equal interactors. 'Identity management is called privacy-enhancing if it does not provide essentially more linkability between partial identities' [13].

By extending [13] we define applications (e.g., Internet communities) where identity management could be used to be designed in a privacy-enhancing identity management enabling way if neither the pattern of actions nor the attributes given to entities (i.e., humans, organizations, computers) acting within the system imply more linkability than is strictly necessary to achieve the purposes of the application. A privacy-respecting application at least tries to respect the privacy of the entities using the application by not necessarily reducing the linkability reached within the application to a minimum but to a level acceptable for all entities involved. This is what our reputation system tries to be because the trust reputation systems try to achieve within an Internet community should still be achievable. Unfortunately trust is something very difficult to measure but we are able to measure at least the anonymity provided with the measures outlined above.

3 Modelling the Internet Community

In the following our model of a centralised Internet community and a privacy-respecting reputation systems that could be established within such a community is outlined.

3.1 Assumptions

We consider an Internet community whose users use global pseudonyms within the system. Linked to the pseudonyms there are specific global reputations. Under certain circumstances users are allowed to give ratings to other users that are added to the global reputation that is associated with the other user's pseudonym. The global reputation has to be updated in a centralized reputation data base.

The circumstances that initiate a rating can be neglected for the model. In example 2 circumstances were sales between pseudonyms.

We limit our model to global reputations and do not consider different views on reputations or inconsistent local storage. Examples of such systems can be found in P2P systems e.g., EigenTrust [12] or [8]. We assume this global and central data base model of reputation systems because it allows to consider a global attacker who has easy access to all reputation information. Every kind of distributed storage, distribution and views only needs to be protected against weaker attackers. Nevertheless our approach can be extended to analyse local storage of global reputation values that might be realised by coins as suggested in [24]. But their approach needs to guarantee that users cannot get rid of negative reputations. This was already formulated in [2] for negative credentials. A central storage guarantees that the reputations collected under one pseudonym can only be used linked to each other, positive and negative ones.

Nevertheless also central storage does not solve the problem of pseudonym changes without a transfer of (especially negative) reputations or the creation of new pseudonyms in Internet communities. Friedman and Resnick [10] propose to charge every newcomer an entrance fee or to use cryptographic mechanisms for anonymous credentials usable for specific purposes in every Internet community. A person using such a pseudonym is not able to change the pseudonym without transferring the reputation collected under this pseudonym.

Anonymity measurement within a reputation system needs the distribution of reputations on all pseudonyms. In the case of local storage these numbers can only be estimated while central storage allows an easy query from the reputation data base.

Let the set of global pseudonyms at time t be $\mathcal{P}_t = \{p_{t,1}, \ldots, p_{t,m}\}$ and the set of possible reputations that might be associated with $\mathcal{P}_t$ be R with $(R, +)$ a commutative group and $+$ an operator to combine elements from R and R independent of t.

At time t_1 every pseudonym $p_{t_1,l}$ ($l \in \{1, \ldots, m\}$) has a reputation $rep(t_1, p_{t_1,l}) \in R$. Let R' be a subset of R that contains the possible ratings that might be given to pseudonym $p_{t_1,i}$ by pseudonym $p_{t_1,j}$.

Then as long as the pseudonym $p_{t_1,i}$ exists globally and the rating r_{j,i,t_1} that $p_{t_1,i}$ has received at time t_1 from p_{j,t_1} was the only one since t_1 at time $t_2 \geq t_1$ the pseudonym $p_{t_1,i}$ has the new reputation $rep(t_2, p_{t_1,i}) = rep(t_1, p_{t_1,i}) + r_{j,i,t_1} \in R$.

We do not consider the concrete implementation of R, R' and $+$ here but this general model is applicable to many existing reputation systems.

Example 3 (eBay's reputation system). In eBay's reputation system an element of the set R' consists of several elements: a value from $\{-1,0,1\}$, a limited free-text field, the time the rating was given and possibly the annotator and the trade considered. The operator $+$ is the simple succession of elements from R' and accordingly it holds $R = R'^*$.

To assure the authenticity of ratings given either each rating could be signed by its issuer's pseudonym. This needs a public-key infrastructure to be established. Or the provider of the community needs to assure authentic ratings by appropriate authentication methods for the pseudonymous accounts established within the community. This needs appropriate trust in the community provider. Note both measures do not prevent an issuer from giving wrong ratings.

3.2 Usage of pseudonyms

All ratings given to the same pseudonym are linkable to each other globally because they build the reputation of one pseudonym. To increase privacy (or especially anonymity of users or unlinkability of their actions) in Internet communities the usage of pseudonyms and the possibility of changing them should follow specific rules which are explained in this section. These rules have effects on the reputation associated with these pseudonyms as also outlined in the following.

Parallel usage of pseudonyms Unlinkability between different contexts (or context types) a member of the community is involved in can be reached by using role pseudonyms regarding to the roles he has in these contexts.

Example 4 (Different contexts in Internet Communities). By the parallel usage of unlinkable pseudonyms the contexts 'offering goods within the community' or 'giving advice regarding a specific topic' or 'chatting about a hobby' could be separated.

This has the positive side effect that reputations for different roles are collected separately. This should even increase the trust in the reputation system because members might be different trustworthy depending on the context. The definition of a context and the distinction between contexts has to be made in the reputation system to make the reputations collected under a pseudonym sensible. All members with access to the reputation system have the opportunity to link all context information regarding the respective pseudonym.

Consecutive usage of pseudonyms Beneath using role pseudonyms for different contexts users should change the pseudonyms they use within these contexts from time to time. This gives members the possibility to determine the linkability of their actions within the community. They might even use their reputation with different sequenced pseudonyms. In a global system like in our model there are several attacker models imaginable under which unlinkability can be guaranteed that are similar to the attacker models of anonymous communication:

The users might trust the provider of the reputation data base that he changes his pseudonym on demand, then for outsiders the pseudonyms are unlinkable but for the provider they are still linkable.

Example 5 (eBays reputation system). eBays reputation system already allows users to change pseudonyms but the history of all previous pseudonyms is available globally as well. The minimum necessary to reach unlinkability against outsiders would mean that eBay keeps this history secret.

A stronger attacker model (that tries to limit the trust in the provider) would be to include several third parties in the change of a pseudonyms that make several consecutive changes. But this still needs trust that the third parties do not collaborate resp. none observes the communication between them. This is similar to the use of anonymous proxies for anonymous communication.

The use of convertible credentials [2] issued by identity providers enables users to transform statements made about one of his pseudonyms to statements about another one of his pseudonyms while the pseudonyms are still unlinkable to each other for everyone except himself. But in the case of a misuse the identity providers can reveal a pseudonym's user. This would mean that in the case of a pseudonym change the user asks the identity provider to issue a credential on his reputation value that he can convert to another credential himself and send it to the provider of the global reputation data base.

3.3   Frequency of pseudonym changes

Pseudonym changes naturally only make sense if the reputation related to the pseudonym is the same many other members have as well, the pseudonym's possible anonymity set for the pseudonym change. Usually the possible anonymity sets in Internet communities are quite large. If the number of possible reputations is limited, e.g. by a numerical sum of ratings many members will have the same reputation and thus the anonymity set of one single member could contain all members with the same reputation after a pseudonym change of all members with the same reputation. If the reputation system allows the members to give additional comments regarding their rating, the possibility for the formulation of comments has to be limited as well to guarantee appropriate anonymity sets. Especially digital signatures of issuers have to be omitted but be substituted by signatures of the community provider or identity providers.

Because the change of a pseudonym and the corresponding reputation usually is costly and needs many members to participate, there has to be made a trade-off between the costs of a pseudonym change and the linkability of information regarding a pseudonym. In the following measurement of anonymity for pseudonym changes we concentrate on the optimal points for pseudonym changes regarding the anonymity sets considered. Note that we could also measure unlinkability of pseudonyms instead of anonymity regarding a pseudonym change. Due to the lack of space we omit this measurement and also neglect that and how the number and kind of ratings collected under one pseudonym will influence the times of pseudonym changes as well.

4   Measuring Anonymity within an Internet Community

Using the terms common in identity management reputation is an attribute that in contrast to many other attributes varies frequently over the time. Regarding this attribute we analyse the user's unlinkability regarding parallel usage of pseudonyms and his anonymity regarding pseudonym changes, the measures suggested above to reach a privacy-respecting design of reputation systems. For many applications this examination should be extended to more attributes a user might have.

Unlinkability of parallel used pseudonyms If users do not reveal additional information the parallel usage of pseudonyms is not linkable, this means for all linkability relations $\sim_{r(\mathcal{P}_{t_1})}$, pseudonyms $p_{t_1,i}, p_{t_1,j} \in \mathcal{P}_{t_1}$ and $i \neq j$ the (i,j)-unlinkability $d(i,j)$ the reputation system provides is

$$d(i,j) = -P(p_{t_1,i} \sim_{r(\mathcal{P}_{t_1})} p_{t_1,j}) \cdot \log_2(P(p_{t_1,i} \sim_{r(\mathcal{P}_{t_1})} p_{t_1,j}))$$

$$-P(p_{t_1,i} \not\sim_{r(\mathcal{P}_{t_1})} p_{t_1,j}) \cdot \log_2(P(p_{t_1,i} \not\sim_{r(\mathcal{P}_{t_1})} p_{t_1,j})) = \frac{1}{2}.$$

As far as no additional information becomes known (e.g. how many users have a specific number of pseudonyms) the unlinkability has the maximum value above.

Anonymity of a pseudonym change Usually the set of pseudonyms at time t_1 is split into several subsets regarding the relation 'has the same reputation'. Now we consider one of these subsets, the set $\mathcal{P}_{t_1,r}$ with the pseudonyms having the reputation $r \in R$:

$$\mathcal{P}_{t_1,r} = \{p_{t_1,i} \mid rep(t_1, p_{t_1,i}) = r.\}$$

If a global pseudonym change within this group is announced a subset of this set will change its pseudonyms with the function $c : \mathcal{P}_{t_1,r} \rightarrow \mathcal{P}_{t_2,r}$ with $\mathcal{P}_{t_2,r}$ the resulting pseudonym set after the pseudonym change. None of the members has an advantage regarding the anonymity of his own profile in not participating in the pseudonym change but concurrently he decreases the other pseudonyms' anonymity. This might be a motivation for an attacker.

Every pseudonym in $\mathcal{P}_{t_2,r}$ is 'related' to exactly one pseudonym in $\mathcal{P}_{t_1,r}$ because no new pseudonym could be added to $\mathcal{P}_{t_2,r}$ without having reached reputation r at time t_1 and thus belonging to $\mathcal{P}_{t_1,r}$. If there exist users who have not participated in the pseudonym change phase it holds $\mathcal{P}_{t_2,r} \cap \mathcal{P}_{t_1,r} \neq \emptyset$.

According to section 2 the effective size of the anonymity set probability distribution regarding the anonymity $p_{t_2,j}$ has for the pseudonym change c can be calculated (for X the random variable that $p_{t_2,j}$ resulted from $p_{t_1,i}$ through c):

$$H(X) = - \sum_{p_{t_1,i} \in \mathcal{P}_{t_1,r}} P(c(p_{t_1,i}) = p_{t_2,j}) \log_2(P(c(p_{t_1,i}) = p_{t_2,j}))$$

The continual growth of reputations within the system produces different sizes of anonymity sets.

If the pseudonym change is initiated for all $r \in R$ at the same time, the same degree of anonymity for all pseudonyms is reachable at time t_1 when it holds $|\mathcal{P}_{t_1,r_1}| = |\mathcal{P}_{t_1,r_2}|$ $\forall r_1, r_2 \in R$ and all pseudonyms participate in the pseudonym change.

But the goal of every user is to maximise his own degree of anonymity of a pseudonym change. He is interested in maximising his own anonymity set.

The other possibility for the provider is to fix minimal sizes of the anonymity sets as security parameter that should be reached for a pseudonym change and initiate pseudonym changes for each anonymity group separately. But this may lead to more pseudonym changes for single pseudonyms who change the anonymity set meanwhile while other pseudonyms often might 'miss' the pseudonym changes by changing the anonymity set.

5 Summary and Future Work

We have presented privacy-respecting design options of centralised reputation systems for Internet communities that keep the level of trust provided to the members by the use of reputations. Common information-theoretic models were used to evaluate the unlinkability/anonymity of user reputation profiles the proposed privacy measures provide. The proposed measurements allow to study similar aspects of privacy in other systems, especially single changing user attributes in privacy-enhancing identity management systems.

In the near future we will study the linkability regarding the information collected under one pseudonym in interplay with the provider-initiated points of pseudonym changes that are determined by the anonymity sets regarding reputation. Especially we will make simulations on the privacy-enhancing reputations systems to allow the user scalability of reputation and privacy and especially give him feedback and suggestions on both factors. Further in future research the model has to be extended for privacy-enhancing identity management to allow the measurement of combinations from more than one user attribute than just reputation.

References

1. Oliver Berthold, Hannes Federrath, and Stefan Köpsell. Web mixes: A system for anonymous and unobservable internet access. Designing Privacy Enhancing Technologies. Proc. Work-

shop on Design Issues in Anonymity and Unobservability, LNCS 2009, Springer-Verlag, Heidelberg 2001, pp. 115–129.

2. David Chaum. Showing credentials without identification - signatures transferred between unconditionally unlinkable pseudonyms. Advances in Cryptology - EUROCRYPT 85, LNCS 219, Springer-Verlag Berlin 1986, pp. 241–244.

3. David Chaum. Untraceable electronic mail, return addresses and digital pseudonyms. Communications of the ACM, 24(2), 1981, pp. 84–88.

4. Sebastian Clauß, Andreas Pfitzmann, Marit Hansen, and Els Van Herreweghen. Privacy-enhancing identity management. The IPTS Report 67 (September 2002), pp. 8-16.

5. Sebastian Clauß and Marit Köhntopp. Identity management and its support of multilateral security. Computer Networks 37 (2001), Special Issue on Electronic Business Systems; Elsevier, North-Holland 2001; 205-219.

6. Chrysanthos Dellarocas. Immunizing online reputation reporting systems against unfair ratings and discriminatory behavior. ACM Conference on Electronic Commerce, 2000, 150-157.

7. Claudia Díaz, Stefaan Seys, Joris Claessens, and Bart Preneel. Towards measuring anonymity. In Roger Dingledine and Paul Syverson, editors, Proceedings of Privacy Enhancing Technologies Workshop (PET 2002). Springer-Verlag, LNCS 2482, April 2002.

8. Roger Dingledine, Nick Mathewson, and Paul Syverson. Reputation in P2P Anonymity Systems. In Proceedings of Workshop on Economics of Peer-to-Peer Systems, June 2003.

9. Roger Dingledine, Nick Mathewson, and Paul Syverson. Tor: The second-generation onion router. In Proceedings of the 13th USENIX Security Symposium, August 2004.

10. Eric Friedman and Paul Resnick. The social cost of cheap pseudonyms. Journal of Economics and Management Strategy, Aug. 1999.

11. Dominic Hughes and Vitaly Shmatikov. Information hiding, anonymity and privacy: A modular approach. Journal of Computer Security, 12(1):3–36, 2004.

12. Sepandar D. Kamvar, Mario T. Schlosser, and Hector Garcia-Molinal. The eigentrust algorithm for reputation management in p2p networks. Proceedings of the Twelfth International World Wide Web Conference, May, 2003.

13. Marit Köhntopp and Andreas Pfitzmann. Anonymity, unobservability, and pseudonymity - a proposal for terminology. Draft v0.26, December 2005, http://dud.inf.tu-dresden.de/Literatur_V1.shtml.

14. Peter Kollock. The production of trust in online markets. Advances in Group Processes (Vol. 16), Greenwich, CT: JAI Press., 1999.

15. Tobias Mahler and Thomas Olsen. Reputation systems and data protection law. eChallenges e-2004 Conference, Vienna, October 2004.

16. M. K. Reiter and A. D. Rubin. Crowds: Anonymity for web transactions. ACM Transactions on Information and System Security 1(1), November 1998, pp. 66–92.

17. Steve Schneider and Abraham Sidiropoulos. CSP and anonymity. ESORICS 1996, LNCS 1146, Springer-Verlag Berlin 1996, pp. 198–218.

18. Andrei Serjantov and George Danezis. Towards an information-theoretic metric for anonymity. Privacy Enhancing Technologies 2002, LNCS 2482, Springer-Verlag Berlin.

19. Vitaly Shmatikov. Probabilistic analysis of anonymity. Proc. 15th IEEE Computer Security Foundations Workshop (CSFW) 2002, pp 119–128.

20. Sandra Steinbrecher. Balancing privacy and trust in electronic marketplaces. DEXA Conference on Trust and Privacy in Digital Business 2004, LNCS 3184, Springer Verlag Berlin, pp. 70-79.

21. Sandra Steinbrecher and Stefan Köpsell. Modelling unlinkability. In Roger Dingledine, editor, Proceedings of Privacy Enhancing Technologies workshop (PET 2003). Springer-Verlag, LNCS 2760, March 2003.

22. Paul F. Syverson and Stuart G. Stubblebine. Group principals and the formalization of anonymity. FM'99 – Formal Methods, Vol. I, LNCS 1708, Springer-Verlag Berlin 1999, pp. 814–833.
23. Gergely Tóth, Zoltán Hornák, and Ferenc Vajda. Measuring anonymity revisited. In Sanna Liimatainen and Teemupekka Virtanen, editors, *Proceedings of the Ninth Nordic Workshop on Secure IT Systems*, pages 85–90, Espoo, Finland, November 2004.
24. Marco Voss. Privacy preserving online reputation systems. In *International Information Security Workshops*, pages 245–260. Kluwer, 2004.
25. Graeme Wearden. Judge raps ebay over fraud. December 7, 2004, available from http://news.com.com/2102-1038_3-5481601.html.

Protecting (Anonymous) Credentials with the Trusted Computing Group's TPM V1.2*

Jan Camenisch

IBM Research, Zurich Research Lab
Säumerstrasse 4, CH-8803 Rüschlikon, Switzerland
jca@zurich.ibm.com

Abstract. Digital credentials and certificates can easily be shared and copied. For instance, if a user possesses a credential that allows her to access some service, she can easily share it with her friends and thereby let them use the service as well. While with non-anonymous credentials, this sharing can to some extend be detected by the fact that some credentials get used too often, such detection is not possible with anonymous credentials. Furthermore, the honest user is also at risk of identity theft: malicious software such as viruses and worms or phishing attacks can without too much difficulty steal her credentials.
One solution to the problem is to use tamper-resistant hardware tokens to which a credential is bound such that a credential can only be used in connection with the token. Although this approach is sometimes taken for isolated high security applications, it is not used widely because of the organizational overhead to distribute such tokens. Moreover, such tokens are usually very application specific and hence cannot be used with different applications (from different service providers).
Recently, however, manufacturers have started to embed into computers a tamper-resistant piece of hardware, called trusted platform modules (TPM), as specified by the Trusted Computing Group. In this paper we show that this module can in fact be used to secure anonymous as well as non-anonymous credentials. We provide a mechanism to insure that credentials can only be used with the TPM it got issued to. We then extend our solution to one that allows the use of credentials not only with the TPM they got issued to but also with other TPMs of the *same* user. Finally, we show how to secure a full-fledged anonymous credential system.

1 Introduction

Due to their nature, digital credentials can easily be copied and distributed. Thus, on the one hand, a computer virus or worm, for instance, can easily steal a user's credentials and, on the other hand, a user can even easier share her credentials (illegitimately) with her friends. In case credentials are used to protect access to valuable resources or services, such things should obviously be prevented and the credentials themselves be protected as well.

Although one can obtain some protection by software (such as storing credentials only in encrypted form and trying to secure the operating system), containment of credentials in a hardware token offers much better protection. While such protection is in

---

* A full version of this paper is available at www.zurich.ibm.com/~jca/publications.

Please use the following format when citing this chapter:
Author(s) [insert Last name, First-name initial(s)], 2006, in IFIP International Federation for Information Processing, Volume 201, Security and Privacy in Dynamic Environments, eds. Fischer-Hubner, S., Rannenberg, K., Yngstrom, L., Lindskog, S., (Boston: Springer), pp. [insert page numbers].

principle possible also for credentials consisting of username and password (e.g., using so-called password-based key exchange protocols [3, 2, 17]), one would rather use public key cryptography because passwords have low entropy (so that they can be stored in a human brain). Credentials based on public key cryptography work as follows: A public/private key pair is generated (inside the hardware token) and the public key is sent to the issuer of the credential. The issuer either just stores the public key in a list of authenticated keys or actually issues a certificate on the public key, i.e., signs the public key together with some further (access) information or attributes. When the user then wants to access the service service or resource using her credentials, she sends the public key (and, if necessary, also the certificate) to the resource or service provider. The provider then either checks whether the public key is in the list of authorized keys or verifies the validity of certificate. Finally, using the secret key, the user (or the hardware token) identifies as the owner of the public key, and then will obtain access to the requested service or resource. If one uses so-called zero-knowledge protocols for this identification process (e.g., [15, 20]), this process does not divulge the secret key. Thus, if the only interface the hardware token offers is to generate a key pair, output the public key, and to run a zero-knowledge identification protocol w.r.t. this key pair, no information about the secret key is leaked from the hardware token and the credential cannot be used without the hardware token. Thus, the access credentials are protected from malicious software such as viruses and worms. Furthermore, assuming that the hardware token is tamper-resistant and it is ensured that the secret key is indeed held in the hardware token, users can no longer share credentials without sharing the token as well.

We note that this kind of protection is also applicable to so-called anonymous or private credentials [11, 6].

Today, credentials are only rarely protected by hardware tokens. One reason for this is that the cost of the deployment of such tokens is still too high, in particular as the tokens are not interoperable and can hence only be used for isolated applications. As a result, weak authentication is used, which in combination with the growing rate of frauds such as phishing attacks seriously hinder the growth of e-commerce on the Internet and even turn people away from using the Internet for financial transactions.

TCG's Trusted Platform Module. Recently, manufacturers have started to embed so-called trusted platform modules (TPM) [21] into computers. These modules are one of the building blocks for trusted computing that are specified by the Trusted Computing Group (TCG). They are essentially smartcard chips build into a computing device. These modules can, among other things, generate public and secret key pairs. Moreover, they have a mechanism to remotely convince another party that a key pair was indeed generated by them and that the secret is protected by the module (i.e., cannot not be extracted from the module except by physically breaking it open). The mechanism is called direct anonymous attestation (DAA) [21, 5] and can be seen as a group signature scheme without the capability to open signatures (or anonymity revocation) but with a mechanism to detect rogue members (TPMs in this case). In a group signature scheme, there is a group manager (the manufacturer of TPMs in our case) who controls who are the members of the group (all TPMs produced by the manufacturer). Group signatures allow member of the group to sign anonymously on behalf of the group. Thus, the capability to sign proves group membership and hence, as TPMs are instructed to sign only public keys to which they holds the secret key, the desired mechanism results.

Our Contribution. In principle one could use the TPM to secure credentials by having the TPM generate a key pair, proving that the key pair was indeed generated by the TPM (using the DAA protocol), and then issue a certificate on the signed public key. However, this approach does not protect the user's privacy as the issuing and each use of the certificate can be linked.

In this paper we show how the TPM's functionalities can be used to secure credentials and how to do it in a privacy friendly way. More precisely, we analyze the DAA protocol and show how the TPM's part of that protocol can be used to obtain a new, DAA-like protocol that allows one to issue (anonymous) credentials to users in such a way that they can only be used in conjunction with the TPM they got issued to. This protocol provides privacy to users, i.e., the issuer of the credential and the provider of the service or resource cannot link the two transactions. Essentially, we obtain an anonymous credential system where a user can only use her credentials in cooperation with her TPM. We note that our new protocol does not require any modification of the TPM and hence our solution can be realized with the TPM following the V1.2 specification which are already found in some computing devices today.

While our solution offers users protection against viruses and service providers protection against fraudulent users, it has the drawback that users can use a credential only with the device (resp., the TPM embedded into this device) the credential was issued to. Thus, credentials are not portable as they would for instance be if they were tied to a smartcard or a USB key. We therefore extend our solution to allow each user to use all *her* credentials with all *her* devices. We also show how to protect conventional (i.e., non-anonymous) credentials as well how to extend our scheme to a full-fledged anonymous credential system.

We believe that once TPMs according to the V1.2 specification [21] become widely available, our solution can enable widespread strong authentication and privacy protection for electronic transactions and help ignite the staggering growth of e-commerce on the Internet.

2   Model and Security Requirements of Our Scheme

A system for protecting anonymous credentials for use with all of a user's devices and *only* with those is a follows. It consists of five kinds of parties, device-credential issuers, application-credential issuers, service (or resource) providers, devices, and users. For simplicity we will consider only a single device-credential issuer, a single application-credential issuer and a single provider. We stress, however, that our scheme will also achieve all security properties if multiple such parties participate. The system features the following procedure.

KeyGenDevCredI and KeyGenAppCredA. These are the key generators for the device-credential and the application-credential issuer. On input a security parameter λ, they output a public/secret key pair (PK_D, SK_D), resp., (PK_A, SK_A), for the device-credential and the application credential issuer, respectively.

GetDevCred. This is a protocol between a user's device and a device-credential issuer. The input to both parties are the latter's public key, PK_D, and the user's identity ID_U. The issuer's additional input is his secret signing key SK_D. In case the user is eligible to register the device (e.g., because she has not yet registered too many devices), the user's device's output of the protocol is a device credential and some related secret keys (which will be held inside the device's TPM).

GetAppCred. This is a protocol between a user's device and an application-credential issuer. The input to both parties are the latter's public key PK_A. The user's device gets as additional input the identity ID_U. The application-credential issuer's additional input is his secret signing key SK_A. In case the user is eligible to obtain an application credential, the user's device's output of the protocol is an application credential and some related secret keys, all of which the device outputs.

UseAppCred. This is a protocol between a user's device and a service provider. The input to both parties are the public keys PK_A and PK_D of the device- and application-credential issuers, respectively. The device's input consists of its device credential and the related secret keys (the latter are kept in the device's TPM), the user's identity, as well as an application credential the user has obtained with one of her devices and the related secret keys. The output of the service or resource provider is either accept or reject.

The registration of a user's device does not necessarily require the user's identity – it can in principle also be done anonymously. We discuss this issue in §4.2, but for now require the user to identify herself to register a device.

The security requirements are as follows:

Unforgeability. We require that no adversary, who can register as many devices and retrieve as many application credentials as he wishes, can successfully run the protocol UseAppCred with a service-provider with an unregistered device or can successfully run the protocol UseAppCred with more (hidden) identities that he has obtained application credentials.

Anonymity. We require that even if the device-credential issuer, the application-credential, and the service provider collude, they cannot link different transactions by the same user except those transactions to register devices that were conducted under the same identity.

We note that the unforgeability property ensures that an adversary can only use an application credential with devices that were registered w.r.t. some particular user.

3 Preliminaries

3.1 Known Discrete-Logarithm-Based, Zero-Knowledge Proofs

In the common parameters model, we use several previously known results for proving statements about discrete logarithms, such as (1) proof of knowledge of a discrete logarithm modulo a prime [20] or a composite [16, 14], (2) proof of knowledge of equality of representation modulo two (possibly different) prime [12] or composite [8] moduli, (3) proof that a commitment opens to the product of two other committed values [8,

4], (4) proof that a committed value lies in a given integer interval $[10, 8]$, and also (5) proof of the disjunction or conjunction of any two of the previous [13]. These protocols modulo a composite are secure under the strong RSA assumption and modulo a prime under the discrete logarithm assumption. When referring to the proofs above, we will follow the notation introduced by Camenisch and Stadler [9] for various proofs of knowledge of discrete logarithms and proofs of the validity of statements about discrete logarithms. For instance,

$$PK\{(\alpha, \beta, \delta) : y = g^\alpha h^\beta \wedge \tilde{y} = \tilde{g}^\alpha \tilde{h}^\delta \wedge (u \le \alpha \le v)\}$$

denotes a *"zero-knowledge Proof of Knowledge of integers α, β, and δ such that $y = g^\alpha h^\beta$ and $\tilde{y} = \tilde{g}^\alpha \tilde{h}^\delta$ holds, where $u \le \alpha \le v$,"* where $y, g, h, \tilde{y}, \tilde{g}$, and $\tilde{h}$ are elements of some groups $G = \langle g \rangle = \langle h \rangle$ and $\tilde{G} = \langle \tilde{g} \rangle = \langle \tilde{h} \rangle$. We apply the Fiat-Shamir heuristic [15] to turn such proofs of knowledge into signatures of knowledge on some message m; denoted as, e.g., $SPK\{(\alpha) : y = g^\alpha\}(m)$.

3.2 Direct Anonymous Attestation

The direct anonymous attestation (DAA) protocol [5,21] applies the Camenisch-Lysyanskaya signature scheme [7] and the related protocols to issue a certificate (attestation) to a computing platform that it is genuine and to allow a platform to remotely prove to a service provider that it is indeed genuine while protecting the platform user's privacy. More precisely, the attestation is issued to the trusted platform module (TPM) embedded into the platform. Let us describe the DAA protocol in more detail.

The involved parties are an attester, a device, a platform, a TPM embedded into the device, and a verifier who wants to get convinced by the platform that it got attestation. To communicate with the outside world, the TPM is dependent on the other components of the device. We call all these other components the platform, i.e., a device consist of two (separate) parties, a TPM and a platform. the TPM communicates only with the platform.

The idea underlying DAA is to use Camenisch-Lysyanskaya (CL) signature [7] and the related protocols to sign as attestation secret messages, i.e., "messages" m_0 and m_1 chosen by the TPM. The reason that the TPM chooses two instead of just a single secret message is technical – it allows one to keep the message space small and thus to keep small the primes e that need to be generated for each signature by the attester which in turn makes generating them during signature generation much more efficient) while guaranteeing sufficient entropy in the TPM's secret.

Now, when the platform wants to prove to the verifier that it has embedded an attested TPM, the TPM generates a commitment (pseudonym) N_V on (m_0, m_1) and then proves that it has gotten a signature from the attester on the committed messages. This proof is done using the protocol provided together with CL signature [7] with the difference that N_V is a special commitment, i.e., $N_V = \zeta^{m_0 + 2^\ell m_1}$ for some given ζ and ℓ. We refer to [5] for more details on N_V.

To keep the TPM as small a chip as possible, the direct anonymous attestation protocol was designed such that all operations for retrieving a signature and proving possession of a signature that are not security critical are be outsourced to the platform and computed there. In particular, as a platform could always destroy the privacy of its TPM, all operations that are necessary for privacy but not for security are performed by the platform. For instance, in the protocol to prove possession of a signature (attestation), the TPM computes the "commitment" N_V and the prover's part of the proof protocol

$$PK\{(m_0, m_1, v) : \quad U \equiv R_0^{m_0} R_1^{m_1} S^v \pmod{n} \wedge N_V \equiv \zeta^{m_0 + m_1 2^\ell} \wedge$$
$$m_0, m_1 \in \{0, 1\}^{\ell_m + \ell_\varnothing + \ell_\mathcal{H} + 2}\} \ ,$$

where ℓ, ℓ_m, $\ell_\varnothing + \ell_\mathcal{H}$ are security parameters (cf. [5]). Note that this proof reveals U, i.e., does not hide the TPM's (and thus the platform's) identity. The platform then transform the TPM's messages of that proof, using its knowledge of A and e, into the prover's messages of the following proof protocol

$$SPK\{(m_0, m_1, \tilde{v}, e) : \quad Z \equiv \pm A'^e S^{\tilde{v}} R_0^{m_0} R_1^{m_1} \pmod{n} \wedge N_V \equiv \zeta^{m_0 + m_1 2^\ell} \wedge$$
$$m_0, m_1 \in \{0, 1\}^{\ell_m + \ell_\varnothing + \ell_\mathcal{H} + 2} \wedge (e - 2^{\ell_e}) \in \{0, 1\}^{\ell'_e + \ell_\varnothing + \ell_\mathcal{H} + 1}\} \ ,$$

where $A' := A S^r$ for a randomly chosen r.

4   Securing Credentials with a TPM

The fact that the operation of the "signature receiver" in the protocols to obtain a signature and to prove knowledge of a signature are split between the TPM and the platform and the fact that the platform's operations in the protocol are implemented in software, allow us to "abuse" the DAA protocol and to extend it for our purposes by modifying the software parts of the protocol.

In this section, we first describe how to extend the DAA-protocol such that a DAA-certificate can include attributes while keeping the TPM-part of the protocol unaltered. That is, the modified protocol will allow one to obtain a DAA-certificate containing, besides the secret messages m_0 and m_1 (that will only be known by the TPM), messages $m_2, \ldots m_{L-1}$ that are potentially only known to the platform. The issuer will only learn a commitment to these messages unless the (user of the) platform decides to reveal some of them. Similarly, the modified protocol will allow the platform to prove that the DAA-certificate contains further messages $m_2, \ldots m_{L-1}$ where the individual messages can either be revealed to the verifier, be given in a commitment to him, or be hidden from him. Both protocols will require the cooperation of the TPM to be successfully executed. In particular, the protocols maintain the fact that one cannot prove possession of a DAA-certificate without involving the TPM to which the certificate has been issued. Thus, the user is protected from malicious code such as viruses aiming to steal her certificates and a credential issuer is protected from malicious users because as the certificate can not longer be shared by different users (or at least only by the users of the same platform).

However, as a TPM itself is tied to a particular device, this is not very convenient for users who use a number of devices (e.g., laptop, PDA, mobile phone, home-computer, office-computer, etc) and want to use their credentials with all their devices as this would mean retrieving a particular credential for each of these platforms. Indeed, users would like to have their credentials portable as it would for instance be the case if the credentials were tied to token such as a smartcard or a USB-token. To overcome this drawback, we present a scheme that allows a user to use a credential issued to her with all *her* devices.

Finally, we will show how our basic schemes can be extended to full-fledged credential system and to traditional (non-privacy protecting) certificates and credentials.

Let the public key of the signer consist of an ℓ_n-bit RSA modulus n and elements $R_0, \ldots, R_{L-1}, S, Z \in QR_n$ for some L and the secret key consists of Also let g_i be random group elements of QR_n such that $g_i \in \langle g_0 \rangle$ and such that $\log_{g_0} g_i$ is unknown.

4.1 Extending DAA-Credentials to Include Attributes

A DAA-certificate entails values (A, v, e) such that $Z \equiv A^e S^v R_0^{m_0} R_1^{m_1} \pmod{n}$, where v, m_0, and m_0 are only known to the TPM [21,5]. We now want to extend the DAA protocols to retrieved a signature and to prove knowledge of a signature such that (A, v, e) will be a signature on additional messages such that the TPM's part of the DAA protocols remain unchanged.

Obtaining a Credential That is Tied to a TPM The DAA-join protocol can be extended as follows to have the issuer in addition sign the messages $m_2, \ldots, m_{L-1} \in \pm\{0,1\}^{\ell_m}$, where the issuer is given the m_i's only as a commitment (should an application require the issuer to learn some of the m_i, they can just be reveal and then it can be proven that one has revealed in indeed to correct ones).

It is often useful that the issuer or the verifier do not learn all of the messages $m_2, \ldots, m_{L-1}$. In the following we assume that the issuer learns the messages $m_{L'}, \ldots, m_{L-1}$ and is given a commitment C to the other messages so that, if needed, the platform could prove properties about them using C independently of our protocol.

In the DAA protocol, the TPM sends the issuer (attester) a values $U = S^{v'} R_0^{m_0} R_1^{m_1}$ and proves to the issuer knowledge of v', m_0, m_1, and then the issuer will use U to produce the signature. Now, the idea to extend the DAA-certificate is to send the issuer a second values U' that contains the messages $m_2 \ldots, m_{L'-1}$ and then have the issuer to use that value as well in the signature generation. Let us describe this in more details. Let $C = \mathsf{Com}(m_2, \ldots, m_{L'-1}; r)$ for some suitably chosen r.

1. While the TPM computes U (and some other value N_I serving as pseudonym with the issuer), the platform chooses a random $\hat{v} \in_R \{0,1\}^{\ell_n + \ell_\varnothing}$, computes $U' := S^{\hat{v}} \prod_{i=2}^{L'-1} R_i^{m_i} \bmod n$ and sends to the signer the value U' together with the U produced by the TPM. Furthermore, the value U is authenticated by the TPM using its endorsement key EK. We refer to [5,21] for the details on how this is achieved.
2. Next, the issuer needs to get convinced that U and U' are constructed correctly and that U' corresponds to C. Using the TPM's prover-messages of the original

protocol, the platform computes the proof

$$SPK\{(m_0,\ldots,m_{L'-1},v',\tilde{v},r):$$

$$U \equiv \pm S^{v'} R_0^{m_0} R_1^{m_1} \pmod{n} \wedge N_I := \zeta_I^{m_0+m_1 2^{\ell_m}} \pmod{\Gamma} \wedge$$

$$U' \equiv \pm S^{\tilde{v}} \prod_{i=2}^{L'-1} R_i^{m_i} \pmod{n} \wedge C \equiv g_0^r \prod_{i=2}^{L'-1} g_{i-1}^{m_i} \wedge$$

$$m_0,\ldots,m_{L'-1} \in \{0,1\}^{\ell_m+\ell_\varnothing+\ell_\mathcal{H}+2} \wedge v',\tilde{v} \in \{0,1\}^{\ell_n+\ell_\varnothing+\ell_\mathcal{H}+2}\} \ .$$

This protocol convinces the issuer that the TPM has computed U and N_I correctly, the platform did build U' correctly and that U' contains the messages committed to in C.

3. Now the signature is generated by the signer as in the DAA protocol with the exception that A is computed as

$$A := \left(\frac{Z}{UU'S^{v''} \prod_{i=L'}^{L-1} R_i^{m_i}}\right)^{1/e} \bmod n \ ,$$

where e is a randomly chosen ℓ_e-bit prime e and v a randomly chosen $(\ell_n + \ell_\varnothing)$-bit integer. The signer sends the values (A, e, v'') to the platform.

4. The signer's proof that A is correctly formed is done in the same way as in the DAA protocol with the adaption to the two values U and U', i.e., the proof protocol becomes

$$SPK\{(d): \quad A \equiv \pm\left(\frac{Z}{UU'S^{v''} \prod_{i=L'}^{L-1} R_i^{m_i}}\right)^d \pmod{n}\} \ .$$

5. The platform forwards v'' to the TPM which sets $v := v'' + v'$, and stores (m_0, m_1, v). The platform stores A, e, $\hat{v}$ and $m_2,\ldots,m_L$.

Proving Possession of a Credential that is tied to a TPM To show possession of an extended DAA-certificate, i.e., a signature by the DAA-issuer that now is not only a signature on the TPM's secret keys m_0 and m_1 but also on the messages $m_2,\ldots,m_{L-1} \in \pm\{0,1\}^{\ell_m}$, we have to modify the DAA-sign protocol as follows. Let I_r, I_c, and I_h be three sets. We assume that the verifier is given the messages m_i with $i \in I_r$ and a commitment C to messages m_i with $i \in I_c$ but that the messages m_i with $i \in I_h$ are hidden from the verifier. As before, we need to build the protocol such that the TPM's part of it are as in the original DAA-sign protocol. Thus, the platform now needs to transform the TPM's proof-protocol messages into ones of a proof that convinces the verifier that the messages $m_2,\ldots,m_{L-1}$ are contained as attributes in the DAA-certificate. That is, the platform receives from the TPM prover-messages for the the original protocol and needs to transform them into the prover-messages of the protocol

$$PK\{(e, \tilde{v}, \{m_i | i \in I_c \cup I_h\}, r') :$$

$$Z \prod_{i \in I_r} R_i^{-m_i} \equiv \pm A'^e S^{\tilde{v}} \prod_{i \in I_c \cup I_h} R_i^{m_i} \pmod{n} \wedge C \equiv g_0^{r'} \prod_{i \in I_c} g_i^{m_i} \wedge$$

$$m_i \in \{0,1\}^{\ell_m + \ell_\varnothing + \ell_\mathcal{H} + 2} (i \in I_c \cup I_h) \wedge (e - 2^{\ell_e}) \in \{0,1\}^{\ell'_e + \ell_\varnothing + \ell_\mathcal{H} + 1}\},$$

where the value A' is derived from A as $A' = AS^r$ for a suitable chosen r (such that A' will be a random element) and I_c and I_h are set of indices of the messages to which the verifier receives the commitments C and which remain hidden from the verifier, respectively.

4.2 Using Credentials with Several Devices

We now describe how to realize our limited transferable anonymous certificate scheme using TPM V1.2 chips. The idea is that a user registers (the TPM's of) all her devices with some authority, that is, the registration authority issues all the user's TPMs an extended DAA-credential that contains as one of the extra messages signed (e.g., m_2) an identifier that is unique to that user, e.g., her identity. We call such a credential an *device credential*. We will call the "real" credentials, i.e., those that will allows the user to access some resource or service, *application credential*. These are then issued to the user as described in [7] except that we always set one of the message includes in the credential, e.g., m_0, to the user's identity. Note that these credentials are not directly tied to the TPM. In case the user's identity should not get known to the issuer of application credentials, the user can provide him with a commitment C to m_0 (her identifier), use the protocol presented in §4.1 to show that she has obtained a device-credential that contains as message m_2 the same value that is committed to by C, and then the two can run the protocol in [7] to obtain a signature on a committed message. Now, whenever a user wants to use an application credential, we require the user to provide a commitment C to her identifier and then to prove that she has obtained a device credential that contains as second message the value committed to by C and that she has further obtained an application credential that contains as 0-th message the value committed to by C. This she can do using the protocols provided in §4.1, respectively.

It is not hard to see that this solution provides what we want: Application credentials cannot be used without having access to a device that got registered w.r.t. the identity that is contained in the application credential. Thus, if the device credential issuer makes sure that only a limited number of devices get registered under the same identity, application credentials can only be used with a limited number of devices. In fact, it is not important that the string encoded into the device credentials and the application credentials is the user's real identifier. The device-credential issuer only needs to make sure that only a limited amount of devices get registered per user/identifier. Depending on the scenarios, one might have different limits here. Thus, the registration of a device could even be pseudonymous. That is, the first time a user registers a device, she would establish a pseudonym with the device credential issuer who would then choose an identifier for the user to be encoded into the device credential.

Depending on the scenario and the limits on how many devices a user can register, one might nevertheless want to ensure that users with few devices register their devices w.r.t. the same identifier. In the non-pseudonymous case, one could achieve this by requiring that the user fully identifies herself. In the pseudonymous case, one would require that the user prove ownership of her pseudonym (of course only after she has registered the first device) and apply one of the known methods to prevent the user from sharing her pseudonym (cf. [6]). One such method is for instance to bind the secret key required to prove ownership of the pseudonym to, e.g., the user's bank account. Thus, if the user would share her pseudonym, she would also share her bank account. The details of all of this, however, are out of the scope of this paper and we assume for simplicity in the following description of our solution that each user has a unique identifier.

Setup. For simplicity we consider only a single issuer of device credentials and a single issuer of application credentials. However, the scheme is easy extendable to several registration authorities. Let $(n, R_0, \ldots, R_{L-1}, S, Z)$ be the former's public key for the CL-signature scheme and $(\hat{n}, \hat{R}_0, \ldots, \hat{R}_{L-1}, \hat{S}, \hat{Z})$ be the one of the latter. That is, the key generation algorithms KeyGenDevCredI and KeyGenAppCredA are the key generation algorithms of the CL-signature scheme. We assume each user is somehow assigned an identity ID_U.

Registering a Device. The procedure GetAppCred to register a device is as follows. The user's device runs the protocol to obtain a signature that is tied to a TPM as described in §4.1 with the parameters $L' = 2$ and $L = 3$ and $m_2 = ID_U$. Thus, the user's device will obtain a device credential, i.e., values (A, e, v) such that

$$ Z \equiv A^e R_0^{m_0} R_1^{m_1} R_2^{ID_U} S^v \pmod{n} $$

holds, where the values m_0, m_1, and v are known only to the TPM of the device the user just has registered. Thus, the user can only prove ownership of this device credential when involving the TPM in this proof.

Obtaining a Credential That is Tied to All of the User's TPMs. We now describe the procedure GetAppCred. To obtain an application credential, the user computes a commitment C to her identity, sends C to the issuer, and then runs with the issuer the protocol to obtain a signature on a committed message as described in [7]. Depending on the applications, the application credential might contain other messages (attributes). Thus, we assume that as a result of this protocol the user obtained a CL-signature $(\hat{A}, \hat{e}, \hat{v})$ (application credential) on the messages $ID_U, \hat{m}_1, \ldots, \hat{m}_{\hat{L}-1}$.

We note that there is per se no need for the application issuer to verify that the user has obtained a device credential nor that she has provided the right identity in C, because later on the user won't be able to use the obtained application credential if she has not obtained a device credential containing the identifier contained in C.

Also note that in practise, a user usually will not obtain an application credential without fulfilling some prerequisite. This might include the need to show the issuer some other (application) credential. In this case it might be important that the credential issued and the one that the user proves possession of all encode the same identifier ID_U and thus that the issuer verifies this.

Anonymously Using a Secured Credential. We now describe the procedure UseApp-Cred. Let $(\hat{A}, \hat{e}, \hat{v})$ be an application credential, i.e., a signature on the messages ID_U, $\hat{m}_1, \ldots, \hat{m}_{\hat{L}-1}$, that the user wants to prove possession of to a service or resource provider (called verifier in the following) using a device she registered, i.e., for which she got the device credential (A, e) (for which that device's TPM keeps secret the corresponding m_0, m_1, and v values).

For simplicity, we assume that all the attributes (messages) $\hat{m}_1, \ldots \hat{m}_{\hat{L}-1}$ contained the application credential are hidden from the verifier. However, it is easy to modify the below protocol as to reveal (some of) the message or to provide the verifier only commitments to (some of) them.

1. The platform computes a commitment C to ID_U: it selects a random $r \in_R$ $\{0,1\}^{\ell_n + \ell_\varnothing}$, computes $C := g_1^{ID_U} g_0^r$, and sends C to the verifier.
2. The platform proves possession of an application credential whose 0-th message is committed to in C. The other attributes (i.e., messages) $\hat{m}_1, \ldots \hat{m}_{\hat{L}-1}$ contained in the application credential can be handled as revealed, committed-to, or hidden messages, depending on the application, we here assume that they are all hidden. That is, the platform
   (a) chooses $\hat{r} \in_R \{0,1\}^{\ell_n + \ell_\varnothing}$, computes $\hat{A}' := \hat{A}\hat{S}^{\hat{r}}$, and sends $\hat{A}'$ to the application-credential issuer.
   (b) and then runs the following

$$SPK\{(\hat{e}, \hat{v}, ID_U, \hat{m}_1, \ldots \hat{m}_{\hat{L}-1}, r):$$

$$\hat{Z} \equiv \pm \hat{A}'^{\hat{e}} \hat{S}^{\hat{v}} \hat{R}_0^{ID_U} \prod_{i=1}^{\hat{L}-1} \hat{R}_i^{\hat{m}_i} \wedge C \equiv \pm g_1^{ID_U} g_0^r \wedge$$

$$\hat{m}_1, \ldots, \hat{m}_{\hat{L}-1}, ID_U \in \{0,1\}^{\ell_m + \ell_\varnothing + \ell_{\mathcal{H}} + 2} \wedge (e - 2^{\ell_e}) \in \{0,1\}^{\ell'_e + \ell_\varnothing + \ell_{\mathcal{H}} + 1}\}$$

3. To prove that it has also obtained a device-credential, the platform proceeds as follows:
   (a) The platform chooses $r \in_R \{0,1\}^{\ell_n + \ell_\varnothing}$, computes $A' := AS^r$, and sends A' to the application-credential issuer.
   (b) The platform as prover (with the help of its TPM) executes the protocol

$$SPK\{(e, \tilde{v}, m_0, m_1, ID_U, r):$$

$$Z \equiv \pm A'^e S^{\tilde{v}} R_0^{m_0} R_1^{m_1} R_2^{ID_U} \pmod{n} \wedge C \equiv \pm g_1^{ID_U} g_0^r \bmod n \wedge$$

$$m_0, m_1, ID_U \in \{0,1\}^{\ell_m + \ell_\varnothing + \ell_{\mathcal{H}} + 2} \wedge (e - 2^{\ell_e}) \in \{0,1\}^{\ell'_e + \ell_\varnothing + \ell_{\mathcal{H}} + 1}\}$$

with the application-credential issuer as verifier. To be able to prove the first term, the platform needs to transform the corresponding prover's messages obtained from the TPM via the DAA-protocol in the way described in §4.1.

5 Conclusion

We have provided means to bind traditional as well as privacy-protecting certificates and credentials to TPM chips such that they cannot be used without access to the particular TPM chip they were issued. We then extended our scheme so that a user can use her certificates and credential with all of *her* devices but not with any other device. Thus, we provide the users protection of their certificates and credentials from theft by, e.g., malware or phishing attacks. We also provide protection for the service providers from malicious users sharing their credentials. We believe that our solutions overcome two of main barriers of electronic commerce: the insecurity of the currently used authentication schemes and their lack of privacy.

References

1. G. Ateniese, J. Camenisch, M. Joye, and G. Tsudik. A practical and provably secure coalition-resistant group signature scheme. In *CRYPTO 2000*, vol. 1880 of *LNCS*, pp. 255–270. Springer Verlag, 2000.
2. M. Bellare, D. Pointcheval, and P. Rogaway. Authenticated key exchange secure against dictionary attacks. In *EUROCRYPT 2000*, vol. 1087 of *LNCS*, pp. 139–155.
3. S. M. Bellovin and M. Merritt. Augmented encrypted key exchange: A password-based protocol secure against dictionary attacks and password file compromise. In *ACM CCS*, pp. 244–250, 1993.
4. S. Brands. Rapid demonstration of linear relations connected by boolean operators. In *EUROCRYPT '97*, vol. 1233 of *LNCS*, pp. 318–333. Springer Verlag, 1997.
5. E. Brickell, J. Camenisch, and L. Chen. Direct anonymous attestation. In *ACM CSS*, pp. 225–234. acm press, 2004.
6. J. Camenisch and A. Lysyanskaya. Efficient non-transferable anonymous multi-show credential system with optional anonymity revocation. In *EUROCRYPT 2001*, vol. 2045 of *LNCS*, pp. 93–118. Springer Verlag, 2001.
7. J. Camenisch and A. Lysyanskaya. A signature scheme with efficient protocols. In *SCN 2002*, vol. 2576 of *LNCS*, pp. 268–289. Springer Verlag, 2003.
8. J. Camenisch and M. Michels. Proving in zero-knowledge that a number n is the product of two safe primes. In *EUROCRYPT '99*, vol. 1592 of *LNCS*, pp. 107–122.
9. J. Camenisch and M. Stadler. Efficient group signature schemes for large groups. In *CRYPTO '97*, vol. 1296 of *LNCS*, pp. 410–424. Springer Verlag, 1997.
10. A. Chan, Y. Frankel, and Y. Tsiounis. Easy come – easy go divisible cash. In *EUROCRYPT '98*, vol. 1403 of *LNCS*, pp. 561–575. Springer Verlag, 1998.
11. D. Chaum. Security without identification: Transaction systems to make big brother obsolete. *Communications of the ACM*, 28(10):1030–1044, Oct. 1985.
12. D. Chaum and T. P. Pedersen. Wallet databases with observers. In *CRYPTO '92*, vol. 740 of *LNCS*, pp. 89–105. Springer-Verlag, 1993.
13. R. Cramer, I. Damgård, and B. Schoenmakers. Proofs of partial knowledge and simplified design of witness hiding protocols. In *CRYPTO '94*, vol. 839 of *LNCS*, pp. 174–187. Springer Verlag, 1994.
14. I. Damgård and E. Fujisaki. An integer commitment scheme based on groups with hidden order. In *ASIACRYPT 2002*, vol. 2501 of *LNCS*. Springer, 2002.
15. A. Fiat and A. Shamir. How to prove yourself: Practical solutions to identification and signature problems. In *CRYPTO '86*, vol. 263 of *LNCS*, pp. 186–194.

16. E. Fujisaki and T. Okamoto. Statistical zero knowledge protocols to prove modular polynomial relations. In *CRYPTO '97*, vol. 1294 of *LNCS*, pp. 16–30.

17. R. Gennaro and Y. Lindell. A framework for password-based authenticated key exchange. In *EUROCRYPT 2003*, vol. 2656 of *LNCS*, pp. 524–543. Springer Verlag,

18. T. P. Pedersen. Non-interactive and information-theoretic secure verifiable secret sharing. In *CRYPTO '91*, vol. 576 of *LNCS*, pp. 129–140. Springer Verlag, 1992.

19. R. L. Rivest, A. Shamir, and L. Adleman. A method for obtaining digital signatures and public-key cryptosystems. *Communications of the ACM*, 21(2):120–126.

20. C. P. Schnorr. Efficient signature generation for smart cards. *Journal of Cryptology*, 4(3):239–252, 1991.

21. Trusted Computing Group. TCG TPM specification 1.2. Available at www.trustedcomputinggroup.org, 2003.

Analysis and Improvement of Anti-Phishing Schemes

Dinei Florêncio and Cormac Herley

Microsoft Research
One Microsoft Way, Redmond, WA, USA

Abstract. The problem of phishing has attracted considerable attention recently, and a number of solutions and enhanced security measures have been proposed. We perform a detailed analysis of several anti-phishing schemes, and attacks and improvements. While several anti-phishing technologies address commonly observed phishing tactics, the space evolves rapidly, and a good prevention technique should be robust to anticipated as well as observed attacks. We present a number of attacks and techniques that might be easily employed by phishers and examine the robustness of a recently proposed password re-use anti-phishing system. We compare with other proposed phishing prevention techniques and find that it withstands several attacks that render current anti-phishing approaches obsolete and fares better in a large scale deployment than others.

1 Introduction

The problem of phishing has been well documented in the popular press. A phisher who wishes to attack, say BigBank.com, spams many users with an email purporting to come from Bigbank. The email says that there is a problem with their BigBank account, and directs them to a website to login and fix the problem. The email and the phishing website look as though they belong to BigBank, but in fact have no affiliation. Users who "login" are parting with their BigBank identity, which can be harvested by the phisher. See [13] for details of recent attacks and statistics on the enormous growth in the number of attacks since the phenomenon first emerged.

The problem differs from many other security problems in that we wish to protect users from themselves. The difficulty of finding a solution is compounded by a number of issues. Both false positives (where we falsely suspect a phishing attack) and false negatives (where we fail to detect one) are very expensive. False positives erode trust in the system and cause inconvenience and possible loss to websites that are erroneously classified as phishing. False negatives allow a phisher to grab a user's credentials in spite of our efforts. Recent approaches to phishing prevention have struggled with the effort to keep both kinds of error rates low.

A further difficulty is that of warning the user (or taking other action when phishing is detected or suspected). Halting the browser connection (*i.e.* refusing to connect to the site) is usually not acceptable unless it is absolutely certain that the site is phishing. Warnings and pop-ups have been found to be of very questionable use in getting users to alter their behavior [15].

We explore some of the proposed solutions to this problem and examine attacks and improvements. An interesting recently proposed scheme [7] claims to address all

Please use the following format when citing this chapter:
Author(s) [insert Last name, First-name initial(s)], 2006, in IFIP International Federation for Information Processing, Volume 201, Security and Privacy in Dynamic Environments, eds. Fischer-Hubner, S., Rannenberg, K., Yngstrom, L., Lindskog, S., (Boston: Springer), pp. [insert page numbers].

of these problems, and stop essentially all phishing attacks. We present some tactics that phishers might employ against this system and explore it's robustness. We also document the strength and weaknesses of other phishing prevention technologies. The next section covers related work. Section 3 gives a brief overview of the Password Re-Use scheme. Section 4 analyzes the attacks on many of the anti-phishing solutions and the PRU scheme. Section 5 concludes.

2   Related Work: Existing Anti-Phishing Approaches

Broadly speaking, solutions divide into those that attempt to filter or verify email, password management systems, and browser solutions that attempt to filter or verify websites.

2.1   Password Management Systems

Since phishing primarily targets the user's password several proposed approaches address the problem by using a password management system. Such systems enable users to manage all of their passwords from a single secure location. An early example proposed by Gaber et al. [8] used a master password when a browser session was initiated to access a web proxy, and unique domain-specific passwords were used for other web sites. These were created by hashing whatever password the user typed using the target domain name as salt. Similarly, Microsoft's Passport [1] allows users to sign in to the Passport site, which remembers their credentials and authenticates them at other sites that participate in the Passport program. Neither of these systems aimed to address phishing directly.

Ross et al. [14] propose a phishing solution that, like [8], uses domain-specific passwords for web sites. A browser plug-in hashes the password salted with the domain name of the requesting site. Thus a phisher who lures a user into typing her BigBank password into the PhishBank site will get a hash of the password salted with the Phish-Bank domain. This, of course, cannot be used to login to BigBank, unless the phisher first inverts the hash. Their system has no need to store any passwords.

Halderman et al. [9] also propose a system to manage a user's passwords. Passwords both for web sites and other applications on the user's computer are protected. In contrast to [14] the user's passwords are stored, in hashed form on the local machine. To avoid the risk of a hacker mounting a brute force attack on the passwords a slow hash [12] is employed.

2.2   Browser Plug-ins

A number of browser plug-in approaches attempt to identify suspected phishing pages and alert the user. Chou et al. [5] present a plug-in that identifies many of the known tricks that phishers use to make a page resemble that of a legitimate site. For example numeric IP addresses or web-pages that have many outbound links (e.g. a PhishBank site having many links to the BigBank site) are techniques that phishers have used frequently. In addition they perform a check on outgoing passwords, to see if a previously used password is going to a suspect site. Earthlink's Scamblocker [2] toolbar maintains a blacklist and alerts users when they visit known phishing sites; however this requires an accurate and dynamic blacklist. Spoofstick [3] attempts to alert users when the sites they visit might appear to belong to trusted domains, but do not. Trustbar [10] by Herzberg and Gbara is a plug-in for FireFox that reserves real estate on the browser to authenticate both the site visited and the certificate authority.

Dhamija and Tygar [6] propose a method that enables a web server to authenticate itself, in a way that is easy for users to verify and hard for attackers to spoof. The scheme requires reserved real estate on the browser dedicated to userid and password entry. In addition each user has a unique image which is independently calculated both on the client and the server, allowing mutual authentication. A commercial scheme based on what appear to be similar ideas is deployed by Passmark Security [4]. The main disadvantage of these approaches is that sites that are potentially phishing targets must alter their site design; in addition users must be educated to change their behavior and be alert for any mismatch between the two images.

3   Review of the Password Re-Use Scheme [7]

3.1   Client Piece: Browser Plugin

The Password Re-Use (PRU) architecture involves a plug-in running in the user's browser that detects when credentials from a *protected list* are entered in the browser, and a server that receives an alert when this has occurred. The credentials are (uid, pwd, dom), where uid, pwd and dom are the userid, password and domain respectively. When the user enters a pwd at any site dom' where $dom' \neq dom$ and dom' is not on the *whitelist*, that fact is reported to the server by sending (hash(uid), dom, dom'). The server is in a position to aggregate the reports from many users, and distinguish a phishing attack from the reports that we expect due to the fact that users commonly re-use a few passwords across all the sites they visit.

The credentials are extracted from the data POST'ed for any page that contains a password. A separate thread tracks the user's keystrokes to detect when a previously POST'ed password is retyped at an unfamiliar site. Whenever a hit is generated, the server is informed. What is reported to the server is the fact that a password from dom_1, on the protected list, was typed at dom_R, which is not on a pre-populated whitelist. Users commonly use the same password at several legitimate sites. This is not a problem, since only an accumulation of reports will generate suspicion at the server.

3.2   The Server Piece

The server's role is that of aggregating information from many users. A Password Re-Use report is in itself of course, not proof that an attack is in progress. It means either that the user is knowingly using the same password at a protected and a non-whitelisted site, or that she has been fooled into entering the data by a phishing site. Thus it is important to distinguish innocent cases of password re-use from phishing attacks. This task is much simplified by the fact that the server aggregates the data across many users.

Having a single user typing her BigBank credentials into an unknown site may not be alarming, but having several users type BigBank credentials into *the same* unknown site within a short period of time is definitely alarming.

One of our goals is to examine how robust this scheme is to evolving attacks, which we examine in the next section.

Notifying the Target A key difference between the PRU scheme and the anti-phishing browser plug-ins [5, 2, 3] is the action taken when a site is suspected of phishing. When a threshold number of users report using their dom_R password at another site dom, the server determines that an attack is in progress. Rather than inform the user, at this point the server notifies the institution under attack. There are two very important components to the information the server can now provide dom_R :

- The attacking domain *dom*
- The hashes h(uid) of already phished victims.

First, by getting the attacking domain to the institution under attack they can proceed with "Cease and Desist" orders or web-site takedown (a process that can involve legal as well as Denial of Service measures). Next, by providing the institution with h(uid) for phishing victims, they can disable withdrawal facilities on the accounts in question.

Since additional victims are likely to be phished in the interval between the server notifying dom_R and the phishing site dom actually going offline. Each of these victims will generate a report to the server, and thus h(uid) for each victim can be routed to dom_R without delay. Thus, even though the scheme provides no notification to users, their accounts are protected.

The mechanism for notifying dom_R that it is under attack is simple. A domain Big-Bank that wishes to be protected under this scheme sets up an email account phish-reports@bigbank.com. Reports will be sent to that address. For verification purposes the email header will contain the time, the domain (*i.e.* "Bigbank") and the time and domain signed with the server's private key. In this manner any spam or other email that does not come from the server can be immediately discarded. Scale of deployment is a key factor here. It is unlikely that BigBank would set up special procedures to save just a few users. However, if the proposed scheme were deployed to a majority of users it is more likely that financial institutions would take the steps to use this information to protect their users. In other words scale works in favor of the scheme, instead of against it.

4 Attacks on Anti-Phishing Schemes

Anti-phishing solutions must observe both security and usability constraints. A peculiarity of the space is that for many solutions the degree of protection it offers is related to the scale of deployment. If the installed base for a particular solution is small enough, it is very likely that phishers will simply ignore those users and target only the bulk of users, i.e., users not using that technology. However, as the installed base grows, phishers will no longer ignore those users. Thus, the efficacy of some technologies decreases with the scale of deployment. We will try to illustrate this in our enumeration of attacks that follows.

A rather obvious objection that is common to the client plug-ins [5, 3, 2], the PRU scheme [7], and password management schemes [14] is that they require the user to instal software or change their behavior. Phishing, as opposed to pharming or keylogging, probably finds most of its victims among the less technically savvy. Once a user understands what phishing is, and how it works she is no longer at great risk. The paradox is that those who know enough to download a plug-in probably no longer need the plug-in. Nonetheless these technologies are worth examining in detail, since those that are effective may become incorporated in the popular browsers.

4.1   Attacks on Anti-Phishing Client Plug-ins

A sample of the client plug-ins that offer protection from phishing schemes are [3, 2, 5].

Broken Links and Delaying Pageload Attack   Client plug-ins that perform some test to determine whether a site is phishing or not are amenable to an attack that delays completion of the pageload. For example, Internet Explorer provides and event handler DocumentComplete, which might seem the perfect place to introduce the test. Spoofguard [5], for example, performs several checks only when this event occurs. However, a phisher then need merely place one broken link on the page to prevent this event from ever occurring. This prevents the plug-in from even executing the phishing test. To avoid this, the plug-in might execute the test a fixed amount of time after the URL was first contacted. This is better, but again open to attack: if the plug-in waits, say 10 seconds, before performing the test, the phishing site need merely delay any items that are likely to cause suspicion until after the test is performed. For example, the part of the page that collects a password can be withheld until after the test is performed.

Thus, quite apart from the question of *what* a phishing detection plug-in should check, there is a considerable question of *when* those checks should be performed. An improvement might be to execute any checks when the user types the first keystroke on the page. This avoids wastefully executing the phishing detection when a user is navigating to sites that involve no typing (which is likely a majority of pages for most users), while allowing the check to be performed before the password is typed (assuming that the phishing page asks for the userid first).

Problems with Blacklist Approaches   Blacklisting approaches attempt to inform clients of phishing sites by either pushing an updated list to the client plug-ins [2] or having the clients check with a server to request information on a URL it is visiting. Both of these approaches have difficulties. If a blacklist server broadcasts updated lists of phishing sites there is a definite latency issue. Even if the broadcasts occur once a day a phisher can have a full 24 hours to harvest passwords without fear of discovery. Greater frequency increases the load on the server; this might be feasible if the plug-in is used by a small percent of the population but becomes unwieldy with scale. If each client contacts a blacklist server for information on each URL the latency issue is moot, but the scale problems for the server are even worse.

Problems with Whitelist Approaches In approaches where the client contacts a black-list server for each url, whitelists (i.e., a pre-compiled list of safe sites) can be used to reduce the traffic to the server. More specifically, if a user visits a site that is in the whitelist, there is no need to contact the blacklist server. Nevertheless, updating white-lists in the client is cumbersome and costly, and white-listing is subject to cross-site scripting, hacking, and personal sites located on large domains. For this reason, whitelisting can only be used in conjunction with sites that have high security stan-dards, and do not host personal pages.

Redirection and Distributed Attacks The distributed phishing attack described in [11] poses an interesting challenge for all phishing protection systems. In this attack the phisher hosts the phishing page at many different sites; in the limiting case each victim might be directed to a page unique to them. If a client plug-in makes use only of information at the client (*e.g.* using rules based on the URL and html) then dis-tributing the site among many pages makes no difference (since the individual clients are not sharing information). Of course protection systems like this are the most easily defeated: rules are easily evaded and these solutions suffer the problems of scale.

For plug-ins where individual clients make use of external information, for example by getting periodic blacklist updates, a distributed attack can destroy the value of the blacklist. Even if blacklists are updated very frequently the phisher can ensure that no victim is ever directed to a site on the blacklist, but rather is sent to the next in a long series of host addresses. A suitably organized botnet can provide the phisher with more than enough hosting sites.

Problem of getting users to alter their behavior A very interesting recent study by Wu [15] confirms that users either tend to ignore or fail to act on security warnings. The study attempted to measure whether users notice the warnings provided by anti-phishing toolbars [3, 2] *even when the toolbar correctly detected the attack*. A large percentage of the participants did not change their behavior based on the warning. This point threatens the underpinning of several anti-phishing solutions. It appears that iden-tifying a site as being a phishing site is not sufficient.

A clear advantage of the PRU scheme [7] is that it does not assume that users alter their behavior based on warnings.

The Problem of Scale Like many security technologies client-side detection systems face the problem of scale. Simple techniques that may work well when employed by only a small portion of the population. For example, each of [5, 3] filter for behaviors that are known to be in common use by phishers. Consider a plug-in phishing detector that is used by only 1% of the population. At that level of penetration phishers are unlikely to go to much effort to avoid the filters, so the 1% may indeed get worthwhile protection. Now consider the same plug-in used by 90% of the population. At this level of deployment phishers will be keenly motivated to evade the filters. In other words there are many rules or heuristics that can appear promising when run on training data. They can even perform successfully and offer worthwhile protection to small fractions of the overall population. However their efficacy is in inverse relation to their scale of deployment: the more people use them the less effective they are. An advantage claimed in [7] is that the efficacy grows rather than decreases with the scale of deployement.

4.2   Attacks on Password Re-Use Anti-Phishing Scheme

The simplicity of the PRU client means that it is relatively hard to prevent it from reporting password re-use events. Nonetheless there are a few approaches that an attacker might take to trick the client software into failing to report. The next four attacks we consider are of this form.

Flushing the protected list   A Phisher might try to circumvent the protection by removing some (or all) of the passwords from the protected list. For example, since the protected list has only 256 entries, a phishing site could submit (using HTML forms) 256 strings as passwords to a random site. This would effectively "flush" everything from the protected list because of the Least Recently Used maintenance rule. To avoid this attack, before accepting a new entry, from the HTML form data, the password is matched with the contents of a keyboard buffer, effectively requiring that the password have been actually typed at the site. It is unlikely that a Phisher can induce a victim to actually type hundreds of password-like strings.

Hosting on a whitelisted domain   A phisher might attempt to host on an existing, legitimate site. For example putting the phishing page up on an ISP member site, like members sites on AOL or MSN, or a small site like a community group association, or by employing a Cross-Site Scripting (CSS) attack. Each of these is handled by proper design of the client whitelist.

It is easy to handle ISP member sites by including the ISP, but excluding certain sub-domains from the whitelist. Small groups like community associations cannot be depended upon to prevent break-ins. Thus the client whitelist should contain only very large commercial domains. Recall that a site can be on a users protected list, without being on the whitelist. CSS attacks actually host the phishers page on a target domain. For this reason, only sites that can be depended upon to maintain basic levels of security should be permitted to populate the client's whitelist.

Tricking the user into mis-typing the password   An earlier version of the algorithm hashed the combined *uid/pwd*. This provided a way for a Phisher to circumvent the system, by forcing the user to mis-type the *uid*. Normally, as you type your userid, the letters show up at the screen. Suppose the Phisher introduces a page with a script where the third character you type do not show up in the screen. You'd think you did not pressed hard enough, and would re-type the character. As you do that, the keyboard buffer will have that character twice, and it will not hash to the protected entry. We note that this attack is not possible with the password, since the password do not show up in the screen as you type (only ****). If something goes wrong, most users simply delete the whole thing and re-start.

Visual Keyboard The PRU scheme only detects passwords type at the browser. Any scheme that obtains the password by other means than typing at the browser would be undetected. For example, a phisher may convince the victim to use a screen keyboard and click on each of the letters corresponding to the password. Or may convince the victim to type the password first on notepad, then copy and paste on the browser window. Or get the Phone and call an 1-800 number. Any of these methods would not trigger the defense. Nevertheless, we believe the further away the attack get from what the user expects, the less likely is the phisher to succeed.

Distributed Attack A possible approach for a phisher who seeks to evade detection is to distribute the attack. Rather than phish BigBank by directing victims to PhishBank the phisher may use many domains, or numeric IP addresses. Thus when clients report sending their BigBank credentials, it fails to trigger an alert at the server. For this reason, we believe the server logic needs to adapt as phishers adapt. For example, while the destination for several BigBank credentials may be distributed, a large increase in the number of reports for a given whitelisted domain is in itself worthy of suspicion.

Redirection Attack Similar to the distributed attack is a Redirection attack where a phisher directs all victims to a single URL, but each victim is redirected to a different (possibly unique) address to be phished. For example the phishing URL might originally redirect to IP_1, but as soon as the first victim is caught it redirects to IP_2 and so on. This might appear to confuse the system by distributing the client reports one at a time among many addresses. To circumvent this the client report to the server includes any URLs visited in the last minute. By intersection, the redirecting (phishing) URL can be detected.

Also, we point out that many competing anti-phishing schemes would be highly susceptible to this kind of attack. In particular, any scheme that relies on blocking visualization of a page that has been detected as phishing would be susceptible to this attack. Similarly, this applies to any technology that relies on users reporting suspicious pages. Of course, the solution used in the PRU scheme can be easily adapted to work with these other anti-phishing schemes as well.

Looking at the Phishing html? Including a site on the block list should be taken only when no doubt remains about a site being a phishing site. For legal and liability reasons it may even be necessary to have a person actually look at a site before making a final determination on block list inclusion. If that's the case, rather than visit the suspect site it is better to receive directly from the reporting client the HTML content that it received. The reason for this is that a phisher might easily present each phishing victim with a unique url, so that the first visitor to the url (the victim) would see the page requesting userid and password, while the second and subsequent visitors (*e.g.* someone at the server checking the site) would see a completely innocent page. This is easily accommodated by adding the HTML as a record to the the *pwd*re-use report.

4.3   Denial of Service on a Site

We now explore the possibility that a vandal tries to fool the PRU system that a legitimate site is phishing. Specifically, suppose a disgruntled MyCornerStore customer types BigBank credentials at the MyCornerStore login site. Recall, the vandal need not use real BigBank credentials, since populating the protected list was very easy. What are the consequences if the server wrongly concludes that MyCornerStore is phishing and places it on the block list?

First, note that the system tracks the IP of the reporting client; a single client reporting the site repeatedly will have no effect. Second, no site that is on the client whitelist (of large institutions) or the server's much larger whitelist can ever be placed on the block list. The most powerful defense, however, is that if MyCornerStore does get on the block list, *it does not mean that nobody can navigate to that site*. Rather, it means that BigBank customers those who login to MyCornerStore for the first time (*i.e.* it is not on their protected list) and use a password already used at at BigBank would have their h(*uid*) sent to BigBank for monitoring. Users who have existing MyCornerStore credentials in their protected list would be unaffected (since the client will not even consult the server). BigBank users logging in for the first time who choose passwords not on their protected list would be unaffected. So, the level of effort required to include a site in the block list seem significantly high for causing a reasonably small inconvenience to users of the site.

4.4   Attacks on other approaches

Two Problems with pwdHash [14] The basic idea behind pwdHash is to detect passwrods, and send hashes, instead of the actual password. A difficulty, however, is that it is by no means simple to know when a password is being typed (*e.g.* phishers may use Javascript rather than HTML forms to gather passwords). To circumvent this problem [14] requires that users prefix all password by some special sequence or key (*e.g.* type 'F8' before any password). Thus, users must be "trained" to adopt the proposed system, and change their behavior. This might be an acceptable solution, but represents a non-trivial change in current practice.

A further difficulty with domain specific passwords is that different web-sites have very different password rules. Some sites require strong passwords, some accept only alphanumeric passwords, and some accept only numeric passwords. Many banks, for example, require that a user's online password be the same as the PIN they use to access their ATM. This creates the difficulty that the domain specific passwords generated will be unacceptable to the target web-site. To address this problem [14] suggests tabulating the password rules that different institutions accept. This is clearly not a very scalable solution.

Attack on Mutual Authentication Scheme [6] A main weakness with the image based mutual authentication scheme is that it represents an unfamiliar use model, and thus is probably more susceptible to social engineering attack. If a bank chooses to authenticate itself to users by presenting a user-chosen image it adds a level of security. It remains open to question whether users notice *an act on* the absence of the authenticating image. But further the problem of phishing derives from the ease with with users are manipulated into parting with sensitive information. For example, a phishing attack on a server using image authentication could involve sending users an email saying there is a problem with their authenticating image and asking to login to fix it.

5 Conclusion

We have examined attacks and improvements on a number of anti-phishing technologies. We found that many of the client plug-in approaches that have been proposed have efficacy that decreases as the scale of the deployment increases. By contrast, we reviewed a powerful new method for detecting phishing attacks and protecting users that has been recently proposed in [7]. That method relies on two independent ideas: aggregating information at the server for detecting an attack, and back channel protection for saving users. The method grows strong with the more users using the system. We examined its ability to withstand various anticipated attacks as compared with other anti-phishing technologies. We find that while several anti-phishing approaches have severe difficulties coping with possible phishing tactics the PRU scheme exhibits great robustness.

References

1. http://www.passport.com.
2. http://www.scamblocker.com.
3. http://www.spoofstick.com.
4. http://www.passmarksecurity.com.
5. N. Chou, R. Ledesma, Y. Teraguchi, D. Boneh, and J. Mitchell. Client-side defense against web-based identity theft. *Proc. NDSS*, 2004.
6. R. Dhamija and J. D. Tygar. The battle against phishing: Dynamic security skins. *Symp. on Usable Privacy and Security*, 2005.
7. Dinei Florêncio and Cormac Herley. Stopping Phishing Attacks Even When the Victims Ignore Warnings. *MSR Tech. Report*. http://research.microsoft.com/users/cormac/papers/NoPhish.pdf.
8. E. Gaber, P. Gibbons, Y. Matyas, and A. Mayer. How to make personalized web browsing simple, secure and anonymous. *Proc. Finan. Crypto '97*.
9. J. A. Halderman, B. Waters, and E. Felten. A convenient method for securely managing passwords. *Proceedings of the 14th International World Wide Web Conference (WWW 2005)*.
10. A. Herzberg and A. Gbara. Trustbar: Protecting (even naïve) web users from spoofing and phishing attacks. 2004. http://eprint.iacr.org/2004/155.pdf.
11. M. Jakobssen and A. Young. Distributed phishing attacks. 2005. http://eprint.iacr.org/2005/091.pdf.
12. J. Kelsey, B. Schneier, C. Hall, and D. Wagner. Secure applications of low-entropy keys. *Lecture Notes in Computer Science*, 1396:121-134, 1998.
13. Anti-Phishing Working Group. http://www.antiphishing.org.
14. B. Ross, C. Jackson, N. Miyake, D. Boneh, and J. C. Mitchell. Stronger password authentication using browser extensions. *Proceedings of the 14th Usenix Security Symposium, 2005*.
15. M. Wu. Users are not dependable: How to make security indicators to better protect them. *Trustworthy Interfaces for Passwords and Personal Information*, 2005.

CAT – A Practical Graph & SDL Based Toolkit for Vulnerability Assessment of 3G Networks

Kameswari Kotapati, Peng Liu, and Thomas F. LaPorta

The Pennsylvania State University
University Park, PA 16802, USA
kotapati@cse.psu.edu, pliu@ist.psu.edu, tlp@cse.psu.edu

Abstract. This paper presents the Cellular Network Vulnerability Assessment Toolkit - CAT, designed for end-to-end vulnerability assessment of 3G networks. It is the first tool of its kind to model and represent 3G network vulnerabilities and attacks as attack graphs. CAT uses freely available 3G telecommunication specifications written in SDL, the standard Specification and Description Language to produce attack graphs. Attack graphs generated by CAT are unique due to their: (1) global representation of the network, (2) independence from physical deployments, and (3) depiction of the 3G attack graph model and cascading effects.

1 Introduction

Third generation (3G) wireless telecommunication provide circuit switched and high speed packet data services for 3G-enabled mobile devices. These networks have evolved from the isolated 1G & 2G networks by integrating with the Internet. This integration imports the inherent vulnerabilities of the Internet to the 3G networks and gives the end subscriber direct access to the control infrastructure of the 3G network. The goal of this research is to assess the vulnerabilities introduced by this merger by development of the Cellular Network Vulnerability Assessment Toolkit - CAT. CAT models 3G network vulnerabilities and attacks as attack graphs.

Attacks on the 3G network are unique because corruption propagates across the network due to normal end-to-end network operation. This feature known as the *cascading effect*, occurs due to the exchange of corrupt data items in signaling messages between 3G servers. Hence the goal of 3G network vulnerability assessment is to not only identify the attack origin but also the cascading effects caused due to the end-to-end system level vulnerabilities and interactions.

Manual deduction of vulnerabilities and attacks in 3G systems is not feasible because vulnerability deduction requires extensive knowledge of thousands of state machines and end-to-end networking of the telecommunication systems. Also standard Internet based vulnerability assessment tools are insufficient for 3G networks because they present physical vulnerabilities which is not the goal of 3G network vulnerability assessment. The goal is to identify end-to-end system level vulnerabilities and interactions that lead to the cascading effect.

Please use the following format when citing this chapter:

Author(s) [insert Last name, First-name initial(s)], 2006, in IFIP International Federation for Information Processing, Volume 201, Security and Privacy in Dynamic Environments, eds. Fischer-Hubner, S., Rannenberg, K., Yngstrom, L., Lindskog, S., (Boston: Springer), pp. [insert page numbers].

CAT works by taking in 3G data parameters called seeds and goals as input, and uses free [2] technical specifications written in the Specification and Description Language (SDL) to identify system interactions that lead to the cascading effect. SDL is developed by the International Telecommunication Union (ITU) and is designated as the formal description language for specifying and describing the functional behavior of telecommunication systems [24], [2] by major international standards bodies.

CAT is the first tool of its kind to present end-to-end vulnerabilities for any system with SDL specifications. CAT is practical because of its universal applicability and its independence from physical deployments. Other contributions in this paper include the definition of cascading effect of attacks, generic model of attack graphs for 3G networks and categorization of attacks on 3G networks. The attack graphs generated by CAT show the global network view and are succinct, loop free with low redundancy.

2   Related Work

Our literature survey comprises of vulnerability assessment in telecommunication networks and attack graphs.

The vulnerabilities of telecommunication networks are well addressed in the literature. Telecommunication standards [4], [5], [6] specify 3G security and identify certain security threats. Howard et al. [7], El-Fishway et al. [8], Lo et al. [9], Welch et al. [10], Clissmann et al. [11] have identified threats or attack scenarios on the 3G network while trying to prove the inadequacy of current security schemes, or present new architectures for 3G security. Brookson in [12] motivates the need for security. Mitchell et al. in [13], and Boman et al. in [14] discuss the security features available in current 3G networks. Kotapati et al in [1] present a taxonomy of cyber attacks in 3G networks. *However, the above literature does not present vulnerability assessment solutions.*

3G system administrators typically use conventional tools to assess the physical implementation vulnerabilities. In the literature there are no known techniques for *system level end-to-end vulnerability assessment in 3G networks.*

CAT adapts the attack graph technology which has been well investigated in the literature. This research has foundation in Swiler and Philips et al. [15], [16], [17]. Their work analyses network vulnerability using the graph based approach. Graphs generated by CAT extend their graphs to show normal network activity and subscriber activity in addition to attack activity and provide the global network view of the adversary action. Swiler and Philips [15], [16], [17] generated their attacks by backward exploration from the goal given atomic attacks as input. Unlike the Swiler and Philips model, CAT does not answer any 'what-if' questions regarding security effects of configuration changes. It does not analyze the graph or assign quantitative metrics. It also identifies atomic attacks.

Ritchey and Amman [18] used model checking for vulnerability analysis of a network. Amman et al. in [19] present a scalable method for representing attack graphs with the assumption of monotonocity. Sheyner et al. [3] have shown that model checking may be applied to automatic generation of attack graphs. Jha et al. [20], [21], [22] present algorithms for analyzing attack graphs. Jha et al. [20] present a minimization analysis technique that allows analysts decide which minimal set of security measures guarantee the safety of the system.

All the aforementioned attack graph research focuses on Internet vulnerability assessment. Schneier [23], states that in general, attacks against system may be represented in a tree structure. The literature surveyed reveals that CAT is the first effort to use SDL specifications to automatically infer possible 3G network attacks in the form of an attack graph. It should be noted that extending the attack graph technology from the Internet to 3G networks is not trivial because Internet case lacks assessment of end-to-end network; and 3G network physical configurations are different between network deployments.

3   Overview

This section gives an overview of the 3G network, SDL and the model of the 3G attack graph.

3.1   3G network

The 3G network is comprised of a number of servers as shown in Fig. 1. The servers in the circuit switched domain of the 3G network include Home Location Register (HLR), Visitor Location Register (VLR), Mobile Switching Center (MSC) and Gateway Mobile Switching Center (GMSC). The 3G network provides service to the subscriber by the exchange of signaling messages among its servers.

All subscribers are permanently assigned to a HLR. The HLR is in the home network and stores permanent subscriber data and current subscriber location (pointer to VLR). VLRs are assigned to a specific administrative area and are associated with one or more MSCs. The VLR acts as a temporary repository and stores data of all mobile stations (user handset) that are currently roaming in its assigned area. The VLR obtains this data from the HLR assigned to the mobile station. The MSC acts as an interface between the radio system and the fixed network. It handles the circuit switched services to and from the mobile stations roaming into its area. The VLR and MSC are either in the home or home network depending on the location of the subscriber.

The *call delivery service* is a *3G service* that delivers incoming calls to the subscriber regardless of the location of the called subscriber and the caller. Calls are sent (signaling message 'IAM' in Fig. 2.) to the GMSC, which is in charge of routing the call to the mobile station and passing voice traffic between different networks. The GMSC checks the called number in the incoming call ('IAM') and resolves it to the assigned HLR of the called party. It signals the HLR of the incoming call using the signaling message 'SRI'. The HLR is aware of the location where the called subscriber is currently visiting and requests the corresponding VLR for a 'roaming number' ('PRN') to route the call and downloads the incoming call profile to the VLR. The VLR assigns a roaming number for routing the call and passes it on to the HLR ('PRN_ACK'). The HLR passes on this 'roaming number' to the GMSC ('SRI_ACK'). The GMSC uses this 'roaming number' to route the incoming call to the MSC where the subscriber is currently visiting. The MSC requests the VLR for the incoming call profile for the called

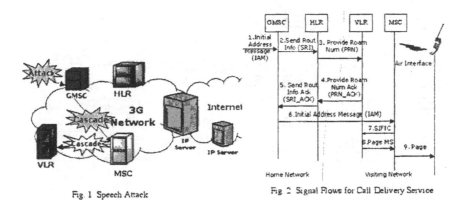

Fig. 1 Speech Attack   Fig 2 Signal Flows for Call Delivery Service

subscriber ('SIFIC') and receives the profile in the 'Page MS' signaling message. The MSC alerts ('Page') the mobile station.

Each of the above signaling messages comprises of two types data elements: (1) parameters to invoke a function in the destination server; and (2) administrative parameters required for communication such as originating server address and destination server address.

3.2 SDL and Mapping to 3G

This section provides a background on SDL and uses the aforementioned 3G network to illustrate the usage of SDL. SDL is an object-oriented, formal language and is intended for the specification of event-driven, real-time, concurrent distributed systems interacting with discrete signals. SDL is a graphical language and SDL specifications do not indicate an implementation structure. In basic SDL the system description is hierarchically structured. It describes the local and remote behavior of telecommunication systems, as Systems, Blocks and Processes.

A *System* is comprised of a number of concurrently running Blocks that communicate by passing signaling messages through a channel. *Blocks* may be of different types and there may be multiple instances of a single block type at a time. The 3G telecommunication network show in Fig. 1 is an *example of the SDL system*. The servers in the 3G network correspond to blocks in SDL.

A *Block* represents a processing unit in a single location. A block is a collection of data and concurrently running processes of same and different types. Blocks provide service and communicate with each other by sending signaling messages through a channel. Data is always associated with or owned by the block. The MSC shown in Fig. 1 is an *example of the block* and it comprises of subscriber data for those roaming in its administrative area.

Processes are basic functional units of SDL systems and perform functions using a service logic and have the capability to change data associated with the block. A Process may be defined as a communicating extended finite state machine (CEFSM)

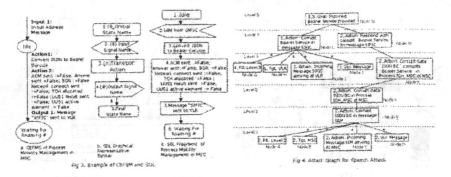

Fig 3. Example of CEFSM and SDL

Fig 4. Attack Graph for Speech Attack

represented by a 6-tuple $(\Theta, \theta_0, \Xi, \delta, \Lambda, \Phi)$. Fig. 3b shows the graphical syntax of the process represented using SDL. A process in an initial state (θ_0) (node 1 in Fig. 3b) receives an input event (Ξ) (node 2), performs certain transition actions (Λ) (node 3), generates an output (Φ) (node 4), and finally transitions (δ) to another state (node 5). Θ represents the set of finite states in CEFSM. The input event comprises of incoming signaling messages from other processes in same or different blocks. Transition actions comprise of the getting or setting certain conditions or variables or functions. The output generated by the process comprises of signaling messages to processes in same or different blocks. At the end of its regular operation, the process transitions into a final state. *Process types within the MSC block may be broadly classified as Mobility Management, Call Handling, Operations and Maintenance, Fault Recovery, Handover and Subscriber Management.* The CEFSM state transition diagram of *Process Mobility Management* is shown in Fig. 3a. Mapping from the CEFSM to the SDL is one-to-one. Fig. 3c shows the actual SDL fragment for the basic CEFSM of Fig. 3a. The SDL diagram in Fig.3c is representative of the SDL diagrams used in telecommunication specifications.

3.3   3G Attack Graph

An *attack* in CAT may be defined as a network state transitions due to adversary action, where the final transition results in the adversary achieving a goal. CAT deduces possible attacks and presents them using attack graphs. *A 3G network specific attack graph, as shown in Fig. 4, is a network state transition showing the paths through a system starting with the conditions of the attack, the attack, continuing with the cascading effect of the adversary's attack action(s) and ending in the adversary's goal.* The state of a 3G network may be defined as the collective state of all its blocks.

The attack graph in Fig. 4 is constructed for the attack shown in Fig. 1. The attack happens by corruption of 'ISDN BC' data parameter in the 'IAM' message. The 3G data parameter 'ISDN BC' is considered as the direct intent of the attack and it is called as the *seed*. CAT builds this graph bottom-up. For description purposes, this attack graph has been divided into levels and assigned node labels followed by an alphabet. Each node has been assigned numbers; these numbers are tree numbers and correspond to the tree to which the node belongs. For example, all the nodes marked with number 2 form the second tree of the graph. Nodes at a particular level with the same tree number(s) are *AND* nodes. Nodes with the same tree number at a layer connected to a node in the layer above indicate AND nodes. For example at Level 0, Nodes A-D are AND nodes, Node L, M at Level 4 are OR nodes. The attack graphs generated by CAT comprise of three types of nodes; condition, action and goal.

Condition Nodes: represent conditions that hold for an attack. *Physical Access* corresponds to adversary's physical access to the network and may be classified as: (1) access to the air interface with the help of a physical device; (2) access to cables connecting central offices; and (3) access to 3G core network blocks in the central office. In the attack example of Fig. 4 the adversary's Physical Access is at Level 2 (Node A). The high level description of an adversary's *target* is described by a block and indicates all the processes and data sources within a block. In the attack example of Fig. 4 the target is MSC (Node B). An adversary takes advantage of *vulnerabilities*: (1) by attacking the data parameters in *signaling messages* exchanged between blocks; (2) by attacking the service logic of a process in a block so that it behaves abnormally; and (3) by corrupting the data sources in a block. In the attack example of Fig. 4 the adversary corrupts data 'ISDN BC' in message IAM. The vulnerability is message (Node D).

Action Nodes may be events or non-events that causes a network transistion. Examples of events include incoming (Node C) and outgoing (Node M) signaling messages. An example of a non-event includes changing data associated with the block (Node F). Non-events cause a change in state of the network, but do not generate an event. Actions may be further classified as *adversary actions, normal network operations and normal subscriber activities*. Adversary actions comprise of insertion, corruption or deletion of data, signaling messages and service logic (Node E and Node L). Normal network operations include sending and receiving signaling messages (Node C). Subscriber activity may comprise of updating personal data and initiating service.

Goal Node are the final nodes in a tree occurring at the highest level (Node N in Fig. 4). They indicate corruption or derivation of data parameters due to the direct corruption of other data parameters (seeds) by the adversary. The goal is achieved when the corrupt data parameters are propagated to other 3G blocks. The goal of the attack graph is an action that comprises of an event (incoming or outgoing message) with corrupt goal parameter(s) or a non-event representing block level corruption.

The attack graph shows through its edges the implicit transition in network state. The *transition due to adversary action* describes the change in the state of the network as a result of the adversary action and is indicated by a edge marked by the letter A. The *network transition* describes the change in the state of the network as a result of any of the action nodes. By inclusion of normal network transitions in addition to the adversary transitions, the proposed attack graph shows not only the adversary's activity but also the global view or cumulative effect of adversary's action. This is a unique feature of the attack graph. Attacks graphs may be represented using a simplified form of CEFSM using a 4 tuple $(\lambda_0, \Lambda, \tau, L)$ where Λ represents nodes. $\lambda_0 \subseteq \Lambda$ represents the set of intial states. τ represents edges in the attack graph. L represents labels (attack A or non-attack $\emptyset$) for the edges/transitions.

4   Features of CAT toolkit

4.1   Architecture

The overall architecture of CAT is shown in Fig. 5a. It is composed of the GUI subsystem, which takes seeds and goals as input from the user, the analysis engine subsystem, which explores the possibility of the seeds reaching the goal, and the SDL database in which the 3G telecommunication specifications are stored. The integrated data structure has structure similar to that of the SDL database described below and holds attack graph results from CAT analysis against the SDL database. Fig. 5b. shows the functional architecture of the toolkit. The toolkit takes in seeds and goals as input and explores for the output. The initial output is a 'Maximum View' of the attack graph which is pruned to remove redundancy to provide a 'Final View' of the attack graph to minimize redundancy.

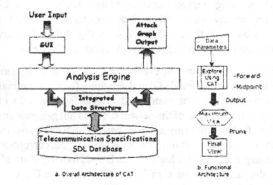

Fig. 5. Architecture of CAT

4.2   User Input

CAT works by taking in 3G data parameter seeds and goals as input from the user. Seeds are data parameters which when corrupted by the adversary may or may not lead to the goal. Seeds may merge at different stages of the attack graph. Goals are data parameters that are derived incorrectly due to the direct corruption of seeds by the adversary.

4.3   SDL System Input

The SDL database comprises of 3G telecommunication specifications [25]. Database contains signaling messages and data parameters they contain. They also contains information regarding processes in blocks. Process information is stored as initial and final states, input and output messages and actions. Unlike other methods, CAT does not require network topology, network configuration, adversary profile information or attacks in atomic form, as input. CAT works for any implementation which follows telecommunication standards. CAT assumes that the adversary has the necessary tools to penetrate the network at the different levels of physical access and vulnerabilities as described in Section 3.

4.4 Attack types

Attacks detected by CAT may be categorized as follows. 1. *1-Level Indirect attacks* are those attacks in which, corruption of $Seed_1$ leads to corruption of the goal hence reaching the goal. $Seed_1 \to Goal$.

2. *N-level indirect attacks* are those attacks in which, given any 'k' *seeds* $\in \{S\}$, $Seed_1, Seed_2, \ldots, Seed_k$ and $Goal$, corruption of $Seed_1$ leads to corruption of some seed $Seed_i$ (where $Seed_i \in \{S\}$), which in-turn leads to corruption of some seed $Seed_j$ (where $Seed_j \in \{S\}$) and so on until the $Goal$ is corrupt. $Seed_1 \to \ldots Seed_i \to Seed_j \to \ldots \to Seed_n \to Goal$.

3. In the *Collaborative attack*, a single seed cannot reach the $Goal$ but the corruption of multiple seeds allows for reaching of the $Goal$ i.e. $Seed_1$ & $Seed_2 \to Goal$.

4. In the *Multi-stage attack*, a first attack is used to gather information to perform a second attack. The second attack gathers information to perform another attack until the $Goal$ is reached.

4.5 Issues with SDL

CAT algorithms trace the flow of data through the network. Corruption of a data parameter may lead to the corruption of other data parameters which may or may not lead to the goal. When converting SDL specification to data used by CAT there are a number of issues that must be taken into consideration.

Message and Message-ACK Pairs: Issues arise with message and the corresponding message-ack pairs *e.g., message SRI and SRI-ACK, PRN and PRN-ACK.* The message typically comprises of a subscriber key for which the destination block assigns a value. The message-ack contains this value but not the subscriber key. The absence of the subscriber key in the message-ack (PRN-ACK) must be taken into consideration or certain attacks may be missed because the algorithm may lose track of data correlations.

Data Dependencies in Action Attributes: Actions in SDL-specifications (Table 2) may comprise of certain procedures such as 'Check Parameters'. SDL may not specify how the subroutine is to be executed. In such cases (1) the input data-parameters to the subroutine and the output parameters must be clearly specified; and (2) the relationship between the input and output parameters must be specified or else the data dependencies will be lost. In many cases SDL does not provide this information. Uncovering multiple seed attacks such as Collaborative and Multi-stage attacks requires knowledge of the input-output parameters and their relationships. If this information is present in the standard SDL specifications (action attribute of Table 2) then the attacks are discovered. If they are not present in the the standard SDL specifications, these attacks may not be discovered.

4.6   Algorithms

CAT algorithms may be used by 3G System Administrators wanting to detect vulnerabilities in scenarios, such as 'inability of subscriber to hear the voice of a caller in incoming calls'. The goal is known i.e. garbled voice of caller and hence the *seeds and goals* may be assigned: *Goal – Bearer Service* (Bearer Service indicates the type of voice transmit signals between subscribers) and *Seed – ISDN Bearer Capability* (ISDN Bearer Capability is one of the many factors used to determine Bearer Service). The goal is a clue to detecting the major problem i.e. *corrupt Bearer Service*. The output of using the *Goal – Bearer Service*; *Seed – ISDN Bearer Capability* in the algorithm is shown in Fig. 4. With more seeds, the algorithm will produce a much more detailed attack graph signifying that there are many ways to reach a goal. Note that by exhaustively trying every possible goal and every possible set of seeds, CAT can be easily extended to automatically identify all the possible (detectable) attacks associated with a certain service such as the *call delivery service*.

Algorithms take seeds as input from the user. Based on the input provided messages and actions of SDL are explored for generating attack graphs. The following conditions must be satisfied to generate and connect nodes in the attack graph. (1) If the seed occurs in messages or actions of SDL, then the condition nodes (Nodes A-D in Fig. 4) and adversary action nodes (Node E) may be generated and connected. (2) When a corrupt seed occurs in a incoming message of a block (action node) and the same seed occurs in the action of the block (action node), it may be assumed that the corrupt seed in the message is used by the block hence corruption spreads from the message to the block (indicated by edge connecting Node E and F). (3) When a corrupt seed occurs in the action of the block (action node - Node F) and another seed or the goal itself occurs in the same action, it may be assumed the corrupt seed corrupts the other seed/goal (action node - Node K) leading to the generation of the edge connecting the two nodes. (4) When a corrupt seed or goal occurs in the action of the block (action node - Node K) and the same seed or goal occurs in the outgoing message from the block (action node - Node M), it may be assumed that the corrupt seed/goal in the block spreads to the message, leading to the edge connecting the two nodes.

1. Exhaustive Forward Exploration Algorithm The Forward Exploration algorithm starts 'bottom-up' from the seed and works towards finding the goal. It is exhaustive and checks each and every possible tuple in the SDL database. The Forward exploration algorithm to detect multi-stage attacks is detailed in Algorithm 1 displayed in Fig. 6a. The algorithm works in two phases.

Phase-1: Building Sub Graphs: In this phase, attacks are detected and attack graphs are built based on seed values and types of attacks. This phase also takes care of garbage collection and assigns levels to aid in pruning the graph. Garbage collection is performed when it is found that the seed fails to reach the goal. Levels are assigned for pruning the graph. The goal node is at level X and nodes 'X' edges away from the goal at level 0. Fig. 4. clearly illustrates the concept of levels. This phase is exhaustive and stops when (i) the seed reaches the goal, or the seed has not reached the goal but (ii) it has stopped propagating, or (iii) all messages upto the terminating message are explored.

```
Algorithm 1 Multi-Stage Forward Exploration Algorithm
{Seed} : Set of Input Seeds; {Goal} : Goal
for every s, ∈ {Seed} loop
   for every CEFSM ∈ {S DI} loop
      if s, in Message .or. Action then
         Add(PA, Tgt,Vul),(Access, Tgt) to Tree
         Call Find-Multistage-Tree(s,)
      end if
   end loop
end loop
procedure Find-Multistage-Tree (s,) is
begin
   while true loop
      for every E, ∈ {Connected – Emity} loop
         if any {Seed} in Action then
            Add(Corrupt Seed) to Tree
            Add(Spy for Next Element) to Tree
         end if
         if {Goal} in Action then
            Add(Corrupt Goal) to Tree
            break
         end if
      end loop
   end loop
end Find-Multistage-Tree
```

(a) Forward Exploration

```
Algorithm 2 Heuristic Based Mid Point Method
{Seed} : Set of Input Seeds; {Goal} : Goal
for every s, ∈ {Seed} loop
   if !Check-Heuristic(s,) then
      continue
   else
      if s, in Message/Action then
         Add(PA,Tgt,Vul) to Tree
      end if
      if Goal in Message/Action then
         Add(Incorrect Goal) to Tree
      end if
      GoalReached=Compare(s,.SeedElement.GoalElement)
      while (! GoalReached) loop
         track-seeds(s,) /*tracks the flow of the seed */
         GoalReached=Compare(s,.SeedElement.GoalElement)
         if !GoalReached then
            /*tracks the flow of the goal */
            track-goal(s,)
         end if
         GoalReached=Compare(s,.SeedElement.GoalElement)
      end loop
   end if
end loop
procedure Compare (s,.se, ge) is
begin
   if se==ge then
      Add(Corrupt Seed s, Corrupts Goal) to Tree
      return true
   else
      return false
   end if
end Compare
```

(b) Heuristic Based Mid-Point

Fig. 6. Algorithms

Phase-2: Integrating and Pruning Sub Graphs: This phase integrates and prunes the graphs built in the previous phase. Low redundancy attack graphs are constructed by collapsing similar nodes and paths at the same level into a single node and path. The Forward exploration is a good approach if the seed actually reaches the goal. Issues arise when the seeds fails to reach the goal.

When the seed cannot reach the goal, the algorithm must *explore all the data sets till the terminating message in that sequence can be reached (via cascading effects)*. This reduces the efficiency of the algorithm. Another issue that arises frequently is the *appearance of loops when the seed fails to reach the goal*. Loops appear frequently due to the unique nature of the SDL data. Looping conditions must be checked at various points to avoid this problem. In the next section the Heuristics based Mid-Point approach is presented. This algorithm does not have some of the efficiency and looping problems evident in the forward exploration algorithm.

2. Heuristics Based Mid-Point Algorithm: This algorithm works 'bottom-up' from the seed and 'top-down' from the goal and terminates when the seed nodes from the bottom meet the goal nodes from the top. When seeds do not meet the goal the given heuristics may be used as a terminating condition to make the algorithm efficient. Algorithm 2 displayed in Fig. 6b shows the Heuristics Based Mid-Point method.

As the network semantics and the SDL data are already known, it possible to assign heuristics as a terminating condition. The following are the heuristics: (1) *Limit Node*

Heuristics states that if the number of nodes in a graph exceeds a set number of nodes (E.g. 20 Nodes) the algorithm must terminate. This is impractical and may not detect attacks with lengthy paths. (2) *1-Level Indirect Attack Checking Heuristic* states that if the goal and the seed appear together in any action and the output signaling message has the goal then the seed causes 1-Level Indirect Attack. However this heuristic is not sufficient to eliminate seeds that do not cause N-Level Indirect Attacks. (3) *N-Level Indirect Attack Checking Heuristic* checks each seed with every other seed and the goal for 1-Level Indirect Attacks. A seed may be eliminated from N-level indirect attacks if any of the other seeds it affects fails to reach the goal. This approach is exhaustive and would require N^2 database queries and is hence inefficient. (4) *Parameter Based Heuristic*: contains lists with sets of related and unrelated data parameters. The list of related parameters contains pairs of associated data parameters. For example, if data X is used to derive data Z, and data Y is not involved in computing the Z, the pair 'X-Z' belongs in the related parameters list and the pair 'Y-Z belongs in the unrelated parameters list. If the seed-goal pair occurs in a 'related parameters' list, the algorithm is executed, else the algorithm is not executed. The advantage of this approach is that it does not require any computation and reduces execution time.

It is not possible to have the perfect heuristic. There is always the problem of mis-detection resulting in Missed seeds and Over-Seeking seeds. Due to inadequate heuristics, seeds that actually reach the goal are assumed to fail to reach the goal resulting in *Missed seeds*. This may result in attacks not being detected and happens because it is not possible to have a complete and exhaustive list of 'related' parameters and 'unrelated' parameters. This may be minimized by picking a heuristic that only checks for 'un-related' Parameters. *Over-Seeking seeds* are those that fail to reach the goal but are assumed to be able to reach the goal carry the algorithm works towards matching the seed nodes and the goal nodes. This may result in unnecessary seeking of the goal with a large number of extraneous nodes and increase in execution time. Thereby reducing the efficiency of the algorithm.

4.7   Results

This section explains some representative results produced by CAT.

1-Level Indirect attacks: $Seed_1 \rightarrow Goal$. $Seed_1$: *ISDN BC* $\rightarrow$ *Goal:Bearer Capability*. Corrupting the ISDN BC in the IAM message leads to incorrect calculation of the Bearer Capability displayed in Fig. 4.

N-level indirect attacks: $Seed_1 \rightarrow Seed_2 \ldots Seed_i \rightarrow Seed_j \rightarrow \ldots \rightarrow Seed_n \rightarrow Goal$. $Seed_1$: *Alerting Pattern* $\rightarrow Seed_2$: *Pre-paging support* $\rightarrow Goal:Page type*. Corrupting the Alerting Pattern in the IAM signaling message leads to the retrieval of incorrect Pre-paging support at the GMSC and hence Incorrect Pre-paging support is provided in the SIFIC signaling message to the VLR. At the VLR incorrect Page type is calculated and the subscriber cannot receive calls.

4.8   Performance Analysis

The performance of algorithms is evaluated on the execution time by varying the *Seed Failure Ratio*. *Seed Failure Ratio* may be defined as the ratio of number of seeds failing to reach the goal to the total number of seeds used by the algorithm. The results are shown in Fig. 7. The algorithm is executed with a single goal, 8 seeds and heuristics varied to match the Seed Failure Ratio. When the Seed Failure Ratio is 0, i.e., all the seeds reach the goal, it is found that all the algorithms perform in a similar manner. With *0% mis-detection* (exact heuristic matching) the Mid-Point algorithm performs best and results in up to a 68% decrease in experiment time, when compared to the Forward exploration algorithm. With the *50% mis-detection rate* the Mid-Point algorithm results in up to 11% decrease in time than when compared to the Forward exploration algorithm.

5 Discussion and Conclusion

The introduction of IP based services into 3G networks increases the possibility of attacks on 3G network. CAT has been developed to detect all possible 1-Level and N-Level Indirect attacks. As the SDL specifications do not capture the data dependencies it is not possible to produce an exhaustive attack graph for multi-seed attacks with strong relationships and dependencies not exhibited in the standard SDL specifications. In the future the existing SDL specifications will be augmented with expert input to capture missing data relationships. Research work will be conducted on detecting new and unknown attacks and finding techniques to reduce the vulnerability of 3G network.

Seed Failure Ratio	Forward Exploration (milli secs)	MidPoint Method 0% Mis-detection Time in milli secs (% Time Saving)	MidPoint Method 50% Mis-detection Time in milli secs (% Time Saving)
0	6224	6185 (1%)	6150 (1%)
0.25	6120	5688 (7%)	5612 (8%)
0.5	6011	4903 (18%)	5567 (7%)
0.75	5295	2017(62%)	4897 (8%)
1	4064	1290 (68%)	3637 (11%)

Fig. 7. Time Analysis of Performance

References

1. K. Kotapati, P. Liu, Y. Sun, T. F. LaPorta, A Taxonomy of Cyber Attacks on 3G Networks, in Proc. IEEE Intl Conf. on Intelligence and Security Informatics (Extended Abstract), 2005. Lecture Notes in Computer Science, Vol. 3495, Springer-Verlag, 2005
2. Third Generation Partnership Projects (3GPP and 3GPP2), http://www.3gpp.org/
3. O. Sheyner, J. Haines, S. Jha, R. Lippmann, J. M. Wing, Automated Generation and Analysis of Attack Graphs, Proceedings of the 2002 IEEE Symposium on Security and Privacy, p.273, May 12-15, 2002
4. 3G TS 21.133 V3.1.0 (1999-12) 3G Security; Security Threats and Requirements version 3.1.0
5. 3G TR 33.900 V1.2.0 (2000-01),A Guide to 3rd Generation Security
6. 3G TS 33.120 V3.0.0 (1999-05) 3G Security; Security Principles and Objectives version 3.0.0

7. P. Howard, M. Walker, T. Wright, Towards a coherent approach to third generation system security, Second International Conference, 3G Mobile Communication Technologies, 2001. on (Conf. Publ. No. 477)

8. N. A. El-Fishway, M. A. Nofal, A. M. Tadros, An Improvement on Secure Communication in PCS,Performance, Computing, and Communications Conference, 2003. Conference Proceedings of the 2003 IEEE International , 9-11 April 2003

9. C. C. Lo and Y. J. Chen, Secure communication mechanisms for GSM networks, IEEE Transactions on Consumer Electronics, Vol. 45, No. 4, pp..

10. D. Welch, S. Lathrop, Wireless Security Threat Taxonomy, June 2003 IEEE Workshop on Information Assurance.

11. C. Clissmann, A. Patel, Security for mobile users of telecommunication services, Universal Personal Communications, 1994. Record., 1994 Third Annual International Conference on , 27 Sept.-1 Oct. 1994,Pages:350 - 353.

12. C. B. Brookson, Security in current systems, IEE Colloquium on Security in Networks (Digest No. 1995024), 3 Feb. 1995, Pages: 3/1 - 3/6.

13. C. J. Mitchell, Security techniques, in Proceedings of the IEE Electronics Division Colloquium on Security in Networks, London, February 1995, IEE (London) Digest No: 1995/024, pp. 2/1-2/6.

14. K. Boman, G. Horn, P. Howard, V. Niemi, UMTS security, Electronics & Communication Engineering Journal, Volume:14, Issue:5, Oct. 2002, Pages:191 - 204

15. L. P. Swiler, C. Philips and T. Gaylor, A Graph-Based Network Vulnerability Analysis System, SandiaReport, SAND97-3010/1, January 1998, Sandia National Laboratories, Albuquerque,New Mexico, U.S.A., 1998.

16. C. A. Phillips, L. P. Swiler, A Graph-Based System for Network-Vulnerability Analysis, Proceedings of the 1998 Workshop on New Security Paradigms (NSPW'98, Charlottsville, VA, USA), pp. 71-79, ACM Press

17. L. Swiler, C. Phillips, D. Ellis, S. Chakerian, Computer-Attack Graph Generation Tool, in Proceedings of the DARPA Information Survivability Conference and Exposition II, June 2001.

18. R.W. Ritchey and P. Ammann, Using model checking to analyze network vulnerabilities. In Proceedings 2000 IEEE Computer Society Symposium on Security and Privacy, pages 156-165, Oakland, CA, May 2000.

19. P. Ammann, D. Wijesekera, S. Kaushik, Scalable, graph-based network vulnerability analysis, Proceedings of the 9th ACM conference on Computer and communications security, November 18-22, 2002, Washington, DC, USA

20. S. Jha, O. Sheyner, J. Wing, Two Formal Analys s of Attack Graphs, Proceedings of the 15th IEEE Computer Security Foundations Workshop (CSFW'02), p.49, June 24-26, 2002

21. S. Jha, O. Sheyner, and J. M. Wing, Minimization and Reliability Analyses of Attack Graphs, CMU-CS-02-109, February 2002. Detailed version of paper to appear in Computer Security Foundations Workshop, Nova Scotia, June 2002.

22. O. Sheyner and J. Wing, Tools for Generating and Analyzing Attack Graphs, Proceedings of Formal Methods for Components and Objects, Lecture Notes in Computer Science, 2005.

23. B. Schneier, Attack graphs, Dr. Dobb's Journal, pp. 21-29, December 1999

24. J. Elisberger, D. Hogrefe, A. Sarma, SDL, Formal Object-oriented Language for Communicating Systems,Prentice Hall, 1997, ISBN 0-13-621384-7, 312 pp.

25. 3GPP TS-23.018 (v3.4.0) Basic Call Handling - Technical realisation, April 99

Protecting Web Services from DoS Attacks by SOAP Message Validation

Nils Gruschka and Norbert Luttenberger

Department for Computer Science
Christian-Albrechts-University of Kiel, Germany
{ngr|nl}@informatik.uni-kiel.de

Abstract. Though Web Services become more and more popular, not only inside closed intranets but also for inter-enterprise communications, few efforts
have been made so far to secure a Web Service's availability. Existing security
standards like e.g. WS-Security only address message integrity and confidentiality, and user authentication and authorization. In this article we present a system
for protecting Web Services from Denial-of-Service (DoS) attacks. DoS attacks
often rely on misformed and/or overly long messages that engage a server in
resource-consuming computations. Therefore, a suitable means to prevent such
kinds of attacks is the full grammatical validation of messages by an application
level gateway before forwarding them to the server. We discuss specific kinds
of DoS attacks against Web Services, show how message grammars can automatically be derived from formal Web Service descriptions (written in the Web
Service Description Language), and present an application level gateway solution
called "Checkway" that uses these grammars to filter Web service messages. The
paper closes by giving some performance figures for full grammatical validation.

1 Introduction

As Web Services become more and more popular, not only inside closed intranets but
also for inter-enterprise communications, security is becoming crucial for operating
Web Services. While the basic Web Service specifications ([4], [10]) themselves do not
address any security topics, a large number of additional specifications (WS-Security
[3], WS-SecurityPolicy [6], WS-Trust [12], WS-SecureConversation [11] etc.) for Web
Services security exists. However all these standards focus on the aspects of message
integrity and *confidentiality* and user *authentication* and *authorization*.

Few efforts have been made so far to secure the Web Service server itself and ensure
a Web Service's *availability*. Of course traditional perimeter protection systems like
packet filters, application level gateways, and intrusion detection systems contribute to
this, but we will show that these are unable to secure a Web Service server's availability
in an adequate manner.

In this article we present an application level gateway system for protecting Web
Services from Denial-of-Service (DoS) attacks. DoS attacks often rely on misformed
and/or overly long messages that engage a server in resource-consuming computations.
For Web Services a suitable means to prevent such kinds of attacks is the full grammatical validation of messages by an application level gateway before forwarding them to

Please use the following format when citing this chapter:

Author(s) [insert Last name, First-name initial(s)], 2006, in IFIP International Federation for Information
Processing, Volume 201, Security and Privacy in Dynamic Environments, eds. Fischer-Hubner, S., Rannenberg,
K., Yngstrom, L., Lindskog, S., (Boston: Springer), pp. [insert page numbers].

the server. Web Service messages are XML documents and these are usually defined by an XML Schema, written in the XML Schema definition language—a grammar language for XML. Our system generates an XML Schema from a Web Service description and validates all Web Service messages against this schema.

This article is organized as follows: The next chapter introduces Denial of Service attacks in general and in the context of Web Services. Chapter 3 discusses the protection of Web Services from DoS attacks and introduces our solution. In chapter 4 the processing of a Web Service description for our Web Service firewall and in chapter 5 the firewall itself are presented. The article closes with an outlook.

2   Attacks on Services

Denial of Service (DoS) attacks aim at reducing or completely eliminating a systems's or service's availability. One can distinguish two kinds of DoS attacks: *Protocol Deviation Attacks* and *Resource Exhaustion* [17]. Protocol Deviation Attacks exploit vulnerabilities in implementations of protocol processing entities. In some cases a single packet that diverges from the intended protocol flow can make the attacked system crash. A well-known example is *Ping of Death*.

Resource Exhaustion attacks consume the resources necessary to provide the service (network bandwidth, memory and computation resources). The simplest attack produces an extremly high network traffic load to the system providing the service (*Dump Flooding*). Using such an attack makes it difficult to completely interrupt a service's availability, even if executed as a *Distributed Denial of Service* (DDoS) attack. More elaborated DoS attacks do not try to occupy all available network capacity by brute force, but send messages that—though comparably small in number—are suited to quickly exhaust the server's memory and cpu resources. A popular example is the *TCP/SYN flooding*, where the server is flooded with (small) TCP/SYN packets. The server must create a complete TCP connection context for each packet and finally crashes due to memory consumption.

With XML and Web Services new kind of attacks arise. The most common message protocol for Web Services is SOAP, an XML based message format. Such a SOAP message is usually transported using the HTTP protocol. Figure 1 shows a simple SOAP message with the most relevant HTTP header lines. The message contains a request for the operation add with 3 parameters named x.

Two of the most important DoS attacks on XML based services like Web Services are *Coercive Parsing* and *Oversize Payload* (see e.g. [18] and [13]). The first one uses a deeply nested XML document, the second one an extremly large XML document to exhaust the service's memory. This is easier than for non-XML protocols due to the nature of XML document processing. An incoming SOAP message is parsed, validated to the Web Service interface specification and bound to programming language objects [14]. The most common and flexible model for XML processing is DOM [2]. When using DOM a DoS attack would indeed be very simple. A DOM based parser reads the complete SOAP message and builds an in-memory representation (called DOM tree), that is much larger than the message itself. The parser can therefore be attacked by an

```
POST /WebServices/MathService.asmx HTTP/1.1
SOAPAction: "http://example.com/add"
Content-Type: text/xml

<soap:Envelope
   xmlns:soap="http://schemas.xmlsoap.org/soap/envelope/"
   xmlns:ns="http://example.com/AddService">
   <soap:Body>
      <ns:add>
         <ns:x>12</ns:x>
         <ns:x>38</ns:x>
         <ns:x>27</ns:x>
      </ns:add>
   </soap:Body>
</soap:Envelope>
```

Fig. 1. Sample SOAP message.

arbitrary SOAP message, e.g. a message with a large total size or with a deeply nested XML structure.

Even if the the parser component of the Web Service uses an event-based processing model (e.g. SAX [15]) and the succeeding components (for validating and language binding) check the correctness of the SOAP message, there are still possibilities for attacks. A simple, yet effective attack can be performed if the Web Service message contains a list of elements (like in the sample shown in figure 1). This is defined in the Web Service interface description (see section 4.1) by an XML Schema element [7] containing an attribute maxOccurs="*number-of-elements*". If this element has a cardinality > 1, the number of elements is nearly always set to "unbounded" to simplify the Web Service processing. If the description is generated by a Web Service framework from an existing implementation (which is a very common proceeding), this value is automatically set for all data arrays. Such a declaration allows documents to contain an unlimited number of elements. It is obvious that such a document can exhaust the server's memory. In practical tests we easily produced deadlocks and crashes, sending a SOAP message with a large number of elements to a .NET and an AXIS Web Service.

Though not a DoS attack, a further important attack on Web Services covered by our solution is *WSDL Scanning*. All operations for a service are described and advertised inside a Web Service description using the *Web Service Description Language* (see section 4.1). If only some of a service's operations are intended to be called from the internet, an attacker is able to call all the service's operations anyway. Packet Filters and HTTP ALG are unable to differentiate operations belonging to the same service, because they all have the same service endpoint (IP address, TCP port and HTTP URL).

The operation is only defined inside the SOAP message[1] (e.g. the operation add in the SOAP message in figure 1).

3   Protecting Web Services

3.1   Web Services and Firewalls

Today it is common practice that hosts and services inside a private network (whether enterprise or home) are protected by a firewall system[2]. The firewall has two tasks: 1. to protect the services from attacks and 2. to prevent access to services, which shall not be reachable from the internet.

The most widespread firewall concept is packet filtering. Packet filters operate on layer 3 and 4 of the ISO/OSI Basic Reference Model and analyse IP and TCP headers. Such firewalls are suitable for protecting against DoS attacks exploiting the TCP or IP protocol, like Ping of Death or the TCP/SYN Flood. It is also capable to filter accesses to services using the target IP adress and the target TCP port.

Application level gateways (ALG) are defined to analyse application level protocols above ISO/OSI layer 4. Actual ALGs understand simple application protocols like HTTP. Such a HTTP ALG protects a service from attacks using malformed HTTP requests and attacks like Cookie Poisoning. It can limit access to services using the HTTP request URL.

But how can Web Services be protected? Packet filters and HTTP ALGs only check the TCP, IP and HTTP protocol header, but not the SOAP message.

A Web Service defines the valid SOAP messages using a Web Service interface description (see section 4.1). Processing of SOAP messages is time and memory consuming for the Web Service server, so every *non-valid* message should be rejected by a Web Service firewall. This can be done by validating the SOAP message in an external application level gateway.

A very simple countermeasure against large *valid* messages is limiting the SOAP message's total size. This can even be done by a simple firewall without checking the SOAP messages itself. On the other hand, this is not very sensible. The amount of memory needed while processing an XML document is usually much larger than the document itself. In order to avoid attacks, the size limit should be low. Unfortunately, this could exclude many valid documents.

A much more sophisticated solution is to restrict the length of single XML elements and also the number of elements inside the SOAP message. These restriction can be enforced by validating the SOAP message against a specially modified XML Schema derived from the Web Service interface description. For details on the kinds of modification see section 4.2.

---

[1] The HTTP header field SOAPAction also includes the operation, but this is only a hint to the actual Web Service operation inside the SOAP message and should not be taken into account (see also [9], 4.3.4)

[2] The term *firewall* is often used for packet filtering systems, that analyse only IP addresses and TCP ports. In this article we use *firewall* generalised for all security systems, which analyse and filter data traffic

In the same way, validating the SOAP message to an XML Schema containing only the allowed operations solves the WSDL Scanning problem.

3.2   Design for a Web Service Firewall

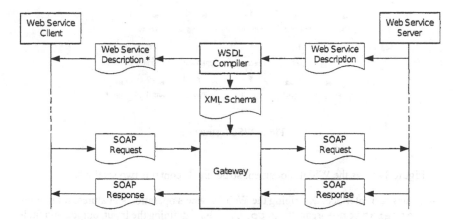

Fig. 2. Integration of the CheckWay Web Service Firewall.

The considerations above regarding SOAP message validation lead to our Web Service firewall, called *CheckWay*. Figure 2 shows the Integration of a Web Service firewall between Web Service client and server. The *CheckWay WSDL Compiler* gets the Web Service server's Web Service description, generates the corresponding XML message Schema, "hardens" the description, and advertises the modified description (marked with *) to a Web Service client. The *CheckWay Gateway* validates all SOAP messages against the Schema, forwards the message if it is valid, and rejects the message if it is not[3].

The next step is now to consider: 1. how to obtain an XML Schema for the message validation and 2. which problems regarding the firewalls performance emerge from the validation process. In order to answer the first question a closer look at Web Service client/server interaction and the Web Service interface description are required.

---

[3] Commercial products like Forum XWall or Datapower XS40 also claim to increase security by XML Schema validation, but with these products it is totally unknown: How do they gain the required XML Schemas? Were any improvements on the Schemas conducted? And which kind of XML validation software is used (which has a large impact on the gateway's performance and robustness; see section 5)?

4   Web Service Interface Description

4.1   WSDL Structure

The Web Service interface description is composed using the *Web Service Description Language* (WSDL) [5].

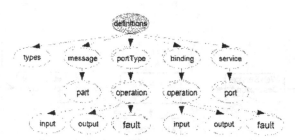

Fig. 3. WSDL structure.

Figure 3 shows the WSDL document structure. It contains two sections:

– an abstract interface, describing the Web Service's operation signatures. It includes the operation—organized in portTypes—defining the input, output, and fault messages composed of parts, which refer to a datatype, defined in the types section.
– a concrete implementation. It includes a binding section—assigning the operations to a wire format and a transport protocol—and the ports—defining the service's network endpoint address.

The WSDL specification [5] either allows a variety of concrete implementations or does not make any regulations at all. This applies for example to the grammar language used for data types (XML Schema, DTD, etc.), the encoding rules (literal, SOAP encoded, etc.) or the transport binding (SOAP, HTTP POST, HTTP GET). This creates a problem in implementing compatible systems. Thus, the WS-I[4] Basic Profile [9] recommends a number of constraints for Web Service descriptions and SOAP messages. Some important restrictions are:

– Only XML Schema is permitted for defining data types.
– The only wire format is "literal" ("SOAP encoded" is not allowed, see also [1]). This means, the data types defined in the abstract section therefore become concrete types.
– Only SOAP/HTTP binding is allowed.

---

[4] The *Web Services Interoperability Organisation* was founded by leading Web Service enterprises to create interoperability guides. In these guides the Web Service specifications are restricted and rendered more precisely to ease the creation of interoperable implementations.

Additionally there exist two different Web Services styles: *RPC* and *document*. In many cases both styles result in similar wire messages, but their definitions inside a Web Service description varies in many ways. This must be taken into consideration when analysing a Web Service description. Due to space limitations, we do not discuss this problem any further.

The next sections shows how a WSDL document is analysed and compiled to an XML Schema representing exactly the messages defined by this document.

4.2   Compiling a Web Service Description

The SOAP message's structure belonging to a Web Service description is defined by informations spread all over the description document. The description must be traversed and the informations necessary for a specific service or operation must be merged into a message definition. The arrow in figure 4 shows how a Web Service description is traversed to determine the SOAP message's structure and to generate the appropriate XML Schema.

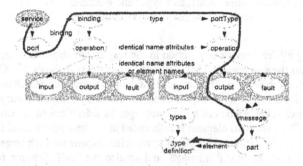

Fig. 4. Traversing a Web Service description while analysing.

Figure 6 shows a simple Web Service description[5] for a sample Web Service belonging to the SOAP message in figure 1. This example illustrates the traversing steps through a Web Service description (printed in italics).

The following WSDL elements are passed in this order:

1. The Web Service contains one or more ports.
   The Web Service AddService contains the port AddServicePort.
2. A port references a binding by the binding-attribute.
   The port is bound to the binding AddServiceBinding.

---

[5] The Web Service description was simplified for the sake of readability: all namespace prefixes and namespace declarations were removed; further on the declaration for the outgoing message was also omitted.

3. A binding decribes the wire format and the network protocol for the Web Service operations. All non-SOAP bindings and non-literal encodings (which do not conform to the WS-I Basic Profile) are ignored. This is also the place, where the service's style (RPC or document) is defined. Finally the binding references to a port type using the `type` attribute.

   The binding `AddServiceBinding` defines a SOAP binding using HTTP transport and literal encoding and furthermore an operation `add` with an input message using literal encoding and it links to the port type `AddServiceType`.

4. For each operation defined in the binding section the referenced port type contains an operation with the same name and the same input, output and fault messages, which reference a message element.

   The port type `AddServiceType` contains also an operation `add`, which references the message `addSoapIn`.

5. The message contains one or more message parts, which reference an XML Schema type or an XML Schema element (depending on the service's style) inside the types section.

   The message `addSoapIn` contains one part that links to the XML Schema element `add`.

6. The types section defines XML data types and elements for the SOAP messages.

   The element `add` is defined as complex type containing a list of elements `x` of type integer.

After passing a Web Service description in the way stated above the CheckWay compiler generates the appropriate XML Schemas. Figure 6 also shows the XML Schemas for the sample Web Service. The first schema defines a common SOAP message skeleton with envelope, header and body. The child of the `body` element in our simple example is just the element referenced by the message, the `add` element (as also can be seen in figure 1). Thus, the `add` element is referenced in the first schema and defined in the second schema. The definition is split into two schemas, one for each target namespace.

For RPC style the SOAP message (and so also the XML Schema for the SOAP message) is more complex and goes beyond this article's scope. For further details on creating XML Schemas from a Web Service description see [19].

To fight DoS attacks effectively—as shown in section 3.1—messages that are to be forwarded to a Web Service server must not only be valid with respect to the XML Schema that can be derived from the Web Service description, but moreover to a "hardened" XML Schema, constructed from the initial XML Schema as follows:

– Replacing `maxOccurs="unbounded"` in complex data types with an adequate number, e.g. `maxOccurs="1000"`. For most practical cases it is easy to determine an upper bound for the number of elements. With this limitation it is no longer possible to "flood" a Web Service with a endless series of elements.
– Replacing simple types without length restriction (e.g. `xsd:string`) with a corresponding data type containing a length restriction. This can be implemented by adding an XML Schema facette [8] to the simple type definition inside the `types` section of the Web Service description. Restricting simple types is easier and more natural than limiting the message's total length (done e.g. when defining input forms or database fields).

- Removing all operations, which are not intended to be called from the internet.

The first two points retrict implicitly the total document length and thereby prevent the *Oversize Payload* attack. It has to be noted that these modifications have to be performed with respect to the concrete Web Service application. There are no universally valid values for the number of elements or the length of simple types.

Now that we have shown, how an effective XML Schema is derived from a Web Service description, we regard how XML Schema validation is implemented in our Web Service firewall.

5   The Web Service Firewall Implementation

The core of the *CheckWay Gateway* (see figure 2) is an XML validation engine, which validates the SOAP message to the appropriate schemas. If the validation is successful, the SOAP message is forwarded. SOAP messages containing an "unlimited" number of elements do not match the (hardened) schema and are rejected. Additionally "ultra long" simple type elements do not match the (restricted) simple type definition and are also refused.

The validator's implementation is crucial for the gateway's efficiency. First of all, if the gateway is vulnerable to the attacks that it is actually supposed to protect against, it is useless. Furthermore, the processing speed is—like for every network intermediary—extremely important. The gateway should not increase the total response time significantly. We developed a special XML validation engine which was designed using the following principals [16]:

- Consistent event-based XML processing
- Support for large cardinalities
- Support for all XML Schema simple types including facets

As stated before, XML parsing and validating can be very memory consuming using an improper implementation. A DOM based parser e.g. builds the complete XML document in memory. This makes it vulnerable for attacks using documents with "unlimited" length. The gateway memory would be exhausted before the validator could even start the validating process. Thus, our validator works entirely event-based, using a SAX [15] interface. The XML document is parsed and sent event per event to the validator. The validator operates directly on these events to validate the document. There is no need, neither for the parser nor the validator, to reconstruct the whole document in memory. In fact the validator has constant memory consumption (only depending on the schema size) and linear runtime.

The gateway can therefore easily process very large documents. If the validator finds a schema violation inside a SOAP message, the gateway has read the document only up to that particular element. The remaining document is in this case never read and can therefore not impact the gateway's function.

Theoretically, the CheckWay gateway can operate completely *on the fly*. It can forward the XML document parts that have already passed the validator. In this case, the gateway's memory usage would be completely independent from the SOAP messages' size. However a security gateway should not forward any document parts before it has stated that the whole document does not contain any malicious parts. Thus, the Check-Way stores the document until the validating process has been successfully completed. This way, only the valid document parts are stored and a Coercive Parsing attack can still not harm the gateway.

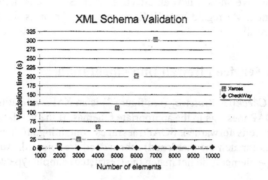

Fig. 5. Validation time.

As stated earlier, the CheckWay compiler replaces maxOccurs="unbounded" cardinalities with a large integer. Thus the validator must be able to cope with such a schema construct, which is not self-evident. We validated documents against a simple schema with increasing maxOccurs value and compared our validator to Xerces[6]. Figure 5 shows the validatation time for both engines. While the CheckWay validator's runtime has linear dependency on the maxOccurs value, the Xerces validator's runtime increases exponentially. The Xerces' time consumption, even for small values, is unacceptable for a network gateway[7]. For values greater than approx. 7500, the Xerces validator aborted throwing an out-of-memory exception.

Together with the checking of length restricted data types created by the CheckWay compiler, the validator is able to detect the attacks pictured above.

6   Summary and Outlook

In this paper we have shown how Web Services open up new possibilities for Denial of Service attacks. We presented a solution that uses XML Schema validation to detect malicious SOAP messages. Our Web Service firewall combines a WSDL compiler to generate the necessary Schemas and an efficient XML validator to filter the potential dangerous SOAP messages.

A further kind of DoS attacks not discussed in this articles forces a server into expensive cryptographic computations. With WS-Security and WS-SecurityPolicy such

---

[6] Xerces2 Java 2.7.1
[7] 2 seconds on a 2 GHz machine for maxOccurs="1000"

attacks can also harm Web Services. We are already working on an extented Web Service firewall with security and policy support to fend off such attacks just as well.

References

1. Frank Cohen. Discover SOAP encoding's impact on Web service performance. *IBM developerWorks*, 2003.
2. Arnaud Le Hors et al. Document Object Model (DOM) Level 3 Core Specification. *W3C Recommendation*, 2004.
3. Bob Atkinson et al. Web Services Security (WS-Security). 2002.
4. David Booth et al. Web Services Architecture. *W3C Recommendation*, 2004.
5. Erik Christensen et al. Web Services Description Language (WSDL). *W3C Note*, 2001.
6. Giovanni Della-Libera et al. Web Services Security Policy Language (WS-SecurityPolicy). 2005.
7. H.S. Thomson et al. XML Schema Part 1: Structures Second Edition. *W3C Recommendation*, 2004.
8. H.S. Thomson et al. XML Schema Part 2: Datatypes Second Edition. *W3C Recommendation*, 2004.
9. Keith Ballinger et al. Basic Profile Version 1.1. *WS-I Organisation*, 2004.
10. Martin Gudgin et al. SOAP Version 1.2 Part 1: Messaging Framework. *W3C Recommendation*, 2003.
11. Steve Anderson et al.   Web Services Secure Conversation Language (WS-SecureConversation). 2005.
12. Steve Anderson et al. Web Services Trust Language (WS-Trust). 2005.
13. Pete Lindstrom. Attacking and Defending Web Service. *A Spire Research Report*, 2004.
14. Brett McLaughlin. *Java and XML Data Binding*. O Reilly, 2002.
15. The SAX Project. Simple API for XML – SAX 2.0.1. 2002.
16. Florian Reuter. Forthcoming dissertation.
17. Günter Schäfer. Sabotageangriffe auf Kommunikationsstrukturen: Angriffstechniken und Abwehrmaßnahmen. *PIK 28*, pages 130–139, 2005.
18. Andre Yee. Protecting Your Web Services Deployment.
19. Jesper Zedlitz. Spezifikation und Implementierung eines Application Level Gateways für Web Service. *Diploma thesis*, 2004.

Sample Web Service Description:

```
<definitions targetNamespace="http://example.com/AddService">
  <types>
    <schema targetNamespace="http://example.com/AddServicey>
      <element name="add">
        <complexType>
          <sequence>
            <element minOccurs="1" maxOccurs="unbounded" name="x" type="int" />
          </sequence>
        </complexType>
      </element>
    </schema>
  </types>
  <message name="addSoapIn">
    <part name="parameters" element="add" />
  </message>
  <portType name="AddServiceType">
    <operation name="add">
      <input message="addSoapIn" />
    </operation>
  </portType>
  <binding name="AddServiceBinding" type="AddServiceType">
    <soap:binding transport="http://schemas.xmlsoap.org/soap/http" style="document" />
    <operation name="add">
      <soap:operation soapAction="http://example.com/AddService/add" style="document" />
      <input>
        <soap:body use="literal" />
      </input>
    </operation>
  </binding>
  <service name="AddService">
    <port name="AddServicePort" binding="AddServiceBinding">
      <soap:address location="http://ws-server.local/AddService/Service1.asmx" />
    </port>
  </service>
</definitions>
```

Resulting XML Schemas:

```
<schema targetNamespace="http://schemas.xmlsoap.org/soap/envelope/">
  <element name="Envelope" type="tn:EnvelopeType" />
  <complexType name="EnvelopeType">
    <sequence>
      <element name="Body" type="tn:BodyType" />
    </sequence>
    <anyAttribute namespace="##other" />
  </complexType>
  <complexType name="BodyType">
    <choice>
      <element ref="add" />
    </choice>
    <s:anyAttribute namespace="##other" /
  </complexType>
</schema>

<schema targetNamespace="http://example.com/AddService">
  <element name="add">
    <complexType>
      <sequence>
        <element maxOccurs="1000" minOccurs="1" name="x" type="s:int" />
      </sequence>
    </complexType>
  </element>
</schema>
```

Fig. 6. Sample Web Service and generated XML Schemas.

A Flexible and Distributed Architecture to Enforce Dynamic Access Control*

Thierry Sans, Frédéric Cuppens, and Nora Cuppens-Boulahia

GET/ENST Bretagne, 35576 Cesson-Sévigné Cedex, France
{thierry.sans,frederic.cuppens,nora.cuppens}@enst-bretagne.fr

Abstract. Avoiding unauthorized access in an information system usually means enforcing access control mechanisms. Traditional access control only aims at deciding if an access can be granted or not. Dynamic access control goes further as it aims at controlling also if an ongoing access is still authorized while it is running. Rights Expression Languages, such as MPEG-REL, take into account dynamic aspects of access control policy. However, existing access control architectures are not adequate to enforce such dynamic access control. In this paper, we first explain what dynamic access control involves and why existing architectures are not appropriate. We then provide a flexible and distributed architecture where different components interact to enforce dynamic access control. Using temporal logic of actions, we specify the different interactions between components in the architecture and specify more precisely the component in charge of giving the decision. Finally, we discuss about technical and security issues about how the architecture can be implemented to enable Digital Rights Management (DRM) applications.

1 Introduction

Securing an information system usually means avoiding that users have unauthorized access to information. To prevent unauthorized access, we need to specify and enforce access control to regulate who may have access and how to have access to resources managed by the information system. Specifying and deploying an access control process can be divided into three steps: (1) specifying the access control policy, (2) designing a decision mechanism to grant access according to the access control policy and (3) enforcing the decision in an access control application of the information system.

The access control policy aims at specifying who may have access to the information system. This policy is usually represented by Access Control List (ACL). Nowadays, we talk about Rights Expression Languages (REL) [6, 10] as structured and high expressive languages to specify security policies. A REL aims at identifying the entities of the information system (subjects, actions[1], objects[2]) and specifying which subject may perform an action on an object. A subject can be a physical person [3] or an external application interacting with the information system.

---

*This work was funded by the "ACI Sécurité Informatique: CASC Project".

[1] also called rights or privileges.

[2] also called resources.

[3] A user who interacts with the information system through a GUI.

Please use the following format when citing this chapter:

Author(s) [insert Last name, First-name initial(s)], 2006, in IFIP International Federation for Information Processing, Volume 201, Security and Privacy in Dynamic Environments, eds. Fischer-Hubner, S., Rannenberg, K., Yngstrom, L., Lindskog, S., (Boston: Springer), pp. [insert page numbers].

When a subject wants to perform an access to a resource, the subject makes a request through the frontend application of the information system. From this request and according to the security policy, a decision mechanism allows or not the subject to have an access to the resource. This decision mechanism is based on the underlying access control model [15] implemented by the Rights Expression Language. The decision mechanism must be reliable, deterministic and reproducible [7].

Finally, an architecture must be designed so that given subject can only have an access to a resource through the access control layer. It means that the architecture must be tamper resistant to bypassing the decision and prevent any uncontrolled access to the information.

Existing access control models [15] provide decision mechanisms to reason on the access control policy. These traditional decision mechanisms only aim at enforcing the decision *before* a given action is launched. However, in more recent applications such as Digital Right Management (DRM) [2, 20], we also want to control if this action is still allowed or not while it is rendering. This is because the access decision can change while the action is running. So, the decision mechanism is no longer static but dynamic.

Why do we need ongoing checks when the access is rendering? Because the environment can change and the conditions to allow an access may not be still satisfied then a previous authorization can then be forbidden. In [17], R.Sandhu and J.Park show up that the traditional approach is not sufficient to deal with dynamic requirements. For instance, "a user can use a free Internet access only if an advertisement bar is on". It means that the bar must be active at the beginning of the Internet access and must remain active during the access is running otherwise the access must end. We agree with [17] that traditional access control cannot enforce this kind of requirement. The *pre* and *ongoing* models of $UCON_{ABC}$ overcome this limitation. Pre-models are sets of rules which have to be satisfied before the access is granted. On-models (ongoing models) are sets of rules which have to be satisfied while an access is running.

However, Rights Expression Languages and access control models such as $UCON_{ABC}$ that support dynamic access control do not define an appropriate architecture to enforce the underlying decision mechanism. Why do we need a new architecture to enforce dynamic access control? Because existing architecture [11, 4] are not sufficient to enforce ongoing decision mechanism implied by dynamic access control. For instance, if we consider the XACML specification[4] and focus on its enforcement in a AAA Architecture [16, 4], the specification does not take into account such a mechanism. In this architecture, a subject who wants to perform an access, makes a request to a PEP (Policy Enforcement Point), the component in charge of granting an access or not. The PEP then sends a request[5] to a PDP (Policy Decision Point), the component in charge of making the decision. According to the XACML access control policy, the PDP sends back the decision to the PEP. The PEP finally enforces the decision of granting or not the access.

Now, if we want to take into account dynamic access control requirements into the AAA architecture, the only way to perform ongoing checks is to send request to the PDP periodically in order to check if the ongoing access is still allowed or not. This

---

[4] An OASIS standard in version 2.0.
[5] This request is embedded in a SAML Token. SAML is another OASIS standard.

approach is not adequate for two reasons. First it creates useless traffic between the
PEP and PDP. Secondly, it is costly in time to periodically check if the conditions to
allow the access are still satisfied or not. It would be more efficient if the PDP can notify
the PEP that the access must be revoked.

Thus, the objective of this paper is to formally define an adequate architecture to enforce dynamic access control mechanism. This architecture takes into account dynamic
interactions between the component in charge of making a decision and the component
in charge of enforcing it. In section 2, we further explain our approach of dynamic access control. In section 3, we present the different components of our architecture and
specify how they interact each other. Using temporal logic we define how the components must behave in the architecture in order to enforce dynamic access control. In
section 4, we focus on the specification of the component in charge of the decision
mechanism. We formally specify how this component makes the decision. Finally in
section 5, we discuss how to implement this architecture with existing technologies and
also what are the security issues we have to face to reliably deploy this architecture.

2 Our approach

Many Access Control List Languages (ACL) and Rights Expression Languages (REL)
has been previously defined [6, 10]. So, this paper does not aim at providing a new
structured language to specify the access control policy. We simply assume that the
expression of the access control policy is based on provisional authorizations [12]. It
means that an access can be allowed if some conditions are satisfied. These conditions
may depend on the system environment [15]. They can change while an access is running and require dynamic access control mechanisms to be implemented.

In order to represent provisional authorizations, we adopt the MPEG-REL[6] approach [10]. Even if the initial specification of MPEG-REL enforcement is not formally defined, it has been formalized in [8]. Enforcement of the access control policy
is divided into two steps. In the first step, called "policy matching", we have to select the authorizations relevant to the requested access. At this step, the access can be
denied if none authorization can match the request. In the second step called "condition validation", the conditions associated with the provisional relevant authorizations
are evaluated with respect to the system environment, and the access is either allowed
if one condition applies or denied if all conditions fail. In dynamic access control, it is
necessary to make a clear separation between policy matching and condition validation.
Indeed, while the access is running, conditions continue to apply and we must check if
they are still satisfied. By contrast, the policy does not need to be matched again, except
when the policy is updated during the access. We deal with this last issue in the policy
update extension specified further in section 4.3.

Once the decision mechanism is defined, we aim at designing an appropriate architecture to enforce dynamic access control. For this purpose, we suggest an approach
based on a mathematical formalism to model interactions between components used to
enforce dynamic access control. We have chosen the Temporal Logic of Actions (TLA)

---

[6] Called XrML before becoming an ISO/IEC Standard.

defined by L.Lamport [14]. TLA is based on first order logic extended with temporal modalities. We briefly introduce here the main concepts of the TLA formalism :

A state is an assignment of values to variables.

A predicate is a boolean expression valuated from a given state :

$$s_i: s_i[\![P]\!] \triangleq P(\forall v : s_i[\![v]\!]/v)$$

An action is a boolean expression representing a transition between an old state and a new state of the system. So, actions are expressed with unprimed and primed variables representing respectively a condition on the old system state and a condition on the new system state. An action can be valuated from two consecutive states: $s_i[\![A]\!]s_{i+1} \triangleq A(\forall v : s_i[\![v]\!]/v, s_{i+1}[\![v]\!]/v')$. The meaning $[\![A]\!]$ of an action A is a relation between states, i.e. a function that assigns a boolean $s_i[\![A]\!]s_{i+1}$ to a pair of states s_i and s_{i+1}.

For a given sequence of states $\langle s_0, s_1, s_2, ..., s_n \rangle$, for A and B actions, TLA defines the following modalities:

$$\langle s_0, s_1, s_2, ..., s_n \rangle[\![A]\!] \quad \triangleq \quad s_0[\![A]\!]s_1$$
$$\textbf{Next} \bigcirc A \quad : \langle s_0, s_1, s_2, ..., s_n \rangle[\![\bigcirc A]\!] \triangleq s_1[\![A]\!]s_2$$
$$\textbf{Always} \,\square\, A \quad : \langle s_0, s_1, s_2, ..., s_n \rangle[\![\square A]\!] \triangleq \forall i \in [0..n]\ s_i[\![A]\!]s_{i+1}$$
$$\textbf{Eventually} \,\lozenge A : \langle s_0, s_1, s_2, ..., s_n \rangle[\![\lozenge A]\!] \triangleq \exists i \in [0..n]\ s_i[\![A]\!]s_{i+1}$$

Then, using first order logic operators, a TLA formula is defined by the following grammar:

Formula F ::= $A \mid \neg F \mid \bigcirc F \mid \square F \mid \lozenge F \mid F \wedge F \mid F \vee F \mid F \rightarrow F$

3   The architecture

In this section, we introduce the different components of our distributed architecture. Using TLA, we show how they interact and behave to enforce dynamic access control.

3.1   The components

We focus on three main components of our access control architecture: (1) The frontend handler, (2) the rendering handler and (3) the policy handler.

The frontend handler is the application layer where a subject can interact with the information system. Using this component, the subject requests execution of actions managed by the system.

The rendering handler is in charge of performing an allowed request. It executes the corresponding action from the action library. The action library is a set of programs in charge of rendering the information to the subject.

The policy handler is in charge of evaluating a request and provides a decision with respect to the access control policy. This component enforces the decision mechanism of the underlying Right Expression Language used to express the policy. It can then allow a subject to perform an action requested from the frontend handler. This decision

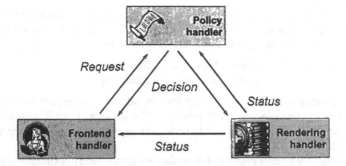

Fig. 1. Distributed Architecture.

message is sent either to the rendering handler or the frontend handler. With dynamic access control, if the decision changes during the rendering, the policy handler notifies the rendering handler that the action is no longer allowed and stops the rendering.

As shown in figure 1, each component interacts with the others by exchanging messages. In order to enforce dynamic access control, we define three message classes:

- Request: When a subject wants to have access to the system, the *request* message is sent from the frontend handler to the policy handler to be evaluated.
- Decision: There are three types of decision messages: *grant*, *deny* and *revoke*. The *grant* message is sent to the rendering handler when a request is allowed. The *deny* message notifies the frontend handler when a request is not allowed. In dynamic access control, we also want to control if an ongoing access is still allowed. If the decision changes during the access, a *revoke* message is sent to the rendering handler to stop the rendering.
- Status: Once a decision is taken, the rendering handler must notify the other handlers that the rendering action is launched or is completed. Thus, we define the *access* message when the action is launched and the *end* message when it is completed.

For a better reading, we have chosen to define data structures with a TLA-like formalism. We formally define these different types of message as follows:

$$\text{TYPE} \qquad MessageType = \{\ \text{``request''}, \text{``grant''}, \text{``deny''},$$
$$\text{``revoke''}, \text{``access''}, \text{``end''}\ \}$$

Every message contains a description of the access. We call *target* a tuple composed of: (1) who wants to access, (2) which object is requested and (3) for which rendering action. The target is denoted α and defined as follows:

$$\text{TYPE} \qquad Target = [Subject \times Action \times Object]$$

A *message* is then formally defined as a tuple with a message type and a target as follows:

$$\text{TYPE} \qquad Message = [MessageType \times Target]$$

Finally, we need to model interaction between components through the network by sending and receiving messages. The network is a set of messages that we denote Φ. We respectively define two predicates snd and rcv like this:

PREDICATE $rcv = [Message \rightarrow Boolean]$
              $snd = [Message \rightarrow Boolean]$

These predicates modify the network state by adding or taking off a message. So, invoking one of these predicates will modify Φ. For instance, $\forall \omega : Message\ \Phi, \Phi' \vdash rcv(\omega)$ means that a message is taken from Φ and now the set of messages, representing the network, is Φ'.

Notice that for a better reading of formulae, we do not need to explicitly specify the sender and the receiver in the snd and rcv predicates. Using the type of the messages, every component knows who is the sender and the recipient.

In the next part, we further explain how the different components interact using messages, and formalize how they enforce dynamic access control policy.

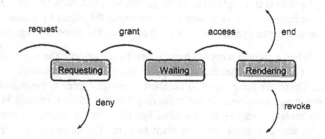

Fig. 2. Dynamic Access Control Enforcement.

3.2   The dynamic access control enforcement

Figure 1 shows what kind of message the different components exchange and figure 2 shows when the different messages are sent.

First, a request message is sent from the frontend layer to the policy handler. This *request* message contains the target representing who wants to access, which object is requested and for which rendering action. Then, the policy handler makes a decision with respect to the access control policy. If the decision is to allow the request, a *grant* message is sent to the rendering handler. If the decision is to not allow the request, a *deny* message is sent to the frontend handler notifying the subject that the request is rejected. So, using temporal logic, we can describe the behavior of the policy handler. When a *request* message is sent, the policy handler has to send a *grant* message or a *deny* message in return. We can formalize it as follows:

The policy handler :
    $\Box\, [\, rcv("request", \alpha) \; \rightarrow \; \Diamond\, (\, snd("grant", \alpha) \; \vee \; snd("deny", \alpha)\,)\,]$

Notice that the formula, used to represent how the policy handler behaves, is indeterministic. The choice between *grant* and *deny* message depends on the decision mechanism implemented by the policy handler. This non determinism will disappear when we shall formally specify the decision mechanism of the policy handler in section 4.

So far, we have described the traditional access control enforcement in our distributed architecture. Now, we want to enforce dynamic access control and check if an ongoing rendering is still allowed or not. When the rendering handler receives a *grant* message, it must perform the corresponding action from the actions library to satisfy the authorized request. The rendering handler then sends an *access* message to the policy handler notifying that the authorized access has been launched. So, when a request is allowed by the policy handler, the action will finally be launched by the rendering handler. For the rendering handler, it means that when a *grant* message is received, it has to send an *access* message in response. Respectively, for the policy handler, when a message *grant* is sent, it expects to receive back an *access* message. We can formalized it as follows:

The rendering handler :
$\square\,[\,rcv("grant",\alpha)\;\rightarrow\;\lozenge\,(snd("access",\alpha)\,)\,]$
The policy handler :
$\square\,[\,snd("grant",\alpha)\;\rightarrow\;\lozenge\,(rcv("access",\alpha)\,)\,]$

With the dynamic approach, while the action is rendering, the policy handler is still evaluating the request until it ends. If the decision changes during the rendering, the policy handler notifies the rendering handler that the action is no longer allowed and stops the rendering. If the decision does not change, the action will eventually end and the rendering handler will send an *end* message to notify the policy handler that it has to stop evaluating the decision for the corresponding request. So, when an action is rendering, the policy handler can revoke the access with a *revoke* message. If the decision does not change, the policy handler will eventually receive the notification with an *end* message that the action has been done. Respectively, we can formalize the corresponding behavior for the rendering handler. The different behaviors can be formalized as follows:

The policy handler :
$\square\,[\,rcv("access",\alpha)\;\rightarrow\;\lozenge\,(\,snd("revoke",\alpha)\;\vee\;rcv("end",\alpha)\,)\,]$
$\Rightarrow\;\square\,[\,rcv("request",\alpha)\;\rightarrow\;\lozenge\,(\,snd("deny",\alpha)$
$\qquad\qquad\qquad\qquad\qquad\vee\,snd("revoke",\alpha)\;\vee\;rcv("end",\alpha)\,)\,]$
The rendering handler :
$\square\,[\,snd("access",\alpha)\;\rightarrow\;\lozenge\,(\,snd("end",\alpha)\;\vee\;rcv("revoke",\alpha)\,)\,]$
$\Rightarrow\;\blacksquare\,[\,rcv("grant",\alpha)\;\rightarrow\;\lozenge\,(\,snd("end",\alpha)\;\vee\;rcv("revoke",\alpha)\,)\,]$

Finally, we can give the behavior of the frontend handler. When it has sent a request, the frontend handler expects to receive either: A *deny* message notifying that the corresponding request has not been allowed. A *revoke* message notifying that the corresponding request has been allowed and launched, but it has not been allowed to complete. An *end* message notifying that the corresponding request has been allowed and has successfully completed.

So, the frontend handler behavior can be formalized like this:

The frontend handler :

$\Rightarrow \Box \left[snd(\text{``request''}, \alpha) \rightarrow \Diamond \left( rcv(\text{``deny''}, \alpha) \right. \right.$
$\left. \left. \vee \ rcv(\text{``revoke''}, \alpha) \vee rcv(\text{``end''}, \alpha) \right) \right]$

4 The policy handler specification

In this section, we focus on the specification of the component that enforces the access control policy: The policy handler. First, we model how to manage provisional conditions to make a decision. Then, using TLA, we formally specify how the policy handler enforces this decision.

4.1 Managing provisional conditions

We denote Γ the access control policy. According to the previous definition of $Target$ given in section 3.1, we define how to match the policy and the target:

PREDICATE $isPermitted = [Target \times Condition \rightarrow Boolean]$

For instance, $\forall \alpha : Target, \ \forall c : Condition \ \Gamma \vdash isPermitted(\alpha, c)$ means that, according to the security policy Γ it is allowed to grant an access α if the condition c is satisfied. Notice that this predicate does not change the access control policy.

We then both check if a condition is satisfied in the environment and also log a message as environment information:

PREDICATE $isSatisfied = [Target \times Condition \rightarrow Boolean]$
$\qquad\qquad\qquad\quad addLog = [Message \rightarrow Boolean]$

For instance, $\forall \alpha : Target, \ \forall c : Condition \ \Sigma \vdash isSatisfied(\alpha, c)$ means that, according to the environment Σ, the condition c that belongs to α is satisfied. In the same way, $\forall \omega : Message \ \Sigma, \Sigma' \vdash addLog(\omega)$ modifies the environment by logging a message ω. Notice that the predicate $isSatified$ does not change the environment whereas $addLog$ modifies it.

4.2 Policy Handler TLA Specification

As shown in figure 3, there are three steps in the decision enforcement: (1) getting a message from the network and log it, (2) making a decision according to the message type and (3) checking ongoing access. The policy handler makes a decision as follows:

- Request: If the policy matches the target and if the corresponding conditions are satisfied then a *grant* message is sent to the rendering handler, else a *deny* message is sent to notify the application handler. This case is defined in the *requesting* action.
- Access: If the policy matches the target then a corresponding $\langle target, condition \rangle$ is added in the *ongoing* set, else a *revoke* message is sent to the rendering handler. This case is defined in the *accessing* action.

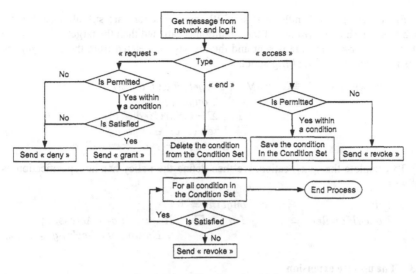

Fig. 3. Policy Handler Algorithm.

- End : The corresponding target is deleted from the *ongoing* set to stop validation of ongoing access. This case is defined in the *ending* action.

In the specification, we need a variable *ongoing* to represent the set of ongoing access and the corresponding condition to be satisfied:

$$\text{VARIABLE} \qquad ongoing : \{[Target \times Condition]\}$$

$$Requesting \triangleq \quad \exists\,\alpha : Target,\ \exists\,c : Condition\ |$$
$$\Phi, \Phi' \vdash rcv(\langle\text{"}request\text{"}, \alpha\rangle)$$
$$\land\ \Sigma, \Sigma' \vdash addLog(\langle\text{"}request\text{"}, \alpha\rangle)$$
$$\land\ If\ (\ \Gamma \vdash isPermitted(\alpha, c) \land \Sigma \vdash isSatisfied(\alpha, c))$$
$$Then\ \Phi, \Phi' \vdash snd(\langle\text{"}grant\text{"}, \alpha\rangle)$$
$$Else\ \Phi, \Phi' \vdash snd(\langle\text{"}deny\text{"}, \alpha\rangle)$$

$$Accessing \triangleq \quad \exists\,\alpha : Target,\ \exists\,c : Condition\ |$$
$$\Phi, \Phi' \vdash rcv(\langle\text{"}access\text{"}, \alpha\rangle)$$
$$\land\ \Sigma, \Sigma' \vdash addLog(\langle\text{"}access\text{"}, \alpha\rangle)$$
$$\land\ If\ (\ \Gamma \vdash isPermitted(\alpha, c))$$
$$Then\ ongoing' = ongoing \cup \{\langle\alpha, c\rangle\}$$
$$Else\ \Phi, \Phi' \vdash snd(\langle\text{"}revoke\text{"}, \alpha\rangle)$$

$$Ending \triangleq \quad \exists\,\alpha : Target,\ \forall\,c : Condition\ |$$
$$\Phi, \Phi' \vdash rcv(\langle\text{"}end\text{"}, \alpha\rangle)$$
$$\land\ \Sigma, \Sigma' \vdash addLog(\langle\text{"}end\text{"}, \alpha\rangle)$$
$$\land\ ongoing' = ongoing \backslash \{\langle\alpha, c\rangle\}$$

Finally, the policy handler checks if all ongoing actions are still allowed. So, for each target in the *ongoingset*, if the condition is satisfied then the target is kept in the set, else a *revoke* message is sent and the message is deleted from the *ongoing* set. This is defined in the *checking* action.

$$
\begin{aligned}
Checking \quad &\triangleq \quad \forall\, \alpha : Target,\ \forall\, c : Condition \mid \\
& \langle \alpha, c \rangle \in ongoing \\
& \wedge If\ (\ \Sigma \vdash isSatified(\alpha, c)) \\
& \quad Then\ \langle \alpha, c \rangle \in ongoing' \\
& \quad Else\ \Phi, \Phi' \vdash snd(\langle \text{"revoke"}, \alpha \rangle)
\end{aligned}
$$

To complete the specification, we then define the policy handler specification as follows:

$$
\begin{aligned}
Init \quad &\triangleq \quad ongoing = \emptyset \\
PolicyHandler \quad &\triangleq \quad Init \wedge \square\,[\quad Requesting \vee Accessing \\
& \qquad\qquad\qquad\quad \vee Ending \vee Checking\,]_{<ongoing>}
\end{aligned}
$$

4.3   The update extension

What happens if the policy changes during an authorized access? This can change the conditions associated with ongoing access. So, we provide an update extension to deal with this problem. We can assume that the policy is managed by a new component: a policy manager. The policy manager can be seen as a rendering handler that enforces updates of the security policy. Therefore, an update must have been previously allowed by an administrative policy. This kind of reflexive architecture can enforce a reflexive access control administration model like [15].

When an update is done, the policy manager (like a rendering handler) sends to the policy handler an end message $\langle \text{"end"}, \langle s, \text{"modify"}, \text{"securityPolicy"} \rangle \rangle$ notifying that the policy has changed. We then need to extend the definition of the "ending" action in order to handle an update. So, we modify the *ending* action as follows:

$$
\begin{aligned}
Ending \quad &\triangleq \quad \exists\, \alpha : Target,\ \forall\, c : Condition \mid \\
& \Phi, \Phi' \vdash rcv(\langle \text{"end"}, \alpha \rangle) \\
& \wedge \Sigma, \Sigma' \vdash addLog(\langle \text{"end"}, \alpha \rangle) \\
& \wedge ongoing' = ongoing \backslash \{\langle \alpha, c \rangle\} \\
& \wedge If\ (\exists\, s : Subject \mid \alpha = \langle s, \text{"modify"}, \text{"SecurityPolicy"} \rangle) \\
& \quad Then\ Updating_{<ongoing>}
\end{aligned}
$$

When an update happens, the *updating* action specifies that for all ongoing access, the policy handler checks the policy again and updates the ongoing set with the corresponding condition. Some access can be revoked if the policy does not authorized them anymore. The *updating* action is defined as follows:

$$
\begin{aligned}
Updating \quad &\triangleq \quad \forall\, \alpha : Target,\ \forall\, c_1, c_2 : Condition \mid \\
& \wedge \langle \alpha, c_1 \rangle \in ongoing \\
& \wedge If\ (\ \Gamma \vdash isPermitted(\alpha, c_2)) \\
& \quad Then\ \langle \alpha, c_2 \rangle \in ongoing' \\
& \quad Else\ \Phi, \Phi' \vdash snd(\langle \text{"revoke"}, \alpha \rangle)
\end{aligned}
$$

Notice that at the *updating* step, the conditions do not need to be validated because they are going to be validated in the next step with the *checking* action as defined previously in the policy handler specification.

5 Technical and security issues

In traditional access control architecture, the data and rendering actions remain on the server side in a secure area. Identification, authentication and access control mechanisms enable a trusted subject to interact with the information system from a (potentially) non secure client. However, information systems are currently getting more complex and distributed. In this context [2, 20], the data and rendering actions are more and more disseminated on the client side. So, we need a flexible and distributed architecture to control the outsourced information.

To deal with new communication models like DRM, our proposal can be implemented as a service oriented architecture (SOA) as defined in [5]. Components of our architecture are independent from each other and can be implemented both on a server side or client side. The implementation of the communication layer can be based on web services [1, 19]. Targets of access control could be wrapped in SAML messages as described in [9]. This architecture enforces security mechanisms, so it must be tamper resistant to different attacks. Let us focus on security issues of this architecture:

Trust management: Only trusted components can interact in the architecture [3], because a rogue policy handler might deliver malicious decision to perform an unauthorized access. To prevent this flaw, authentication mechanism must be enforced between the different components of the trusted architecture.

Integrity: The messages must not be modified by a non authorized entity. Digital signatures must be applied to messages exchanged between trusted components to guarantee the integrity of the access control information. Messages must also not be deleted without control, so non repudiation mechanism [21] must be enforced to guarantee that a message sent will be eventually received.

Confidentiality: At first glance, we can think that confidentiality is not necessary in our architecture. It could not matter if someone can see access control decisions and status. However, confidentiality can be required when the target embeds private or confidential information about subject, action and resource [13].

Availability: For instance, it could be obvious to let the policy handler allows an access and then, performs a denial of service on this component to avoid a *revoke* message. To prevent this intrusion, heartbeats messages must be exchanged between the components during an access.

Now, another security issue can appear regarding the component location in the information system.

On a server-side, we consider that the servers[7] are inside the trusted and secure area. It means that we assume that the underlying Operating System (OS) and program execution is safe from any external threat.

---

[7] When different servers host the different components of our architecture.

On a client-side, we can no longer assume this hypothesis. The component is executed out of the scope of the safe and secure area. On the client side, the running OS and processes execution can be hooked. Existing DRM frameworks usually deal with this issue. Most of the time the application handler and rendering handler are embedded in a program executed in the client side. An obvious solution could be to hide the code of both the OS and the program to avoid modification. Unfortunately this solution is not viable because it cannot be enforced in open source systems, and also because reverse engineering is still possible. The solution could be to use a Trusted Third Party (TTP) in the client. This TTP is a safe area where trusted programs can be executed. New technology like TCPA[8] [18, 2] embeds this TTP as a part of the processor chip.

6 Conclusion

In traditional access control architecture, access control only applies before launching an action. Dynamic access control goes one step further by also controlling if provisional conditions are still satisfied during the access. The main contribution of this paper is to formally define a distributed architecture that supports dynamic access control mechanisms.

Our architecture is based on three components: (1) The request handler is used by an external subject to make a request to the information system, (2) the policy handler is in charge of making a decision and (3) the rendering handler is in charge of enforcing the decision associated with a given allowed request. We first show that existing architectures are not relevant to enforce dynamic access control because interactions between their policy handler and their rendering handler are not efficient.

Our architecture defines new interactions between the policy handler and the rendering handler. When the access is granted, the rendering policy launches the action and notifies it to the policy handler. During the access, the policy handler keeps on checking if the conditions allowing the access are still satisfied. If they are not, the policy handler notifies the rendering handler to revoke the access. Else, if the action ends normally, the rendering handler notifies it to the policy handler in order to stop ongoing checks.

We then formally specify how the policy handler makes a decision using temporal logic of actions. First, we define what the policy handler does when it receives access control messages. Secondly, we define an endless action to check conditions that belongs to ongoing access.

Our architecture can be implemented as a service oriented architecture (SOA). Components can be either distributed on a server side or on a client side. Therefore, our architecture can be used as a framework to enforce Digital Rights Management (DRM) applications.

References

1. G. Alonso, F. Casati, H. Kuno, and V. Machiraju. *Web Services: Concepts, Architectures and Applications.* Springer-Verlag, 2004.

---

[8] Trusted Computing Platform Alliance.

2. Eberhard Becker, Willms Buhse, Dirk Gnnewig, and Niels Rump, editors. *Digital Rights Management: Technological, Economic, Legal and Political Aspects.* Springer-Verlag GmbH, 2003.
3. M. Blaze, J. Feigenbaum, and J. Lacy. Decentralized Trust Management. In *The IEEE Symposium on Security and Privacy (SSP'96)*, Oakland, CA, May 1996.
4. C.T.A.M de Laat, G.M. Gross, L.Gomans, J.R. Vollbrecht, and D.W. Spence. Generic AAA architecture, RFC 2903. Technical report, IETF Internet Working Group, August 2000.
5. Thomas Erl. *Service-oriented Architecture: Concepts, Technology, And Design.* Prentice Hall PTR, 2005.
6. Susanne Guth. *Digital Rights Management: Technological, Economic, Legal and Political Aspects*, volume Volume 2770, chapter 2.3.5 Rights Expression Languages, pages 101–112. Springer-Verlag GmbH, 2003.
7. J.Y. Halpern and V. Weissman. Using First-Order Logic to Reason about policies. In *16th IEEE Computer Security Foundation Workshop (CSFW'03)*, Pacific Grove, California, June 2003.
8. J.Y. Halpern and V. Weissman. A Formal Foundation for XrML. In *17th IEEE Computer Security Foundation Workshop (CSFW'04)*, Pacific Grove, California, June 2004.
9. J. Hughes and E. Maler. Security Assertion Markup Language (SAML) Version 2.0. Technical report, OASIS, February 2005. www.oasis-open.org.
10. International Organization for Standardization (ISO). *ISO/IEC 21000-5:2004 Information technology – Multimedia framework (MPEG-21) – Part 5: Rights Expression Language*, 2004. www.iso.ch/iso/fr/prods-services/popstds/mpeg.html.
11. ISO International Organization for Standardization. Information technology – Open Systems Interconnection – Security Frameworks in Open Systems – Part 3:Access Control, ISO/IEC 10181-3. Technical report, ISO JTC 1, August 2001.
12. S. Jajodia, M. Kudo, and V.S. Subrahmanian. Provisional Authorizations. In A. Ghosh, editor, *Security and Privacy in E-Commerce*, pages 133–159, Athens, Greece,, November 2000. Kluwer Academic Publishers.
13. L. Korba and S. Kenny. Applying Digital Rights Management Systems to Privacy Right Management. *Journal of Computer and Security*, 2002.
14. Leslie Lamport. *Specifying Systems*. Addison-Wesley Professional, July 2002.
15. Alexandre Miège. *Definition of a formal framework for specifying security policies. The Or-BAC model and extensions.* PhD thesis, ENST, 2005.
16. Tim Moses. eXtensible Access Control Markup Language (XACML) Version 2.0. Technical report, OASIS, February 2005. www.oasis-open.org.
17. J. Park and R. Sandhu. The $UCON_{ABC}$ Usage Control Model. *ACM Transactions on Information and System Security*, 7(1), February 2004.
18. Siani Pearson. *Trusted Computing Platforms: TCPA Technology In Context.* Prentice Hall PTR, July 2002.
19. J. Rosenberg and D. Remy. *Securing Web Services With Ws-Security.* Sams, 2004.
20. W. Rosenblatt, B. Rosenblatt, and W. Trippe. *Digital Rights Management: Business and Technology.* Wiley, Decembre 2001.
21. J. Zhou and D. Gollman. A fair non-repudiation protocol. In *SP '96: Proceedings of the 1996 IEEE Symposium on Security and Privacy*, page 55, Washington, DC, USA, 1996. IEEE Computer Society.

A Paradigm for Dynamic and Decentralized Administration of Access Control in Workflow Applications

Andreas Mattas[1], Ioannins Mavridis[2], and Iason Pagkalos[1]

[1]Informatics Laboratory, Computers Division, Faculty of Technology, Aristotle University,
54006, Thessaloniki, Greece,
mattman@gen.auth.gr, pangalos@gen.auth.gr
[2]Department of Applied Informatics, University of Macedonia,
156 Egnatia Street, 54006, Thessaloniki, Greece,
mavridis@uom.gr

Abstract. The administration of authorizations in modern Web-based computing environments has become a primary concern. Application security is characterized by a significant complexity, due to the large number of variations and combinations of objects and operations to be protected. Thus, there is a need for data, processes and context parameters, like time and location, to be combined into a security model that ensures correct decision-making for access. Moreover, access control must often be based on dynamic functional requirements that are capable of embedding the required context information to express application-level access control policies in new application domains, as for example Internet workflow applications. In this work a new paradigm of dynamic and decentralized administration of access control that is based on the DARBAC model is presented. DARBAC concerns access control for a wide-range of collaborative applications and aims to provide fine-grained and dynamic administration of authorizations. The presented implementation assumes Web-based applications to support enforcing of access control at a distributed platform level, and it demonstrates in a step-by-step basis the construction of DARBAC components and their management during run-time.

1 Introduction

Access control ensures in general that accesses to information system's objects occur according to the modes and rules fixed by the corresponding security policies [1]. Subjects request for operations on objects. Their requests are permitted or denied usually by one (or more in distributed systems) reference monitor that is responsible for mediating subject's actions on objects and implementing a particular security policy based on an access control model.

In modern application systems, access control must be based on strictly controlled permissions that are available (through activated roles) just-in-time, only to proper users and until they accomplish specific tasks. To support such control activities, proper mechanisms are needed, which must not overload administrative tasks but

Please use the following format when citing this chapter:

Author(s) [insert Last name, First-name initial(s)], 2006, in IFIP International Federation for Information Processing, Volume 201, Security and Privacy in Dynamic Environments, eds. Fischer-Hubner, S., Rannenberg, K., Yngstrom, L., Lindskog, S., (Boston: Springer), pp. [insert page numbers].

support them in a flexible and effective manner. Access control administration depends mainly on the number of the components that are handled, a parameter that depends on the simplicity of the access control model, as well as to the frequency permissions have are changed. On the other hand, it is the nature of information systems that must reflect the changes of the organization they are serving.

Beyond the traditional mandatory (MAC) [2], [3] and discretionary (DAC) [4], [5], [6] approaches, Role-based access control (RBAC) [1], [7] has received considerable attention and has already been implemented in various operating and database management systems [8] as a convenient way to address the problem of organizing permissions. RBAC's main advantage is the efficient administration of permission assignment to subjects through roles and their hierarchies. Researchers [9], [10] have argued however that one of the main omissions of the RBAC model is the authorization of administration, as well the administration in large scale systems, which must be decentralized and be managed using administrative roles. The ARBAC97 [10] model demonstrates how this can be accomplished using RBAC96 [1] as the underlying model. It is desirable however to develop new standards in the area of access control administration, because it is often the place where security breaks. Other alternate paradigms that have been recently discussed in the literature [10], [11], [12], [13] also address RBAC administration from one point of view.

As Web applications become increasingly available today throughout Internet and corporate intranets, a significant administrative overload is being produced when determining the proper authorization schema [14]. Moreover, additional access control mechanisms are needed to record dynamic changes in the content and context of information that differentiate users' need-to-know requirements, to monitor the system's security state, and to facilitate the carrying out transactional activities [15]. This means that access control models must provide efficient administration of authorizations to ensure that valid users exercise their privileges only during the progress of an official activity of their organization. As a result, new approaches of access control to meet the challenges of these new models of computing are required. An approach in this direction, which is based on the DARBAC (Dynamically Administering Role Based Access Control) model, is presented in this work. More specifically, a paradigm for implementing the DARBAC model in a typical workflow application is demonstrated.

2 Access Control Administration

2.1 Main Approaches - Limitations

The various access control approaches, when examined from an administrative point of view, can be grouped into two main styles of handling subjects: the identity-based and the attribute-based. Traditional identity-based access control models are those also-known as supporting DAC. They restrict access to objects based on the identity of subjects. However, providing fine-grained specification of authorizations on subject's identity entails a significant administrative overload, as the number of subjects becomes huge. For this reason, decentralized administration was selected, where the user who creates an object (its owner) is the one who decides for the authorizations of other users on accessing it, as well as for any possible delegations of his administrative privileges to specific users (named controllers). Such a rather simple model is not however always sufficient for access control administration in modern distributed and collaborative applications, especially for large and dynamically changing organizations. This is mainly due to the lack of supporting dynamic changes of access rights, associating them to subject's credentials when performing an operation, as well as relating them to attribute of resources or other contextual information [16]. Furthermore, the unlimited freedom of owners to delegate administrative privileges often results in a complicated and potentially uncontrolled administration of authorizations. On the other hand, differentiated protection of objects [17] demands for non-stop access control administration that tends to be costly and prone to error.

The use of groups in common implementations of access control lists (ACLs), was an attempt to make their management easier. However, it still remains the question how groups are formed. A widely accepted answer was to define groups based on the subject's responsibility or job function in the organization, which lead to the notion of roles. Roles (RBAC [1], [7]), as well as labels (MAC [2], [3]), are used in attribute-based access control approaches, where usually a centralized style of administration is used. The use of attributes, like roles in RBAC, provides a significant flexibility as far as it concerns the management of permission assignments to subjects. Roles differ from groups because of the role hierarchies and the inheritance they support. A major drawback of traditional RBAC models, which limits their usefulness, is their inability to take into account fine-grained information from the execution context [18]. Pure role-based access control [1] seems to be suitable for session-based operations that take place in function-oriented organization structures usually used in relatively stable environments. The use of roles for grouping authorizations is based however on general organizational terms without incorporating user, object or process attributes [17]. They also lack of fine-grained administration of authorizations, which are specified based on role and object types, while in collaborative applications detailed control on individual role and object instances is often the case. Even the mechanism of roles in RBAC is characterized as static, as opposed to the dynamic changes of context during the progress of collaborative activities [16]. Furthermore, the concept of session in RBAC restricts its applicability in large distributed and cooperative applications where many users are acting asynchronously but under conditions and constraints that are related to the same workflow or mission.

2.2 Design-time and Run-time Administration

The overall administration problem can be separated into the design-time and run-time access control administration. Design-time administration refers to the transformation of organization policies into static components and mechanisms of the access control system. For example, in Core RBAC [7], design-time access control administration (also known as role engineering [19]) may involve specifying roles and permissions, and their assignments. During run-time, users are defined and assigned to roles in order to execute their tasks. Administration of access control during runtime introduces more complex issues, which are related to the need for supporting least-privilege, privacy protection and just-in-time access control. For example, a teller can always register a check but he must take first the approval of his manager in order to proceed with payment. So, the teller's permission set has to be initially poor and be enriched only when needed.

In known access control administration models, as for example the ARBAC family of models ([10], [11]), the main effort was focused on design-time to control distributing of administrative authority in a hierarchical way via administrative roles. Only management of user to role assignment (e.g. URA97, [10]) can be considered as happening in run-time. So, there is no concern on run-time administration of permissions and roles; and runtime means plenty of dynamic factors, like the ability to describe protection of objects depending on the processes accessing them [17].

2.3 Passive and Active Security

The above distinction between design-time and runtime administration has also been expressed as the separation between passive and active security approaches [20], [21]. In passive security models primary concern is given to maintaining permission assignments, providing so a static protection of objects. Trying to differentiate the supported protection, access control administration workload becomes too heavy, because many applications utilize static ACLs that are specified in a process that is characterized as labor intensive, costly and error prone.

In active security models there is a clear distinction between assignments and activations of permissions. Moreover, permissions are activated and deactivated depending on the evolution of the tasks or contextual conditions. For this reason, it is desired the contribution of contextual information that is related to subjects (e.g. place and time of access request, identity and roles) or objects (e.g. storage location, attribute values) to differentiate decisions for access. This is done considering not simply user's need-to-know requirements but the need-to-do requirements of the enterprise mission in which the user is participating as member of a team; a process that requires a significant administrative workload during run-time. So, the point is to eliminate this manual procedure by incorporating automatically driven acquisition and processing of live information of context, goal, environment, etc. Such information must be taken under consideration when specifying the least-privilege that a user needs at a specific time to accomplish a particular task in the context of a workflow or mission. However, this may also involve significant administrative workload, especially due to the complexity of mechanisms needed.

Thomas and Sandhu [20] have argued the need for active authorization models, which are self-administrative. Such models should provide automatically the ability to manage the components of an access control system during run-time. Relative research work that has been developed on this direction considers mainly the definition of temporal constraints [22], [23], [24], [25], while TBAC [20] and TMAC [21] models do not provide particular ways for implementing the concepts they have introduced and which have influenced other researchers. Such a development was the introduction of the C-TMAC model [25], where specific procedures for filtering permissions based on the contextual information are proposed. However, it lacks self-administration and fine-grained administration of entities and assignment relations, as well as multidimensional definition of collaborative contexts [16]. Finally, the PBDM model [26] also addresses the problem of delegation of authority, dealing with the different kinds of delegation: user-to-user, user-to-role, role-to-role. Nevertheless, it introduces a lot of administrative intervention for controlling those delegations.

3   The DARBAC model

A recent effort to form an integrated solution to the above issues has resulted to the introduction of the DARBAC model [27]. The DARBAC model is based on the RBAC [7] and PBDM [26] families of models. It gives priority to the administration of access control during run-time and addresses the problem from a different perspective. More specifically, it considers a distributed Web-based information system wherein a number of missions with possible relationships between them are in progress. The protection state of the system is concerned to be partitioned in particular states that are related to each one mission instance. Moreover, sessions are replaced by the notion of mission instances, which are more suitable for Web-application environments, in order to support enforcement of access control at a distributed platform level. The concept of session, which is used in RBAC-based access control models as a unity wherein the activated roles and permissions, as well as the results of enforcing constraints, are defined on a user basis. A mission instance encompasses the whole effort of a team of users that aims to accomplish a goal through particular tasks and in specific limits (e.g. time, etc). So, various constraints can be enforced regarding specific object-instances, without allowed to users to violate them via multiple sessions. Mission instances are used as a basis for controlling the activation of permissions from subsets of roles to which a user belongs. While sessions are user-oriented, missions are goal-oriented. As a result, the protection state can be checked on collaborative basis rather than on a single user basis. Mission instances can be thought as loose variations of tasks, where instead of operations can be represented states, teams, or co-operations between groups of users. An overview of the DARBAC model is shown in Figure 1.

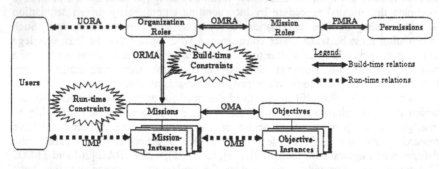

Fig. 1. The DARBAC model.

The DARBAC model aims to satisfy requirements for access control in workflow systems [28], [24] that include the use of task as a factor for differentiating access control, distinction between role and process instance-based user group, dynamic authorization based on access history, privacy protection through user exclusion, permission propagation through temporal role delegation, activation of permissions only during the execution of a task and ability to handle temporal constraints.

4   The DARBAC Structure

The DARBAC model relies on six sets of entities called users, organization and mission roles, permissions, missions and objectives (Figure 1). A *user* is a person that uses a Web-application. *Permissions* are modes of access users can exercise on one or more data objects. In addition, DARBAC incorporates the *role* concept in a slightly different manner. More specifically, it distinguishes between organization-roles (job functions within the context of an organization with some associated semantics, regarding authorities and responsibilities conferred on users assigned to them) and mission-roles (temporarily activated or delegated, and serving the specific needs of a given application). Mission-roles are activated only in the frame of mission-instances. A *mission* is considered as a type of project/process that is carried out by a user or a team/group of users with appropriate roles. In collaborative environments, missions can be thought of as identical to teams of users, while in workflow ones a mission may represent a part (tasks) or an entire workflow. The structure of a mission may represent a temporary project team organization (e.g. adhocracy organization [29]); for a finite period of time the members of project team are acting in order to accomplish specific goals that are determined by a number of objectives. When goals are accomplished, the particular mission instance is ended. The notion of *objective* is similar to that of context in [21], but it is used in a broader sense; an objective may include the particular target/object of an operation. For example, the payment of a check concerns a given check that is identified by the check's number. In general, an objective instance may contain values of time intervals, object identities, and other contextual information that contributes to define a restricted range of exercising generally applied permissions. *Permissions* are assigned to mission-roles with a many-to-many Permission-to-Mission-Role Assignment relation (PMRA). Users are also related to organization-roles with a many-to-many User to Organization-role Assignment relation (UORA). Furthermore, mission-roles are assigned to organization ones with a many-to-many Mission-role to Organization-role relation (OMRA). On the other hand, objectives are assigned to missions with a many-to-many Objective to Mission Assignment relation (OMA). The set of skills needed for a mission to accomplish its goal is specified through an Organization-role to Mission Assignment relation (ORMA), where each role refers to an autonomous activity of mission, thus giving an alternative way to represent tasks in workflows.

During run-time, users with sufficient administrative permissions can bind an objective instance to a mission instance through a many-to-one Objective-instance to Mission-instance Binding relation (OMB). In addition, as users participate in mission instances, new entries are added in a many-to-many User to Mission-instance Participation relation (UMP). Two types of constraints can be defined by security designers during build-time: Separation of Duty Constraints (SDC) and Join of Duty Constraints (JDC). SDC and JDC are examined during run-time to decide the users' participation in mission instances. SDC imposes the rule that no user can participate in a mission-instance with more organization-roles than specified. JDC specifies that a user with a given organization-role can participate in a mission instance, only if a second user with another organization-role is already participating or not. In addition, identity-based inclusions or exclusions of users to participate in a mission instance are specified during run-time with User-Mission Constraints (UMC).

A more formal description of the DARBAC model, which are based on RBAC [7] and PBDM [26] families of models, can be found in [30].

5 The DARBAC Decision-making Process

Decision-making in the presence of a user access request is performed in DARBAC using the permissions gained by mission roles (or possible enrichments from delegations) and the particular values of the objective instances bound to the mission instance, where the user currently participates. Decision-making is accomplished in accordance with the following four-step procedure, which is repeated for every user's access request:

Step 1: Reviewing. In order to perform an operation, the user submits an access request through the Web-application, after he has activated either manually (from a picking list), or automatically (through the application) the prerequisite organization-role to participate in the corresponding mission instance. Then,
1. Given the bound objective instance, the mission instance is sought in OMB.
2. In case there is no such mission instance, the access request is denied. Otherwise the user's participation is sought in UMP. If he already participates in the mission instance, the procedure continues with step 3; otherwise it goes to step 2.

Step 2: Participating. To decide whether the user can participate in the mission instance:
1. UORA is checked to confirm that the required organization-role has been assigned to the user. Otherwise, the access request is denied.
2. ORMA is sought to be determined whether the user is permitted to participate in an instance of that mission.

Step 3: Checking. Verification of user's participation is performed by examining constraints SDC, JDC and UMC, as follows:
1. Based on the values of username, organization-role and mission instance, SDC, JDC and UMC constraints are applied.
2. In case the above constraints are satisfied, the user is allowed to participate in the specific mission instance and UMP is updated.
This step has to be repeated for every new access request, whether or not the user participates already in the mission instance, in order to verify his participation under current dynamically changing conditions.

Step 4: Matching. The final control of whether the user has the right to execute his access request is performed with following actions:
1. Aggregation of permissions the user gains from mission roles, either assigned to his organization role during build-time or delegated during run-time, and
2. Matching the requested operation to the permissions acquired.

6 An Implementation Paradigm

The implementation of DARBAC in a real life situation is demonstrated in this section with an application example from the banking domain. As discussed already, the access control system to be implemented is comprised of two parts: a build-time module for defining and maintaining the components of DARBAC, and a run-time module that enforces all DARBAC security considerations to control user interactions with the banking system. The process of constructing these modules in corresponding phases is briefly described below.

6.1 Build-Time Phase

Access control design during the built-time is carried out in an off-line state. The organization managers in cooperation with the application developers capture the organization's rules and policies to define, name and construct the components of the access control system. Administrative tasks during build-time are quite similar to those specified in ARBAC family of models [10], [11], [12], [13] that address sufficiently distributed administration of role and permission assignments. The demonstrated implementation is focused on a typical banking transaction, known as the "check payment".

Definition of Entities. The security designer defines two missions: MD, as the default mission for all bank's transactions, and MPC for check payments. Additionally, he defines the objective Work_days, for the (working) days the banking system is accessible by users, and Check_ID, which is the identification number of a check. Then he defines the organization-roles Teller (to register and pay checks) and Manager (to approve checks' payments), as well as the mission-roles: regular roles R_teller and R_manager, fixed delegatable role F_manager and temporal delegatable role T_teller (for role delegation purposes). He also defines DPCm, a delegation role owned by F_manager (for use in mission MPC). Permissions are distinguished between regular: Insert, Approve, Pay, and administrative ones: DelegateDPCm, StartMPC, EndMPC.

Definition of Relationships. The security designer assigns (OMRA) mission-roles to Manager and Teller, and permissions (PMRA) to roles, as shown in figure 2. Then he assigns (OMA) objectives Work_days and Check_ID to missions MD and MPC, respectively. He also assigns (ORMA) roles Manager and Teller to missions MD and MPC.

Definition of Constraints. SDC and JDC constraints are declared, as follows:

- SDC_{MPC} = ({Manager, Teller}, 2), which means that the same user may activate, only one of organization-roles Manager and Teller when participating in any mission instance of mission MPC.
- JDC_{MPC} = (Teller, Manager, ||), which means a user with organization-role Manager can participate in any mission instance of mission MPC, only while another user with organization-role Teller is participating.

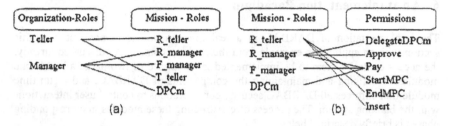

Fig. 2. OMRA (a) and PMRA (b).

6.2 Run-Time Phase

Access control managing during run-time must be able to cope with situations related to any daily or emergency activities in an organization. Administrative operations are performed by the security administrator, as well as a wide variety of users under certain constraints; e.g. a user can start a new mission instance and bind it to an objective instance. The security administrator assigns organization-roles to users, which can then participate in a default mission instance. In order to perform their specific tasks they have to participate firstly in corresponding mission instances.

During build-time, fewer permissions than necessary are assigned to mission roles. However, temporal role-to-role delegation can be used in run-time to provide further functional dependencies in the context of a mission instance. This is useful to ensure that no job can be completed unless permitted by a supervisor role who delegates the necessary additional permissions (through an appropriate delegation role [26]). The type of delegation adopted in DARBAC is temporal, since its term ends automatically when a user with administrative permissions terminates the mission instance. This fact, in conjunction with the required participation of users in mission instances for being able to activate mission roles, results in the revocation of available permissions, either enriched via delegations or initially assigned ones.

A demonstration of the progress of this example during the run-time is depicted in figure 3 where it is assumed that the time is advancing from left to right. Mission-instances are depicted with different shades. Particular operations accomplished during this example are also distinguished with vertical lines.

Fig. 3. Progress of access requests through mission instances.

System initialization. First of all, the security administrator starts up the instance MD#15 of the default mission MD, and binds it (OMB) to the instance (Monday..Friday) of objective Work_Days. Then, he creates user accounts Alice and Bob and assigns them (UORA) to roles Manager and Teller, respectively. Both users can use the banking system (after participate in MD#15) only during working days.

Check registration. Let's assume that Bob has received a check with identification number '960' and proceeds with the check's registration. Check's registration includes two operations: an administrative one (StartMPC) and a regular one (Insert), as follows:
- StartMPC: Bob participates in MD#15 with organization-role Teller and executes operation 'StartMPC' that starts a new mission instance of MPC (e.g. MPC#45) and binds it to an instance of objective Check_ID with value (960).
- Insert: Bob participates in MPC#45 (constraints SDC_{MPC} and JDC_{MPC} are satisfied) as Teller and executes operation 'Insert' to register the check.

Payment approval. Then Bob asks his manager (Alice) to approve the check's payment. Check's approval includes a regular operation (Approve) and an administrative one (DelegateDPCm), as follows:
- Approve: Alice participates in MD#15 and MPC#45 with organization-role Manager (JDC_{MPC} is satisfied because Teller already participates) and executes operation 'Approve'. However, user Bob cannot complete the payment until the permission Pay will be given to him with a role-to-role delegation.
- Delegate_DPC: Alice (still participating in MPC#45) assigns mission-role DPCm to mission-role T_teller (due to administrative permission DelegateDPCm).

Check payment. Bob can now proceed with the check's payment, as follows:
- Pay: Bob (still participating in MPC#45) executes operation 'Pay' that results in completing the check payment.
- EndMPC: Bob terminates MPC#45, giving also an end to any temporal administrative operation that took place during that mission instance. As a result Teller's extended rights are over and his first assigned permissions are restored.

As a result of the above process, it has been possible to apply fine-grained and just-in-time access control using only administrative functions of the access control system. Hence, access control can be clearly distinguished from application logic. Moreover, users can exercise administrative permissions in a really distributed environment.

7 Conclusion

In this paper the application of dynamic administration of role-based access control based on the DARBAC model is demonstrated. DARBAC guides the security designer during build-time and provides an integrated framework for decentralized and temporal administrative activities during runtime.

The DARBAC model is suitable for access control in a wide-range of collaborative applications, usually set-up in Web-based environments. It introduces a distinct structure for defining its components, attributing administrative privileges to a variety of roles and imposing constraints for separation, synchronization and user-based inclusion/exclusion to satisfy the security principles of least-privilege, separation of duties, conflict of interests and privacy protection. DARBAC also preserves the advantages of permission administration that RBAC models offer and yet introduces the concept of mission, in addition to that of roles, as an abstract mechanism to formulate the objective information, which in turn identifies the aim and context of activities to be performed by a group/team of users with prerequisite roles. Dynamic administration is achieved by granting to normal and administrative users the proper administrative permissions to manage missions and their objectives, to perform temporary delegations and to apply constraints governing mission participations; allowing so controlled transfer of role competences and decentralization of authority.

A paradigm of dynamic and decentralized administration of access control based on the DARBAC model has been presented, through an implementation of DARBAC in a real life situation application example from the banking domain. The presented implementation assumes Web-based applications to support enforcing of access control at a distributed platform level and it demonstrates in a step-by-step basis the construction of DARBAC components and their management during run-time. It can therefore be said that DARBAC can provide a promising alternative and an interesting starting point for further research work on new access control administration paradigms for Web applications and services. Future work includes further study on relationships between Web applications and missions, as well as exploiting additional features of Web-services for access control across different administration domains.

References

1. Sandhu, R.: Role-Based Access Control. Advances in Computers. Academic Press (1998).
2. Bell, D.E., LaPadula, L.J.: Secure computer systems: mathematical foundations and model. Technical Report, MITRE (1974).
3. Biba, K.J.: Integrity Considerations for Secure Computers Systems. Bedford, MA: The MITRE Corporation (1977).
4. Lampson, B.W.: Protection. In 5th Princeton Symposium on Information Science and Systems, p. 437-443. Reprinted in ACM Operating Systems, Review 8(1) (1971) 18-24.
5. Graham, G.S., Denning, P.J.: Protection - principles and practice. In AFIPS Spring Joint Computer Conference (1972) 40:417-429.
6. Harrison, M., Ruzzo, W., Ullman, J.: Protection in operating systems. Communications of the ACM 19, 8 (1976) 461-471

7. Ferraiolo, D., Sandhu, R., Gavrila, S., Kuhn, D.R., Chandramouli, R.: A Proposed Standard for Role Based Access Control. Transactions on Information and System Security (2001)
8. Chandramouli, R., Sandhu, R.: Role Based Access Control Features in Commercial Database Management Systems. 21st National Information Systems Security Conference (1998)
9. Sandhu, R.: Future Directions in Role-Based Access Control Models. In conference: International Workshop MMM-ACNS. St. Petersburg, Russia (2001)
10. Sandhu, R., Bhamidipati, V., Munawer, Q.: The ARBAC97 Model for Role-Based Administration of Roles. Transactions on Information and System Security (1999) 105-135
11. Sandhu, R., Munawer, Q.: The ARBAC99 Model for Administration of Roles. Proceedings of the 15th Annual Computer Security Applications Conference (1999) 229
12. Oh, S., Sandhu, R.: A Model for Role Administration Using Organization Structure. 7th ACM Symposium on Access Control Models and Technologies. USA (2002) 155-168
13. Kern, A., Schaad, A., Moffett, J.: An Administration Concept for the Enterprise Role Based Access Control Model. 8th Symposium on Access Control Models and Technologies (2003)
14. Kooker, R., Kane, S.: Identity Management: Role Based Access Control for Enterprise Services. Command and Control Research and Technology Symposium. USA (2004)
15. Joshi, J., Aref, W.G., Ghafoor, A., Spafford, E.H.: Security Models for Web-Based Applications. Communications of the ACM, Vol. 44. No. 2. (2001)
16. Tolone, W., Ahn, G., Pai, T., Hong, S.: Access control in collaborative systems. Source ACM Computing Surveys (CSUR) archive, Vol. 37. No. 1. (2005) 29 – 41
17. Kern, A., Kuhlmann, M., Kuropka, R., Ruthert, A.: A Meta Model for Authorizations in Application Security Systems and their Integration into RBAC Administration. 9th ACM Symposium on Access Control Models and Technologies. USA (2004)
18. Yao, W., Moody, K., Bacon, J.: A Model of OASIS RoleBased Access Control and its Support for Active Security. In SACMAT'01, Chantilly, Virginia, USA (2001)
19. Epstein, P., Sandhu R.: Engineering of Role/Permission Assignments. 17th Annual Computer Security Applications Conference (2001)
20. Thomas, R., Sandhu, R.: Task-based authorization controls (TBAC): A family of models for active and enterprise-oriented authorization Management. In Database Security, XI: Status and Prospects (eds. T.Y.Lin and S. Qian), Chapman and Hall, London (1997)
21. Thomas, R.: Team-Based Access Control: A Primitive for Applying Role-Based Access Controls in Collaborative Environments. 2nd ACM Workshop on RBAC, USA (1997)
22. Bertino, E., Bonatti, P.A., Ferrari E.: TRBAC: A temporal role-based access control model. ACM Transactions on Information and System Security (TISSEC). (2001) 191 – 233
23. Joshi, J., Bertino, E., Latif, U., Ghafoor, A.: Generalized Temporal Role-Based Access Control Model. IEEE Transaction on Knowledge and Data Engineering. (2005) 4 - 23
24. Atluri, V., Huang, W.; An Authorization Model for Workflows. In Lecture Notes in Computer Science, No.1146. Springer-Verlag (1996) 44–64
25. Georgiadis, C., Mavridis, I., Pangalos, G., Thomas, R.: Flexible team-based access control using contexts. 6th ACM Symposium on Access Control Models and Technologies. (2001)
26. Zhang, X., Oh, S., Sandhu, R.: PBDM: a flexible delegation model in RBAC. Proceedings of 8th ACM Symposium on Access Control Models and Technologies, Como, Italy (2003)
27. Mattas, A., Mavridis, I., Pangalos, G.: Towards Dynamically Administered Role-Based Access Control. 14th Int.Workshop on Database and Expert Systems Applications. (2003)
28. Wu, S., Sheth, A.P., Miller, J.A., Luo, Z.: Authorization and Access Control of Application Data in Workflow Systems. Journal of Intelligent Information Systems (JIIS) (2002) 71-94
29. Shim, W.B., Park, S.: Toward an Improved RBAC Model for the Organic Organization. 9th International Conference on Parallel and Distributed Systems, Taiwan (2002)
30. Mattas, A., Mavridis, I., Pangalos, G.: The DARBAC Model, Technical Report INFOLAB-TR01-2005 (2005) URL: http://infolab.gen.auth.gr/TR/INFOLAB-TR01-2005.pdf

CAS++: An Open Source Single Sign-On Solution for Secure e-Services

Claudio Agostino Ardagna, Ernesto Damiani,
Sabrina De Capitani di Vimercati, Fulvio Frati, and Pierangela Samarati

Dipartimento di Tecnologie dell'Informazione
Università degli Studi di Milano
Via Bramante 65 - Crema - Italy
{ardagna,damiani,decapita,frati,samarati}@dti.unimi.it

Abstract. Business and recreational activities on the global communication infrastructure are increasingly based on the use of remote resources and services, and on the interaction between different, remotely located parties. On corporate networks as well as on the open Web, the huge number of resources and services often requires to multiple log-ons leading to credential proliferation and, potentially, to security leaks. An increasingly widespread approach to simplify and secure the log-on process is Single Sign-On (SSO) that allows automatic access to secondary domains through a single log-on operation to a primary domain. In this paper, we describe the basic concepts of SSO architecture focusing on the central role of open source implementations. We outline three major SSO trust models and the different requirements to be addressed. We then illustrate CAS++, our open source implementation of a Single Sign-On service. Finally, we illustrate the application of CAS++ to a real case study concerning the development of a multi-service network management system. The motivation for our work has been raised in response to the requirements of such case study within the Pitagora project.

1 Introduction

Applications running on the Global Information Infrastructure are increasingly designed by composing individual *e-services* such as e-Government services, remote banking, and airline reservation systems [12], providing various kind of functionalities such as paying fines, renting a car, releasing authorizations, and so on. From the architectural point of view, service-oriented distributed applications follow a layered software structure composed of three layers [16]: *i) e-Service components,* software components implementing e-services; *ii) Application server,* a middleware layer over which the components will be deployed and that provides some additional functionalities such as management of security and persistence; *iii) Operating System platform,* over which the application will be distributed. While there is an increasing need for authenticating clients of these applications before granting them access to services and resources, individual e-services are rarely designed in such a way to handle the authentication process. The reason e-services do not include functionalities for checking the client's credentials is that they assume a unified directory system to be present, making suitable authentication interfaces available to client components of network applications. On some corporate networks, all users have a single identity across all services and all applications are directory enabled. As a result, users only log in once to the network, and all applications across the network are able to check their unified identities and credentials when granting access to their services. However, on most Intranet and on the open network users have multiple identities, and a solution is needed to give them the illusion of having a single identity and a single set of credentials. Single Sign-On (SSO) systems are aimed at providing this functionality, managing the multiple identities of each user and presenting their credentials to network applications for authentication. In this paper, we describe a fully functional *open source* Single Sign-On [7] solution, that allows users to enter a single username and password to access systems and resources, to be used in the framework of an open source e-service scenario. Indeed, open specifications for inter-organizational SSO do exist; for example, the Liberty Alliance (LA) project, started in 2001 and involving more than 130 organizations, is aimed at providing a framework for protecting business transaction, and its scope clearly includes open standards for *federated network identity*. However, here we shall focus on specific open source implementations of SSO systems, which may or may not fully comply to open specifications like LA. As a matter of fact, in many application fields open source products are increasingly being adopted as an alternative to proprietary solutions. In particular, our work has been driven by the requirements for an open source Single Sign-On solution raised within the Pitagora project, where we are collaborating with Siemens Mobile for the development of a multi-service network management system.

2 Single Sign-On: Basic Concepts

The huge amount of services available on the Net is causing a proliferation of user accounts. Users typically have to log-on to multiple systems, each of which may require different usernames and authentication information. All these accounts may be managed independently by local administrators within each individual system [20].

In a multiservice domain, each system acts as an independent domain. The user first interacts with a *primary domain* to establish a session with that domain. This transaction requires the user to provide a set of credentials applicable to the primary domain. The primary domain session is usually represented by an operating system shell executed on the user's workstation. From this primary domain session shell, the user can require services from other *secondary domains*. For each of such requests the user has to provide another set of credentials applicable to the interested secondary domain.

From the account management point of view, this approach requires independent management of accounts in each domain and use of different authentication mechanisms. In the course of time, several usability and security concerns have been raised leading to a rethinking of the log-on process aimed at co-ordinating and, where possible, integrating user log-on mechanisms of the different domains.

A service/architecture that provides such a co-ordination and integration is called *Single Sign-On* [13]. In the SSO approach the primary domain is responsible for collecting and managing all user credentials and information used during the authentication process, both to the primary domain and to each of the secondary domains that the user may potentially require to interact with. This information is then used by Single Sign-On services within the primary domain to support the transparent authentication by each of the secondary domains with which the user requests to interact. The advantages of the SSO approach include [11, 20]:

- *reduction* of *i)* the *time spent* by the users during log-on operations to individual domains, *ii) failed log-on* transactions, *iii)* the *time used to log-on* to secondary domains, *iv) costs and time* used for users profiles administration;
- *improvement to users security* since the number of username/password each user has to manage is reduced;[1]
- *secure and simplified administration* because with a centralized administration point, system administrators reduce the time spent to add and remove users or modify their rights;
- *improved system security* through the enhanced ability of system administrators to maintain the integrity of user account configuration including the ability to change an individual user's access to all system resources in a co-ordinated and consistent manner;
- *improvement to services usability* because the user has to interact with the same login interface.

SSO provides a uniform interface to user accounts management thus enabling a coordinated and synchronized management of the component domains.

3   Trust Models and Requirements of Single Sign-On Solutions

The definition of different trust models is important for the evaluation of different SSO solutions, which could slightly differ in their purposes depending on the business and trust scenario in which they act. For the goal of our analysis, we define three trust models over which the requirements, defined in Section 3.2, will be categorized.

3.1   Trust Models

A trust model describes a system through the definition of the underlying environment and of its behaviors, components, and rules. In particular, the model defines the entities involved in the system, the rules that regulate the interactions between the entities and the peculiarities of the overall system. Trust models are the basis for interoperability. For our goals, we focus on the definition of trust models in SSO environments based on the services that these environments support. We have identified three models.

Authentication and Authorization Model (AAM). This model represents one of the traditional security/trust models describing all the frameworks that provide authentication and authorization features [10]. It represents the basic mechanism in which

---

[1] It is important to note that, while improving security since the user has less accounts to manage, SSO solutions imply also a greater exposure from attacks; an attacker getting hold of a single credential can in principle compromise the whole system.

a user requires an access to a service that checks the users' credentials to decide whether access should be granted or denied. This model identifies two major entities: *users*, which request accesses to resources, and *services*, potentially composed by a set of intra-domain services, which share these resources. This model is based on the classic client-server architecture and provides a generic protocol for authentication and authorization processes.

Federated Model (FM). This model represents one of the emergent security/trust models in which several homogeneous entities interact to provide security services, such as identity privacy and authentication. This model identifies two major entities: *users*, which request accesses to resources, and *services*, which share these resources. The major difference with the previous model resides in the service definition and composition: in federated systems the services are distributed on different domains and they are built on the same level allowing mutual trust and providing functionalities as cross-authentication [17].

Full Identity Management Model (FIMM). This model represents one of the most challenging security and privacy/trust models that, potentially, could merge the previous two models. In addition, it provides mechanisms for identity and account management and privacy protection [3, 18]. This model identifies three major entities: *users*, which request accesses to resources, *services*, which share these resources, and *identity manager*, which gives functionalities to manage users identities. The major difference with the previous models is that FIMM tries also to fulfill the needs of privacy that arise in emerging scenarios.

3.2 Requirements

The requirements that a Single Sign-On solution should satisfy are more or less well known within the security community, and several SSO projects published partial lists. [2] However, to the best of our knowledge no complete discussion of high-level functional requirements for SSO has been published yet. A first step before implementing an open source innovative SSO system consists in spelling out these requirements, taking lessons learned from previous projects into account. Our analysis brought us to formulating the following requirements (for each requirement we report the trust model (AMM, FM, FIMM) to which it refers). [3]

Authentication (AAM,FM,FIMM). The main feature of a SSO system is to provide an authentication mechanism. Usually the authentication is performed through the classic username/password log-in, whereby a user can be unambiguously identified. Authentication mechanisms should usually be coupled with a logging and auditing process to prevent and, eventually, find out malicious attacks and unexpected behaviors. From a software engineering point of view, authentication is the only "necessary and sufficient" functional requisite for a SSO architecture.

---

[2] For an early attempt at a SSO requirements list, see middleware.internet2.
edu/webiso/docs/draft-internet2-webiso-requirements-07.html

[3] Note that, different models fulfill a different set of requirements (see Table 3.2). SSO solution should be evaluated therefore by taking into consideration only the requirements supported by the corresponding trust model.

Table 1. Requirements categorization basing on the specific trust model.

Requirement	AAM Model	FM Model	FIMM Model
Authentication	X	X	X
Strong Authentication	X	X	X
Authorization	X		X
Provisioning	X		X
Federation		X	X
C.I.M. (Centralized Identity Management)	X		X
Client Status Info	X	X	X
Single Point of Control	X		
Standard Compliance	X	X	X
Cross-Language availability	X	X	X
Password Proliferation Prevention	X	X	X
Scalability	X	X	X

Strong Authentication (AAM,FM,FIMM). For high security environments, the traditional username/password authentication mechanism is not enough. Malicious users can steal a password and act in place of the user. New approaches are therefore required to better protect services against unauthorized accesses. A good solution to this problem could integrate username/password with strong authentication mechanism based on two-factor authentication such as a smartcard and biometric properties of the user (fingerprints, retina scan, and so on).

Authorization (AAM,FIMM). After the authentication process, the system can determine the level of information/services the requestor can see/use. While application based on domain specific authorizations can be defined and managed locally at each system, the SSO system can provide support for managing authorizations (e.g. role or profile acquisitions) that apply to multiple domains.

Provisioning (AAM,FIMM). Provisions are those conditions that need to be satisfied or actions that must be performed before a decision is taken [6]. A provision is as a pre-condition; it is responsibility of the user to ensure that a request is sent in an environment satisfying all the pre-conditions. The non-satisfaction of a provision implies a request to the user to perform some actions.

Federation (FM,FIMM). The concept of *federation* is strictly related to the concept of *trust*. A user should be able to select the services that she wants to federate and de-federate to protect her privacy and to select the services to which she will disclose her own authorization assertions.

C.I.M. (Centralized Identity Management) (AAM,FIMM). The centralization of authentication and authorization mechanisms and, more generally, the centralization of identity management implies a simplification of the user profile management task. User profiles should be maintained within the SSO server thus removing such a burden from local administrators. This allows a reduction of user-profile administration cost and time and improves administrators' control on user profiles and authorization policies.

Client Status Info (AAM,FM,FIMM). The SSO system architecture implies the exchange of user information between SSO server and services to fulfill authentication and authorization processes. In particular, when the two entities communicate, they have to be synchronized on what concern the user identity; privacy and security issues need to be addressed. Different solutions of this problem could be adopted involving either the transport (e.g. communication can be encrypted) or the application layer.

Single Point of Control (AAM). The main objectives of a SSO implementation are to provide a unique access control point for users who want to request a service, and, for applications, to delegate some features from business components to an authentication server. This point of control should be unique to clearly separate the authentication point from business implementations, avoiding the replication and the ad-hoc implementation of authentication mechanisms for each domain. Note that every service provider will eventually develop its own authentication mechanism.

Standard Compliance (AAM,FM,FIMM). It is important for a wide range of applications to support well-known and reliable protocols to make possible communication and integration between different environments. In a SSO scenario, there are protocols for exchanging messages between authentication servers and service providers, and between technologies, within the same system, that can be different. Hence, every entity can use standard technologies (e.g. X.509, SAML for expressing and exchanging authentication information and SOAP for data transmission) to interoperate with different environments.

Cross-Language availability (AAM,FM,FIMM). The widespread adoption of the global Internet as an infrastructure for accessing services has consequently influenced the definition of different languages/technologies used to develop these applications. In this scenario, a requisite of paramount importance is the development of SSO solutions that permit the integration of service implementations based on different languages, without substantial changes to service code. The first step in this direction is the adoption of standard communication protocols based on XML.

Password Proliferation Prevention (AAM,FM,FIMM). A well-known motivation for the adoption of SSO systems is the prevention of password proliferation so to improve security and simplify user log-on actions and system profile management.

Scalability (AAM,FM,FIMM). An important requirement for SSO systems is to support and correctly manage a continuous growth of users and subdomains that rely on them, without substantial changes to system architecture.

4 Our Solution: CAS++

We have developed our open source SSO system with the goal of addressing the AAM requirements identified in the previous section by properly extending an existing open source SSO implementation, named *Central Authentication Service* (CAS) [5, 8]. In this section, we briefly describe CAS and then illustrate our solution, called *CAS++*, developed as an extension to CAS. Note that, CAS++ is not the only implementation available on the Net. In particular, *SourceID* [21], an Open Source implementation of the SSO Liberty Alliance, *Java Open Single Sign-On* (JOSSO) [15], and *Shibboleth* [19] stand out as the most complete available SSO solutions.

4.1 Central Authentication Service (CAS)

Central Authentication Service (CAS) [5, 8] is an open source framework developed by Yale University and implements a SSO mechanism to provide a *Centralized Authentication* to a single server and *HTTP redirections*. CAS authentication model is loosely based on classic Kerberos-style authentication. When an unauthenticated user sends a service request, this request is redirected from the application to the authentication server (CAS Server), and then back to the application after the user has been authenticated. The CAS Server is therefore the only entity that manages passwords to authenticate users and transmits and certifies their identities. The information is forwarded by the authentication server to the application during redirections by using session cookies (see data flow in Figure 2).

CAS is composed of pure-Java servlets running over any servlet engine and provides a very basic web-based authentication service. In particular, its major security features are:

1. passwords travel from browsers to the authentication server via an encrypted channel;
2. re-authentications are transparent to users if they accept a single cookie, called *Ticket Granting Cookie* (TGC). This cookie is opaque (i.e., TGC contains no personal information), protected (it uses SSL) and private (it is only presented to the CAS server);
3. applications know the user's identity through an opaque one-time Service Ticket (ST) created and authenticated by the CAS Server, which contains the result of a hash function applied to a randomly generated value.

Also, CAS credentials are *proxiable*. At start-up, distributed applications get a *Proxy-Granting Ticket* (PGT) from CAS When the application needs access to a resource, it uses the PGT to get a proxy ticket (PT). Then, the application sends the PT to a back-end application. The back-end application confirms the PT with CAS, and also gains information about who proxied the authentication. This mechanism allows "proxy" authentication for Web portals, letting users to authenticate securely to untrusted sites (e.g., student-run sites and third-party vendors) without supplying a password. CAS works seamlessly with existing Kerberos authentication infrastructures and can be used by nearly any Web-application development environment (JSP, Servlets, ASP, Perl, mod_perl, PHP, Python, PL/SQL, and so forth) or as a server-wide Apache module. Also, it is freely available from Yale University (with source code).

4.2 CAS++

We developed an open source SSO system, called CAS++, based on the use of identity certificates and fully integrated with the JBoss security layer. Our solution integrates the CAS system with the authentication mechanism implemented by a Public Key Infrastructure (PKI). CAS++ implements a fully multi-domain stand-alone server that provides a simple, efficient, and reliable SSO mechanism through HTTP redirections, focused on user privacy (opaque cookies) and security protection. CAS++ permits a

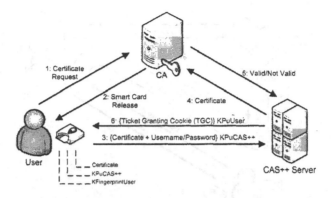

Fig. 1. CAS++ certificate-based authentication flow.

centralized management of user profiles granting access to all services in the system with a unique pair username/password. The profiles repository is stored inside the SSO server application and is the only point where users credentials/profiles are accessed, thus reducing information scattering. In our implementation, services do not need an authentication layer because this feature is managed by CAS++ itself.

CAS++ relies on standard protocols such as SSL, for secure communications between the parties, and X.509 digital certificates for credentials exchange. Besides being a "pure-Java" module like its predecessor, CAS++ is a fully J2EE compliant application integrable with services coded with every web-based implementation language. It enriches the traditional CAS authentication process through the integration of biometric identification (by fingerprints readers) and smart card technologies in addition to traditional username/password mechanism, enabling two authentication levels. Our strong authentication process flow is composed of the following steps (see Figure 1):[4]

1. the user requests an identity certificate to the CA (Certification Authority);
2. the user receives from the CA a smart card that contains a X.509 identity certificate, signed with the private key of the CA, that certifies the user identity. The corresponding user private key is encrypted with a symmetric algorithm (e.g., 3DES) and the key contained inside the smart card can be decrypted only with a key represented by user fingerprint (KFingerprintUser)[14];
3. to access a service the public key certificate, along with the pair username/password, is encrypted with the CAS++ public key (KPuCAS++) and sent to CAS++;
4. CAS++ decrypts the certificate with its private key, verifies the signature on the certificate with the CA public key, and verifies the validity of this certificate by interacting with the CA;
5. CAS++ retrieves from the CA information about the validity of the user certificate encrypted with KPuCAS++;

---

[4] Note that, the first two actions are performed only once when the user requests the smart card along with an identity certificate.

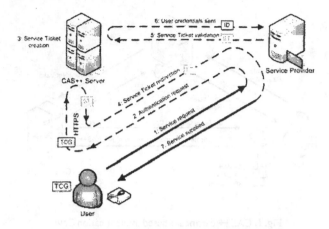

Fig. 2. CAS++ information flow for service request evaluation.

6. if the certificate is valid, CAS++ extracts the information related to the user, creates the ticket (TGC, Ticket Granting Cookie) and returns it to the user encrypted with the public key of the user (KPuUser). At this point, to decrypts the TGC, the user must retrieve the private key stored inside the smart card by mean of her fingerprint. As soon as the card is unlocked, the private key is extracted and the TGC decrypted. This ticket will be used for every further access, in the same session, to any application managed by the CAS++ Single Sign-On server.

At this point, for every further access in the session, the user can be authenticated by the service providing only the received TGC without any additional authentication action.[5]

The service access flow, that takes place over secure channels and is similar to the one in CAS, is composed of the following steps (see Figure 2):

1. the user, via a web browser, requests access to the service provider;
2. the service provider requests authentication information through a HTTP redirection to the CAS++ Server;
3. the CAS++ Server retrieves the user TGC and the service requested URL. If the user has been previously authenticated by CAS++ and has the privilege to access the service a Service Ticket is created;
4. the CAS++ Server redirects the user browser to the requested service along with the ST;
5. service receives the ST and check its validity sending it to the CAS++ Server;
6. if the ST is valid the CAS++ Server sends to the Service an XML file with User's credentials;
7. the user gains the access.

---

[5] Note that the TGC lifetime should be relatively short to avoid conflicts with the CA's certificate revocation process, which could cause unauthorized accesses.

Table 2. Evaluation of CAS++ with respect to the requirements of the AAM model.

Requirement	CAS++
Authentication	yes
Strong Authentication	yes
Authorization	yes
Provisioning	planned
C.I.M. (Centralized Identity Management)	yes
Client Status Info	yes (opaque)
Single Point of Control	yes
Standard Compliance	partial (HTTP, SSL, X.509)
Cross-Language Availability	yes
Password Proliferation Prevention	yes
Scalability	planned

4.3 Evaluating CAS++ Against the AAM Requirements

CAS++ is based on the Authentication and Authorization Model. Table 4.3 reports the results of the evaluation of CAS++. As it is visible from this table, CAS++ fulfills most of AAM requirements; it provides a central point of control to manage authentication, authorization, and user profiles.[6] Furthermore, CAS++ enriches the traditional CAS authentication process with the integration of biometric identification (via fingerprints readers) and smart card technologies and it is planned to include provisioning features in future releases. Note that, the lower level of CAS++ system is language independent and relies on traditional established standards, such as HTTP, SSL and X.509, without adopting emerging ones, such as SOAP and SAML. Finally, focusing on client status info, all communications between user browser, services providers and authentication server in CAS++ scenario are managed by the exchange of opaque cookies and by the use of encrypted channels.

5 A Case Study: the Pitagora Project

The increasing usage of GSM mobile phones and the upcoming of a new generation of mobile system (called third-generation or 3G) have lead to the development of applications that manage the mobile network and provide new services to users. In this scenario, every network technician that has to use multiple parallel services must manage several pairs username/password, raising all the problems discussed in the previous sections of this paper. In particular, the adoption of SSO, with strong authentication mechanisms through smart card and fingerprint readers, allows also the restriction of simultaneous multi-accesses for security reasons; in our scenario, in fact, we manage very sensitive data and, in some cases, we want to avoid any kind of data correlation.

---

[6] The centralization of users profiles affects system scalability. A solution that provides a balance between centralization and scalability needs is under study.

Focusing on this scenario, we show a case study example that involved our SSO implementation integrated with the research and development project "Pitagora", carried out by our group in cooperation with Siemens Mobile. Currently, the Pitagora Project is composed of the following applications:

Web-based MultiProtocol User Interface (IMW): is the application tool that provides and controls the access to OMC (Operation and Maintenance Center) system requested by users/ technicians. In particular, users are able to manage, configure, and check OMC mobile network using different technologies and devices, such as traditional PCs/laptops, PDAs, mobile phones. Hence, IMW manages all the communication process between users and OMC system, through different technologies as web browser and HTTP/HTTPS protocol, WAP browser, SMS. IMW keeps network technicians up-to-date on the network state, notifying alarms and warnings, at which the users are previously registered, happened on the supervised network.

Geo-location Applications (i-Geo): is the application involved in the geo-location of the customers mobile [2]. In particular, our solution locates mobile phones taking into account real and estimated path-loss with all information that can be extracted from a GIS map of the interested area rather than compute the mobile position only through real and estimated path-loss as in classical approaches.

Geographical Electromagnetic Field Information System (GEMFIS): is an open source application used to monitor the network usage focusing on maximizing performance and checking electric pollution levels, in accordance with the current legislation. GEMFIS includes functionalities for storing, displaying and managing environmental data.

In the scenario depicted above, without a SSO solution, the technicians that wished to access Pitagora's tools had to manage several username/password pairs and log-on separately to each service. The adoption of CAS++ solution has brought several advantages. In current Pitagora's architecture, individual services are not stand-alone modules, each with its own access control layer; rather, they are fully integrated in a single security domain. Technicians needing to use multiple applications can perform a single log-on operation and all profile information requested by the application is transparently provided by CAS++. The adoption of CAS++ also improved user profile management, since our profiles repository and administration point are fully integrated within CAS++. Another important requirement fulfilled by CAS++ is strong authentication, a fundamental aspect in our scenario. Finally, CAS++ allowed Siemens developers to freely choose the programming language used to implement individual services.

6 Conclusions

We described some trust models representing different systems behaviors and goals for Single Sign-On services, and identified the requirements that an open source Single Sign-On solution should satisfy. We then illustrated our open source SSO system, called CAS++ and its application to a real case study. Issues to be investigated include an extension of CAS++ to fully support the requirements of a full identity management model.

Acknowledgments

We thank the anonymous reviewers and Tuomas Aura for comments and suggestions which considerably improved the paper. This work was supported in part by the European Union within the PRIME Project in the FP6/IST Programme under contract IST-2002-507591 and by the Italian MIUR within the KIWI and MAPS projects.

References

1. M. Anisetti, V. Bellandi, E. Damiani, M. Montel, and S. Reale. Open Source Electromagnetic Field Monitoring as e-Government Service. *Proc. of the International Symposium on Telecommunications*, Shiraz, Iran, September 2005.
2. M. Anisetti, V. Bellandi, E. Damiani, and S. Reale. Localize and tracking of mobile antenna in urban environment. *Proc. of the International Symposium on Telecommunications*, Shiraz, Iran, September 2005.
3. C.A. Ardagna, E. Damiani, S. De Capitani di Vimercati, and P. Samarati. Towards Privacy-Enhanced Authorization Policies and Languages. *Proc. of the 19th IFIP WG11.3 Working Conference on Data and Application Security*, Nathan Hale Inn, University of Connecticut, Storrs, USA, August 2005.
4. C.A. Ardagna, E. Damiani, F. Frati, and M. Montel. Using Open Source Middleware for Securing e-Gov Applications. *Proc. of the First International Conference on Open Source Systems (OSS 2005)*, Genova, Italy.
5. P. Aubry, V. Mathieu, and J. Marchal. ESUP-Portal: open source Single Sign-On with CAS (Central Authentication Service). *Proc. of EUNIS04 - IT Innovation in a Changing World*, Bled (Slovenia), July 2004
6. C. Bettini, S. Jajodia, X. Sean Wang, and D. Wijesekera. Provisions and obligations in Policy Management and Security Applications. *Proc. of the 28th VLDB Conference*, Honk Kong, China, 2002.
7. D.A. Buell, and R. Sandhu. Identity Management. *IEEE Internet Computing*, November-December 2003.
8. Central Authentication Service, http://jasigch.princeton.edu:9000/display/CAS
9. A. Corallo, M. Cremonini, E. Damiani, S. De Capitani di Vimercati, G. Elia, and P. Samarati. Security, Privacy, and Trust in Mobile Systems. *Mobile and Wireless Systems Beyond 3G: Managing New Business Opportunities*, Idea Group Inc., (2005).
10. S. De Capitani di Vimercati, and P. Samarati. *Access control: Policies, models, and mechanisms*, Foundations of Security Analysis and Design, 2001.
11. J. De Clercq. Single sign-on architectures. *International Conference on Infrastructure Security (InfraSec 2002)*, Bristol, UK, October 2002.
12. S. Feldman. The Changing Face of e-Commerce. *IEEE Internet Computing*, 4(3):82–84, May/June (2000).
13. B. Galbraith et al. Professional Web Services Security. Wrox Press, 2002.
14. F. Hao, R. Anderson, and J. Daugman. Combining cryptography with biometrics effectively. Technical report, Cambridge University - Computer Laboratory Technical Report UCAM-CL-TR-640.
15. Java Open Single Sign-On (JOSSO), http://www.josso.org/.
16. R. Khosla, E. Damiani, and W. Grosky. Human-Centered E-Business. Kluwer Academic Publishers, Massachusetts, USA, 315 pages, April 2003.
17. Liberty Alliance Project, http://www.projectliberty.org/

18. PRIME (Privacy and Identity Management for Europe), http://www.prime-project.eu.org.
19. Shibboleth Project, http://shibboleth.internet2.edu/.
20. Single Sign-On, The Open Group, http://www.opengroup.org/security/sso/.
21. SourceID Open Source Federated Identity Management, http://www.sourceid.org/index.html

A Synchronous Multi-Party Contract Signing Protocol Improving Lower Bound of Steps

Jianying Zhou[1], Jose A. Onieva[2], and Javier Lopez[2]

[1] Institute for Infocomm Research
21 Heng Mui Keng Terrace, Singapore 119613
jyzhou@i2r.a-star.edu.sg
[2] Computer Science Department
University of Malaga
29071 - Malaga, Spain
{onieva,jlm}@lcc.uma.es

Abstract. Contract signing is a fundamental service in doing business. The Internet has facilitated the electronic commerce, and it is necessary to find appropriate mechanisms for contract signing in the digital world. A number of two-party contract signing protocols have been proposed with various features. Nevertheless, in some applications, a contract may need to be signed by multiple parties. Less research has been done on multi-party contract signing. In this paper, we propose a new synchronous multi-party contract signing protocol that, with n parties, it reaches a lower bound of $3(n-1)$ steps in the all-honest case and $4n-2$ steps in the worst case (i.e., all parties contact the trusted third party). This is so far the most efficient synchronous multi-party contract signing protocol in terms of the number of messages required. We further consider the additional features like timeliness and abuse-freeness in the improved version.

1 Introduction

The Internet has facilitated the electronic commerce. Many business transactions have been shifted to the Internet. The motivation for such a trend is the efficiency and cost-saving. However, as new risks may arise in the digital world, sufficient security measures should be taken. This will help users to establish the confidence for doing business on the Internet.

Contract signing is a fundamental service for business transactions, and has been well practiced in the traditional paper-based business model. Now, it is necessary to find appropriate mechanisms for contract signing in the digital world. Consider several parties on a computer network who wish to exchange some digital items but do not trust each other to behave honestly. *Fair exchange* is a problem of exchanging data in a way that guarantees either all participants obtain what they want, or none does. From a designing point of view, contract signing is a particular form of fair exchange, in which the parties exchange commitments to a contract (typically, a text string spelling out the terms of a deal). That is, a contract is a non-repudiable agreement on a given text such that after a contract signing protocol instance, either *each* signer can prove the

Please use the following format when citing this chapter:

Author(s) [insert Last name, First-name initial(s)], 2006, in IFIP International Federation for Information Processing, Volume 201, Security and Privacy in Dynamic Environments, eds. Fischer-Hubner, S., Rannenberg, K., Yngstrom, L., Lindskog, S., (Boston: Springer), pp. [insert page numbers].

agreement to any verifier *or none* of them can. If several signers are involved, then it is a *multi-party contract signing* (MPCS) protocol.

There are some two-party contract signing protocols in the literature. Nevertheless, less research has been done on multi-party contract signing. In this paper, we propose a new synchronous multi-party contract signing protocol that, with n parties, it reaches a lower bound of $3(n - 1)$ steps in the all-honest case and $4n - 2$ steps in the worst case (i.e., all parties contact the trusted third party). This is so far the most efficient synchronous multi-party contract signing protocol in terms of the number of messages required. We further consider the additional features like timeliness and abuse-freeness in the improved version.

The rest of this paper is organized as follows. In Section 2, we review the previous work related to contract signing, outline the properties to be satisfied when designing an optimistic contract signing protocol, and give explicit definitions for some terms used along the descriptions of these protocols. In Section 3, we describe a simple synchronous protocol for multi-party contract signing, then improve the simple version to an optimal multi-party contract signing protocol. After that, we further consider the additional features like timeliness and abuse-freeness in Section 4, and conclude the paper in Section 5.

2   Related Work

As contract signing is a particular case of fair exchange, any fair exchange protocol found in the literature in which digital signatures are exchanged can be considered as the related work. In all practical schemes, contract signing involves an additional player, called *trusted third party* (TTP). This party is (at least to some extent) trusted to behave correctly, thus playing the role of a notary in paper-based contract signing and somehow sharing the legal duties the former ones have. In fact, designing and implementing a contract signing protocol using an on-line TTP should not be a complicated task. In this case, if Alice and Bob wish to enter into a contract, they each sign a copy of the contract and send it to the TTP through a secure channel. The TTP will forward the signed contracts only when it has received valid signatures from both Alice and Bob.

Nevertheless, in our continuous search for speeding up our daily life activities, it is desirable not using a TTP in a contract signing protocol. Additionally, if the TTP is not involved, the notary fee could be avoided. Some protocols appear in the literature trying to eliminate the TTP's involvement using *gradual exchange* of signatures [9, 10]. But these solutions are not deterministic, thus may not be accepted by signatories. Our objective is to focus on contract signing protocols that necessarily use a TTP only in those cases in which an exception occurs (i.e., a network communication failure or a dishonest party's misbehavior). Otherwise (all-honest-case), the TTP will not be contacted, and parties will bring the protocol to its end by themselves. In the literature, these protocols are called *optimistic contract signing* protocols [2–4, 14–17].

Some properties extracted from the different previous work on optimistic contract signing are summarized as follows.

- *Effectiveness* - if each party behaves correctly, the TTP will not be involved in the protocol.

- *Fairness* - no party will be in an advantageous situation at the end of the protocol.
- *Timeliness* - any party can decide when to finish a protocol run without loosing fairness.
- *Non-repudiation* - no party can deny its action.
- *Verifiability of TTP* - if the TTP misbehaves, all harmed parties will be able to prove it.
- *Transparency of TTP* - if the TTP is contacted to resolve the protocol, the resulting contract will be similar to the one obtained in case the TTP is not involved.
- *Abuse-Freeness* - it is not possible for an attacker (either a legitimate participant or an outsider) to show a third party that the contract final state is under its control.

In [8], Ben-Or *et al.* presented an optimistic contract signing protocol based on a *probabilistic approach*. Such a contract signing protocol is said to be (ν, ϵ)-fair if for any contract C, when signer A follows the protocol properly, if the probability that signer B is privileged to validate the contract with the TTP's help is greater than ν, the conditional probability that "A is not privileged", given that "B is privileged", is at most ϵ.

Previous work in which several signatories are involved in a contract can be found in [1, 6, 11, 12]. Only Asokan *et al.* addressed the MPCS problem in synchronous networks [1]. As they stated, this solution clearly improves the efficiency of those asynchronous protocols previously presented with respect to the number of messages; $4(n - 1)$ messages in the all-honest-case and $6n - 4$ messages in the worst case. This is possible due to a better reliability of the underlaying network as we can see in Definition 1 below.

Some authors considered the abuse-freeness property in [7, 13]. Baum-Waidner proposed new protocols in [6] that improve the solutions presented for asynchronous networks in [7] such that the number of rounds is significantly reduced in the case that the number of dishonest participants t is considerably less than the total number of participants n - the smaller t is, the better results the new protocols achieve.

Definition 1. *A "synchronous" contract signing protocol is used in synchronous networks in which there is a limited time for a message to reach its destination (otherwise it has been lost and the appropriate transport layer manages these events) even if an attack occurs. Thus a party can determine that a message has not been sent by other party if it did not arrive within the limited time. Users' clocks are assumed to be synchronized.*

Definition 2. *An "asynchronous" contract signing protocol is used in asynchronous networks in which there is no limited time for a message to reach its destination. Loss and unsorted arrival of messages are possible and have to be managed by the contract signing protocol itself. Clocks are not assumed to be synchronized among users.*

A number of protocols exist in the literature which use an asynchronous model of network (i.e., messages can be reordered and lost) with deadline parameters. But when a deadline is introduced, and thus, synchronized clocks among users are assumed (at least when the deadline is approaching), these protocols are converted into synchronous protocols.

In the literature, MPCS protocols make use of either a ring or a matrix topology. Throughout these solutions, authors use the terms *round* and *step* without clearly defining them, which often brings on confusion with respect to the metric to be used for its efficiency evaluation. For this reason we explicitly define these terms as follows:

- *Round* is understood as the existing time slot in which messages are distributed in synchronous networks. In asynchronous networks, the entities need to wait for a local timeout before going to the next round (in case the round is not completed).
- *Step* refers to the action of sending or receiving a message. It is the operation performed by a participating entity. Each round means one step (when all the messages from all entities are distributed or broadcasted in the same time slot, usually in matrix topologies) or several steps (when messages from the same round are distributed from one entity to another, usually in ring topologies).

Some confusion exists in the literature with respect to the term 'round'. Some authors explain that when the next message to be sent depends on the previous one, that is a different round. But we claim two different cases can be found (1) message to be sent depends on the previous one because the entity needs to compute/verify it before sending the next one or (2) message to be sent depends on the previous one because there is a distribution order to be respected (as in ring topologies). We consider a round occurs in Case (1).

All of previous solutions to the asynchronous multi-party contract signing problem reach the lower bound on the number of rounds described in Theorem 3 given in [13]:

Any complete and optimistic asynchronous contract-signing protocol with n participants requires at least n rounds in an optimistic run.

Describing the theorem, Garay *et al.* stated that for each party P_i, when it sends a message that can be used (together with other information) by other entities to obtain a valid contract, as the protocol is fair, it must have received in a previous round, a message from the rest of participants in order to be able to get a valid contract too (probably with the TTP's help), no matter how others behave. By an inductive argument, they showed the number of rounds is at least n.

Ferrer's asynchronous protocol presented in [11] with only three rounds is an exception. It claimed to use a number of rounds independent from the number of participants. However, the protocol is flawed [18].

In our proposal to be presented below, we use a synchronous model, in which we assume messages sent among participants can be lost in the network, but a message from a participant reaches the TTP in a finite and known amount of time. Attackers can insert, delete and modify messages, but it is assumed that attackers cannot break the clock synchronization of the network and cannot forge digital signatures. Under this model, the number of rounds can be made independent of the number of participants.

3   A New Synchronous MPCS Protocol

Here we first present a simple synchronous protocol for multi-party contract signing. As stated before, the only protocol in a synchronous model that we can compare with is Asokan's approach [1]. Our approach is also based on two differentiated phases: a promise to sign, and a real signature that a party releases only after receiving all promises from the rest of participants. Again, in the same manner, we reach a lower bound of $4(n-1)$ steps in the all-honest case and $5n-3$ steps in the worst case that all parties contact the TTP. This result will be further improved in the optimal version by reducing the number of steps to $3(n-1)$ in the all-honest case and $4n-2$ in the worst case.

3.1   A Simple Version

Let us consider the following simple solution which uses verifiable encryption of signatures based on a ring architecture for achieving *transparency* of the TTP. Assume that the channel between any participant and the TTP is functional and not disrupted. The following notation is used in the protocol description.

- $C = [M, P, id, t]$: a contract text M to be signed by each party $P_i \in P (i = 1, \cdots, n)$, a unique identifier id for the protocol run, and a deadline t agreed by all parties to contact the TTP.
- $e_P(X)$: encryption of message X with P's public key.
- $S_P(X)$: P's digital signature on X.
- $Cert_i$: a certificate with which anyone can verify that the ciphertext is the correct signature of the plaintext, and can be decrypted by the TTP (see CEMBS - *Certificate of an Encrypted Message Being a Signature* in [5]).

A simple linear protocol for multi-party contract signing is sketched as follows:

1.	$P_1 \to P_2$	: $m_1[= C, e_{TTP}(S_{P_1}(C)), Cert_1]$
2.	$P_2 \to P_3$	: $m_1, m_2[= C, e_{TTP}(S_{P_2}(C)), Cert_2]$
$n-1.$	$P_{n-1} \to P_n$	: $m_1, .., m_{n-1}[= C, e_{TTP}(S_{P_{n-1}}(C)), Cert_{n-1}]$
$n.$	$P_n \to P_{n-1}$	: $m_n[= C, e_{TTP}(S_{P_n}(C)), Cert_n]$
$n+1.$	$P_{n-1} \to P_{n-2}$	: m_{n-1}, m_n
$2(n-1).$	$P_2 \to P_1$	: $m_2, m_3, .., m_n$
$2n-1.$	$P_1 \to P_2$	: $S_{P_1}(C)$
$2n.$	$P_2 \to P_3$	: $S_{P_1}(C), S_{P_2}(C)$
$3(n-1).$	$P_{n-1} \to P_n$	: $S_{P_1}(C), S_{P_2}(C), .., S_{P_{n-1}}(C)$
$3n-2.$	$P_n \to P_{n-1}$	: $S_{P_n}(C)$
$3n-1.$	$P_{n-1} \to P_{n-2}$	: $S_{P_{n-1}}(C), S_{P_n}(C)$
$4(n-1).$	$P_2 \to P_1$	: $S_{P_2}(C), S_{P_3}(C), .., S_{P_n}(C)$

The above main protocol is divided into two phases. The parties first exchange their commitments in an "in-and-out" manner. Note that P_1 can choose t in the first message (and others can halt if they do not agree). Only after the first phase is finished at step

$2(n - 1)$, the final signatures are exchanged. Following this simple approach, only $4(n - 1)$ steps are needed.

If there is no exception (e.g., network failure or misbehaving party), the protocol will not need the TTP's help. Otherwise, the following resolve sub-protocol helps to drive the contract signing process to its end. P_i can contact the TTP before the deadline t.

1. $P_i \rightarrow TTP : resolve_{P_i} = C, m_1, .., m_n, S_{P_i}(C, m_1, .., m_n)$
2. TTP : IF $resolve_{P_i}$ is received before t THEN
            decrypts $m_1..m_n$
            publishes $S_{P_1}(C), .., S_{P_n}(C)$

If the main protocol is not completed successfully, some parties may not hold all the commitments $(m_1, .., m_n)$. Then, they just wait until the deadline t and check with the TTP whether the contract has been resolved by other parties. If not, the contract is cancelled. Otherwise, they get the valid contract $(S_{P_1}(C), .., S_{P_n}(C))$ from the TTP.

If a party has all the commitments when the main protocol is terminated abnormally, it could initiate the above sub-protocol. Then the TTP will help to resolve the contract if the request is received before the deadline t, and the contract will be available to all the participants (even after the deadline t). After the deadline, the TTP will not accept such requests any more. In other words, the status of the contract will be determined the latest by the deadline t.

3.2 Security Analysis

Here we informally analyze our protocol regarding the security properties outlined in Section 2.

- *Effectiveness*: If all parties send all the needed messages correctly, the TTP will not have to decrypt any commitment since after the $4(n - 1)$ steps all parties have the contract signed (with n signatures).
- *Fairness*: No party will be in an advantageous situation at the end of the protocol. That is, either all of them possess the contract (or have access to it), or none of them obtains it.
- *Timeliness*: The status of a contract will be finalized either at the end of the main protocol or the latest by a pre-defined deadline t. As the participants not holding all the commitments cannot determine the status of the contract before the deadline t, the property of timeliness is not satisfied. We will further discuss timeliness in Section 4.2.
- *Non-repudiation*: No party can deny its action since each message it sent bears its digital signature.
- *Transparency of TTP*: We use a cryptographic primitive (CEMBS), which allows the users to verify that a bit string is actually the encryption (with the TTP's public key) of the sender's digital signature over the contract C. If the TTP is invoked, it only decrypts the digital signatures and makes them available to all participants. Therefore, after a successful protocol instance, no evidence of the TTP's participation exists.

- *Verifiability of TTP*: Let us identify the possible dishonest behaviors of the TTP: (1) the TTP simply does not reply to participants' requests, or replies with invalid messages; (2) the TTP resolves the protocol but does not publish the contract.

  In the first case, some parties could be beneficiated if they got the contract from the main protocol while others did not. A possible solution is using multiple TTPs and a secure media storage. TTPs have only the write privilege over the media storage but do not control it while participants in the contract signing protocol have only the read privilege over the media storage. A participant can multi-cast his request to the TTPs before the deadline t. As long as one of the TTPs does not misbehave, the correct response will be available from the secure media storage.

  In the second case, the TTP could collude with some parties and resolve the contract for them but does not publish the contract for other parties. That means some parties not holding all the commitments will not get the valid contract. To detect the TTP's cheating, the TTP is required to sign the contract when it is resolved, but this overrides the TTP's transparency. It is difficult to reach a trade-off between transparency and verifiability.

- *Abuse-freeness*: In our protocol, the last participant (P_n) in the ring can decide whether to resolve the protocol after receiving all the commitments from other parties However, as stated in [7] it is not possible to avoid this participant to control whether the normal flow of the protocol continues or not, but all we can aim to is to avoid that it is able to provide evidence to an outsider about its control over the result of the contract. So, for P_n holding $m_1, \cdots, m_{n-1}$, due to the presence of $Cert_i$ in m_i that anyone can verify, it is possible for P_n to *abuse* about the state of the contract. Nevertheless, we show in Section 4.1 that the property of abuse-freeness can be achieved.

3.3 An Optimal Version

The protocol in Section 3.1 has two clearly differentiated phases: exchange of commitments and exchange of digital signatures. The number of steps can be further reduced if we send more available information at each step and thus merge both phases. This will result in an improvement to the previous simple version protocol.

Using the same notation, an optimal synchronous protocol for multi-party contract signing is outlined as follows:

$$
\begin{array}{lll}
1. & P_1 \to P_2 & : m_1[= C, e_{TTP}(S_{P_1}(C)), Cert_1] \\
2. & P_2 \to P_3 & : m_1, m_2[= C, e_{TTP}(S_{P_2}(C)), Cert_2] \\
n-1. & P_{n-1} \to P_n & : m_1, .., m_{n-1}[= C, e_{TTP}(S_{P_{n-1}}(C)), Cert_{n-1}] \\
n. & P_n \to P_{n-1} & : m_n[= C, e_{TTP}(S_{P_n}(C)), Cert_n], S_{P_n}(C) \\
n+1. & P_{n-1} \to P_{n-2} & : m_{n-1}, m_n, S_{P_{n-1}}(C), S_{P_n}(C) \\
2(n-1). & P_2 \to P_1 & : m_2, m_3, .., m_n, S_{P_2}(C), S_{P_3}(C), .., S_{P_n}(C) \\
2n-1. & P_1 \to P_2 & : S_{P_1}(C) \\
2n. & P_2 \to P_3 & : S_{P_1}(C), S_{P_2}(C) \\
3(n-1). & P_{n-1} \to P_n & : S_{P_1}(C), S_{P_2}(C), .., S_{P_{n-1}}(C)
\end{array}
$$

The resolve sub-protocol used by participants to request the TTP's help is the same as presented in Section 3.1. Note that even though the two phases are merged, no party releases its plaintext signature of the contract without having first received all the commitments. If any party decides to quit after releasing its plaintext signature of the contract, the rest of participants can obtain the plaintext signatures of the contract with the TTP's help. As the protocol is similar to the previous one, the same security properties are fulfilled.

This optimal version permits overlapping the dispatch of promises with real signatures without loosing fairness. It improves the simple version presented in Section 3.1 by reducing the number of steps to $3(n-1)$ in the all-honest case and $4n-2$ in the worst case. Note that for $n=2$, three messages are sufficient, as shown in [17].

4 Further Discussions

The MPCS protocol presented in the previous section improved the lower bound of steps. However, as we pointed out in the security analysis that it does not satisfy the properties of abuse-freeness and timeliness. Here we further improve our MPCS protocol to address these properties.

4.1 Achieving Abuse-Freeness

Although it is not possible to force a participant to keep on following the steps of the protocol, we can design the protocol in such a manner that it has no way to demonstrate to an outsider the contract is under its control. For this purpose, we use a *blind commitment* that only the TTP can verify. With this concept of design in mind, we modify the previous protocol to eliminate the *illustrative* information. The main protocol remains the same, but $Cert_i$ is not included in m_i. Instead, the evidence of origin of the blind commitment $Commit_i$ is generated:

$$Commit_i = S_{P_i}(h(C), e_{TTP}(S_{P_i}(C)))$$

where $h(C)$ is the hash value of C to be used to establish a unique link between $Commit_i$ and C.

1.	$P_1 \rightarrow P_2$	$: m_1[= C, e_{TTP}(S_{P_1}(C)), Commit_1]$
2.	$P_2 \rightarrow P_3$	$: m_1, m_2[= C, e_{TTP}(S_{P_2}(C)), Commit_2]$
$n-1$.	$P_{n-1} \rightarrow P_n$	$: m_1, .., m_{n-1}[= C, e_{TTP}(S_{P_{n-1}}(C)), Commit_{n-1}]$
n.	$P_n \rightarrow P_{n-1}$	$: m_n[= C, e_{TTP}(S_{P_n}(C)), Commit_n], S_{P_n}(C)$
$n+1$.	$P_{n-1} \rightarrow P_{n-2}$	$: m_{n-1}, m_n, S_{P_{n-1}}(C), S_{P_n}(C)$
$2(n-1)$.	$P_2 \rightarrow P_1$	$: m_2, m_3, .., m_n, S_{P_2}(C), S_{P_3}(C), .., S_{P_n}(C)$
$2n-1$.	$P_1 \rightarrow P_2$	$: S_{P_1}(C)$
$2n$.	$P_2 \rightarrow P_3$	$: S_{P_1}(C), S_{P_2}(C)$
$3(n-1)$.	$P_{n-1} \rightarrow P_n$	$: S_{P_1}(C), S_{P_2}(C), .., S_{P_{n-1}}(C)$

Note each party needs to check whether all the blind commitments it has received are valid before releasing its real signature of the contract. A *valid* blind commitment $Commit_i$ means it is from P_i (by checking its signature), linked to C (by checking $h(C)$), but does not guarantee that $e_{TTP}(S_{P_i}(C))$ in $Commit_i$ matches $S_{P_i}(C)$. $Commit_i$ is *correct* if it is valid and also matches $S_{P_i}(C)$.

If there is no exception (e.g., network failure or misbehaving party), the protocol will not need the TTP's help. Otherwise, a modified resolve sub-protocol helps to drive the contract signing process to its end. P_i can contact the TTP before the deadline t.

1. $P_i \rightarrow TTP : resolve_{P_i} = C, m_1, .., m_n, S_{P_i}(C, m_1, .., m_n)$
2. TTP : IF $resolve_{P_i}$ is received before t
         AND all $Commit_i$ are valid THEN
         decrypts & verifies $m_1..m_n$
         IF $S_{P_1}(C), .., S_{P_n}(C)$ ok THEN
         publishes $S_{P_1}(C), .., S_{P_n}(C)$
         ELSE IF $P_i \notin group_f$
         publishes $fail, group_f, S_{TTP}(fail, C, group_f)$

When a party holding all the *valid* blind commitments initiates the above sub-protocol, the TTP will help to resolve the contract if the request is received before the deadline t. The TTP decrypts and verifies $m_1, \cdots, m_n$. If they are all correct, the TTP will publish $S_{P_1}(C), \cdots, S_{P_n}(C)$. Otherwise, the TTP will invalidate the contract by publishing a *fail* token $S_{TTP}(fail, C, group_f)$ where $group_f$ indicates the parties misbehaved in generating their commitments.

The dispute resolution process is changed when the *fail* token is introduced. If a party can show this token, the contract is invalid. Therefore, at the end of the main protocol, each party needs to check whether $e_{TTP}(S_{P_i}(C))$ in $Commit_i$ matches $S_{P_i}(C)$ for $i = 1, \cdots, n$ (assuming the encryption algorithm is deterministic). If not, it should initiate the above sub-protocol to get the *fail* token. Note, a party P_i cannot get any advantage by providing different $Commit_i$ in the main protocol and the resolve sub-protocol. If P_i provides correct $Commit_i$ in the main protocol but incorrect $Commit'_i$ in the sub-protocol, P_i will not get the *fail* token, i.e., cannot cancel a protocol instance whose final state is signed. On the other hand, if P_i provides incorrect $Commit_i$ in the main protocol but correct $Commit'_i$ in the sub-protocol, P_i may get the signed contract if other parties did not misbehave in generating their commitments, but any other honest party can initiate the resolve sub-protocol to get the *fail* token, thus the contract is still invalid.

The blind commitment does not allow a participant to demonstrate that the protocol state is under its control. In fact, in this case, getting all m_i does not mean being able to solve the protocol as in previous protocols presented in this paper. Thus it provides an abuse-freeness feature. Proof is straightforward, since there is no point in the protocol in which an entity can ensure, even to itself, that the contract is signed till plaintext signatures are obtained. The solution allows to maintain the same number of steps as the optimal protocol in Section 3.3. Furthermore, the TTP is still transparent in this sub-protocol as the signed contract published by the TTP is the same as obtained in the main protocol.

4.2 Achieving Timeliness

In the previous protocols just presented, a deadline t is selected by the first participant. If other participants disagree with the deadline, they can simply abort the execution of

the protocol. Of course, this deadline could be negotiated among the participants before
the contract signing protocol is initiated.

If the main protocol is not completed successfully, some participants may hold all
the commitments while the others may only hold part of the commitments. For those
holding all the commitments, they have the freedom to either resolve the contract with
the TTP's help before the deadline t, or take no action and just let the contract being
automatically cancelled after the deadline t.

However, for those only holding part of the commitments, they have no options
but only wait until the deadline t to know the status of the contract. Obviously, this
is unfavorable to these participants in term of timeliness. They should also have the
right to decide the status of the contract before the deadline t. As they only hold part of
commitments, they are not able to resolve the contract, so they can only choose to cancel
the contract. (Note that in our "in-and-out" architecture of commitment exchange, for
those participants only holding part of the commitments, even if all of them collaborate,
their combined commitments are still incomplete to resolve the contract.)

Here we present a (j, n)-threshold cancel sub-protocol. As long as there are at least
j out of n participants that wish to cancel the contract before the deadline t, the contract
could be cancelled. The cancel sub-protocol is as follows, where counter records the
number of cancel requests received by the TTP, and $group_c$ records the participants
which made cancel requests. For simplicity of description, it is built based on the main
protocol in Section 3.3 without considering abuse-freeness.

1. $P_i \rightarrow TTP$: $cancel_{P_i} = C, cancel, S_{P_i}(C, cancel)$
2. TTP : IF $cancel_{P_i}$ is received before t
    AND C is not resolved THEN
        stores $cancel_{P_i}$; $group_c = group_c + P_i$;
        $counter + +$;
        IF $counter \geq j$ THEN
            sets C as cancelled
            publishes $cancel, group_c, S_{TTP}(cancel, C, group_c)$

The resolve sub-protocol is modified as follows.

1. $P_i \rightarrow TTP$: $resolve_{P_i} = C, m_1, .., m_n, S_{P_i}(C, m_1, .., m_n)$
2. TTP : IF $resolve_{P_i}$ is received before t
    AND C is not cancelled THEN
        decrypts $m_1..m_n$
        sets C as resolved
        publishes $S_{P_1}(C), .., S_{P_n}(C)$

With the above cancel and resolve sub-protocols, each participant has at least one
option to determine the status of the contract before deadline t if the main protocol is
not completed successfully. Thus timeliness is achieved, and the extent of timeliness
depends on the threshold value j: strong timeliness when $j = 1$, and weak timeliness
when $j = n$.

However, the threshold value j should be selected carefully. If j is too small, a few
parties may collude to invalidate a contract. If j is too big, it might be hard to establish

a valid cancel request among j parties. A possible option is $j = \lceil n/2 \rceil + 1$, with a weak majority to "vote" for the validity of a contract.

In the dispute resolution, the *cancel* token issued by the TTP has the top priority. In other words, if a participant presents the *cancel* token, then the contract is invalid. That implies if there are at least j out of n participants who want to cancel the contract before the deadline, even if they have released their plaintext signatures in the main protocol, they together can still change their mind before that deadline. This is a reasonable scenario in the real world because the situation defined in the contract may change with time, even during the process of contract signing, and each participant wishes to pursue the maximum benefit by taking appropriate actions (resolve or cancel).

As the *cancel* token from the TTP has higher priority than the signed contract, those parties that have got the signed contract in the main protocol may need to double check with the TTP about the status of the contract by the deadline t. (Note that the double check does not mean the involvement of the TTP itself, but just a query to a public file maintained by the TTP.) If they do not want to wait until that deadline, they can send the resolve request to the TTP instead, thus blocking other parties to enable the TTP to issue the *cancel* token.

5 Conclusions

Contract signing is a fundamental service for business transactions. Previous work mainly focused on two-party contract signing. In some applications, however, a contract may need to be signed by multiple parties.

In this paper, we presented a new multi-party contract signing protocol that reaches a lower bound of $3(n-1)$ steps in the all-honest case and $4n-2$ steps in the worst case (i.e., all parties contact the TTP). The result improves the lower bound of $4(n-1)$ steps for the all-honest case and $6n-4$ steps for the worst case in Asokan *et al.*'s protocol [1]. Actually, our protocol is so far the most efficient synchronous multi-party contract signing protocol in terms of the number of messages required.

We further considered the additional features like abuse-freeness and timeliness in our protocol. With no special requirements and more importantly without introducing additional steps in the protocol, we achieved the abuse-freeness property which is very important for contract signing protocols. In addition, by introducing the concept of threshold cancel sub-protocol, we achieved the timeliness property. Achieving the TTP's strong verifiability while keeping its transparency is an open issue to be further investigated. Future work also includes formal security analysis of our protocol.

Acknowledgements

We thank the anonymous reviewers for their valuable comments and suggestions on the improvement of this paper. The second author has been funded by the Consejeria de Innovacion, Ciencia y Empresa (Junta de Andalucia) under the III Andalusian Research Plan.

References

1. N. Asokan, Birgit Baum-Waidner, Matthias Schunter, and Michael Waidner. Optimistic synchronous multi-party contract signing. Technical Report RZ 3089, IBM Zurich Research Lab, 1998.
2. N. Asokan, Matthias Schunter, and Michael Waidner. Optimistic protocols for multi-party fair exchange. Technical Report RZ 2892, IBM, Zurich Research Laboratory, 1996.
3. N. Asokan, Matthias Schunter, and Michael Waidner. Optimistic protocols for fair exchange. In *Proceedings of 4th ACM Conference on Computer and Communications Security*, pages 7–17. ACM Press, 1997.
4. N. Asokan, Victor Shoup, and Michael Waidner. Optimistic fair exchange of digital signatures. *IEEE Journal on Selected Areas in Communications*, 18(4):593–610, 2000.
5. Feng Bao, Robert Deng, and Wenbo Mao. Efficient and practical fair exchange protocols with off-line TTP. In *Proceedings of 1998 IEEE Symposium on Security and Privacy*, pages 77–85. IEEE, May 1998.
6. Birgit Baum-Waidner. Optimistic asynchronous multi-party contract signing with reduced number of rounds. In *Proceedings of 28th International Colloquium on Automata, Languages and Programming*, pages 898–911. Springer, 2001.
7. Birgit Baum-Waidner and Michael Waidner. Round-optimal and abuse-free multi-party contract signing. In *Proceedings of 27th International Colloquium on Automata, Languages and Programming*, LNCS 1853, pages 524–535. Springer, 2000.
8. M. Ben-Or, O. Goldreich, S. Micali, and R. Rivest. A fair protocol for signing contracts. *IEEE Transactions on Information Theory*, volume 36, pages 40–46, 1990.
9. M. Blum. Three applications of the oblivious transfer. Technical Report, Department of EECS, University of California, Berkeley, CA, 1981.
10. S. Even, O. Goldreich, and A. Lempel. A randomized protocol for signing contracts. *Communications of the ACM*, volume 28, pages 637–647, 1985.
11. Josep Lluís Ferrer-Gomila, Magdalena Payeras-Capellà, and Llorenç Huguet-Rotger. Efficient optimistic n-party contract signing protocol. In *Proceedings of 4th International Conference on Information Security*, pages 394–407. Springer, 2001.
12. Josep Lluís Ferrer-Gomila, Magdalena Payeras-Capellà, and Llorenç Huguet-Rotger. Optimality in asynchronous contract signing protocols. In *Proceedings of 1st International Conference on Trust and Privacy in Digital Business*, LNCS 3184. Springer, August 2004.
13. Juan A. Garay and Philip D. MacKenzie. Abuse-free multi-party contract signing. In *Proceedings of 13th International Symposium on Distributed Computing*, pages 151–165. Springer, 1999.
14. N. González-Deleito and O. Markowitch. An optimistic multi-party fair exchange protocol with reduced trust requirements. In *Proceedings of 4th International Conference on Information Security and Cryptology*, LNCS 2288, pages 258–267. Springer, December 2001.
15. O. Markowitch and S. Saeednia. Optimistic fair-exchange with transparent signature recovery. In *Proceedings of Financial Cryptography 2001*. Springer, February 2001.
16. Silvio Micali. Simple and fast optimistic protocols for fair electronic exchange. In *Proceedings of 22nd Annual Symposium on Principles of Distributed Computing*, pages 12–19. ACM Press, 2003.
17. Birgit Pfitzmann, Matthias Schunter, and Michael Waidner. Optimal efficiency of optimistic contract signing. In *Proceedings of 17th Annual ACM Symposium on Principles of Distributed Computing*, pages 113–122. ACM Press, 1998.
18. Jose Onieva, Jianying Zhou, and Javier Lopez. Attacking an asynchronous multi-party contract signing protocol. In *Proceedings of 6th International Conference on Cryptology in India*, LNCS 3797, pages 311–321. Springer, December 2005.

On the Cryptographic Key Secrecy of the Strengthened Yahalom Protocol*

Michael Backes[1] and Birgit Pfitzmann[2]

[1] Saarland University, Germany
[2] IBM Zurich Research Laboratory, Switzerland
{mbc,bpf}@zurich.ibm.com

Abstract. Symbolic secrecy of exchanged keys is arguably one of the most important notions of secrecy shown with automated proof tools. It means that an adversary restricted to symbolic operations on terms can never get the entire key into its knowledge set. Cryptographic key secrecy essentially means computational indistinguishability between the real key and a random one, given the view of a much more general adversary.
We analyze the cryptographic key secrecy for the strengthened Yahalom protocol, which constitutes one of the most prominent key exchange protocols analyzed symbolically by means of automated proof tools. We show that the strengthened Yahalom protocol does not guarantee cryptographic key secrecy. We further show that cryptographic key secrecy can be proven for a slight simplification of the protocol by exploiting recent results on linking symbolic and cryptographic key secrecy in order to perform a symbolic proof of secrecy for the simplified Yahalom protocol in a specific setting that allows us to derive the desired cryptographic key secrecy from the symbolic proof. The proof holds in the presence of arbitrary active attacks provided that the protocol is relying on standard provably secure cryptographic primitives.

1 Introduction

Cryptographic protocols for key establishment are an established technology. Nevertheless, most new networking and messaging stacks come with new protocols for such tasks. Since designing cryptographic protocols is known to be error-prone and, owing to the distributed-system aspects of multiple interleaved protocol runs, security proofs of such protocols are awkward to make for humans, automation of such proofs has been studied almost since cryptographic protocols first emerged. From the start, the actual cryptographic operations in such proofs were idealized into so-called Dolev-Yao models after the first authors [17], e.g., see [24,1,29,31]. These models replace cryptography by term algebras, e.g., encrypting a message m twice does not yield a different message from the basic message space but the term $E(E(m))$. A typical cancellation rule is $D(E(m)) = m$ for all m. It is assumed that even an adversary can only operate on terms by the given operators and by exploiting the given cancellation rules. This assumption, in other words the use of initial models of the given equational specifications,

---

* An extended version of this paper is available at [7].

Please use the following format when citing this chapter:

Author(s) [insert Last name, First-name initial(s)], 2006, in IFIP International Federation for Information Processing, Volume 201, Security and Privacy in Dynamic Environments, eds. Fischer-Hubner, S., Rannenberg, K., Yngstrom, L., Lindskog, S., (Boston: Springer), pp. [insert page numbers].

makes it highly nontrivial to know if results obtained over a Dolev-Yao model are also valid over real cryptography. One therefore calls properties and actions in Dolev-Yao models *symbolic* in contrast to *cryptographic*.

Arguably the most important and most common properties proved symbolically are secrecy properties, as initiated in [17], and in particular key secrecy properties. Symbolically, the secrecy of a key is represented by knowledge sets: The key is secret if the adversary can never get the corresponding symbolic term into its knowledge set. Cryptographically, key secrecy is defined by computational indistinguishability between the real key and a randomly chosen one, given the view of the adversary. Hence symbolic secrecy captures the absence of structural attacks that make the secret as a whole known to the adversary, and because of its simplicity it is accessible to automated proofs tools, while cryptographic secrecy constitutes a more fine-grained notion of secrecy that is much harder to establish.

The Yahalom protocol [14, 32] is one of the most prominent key exchange protocols. Paulson discovered that the original protocol from [14] is insecure and proposed a strengthened variant [32]. This was extensively investigated, e.g., in [32, 19, 11]. However, all existing security proofs are restricted to the Dolev-Yao model. We first remark that the protocol does not satisfy the definition of cryptographic key secrecy because of the (essentially) well-known fact that computing an encryption with the key as a form of confirmation which becomes known also to the adversary (as is the case for the Yahalom protocol) already makes the key distinguishable from a fresh random key. We show that a simplified version of the protocol obtained by removing the encryption computed with the exchanged key allows for a proof of cryptographic key secrecy, i.e., we show that keys exchanged between two honest users are secret in the strong sense of indistinguishability from random keys. This holds in the presence of arbitrary active attacks, provided that the Dolev-Yao abstraction of symmetric encryption is implemented by a symmetric encryption scheme that is secure against chosen-ciphertext attacks and additionally ensures integrity of ciphertexts. This is the standard security definition of authenticated symmetric encryption [13, 12]. Efficient symmetric encryptions schemes provably secure in this sense exist under reasonable assumptions [18, 23].

We achieve this result by analyzing the simplified version of the strengthened Yahalom protocol based on the *cryptographic library* of Backes, Pfitzmann, and Waidner [9, 10, 6], which corresponds to a slightly extended Dolev-Yao model that can be faithfully realized using provably secure cryptographic primitives in the standard model of cryptography. In combination with a recent result on linking symbolic and cryptographic key secrecy [8], this allows us to perform a proof of secrecy for the simplified Yahalom protocol in a specific, symbolic setting and to derive the desired cryptographic key secrecy from that. This is the first symbolic proof of a cryptographic protocol that can be exploited to derive cryptographic secrecy for the exchanged keys. (Another such proof was conducted concurrently and independently by Canetti and Herzog, cf. below.)

Further Related Work. Early work on linking Dolev-Yao models and cryptography [3, 2, 20, 25] only considered passive attacks, and therefore cannot make general statements about protocols. A cryptographic justification for a Dolev-Yao model in the sense of simulatability [33], i.e., under active attacks and within arbitrary surrounding interactive protocols, was first given in [9] with extensions in [10, 6]. Based on that Dolev-

Yao model, the well-known Needham-Schroeder-Lowe and Otway-Rees protocols were proved in [5, 4]. The former is entirely an authentication proof and hence does not have to reason about secrecy aspects. The latter contains a key secrecy property but this was reformulated by hand into a (considerably weaker) integrity property so that the integrity preservation theorem could be used.

Laud [26] has presented a cryptographic underpinning for a Dolev-Yao model of symmetric encryption under active attacks. His work is directly connected with a formal proof tool, but it is specific to certain confidentiality properties and protocol classes. Herzog et al. [21] and Micciancio and Warinschi [30] have also given a cryptographic underpinning under active attacks. Their results are narrower than that in [9] since they are specific for public-key encryption and certain protocol classes, but consider slightly simpler real implementations. Efforts are also under way to formulate syntactic calculi for dealing with probabilism and polynomial-time considerations, in particular [27, 22] and, as a second step, to encode them into proof tools. This approach can not yet handle protocols with any degree of automation.

Cortier and Warinschi [16] have shown that symbolically secret nonces are also computationally secret, i.e., indistinguishable from a fresh random value given the view of a cryptographic adversary. Backes and Pfitzmann [8] and Canetti and Herzog [15] have established new symbolic criteria for proving a key cryptographically secret.

2   The Strengthened Yahalom Protocol

The Yahalom protocol [14] and its strengthened variant [32] are four-step protocols for establishing a shared secret encryption key between two users. The protocol relies on a distinguished trusted party T, and it is assumed that every user u initially shares a secret key K_{ut} with T. Expressed in the typical protocol notation as in, e.g., [28], the strengthened Yahalom works as follows.

$$
\begin{aligned}
&1. \quad u \rightarrow v : u, N_u \\
&2. \quad v \rightarrow \mathsf{T} : v, N_v, (u, N_u)_{K_{vt}} \\
&3. \quad \mathsf{T} \rightarrow u : N_v, (v, K_{uv}, N_u)_{K_{ut}}, (u, v, K_{uv}, N_v)_{K_{vt}} \\
&4. \quad u \rightarrow v : (u, v, K_{uv}, N_v)_{K_{vt}}, (N_v)_{K_{uv}}.
\end{aligned}
$$

User u seeks to share a new session key with user v. It generates a nonce N_u and sends it to v together with its identity (first message). Next, v generates a new nonce N_v, creates a new message containing the identity u and the nonce N_u, and encrypts it with the key it shares with T. Then v sends its identity, its nonce N_v, and the encryption to the trusted party (second message). Now T decrypts the encryption yielding the identity of u and the nonce N_u, generates a fresh key K_{uv} for u and v, generates a message according to the protocol description, and sends it to u (third message). Then u decrypts the first encryption and tests whether the contained nonce is the one it sent to v before, i.e., to the identity that is contained in this encryption. If so, it forwards the second encryption to v (fourth message) together with an encryption of N_v with the shared key K_{uv} and terminates the protocol by outputting a handle to the shared secret key K_{uv} to its user. Finally v decrypts the first encryption contained in this message, obtains the shared key K_{uv}, and tests if the message contains its own identity and the contained nonce was previously sent to T. If so, it further decrypts the second encryption and checks if the obtained nonce matches N_v. It then outputs a handle to the shared key K_{uv} to its user and terminates the protocol. Note that the fourth message of the strengthened Yahalom protocol contains an encryption of the nonce N_v with the shared key K_{uv}. We show below that this encryption destroys cryptographic key secrecy. We subsequently analyze the protocol obtained by removing this encryption, and we show cryptographic key secrecy for this protocol. We only briefly note that the authenticity guarantees of the Yahalom protocol [32] still hold in our setting if we omit this encryption from the fourth message, since our cryptographic implementation is already based on an authenticated symmetric encryption scheme; authenticated encryption is necessary for exploiting the underlying proof of cryptographic soundness of the Dolev-Yao model.

2.1 Why the Strengthened Yahalom Protocol does not offer Cryptographic Key Secrecy

We now briefly sketch why the unmodified strengthened Yahalom protocol cannot achieve cryptographic key secrecy. The argument is general (and obvious for a cryptographer) and applies to *all* key exchange protocols that already use the exchanged key to compute an encryption that becomes known to the adversary. The reason is that symmetric encryptions provide partial information about a symmetric secret key, at least if one also has partial information about the message encrypted. This partial information already allows an adversary to distinguish the exchanged key from a random key that has been chosen independently of the protocol. To distinguish the keys, the adversary first completes a regular execution of the protocol between two honest parties, thus learning the nonce N_v and the encryption $(N_v)_{K_{uv}}$. A bit b is then flipped, and the adversary receives a key K, which equals the (unknown) key K_{uv} if $b = 0$ or a fresh random key if $b = 1$. The adversary then decrypts $(N_v)_{K_{uv}}$ with K yielding N and outputs $b^* := 0$ as its guess on b if $N = N_v$, and $b^* := 1$ otherwise. The probability of a correct guess is then given by $1 - \epsilon$, where ϵ denotes the probability that for a randomly chosen nonce N_v and randomly chosen keys K_{uv}, K, we have that $(N_v)_{K_{uv}}$ decrypted with K yields N_v again, which is negligible. The adversary has thus a non-negligible advantage of distinguishing the keys. Hence cryptographic key secrecy does not hold.

2.2 Protocol Details with the Dolev-Yao-style Cryptographic Library

We now capture the simplified version of the strengthened Yahalom protocol, i.e., without the encryption $(N_v)_{K_{uv}}$ in its fourth step, using the Dolev-Yao-style cryptographic library from [9]. For simplicity, we speak of the Yahalom protocol again in the following. Almost all formal proof techniques for protocols first need a reformulation of the protocol into a more detailed version than the four steps above. These details include necessary tests on received messages, the types and generation rules for values like u and N_u, and a surrounding framework specifying the number of participants, the possibilities of multiple protocol runs, and the adversary capabilities. We now present the protocol details when using the Dolev-Yao-style cryptographic library from [9] as well as general aspects of this framework.

Algorithm 1 Evaluation of User Inputs in M_u^{Ya} with $u \neq T$ (Protocol Start)

Input: $(\text{new\_prot}, \text{Yahalom}, v)$ at $\text{KE\_in}_u?$ with $v \in \{1, \ldots, n\} \setminus \{u\}$.

1: $n_u^{hnd} \leftarrow \text{gen\_nonce}()$.
2: $Nonce_u := Nonce_u \cup \{(n_u^{hnd}, v, 1)\}$.
3: $u^{hnd} \leftarrow \text{store}(u)$.
4: $m_1^{hnd} \leftarrow \text{list}(u^{hnd}, n_u^{hnd})$.
5: $\text{send\_i}(v, m_1^{hnd})$.

We write ":=" for deterministic assignment, and $\downarrow$ is an error element available as an addition to the domains and ranges of all functions and algorithms. The framework is automata-based, i.e., protocols are executed by interacting machines, and event-based, i.e., machines react on received inputs. By M_i^{Ya} we denote the Yahalom machine for a participant i; it can act in the roles of both u and v above.

The first type of input that M_i^{Ya} can receive is a start message $(\text{new\_prot}, \text{Yahalom}, v)$ from its user denoting that it should start a protocol run with user v. The number of users is called n.[1] User inputs are distinguished from network inputs by arriving at a so-called port $\text{KE\_in}_u?$. The "?" for input ports follows the CSP convention, and "KE" stands for key exchange because the user interface is the same for all key exchange protocols. The reaction on this input, i.e., the sending of the first message, is described in Algorithm 1. The command gen_nonce generates the nonce. M_u^{Ya} stores the resulting so-called *handle* n_u^{hnd} (a local name that this machine has for the corresponding term) in a set $Nonce_u$ for future comparison together with the identity v and an indicator that this nonce was generated and stored by u in the first step. The set $Nonce_u$ formally consists of triples (n^{hnd}, w, j) where n^{hnd} is a handle, $w \in \{1, \ldots, n\} \setminus \{u\}$, and $j \in \{1, 2, 3, 4\}$. A triple (n^{hnd}, w, j) means that M_u^{Ya} stored the handle n^{hnd} in the j-th protocol step in a session with w. The command store inputs arbitrary application data into the cryptographic library, here the user identity u. The command list forms a list, and the final command send_i means that M_u^{Ya} sends the resulting term to v over an insecure channel. The effect is that the adversary obtains a handle to the term and can decide what to do with it (such as forwarding it to M_v^{Ya} or performing Dolev-Yao-style algebraic operations on the term). The superscript ^{hnd} on most parameters denotes that these are handles, i.e., the users obtain local names for the corresponding terms. This is an important aspect of [9] because it allows the same protocol description to be implemented once with Dolev-Yao-style idealized cryptography and once with real cryptography. The four commands we saw so far and their input and output domains belong to the interface (in the same sense as, e.g., a Java interface) of the underlying cryptographic library. This interface is implemented by both the idealized and the real version. In the first case, the handles are local names of Dolev-Yao-style terms, in the second case of real cryptographic bitstrings, on which the adversary can perform arbitrary bit manipulations. We say more about these two implementations below.

---

[1] The set of users is $\{1, \ldots, n\}$ and the Yahalom protocol is designed such that $T \notin \{1, \ldots, n\}$ where T denotes the trusted party.

Algorithm 2 Behavior of the Trusted Party M_T^{Ya}

Input: $(v, \mathsf{T}, \mathsf{i}, m^{\mathsf{hnd}})$ at $\mathsf{out_T}?$ with $v \in \{1, \ldots, n\}$.

1: $t_i^{\mathsf{hnd}} \leftarrow \mathsf{list\_proj}(m^{\mathsf{hnd}}, i)$ for $i = 1, 2, 3$.

2: $t_1 \leftarrow \mathsf{retrieve}(t_1^{\mathsf{hnd}})$. $\{t_1 \approx v\}$

3: $type_{t_2^{\mathsf{hnd}}} \leftarrow \mathsf{get\_type}(t_2^{\mathsf{hnd}})$.

4: $l^{\mathsf{hnd}} \leftarrow \mathsf{sym\_decrypt}(skse_{\mathsf{T},v}^{\mathsf{hnd}}, t_3^{\mathsf{hnd}})$. $\{l^{\mathsf{hnd}} \approx (u, N_u)\}$

5: $x_i^{\mathsf{hnd}} \leftarrow \mathsf{list\_proj}(l^{\mathsf{hnd}}, i)$ for $i = 1, 2$.

6: $x_1 \leftarrow \mathsf{retrieve}(x_1^{\mathsf{hnd}})$. $\{x_1 \approx u\}$

7: $type_{x_2^{\mathsf{hnd}}} \leftarrow \mathsf{get\_type}(x_2^{\mathsf{hnd}})$.

8: **if** $type_{t_2^{\mathsf{hnd}}} \neq \mathsf{nonce} \vee type_{x_2^{\mathsf{hnd}}} \neq \mathsf{nonce} \vee t_1 \neq v \vee x_1 \notin \{1, \ldots, n\} \setminus \{v\}$ **then** Abort **end if**

9: $skse^{\mathsf{hnd}} \leftarrow \mathsf{gen\_symenc\_key}()$. $\{skse^{\mathsf{hnd}} \approx K_{uv}\}$

10: ${l_3^{(1)}}^{\mathsf{hnd}} \leftarrow \mathsf{list}(t_1^{\mathsf{hnd}}, skse^{\mathsf{hnd}}, x_2^{\mathsf{hnd}})$. $\{{l_3^{(1)}}^{\mathsf{hnd}} \approx (v, K_{uv}, N_u)\}$

11: ${c_3^{(1)}}^{\mathsf{hnd}} \leftarrow \mathsf{sym\_encrypt}(skse_{\mathsf{T},x_1}^{\mathsf{hnd}}, {l_3^{(1)}}^{\mathsf{hnd}})$. $\{{c_3^{(1)}}^{\mathsf{hnd}} \approx (v, K_{uv}, N_u)_{K_{ut}}\}$

12: ${l_3^{(2)}}^{\mathsf{hnd}} \leftarrow \mathsf{list}(x_1^{\mathsf{hnd}}, t_1^{\mathsf{hnd}}, skse^{\mathsf{hnd}}, t_2^{\mathsf{hnd}})$. $\{{l_3^{(2)}}^{\mathsf{hnd}} \approx (u, v, K_{uv}, N_v)\}$

13: ${c_3^{(2)}}^{\mathsf{hnd}} \leftarrow \mathsf{sym\_encrypt}(skse_{\mathsf{T},v}^{\mathsf{hnd}}, {l_3^{(2)}}^{\mathsf{hnd}})$. $\{{c_3^{(2)}}^{\mathsf{hnd}} \approx (u, v, K_{uv}, N_v)_{K_{vt}}\}$

14: $m_3^{\mathsf{hnd}} \leftarrow \mathsf{list}(t_2^{\mathsf{hnd}}, {c_3^{(1)}}^{\mathsf{hnd}}, {c_3^{(2)}}^{\mathsf{hnd}})$. $\{m_3^{\mathsf{hnd}} \approx (N_v, (v, K_{uv}, N_u)_{K_{ut}}, (u, v, K_{uv}, N_v)_{K_{vt}})\}$

15: $\mathsf{send\_i}(x_1, m_3^{\mathsf{hnd}})$.

The treatment of network inputs by protocol machines and by the trusted third party is defined similar to Algorithm 1. Network inputs of user u arrive at port $\mathsf{out}_u?$ and are of the form $(v, u, \mathsf{i}, m^{\mathsf{hnd}})$ where v is the supposed sender, i denotes that the channel is insecure, and m^{hnd} is a handle to a list. The port $\mathsf{out}_u?$ is connected to the cryptographic library, whose two implementations represent the obtained Dolev-Yao-style term or real bitstring, respectively, to the protocol in a unified way by the handle m^{hnd}. Due to space constraints, we omit an informal description of how these inputs are processed; this should already be clear from the preceding protocol description. Moreover, we only give the algorithmic description how the trusted third party reacts on network inputs in Algorithm 2 and postpone the algorithmic description how the protocol machines react on network inputs to [7].

We furthermore use the convention that every machine should immediately abort the handling of the current input if a cryptographic command does not yield the desired result, e.g., if a decryption fails.

2.3 Overall Framework and Adversary Model

The framework that determines how machines such as our Yahalom machines and the machines of the idealized or real cryptographic library execute is taken from [33]. The basis is an asynchronous probabilistic execution model with distributed scheduling and with a well-defined Turing-machine refinement for complexity considerations. We already used implicitly above that for term construction and parsing commands to the cryptographic library, so-called local scheduling is defined, i.e., a result is returned immediately. The idealized or real network sending via this library, however, is scheduled by the adversary.

When protocol machines such as M_u^{Ya} are defined there is no guarantee that all these machines are correct. A trust model determines for what subsets $\mathcal{H}$ of $\{1, \ldots, n, T\}$ we want to guarantee anything; here these are the subsets that contain at least the trusted party: We prove secrecy of keys shared by u and v whenever $u, v \in \mathcal{H}$ and thus whenever M_u^{Ya} and M_v^{Ya} are correct. Incorrect machines disappear and are replaced by the adversary. Each set of potential correct machines together with its user interface is called a structure, and the set of these structures is called the system. When considering the security of a structure, an arbitrary probabilistic machine H is connected to the user interface to represent all users, and an arbitrary probabilistic machine A is connected to the remaining free ports (typically the network) and to H to represent the adversary. In polynomial-time security proofs, H and A are polynomial-time. This setting implies that any number of concurrent protocol runs with the honest participants and the adversary are considered because H and A can arbitrarily interleave protocol start inputs (new_prot, Yahalom, v) with the delivery of network messages.

For a set $\mathcal{H}$ of honest participants, the user interface of the Yahalom protocol machines is $S_{\mathcal{H}}^{KE} := \{KE\_in_u?, KE\_out_u! \mid u \in \mathcal{H} \setminus \{T\}\}$. The ideal and real Yahalom protocol serving this interface differ only in the cryptographic library, i.e., the Yahalom machines either rely on a set $\hat{M}_{\mathcal{H}}^{cry} := \{M_{u,\mathcal{H}}^{cry} \mid u \in \mathcal{H}\}$ of real cryptographic machines or an ideal machine $TH_{\mathcal{H}}^{cry}$ called *trusted host*. With $\hat{M}_{\mathcal{H}}^{Ya} := \{M_u^{Ya} \mid u \in \mathcal{H}\}$, the ideal system is $Sys^{Ya,id} := \{(\hat{M}_{\mathcal{H}}^{Ya} \cup \{TH_{\mathcal{H}}^{cry}\}, S_{\mathcal{H}}^{KE}) \mid \{T\} \subseteq \mathcal{H} \subseteq \{1, \ldots, n, T\}\}$, and the real system is $Sys_{S\mathcal{E}}^{Ya,real} := \{(\hat{M}_{\mathcal{H}}^{Ya} \cup \hat{M}_{\mathcal{H}}^{cry}, S_{\mathcal{H}}^{KE}) \mid \{T\} \subseteq \mathcal{H} \subseteq \{1, \ldots, n, T\}\}$, where $S\mathcal{E}$ denotes the symmetric encryption scheme used.

3 The Key Secrecy Property

In the following, we formalize the key secrecy property of the ideal and real Yahalom protocols. The property is an instantiation of a general symbolic key secrecy definition for arbitrary protocols based on the ideal cryptographic library from [8], which is based on the typical notion that a term is not an element of the adversary's knowledge set. In the given Dolev-Yao-style library, the adversary's knowledge set is the set of all terms to which the adversary has a handle.

3.1 Overview and States of the Ideal Cryptographic Library

The ideal cryptographic library administrates Dolev-Yao-style terms and allows each user to operate on them via handles, i.e., via local names specific to this user. The handles also contain the information that knowledge sets give in other Dolev-Yao formalizations: The set of terms that a participant u knows, including $u =$ a for the adversary, is the set of terms with a handle for u. The terms are typed; for instance, decryption only succeeds on ciphertexts and projection only on lists. Moreover, the terms are globally numbered by a so-called index. Each term is represented by its type (i.e., root node) and its first-level arguments, which can be indices of earlier terms. This enables easy distinction of, e.g., which of many nonces is encrypted in a larger term. These global indices are never visible at the user interface. The indices and the handles for each participant are generated by one counter each.

The data structure storing the terms in [9] is a database D. Generally, a database D is a set of functions, called entries, each over a finite domain called attributes. For an entry $x \in D$, the value at an attribute att is written $x.att$. For a predicate $pred$ involving attributes, $D[pred]$ means the subset of entries whose attributes fulfill $pred$. If $D[pred]$ contains only one element, we use the same notation for this element. Adding an entry x to D is abbreviated $D :\Leftarrow x$. Moreover, we write the list operation as $l := (x_1, \ldots, x_j)$, and argument retrieval as $l[i]$ with $l[i] = \downarrow$ if $i > j$.

In the specific term database D, each entry x can have the following arguments (with domains omitted for brevity): $x.ind$ is the global index of an entry, which is used as a primary key attribute of the database, i.e., we write $D[i]$ for the selection $D[ind = i]$. $x.type$ denotes the $type$ of x and $x.arg = (a_1, a_2, \ldots, a_j)$ is a possibly empty list of arguments. $x.hnd_u$ for $u \in \mathcal{H} \cup \{a\}$ are handles, where $x.hnd_u = \downarrow$ means that u does not know this entry. Finally, $x.len$ denotes the length of the entry. The machine $\mathsf{TH}_{\mathcal{H}}$ has a counter $size \in \mathcal{INDS}$ for the current size of D and counters $curhnd_u$ (current handle) for the handles, all initialized with 0.

In order to capture that keys shared between users and the trusted party have already been generated and distributed, we assume that suitable entries for the keys already exist in the database. We denote the handle of u to the secret key shared with v, where either $u \in \{1, \ldots, n\}$ and $v = \mathsf{T}$ or vice versa, by $skse^{\mathsf{hnd}}_{u,v}$.

3.2 The Real Cryptographic Library

In the real cryptographic library, each user has its own machine. This machine contains a database D_u with only three main attributes: the handle hnd_u for this user u, the real cryptographic bitstring $word$, and the type $type$. The users can use the same commands as with the ideal library, e.g., en- or decrypt a message etc. These commands now trigger real cryptographic operations. The operations use standard cryptographically secure primitives, but with certain additional tagging, randomization etc. Send commands now trigger the actual sending of bitstrings between machines and/or to the adversary.

3.3 Definition of the Key Secrecy Property

The first step towards defining symbolic key secrecy is to consider one state of the ideal Dolev-Yao-style library and to define that a handle points to a symmetric key, that the key is symbolically unknown to the adversary, and that it has not been used for encryption or authentication. These are the symbolic conditions under which we can hope to prove that the corresponding real key is indistinguishable from a fresh random key for the adversary. Note that the operations that the Yahalom protocol performs on new keys are allowed in this sense. For Condition (3) in the definition, note that the arguments of a ciphertext term are (l, pk) where l is the plaintext index and pk the index of the public tag of the secret key, with $pk = sk - 1$ for the secret key index.

Definition 1. *(Symbolically Secret Encryption Keys [8])* Let $\{\mathsf{T}\} \subseteq \mathcal{H} \subseteq \{1, \ldots, n, \mathsf{T}\}$, a database state D of $\mathsf{TH}^{\mathsf{cry}}_{\mathcal{H}}$, and a pair $(u, l^{\mathsf{hnd}}) \in \mathcal{H} \times \mathcal{HNDS}$ of a user and a handle be given. Let $i := D[hnd_u = l^{\mathsf{hnd}}].ind$ be the correspond- ing database index. The *term under* (u, l^{hnd}) (1) *is a symmetric encryption key* iff

$D[i].type = $ skse, (2) *is symbolically unknown (to the adversary)* iff $D[i].hnd_a = \downarrow$, (3) *has not been used for encryption*, or short *is unused*, iff for all indices $j \in \mathbb{N}$ we have $D[j].type = $ symenc $\Rightarrow D[j].arg[2] \neq i - 1$, and (4) *is a symbolically secret key* iff it has the three previous properties. $\diamond$

A secret-key belief function is a general way to designate the keys whose secrecy should be proved. The underlying theory from [8] is based on such functions. We instantiate them for the Yahalom protocol and thus essentially for all individual key exchange protocols. A secret key belief function maps the user view to a set of triples (u, l^{hnd}, t) of a user, a handle, and a type, pointing to the supposedly secret keys. For the Yahalom protocol, we define secret-key belief functions seckeys_initiator_Ya for the initiator and seckeys_responder_Ya for the responder that designate the exchanged keys.

Definition 2. *(Secret-key Belief Functions for the Yahalom Protocol)* A *secret-key belief function* for a set $\mathcal{H}$ is a function seckeys that maps each view *view* of the user to an element of $(\mathcal{H} \times \mathcal{HNDS} \times \{$skse$\})^*$.
   The *secret-key belief functions* seckeys_initiator_Ya and seckeys_responder_Ya of the Yahalom protocol map each element (ok_initiator, Yahalom, v, $skse^{hnd}$) respectively (ok_responder, Yahalom, v, $skse^{hnd}$) of *view* arriving at port KE_out$_u$? in the users view to $(u, skse^{hnd}, $ skse$)$ if $u \in \mathcal{H}$, and to ϵ otherwise. Elements of *view* that are not of this form are also mapped to ϵ. $\diamond$

We now define symbolic key secrecy for such a function. In addition to the conditions for individual keys, we require that all elements point to different terms, so that we can expect the corresponding list of cryptographic keys to be entirely random.

Definition 3. *(Symbolic Key Secrecy Generally and for the Yahalom Protocol)* Let a user H* suitable for a structure $(\{\mathsf{TH}_{\mathcal{H}}^{cry}\}, S_{\mathcal{H}}^{cry})$ of the cryptographic library $Sys^{cry,id}$ and a secret-key belief function seckeys for $\mathcal{H}$ be given. The ideal cryptographic library with this user *keeps the keys in* seckeys *strictly symbolically secret* iff for all configurations $conf = (\{\mathsf{TH}_{\mathcal{H}}^{cry}\}, S_{\mathcal{H}}^{cry}, \mathsf{H}, \mathsf{A})$ of this structure, every $v \in view_{conf}(\mathsf{H})$, and every element (u_i, l_i^{hnd}, t_i) of the set seckeys(v), the term under (u_i, l_i^{hnd}) is a symbolically secret key of type t_i, and $D[hnd_{u_i} = l_i^{hnd}].ind \neq D[hnd_{u_j} = l_j^{hnd}].ind$ for all $i \neq j$.
   The ideal Yahalom protocol *keeps the exchanged keys of honest users strictly symbolically secret* iff the ideal cryptographic library keeps the keys in seckeys_initiator_Ya and seckeys_responder_Ya strictly symbolically secret with all users H* that are the combination of the machines M_u^{Ya} for $u \in \mathcal{H}$ and a user H of those machines. $\diamond$

General cryptographic key secrecy requires that no polynomial-time adversary can distinguish the keys designated by the function seckeys from fresh keys. The cryptographic key secrecy of the Yahalom protocol is the instantiation for seckeys_initiator_Ya and seckeys_responder_Ya and the configurations of the Yahalom protocol.

Definition 4. *(Cryptographic Key Secrecy Generally and for the Yahalom Protocol)* Let a polynomial-time configuration $conf = (\hat{M}_{\mathcal{H}}^{cry}, S_{\mathcal{H}}^{cry}, \mathsf{H}, \mathsf{A})$ of the real cryptographic library $Sys_{SE}^{cry,real}$ and a secret-key belief function seckeys for $\mathcal{H}$ be given. Let gen$_{SE}$

denote the key generation algorithm. This configuration *keeps the keys in* seckeys *cryptographically secret* iff for all probabilistic-polynomial time algorithms Dis (the distinguisher), we have

$$|\Pr[\text{Dis}(1^k, va, keys_{real}) = 1] - \Pr[\text{Dis}(1^k, va, keys_{fresh}) = 1]| \in NEGL$$

where $NEGL$ denotes the negligible function of the security parameter k and the used random variables are defined as follows: For $r \in run_{conf}$, let $va := view_{conf}(\text{A})(r)$ be the view of the adversary, let $(u_i, l_i^{hnd}, t_i)_{i=1,\dots,n} := \text{seckeys}(view_{conf}(\text{H})(r))$ be the user-handle-type triples of presumably secret keys, and let the keys be $keys_{real} := (sk_i)_{i=1,\dots,n}$ with

$$sk_i := D_{u_i}[hnd_{u_i} = l_i^{hnd}].word \text{ if } D_{u_i}[hnd_{u_i} = l_i^{hnd}].type = t_i, \text{ else } \epsilon;$$

and $keys_{fresh} := (sk_i')_{i=1,\dots,n}$ with $sk_i' \leftarrow \text{gen}_\text{A}(1^k)$ if $t_i = $ ska, else $sk_i' \leftarrow \epsilon$.

A polynomial-time configuration $(\hat{M}_\mathcal{H}^{cry} \cup \hat{M}_\mathcal{H}^{Ya}, S_\mathcal{H}^{KE}, \text{H}, \text{A})$ of the real Yahalom protocol $Sys^{Ya,real}$ *keeps the exchanged keys of honest users cryptographically secret* iff the configuration $(\hat{M}_\mathcal{H}^{cry}, S_\mathcal{H}^{cry}, \{\text{H}\} \cup \hat{M}_\mathcal{H}^{Ya}, \text{A})$ keeps the keys in seckeys_initiator_Ya and seckeys_responder_Ya cryptographically secret.   ◇

Theorem 1. *(Security of the Yahalom Protocol)* The ideal Yahalom system $Sys^{Ya,id}$ from Section 2.3 keeps the exchanged keys of honest users strictly symbolically secret, and all polynomial-time configurations of the real system $Sys^{Ya,real}$ keep the exchanged keys of honest users cryptographically secret.   □

4   Proof of the Cryptographic Realization from the Idealization

As discussed in the introduction, the idea of our approach is to prove Theorem 1 for the protocol using the ideal Dolev-Yao-style cryptographic library. Then the result for the real system follows automatically. The notion that a system Sys_1 securely implements another system Sys_2 in the sense of reactive simulatability [33], is written $Sys_1 \geq_{sec}^{poly} Sys_2$ (in the computational case). The main result of [9, 10, 6] is therefore

$$Sys^{cry,real} \geq_{sec}^{poly} Sys^{cry,id}. \tag{1}$$

If symmetric encryption is present, this result is additionally subject to the condition that the surrounding protocol, in our case the Yahalom protocol, does not raise a so-called commitment problem for symmetric encryption. It is a nice obseration that this condition can be immediately concluded from the overall proof; the formal argument is contained in the long version [7]. For technical reasons, one further has to ensure that the protocol does not create encryption cycles (such as encrypting a key with itself); this is needed even for much weaker properties than simulatability, see [3]. This property clearly holds for the Yahalom protocol.

Once we have shown that the considered keys are symbolically secret and that the commitment problem does not occur for the Yahalom protocol, we can exploit the key-secrecy preservation theorem of [8]: If for certain honest users H and a secret-key belief function seckeys the ideal cryptographic library keeps the keys in seckeys strictly symbolically secret, then every configuration of H with the real cryptographic library keeps the keys in seckeys cryptographically secret.

5 Proof in the Ideal Setting

It remains to prove the ideal part of Theorem 1. The proof idea is the following: If an honest user u successfully terminates a session run with another honest user v, we first show that the established key has been created by the trusted party. Then we exploit that the trusted party and the honest users only send this key within an encryption generated with a key shared between u and T respectively v and T, and we conclude that the adversary never gets a handle to the key. The main challenge is to find suitable invariants on the state of the ideal Yahalom system $Sys^{\mathsf{Ya,id}}$. We now present these invariants. Their proof and the proof of Theorem 1 is postponed to [7] due to space constraints.

The first invariants, *correct nonce owner* and *unique nonce use*, are easily proved. They essentially state that handles n^{hnd} where $(n^{\mathsf{hnd}}, \cdot, \cdot)$ is contained in a set $Nonce_u$ point to entries of type nonce and that no nonce is in two such sets.

Invariant 1 *(Correct Nonce Owner)* For all $u \in \mathcal{H} \setminus \{\mathsf{T}\}$, $v \in \{1, \ldots, n\}$, $j \in \{1, 2, 3, 4\}$ and $(n^{\mathsf{hnd}}, v, j) \in Nonce_u$, we have $D[hnd_u = n^{\mathsf{hnd}}] \neq \downarrow$ and $D[hnd_u = n^{\mathsf{hnd}}].type = \mathsf{nonce}$.

Invariant 2 *(Unique Nonce Use)* For all $u, v \in \mathcal{H} \setminus \{\mathsf{T}\}$, all $w, w' \in \{1, \ldots, n\}$, all $j, j' \in \{1, 2, 3, 4\}$, and all $i \leq size$: If $(D[i].hnd_u, w, j) \in Nonce_u$ and $(D[i].hnd_v, w', j') \in Nonce_v$, then $(u, w) = (v, w')$.

The invariant *encrypted-key secrecy* states that a key shared between honest u and v as well as all lists containing this key can only be known to u, v, and T. Moreover, such lists only occur within "suitable" symmetric encryptions.

Invariant 3 *(Encrypted-Key Secrecy)* For all $u, v \in \mathcal{H} \setminus \{\mathsf{T}\}$ and all $i \leq size$ with $D[i].type = \mathsf{symenc}$: Let $l^{\mathsf{ind}} := D[i].arg[1]$, $pkse^{\mathsf{ind}} := D[i].arg[2]$, $x_t^{\mathsf{ind}} := D[l^{\mathsf{ind}}].arg[t]$, and $x_t := D[x_t^{\mathsf{ind}}].arg[1]$ for $t = 1, 2, 3$. If $D[l^{\mathsf{ind}}].type = \mathsf{list} \wedge pkse^{\mathsf{ind}} = pkse_u \wedge x_1 = v \wedge D[x_t^{\mathsf{ind}}].type = \mathsf{skse}$ for some $t \in \{1, 2, 3\}$ then

a) $D[x_t^{\mathsf{ind}}].hnd_w = \downarrow$ and $D[l'^{\mathsf{ind}}].hnd_w = \downarrow$ for $(\mathcal{H} \setminus \{u, v, \mathsf{T}\}) \cup \{\mathsf{a}\}$ and for all l'^{ind} with $x_t^{\mathsf{ind}} \in D[l'^{\mathsf{ind}}].arg$.

b) For all $l', k \leq size$ such that $D[l'].type = \mathsf{list} \wedge x_t^{\mathsf{ind}} \in D[l'].arg$, we have that $l' \in D[k]$ only if $D[k].type = \mathsf{symenc}$ and $D[k].arg[2] \in \{pkse_u, pkse_v\}$.

The invariant *correct encryption owner* finally states that certain protocol messages can only be constructed by the "intended" users or by the trusted party, respectively.

Invariant 4 *(Correct Encryption Owner)* For all $u \in \mathcal{H} \setminus \{\mathsf{T}\}$ and all $i \leq size$ with $D[i].type = \mathsf{symenc}$: Let $l_k^{\mathsf{ind}} := D[i].arg[2k-1]$ and $pkse_k^{\mathsf{ind}} := D[i].arg[2k]$ for $1 \leq k \leq \frac{|D[i].arg|}{2}$ (entries of type symenc have an even number of arguments by construction). Let further $x_{k,t}^{\mathsf{ind}} := D[l_k^{\mathsf{ind}}].arg[t]$ and $x_{k,t,u}^{\mathsf{ind}} := D[x_{k,t}^{\mathsf{ind}}].hnd_u$ for $t = 1, 2, 3, 4$, and $x_{k,t} := D[x_{k,t}^{\mathsf{ind}}].arg[1]$ for $t = 1, 2$.

a) If $pkse_k^{\mathsf{ind}} = pkse_u$, $x_{k,1} \in \mathcal{H}$, $D[x_{k,2}^{\mathsf{ind}}].type = \mathsf{skse}$, and $(x_{k,3,u}^{\mathsf{hnd}}, x_{k,1}, j) \in Nonce_u$ for some $j \in \{1, 3\}$ and some $k \in \{1, \ldots, \frac{|D[i].arg|}{2}\}$, then $D[i]$ was created by $\mathsf{M_T^{Ya}}$ in Step 11 of Algorithm 2.

b) If $pkse_k^{\text{ind}} = pkse_u$, $x_{k,1} \in \mathcal{H}$, $x_{k,2} = u$, $D[x_{k,3}^{\text{ind}}].type = $ skse, and $(x_{k,4,u}^{\text{hnd}}, x_{k,1}, j) \in Nonce_u$ for some $j \in \{2,4\}$ and some $k \in \{1, \ldots, \frac{|D[i].arg|}{2}\}$, then $D[i]$ was created by M_T^{Ya} in Step 13 of Algorithm 2.

6 Conclusion

We have analyzed the key secrecy property of the strengthened Yahalom protocol. After showing that the protocol does not guarantee cryptographic key secrecy in the sense of computational indistinguishability of the exchanged key from a random one, we have proven cryptographic key secrecy of a slightly simplified version of the protocol via a deterministic, provably secure abstraction of a real cryptographic library. Together with composition and preservation theorems from the underlying model, this library allowed us to perform the actual proof effort in a deterministic setting corresponding to a slightly extended Dolev-Yao model. Besides establishing the cryptographic security of the strenghtened Yahalom protocol, our result also serves an an exemplification of the potential of the cryptographic library and the recent secrecy preservation theorem for symbolic, cryptographically sound proofs of security protocols.

References

1. M. Abadi and A. D. Gordon. A calculus for cryptographic protocols: The spi calculus. In *Proc. 4th ACM CCS*, pages 36–47, 1997.
2. M. Abadi and J. Jürjens. Formal eavesdropping and its computational interpretation. In *Proc. 4th TACS*, pages 82–94, 2001.
3. M. Abadi and P. Rogaway. Reconciling two views of cryptography: The computational soundness of formal encryption. In *Proc. 1st IFIP TCS*, volume 1872 of *LNCS*, pages 3–22. Springer, 2000.
4. M. Backes. A cryptographically sound Dolev-Yao style security proof of the Otway-Rees protocol. In *Proc. 9th ESORICS*, volume 3193 of *LNCS*, pages 89–108. Springer, 2004.
5. M. Backes and B. Pfitzmann. A cryptographically sound security proof of the Needham-Schroeder-Lowe public-key protocol. In *Proc. 23rd FSTTCS*, pages 1–12, 2003.
6. M. Backes and B. Pfitzmann. Symmetric encryption in a simulatable Dolev-Yao style cryptographic library. In *Proc. 17th IEEE CSFW*, pages 204–218, 2004.
7. M. Backes and B. Pfitzmann. Cryptographic key secrecy of the strengthened Yahalom protocol via a symbolic security proof. Research Report 3601, IBM Research, 2005. http://domino.research.ibm.com/library/cyberdig.nsf/index.html.
8. M. Backes and B. Pfitzmann. Relating symbolic and cryptographic key secrecy. In *Proc. 26th IEEE S & P*, 2005. Extended version accepted for *IEEE Transactions on Dependable and Secure Computing*.
9. M. Backes, B. Pfitzmann, and M. Waidner. A composable cryptographic library with nested operations (extended abstract). In *Proc. 10th ACM CCS*, pages 220–230, 2003. Full version in IACR ePrint Archive 2003/015, Jan. 2003.
10. M. Backes, B. Pfitzmann, and M. Waidner. Symmetric authentication within a simulatable cryptographic library. In *Proc. 8th ESORICS*, volume 2808 of *LNCS*, pages 271–290. Springer, 2003.
11. D. Basin, S. Mödersheim, and L. Viganò. OFMC: A symbolic model checker for security protocols. *International Journal of Information Security*, 2004.

12. M. Bellare and C. Namprempre. Authenticated encryption: Relations among notions and analysis of the generic composition paradigm. In *Proc. ASIACRYPT 2000*, volume 1976 of *LNCS*, pages 531–545. Springer, 2000.
13. M. Bellare and P. Rogaway. Encode-then-encipher encryption: How to exploit nonces or redundancy in plaintexts for efficient constructions. In *Proc. ASIACRYPT 2000*, volume 1976 of *LNCS*, pages 317–330. Springer, 2000.
14. M. Burrows, M. Abadi, and R. Needham. A logic for authentication. Technical Report 39, SRC DIGITAL, 1990.
15. R. Canetti and J. Herzog. Universally composable symbolic analysis of cryptographic protocols (the case of encryption-based mutual authentication and key exchange). Cryptology ePrint Archive, Report 2004/334, 2004.
16. V. Cortier and B. Warinschi. Computationally sound, automated proofs for security protocols. In *Proc. 14th ESOP*, pages 157–171, 2005.
17. D. Dolev and A. C. Yao. On the security of public key protocols. *IEEE Transactions on Information Theory*, 29(2):198–208, 1983.
18. V. D. Gligor and P. Donescu. Fast encryption and authentication: Xcbc encryption and xecb authentication modes. In *Proc. 8th FSE*, pages 82–108, 2001.
19. J. Guttman. Key compromise and the authentication tests. In *Proc. MPFS*, volume 17 of *ENTCS*, pages 1–21, 2001.
20. J. D. Guttman, F. J. Thayer Fabrega, and L. Zuck. The faithfulness of abstract protocol analysis: Message authentication. In *Proc. 8th ACM CCS*, pages 186–195, 2001.
21. J. Herzog, M. Liskov, and S. Micali. Plaintext awareness via key registration. In *Advances in Cryptology: CRYPTO 2003*, volume 2729 of *LNCS*, pages 548–564. Springer, 2003.
22. R. Impagliazzo and B. M. Kapron. Logics for reasoning about cryptographic constructions. In *Proc. 44th FOCS*, pages 372–381, 2003.
23. C. Jutla. Encryption modes with almost free message integrity. In *Advances in Crptology: EUROCRYPT 2001*, volume 2045 of *LNCS*, pages 529–544. Springer, 2001.
24. R. Kemmerer, C. Meadows, and J. Millen. Three systems for cryptographic protocol analysis. *Journal of Cryptology*, 7(2):79–130, 1994.
25. P. Laud. Semantics and program analysis of computationally secure information flow. In *Proc. 10th ESOP*, pages 77–91, 2001.
26. P. Laud. Symmetric encryption in automatic analyses for confidentiality against active adversaries. In *Proc. 25th IEEE S & P*, pages 71–85, 2004.
27. P. Lincoln, J. Mitchell, M. Mitchell, and A. Scedrov. A probabilistic poly-time framework for protocol analysis. In *Proc. 5th ACM CCS*, pages 112–121, 1998.
28. G. Lowe. An attack on the Needham-Schroeder public-key authentication protocol. *Information Processing Letters*, 56(3):131–135, 1995.
29. G. Lowe. Breaking and fixing the Needham-Schroeder public-key protocol using FDR. In *Proc. 2nd TACAS*, volume 1055 of *LNCS*, pages 147–166. Springer, 1996.
30. D. Micciancio and B. Warinschi. Soundness of formal encryption in the presence of active adversaries. In *Proc. 1st TCC*, volume 2951 of *LNCS*, pages 133–151. Springer, 2004.
31. L. Paulson. The inductive approach to verifying cryptographic protocols. *Journal of Cryptology*, 6(1):85–128, 1998.
32. L. Paulson. Relations between secrets: Two formal analyses of the yahalom protocol. *Journal of Computer Security*, 9(3):197–216, 2001.
33. B. Pfitzmann and M. Waidner. A model for asynchronous reactive systems and its application to secure message transmission. In *Proc. 22nd IEEE S & P*, pages 184–200, 2001. Extended version of the model (with Michael Backes) IACR Cryptology ePrint Archive 2004/082.

Sealed-Bid Micro Auctions

Kun Peng, Colin Boyd, and Ed Dawson

Information Security Institute
Queensland University of Technology, Australia
{k.peng, c.boyd, e.dawson}@qut.edu.au

Abstract. In electronic auction applications, small-value merchandise is often distributed. We call this kind of auction micro auction. Compared to traditional general-purpose electronic auction, micro electronic auction has its own special requirements. Especially, micro auction must be very efficient: the cost of the auction protocol must not be over the cost of the merchandise for sale. Although the merchandise to distribute are of small value in micro auctions, bid privacy is still needed in many circumstances. So sealed-bid auction mechanism has to be employed in micro auction. Therefore, a question is raised: how to balance between the high efficiency requirement of micro auction and the high cost needed to keep bid privacy. In this paper, the traditional sealed-bid e-auction techniques are modified to satisfy the special requirements of sealed-bid micro auction. Two existing general-purpose electronic sealed-bid auction schemes are modified into micro sealed-bid auction schemes. The new schemes are secure and suitable for micro auction. One of them is further improved in efficiency to meet more critical requirements in certain micro auction applications.

1 Introduction

Auctions have a long history as an effective method to distribute goods fairly. In recent years, electronic auctions on the Internet are becoming more and more popular. Due to security concerns for the network environment and payment method (often through the Internet too), electronic auction is more often used to distribute small-value merchandise. We call auction of small-value merchandise micro auction, which needs studying in the electronic form (through computer network). In any kind of auction, a basic principle should be followed: the cost of the auction protocol must not be over the value of the merchandise to distribute. So high efficiency is a key requirement for micro auction.

In this paper, after detailed analysis sealed-bid auction is chosen as an appropriate mechanism to implement micro auction. Unfortunately, all the existing sealed-bid auction schemes with bid privacy are only suitable for large-value merchandise. Although they are more efficient than double auction, they are still too inefficient for micro auction. They need a large number of exponentiations in computation, whose cost may be over the value of merchandise in micro auctions. So special sealed-bid auction schemes suitable for micro auction must be designed. To our knowledge there is no research work focused on sealed-bid micro auctions. In this paper, security and efficiency of sealed-bid micro auction are discussed and sealed-bid micro auction schemes with satisfactory security properties are designed.

Please use the following format when citing this chapter:

Author(s) [insert Last name, First-name initial(s)], 2006, in IFIP International Federation for Information Processing, Volume 201, Security and Privacy in Dynamic Environments, eds. Fischer-Hubner, S., Rannenberg, K., Yngstrom, L., Lindskog, S., (Boston: Springer), pp. [insert page numbers].

A simple and practical solution to efficient secure micro sealed-bid e-auction is to modify and optimize appropriate existing secure general-purpose sealed-bid e-auction into micro auction schemes. Among the two common methods to design secure sealed-bid e-auction, secure evaluation and one-choice-per-price strategy, one-choice-per-price strategy is more suitable for micro auction as it can more easily achieve high efficiency in micro auction. In this paper two secure micro sealed-bid e-auction schemes are designed based on existing sealed-bid auction schemes employing one-choice-per-price strategy. Both schemes can satisfy the security requirements for micro auction and are efficient, thus are suitable for auction of small-value merchandise. The second scheme is especially efficient as it is improved in efficiency by using the idea of batch proof. Batch proof in this paper employs an idea similar to efficiency improvement measures in some micro payment systems [1]. It aggregates proves validity of a few random subsets of bid opening operations to publicly prove validity of bid opening with a large probability. After the improvement, only a small constant number of exponentiations are needed in the second scheme. Although the improvement sacrifices instant verifiability and cannot detect invalid operation by the auctioneers until a final verification, the sacrifice is tolerable in micro auctions.

2 Requirements

As stated in Section 1, high efficiency is a very important requirement for micro auction. The most efficient auction in computation is open cry auction. In the open cry auctions, the bids are cried out openly and the auction result is publicly decided. As no bid is sealed, it is very efficient in computation. However, open cry auction cannot satisfy many micro auction applications as it is inefficient in communication and reveals all the bids. The open cry mechanism requires each bidder to remain on-line and repeatedly communicate with the auctioneer to update their bids. Very few bidders are willing to pay such a communicational cost for low-value merchandise. There are many reasons to keep bids secret. For example, a bidder may not want to permit other bidders to choose their bids according to his bid; the bidders may not want to permit the seller (or auctioneer) to design selling strategy in the future according to their bids; a bidder may want to keep his bid secret for personal privacy. All these reasons are independent of the value of the merchandise to sell. So like in auctions with large-value merchandise, confidentiality (or privacy) of bids are often required in micro auctions. An auction mechanism to achieve efficient communication and conceal the bids is double auction, which supports multiple sellers and bidders and a deal is made once a bid is no lower than a seller's offer. Double auction supports real-time deal, which may be preferred in micro auction. However, double auction is too inefficient in computation for micro auction.

Sealed-bid auction seems to be a good auction mechanism for micro auction, especially when high efficiency (both in computation and communication) and bid privacy are required. In a sealed-bid auction, a bidder has to submit a sealed bid before a closing time. After the closing time one or more auctioneers open the bids to decide the winners according to a pre-defined rule. Sealed-bid auction is more efficient than double auction while many existing sealed-bid auction schemes conceal the bids. Most security requirements in existing sealed-bid e-auction [3, 4] are also desired in micro auction. They are as follows.

1. Correctness: the auction result must be determined exactly according to the auction rule.
2. Public Verifiability: correctness of the auction must be publicly verifiable.
3. Fairness: no bidder can get more information than other bidders at each stage of the auction.
4. Bid confidentiality: each bid must remain confidential to other bidders and the auctioneer(s) before the bid opening phase starts.
5. Non-repudiation: no bidder can deny his bid.
6. Robustness: the auction can still work properly in abnormal situations
7. Rule Flexibility: various auction rules must be supported.
8. Bid Privacy: the losing bids are kept secret even after the auction.

As the cost of an auction protocol must not be over the value of the merchandise on sale, high efficiency is very important to micro auction. Implementation of any security property must be efficient. When necessary, appropriate trade-off must be made between security and efficiency. For example, correctness and public verifiability of micro auction may be achieved only with a large probability instead of absolutely, so that high efficiency is not compromised. On the condition that any incorrect operation can be publicly detected with a large probability, it is reasonable to assume that nobody will risk his reputation and qualification for a small-value merchandise. This idea has been used in some micro payment systems [1], where only a small subset of operations are verified. As these verified operations are randomly chosen, their validity can guarantee that the whole protocol is correctly carried out with a large probability. This idea of partial verification is also adopted in this paper, with different implementation of course.

As the merchandise to sell in micro auctions are of small value, the number of biddable prices is often not very large in micro auctions. Especially when multiple copies of the merchandise are available (e.g. when they are merchandise in electronic form like music, newspaper and document) and thus tie is not a problem, a small number of biddable prices are enough in micro auctions. So efficient auction mechanisms only dealing with a small number of biddable prices can be employed to achieve high efficiency in many micro auction applications.

3   Bid Privacy and Two Strategies

Bid privacy has a great influence on implementation of sealed-bid auctions including sealed-bid micro auctions. Without bid privacy the other properties can be easily achieved in a sealed-bid auction. Bid privacy actually implies that sealed-bid auction should be an application of secure computation, which evaluates a function with encrypted inputs without revealing the inputs. As secure computation is usually complex, sealed-bid auction is more difficult to design when bid privacy is required. However, bid privacy is necessary in many sealed-bid auction applications including micro auction. No matter whether the merchandise to sell is of small value or not, the following two reasons support the need of bid privacy.

1. Bidders want their bidding behaviours to be untraceable. Especially a bidder does not want other people to know that he submits a certain bid in a certain auction, which is a violation of his personal privacy and may violate his benefit in a later auction.

2. Sellers should be prevented from knowing the bids or their distribution. Otherwise they may gain some advantage when selling an identical or similar merchandise in the future.

Currently, there are two methods to implement bid privacy: secure evaluation and one-choice-per-price strategy. Secure evaluation is also called multiparty computation, which employs an evaluation circuit composed of a few logic gates to evaluate the encrypted bids and output the auction result. All of the auction schemes in this category seal the bid bit-by-bit and employ an evaluation circuit composed of a large number of logic gates to evaluate the sealed bids. A drawback of secure computation is low efficiency.

One-choice-per-price strategy is also frequently applied in sealed-bid auctions [6, 5, 3, 4] to achieve bid privacy. Under this strategy, each bidder must make a choice (indicating willingness or unwillingness to pay) at every biddable price while all his choices form his bidding vector. If a bidder is willing to pay a price, he chooses an integer standing for "YES" as his choice at that price. If a bidder is unwilling to pay a price, he chooses an integer standing for "NO" as his choice at that price. Two common bid opening functions in one-choice-per-price auction are downward searching function [5] and binary searching function [6, 3, 4]. Downward searching function unseals the sealed choices price by price downwards from the highest biddable price until a "YES" choice is unsealed at a price. With binary searching function, a much shorter binary route is searched.

4 Micro Sealed-bid Auction

Note that the most important requirement for micro auction is low cost. So one-choice-per-price strategy is chosen to implement micro auction as it is more efficient. Our idea is choosing appropriate existing secure sealed-bid auction schemes and optimize them into secure sealed-bid micro auction schemes. As the first paper about micro auction, this paper only considers first bid auction for simplicity. Namely, the bidder with the highest bid wins and pays the highest bid. Solutions to more complex auction rules are left as a future work. Two such attempts are made in this section. The first one employs binary search while the second employs downward search.

4.1 Protocol 1 — Micro Sealed-bid Auction Employing Binary Search

As pointed out in [3, 4], most existing first-bid sealed-bid auction schemes employing binary search are vulnerable to attacks and cannot guarantee correctness when there is invalid bid. On the other hand, proof and verification of bid validity are too costly (at least $4w$ exponentiations for a bidder and $4nw$ exponentiations for an auctioneer). So although bid opening through binary search is efficient, there was not any efficient and publicly verifiable sealed-bid auction scheme employing binary search until very recently two new sealed-bid auction scheme employing binary search [3,4] were proposed. These two schemes can publicly guarantee correctness of auction without bid validity check. So these two schemes [3,4] can be used as prototype when sealed-bid micro auction is designed. As [3] is more complex than [4] and has no advantage in efficiency when the number of biddable prices is small, [4] is chosen as a prototype, which is simplified and optimized into a secure sealed-bid micro auction scheme called Protocol 1. The two-round submission in [4] is too complex and costly for a low-cost micro auction. So it is simplified into one round. As a result, unconditional bid confidentiality and fairness in [4] become dependent on a threshold trust on the auctioneers. Bid confidentiality and fairness based on threshold trust should be strong enough for micro auction. Threshold secret sharing in [4] is replaced by simpler and more efficient ElGamal encryption with threshold distributed decryption to seal the bids. Suppose there are w biddable prices $p_1, p_2, \ldots, p_w$ in decreasing order, n bidders $B_1, B_2, \ldots, B_n$ and m auctioneers $A_1, A_2, \ldots, A_m$. Protocol 1 is as follows.

1. **Preparation phase**
   A bulletin board is set up as a broadcast communication channel. An ElGamal encryption system is set up. Large primes p and q are chosen such that q is a factor of $p - 1$. The cyclic group with order q modulo p is denoted as Q. Integer g is a generator Q. Private key x is randomly chosen from Z_q. Public key $y = g^x$ is published. The private key is shared among the auctioneers using threshold secret sharing such that any set of auctioneers can cooperate to perform decryption if and only if the number of cooperating auctioneers is over the sharing threshold. See [2] for more details about ElGamal encryption algorithm with distributed decryption.

2. **Bidding phase**
   Each bidder B_i selects his bidding vector $(b_{i,1}, b_{i,2}, \ldots, b_{i,w})$ as his choices at $p_1, p_2, \ldots, p_w$ where $b_{i,l} \in Z_q$ for $l = 1, 2, \ldots, w$. If he is willing to pay p_l, $b_{i,l}$ is a random integer in Q; if he is unwilling to pay p_l, $b_{i,l} = 1$. Then he encrypts and signs his bid vector and publishes the encrypted bid vector $(c_{i,1}, c_{i,2}, \ldots, c_{i,w})$ and signature on it on the bulletin board where $c_{i,j} = (g^{r_{i,j}}, b_{i,j} y^{r_{i,j}})$ and $r_{i,j}$ is randomly chosen from Z_q.

3. **Bid opening phase**
   The auctioneers cooperate to perform a binary search among the biddable prices. At a price p_l on the searching route, the auctioneers perform as follows.
   (a) Bid randomization and combination
       Each auctioneer A_j publishes a commitment (e.g. one-way hash function) of random integer $R_{j,i,l}$ from Z_q for $i = 1, 2, \ldots, n$. After all the commitments have been published, the auctioneers publish $R_{j,i,l}$ for $i = 1, 2, \ldots, n$ as randomizing factors of $b_{i,l}$. Finally, they compute $R_{i,l} = \sum_{j=1}^{m} R_{j,i,l}$ for $i = 1, 2, \ldots, n$ and $c_l = \prod_{i=1}^{n} c_{i,l}^{R_{i,l}}$.
   (b) Decryption
       The auctioneers cooperate to decrypt c_l and gets the decryption result d_l. If $d_l = 1$, the search goes downwards. If $d_l > 1$, the search goes upwards.
   Finally, the largest l satisfying $d_l > 0$ is found, which is denoted as L. p_L is declared as the winning price.

4. Winner identification phase

All the bid choices at $p_L, c_{1,L}, c_{2,L}, \ldots, c_{n,L}$, are decrypted by the auctioneers into $d_{1,L}, d_{2,L}, \ldots, d_{n,L}$ Any bidder submitting a bid choice larger than 1 at p_L is the winner. The winner's signature is verified and his identity is published.

Theorem 1. *Protocol 1 is correct. More precisely, with an overwhelmingly large probability $d_l > 0$ if and only if there is at least a bid choice indicating the willingness to pay at p_l.*

Proof: Suppose $D()$ is the decryption function of the employed ElGamal encryption. If $b_{1,l}, b_{2,l}, \ldots, b_{n,l}$, all the bid choices at p_l, are 1, $d_l = D(c_l) = D(\prod_{i=1}^{n} c_{i,l}^{R_{i,l}}) = \prod_{i=1}^{n} d_{i,l}^{R_{i,l}} = 1 \bmod p$. If at least one of $b_{1,l}, b_{2,l}, \ldots, b_{n,l}$ is a random integer uniformly distributed in Q, $d_l = D(c_l) = D(\prod_{i=1}^{n} c_{i,l}^{R_{i,l}}) = \prod_{i=1}^{n} d_{i,l}^{R_{i,l}} \bmod p$ is uniformly distributed in Q. So the probability that $d_l = 1$ when there is a bid choice indicating the willingness to pay at p_l is $1/q$, which is overwhelmingly small. $\square$

Theorem 2. *Protocol 1 achieves bid privacy. More precisely, no information about the losing bids is revealed except what can be deduced from the auction result if the number of colluding auctioneers is not over the sharing threshold of the private key.*

Proof: When all the bid choices at p_l are 1, the only revealed information about these bid choices is $d_l = 1$ if the number of colluding auctioneers is not over the sharing threshold of the private key. From the knowledge that $d_l = 1$, it can be deduced that with an overwhelmingly large probability all the bid choices at p_l is 1. However this revealed information can be deduced from the auction result. So bid privacy is not compromised.

When there is at least one bid choice uniformly distributed in Q at p_l, if the number of colluding auctioneers is not over the sharing threshold of the private key the only revealed information about these bid choices is d_l, which is uniformly distributed in Q. In this case the value of d_l reveals that there is at least one none-one bid choice at p_l with an overwhelmingly large probability. However this revealed information can be deduced from the auction result. No other information is revealed if the number of colluding auctioneers is not over the sharing threshold of the private key as given two different sets of bid choices at p_l from Q^n, the two distributions of d_l are indistinguishable (both are uniformly distributed in Q). $\square$

Protocol 1 is publicly verifiable and achieves bid confidentiality and fairness with a threshold trust on the auctioneers. If a reliable digital signature scheme is employed for the bidders to sign their bids, this scheme achieves non-repudiation. If a bid choice indicating willingness to pay is randomly chosen from $Q - \{1\}$, the auction scheme is correct with an even larger probability.

4.2 Protocol 2 — Micro Sealed-bid Auction Employing Downward Search

Usually downward search needs much more searching rounds than binary search, so often compromises efficiency. However, as mentioned in Section 2, only a small number of biddable prices are needed in micro auction when tie is not a problem (e.g. when multiple copies of the merchandise are available). In this case there is not a great difference between w and $\log_2 w$ as w, the number of biddable prices, is very small. So, if each searching round is very efficient, downward search can also achieve high efficiency. To our knowledge, it is very difficult to achieve high efficiency in each searching round with binary search (a few exponentiations are always needed as no bidding choice can be revealed), while it is possible to achieve high efficiency in each searching round with downward search (computation of exponentiation may be avoided as the bid choices can be simply directly decrypted). Therefore a downward search mechanism with efficient computation in each round is needed to design a micro sealed-bid auction with a small number of biddable prices. At the same time, communication must be efficient and non-interactive bid opening (without communication between the bidders and auctioneers) must be employed.

Unfortunately, none of the existing sealed-bid auction schemes employing downward search can provide this searching mechanism as they are inefficient either in computation or communication. So none of the existing sealed-bid auction schemes employing downward search can be used as a prototype.

However, a solution can still be found to design an efficient micro sealed-bid auction scheme with downward search: modify the auction scheme in [3] and replace the binary search in [3] with downward search. In the auction scheme in [3], bid sealing and bid opening are very efficient. Goldwasser-Micali encryption is employed in [3] for bid sealing, which averagely only costs 1.5 multiplications. Goldwasser-Micali decryption is employed in [3] for bid opening, which costs no more than several multiplications. However, to implement binary search without revealing any bid, complex and costly cut-and-choose strategy and zero knowledge proof are implemented in each round of search. So the binary search in [3] is complex and not very efficient. As the number of biddable prices is small in micro auction, the auction scheme in [3] can be optimized by replacing binary search with downward search, during each round of which all the bid choices at the corresponding price are simply decrypted. The new opening function is very simple and efficient as in each round only n instances of Goldwasser-Micali decryption are employed. After the optimization, the new auction scheme is very simple and efficient in both bid sealing and bid opening. The new micro sealed-bid auction scheme is called Protocol 2 and described as follows.

1. **Preparation phase**

   A bulletin board, acting as a broadcast communication channel, is set up, where the auction rule is published. m auctioneers $A_1, A_2, \ldots, A_m$ are employed. Each A_k sets up a Goldwasser-Micali encryption scheme with modulus N_k, public key y_k, encryption function $E_k()$ and decryption function $D_k()$ for $k = 1, 2, \ldots, m$ where N_k is the product of two secret large primes and y_k is a quadratic non-residue modulo N_k with Jacobi symbol 1. The existing Goldwasser-Micali encryption algorithm is slightly modified as follows.

   - Message space and ciphertext space: $\{1, -1\} \longrightarrow Q$ where Q contains all the integers with Jacobi symbol 1.
   - Encryption
     - If the message is 1, a ciphertext for the kth auctioneer is $x^2 \bmod N_k$ where x is randomly chose from $Z_{N_k}^*$.

- If the message is -1, the ciphertext for the kth auctioneer is $yx^2 \bmod N_k$ where x is randomly chose from $Z^*_{N_k}$.
  - Decryption: If an integer with Jacob symbol -1 is given as the ciphertext, the decryption fails and the integer is declared as an invalid ciphertext[1]. If a valid ciphertext is given, output the Legendre symbol of the ciphertext. When necessary, validity of decryption can be publicly proved: publishing a square root of the ciphertext when the decryption outputs 1 or publishing a square root of product of the ciphertext and the public key when the decryption outputs -1.

The modified Goldwasser-Micali encryption algorithm is semantically secure like the original Goldwasser-Micali encryption algorithm as the only change in the modification is replacing 0 with -1 in the message space.

2. **Bidding phase**
   Each bidder B_i chooses $b_{i,j}$, his bidding choice at the jth biddable price for $j = 1, 2, \ldots, w$. If he is willing to pay p_j, B_i chooses $b_{i,j} = -1$. If he is not willing to pay p_j, B_i chooses $b_{i,j} = 1$. Then B_i randomly chooses $b_{i,j,k}$ from $\{1, -1\}$ for $k = 1, 2, \ldots, m$ such that $b_{i,j} = \prod_{k=1}^{m} b_{i,j,k}$. Finally, B_i calculates $c_{i,j,k} = E_k(b_{i,j,k})$ for $j = 1, 2, \ldots, w$ and $k = 1, 2, \ldots, m$, then signs and publishes them on the bulletin board.

3. **Bid opening phase**
   At price p_1, each auctioneer A_k calculates $d_{i,1,k} = D_k(c_{i,1,k})$ for $i = 1, 2, \ldots, n$ and proves validity of decryption. Then $d_{i,1} = \prod_{k=1}^{m} d_{i,1,k}$ is calculated for $i = 1, 2, \ldots, n$. If there is any bid choice $d_{i,1}$ equivalent to -1, it is the winning bid. If $d_{i,1} = 1$ for $i = 1, 2, \ldots, n$, there is no bidder willing to pay p_1 and $c_{i,2,k}$ for $i = 1, 2, \ldots, n$, the bid choices at p_2, are opened with proof of validity of decryption. The search goes downwards until bid choice equivalent to -1 is found as the winning bid.

4. **Winner identification phase**
   The signature on the winning bid is verified and the winner is identified.

Theorem 3. *Protocol 2 is correct. More precisely, there exist i in $\{1, 2, \ldots, n\}$ such that $d_{i,j} = -1$ if and only if there is at least a bid choice indicating the willingness to pay at p_j.*

Proof: $d_{i,j} = \prod_{k=1}^{m} d_{i,j,k} = \prod_{k=1}^{m} D_k(c_{i,1,k}) = \prod_{k=1}^{m} D_k(E_k(b_{i,1,k})) = \prod_{k=1}^{m} b_{i,1,k} = b_{i,j}$ So there exist i in $\{1, 2, \ldots, n\}$ such that $d_{i,j} = -1$ if and only if there is at least a bid choice indicating the willingness to pay at p_j. □

Theorem 4. *Protocol 2 achieves bid privacy. More precisely, no information about the losing bids is revealed except what can be deduced from the auction result if at least one auctioneer does not conspire.*

Proof: As downward search is employed, only the bid choices no lower than the winning price are opened. Every bid choice lower than the winning price is shared

---

[1] Computation for Jacob symbol is efficient and comparable to a multiplication, so invalid ciphertext can be discovered easily.

among the auctioneers. Every bid choice is the product of its shares, which are randomly chosen. Also note that the modified Goldwasser-Micali encryption algorithm is semantically secure and no information is revealed from an encrypted bid choice or bid choice share. So at a price p_j lower than the winning price, even if $m - 1$ colluding auctioneers put their shares together, they get no information about any $b_{i,j}$ as no matter whether $b_{i,j} = 1$ or $b_{i,j} = -1$, the $m - 1$ shares of it are uniformly distributed in $\{1, -1\}^{m-1}$, which is indistinguishable. So no bid choice lower than the winning price is revealed except what can be deduced from the auction result if at least one auctioneer does not conspire.   □

Protocol 2 is publicly verifiable and achieves bid confidentiality and fairness with a m-out-of-m trust on the auctioneers. If a reliable digital signature scheme is employed for the bidders to sign their bids, this scheme achieves non-repudiation. As no exponentiation computation is needed in bid sealing and bid opening, this auction scheme is efficient, especially when the number of biddable prices is small.

5   Further Improvement

Protocol 1 is more efficient than the existing sealed-bid auction schemes with bid privacy and is suitable for micro auction. Protocol 2 provides an efficient solution to micro auction as well when the number of biddable prices is small. However they still have drawbacks. Firstly, they are still not efficient enough for micro auction with a computational cost of at least $O(m(n + (n + 1) \log_2 w))$ exponentiations and $O(wmn)$ exponentiations respectively. So their cost may still be higher than the value of the merchandise in some micro auction applications. Secondly, Protocol 2 is only efficient when the number of biddable prices is small. When tie is concern and the number of biddable prices cannot be too small, Protocol 2 is not efficient enough for micro auction.

So further improvement work (especially in efficiency) is still needed in these two protocols. Unfortunately, efficiency improvement is difficult in Protocol 1. However, in Protocol 2 a dramatic efficiency improvement can be made. The efficiency bottleneck in Protocol 2 lies in proof of validity of decryption of the bid choices in Step 3 (bid opening phase): to publicly prove validity of a decryption, a square root must be calculated, whose cost approximately equals $O(1)$ exponentiations. A solution to this efficiency bottleneck is to batch prove validity of multiple decryptions, which is similar to the idea of aggregate verification in micro payment system [1]. Namely, when M integers $c_1, c_2, \ldots, c_M$ need proving to be quadratic residues, a batch proof instead of M separate proofs can be used, so that invalid decryption by the auctioneers can be detected. The batch proof is described in Figure 1.

---

1. S, a random subset of $\{1, 2, \ldots, M\}$, is chosen.
2. Square root of $\prod_{i \in S} c_i$ is provided.
3. Repeat the operations above T times.

Fig. 1. Batch proof of quadratic residues.

Theorem 5. *If there is at least one quadratic non-residue among* $c_1, c_2, \ldots, c_M$, *the proof in Figure 1 can succeed with a probability no more than* 2^{-T}.

Proof: Suppose c_v is a quadratic non-residue where $1 \leq v \leq M$ Note that half of the subsets of $\{c_1, c_2, \ldots, c_M\}$ contain c_v and the other half do not contain c_v. So all the subsets of $\{c_1, c_2, \ldots, c_M\}$ can be divided into pairs such that in each pair the only difference between the two subsets is that one of them contains c_v and the other does not contain c_v. Note that in each pair of the subsets, the product of one subset's elements must be a quadratic residue while the product of the other subset's elements must be a quadratic non-residue. Namely, half of the subsets of $\{c_1, c_2, \ldots, c_M\}$ contain elements whose product is a quadratic residue and the other half of the subsets of $\{c_1, c_2, \ldots, c_M\}$ contain elements whose product is a quadratic non-residue. So square root of $\prod_{i \in S} c_i$ can be provided with a probability 0.5 when S is randomly chosen from $\{1, 2, \ldots, M\}$. Therefore, if there is at least one quadratic non-residue among $c_1, c_2, \ldots, c_M$, proof in Figure 1 can succeed with a probability no more than 2^{-T}. $\qquad\qquad\square$

The batch proof technique in Figure 1 can be employed to improve efficiency of Protocol 2, where each auctioneer acts as a prover and the random subsets are chosen according to a one-way hash function of the decryption result[2]. In Protocol 2, each auctioneer has to perform $O(nw)$ decryptions, so has to give $O(nw)$ instances of proof of quadratic residue. Normally, computation of $O(nw)$ square roots (costing $O(nw)$ exponentiations) is needed in every auctioneer's proof of decryption validity. When the batch proof technique in Figure 1 is applied to prove validity of decryption, only T square roots need calculating for each auctioneer. Although each auctioneer has a probability of 2^{-T} to cheat successfully, it is worthless for him to risk his reputation or qualification with so low a success rate for a small-value merchandise. Actually, when T is larger than 20, the success rate is less than 0.000001 when there is incorrect decryption, which is small enough to deter an auctioneer from cheating in a micro auction. So this efficiency improvement by batch proof is appropriate in micro auction. After this improvement, only a small constant number of exponentiations are needed in protocol 2. Besides greatly improving efficiency, this optimisation is not affected by the number of biddable prices. Namely, even when tie is a concern and a large number of biddable prices is needed, high efficiency can still be achieved. Moreover, batch proof can be further extended so that each auctioneer's proof of quadratic residue in multiple micro auction processes during a fixed period can be batched into computation of T square roots.

6 Conclusion

Requirements for micro auctions and methods to design sealed-bid micro auctions are surveyed in this paper. The first two secure micro sealed-bid e-auctions schemes are

---

[2] For example, the hash function has an N-bit output $z = z_1 z_2 \ldots z_N$ while an auctioneer has to prove N quadratic residues $c_1, c_2, \ldots, c_N$. c_i is chosen into the random subset if and only if $z_i = 1$.

proposed in this paper. They can satisfy all the security requirements necessary for micro auction. Moreover, these two schemes are efficient, especially when the number of biddable prices is small (as in most micro auctions). The second scheme is further improved in efficiency by batch proof such that only a small constant number of exponentiations are needed. Although instant verification is sacrificed after the optimisation, the sacrifice is tolerable in micro auctions.

Efficiency of the micro auction schemes in this paper and their prototypes are compared in Table 1, where ElGamal encryption and RSA signature are employed and the number of exponentiations are counted. An example is given in Table 1, where $w = 16$, $n = 200$, $m = 5$ and $T = 20$. Table 1 clearly demonstrates that the micro auction schemes proposed in this paper (especially the optimised Protocol 2) are very efficient. Contributions of the paper are illustrated in Table 2. It is clearly demonstrated in Table 2 that very high efficiency can be achieved for micro auction without compromising bid privacy by sacrificing unconditional fairness and instant verification, which can be tolerated in micro auction.

Table 1. Efficiency of Micro Auction Schemes.

Schemes	Computation			
	bidder	example	auctioneer	example
[4]	$(3m + 3)w + 1$	289	$1 + 5n + 5n \log_2 w$	5001
Protocol 1	$2w + 1$	33	$(n + 2) \log_2 w + 2n + 1$	1209
[3]	1	1	about $(mn + 4m + n) \log_2 w$	4880
Protocol 2	1	1	$0.5wn$	1600
Optimised Protocol 2	1	1	T	20

Table 2. Contribution of the Micro Auction Schemes.

Schemes	Fairness	Communi--cation	Search style	Biddable prices	Verification	Computation efficiency
[4]	Unconditional	2 rounds	Binary	Limited	Instant	Normal
Protocol 1	Trust-based	1 round	Binary	Limited	Instant	High
[3]	Trust-based	1 round	Binary	Limited	Instant	Normal
Protocol 2	Trust-based	1 round	Downward	Limited	Instant	High
Optimised Protocol 2	Trust-based	1 round	Downward	Unlimited	Batched	Very high

References

1. Silvio Micali and Ronald Rivest. Micropayments revisited. In *CT-RSA*, volume 2271 of *Lecture Notes in Computer Science*, pages 149–163, Berlin, 2002. Springer.
2. Torben P. Pedersen. *Distributed Provers and Verifiable Secret Sharing Based on the Discrete Logarithm Problem*. PhD thesis, Computer Science Department, Aarhus University, Aarhus, Denmark, 1992.
3. Kun Peng, Colin Boyd, and Ed Dawson. A multiplicative homomorphic sealed-bid auction based on Goldwasser-Micali encryption. In *ISC 2005*, volume 3650 of *Lecture Notes in Computer Science*, pages 374–388, Berlin, 2005. Springer-Verlag.
4. Kun Peng, Colin Boyd, and Ed Dawson. Optimization of electronic first-bid sealed-bid auction based on homomorphic secret sharing. In *Mycrypt 2005*, volume 3715 of *Lecture Notes in Computer Science*, pages 84–98, Berlin, 2005. Springer-Verlag.
5. Kun Peng, Colin Boyd, Ed Dawson, and Kapali Viswanathan. Non-interactive auction scheme with strong privacy. In *5th International Conference of Information Security and Cryptology - ICISC 2002*, volume 2587 of *Lecture Notes in Computer Science*, pages 407 – 420, Berlin, 2002. Springer.
6. Kun Peng, Colin Boyd, Ed Dawson, and Kapali Viswanathan. Robust, privacy protecting and publicly verifiable sealed-bid auction. In *4th International Conference of Information and Communications Security, ICICS 2002*, volume 2513 of *Lecture Notes in Computer Science*, pages 147 – 159, Berlin, 2002. Springer.

Detecting Known and Novel Network Intrusions

Yacine Bouzida[1]* and Frédéric Cuppens[2]

[1] Mitsubishi Electric ITE-TCL 1, allée de Beaulieu CS 10806 F-35708, Rennes, France
Bouzida@tcl.ite.mee.com
[2] ENST Bretagne 2, rue de la Châtaigneraie F-35576, Cesson Sévigné, France
Frederic.Cuppens@enst-bretagne.fr

Abstract. It is well known that signature based intrusion detection systems are only able to detect known attacks. Unfortunately, current anomaly based intrusion detection systems are also unable to detect all kinds of new attacks because they are designed to restricted applications on limited environment. Current hackers are using new attacks where neither access control systems nor current signature based systems can prevent the devastating results of these attacks against information systems. We enhance the notion of anomaly detection, introduce necessary conditions that should be taken into account by the building detection models and propose a new machine learning algorithm based on decision trees to discover known and unknown attacks in real time. Experimental results demonstrate that the proposed method is highly successful in detecting new attacks and significantly outperforms previous work.

1 Introduction

Anomaly intrusion detection systems are not as well studied or explored as misuse detection ones. Misuse detection consists in using patterns of well known intrusions to match and identify known labels for unlabeled data sets. In fact, many commercial and open source intrusion detection systems are misuse based ones. Recently, attackers have explored serious break-ins to many commercial and government sites where serious damages have occurred. The different intrusions that have been used were new. This situation was foreseeable because the attackers are attempting to develop new attacks forms where neither misuse detection tools nor access control tools installed in our networks may detect or stop these new attacks forms.

By contrast, anomaly detection consists in building profiles of normal behaviors then detecting any deviation of a new behavior from the learned normal profiles. This definition of anomaly detection is restrictive because only one class which corresponds to the normal behavior is learned.

In this paper, we extend the definition of anomaly detection to not only take into account normal profiles but also handle known attacks and explore supervised machine learning techniques, particularly decision trees. These techniques have proven their efficiency in predicting the different classes of the unlabeled data in the test data set for the KDD99 intrusion detection contest. Since machine learning techniques, generally,

---

* This work was completed when the author was a PhD student at ENST Bretagne.

Please use the following format when citing this chapter:

Author(s) [insert Last name, First-name initial(s)], 2006, in IFIP International Federation for Information Processing, Volume 201, Security and Privacy in Dynamic Environments, eds. Fischer-Hubner, S., Rannenberg, K., Yngstrom, L., Lindskog, S., (Boston: Springer), pp. [insert page numbers].

cannot find boundaries between known and unknown classes, an extension of decision trees is introduced to deal with new unknown anomalies.

The rest of the paper is organized as the following. Section 2 presents our motivations for extending the notion of anomaly detection. Section 3 enhances machine learning techniques, particularly decision trees, to handle new instances that are not considered in all current supervised machine learning techniques. Using the improvement of decision trees suggested in Section 3, Section 4 describes the experimental results obtained, using the decision trees algorithm and the modified algorithm, over the DARPA98 intrusion detection data set [3]. The KDD99 intrusion detection contest [5] uses a version of this data set. The data set provided in DARPA98 has been severely criticized in several previous works. However, we explain why this data set remains interesting to experiment our proposal. The first results obtained with our enhanced algorithm over KDD99 do not correspond to what we expect. This is due, in reality, to the transformation of DARPA98 to KDD99. Section 5 explains why KDD99 is not an appropriate transformation of DARPA99 and suggests necessary conditions a transformation technique should satisfy in order to keep maximum data information while transforming *tcpdump* traffic into connection records. Section 6 presents the results we obtained when considering new attacks not present in DARPA98 and Section 7 offers conclusive remarks and discusses future work.

2 Motivations

Anomaly intrusion detection is the first intrusion detection method that was introduced to monitor computer systems by Anderson [1] in 1980. At that time, intrusion detection was immature since only user behavior and some system events were taken into account. In fact, this approach consisted in establishing normal behavior profile for user and system activity and observing significant deviations of the actual user activity with respect to the established habitual profile. Significant deviations are flagged as anomalous and should raise suspicion. This definition did not take into account the expert knowledge of known vulnerabilities and then known attacks. This is why we enhance the notion of anomaly detection not only by considering normal profiles but also by taking into account abnormal behaviors that are extracted from known attacks.

Since we have knowledge about known vulnerabilities and their corresponding attacks, we may enhance the anomaly detection by adding to the learning step the abnormal behavior corresponding to known attacks. Therefore anomaly detection would consists in learning all known *normal* and *attacks* profiles. Based on this knowledge, anomaly detection has then to detect whether a new observed profile is normal or abnormal and its corresponding known attack is determined or the observed profile is new and therefore is considered as a novel unknown behavior. Thereafter, we suggest that a diagnosis should be done on the observed traffic that has caused the detection of the new anomaly in order to find out the reason of this new observation. If it corresponds to a normal new activity that was never observed before it is flagged as a normal profile or as a new attack. The new observations with their real classification would then be considered for further investigation. We note that the diagnosis of new observed behaviors is not an objective of this paper. This will be discussed in a forthcoming paper.

Current supervised machine learning and classification techniques are not written to detect new classes that are not present in the training data set (new profiles that are not seen before in our case). Therefore, we investigate in the following section the decision trees induction algorithm and improve it in order to deal with these new classes. We choose to use decision trees induction algorithm to best clarify the idea of new cases since it is such an illustrative technique. In addition, it is the best winning entry [4] for KDD99 intrusion detection contest. Added to this the fact that we are familiar with this technique since we used it to detect intrusions by combining it with principal component analysis for space and time reduction [2].

3 Decision Trees Enhancement

Decision trees classifiers are based on the *"divide and conquer"* strategy to construct an appropriate tree from a given learning set S containing a finite and not empty set of labeled instances. In the following, we are interested in the C4.5 Quinlan algorithm [7].

Most of the decision trees algorithms use a top down strategy; i.e. from the root to the leaves. Two main processes are necessary to use the decision tree, respectively called the building process and classification process.

3.1 Building process

It consists in building the tree by using the labeled training data set. An attribute is selected for each node based on how it is more informative than others. Leaves are also assigned to their corresponding class during this process.

To measure how informative a node is, Shanon entropy is used to construct the decision trees. The selection of the best attribute node is based on the gain $Gain(S, A)$ where S is a set of records and A a non categorical attribute. This gain defines the expected reduction in entropy due to sorting on A. It is calculated as the following [7]:

$$Gain(S, A) = Entropy(S) - \sum_{v \in Values(A)} \frac{|S_v|}{|S|} Entropy(S_v) \qquad (1)$$

If we consider only $Gain(S, A)$ then an attribute with many values will be automatically selected. One solution is to use $GainRatio$ instead [7]

$$GainRatio(S, A) = \frac{Gain(S, A)}{-\sum_{i=1}^{c} \frac{|S_i|}{|S|} log_2 \frac{|S_i|}{|S|}} \qquad (2)$$

where S_i is a subset of S for which A has a value v_i.

3.2 Classification process

A decision tree is important not because it summarizes what we know, i.e. the training set, but because we hope it will classify correctly new cases. Thus, when building classification models, one should have both training data to build the model and test data to verify how well it actually works. New instances are classified by traversing the tree from the up to down based on their attribute values and the node values until one leaf is reached that corresponds to the class of the new instance.

3.3 Improving the classification process

The decision trees C4.5 algorithm written by Quinlan presents a drawback toward the set of instances that are not covered by any of the rules generated from the decision tree. He proposes a default class for those instances. The default class is defined as the one with most items not covered by any rule. In the case of conflict, ties are resolved in favor of more frequent classes.

Using this principle, a default class from the learning data set is assigned to any observed instance that may be normal, known or unknown attack.

The default class is assigned to any new instance which is not covered by any rule generated from the training data set. This classification is useful only in the case of an exclusive classification; i.e. there is a class for any given instance and the assigned class has at least one instance in the learning data set. Since we are interested in detecting novel attacks this classification kind would not be able to detect new attacks that normally are not covered by any rule from the tree built during the learning step.

To resolve this problem, we introduce the following principle: A default class denoted *new class* is assigned to any new class that does not have a corresponding class in the training data set. Therefore, if any new instance does not match any of the rules generated by the decision tree then this instance is classified as a new class instead of assigning it to a default class.

To illustrate the effectiveness of this new idea, in Section 4, we conduct our experiments on the KDD99 database since it contains many new attacks in the test data set that are not present in the training data set and on real traffic in our laboratory network where some new attacks that were not available when DARPA98 was built such as the slammer worm and the different DDoS attacks are presented in Section 6.

4 Experimental Analysis of KDD99

The main task for the KDD99 classifier learning contest was to provide a predictive model able to distinguish between legitimate and illegitimate connections in a computer network. The training data set contained about $5,000,000$ connection records, and the training 10% data set consisted of $494,021$ records among which there are $97,278$ normal connections (i.e. 19.69%). Each connection record consists of 41 different attributes that describe the different features of the corresponding connection, and the value of the connection is labeled either as an attack with one specific attack type, or as normal. There are 39 different attack types present in the 10% data sets. We notice that there are many attacks that are present in the test data set but do not have any occurrence in the learning data set such as *saint, mailbomb, htttptunnel, snmpguess*, etc.

Each attack type falls exactly into one of the following four categories: *probing, DoS, U2R* and *R2L*.

The task was to predict the type of each connection in the test data set containing $311,029$ connections.

There are many occurrences of new attack forms for the two classes U2R and R2L in the test data set. The Probing class presents also many occurrences of new attacks forms in the test data set. However, for this class the difference is in the name of the tool used for the scan operation, not in the method with which the probing is performed.

We should mention that the different attacks present in the test data set that do not have any occurrence in the training data set cannot be easily classified into their appropriate class and will be classified in the class that has a form close to theirs and generally to the normal class. However, if the connection form does not characterize precisely the corresponding attack or the normal traffic as its initial *tcpdump* form then the classification of the new attacks would be unforeseeable.

To rank the different results a cost matrix C is defined. A cost per test (CPT) was calculated using the formula given in Equation 3.

$$CPT = \frac{1}{N} \sum_{i=1}^{5} \sum_{j=1}^{5} C_{i,j} * CM_{i,j} \tag{3}$$

where C corresponds to the cost matrix, N is the number of instances in the test data set and CM corresponds to the confusion matrix.

In the following, we present the different experiments and results obtained when using the different rules generated from the standard C4.5 algorithm. In the second step, the enhanced C4.5 algorithm, as explained in Section 3 to handle new instances, is used.

The accuracy of each experiment is based on the cost per test and the percentage of successful prediction (PSP) on the test data set.

$$PSP = \frac{number\ of\ successful\ instance\ classification}{number\ of\ instances\ in\ the\ test\ set} \tag{4}$$

Table 1 presents the confusion matrix for the 5 classes when using the rules from the decision trees generated by the standard C4.5 algorithm of Quinlan [7].

Table 1. Confusion Matrix relative to the five classes using the rules generated by the standard C4.5.

Predicted / Actual	%Normal	%Probing	%DoS	%U2R	%R2L
Normal(60,593)	**99.47**	0.40	0.12	0.01	0.00
Probing (4,166)	18.24	**72.73**	2.45	0.00	6.58
DoS (229,853)	2.62	0.06	**97.14**	0.00	0.18
U2R (228)	82.89	4.39	0.44	**7.02**	5.26
R2L (16.189)	81.60	14.85	0.00	0.70	**2.85**
$PSP = 92.30\%, CPT = 0.23425$					

From Table 1, the two classes R2L and U2R are badly predicted. On the other hand, many probing and DoS instances are misclassified within the normal class. Most misclassified instances are predicted as normal. This is due to the supervised C4.5 algorithm that assigns a default class among known classes as explained in Section 3.

Hence, if a new instance is presented (different from all other known normal or abnormal instances), it is automatically classified as the default class *normal* since it has the highest number of uncovered instances.

Table 2 shows the confusion matrix obtained when using the enhanced C4.5 algorithm that we have modified to affect a class labeled *new* to any uncovered or unseen instance.

Table 2. Confusion matrix when using the generated rules from the enhanced C4.5 algorithm.

Predicted Actual	%Normal	%Probing	%DoS	%U2R	%R2L	%New
Normal(60,593)	**99.43**	0.40	0.12	0.01	0.00	**0.04**
Probing (4,166)	8.19	**72.73**	2.45	0.00	6,58	**10.06**
DoS (229,853)	2.26	0.06	**97.14**	0.00	0.18	**0.36**
U2R (228)	21.93	4.39	0.44	**7.02**	5.26	**60.96**
R2L (16,189)	79.41	14.85	0.00	0.70	**2.85**	2.20
$PSP = (92.30 + (0.57))\%, CPT = 0.2228$						

Using the new enhanced C4.5 algorithm, we have increased the detection rate of the $U2R$ class by 60.96% which decreases the false negative rate of this class from 82.89%(189/228) to $21,93\%(50/228)$. The detection rate of the Probing class is also enhanced by 10,06% corresponding to 413 instances which are not classified as a normal traffic but as a new class, hence as a new attack.

We should mention that the highest ratio for the U2R class has never exceeded 14% according to the different results available in the literature. Using our approach this attack is detected as an abnormal traffic with a detection rate of 67.98%.

However, the false negative rate of the R2L class remains stable. In addition, even if we count the detection ratio of the new instances that are classified as new attack the PSP (92.30% + 0.57% = 92.87%) ratio remains far from 100%.

The cost per test obtained by our method is much more better than the Pfahringer's winning entry [4] by performing a $CPT = 0.2228$.

In our knowledge, there is not any work in the literature that has exceeded the Pfahringer's [4] winning entry.

Most R2L instances are predicted as normal connections. In the following, we explain why this class is misclassified in the normal type. The main reason is the transformation done over DARPA98 to obtain KDD99 where most attacks of type R2L in the test data set are not different from many normal connections in the training data set.

In order to construct valuable behavior models, many features should be gathered to characterize the considered behavior. However, the raw "unstructured" data collected from a network or other sources are not easy to analyze by different classification techniques which need more structured data format to work well. A data preprocessing phase of the gathered raw data must be performed to extract meaningful features and measures.

5   Why KDD99 is Not an Appropriate Transformation?

The intrusion detection database KDD99 is a result of a transformation, into connection records using some data mining techniques [6], of a *tcpdump* traffic DARPA98 collected in a local area network, during nine weeks, simulating a typical U.S. Air Force LAN. The MIT Lincoln Laboratories operated this simulated LAN as if it were a true Air Force environment, but peppered with the 39 different attacks types. However, we should mention that the transformation done in MADAM ID [6] presents some drawbacks due to some limitations of the tools used for this task and the lack of some basic definitions and necessary conditions that must be satisfied by this transformation.

In the following, we introduce some definitions and conditions that a good transformation should satisfy without losing meaningful information from the initial form of the data.

The transformation task may be formalized as the following. Let R be the raw data set collected from the network traffic or other sources depending on the environment we are interested in analyzing to discover known or new computer security attacks. We can formalize audit data preprocessing by a transformation function T from the raw data set R to a well featured data item set I. This last data set denotes the whole possible values of the different considered features. An item x of I is a vector of the form $(v_1, v_2, ..., v_n)$ where each value v_i is either discrete or continuous. Let $C = \{c_1, c_2, ..., c_m\}$ be a set of the different known classes to which a behavior (an item) may fall.

The classification function, that we denote F, is then used to assign a class label to an input item vector.

5.1   What is an appropriate transformation function

1. The transformation model which consists in transforming the raw data set into their corresponding items in I should be *rich* enough to distinguish between the different behaviors in the new feature space after transformation. A *poor* transformation model T may occur when some attribute values are the same in different data items that have different class labels. This means that if we consider $r_i, r_j \in R$ and $T(r_i) = x_i, T(r_j) = x_j$ where $x_i, x_j \in I$ then if $F(r_i) \neq F(r_j)$ the transformations of r_i and r_j should be different, i.e $x_i \neq x_j$. If this is not the case then the data items that share the same attribute values but have different class labels are considered as noise data and their number must be reduced so that accurate classification models may be learned from I.

2. If two items $T(r_i) = x_i$ and $T(r_j) = x_j$, issued from a transformation T, have two distinct classes and have similar values for all considered attributes then two cases are present:

   (a) either the set of the considered attributes issued from transformation T is not sufficient to characterize and then differentiate them; i.e the transformation function T is *poor*. Then we should add new attributes that can render this transformation *rich*, hence the problem is resolved.
   More formally: if $r_i \neq r_j$, $real\_class(r_i) \neq real\_class(r_j)$ and $T(r_i) = T(r_j)$; then the function T is poor. If this case occurs then the corresponding records present incoherence with the real traffic. Therefore, the number

of attributes which is not sufficient should be increased to distinguish the two distinct records in the new feature space.

(b) or we cannot distinguish between the raw traffic of the two connections r_i et r_j having two distinct classes. In this case we cannot find a transformation function T that may distinguish the two connections form in the new feature space. More formally: If $r_i = r_j$ and $real\_class(r_i) \neq real\_class(r_j)$ then $\nexists\ T$ such that $T(r_i) \neq T(r_j)$.

This last case is possible if we consider a subject b that knows the password of another subject a. The generated data by the intruder b who is using the account of the user a, during a *telnet* authentication session for example, would not be different from that data generated by the legitimate user a. In this situation, there is no intrusion detection method that can find this intrusion without using any additional information.

In the following, we verify the satisfaction of these different necessary conditions on the transformation performed by W. Lee et al. [6] and demonstrate that it is not the case and some attacks, having high occurrence number, belonging to the $R2L$ class do not satisfy the first condition presented above. The bad classification of class $R2L$ is particularly due to the transformation performed over DARPA98 data sets.

5.2 Discussions

In this section, we show that the different KDD99 data sets issued from the transformation T implemented in MADAM/ID [6] is *poor* and the high false negative rate for the R2L class is due to this poor transformation.

In the following, a comparative study between the confusion matrices obtained in two tests, is presented, where in the first case we use the default training data set of KDD99 as the training data set and in the second test we use the test data set as the training set. In each test, we examine the percentage of successful prediction (PSP) using the learning data set of each test as a test set. The objective of this analysis is to help us discover whether the two databases are coherent. Therefore, the different prediction ratios of the different databases may help us to find out whether the transformation done by W. Lee et al. [6] is *poor* or not.

The learning data set coherence Let us examine now Table 3 that corresponds to the confusion matrix obtained from initial learning database when using our enhanced C4.5 induction decision trees algorithm.

We notice that the different classes are predicted with high rates using the learning database to construct the tree and to generate the different rules. The successful prediction ratio is $PSP = 99.99\%$. However, the lowest prediction ratio is that of the $U2R$ classes because there are not enough instances (52) of this class in the learning set. Our enhanced C4.5 algorithm (see Table 3) has proven its ability to classify the least frequent classes, which are not covered by any of the rules generated by the decision tree algorithm, as novel attacks rather than as normal traffic.

In the field of supervised machine learning techniques, a method is said powerful if it learns and predicts easily the different instances of the training set with a low

Table 3. Confusion matrix obtained using the enhanced C4.5 algorithm on the initial KDD99 learning database.

Predicted / Actual	%Normal	%Probing	%DoS	%U2R	%R2L	%New
Normal(97,278)	**99.94**	0.01	0.00	0.00	0.00	**0.05**
Probing (4,107)	0.17	**99.78**	0.00	0.00	0.00	**0.05**
DoS (391,458)	0.00	0.00	**99.99**	0.00	0.00	**0.01**
U2R (52)	1.92	1.92	0.00	**90.39**	0.00	**5.77**
R2L (1,126)	0.62	0.00	0.00	0.09	**98.93**	**0.36**

$$PSP = 99.99\%$$

error detection and then generalizes its knowledge to predict the class of new instances. Unfortunately, the results obtained in Table 3, C4.5 induction algorithm has efficiently learned the different instances of the training set but could not classify new instances, for the moment, into their appropriate category (see for instance Table 1).

The confusion matrix presented in Table 1 shows that the two classes U2R and R2L are badly classified into the normal class. We have expected this result because the standard C4.5 is not designed to detect novel classes that are not present in the training set. We have improved this algorithm to handle these new instances but the R2L class, as showed in Table 2, remains badly classified. Hence, three cases are possible; either the enhanced algorithm failed to detect these new attacks or some KDD99 data are false or some conditions presented in Section 5.1 are possibly not satisfied. If the second case is true, then these data should be analyzed to verify their exactitude. The first assumption is not possible because if a new instance is totally distinct from all other instances of the learning set if there is not any rule issued from the decision tree generated from the learning set that can classify it (but the default rule that can classify it as a *new* instance with the enhanced algorithm) else it is not totally distinct and then belongs certainly to a known class.

The results of Table 2 showed that the enhanced C4.5 algorithm detected more new attacks of type U2R in the test data set. However, the new R2L attacks are predicted as normal connections. We have investigated those new attacks of type R2L that are predicted as normal traffic. There are exactly 7 new R2L classes namely {*named, sendmail, snmpgettattack, snmpguess, worm, xlock, xsnoop*}. Most of these attacks are predicted as normal.The false negative rate is about 99.10% (resp. 99.97%) using the enhanced C4.5 algorithm (resp. the standard C4.5 algorithm). We focus on two of them; *snmpget-tattack, snmpguess* since they present 74.79%(12108/16189) out of the R2L attacks in the test data set. All instances of these two attacks are predicted as normal connections (within R2L class in Table2).

These results show that these new R2L connections are not *distinct* from the normal connections issued after transformation.

In the following paragraph, we investigate the test data set from which we construct a decision tree in order to see if it is coherent and whether the new R2L instances are classified as normal or new from the tree generated by the test data set. After the test, we may conclude that our hypothesis of transformation done over DARPA98 to KDD99 is poor and should be improved.

The test data set incoherence In this second test, we invert the two databases. Hence, the learning database consists of 311, 029 connections and the test database contains 494, 021 connections.

Using the standard and the enhanced C4.5 algorithms, we obtained the confusion matrix presented in Table 4 of the learning instances classification for this second test.

Table 4. Confusion matrix relative to five classes using the rules generated by the enhanced C4.5 algorithm over the learning database of the second test.

Predicted Actual	%Normal	%Probing	%DoS	%U2R	%R2L	%New
Normal(60,593)	**98.34**	0.02	0.03	0.01	1.50	**0.11**
Probing (4,166)	0.19	**99.35**	0.07	0.00	0.00	**0.38**
DoS (229,853)	0.01	0.00	**99.99**	0.00	0.00	**0.00**
U2R (228)	2.19	0,00	0.00	**96.93**	0.00	**0.88**
R2L (16,189)	36.40	0,02	0.01	0.05	**63.33**	**0.19**
$PSP = 97.70\%$						

Although the percentage of successful prediction rate, from confusion matrix 4, is $PSP = 97.70\%$, it is considered very low since it consists in classifying the labeled (known) instances of the learning data set. This means that the C4.5 algorithm failed to learn instances with their appropriate labels. This rate is considered very low in the machine learning domain because it could not learn the instances whose classes are known a priori. On the other hand, The R2L class is highly misclassified. The classifier has learned only 63.33% from all the R2L labeled instances.

Most misclassified R2L instances are predicted as normal connections. This result justifies our observation stated in the above subsection i.e the new R2L attacks are not distinct from the normal connections, issued after transformation.

We investigated the different ratios of misclassified attacks of type R2L, we find out that these misclassified attacks are of type *snmpgettattack* or *snmpguess*.

The *snmpgetattack* type is the most frequent class type present in the $R2L$ category $(7, 741/16, 189)$. The decision rules generated from the decision tree constructed from the second database could not classify 71.85% of *snmpgetattack* instances that correspond to 5, 562 instances; this presents a high false negative rate. Then the test data set of KDD99 is considered incoherent.

In this case, it is not interesting to test the new test database of the second test since the learning set is not learned.

From this, we are sure that these data are false or poor due to the transformation function done by W. Lee et al. in the MADAM/ID tool [6].

The new two attacks *snmpguess* and *snmpgetattack* that are present only during the two test weeks correspond in reality to an attack scenario. In this scenario an attacker guesses the SNMP community password and then remotely monitors the router activity. The SNMP password is set to "public" by default, and is often never changed from this default value.

In the DARPA98 and then KDD99, the SNMP community password remains by default (*"public"*). Hence, during the first day of the first test week, there is an attack, against an internal router of the SNMP community password by sending SNMP requests to that router using different passwords until receiving a response from that router indicating that the password is correct. This attack is similar to the dictionary attack for password guessing. We should mention that there were more than $30,000$ SNMP requests, in the DARPA98 *tcpdump* traffic, to find out the correct password. This attack corresponds to *snmpguess* that is considered as an $R2L$ attack presenting 26.75% $(4,367/16,189)$ connections in the $R2L$ class. Once the attacker has guessed the password, he may easily monitor the router without being detected. Moreover, this attacker has come back many times to monitor this community during the two test weeks by using the guessed password. The attacker monitoring traffic corresponds to the the $R2L$ *snmpgetattack* in the KDD99 database that presents 47.82% $(7,741/16,189)$ of the whole $R2L$ connections in this test database.

All instances of this last attack (*snmpgetattack*) are predicted as normal (within R2L class in Table 4). This result is expected and corresponds exactly to the situation presented in the point *2.b* in Section 5.1. Indeed, this traffic will be recognized as normal because the password is guessed by an attacker. However, the *snmpguess* category should be recognized as a new attack or as a dictionary attack like guess passwd category. Unfortunately, there is not any attribute among the 41 attributes to test the SNMP community password in the SNMP request as it is the case with some attributes that verify if it is a root password or a guest password but this is considered only in the case of *telnet, rlogin*, etc. services. Hence one interesting information is lost after transformation with which we cannot distinguish the traffic generated by the *snmpguess* attack with the normal traffic. This situation corresponds exactly to the necessary condition a transformation function T should satisfy as described in point *2.a* in Section 5.1. Therefore, this transformation function is poor and some attributes should be added to differentiate some attacks using the dictionary from other traffic.

The R2L could never be predicted with high rates exceeding the Pfahringer [4] results since the transformation function T introduced by W. Lee et al. [6] is poor where normal SNMP connections are similar to *snmpguess* and *snmpgettattack* connections after transformation into 41 attributes.

6   Other experiments of *new* attacks detection

In this section, we verify the efficiency of the enhanced C4.5 algorithm in detecting new attacks that are not present when DARPA98 was built.

The transformation and the different programs (MADAM/ID [6]) done at the Columbia University are not available[3]. We did write our own programs that permit to transform the network traffic into connection records but respecting the different

---

[3] These programs are licensed to a company who now is developing it commercially.

rules and conditions that should be taken into account as explained in Section 5.1. The new attacks we investigate are those flooding attacks generated by the different known DDoS tools such as Trinoo, TFN, TFN2K, etc., used during the year 2000 against many servers over Internet. The second attack category is the Slammer DoS worm that infected thousand vulnerable servers over internet in 2003.

We tried to detect the new DDoS and Slammer attacks that were not known when the DARPA98 was constructed as new attacks. Fortunately, they have been classified as DoS attacks. In reality, the traffic form generated from the DDoS agents is not different from that of DoS traffic which is already present in the DARPA98 database. We mention that there is not any signature based IDS that could detect the flooding DDoS traffic. On the other hand, a signature based IDS cannot detect the traffic generated by the Slammer worm without adding appropriate signatures in their database.

We have improved our method as the following. If a new connection is detected as new or as a known attack, we add its corresponding connection record in the learning database if there is not any connection that is similar to the current detected attack in the learning set and then remake the learning step with the presence of these new attacks in the learning database. This idea permits the C4.5 classifier learn the new attacks in an incremental fashion. However, the new connections that are classified in the new category (see instance Table 2 particularly the new R2L attacks detected as new traffic) are considered temporarily abnormal for launching an appropriate countermeasure. However, a thorough diagnosis should be performed to find out whether it is a new traffic corresponding to a new normal activity or it is a new attack that should be added to the learning database for further investigation.

7 Conclusion

In this paper, a new anomaly intrusion detection based on decision trees is investigated and tested over the KDD99 data sets and over real network traffic in real time. We have proven its efficiency and its application has exceeded the winning entry of the KDD99 data intrusion detection contest. Since the different MADAM/ID programs are not available and present many shortcomings, we have written the different programs that transform *tcpdump* traffic into connection records following some necessary conditions we defined. The objective of our contribution is threefold. The first consists in extending the notion of anomaly intrusion detection. The second is the necessity to improve machine learning methods by adding a new class into which novel instances should be classified since they should not be classified as any of the known classes in the learning data set. The third contribution consists in introducing some necessary conditions that should be verified by a rich transformation function. This last point was not taken into account during the transformation of the DARPA98 into KDD99 data sets. As a result many attacks traffic became identical to normal traffic after transformation. Our tool is written in C/C++ for GNU/GPL and works in real time. As future work, we are investigating its use with many correlation tools such as CRIM or CARDS and any other explicit or semi explicit correlation tool. Since these tools do not deal with unknown attacks, we are currently investigating their extension to handle these new attacks generated by our new anomaly detection to integrate them in the ongoing correlation attack scenarios.

270   Yacine Bouzida and Frédéric Cuppens

Acknowledgments

This work was funded by the French ministry of research under the ACI DADDi project.

References

1. J. P. Anderson. Computer Security Threat Monitoring and Surveillance. Technical report, James. P. Anderson Co., Fort Washington, Pennsylvania, 1980.
2. Y. Bouzida and S. Gombault. Eigenconnections to Intrusion Detection. In 19th IFIP International Information Security Conference (SEC'2004), pages 241–258, Toulouse, France, August 2004. Kluwer Academic Publishers.
3. DARPA Intrusion Detection Evaluation. Available at: http://www.ll.mit.edu/IST/ideval/data/data_index.html, 1998.
4. C. Elkan. Results of the KDD'99 Classifier Learning. ACM SIGKDD, 1:63–64, 2000.
5. S. Hettich and S. D. Bay. The UCI KDD Archive. Available at: http://kdd.ics.uci.edu/, 1999.
6. W. Lee and S. Stolfo. A Framework for Constructing Features and Models for Intrusion Detection Systems. ACM Transactions on Information and System Security, 3(4), November 2000.
7. J. R. Quinlan. C4.5: Programs for machine learning. Morgan Kaufmann Publishers, 1993.

Evaluating Classifiers for Mobile-Masquerader Detection*

Oleksiy Mazhelis[1], Seppo Puuronen[1], and Mika Raento[2]

[1] University of Jyväskylä, Finland
{mazhelis,sepi}@it.jyu.fi
[2] University of Helsinki and Helsinki Institute for Information Technology, Finland
Mika.Raento@cs.Helsinki.FI

Abstract. As a result of the impersonation of a user of a mobile terminal, sensitive information kept locally or accessible over the network can be abused. The means of masquerader detection are therefore needed to detect the cases of impersonation. In this paper, the problem of mobile-masquerader detection is considered as a problem of classifying the user behaviour as originating from the legitimate user or someone else. Different behavioural characteristics are analysed by designated one-class classifiers whose classifications are combined. The paper focuses on selecting the classifiers for mobile-masquerader detection. The selection process is conducted in two phases. First, the classification accuracies of classifiers are empirically evaluated, and inaccurate classifiers are excluded. After that, the accuracies of different classifier combinations are explored, and the combination with the best classification accuracy is identified. The experimental results suggest that, in order to achieve better accuracy, the individual classifiers with both high classification accuracy and a small number of non-classifications need to be selected.

1 Introduction

An impersonation of the user of a contemporary mobile terminal, such as a smart-phone or PDA, may result in an abuse of critical private or corporate information. Impersonating the legitimate user (later called *user*) to obtain an unauthorised access to sensitive data or services authorised for that user is referred to as the *masquerade attack*. In order to resist such attack, the so-called *detective* security means [1] can be implemented (in addition to preventive security means) to perform *masquerader detection*. During last years, great efforts have been devoted to the problem of detecting masquerade attacks, e.g. [2–5], also in the context of mobile terminals [6].

In this paper, the problem of mobile-masquerader detection is approached as an anomaly detection problem [2]. To detect anomalies, a user model is learnt through the monitoring of the user behaviour during the so-called learning phase, and the learnt

---

* This work was partly supported by the COMAS Graduate School of the University of Jyväskylä. The Context project was funded by the Academy of Finland under the PROACT research program. The authors would like to thank Hannu Toivonen, as well as anonymous reviewers for valuable comments and suggestions.

Please use the following format when citing this chapter:

Author(s) [insert Last name, First-name initial(s)], 2006, in IFIP International Federation for Information Processing, Volume 201, Security and Privacy in Dynamic Environments, eds. Fischer-Hubner, S., Rannenberg, K., Yngstrom, L., Lindskog, S., (Boston: Springer), pp. [insert page numbers].

model is stored in a *user profile*. The detection may be performed by matching a currently observed behaviour of a claimant (a person whose identity claim is being verified) against the model. Multiple behavioural characteristics have been proposed as potentially useful in masquerader detection [6, 7, 3]. Recently, a set of characteristics for mobile-masquerader detection have been suggested [8]; however, an empirical evidence indicating how well these characteristics can be used in practise has not been provided so far.

We formulate the problem of anomaly detection as a one-class classification problem [9], where a claimant's behaviour, represented by a set of feature values, is classified as belonging to the *user class* reflecting the behaviour of the user, or not. In the latter case, the decision is made that the behaviour belongs to the *impostor class* summing up the behaviours of all other individuals but the user.

In anomaly detection, one-class classifiers are often based on probability estimation [10, 2, 4], and they often analyze the whole set of features simultaneously. However, due to difficulties with learning when the features are lumped into a single high-dimensional vector, difficulties with the normalization of features having different physical meaning, and partial availability of the feature values at the time the detection is performed, the use of an alternative approach based on combining classifiers is justified [11]. Following this approach, the features can be divided into subgroups processed by individual one-class classifiers. Each of them is aimed at classifying the current values of assigned features. By employing a *combining rule*, the final classification is produced based on the classifications of the individual classifiers.

In this paper, we empirically evaluate one-class classifiers to be used in mobile-masquerader detection. For the purposes of the evaluation, the dataset describing the behaviour of nine mobile users was employed. The selection of features and classifiers was constrained by the attributes available in this dataset. The authors are not aware of any other empirical study on mobile-masquerader detection, where more than one behavioural aspect is taken into account.

The evaluation was conducted in two phases. In the first phase, classification accuracies of classifiers were evaluated, and the classifiers with low accuracy were filtered. In the second phase, we investigated which of the remaining classifiers are reasonable to use in combination so that the accuracy of final classification would increase. For this, the accuracies of different classifier combinations were compared. When selecting the classifiers to add to the combination, a variety of criteria can be used; some of them were tested. The best results were achieved, when the classifiers selected had both high classification accuracy and a low number of non-classifications.

The paper is organised as follows. In the next Section, the features employed are described, the design of individual classifiers is discussed, and the details of the utilised combining scheme are provided. The employed dataset is described in Section 3. The experimental settings and the results of experiments are presented in Section 4. Finally, in Section 5, the experimental findings and their limitations are discussed, and the topics for further work are outlined.

2   Design of individual classifiers and their combination

In this section, the measures employed for masquerader detection and the design of individual classifiers to process these measures are considered, and the scheme for combining individual classifications is described.

2.1   Design of individual classifiers

In our approach, the anomaly detection problem is seen as a classification problem, where the object Z (claimant) is to be classified as belonging either to the user class ($Z \in C_U$) or to the class of impostors ($Z \in C_I$), but not to both of them, i.e. $\{Z | Z \in C_U\} \cup \{Z | Z \in C_I\} = \emptyset$. The object Z is represented by the set of n_f features $\{x_1, \ldots, x_{n_f}\}$ from the feature space $\mathcal{X}$, and is analysed by the set of R individual classifiers. Classifier i takes as input the observation vector $\mathbf{x}_i \equiv (x_1^{(i)}, \ldots, x_{n_{f_i}}^{(i)})$, $x_j^{(i)} \in \mathcal{X}_i \subset \mathcal{X}$.

The classification process consists of the learning and the classification phases. In the learning phase, using a training set $\mathcal{DS}_T$, the classifier i learns the set of parameters Θ_i constituting the *model* of the classifier. $\mathcal{DS}_T$ includes the vectors of feature values of the user: $\mathcal{DS}_T = \{((x_1, \ldots, x_{n_f})_j, y_j) | j = 1, \ldots, |\mathcal{DS}_T|\}$, where $y_j = C_U$ is the class label. In the classification phase, the learnt model is used to classify into the user class or the impostor class unlabeled observation vectors from a dataset $\mathcal{DS}_C = \{((x_1, \ldots, x_{n_f})_j) | j = 1, \ldots, |\mathcal{DS}_C|\}$.

Observation vectors of individual classifiers are initialised with available feature values gathered by employing a sliding window $[\tau_1, \tau_2]$ of the length $l_\tau = \tau_2 - \tau_1$ (determining the time interval, within which the feature values are collected), with an increment for the window δ_τ. Given an unlabeled observation vector $\mathbf{x}_i$, each classifier outputs the individual classification $u_i = u_i(\mathbf{x}_i, \Theta_i)$ indicating how likely $Z \in C_U$. Below, the descriptions of the employed features and the individual classifiers are provided.

In [8], the authors considered personality factors in order to identify suitable characteristics and measures for mobile-masquerader detection. They suggest that, while personality factors are latent, they are reflected in different *aspects* of user *behaviour* and *environment*. The characteristics describing these aspects can be directly observed. It is hypothesized that the superposition of characteristics describing one's behaviour and environment is also individual, and can be used to verify the identity of a person.

To measure quantitatively the characteristics of user behaviour and environment, one or more appropriate observable variables, or *measures* should be assigned to each of them. A list of tentative characteristics and measures has been proposed; the interested reader may consult [8] for the detailed description of these characteristics. Some of the measures described in [8] are not available in the dataset (described in Section 3) which was employed in the experiments. The available measures were assigned as features to individual classifiers. To each of the measures, an individual classifier was assigned as described below.

Type of program or service evoked. Active applications evoked by the user are registered in the dataset. This measure is referred to as *active applications* (ACT_APP).

For each application j, the classifier based on active applications maintains a counter a_{app_j} that stores the number of times the user evokes the application. The probability of an application j being evoked out of m applications is approximated as $\hat{P}(\mathrm{app}_j|U) = (a_{\mathrm{app}_j} + 1)/(\sum_m a_{\mathrm{app}_m} + 1)$. Assuming the independence of consequent application evocations, the probability of application evocations within a time window $[\tau_1, \tau_2]$ is approximated as

$$\hat{P}(\mathrm{app}_{i-n_{app}+1}, \ldots, \mathrm{app}_i|U) = \prod_{j=i-n_{app}+1}^{i} \hat{P}(\mathrm{app}_j|U), \tag{1}$$

where app_i is the last application evoked within the time window, and n_{app} is the average number of applications evoked within the window. The application evocations within previous window(s) can be taken into account if needed (the same is valid for the other classifiers, too). Given the current active applications to be classified, the classifier outputs the classification $u_i = \hat{P}(\mathrm{app}_{i-n_{app}+1}, \ldots, \mathrm{app}_i|U)$.

Sequence of cells traversed. The dataset records the identifiers of the cells (Cell IDs) wherein the mobile terminal is registered. The information about consecutive Cell IDs can be utilised in order to create the *sequences of cells traversed* measure ($MOVE$).

The model of the assigned classifier includes the matrix of cell-to-cell transition probabilities, and, in fact, represents a first-order Markov model. An element $a_{\mathrm{cell}_i\ \mathrm{cell}_j}$ of the matrix is a counter that stores the number of times the terminal's Cell ID changed from cell i to cell j. The matrix values are used in approximating the probability $\hat{P}(\mathrm{cell}_j|\mathrm{cell}_i, U)$ of a handover:

$$\hat{P}(\mathrm{cell}_j|\mathrm{cell}_i, U) = \frac{a_{\mathrm{cell}_i\ \mathrm{cell}_j} + 1}{\sum_m a_{\mathrm{cell}_i\ \mathrm{cell}_m} + n_{neighbour\ i}}, \tag{2}$$

where cell_m are the cells to which traversals from cell_i were registered, and $n_{neighbour\ i}$ is the number of such cells. Given the parameters l_τ and δ_τ of sliding windows, the average number of handovers n_{ho} within a window was estimated. Assuming the independence of consequent handovers, the probability of a sequence of cell changes within a time window $[\tau_1, \tau_2]$ was approximated as

$$\hat{P}(\mathrm{cell}_{i-n_{ho}}, \ldots, \mathrm{cell}_i|U) = \prod_{j=i-n_{ho}}^{i-1} \hat{P}(\mathrm{cell}_{j+1}|\mathrm{cell}_j, U), \tag{3}$$

where cell_i is the last cell registered within the time window. In the classification phase, given the current route to be classified, the classifier outputs the classification $u_i = \hat{P}(\mathrm{cell}_{i-n_{ho}}, \ldots, \mathrm{cell}_i|U)$.

Speed of move. The speed of terminal movements is not available in the dataset. However, the timestamps of the Cell ID records can be used to estimate the time the terminal spends in a cell, which, in turn, can be used to roughly estimate the terminal's speed (e.g. in terms of "cell per second") referred as *speed* ($SPEED$) measure.

The speed-based classifier was constructed as follows. For each cell, the user speed is modelled separately based on the empirical distribution of the user speed in this cell. The value of the speed can be approximated as a ratio of the length of the user's path within the cell to the time the user spent in the cell. The time spent in the cell is estimated as the time interval $[\tau_{ho1}, \tau_{ho2}]$ between consequent handovers. It is assumed that the user follows the same path within the cell; hence, the length of the path is assumed constant and is omitted from the expression for speed calculation, i.e. the speed in the cell is estimated as $v_{\text{cell}_i} = 1/(\tau_{ho2} - \tau_{ho1})$ (in "cell per second"). Only smaller values ($\tau^{stay} < 11$ minutes) are processed by the speed-based classifier, while greater values are assumed to indicate that the terminal is not moving. Using the accumulated empirical distribution function (EDF) of v_{cell_i}, the probability density $p(v_{\text{cell}_i})$ of the current speed for cell i is evaluated by using k-Nearest-Neighbours method [12]. Assuming independence of the speed in subsequent cells, the likelihood of a user speed within a time window $[\tau_1, \tau_2]$ is approximated as

$$L_{speed}(\text{cell}_{i-n_c+1}, \ldots, \text{cell}_i | U) = \prod_{j=i-n_c+1}^{i} p(v_{\text{cell}_j}), \tag{4}$$

where cell_i is the last cell registered within the time window, and n_c is the average number of cell changes within a window. Given the current speed values, the classifier outputs the classification $u_i = L_{speed}(\text{cell}_{i-n_c+1}, \ldots, \text{cell}_i | U)$.

Locations where prolonged stops were made. The information about the Cell IDs and the time spent in cells can be used to identify those locations (in terms of Cell IDs) where the terminal stays for a relatively long period of time. This measure is named *places visited* ($PLACES$).

The design of the classifier based on this measure is similar to the design of the classifier based on active applications. The difference is that the locations (Cell IDs) of prolonged stops, as defined in the description of the speed-based classifier, are taken as input instead of the application identifiers.

Temporal interval between two consecutive evocations of a program or service of a same type. In the dataset, the evocations of services (calls and SMS) are recorded and time-stamped; using this information, the intervals between evocations of these services can be evaluated. These measures will be referred to as *arrival of calls* (ARR_CALL) and *arrival of SMS* (ARR_SMS).

For both services, classifiers of the same type are employed. These classifiers analyse the mean inter-arrival time $\overline{\tau}^{ia}$ within a window $[\tau_1, \tau_2]$ for a given service type. The value of $\overline{\tau}^{ia}$ is calculated as $\overline{\tau}^{ia} = \frac{1}{n_{sa}} \sum_{j=i-n_{sa}+1}^{i} \tau_j^{ia}$, where τ_i^{ia} is the last inter-arrival time observed within the window, and n_{sa} is the average number of service arrivals within windows. Using the accumulated EDF of the $\overline{\tau}^{ia}$ values, the probability density $p(\overline{\tau}^{ia})$ of the current mean inter-arrival time is evaluated using k-Nearest-Neighbours method. Given the current inter-arrival time values, the classifier outputs the classification $u_i = p(\overline{\tau}^{ia})$.

Temporal lengths of actions. In the dataset, the durations of calls are recorded; they are used as a *call duration* (DUR_CALL) measure. The design of the classifier based on call duration time is similar to the design of the previous classifier. The difference is that the durations of calls are taken as input instead of the service inter-arrival times.

Address information of the people contacted. Phone numbers contacted via calls or SMS are available in the dataset. This measure is referred to as *contact numbers*

$(CONT\_NUM)$. Besides, the identifiers (MAC-addresses) of neighbouring Bluetooth-devices are logged in the dataset and are employed as *neighbouring Bluetooth devices* (BT_DEV) measure.

The classifier based on the phone numbers of contacted people, and the classifier based on the MAC-addresses of neighbouring Bluetooth devices are designed similarly to the classifier based on active applications. The difference is that contact numbers or MAC-addresses, respectively, are taken as input instead of the application identifiers.

2.2 Combining individual classifications

Combining the classifications produced by several classifiers has been extensively explored as a mean to compensate the weaknesses of individual classifiers. Different combining rules have been investigated [11, 13], and it has been shown that combining may result in a significant reduction of classification errors [13, 14]. However, in combining one-class classifiers, where only the knowledge regarding one class is available, relatively few rules can be used. Among them are different modifications of voting rules as investigated by Xu et al. [11]. Tax [9] reported the applicability of mean vote, mean weighted vote, product of weighted votes, mean of the estimated probabilities, and product combination of probabilities as combining rules for one-class classifiers. In [15], the mean of the estimated probabilities (MP) rule was justified to be among the most suitable ones in the context of mobile masquerader detection, and an improved version of it (modified MP rule) was proposed. This modified MP rule is adopted in the experiments as a scheme for combining individual classifications. Below, the details of this rule are provided.

The modified MP rule assumes that each classifier i outputs its classification as an estimation of the probability density function (pdf) for the user class $p(\mathbf{x}_i|C_U)$. Given R classifiers to be combined, the rule represents the average of the classifier confidences u_i^c:

$$u_{mc}(\mathbf{x}_1, \ldots, \mathbf{x}_R) = R^{-1} \sum_{i=1}^{R} u_i^c(p(\mathbf{x}_i|C_U)), \qquad (5)$$

where u_i^c reflects the degree of the classifier's confidence in the hypothesis that an object Z belongs to the user class. The confidence values can be calculated as [15]:

$$u_i^c(p(\mathbf{x}_i|C_U)) = \frac{1}{1 + \exp\left(-\ln\frac{p(\mathbf{x}_i|C_U)}{\overline{p}(\mathbf{x}_i|C_U)}\right)} = \frac{p(\mathbf{x}_i|C_U)}{p(\mathbf{x}_i|C_U) + \overline{p}(\mathbf{x}_i|C_U)}, \qquad (6)$$

where $\overline{p}(\mathbf{x}_i|C_U)$ is the mean value of the estimated probability $p(\mathbf{x}_i|C_U)$. This mean value is equal to the probability of a random variable uniformly distributed in the feature space $\mathcal{X}_i$.

The final classification result using the modified MP combining rule is made by comparing the obtained u_{mc} value with a threshold t_{mc}:

$$\text{Decide } Z \in C_U \text{ if } u_{mc} \geq t_{mc},$$
$$\text{otherwise decide } Z \in C_I. \qquad (7)$$

3 Dataset

The dataset used in this study was obtained from the Context project at the University of Helsinki and was gathered using the ContextPhone software [16]. ContextPhone runs in the background on Series 60 smartphones, collects data and sends it to a server automatically, without the need for user interaction. The data describes the users' movements (GSM cell changes), phone usage (phone profile, application use, idle and active time, charger), physical social interaction (bluetooth environment) and mobile phone communication (phone calls and text messages).

The data comes from two field studies conducted to test ContextContacts, a social awareness service [17]. The first study was done with a family of four: mother and three children aged 10 to 16. The second group consisted of five high-school students, aged 16 to 18, who ran a small company together. Both studies lasted approximately three months. All subjects were Finns living in the greater Helsinki area. The anonymized version of the dataset is available from http://www.cs.helsinki.fi/group/context/data/.

4 Experimental results

In this section, the experimental settings are described, and the results of the experiments are presented.

4.1 Experimental settings

The experiments were conducted in two phases. The purpose of the first phase was to evaluate the classification accuracy of the individual classifiers and to exclude the classifiers with low accuracy. In turn, the experiments in the second phase were aimed at identifying the classifiers, the combination of which would allow the final classification accuracy to be improved, as compared with the accuracies of individual classifiers. To identify the individual classifiers to be combined, the classifiers were ranked according to several criteria. After that, the best classifiers (according to the ranks) were added one by one to the classifier combination, and the resulting classification accuracy was estimated.

The holdout cross-validation [18] was used in the experiments to assess the accuracies. The model of each classifier was learnt using the training data-set DS_T, and was subsequently used to classify the instances of the classification data-set DS_C. In general, the classification data-set DS_C should include both the instances originated from the user and the instances originated from impostors. However, since the data originated from impostors was not available, the other users' data was employed as the impostor's data.

For each user, the data was split into two parts in the relation 2 : 1 commonly used in classifier evaluation [18]. The first part formed the training data-set DS_T that was used to learn the model for this user only. The second part was included into the classification data-set DS_C that was used by all the classifiers within the same user group in the classification phase. The sliding window of the length of $l_\tau = 1800$ seconds with the increment of $\delta_\tau = 900$ seconds was used.

In order to evaluate the accuracy of a classifier distinguishing between a user and impostors, the values of the probability of correct detection P_D and false rejection (FR) error rates P_{FR} are usually employed. A correct detection happens if an impostor is correctly classified as belonging to the impostors, and a false rejection occurs when a legitimate user is classified as an impostor. The ideal accuracy, corresponding to the values $P_D = 1$ and $P_{FR} = 0$ is extremely difficult, if at all possible, to achieve. Therefore, in practice, a trade-off between P_{FR} and P_D is set as a goal. The dependence between P_D and P_{FR} values can be represented by a so-called receiver-operating curve (ROC-curve) depicting the P_D values as a function of P_{FR}. The area under the curve (AUC) [19] was employed in the experiments, as it reflects the classifier accuracy; in general, the greater area corresponds to the classifier with the better accuracy.

Base ROC-curves, along with corresponding AUCs, reflect how accurate single classifications are, provided that the classifications can be made by the classifier. However, they do not take into account those observation vectors, for which no classification can be provided by the classifier, due to the absence of corresponding feature values in a particular window. The number of such non-classifications is different for different individual classifiers; therefore, their classification accuracies cannot be compared using such base ROC-curve and AUC.

Therefore, along with the base ROC-curve, a normalised ROC-curve and normalised AUC were introduced. A normalised ROC-curve depicts P_D^{norm} as a function of P_{FR}^{norm}, where P_D^{norm} and P_{FR}^{norm} represent respectively the normalisations of P_D and P_{FR}, wherein the cases of non-classifications are taken into account. For classifier i, the values of P_{FR}^{norm} and P_{FR}^{norm} are calculated as:

$$P_{D_i}^{norm} = P_{D_i}\, n_{C_i}/n_{C\ max}, \quad P_{FR_i}^{norm} = P_{FR_i}\, n_{C_i}/n_{C\ max}, \tag{8}$$

where n_{C_i} denotes the number of classifications made by classifier i, and $n_{C\ max}$ is the maximum number of classifications that can be made by individual classifiers or combinations thereof. Furthermore, for the values of $P_{D_i}^{norm}$ and $P_{FR_i}^{norm}$ greater than $n_{C_i}/n_{C\ max}$, we assume $P_{D_i}^{norm} = P_{FR_i}^{norm}$; this reflects the behaviour of a classifier randomly guessing whenever it is unable to make a classification. Given the value of base AUC_i, the normalised AUC can be calculated as:

$$AUC_i^{norm} = 0.5 + \frac{(n_{C_i})^2}{(n_{C\ max})^2}(AUC_i - 0.5) \tag{9}$$

Thus, the base AUC reflects how accurate a single classification is provided that the classification can be made, while the normalised AUC reflects how many accurate classifications can be made in general, taking into account both classifications made and non-classifications.

4.2 Evaluating classifiers' accuracy

In this subsection, the accuracy of individual classifiers is considered. For each user, the accuracy is evaluated individually by using base and normalised AUCs. In Table 1, the base AUCs for individual classifiers averaged over all users are presented. As can be seen from the table, the ARR_CALL and ARR_SMS classifiers had low accuracy ($\overline{AUC} \approx 0.5$), and hence they were excluded from further consideration. The low accuracy of these classifiers suggests that the service inter-arrival times are similar across different users, and hence neither of them is a good differentiator between users. On the other hand, the relatively low accuracy of the $SPEED$ classifier might be attributed to the fact that the Cell IDs, on which this classifier relies, may change sporadically [20], e.g. due to the effect of interference. As a result, the produced estimation of the speed is both biased and noisy.

Table 1. Averaged base and normalised AUCs for individual classifiers.

Classifier	ARR_CALL	ARR_SMS	DUR_CALL	PLACES	SPEED	MOVE	CONT_NUM	BT_DEV	ACT_APP
AUC	0.5006	0.5007	0.5036	0.7429	0.5370	0.5775	0.8062	0.7090	0.5436
AUC^{norm}	–	–	0.5003	0.5429	0.5059	0.5489	0.5176	0.5358	0.5125

The normalised AUCs for remaining seven classifiers are also provided in Table 1. As could be seen, should the classifiers be ranked according to their accuracy, the produced accuracy ranks would differ significantly depending on whether the base or normalised AUC is taken into account. Specifically, while $CONT\_NUM$ is the most accurate classifier according to the base AUC, it is rather poor according to the normalised AUC. On the contrary, the $MOVE$ classifier, while not performing well according to the base AUC, is the most accurate classifier according to the normalised AUC. This is due to the difference in the number of classifications that different classifiers are able to produce. For example, the abovementioned $MOVE$ classifier in average produced 4840 classifications per user, while the $CONT\_NUM$ classifier was able to produce in average only 1237 classifications. Consequently, for a same number of windows, more true detections can be produced by (generally less accurate) $MOVE$ classifier.

4.3 Selecting classifiers to combine

In this phase of the experiments, different combinations of classifiers were explored. The classifiers were added to the combination on a one-by-one basis. In order to select the next classifier to add, the individual classifiers were ranked according to several criteria, including:

- Classification accuracy according to the base AUC;
- Classification accuracy according to the normalised AUC;
- Heuristic accuracy measure $\overline{AUC} \times n_{C_i}$ taking into account both the classification accuracy (base AUC) and the number of classifications the classifier is able to produce.

The resulting ranks are shown in Table 2. As reflected in the table, in many cases, classifiers' ranks differ depending on the criteria used. Therefore, several configurations

Table 2. Ranks of individual classifiers.

Classifier	DUR_CALL	PLACES	SPEED	MOVE	CONT_NUM	BT_DEV	ACT_APP
Rank acc. AUC	7	2	6	4	1	3	5
Rank acc. $\overline{AUC}_{norm}$	7	2	6	1	4	3	5
Rank acc. $\overline{AUC} \times n_{C_i}$	7	1	6	4	3	2	5

Table 3. Averaged base and normalised AUCs for classifier combinations.

Classifiers combined	AUC	AUC_{norm}
PLACES+CONT_NUM	0.7490	0.5742
PLACES+BT_DEV	0.7521	0.6080
CONT_NUM+BT_DEV	0.7316	0.5719
PLACES+MOVE	0.6119	0.5738
PLACES+MOVE+BT_DEV	0.6788	0.6397
PLACES+CONT_NUM+BT_DEV	0.7637	0.6452
PLACES+CONT_NUM+BT_DEV+ACT_APP	0.7139	0.6673
PLACES+MOVE+CONT_NUM+BT_DEV	0.6904	0.6687
PLACES+MOVE+CONT_NUM+BT_DEV+ACT_APP	0.6854	0.6849
DUR_CALL+PLACES+SPEED+MOVE+CONT_NUM+BT_DEV+ACT_APP	0.6658	0.6658

of classifier combinations were tried, and better configurations were subsequently selected. The resulting classification accuracy for different configurations is reported in Table 3.

As indicated by the normalised AUCs, the best combinations of two, three, and four classifiers are produced by adding sequentially $PLACES$, BT_DEV, $CONT\_NUM$, and $MOVE$. Thus, for two-, three-, and four-classifier combinations, the best configurations of classifiers is produced, when the classifiers are added to the combination in accordance with the heuristic accuracy measure $\overline{AUC} \times n_{C_i}$ introduced above. This suggests that the best resulting classification accuracy may be achieved, when the classifiers to be added both i) have high individual classification accuracy (manifested in the base AUC) and ii) produce few non-classifications (manifested in n_{C_i} value).

Note that the best base AUCs increase when the second and the third classifier are added, while adding subsequent classifiers reduces the resulting base AUCs. Meanwhile, the best normalised AUCs increase also when the forth and the fifth classifiers are added, and deteriorate when the sixth and the seventh are included. This indicates that the benefits from being able to make more classifications with the forth and the fifth classifier overweigh the decrease in the accuracy of separate classifications. It should be also noted that, while the normalised AUCs increase when the forth and the fifth classifiers are added, the analysis of the normalised ROC-curves reveals, that the ROC-curves for the four- and five-classifier combinations surpass the ROC-curves for the best three-classifier combination only for high values of FR rate (greater than 0.5). The three-classifier combination was also found superior by analysing partial AUCs, produced by restricting the ROC-curves to the FR rate lower than 0.4. Thus, for the applications where low values of FR rate are important, the use of the three-classifier combination may in fact be a better choice.

5 Discussion and concluding remarks

The means of masquerader detection can be used to resist unauthorised use of sensitive information accessible on mobile terminals. In this paper, the problem of mobile-masquerader detection is approached as an anomaly detection problem. The profile of normal user behaviour is built by monitoring the user over a long period of time. After that, the current user behaviour is matched against the profile, and, should significant discrepancies be found, they are flagged as potential masquerade attacks.

A number of measures have been proposed as potentially useful for mobile-masquerader detection. In this paper, the appropriateness of some of them was empirically tested by using the data describing the behaviour of nine mobile users. Individual one-class classifiers were constructed for each of the measures being verified, and the accuracy of these classifiers and combinations thereof was empirically compared. As a result of experiments, two classifiers (ARR_CALL, ARR_SMS) were found inaccurate; this suggests that the corresponding measures are not useful in mobile-masquerader detection. The accuracies of classifiers and their combinations were compared by using normalised AUCs. The best accuracy was achieved when several classifiers were combined. Furthermore, the best classifier combination was produced when the classifiers both i) produced accurate individual classifications (as reflected in the values of the base AUC) and ii) were able to make many classifications (as reflected in the average numbers of classifications made).

For smaller values of FR rate, the best accuracy was found to be produced by the combination of $PLACES$, $CONT\_NUM$, and BT_DEV classifiers. Noteworthy, the corresponding measures describe the environment of a mobile user from different viewpoints: locations of visited places describe a user's global physical environment, the contacted numbers describe a user's global virtual (social) environment, and neighbouring Bluetooth devices describe a user's local virtual (social) environment. The involvement of several measures into the process of masquerader detection makes the detection more difficult to subvert, since several aspects of the legitimate user's environment need to be mimicked simultaneously by a masquerader. The personal data employed for masquerader detection can be collected, stored, and processed directly on the terminal, without the need to be transmitted and stored on a remote server, and, therefore, this data does not need to be disclosed to a trusted party.

Due to the use of real data in the experiments, the results are likely to be generalisable. On the other hand, due to the peculiarities of the employed dataset, used classifiers, etc., some bias may be contained in the results obtained. Below, these peculiarities are discussed.

First, in the experiments, an attempt was made to distinguish users within groups, wherein the users were acquainted with each other and, hence, shared some of the characteristics (e.g. places visited). Therefore, for some of the classifiers the task of distinguishing between users was more challenging, and their classification accuracy might be underestimated. Second, the design of some of the individual classifiers is likely to be suboptimal. For instance, the low accuracy of the $SPEED$ classifier may be attributed to the inaccurate estimation of the speed that was based on the Cell ID changes; the use of a location recognition algorithm [20] to pre-process the data might improve the classifier's accuracy significantly. Third, in the experiments, it was assumed that the behaviour of impostors may be approximated by the behaviour of other users. Whether such approximation is accurate enough remains to be a question for further study.

In addition to the classification accuracy, the memory requirements and the computational overhead imposed by the proposed masquerader detection approach, need to be evaluated. Their evaluation, however, depends on the number and type of classifiers used, among other parameters. Since the current work was focused on the evaluation of individual classifiers and combinations thereof, the evaluation of the required computational resources was left for further work.

Finally, the behaviour of a limited number of users was described by the dataset, and these users may not reflect accurately the behaviour of mobile users in general. Therefore, the reported results may need to be refined in further research, using bigger datasets describing the behaviour of a larger population of mobile users.

References

1. Straub, D.W., Welke, R.J.: Coping with systems risk: Security planning models for management decision making. MIS Quarterly 22(4) (1998) 441–469
2. Schonlau, M., DuMouchel, W., Ju, W., Karr, A., Theus, M., Vardi, Y.: Computer intrusion: Detecting masquerades. Statistical Science 16(1) (2001) 58–74
3. Lane, T., Brodley, C.E.: An empirical study of two approaches to sequence learning for anomaly detection. Machine Learning 51(1) (2003) 73–107
4. Shavlik, J., Shavlik, M.: Selection, combination, and evaluation of effective software sensors for detecting abnormal computer usage. In: Proceedings of the 2004 ACM SIGKDD international conference on Knowledge discovery and data mining, ACM Press (2004) 276–285
5. IndrajitRay, NayotPoolsapassit: Using attack trees to identify malicious attacks from authorized insiders. In de Capitani di Vimercati, S., Syverson, P., Gollmann, D., eds.: Proceedings of ESORICS 2005. Volume 3679 of Lecture Notes in Computer Science., Springer-Verlag GmbH (2005) 231–246
6. Clarke, N.L., Furnell, S.M., Lines, B., Reynolds, P.L.: Keystroke dynamics on a mobile handset: A feasibility study. Information Management and Computer Security 11(4) (2003) 161–166
7. Hollmen, J.: User Profiling and Classification for Fraud Detection in Mobile Communications Networks. PhD thesis, Helsinki University of Technology (2000)
8. Mazhelis, O., Puuronen, S.: Characteristics and measures for mobile-masquerader detection. In Dowland, P., Furnell, S., Thuraisingham, B., Wang, X.S., eds.: Proc. IFIP TC-11 WG 11.1 & WG 11.5 Joint Working Conference on Security Management, Integrity, and Internal Control in Information Systems, Springer Science+Business Media (2005) 303–318
9. Tax, D.: One-class classification. Ph.D. thesis, Delft University of Technology (2001)
10. Anderson, D., Lunt, T., Javitz, H., Tamaru, A., Valdes, A.: Detecting unusual program behavior using the statistical components of NIDES. SRI Technical Report SRI-CRL-95-06, Computer Science Laboratory, SRI International, Menlo Park, California (1995)
11. Xu, L., Krzyzak, A., Suen, C.Y.: Methods for combining multiple classifiers and their applications to handwriting recognition. IEEE Transactions on Systems, Man, and Cybernetics 22(3) (1992) 418–435

12. Duda, R.O., Hart, P.E., Stork, D.G.: Pattern Classification. Second edn. John Wily & Sons, Inc., New York (2000)

13. Kittler, J., Hatef, M., Duin, R.P., Matas, J.: On combining classifiers. IEEE Transactions on Pattern Analysis and Machine Intelligence 20(3) (1998) 226–239

14. Kuncheva, L.: A theoretical study on six classifier fusion strategies. IEEE Transactions on Pattern Analysis and Machine Intelligence 24(2) (2002) 281–286

15. Mazhelis, O., Puuronen, S.: Combining one-class classifiers for mobile-user substitution detection. In Seruca, I., Filipe, J., Hammoudi, S., Cordeiro, J., eds.: Proceedings of the 6th International Conference on Enterprise Information Systems (ICEIS 2004). Volume 4., Portugal, INSTICC Press (2004) 130–137

16. Raento, M., Oulasvirta, A., Petit, R., Toivonen, H.: Contextphone, a prototyping platform for context-aware mobile applications. IEEE Pervasive Computing 4(2) (2005)

17. Oulasvirta, A., Raento, M., Tiitta, S.: Contextcontacts: Re-designing smartphone's contact book to support mobile awareness and collaboration. In: Proceedings of the 7th International Conference on Human Computer Interaction with Mobile Devices and Services, MOBILE-HCI'05, ACM (2005) 167–174

18. Witten, I.H., Frank, E.: Data Mining: Practical Machine Learning Tools and Techniques. Morgan Kaufmann Publishers (2000)

19. Hanley, J.A., McNeil, B.J.: The meaning and use of the area under a receiver operating characteristic (ROC) curve. Radiology 143 (1982) 29–36

20. Laasonen, K., Raento, M., Toivonen, H.: Adaptive on-device location recognition. In Ferscha, A., Mattern, F., eds.: PERVASIVE 2004, LNCS 3001, Springer-Verlag Berlin Heidelberg (2004) 287–304

VisFlowCluster-IP: Connectivity-Based Visual Clustering of Network Hosts*

Xiaoxin Yin, William Yurcik, and Adam Slagell

National Center for Supercomputing Applications (NCSA)
University of Illinois at Urbana-Champaign
{xiaoxin,byurcik,slagell}@ncsa.uiuc.edu

Abstract. With the increasing number of hostile network attacks, anomaly detection for network security has become an urgent task. As there have not been highly effective solutions for automatic intrusion detection, especially for detecting newly emerging attacks, network traffic visualization has become a promising technique for assisting network administrators to monitor network traffic and detect abnormal behaviors.

In this paper we present *VisFlowCluster-IP*, a powerful tool for visualizing network traffic flows using network logs. It models the network as a graph by modeling hosts as graph nodes. It utilizes the force model to arrange graph nodes on a two-dimensional space, so that groups of related nodes can be visually clustered in a manner apparent to human eyes. We also propose an automated method for finding clusters of closely connected hosts in the visualization space. We present three real cases that validate the effectiveness of *VisFlowCluster-IP* in identifying abnormal behaviors.

1 Introduction

There has been tremendous growth of network applications and services in the last two decades. At the same time, the number of hostile attacks is increasing, and these attacks are hidden by the vast majority of legitimate traffic. There have been many studies on intrusion detection systems (IDS) which fall into the following two categories. The first category is *misuse detection systems* [6, 7, 14, 18], which use predefined signatures to detect intrusions. However, they are not effective for detecting new intrusions and viruses, and the ever growing signature database becomes problematic. The second category is *anomaly detection systems* [15, 17], which attempt to model normal behaviors and give alerts for any behavior that deviates from the model. However, the "normal behaviors" of different persons and tasks may not be similar, so it is difficult to accurately profile normal network traffic. Attempts to detect anomalies based on profiles of network traffic often suffer from unacceptable false positive rates.

As fully automated intrusion detection systems have not been able to provide a highly effective solution to protect network systems, humans are still in-the-loop of

---

* This research was supported in part by a grant from the Office of Naval Research (ONR) under the auspices of the National Center for Advanced Secure Systems Research (NCASSR) <http://www.ncassr.org>.

inspecting large numbers of alerts to identify real threats. In comparison with automated systems, the human mind is capable of rapid visual processing, especially for detecting abnormal or extraordinary visual patterns. Tools that visually depict network traffic patterns leverage this capability for anomaly detection. They can provide a user with the capability to drill down into the data to extract information about potential attacks. Almost all security events leave traces in network traffic. It is a highly challenging task to find these traces in high-volume traffic. Visualization tools can represent high-volume traffic as static graphs or dynamic animations, in order to help network administrators sift through gigabytes of daily network traffic to identify anomalous patterns.

In this paper we propose *VisFlowCluster-IP*, a tool that visualizes network connectivity using visual clustering techniques to assist network administrators with monitoring abnormal behaviors. There have been many studies on visualizing network traffic and connectivity [2, 4, 23, 25]. In these approaches, hosts in a network are represented as nodes and traffic as edges or flows in a graph. However, they fix hosts in certain locations according to their IP addresses, without considering relationships and interactions between different hosts.

In [9] and [13], approaches have been proposed to arrange graph nodes with a *force model* in order to better capture the relationships and patterns among the nodes. This technique has been widely used in graph drawing and visualization [19, 24]. *VisFlow-Cluster-IP* uses this model for arranging hosts in network visualization. It models each host in a network as a particle in a two-dimensional space, and defines the attraction (or repulsion) force between two hosts according to their relationship. Then it lets particles interact with each other until a reasonably stable arrangement is achieved. In the force model method, related hosts can be visually clustered and certain traffic patterns will thus become apparent to human eyes. *VisFlowCluster-IP* can also detect clusters of particles that are located close to each other in the space of visualization, which correspond to groups of hosts that are closely related to each other.

Another shortcoming of most existing approaches for visualizing network traffic [2, 4, 23, 25] is that most of them only use the traffic volume between two hosts to measure the relationship between them. Although this model can identify hosts that communicate with each other, it is not good at finding hosts that exhibit similar behaviors, because two hosts with similar behaviors may not have traffic between them. For example, two hosts in a group often both have high traffic volume to some servers in that group, but usually do not have much traffic between them. Another example is that two basketball fans often have high traffic to web sites of NBA, NCAA, and ESPN, but they seldom communicate with each other. *VisFlowCluster-IP* provides functionality to address this problem. It defines the relationship between two hosts based the external hosts they access, as well as traffic between them.

With the above techniques, *VisFlowCluster-IP* can visualize the network hosts and connections in a 2-D space, so that hosts that exhibit similar behaviors will be arranged close to each other and form visual clusters. This capability is not available in existing visualization systems for anomaly detection. We apply *VisFlowCluster-IP* to the traffic logs from our network. Some abnormal visual patterns are identified from the visualizations, with which we easily find the corresponding abnormal patterns in network traffic. These experiments show that *VisFlowCluster-IP* is able to convert certain abnormal traffic patterns into abnormal visual patterns that are apparent to human eyes. Our experiments also show that *VisFlowCluster-IP* can automatically identify these abnormal visual patterns as visual clusters and report such clusters to users. However, *VisFlowCluster-IP* also reports some clusters that correspond to normal behaviors and are false alerts. The user still needs to make judgments for each cluster based on both the visualization and the network traffic data.

The remainder of this paper is organized as follows. Section 2 summarizes related work. We present background information in Section 3. Section 4 describes the visualization approach of *VisFlowCluster-IP* and the approach for identifying clusters of closely related hosts. Section 5 presents experimental results that validate the capability of *VisFlowCluster-IP* for security monitoring. We end with a summary and conclusions in Section 6.

2 Related Work

Currently, there are two main approaches to intrusion detection: *misuse detection* and *anomaly detection*. Misuse detection [6, 7, 14, 18] finds intrusions by directly matching known attack patterns. The major drawback of this rule-based approach is that it is only effective at finding known attacks with predefined signatures. In anomaly detection [15, 17], the normal behavior of a system is stored as a profile. Any statistically significant deviations from this profile are reported as possible attacks. However, these alarms may also be legitimate but atypical system activity, which often leads to unacceptable false positive alarm rates.

Because of the limited density of information conveyed through text, visualization techniques to present computer network data sets to humans have been a growing area of research. It is well-known that seeing enables humans to glean knowledge and deeper insight from data. Early work on visualizing networks has been motivated by network management and analysis of bandwidth characteristics [3, 5, 10]. A wide spectra of knowledge about visualization of cyberspace is provided in [8], such as topology of connectivity and geography of data flows.

In [20], the authors present a visualization of network routing information that can be used to detect inter-domain routing attacks. In [21, 22], they explore further in this field and propose different ways for visualizing routing data in order to detect intrusions. An approach for comprehensively visualizing computer network security is presented in [11], where the authors visualize the overall behavioral characteristics of users for intrusion detection. They represent the substantial characteristics of user behavior with a visual attribute mapping capable of identifying intrusions that otherwise would be obscured. However, the host representation employed in [11] is not scalable in terms of the number of hosts and traffic volume. In [1], parallel axes are used to visualize network logs about traffic involving a single machine (web server). In [16], the authors present NVisionIP, which shows network traffic in a host-centric view, providing both an overview and detailed views with its on-demand zoom and filtering capabilities.

Linkages among different hosts and events in a computer network contain important information for traffic analysis and intrusion detection. Approaches for link analysis are proposed in [2, 4, 25]. [2] focuses on visualizing linkages in a network, and [4] focuses on detecting attacks based on fingerprints. In [25], the authors present VisFlowConnect-IP, a tool for visualizing connectivity between internal and external hosts using animation. It uses animation to visualize network traffic in real-time and focuses on short-term link analysis. In contrast, *VisFlowCluster-IP* is a complementary, static off-line visualization tool, which uses visual clustering techniques to highlight clusters of hosts closely related to each other. It focuses on long-term link relationships among the hosts.

These tools provide effective ways to visualize hosts and traffic in a network. However, they all use approaches where all nodes are fixed on certain locations or lines, and the locations of nodes are independent from their relationships with other nodes. This prevents the visualization tool from arranging hosts in a nice layout that captures the relationships among them. This problem is discussed in [23], which first performs hierarchical clustering on hosts and then visualizes the clusters. However, the visualization approach in [23] simply shows the hierarchical structures of clusters, instead of arranging them for better understanding.

3 Preliminaries

3.1 NetFlow Source Data

The source data used by *VisFlowCluster-IP* is NetFlow data. We consider two formats of NetFlow data, one from Cisco routers and the other from a freely available software named *Argus* (<http://www.qosient.com/argus/>). A distinct flow is defined as either a unidirectional TCP connection (where a sequence of packets take the same path) or individual UDP packets with the same IP and port in a short period of time.

The input to *VisFlowCluster-IP* is a stream of NetFlow records either from a log file or a streaming socket. A NetFlow agent is used to retrieve the NetFlow records and feed them into *VisFlowCluster-IP*. Each record contains the following information: (1) IP addresses and ports of the source and destination, (2) number of bytes and packets, (3) start and end times, and (4) protocol type.

3.2 Problem Settings

The goal of *VisFlowCluster-IP* is to visualize hosts and network traffic in a way that groups of related hosts can be easily identified by humans. Each host in the network is modeled as a node in a graph, and an edge is added between two nodes if there is certain relationship between them. In *VisFlowCluster-IP*, two nodes are related if they communicate with each other, or they both access the same server(s) outside the network. We translate relationships between nodes into attraction/repulsion forces, which are used to arrange nodes in our visualization.

4 Visualizing Network Flows

4.1 Constructing Graph

Given a network log containing a list of NetFlow records, *VisFlowCluster-IP* constructs a graph with the following procedure.

VisFlowCluster-IP first creates a graph node for each host in the network to be visualized (e.g., each host in NCSA in our visualization), which is called a *particle node*. It also creates a graph node for each host outside the target network, which is called a *hub node*. A hub node is only for visualization and does not participate in the arrangements of graph nodes.

Suppose a graph contains particle nodes $p_1, \ldots, p_n$, and hub nodes $h_1, \ldots, h_m$. The volume of traffic between two nodes x and y (in either direction) is represented by $T(x, y)$. Two nodes are considered to be highly related if there is high traffic volume between them, or they both have high traffic volume to many hub nodes. Thus we define the edge weight between two particle nodes p_1 and p_2 as a combined function of the traffic volume between them and the traffic volume between them and their common neighbor nodes.

$$w(p_1, p_2) = \alpha \cdot \log T(p_1, p_2) + (1 - \alpha) \cdot \log \left(\sum_{j=1}^{m} T(p_1, h_j) \cdot T(p_2, h_j) \right) \quad (1)$$

The user may adjust the weights of internal traffic and external traffic by choosing an appropriate value for α.

4.2 Arranging Nodes

VisFlowCluster-IP uses the *force model* [9, 13] to arrange particle nodes in a graph, in order to reorganize the graph so that groups of nodes related to each other can be clustered on the screen and made apparent to humans. In such a model, two particles attract each other if they have an edge between them, and repulse each other if not. All particle nodes keep interacting with each other in many iterations, until a reasonably stable arrangement is achieved. The following procedure is used for arranging nodes.

Initially, *VisFlowCluster-IP* assigns a default location for each particle node. Because some parts of an IP address may indicate information about the host, the location of each host is determined by its IP. Suppose the IP of a host h is $a.b.c.d$. Suppose H_w and H_h are two hash functions whose input domains are all integers and value ranges are the width and height of the visualization panel respectively. In *VisFlowCluster-IP*, the x coordinate of h is $H_w(256 \times ((256 \times a) + b) + c)$, and the y coordinate is $H_h(d)$. Since hosts belonging to the same group or cluster often belong to the same class C, they will be located on one or a few vertical lines. Some hosts that are certain types of servers often have the same values on last byte of IP (e.g., gateway or DNS server), and thus they will be located on certain horizontal lines.

After the initial assignments, *VisFlowCluster-IP* lets the particle nodes interact with each other in order to achieve an arrangement in which groups of related hosts are visually clustered. As in previous approaches of force models [9, 13, 24], *VisFlowCluster-IP* adjusts the location of each particle according to the attraction and repulsion forces it receives in each iteration, and it performs many iterations until achieving a reasonably stable arrangement.

Suppose the location of a particle node p_i is $\mathbf{p}_i$. The force between two particle nodes p_1 and p_2 is defined as follows.

- **Repulsion:** There is a repulsion force between any two particle nodes, which is a decreasing function of the distance between them. The magnitude of the repulsion force is

$$Repul(p_1, p_2) = \frac{C_{repul}}{\sqrt{\|p_1 - p_2\|}} \qquad (2)$$

in which C_{rep} is a constant. The direction of the repulsion force received by p_1 from p_2 is same as the vector $p_1 - p_2$.
- **Attraction:** If there is an edge between p_1 and p_2, there is an attraction force between them. The magnitude of the attraction force is proportional to the weight of the edge between p_1 and p_2.

$$Attr(p_1, p_2) = C_{attr} \times w(p_1, p_2) \qquad (3)$$

in which C_{attr} is a constant. The direction of the attraction force received by p_1 from p_2 is the same as the vector $p_2 - p_1$.

In each iteration, each particle node p_i receives a force F_i that is the sum of all the repulsion and attraction forces it receives. The movement of p_i in this iteration is δF_i, where δ is the step length. The stability of an arrangement is defined as the average movement of each particle node in an iteration. In most cases, a fairly stable arrangement can be achieved in ten to fifty iterations, and each iteration usually takes several seconds on a graph of a few thousand nodes.

4.3 Visualization

VisFlowCluster-IP assigns a color[1] to each host, which is based on its IP address. The color is determined in a way that hosts with similar IP addresses have similar colors. As the horizontal location of a host is determined by the first three bytes of its IP, and the vertical location by the last byte, we also assign a unique color for each host. The hue of the color is determined by the first three bytes of its IP, and the brightness is determined by the last byte. In this way all hosts from same class C will have similar colors (same hue) but with different brightnesses.

We use an example to show how we determine colors of hosts. The network in NCSA is a class B, which contains 65536 distinct IP addresses. Suppose the IP of a host is $a.b.c.d$. Its hue is set to $360 \cdot c/256$, which ranges from 0 to 360. Its brightness is set to $d/512 + 0.5$, which ranges from 0.5 to 1. Its saturation is set to 1, so that each host has a vivid color (white, gray, and black will not appear here).

In the visualization, each particle node is represented by a circle filled with its color. Each hub node is also represented by a circle, but with the color of light gray. We define the weight of a node n, $w(n)$, as the logarithm of the total traffic volume involving that node. The diameter of a circle is proportional to the weight of the corresponding node. There is a line between two nodes if there is traffic between the two corresponding hosts. The location of each hub node h_i is a weighted average of locations of all particle nodes connected to it, based on the edge weights between h_i and the particle nodes.

---

[1] We note that some visualizations may be hard to understand if this paper is printed in black-and-white. They are clear in electronic versions of this paper.

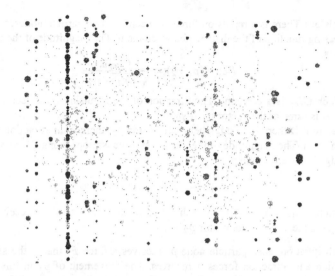

Fig. 1. Initial Arrangement of VisFlowCluster-IP.

The initial assignment of an example NetFlow log file is shown in Fig. 1. This file is an Argus log file that only contains traffic between internal hosts and external hosts. *VisFlowCluster-IP* repeatedly rearranges the particle nodes in Fig. 1. A stable arrangement is achieved after 32 iterations, which takes 11.52 seconds in total. The final arrangement is shown in Fig. 2, in which two clusters of hosts are automatically detected. The approach for detecting clusters will be introduced in Section 4.4, and the sematic meanings of the visualization results will be discussed in Section 5.

4.4 Finding Clusters

During the iterative arrangements of nodes, the sets of particle nodes that are closely related to each other will be grouped together because of the attractions among them, and the particle nodes that are not related to each other will seldom be located close to each other because of the repulsions. Therefore, the dense regions on the plane of visualization correspond to groups of closely related nodes.

VisFlowCluster-IP uses DBSCAN [12], a popular density-based clustering approach to find clusters of related nodes. DBSCAN considers every point as a node in a graph. An edge exists between two nodes if their corresponding points are very close to each other. A cluster is a connected component in such a graph. Because we are only interested in dense regions on the plane of visualization, we slightly modify the algorithm to ignore sparse regions. We first divide the space into many small grids. The density of a grid is defined as the total weights of particle nodes in this grid. We only consider grids whose densities are above a certain threshold, which is β times the average density of all grids ($\beta > 1$). Then we use each dense grid as a point and use DBSCAN to identify clusters of dense grids. Because we are only interested in clusters of significant sizes, we ignore a cluster if the total weight of its particle nodes is less than γ times the

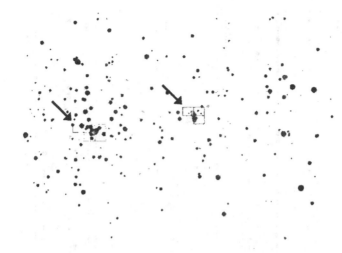

Fig. 2. Stable Arrangement of VisFlowCluster-IP.

total weight of all particle nodes ($0 < \gamma < 1$). Fig. 2 shows two clusters identified by *VisFlowCluster-IP*, which are highlighted by black arrows.

5 Experiments

Experiments are performed to show the effectiveness of *VisFlowCluster-IP* in assisting network administrators to detect abnormal behaviors in a network. We ran *VisFlowCluster-IP* on an Intel PC with 2.4GHz Pentium 4 CPU, 1GB memory, and running Windows XP Professional. In order to show its capability of visual clustering based on communications between internal and external hosts, we set $\alpha = 0$ in *VisFlowCluster-IP* to ignore internal traffic. After trying different values for parameters, we use $\beta = 5$ and $\gamma = 0.02$ when detecting clusters. Thus a region will be detected as a cluster if its density is at least five times the average density and the total weight of its particle nodes is at least 2% of the total weight of all particle nodes.

5.1 Blaster Worms

The Blaster worm spreads quickly between hosts. Once a host is infected, it will send out packets to all hosts known to it. Fig. 3 shows the pattern of Blaster worms, from a real Cisco NetFlow log file. The abnormal behavior is already apparent without re-arranging nodes. The infected hosts can be easily detected using *VisFlowCluster-IP* (which are highlighted by an arrow in Fig. 3).

5.2 Communications with RIPE NCC

In one Cisco NetFlow log file we find that a large number of hosts in NCSA have high-volume communication with a small number of external hosts. This is shown in

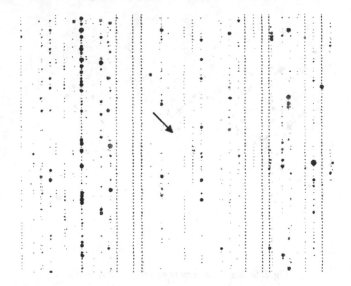

Fig. 3. Pattern of Blaster Worms.

Fig. 4, in which the biggest cluster shows these hosts in NCSA. We find that these hosts are from several clusters of computers, and they connect intensively to the following external hosts as shown in Fig. 4: 131.188.3.221, 153.107.47.81, 192.136.143.150, 192.136.143.151. We used the 'whois' command to check the domains of the above three hosts and we found that they are all from RIPE NCC, a Regional Registry (RIR) providing global Internet resources and related services. We feel that it is not surprising that many hosts connect to RIPE NCC, and this traffic pattern is benign. Therefore, we use filters to filter out traffic involving the domain of RIPE NCC in future visualizations.

5.3 Web Servers

From another Cisco NetFlow log file, we found a group of hosts with high traffic volume that are clustered together, as highlighted in Fig. 5. We found that they are all web servers in NCSA. It is not strange that the web servers are grouped together. However, we find that almost every server in that visual cluster is accessed by about ten hosts from the class C network of 64.68.82.*. This is strange because usually traffic to web servers should come from hosts whose IP addresses are quite random. Again with the "whois" command we find that 64.68.82.* is owned by Google.com. It is clear that Google is crawling our web servers.

6   Conclusions

In this paper we present *VisFlowCluster-IP*, a powerful tool for visualizing network traffic flows. It models the network as a graph by modeling hosts as nodes. It utilizes the force model [9, 13] to arrange graph nodes on a two-dimensional space, so that groups

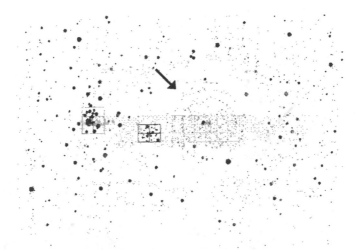

Fig. 4. Communications with RIPE NC.

of related nodes can be visually clustered in a manner apparent to human eyes. We also propose a method based on DBSCAN [12] to automatically detect dense regions on the plane of visualization. We present three real cases that validate the effectiveness of *VisFlowCluster-IP* in identifying abnormal behaviors.

We believe *VisFlowCluster-IP* will be useful for intrusion detection based on preliminary experiments in a laboratory environment. In the short-term we will continue testing *VisFlowCluster-IP* in laboratory environments to identify the types of behaviors it can detect and leverage machine learning techniques for models of normal behavior as well as deviate behaviors. In the future we seek to employ this tool in real networks where accuracy can be statistically measured. *VisFlowCluster-IP* will be distributed at: <http://security.ncsa.uiuc.edu/distribution/VisFlowCluster-IPDownLoad.html>

7 Acknowledgement

We thank fellow members of SIFT research group at NCSA who contributed indirectly to this work: (in alphabetical order) Ratna Bearavolu, Charis Ermopoulos, Kiran Lakkaraju, Yifan Li, and Ramona Su. We thank the anonymous reviewer whose insightful feedback we have incorporated to improve this paper.

References

1. S. Axelsson. Visualisation for Intrusion Detection - Hooking the Worm. *Eighth European Symposium on Research in Computer Security (ESORICS)*, Lecture Notes in Computer Science (LNCS) 2808 , Springer, 2003.
2. R. Ball, G. A. Fink, C. North. Home-Centric Visualization of Network Traffic for Security Administration. *ACM CCS Workshop on Visualization and Data Mining for Computer Security (VizSEC/DMSEC)*, 2004.

294   Xiaoxin Yin, William Yurcik, and Adam Slagell

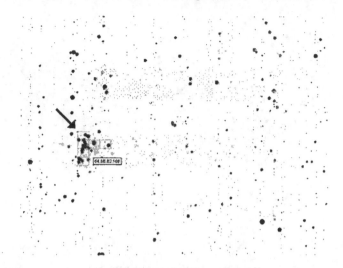

Fig. 5. Patterns with Web Servers.

3. R. Becker, S. Eick, A. Wilks. Visualizing network data. *IEEE Transactions on Visualization and Computer Graphics*, 1(1):16–28, 1995.
4. G. Conti, K. Abdullah. Passive Visual Fingerprinting of Network Attack Tools. *ACM CCS Workshop on Visualization and Data Mining for Computer Security (VizSEC/DMSEC)*, 2004.
5. K. Cox, S. Eick, T. He. 3D Geographic Network Displays. *ACM SIGMOD Record*, 25(4):50–54, 1996.
6. F. Cuppens, A. Miege. Alert Correlation in a Cooperative Intrusion Detection Framework. *IEEE Symp. on Security and Privacy*, 2002.
7. H. Debar, A. Wespi. Aggregation and Correlation of Intrusion Detection Alerts. *Int'l. Symp. on Recent Advances in Intrusion Detection (RAID)*, 2001.
8. M. Dodge, R. Kitchin. *Atlas of Cyberspace*. Addison-Wesley, 2001.
9. P. Eades. A Heuristic for Graph-Drawing. *Congressus Numerantium*, Vol 42, pp 149-160, 1984.
10. S. Eick, G. Wills. Navigating Large Networks with Hierarchies. *IEEE Visualization*, 1993.
11. R. Erbacher, K. Walker, D. Frincke. Intrusion and Misuse Detection in Large-Scale Systems. *IEEE Comp. Graphics and Applications*, 22(1):38–48, 2002.
12. M. Ester, H.-P. Kriegel, J. Sander, X. Xu. A Density-Based Algorithm for Discovering Clusters in Large Spatial Databases with Noise. *ACM Int'l. Conf. on Knowledge Discovery and Data Mining (KDD)*, 1996.
13. T. Fruchterman, E. Reingold. Graph-Drawing by Force-Directed Placement. *Software-Practice and Experience*, Vol 21, pp 1129-1164, 1991.
14. C. Krugel, T. Toth, C. Kerer. Decentralized Event Correlation for Intrusion Detection. *Int'l. Conf. on Info. Sec. and Cryptology (ICISC)*, 2001.
15. C. Krugel, T. Toth, E. Kirda. Service Specific Anomaly Detection for Network Intrusion Detection. *ACM Symp. on Applied Computing*, 2002.
16. K. Lakkaraju, W. Yurcik, A. J. Lee, R. Bearavolu, Y. Li, X. Yin. NVisionIP: NetFlow Visualizations of System State for Security Situational Awareness" *ACM CCS Workshop on Visualization and Data Mining for Computer Security (VizSEC/DMSEC)*, 2004.

17. W. Lee, D. Xiang. Information-Theoretic Measures for Anomaly Detection. *IEEE Symp. on Security and Privacy*, 2001.
18. W. Lee, S. J. Stolfo, K. W. Mok. A Data Mining Framework for Building Intrusion Detection Models. *IEEE Symp. on Security and Privacy*, 1999.
19. A. Noack. An Energy Model for Visual Graph Clustering. *Graph Drawing*, 2003.
20. S. T. Teoh et al. Elisha: a Visual-based Anomaly Detection System. *Int'l. Symp. on Recent Advances in Intrusion Detection (RAID)*, 2002.
21. S. T. Teoh, K. Ma, S. F. Wu. A Visual Exploration Process for the Analysis of Internet Routing Data. *IEEE Visualization*, 2003.
22. S. T. Teoh, K. Ma, S. F. Wu, X. Zhao. Case Study: Internet Visualization for Internet Security. *IEEE Visualization*, 2002.
23. J. Tölle, O. Niggemann. Supporting Intrusion Detection by Graph Clustering and Graph Drawing. *Int'l. Symp. on Recent Advances in Intrusion Detection (RAID)*, 2000.
24. F. van Ham, J. J. van Wijk. Interactive Visualization of Small World Graphs. *IEEE InfoVis*, 2004.
25. X. Yin, W. Yurcik, A. Slagell. The Design of VisFlowConnect-IP: a Link Analysis System for IP Security Situational Awareness. *IEEE Int'l. Workshop on Information Assurance (IWIA)*, 2005.

A Usability Study of Security Policy Management

Almut Herzog and Nahid Shahmehri

Department of Computer and Information Science
Linköpings universitet, Sweden
{almhe,nahsh}@ida.liu.se

Abstract. Security policy management is a difficult and security-critical task. We have evaluated Java's policytool with a usability study to see how well it can support users in setting up an appropriate security policy. The Java policytool is a graphical user interface tool integrated into Sun Microsystem Inc.'s Java 5.0 distribution for setting up security policies that can enable e.g. applets with more permissions than the default sandbox.

Results show that policytool is in line with other security tools, namely usability is poor. Policytool provides a certain degree of syntax help to novice users but it does not help with semantics, does not cater to expert users and actually does promote the accidental set-up of too lenient a policy. We show specific usability problems in policytool, comment on the differences in the policy files created by our study users, explore ways of solving the error-prone task of setting up a Java policy and relate this to the general subject of usability of security tools.

1 Introduction

Security policies come in many different shapes and sizes. They may be long, written documents on how employees must choose passwords, protect their office keys or handle documents. They may be short but intricate rules in a proprietary language to configure a firewall. What they all have in common is that the policy is highly specific to the environment (the company, the household, the user, the network etc.) in which it is used. There is no "one size fits all".

Our interest is in the area of security policies for software. In that area the property of "one size does not fit all" has especially dire implications. It means that the end user, be it a system administrator or regular home user, must be highly involved in the task of setting up a policy because only the end user knows "which size will fit". However, all too often end users do not perform such a setup because security is seldom a main user goal but rather a secondary exercise to the user's primary goal, which is to make the application work. Also, policy setup *is* difficult and time-consuming. "Finding the size that will fit" is a lengthy procedure.

Clearly, applications that target security need to be carefully designed to be useful and usable because "there is already plenty of evidence to suggest that end users do not need a great deal of excuse or encouragement to neglect their security responsibilities"[1]. Security software is usable if "the people who are expected to use it (1) are reliably made aware of the security task they need to perform; (2) are able to figure out

Please use the following format when citing this chapter:

Author(s) [insert Last name, First-name initial(s)], 2006, in IFIP International Federation for Information Processing, Volume 201, Security and Privacy in Dynamic Environments, eds. Fischer-Hubner, S., Rannenberg, K., Yngstrom, L., Lindskog, S., (Boston: Springer), pp. [insert page numbers].

```
1 keystore "file:///tmp/keys.data";

2 grant codeBase "file:///tmp/xx.jar" {
3   permission java.lang.RuntimePermission "getProtectionDomain";
4   permission java.net.SocketPermission "www.ida.liu.se:80", "connect, resolve";
5   permission java.util.PropertyPermission "user.dir", "read";
6   permission java.io.FilePermission "/tmp", "read";
7   permission java.io.FilePermission "/tmp/a", "write, read, delete";
8 };

9  grant signedBy "alice",  codeBase "file:///tmp/yy.jar" {
10    permission yy.YPermission "x", "set", signedBy "bob";
11 };
```

Fig. 1. A policy file with certificate database and two policy entries or grant statements.

how to successfully perform those tasks; (3) do not make dangerous errors; and (4) are sufficiently comfortable with the interface to continue using it."[2]. We will come back to this definition in the conclusion.

This paper examines how well the end user is supported in the task of setting up a security policy for Java applications. Sun Microsystems Inc. provides policytool [3], a tool with a graphical user interface (GUI) that aims at supporting the novice user in the task of setting up a security policy for a Java application or component.

We have evaluated the version of policytool that comes with Java 5.0. For the evaluation we used the think-aloud method [4] with ten graduate and undergraduate students from the area of computer science and with some degree of experience in Java programming. They were asked to individually set up a Java security policy using policytool while thinking aloud about what they were doing and about problems encountered. At the end of each evaluation the user was invited to comment on the difficulty of the tasks and the support that policytool had provided. Users found a total of 23 specific usability problems. Astonishing differences in the resulting policy could be seen. We have used the user observations to draw up suggestions and we comment on how to mitigate the difficulty of setting up Java security policies using examples from other security applications.

The paper is divided into the following sections. Section 2 describes the security architecture and policy files of Java. Section 3 describes the GUI of policytool that is used to set up a Java policy. Section 4 contains the study design. Results are shown in section 5. We discuss related studies and usability solutions in section 6 and conclude the paper with section 7.

2   Security Manager and Java policy files

All Java applications as well as other Java components such as servlets, Enterprise Java Beans (EJBs) or OSGi bundles (www.osgi.org) can be forced to execute under a so-called Security Manager. As of Java 2 the Security Manager can be set up with a set of permissions that modify the default policy of the Security Manager. Since the introduction of that new Security Manager it has been possible to allow fine-grained access control based on *where* the code was downloaded from (the so-called code base) and who has signed the code. Since the introduction of JAAS (Java Authorization and Authentication Service) it has also been possible to set up access control rules based on *who* executes the code. In Sun's Java version, the security policy is by default put in policy files. These are text files that contain the permissions that are explicitly granted to code bases, the location from which a Java class is loaded.

An example of a policy file is shown in fig. 1. The file may start with the definition of the so-called *keystore*, a URL to a file that contains public key certificates for verifying signed Java bytecode (see line 1 in fig. 1). The policy file consists further of *policy entries* (also called *grant statements*) that define positive permissions given to the named code base. In fig. 1 there are two policy entries—one for code base /tmp/xx.jar (lines 2–8), one for code base /tmp/yy.jar with signer alice (lines 9–11). Each policy entry consists of one or more *permission statements*. A permission statement consists of the keyword permission, the permission class such as java.io.FilePermission, a target such as /tmp and an action such as read (line 6). *Basic permissions* such as RuntimePermissions do not have actions, only targets (in this case getProtectionDomain (line 3)).

Java's security architecture is thoroughly described in [5].

3   Java policytool

The Java policytool is a simple GUI application included in every Java distribution and written in Java. The policytool consists of three major windows. The first window named *Policy Tool* (see fig. 2(a)) shows information about where in the file system the policy file resides, where the keystore is located and which policy entries are present in the file. The *File* menu contains the items *Open, Save, Save As, View Warning Log, Exit*. The *Edit* menu contains the items *Add Policy Entry, Edit Policy Entry, Remove Policy Entry* (which are also available as buttons) and *Change KeyStore*. For details about each policy entry one must mark a policy entry and then press *Edit Policy Entry*. This opens the window called *Policy Entry* (see fig. 2(b)) where all details about the policy entry and its permissions are shown. Creating or editing permissions (*Add Permission* or *Edit Permission* buttons in fig. 2(b)) requires a third window titled *Permissions* (see fig. 2(c)) where one specific permission is set up.

4   Study design

The method of our evaluation was a think-aloud study [4] where end users are using the application with a given scenario and tell the evaluator what they are thinking while working with the application and how they reason about problems they encounter.

There were 10 users* in the study (graduate and undergraduate students in the area of computer science) who had all worked with Java before. Only one person had previously set up a Java security policy. The other nine users had heard of Java security policies but had never actually worked with them.

The scenario for the users in this think-aloud study was that they had just downloaded two Java components from the Internet. The advertisement for the components

---

* Literature [6, 4] suggests that 3-5 users are enough to identify the most important usability problems.

described certain functionality but users were told not to trust the components and thus to subject them to the Security Manager to see which permissions the components would actually need and to set up the components with minimal permissions (according to the principle of least privilege). Users were not given access to the source code.

The first component required permissions as shown in the first policy entry (fig. 1, lines 2–8).

The second component involved signed code, i.e. the code that arrived at the end user was signed by Alice and accompanied by Alice's certificate. This task required only one permission, but the difficulty was that it was not a standard permission but rather one that we had developed for this study (called yy.YPermission, fig. 1, line 10). This second task also required the set-up of the keystore (fig. 1, line 1).

The typical procedure was that users ran the component under a Security Manager until an access control exception occured (due to the lack of an appropriate permission). Then they examined the access control exception message, set up the policy file with the required permission and restarted the component.

While solving the two tasks users were encouraged to give feedback, to think aloud. When users could not proceed with their tasks because they did not know how, they were instructed to ask the evaluator, rather than searching for on-line documentation. As the tool did not provide any help features, this shortcut was chosen to keep end user frustration low and to focus the study on the tool and not on the end users' capabilities of browsing for suitable documentation on the Internet.

At the end of the evaluation, users were asked to summarise their experience with policytool. If they were not satisfied with it they were asked to give suggestions for additions or improvements or to propose different ideas for solving the task of setting up a security policy for Java applications.

5 Results

We present the results of the user trials in two groups: feedback that relates to policytool in terms of specific GUI problems and more general usability metrics; and feedback that is oriented towards finding more usable ways of setting up Java security policies.

5.1 Problems with the graphical user interface

Shneiderman and Plaisant [7] provide the following eight golden rules of interface design by which we categorised the usability problems encountered in the user interface.

1. *Strive for consistency* across the application wrt. terminology, colour, layout, fonts, etc.
2. *Cater to universal usability*, design for both novice and expert users.
3. *Offer informative feedback* for every user action by e.g. visual presentation.
4. *Design dialogs to yield closure* so that users know which steps must be accomplished and where in the process they are currently situated.
5. *Prevent errors* by disabling inappropriate fields, checking user input and supplying constructive error feedback.
6. *Permit easy reversal of actions* to relieve user anxiety and to encourage exploration.
7. *Support internal locus of control* by making the user initiate actions, not respond to system output.
8. *Reduce short-term memory load* by e.g. providing online access to syntax help, abbreviations, codes.

Table 1 contains the 23 specific problems that the users found. The problems are grouped by window in which they appear and categorised according to the above mentioned golden rules.

Table 1. Usability details found during the evaluation categorised by the golden rules of Shneiderman and Plaisant [7].

No.	Problems	Category

The following issues were taken up for the main window (fig. 2(a)):

1. At start-up without command line parameters policytool tries to read the user default policy file from $HOME/.java.policy. If this file does not exist (which will rarely be the case) a warning is generated. This puzzles the users. They have done nothing except starting policytool and already a warning is issued. **7**

2. As a reaction many users wanted to enter the name of the policy file in the field labelled `Policy File`. But this field is not editable even though the user interface suggests it by using a text field with sunken relief. Its contents can only be changed through menu options (open an existing file, save a newly edited policy) or by starting policytool with a command line option that specifies the policy file. **1**

3. After returning from the set-up of policy entries, one must save the policy file (and then start the Java application with the newly saved policy file). Every *Save*-operation results in a popup-window that informs the user that the *Save* completed successfully. Some users were annoyed by this. One user suggested that there should be a status bar at the bottom of the window that shows the result of the *Save*-operation and whether there are unsaved changes. **1**

4. Sometimes users forgot to save their changed policy and restarted the application with an old policy file. When they went back to the policytool window, there was no hint to indicate whether or not the user had saved the file. A status bar or greyed-out menu item would have helped here. **3**

5. There are no keyboard shortcuts for menu items, e.g. Ctrl-S for *Save* is not implemented. This annoys proficient programmers because they must make use of the mouse. **2**

6. When users had to set up the second permission they were tempted to create a new policy entry (Button labelled *Add Policy Entry*), when the correct action would have been to add a permission to an existing policy entry (Button labelled *Edit Policy Entry*). In two cases, users created additional policy entries without any code bases (thus granting the permissions to all code), because they assumed that they *were* in fact editing the existing policy entry. Users suggested that showing the complete policy in the main window would be an advantage. Large policy files could be addressed by using collapsing trees (as found in file system browsers). **4**

7. In the second task, it was necessary to also set up a keystore entry. Most users forgot that. The warning that a public key is not known when closing the policy entry window (fig. 2(b)) was not enough to remind people that the keystore was needed. Thus they would restart the application only to get the very same access control exception. This resulted in user bewilderment and frustration because they thought they had made a mistake in the permission definition but could not find any such error. However, while the permission statement was correct, the reference to the certificate database (the keystore) was missing. This would cause the code to fail with the same access control exception as if the policy entry was not there at all. **5**

8. When entering the keystore location one user noticed that it did not matter if the location was entered as a URL or not. Policytool would automatically convert a non-URL location to URL notation. This behaviour is inconsistent with how the code base URL in the *Policy Entry* window is treated. **1**

The following issues were taken up for the policy entry window (fig. 2(b)):

9. Even though users had understood that permissions are granted per code base, the text field CodeBase was sometimes misunderstood. One user wanted to fill in the host name needed for the socket permission. **5, 8**

10. The code base must be filled in as a URL. If this is not done, an error message pops up when trying to close this window. An example of a code base would lead to less user frustration in this issue. **5, 8**

11. Many users were confused by the *SignedBy* text field and did not know whether it was relevant to task 1 or not (it was not). **4, 8**

12. The *SignedBy* text field was relevant in task 2 but many users hesitated what to put there: Should it be alice. Alice or yy.jar? **8**

13. All users wondered about principals and whether they had to deal with them or not (principals are needed in JAAS which we did not use in this study). The UI should clarify how code bases, signers and principals interact. **4**

The following issues were taken up in the window for permission setting (see fig. 2(c)):

14. A number of users were confused by the concepts of permission, target and action. One user was looking for the target *getProtectionDomain* in the permission list. All users were looking for targets such as */tmp/a* or *www.ida.liu.se:80* in the target list and did not expect to type the text themselves. Many users remarked that examples would have helped greatly. **4, 8**

15. While permission names (FilePermission, SocketPermission etc.) are listed in alphabetical order, target names are not. Users were confused when *getProtectionDomain* was not readily visible in the list. **1**

16. It is not possible to get through the lists for permissions, targets or actions more quickly by typing the first letter(s) of the permission, target or action that one wants to find in the list. **2**

17. Most users did not understand that there are both basic permissions (such as a RuntimePermission at line 3 of fig. 1), which consist of a target (in this case *getProtectionDomain*) only, and regular permissions, which consist of target *and* action (see all other permissions in fig. 1). Using target for basic permissions was considered misleading by one user. **4**

18. Many users did not understand that the action list would append its items to the text field. They would enter additional actions by typing the action text in the text field or by creating a new permission for the additional action. **1**

19. Many permissions allow wildcards in their target and action strings. But this is represented in the graphical user interface. Only the `<<ALL FILES>>` keyword is shown for file permissions. However, hints for the wildcards + and − are missing. **8**

20. Users did not understand what the text field *SignedBy* in the *Permission* window was about. **4**

21. Entering a non-standard permission (the yy.YPermission) was difficult for all users. All were spending time in browsing the interface in search of a YPermission. When they entered the text manually, it could happen that the action field was greyed out and thus uneditable because users had chosen a basic permission previously. When they had entered the required text manually and closed the window for permission setting, a warning was issued that a YPermission was not known to the system. However, it was not possible to start policytool with a classpath set that would remedy this warning. This was annoying. **1, 4**

22. Even users that had understood the concepts of permission, target and action were confused when these concepts were applied on a self-defined permission, even though the error message text is completely analogous (...AccessControlException: access denied (yy.YPermission x set), cf. fig. 3). **4**

23. When adding the non-standard YPermission, user were tempted to forget to put the full class name yy.YPermission and would only put YPermission. **5**

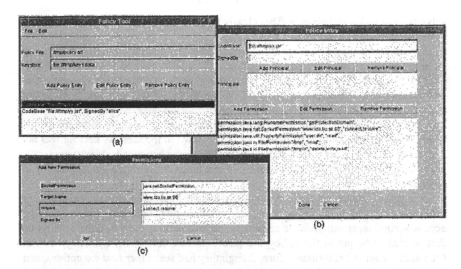

Fig. 2. (a) Main window of the Java policytool (b) Permission entries for the code base /tmp/xx.jar (c) Set-up of permissions.

```
Exception in thread "main" java.security.AccessControlException:
 access denied (\textit{java.net.SocketPermission www.ida.liu.se:80 connect,resolve})
    at java.security.AccessControlContext.checkPermission(AccessControlContext.
    java:264)
    at java.security.AccessController.checkPermission(AccessController.java:427)
    ...
    at java.net.URLConnection.getContentType(URLConnection.java:479)
    at xx.XX.main(XX.java:113)
%\end{alltt}
```

Fig. 3. Error message when executing the code for the first task without the proper socket permission. The text in italics shows the permission that is needed but not currently given. This is the text that corresponds almost verbatim to what must be put in the policy file, see line 4 in fig. 1.

The most frequent user problem was that users simply did not know how to proceed (categorised as no. 4—Design dialogs to yield closure): Users did not know which steps they had to accomplish now nor where in the process of policy set-up they were currently situated—and policytool offered no help. This is most serious and cannot be remedied easily. Categories 1 (inconsistencies) and 8 (reduce memory load) are runners-up. Subjects found a number of inconsistencies within the application (e.g. URL checking is handled differently in two different windows; some lists are ordered alphabetically, some are not) and with general GUI guidelines (e.g. successfully saving a policy causes a pop-up window to appear that must be acknowledged by the user).

It cannot be stressed enough that there was no help feature at all included in the GUI of policytool, not an example, not a pointer to a web page, no help on how to use policytool. No user could complete the task without help from the evaluator. Many said that they would have had to study the documentation extensively before being able to solve the two tasks on their own. This clearly violates items 2 (universal usability) and 8 (reduce short-term memory load).

Working with signed files was considered difficult by all users, which is in line with other studies [2, 8] involving digital signatures. This task required a good understanding of the concepts of public key infrastructure and certificate databases. However, this understanding was made even more difficult due to the fact that keystore creation and import of certificates are not integrated into policytool but done in a separate command line tool called keytool. Users found this switch between applications most confusing. Also, keytool uses a lot of options that must be known to the user. As keytool was not part of the evaluation, users were supplied with the correct commands. Many users commented that it would probably have taken them a long time to figure out the command chain by themselves.

The lack of integration between policytool and the runtime environment also caused problems. Even reasonably experienced programmers did not realize—at first—that the access control exception message caused by the Java runtime contained the permission that needed to be put in the policy file (see bold face text of fig. 3). They had not seen access control exceptions before, though they had seec other Java exceptions, and started examining the stack output rather than the access control exception message.

After evaluating this tool, it is clear why applets as a substitute for plugins or for applications never had a breakthrough—managing their required permissions is an insurmountable task for non-Java security experts given a tool like policytool, especially when working with signed code.

5.2 Differences in the policy files

Of the ten created policy files, four show interesting deviations that have an impact on security and performance.

One user created three permissions where one would have been enough. Instead of the compact

```
permission java.io.FilePermission "/tmp/a", "read, write, delete";
```

the user created three permission entries: one for read, one for write, one for delete. This is not a security problem but an inefficient way of stating policies. Other users started out with this approach but realised what they were doing and changed their policy to the more compact way of stating the permission.

One user became impatient when setting up the required permissions for file access to /tmp/a and chose all actions. This gave the code the unneeded and dangerous permission to *execute* /tmp/a.

One user did not supply the port for the socket permissions, thus allowing the code to connect to any port at www.ida.liu.se (instead of port 80).

Two users mistakenly created policy entries that gave permissions to any code because they had not actively chosen the code base to which they wanted to add a permission:

```
grant {
  permission java.io.FilePermission "/tmp/a", "write";
};
```

Both users mistook the *Add Policy Entry* button for the *Edit Policy Entry* → *Add New Permission* sequence. This serious mistake is a direct result of the GUI design of policytool. In a hand-typed policy file this problem would not have arisen.

5.3   Effectiveness, efficiency, user satisfaction

The previous sections describe specific problems of policytool. This section summarises these findings and comments on the general usability of policytool following the usability-defining keywords of the ISO standard 9241-11: effectiveness, efficiency, and user satisfaction.

Effectiveness judges how well policytool supports the user in setting up a policy. If the user has all the knowledge about how Java security works, policytool may be quite a good syntax helper. However, novice users do not have that knowledge and are left on their own to find guidance in how to proceed to set up a policy. Effectiveness could be increased by guidance features such as wizards or safe staging (see section 6) that help identify the steps that must be taken to arrive at a functional policy. To arrive at a holistic solution, keytool must also be integrated.

Efficiency judges how resource-consuming (both computer and human) policytool is while accomplishing its task. Policytool fails on the human side. Users had to spend a lot of time and effort in figuring out what had to be done and received no help from policytool on this issue. Efficiency for novice users could be increased with wizards and help features; efficiency for expert users could be increased by keyboard shortcuts for buttons and menu items and a view that allows direct editing of the policy file.

User satisfaction judges how acceptable policytool is to the users and if there is a fun factor or enriching experience associated with using policytool. The study users were not that negative towards policytool as a tool for editing a policy file, but they were very negative in their satisfaction with setting up security policies. They would have prefered a tool that was integrated into the Java runtime, a tool that would automatically collect required permissions and interact with the user only to ask whether a permission should be allowed or not.

5.4   Suggestions for improvement

This section contains user suggestions for improving the usability (and security) of setting up Java security policies and comments about the feasibility of the suggestions . The suggestions are categorised into new language features, help for end users and help for developers.

Help for end users As one user suggested: "There should be a -learn option to the Java runtime so that I do not have to be the parser for the system. My task [of putting required permissions in the policy file] could have been automated."

Another user pointed out that there is a mismatch between the syntax of the policy file and the syntax of the access control exception text (see figures 1 and 3). It should be possible to create a smart copy-and-paste function that correctly pastes an access control exception text into a policy file.

One user suggested helplessly that there should be a check that ensures "that one does not allow too much". He had realised during the debriefing that his policy file allowed too much.

It is definitely possible to set up Java security policies at runtime. JSEF [9] has done this with direct user interaction through a GUI. The user is prompted to decide whether to accept the required permission or not. However, using a GUI is not always possible, especially not in container environments where no display is associated with a piece of code. We therefore suggest the implementation of a "policy learner" that will either grant all required permissions by default and write them to a policy file for post mortem analysis or that will interact with user preferences. An analyzer component, much like an intrusion detection module, could react to flaws in the policy and trigger an alert if a piece of code has read a file in the file system and then opens a network connection (implying a breach of confidentiality because data may leave the host system and be transmitted somewhere else without the consent of the host or material owner). A policy learner could have prevented all of the deviations described in 5.2.

Help for developers A tool could be created that semi-automatically detects required permissions in Java code (along the lines of C-tools like IBM Rational Purify, which detects runtime memory leaks). It must be ensured that all code is run (as with IBM Rational PureCoverage) so that even permissions for error situations (writing to an error log file) are detected. A problem is that e.g. automatically generated file names (e.g. date+time.txt) are then difficult to put in a policy.

New language features One user proposed that the Java language could enforce that permissions must be declared in the same way as exceptions are declared today. As in the previous item, dynamic targets would be difficult to handle. It would be possible to require declaration of permissions within the code or that a JIT(Just In Time)-Compiler could produce a footprint of required permissions at early-execution time. It would not be too difficult to find out which *classes* of permissions a piece of code needs, but the problem resides with the targets that could be dynamically created at runtime, e.g. a program may ask the user to supply the hostname of the computer to which it wants to connect. It is obvious at compile time that a socket permission is needed, but the target of the socket permission, the actual host address, is not known before runtime. Koved and others [10] have addressed static analysis of Java code in order to find required permissions. Their approach examines Java bytecode prior to execution and, using invocation graphs, finds required permissions. However, such a solution will not help for targets created at runtime (as described above).

One user suggested permissions that allow the deletion of the files that the program has created. This could be either a new permission class or an additional action for standard FilePermissions. A lot of work exists to make Java security policies more expressive, e.g. [11–13], allowing policies like e.g. "no write after a confidential read". However, none of the existing solutions have addressed usability issues. It is not likely that users would be able to handle more expressive security policies easily.

6 Related work

It may seem that it is rather lopsided to evaluate a small application, find a lot of usability problems and draw general conclusions about usability of security tools from that. Unfortunately, policytool is just one in a long line of security tools that display an astonishing lack of user focus even though they are targeted at novice users. E-mail software with encryption [2, 8], Internet banking [14, 15], Internet Explorer [1], MS Word [16] and firewalls [17, 18]—all these applications show severe shortcomings in the usability of their security functions.

Currently suggested ways for improving the usability of security functions comprise "good-enough security" [19] or "if we put usability first, how much security can we get" [20]. These approaches do not strive for perfect security, but for security that works in many cases. *Safe staging* [21] slowly and safely introduces the security novice to a security application through several stages. Also the concept of *social navigation*—showing how previous users have interacted or should interact with a user interface by leaving traces of earlier use on the artefact—has been used to enhance users' perception of security features [22]. Yee [23] proposes *security by designation*: User action designates what the user wants to do and thus also authorises an action.

In the end, there is a lot to be gained by following professional usability guidelines such as Jonston, Eloff and others [17, six criteria for successful human-computer interaction in security applications], Leveson [24, 60 guidelines for safe HMI design], Nielsen [4, 10 design slogans], Garfinkel [25, 6 general principles], ISO standard 9241 (parts 10–17), Shneiderman and Plaisant [7, 8 golden rules of interface design] and by subjecting the security product to usability testing, again and again.

7 Conclusion

In this paper we have evaluated the usability of the Java policytool for setting up security policies for Java applications or components. We have found a number of problems—some small and some larger—in the GUI of policytool. The small ones violate GUI design guidelines and thus easily annoy users. The larger problems lead to serious lapses in the policy, thus endowing a Java application with more rights than it should have.

The study users suggested a number of improvements that range from more expressive permissions to runtime policy setup with or without user interaction and to issues in static analysis such as changing the Java language in order to support the declaration of permissions.

According to the definition of usable security software (see introduction), the Java policytool is not usable. (1) Users are *not* reliably made aware of their security tasks because policytool is not integrated with the actual Java application. (2) Figuring out how to perform the policy setup takes a lot of help from web resources and is not explained explicitly or implicitly within policytool. (3) Dangerous errors can easily be made as was shown in our evaluation. (4) Expert users are quicker in directly editing the policy file than handling the somewhat cumbersome policytool.

Obviously there is a great potential for improvement and our future work will make use of findings from work in the field of usable security to improve the user task of setting up security policies.

References

1. Furnell, S.M.: Using security: easier said than done. Computer Fraud & Security 2004(4) (2004) 6–10
2. Whitten, A., Tygar, J.D.: Why Johnny can't encrypt: A usability evaluation of PGP 5.0. In: Proceedings of the 8th USENIX Security Symposium (Security'99), Usenix (1999)
3. Sun Microsystems Inc.: Policy tool—policy file creation and management tool. http:// java.sun.com/j2se/1.5.0/docs/tooldocs/solaris/policytool.html (2002)
4. Nielsen, J.: Usability Engineering. Morgan Kaufmann Publishers, Inc (1993)
5. Oaks, S.: Java Security. 2nd edn. O'Reilly & Associates, Inc. (2001)
6. Faulkner, X.: Usability Engineering. Macmillan Press Ltd (2000)
7. Shneiderman, B., Plaisant, C.: Designing the User Interface. 4th edn. Addison Wesley (2004)
8. Gerd tom Markotten, D.: Benutzbare Sicherheit in informationstechnischen Systemen. Rhombos Verlag, Berlin (2004) ISBN 3-937231-06-4.
9. Hauswirth, M., Kerer, C., Kurmanowytsch, R.: A secure execution framework for Java. In: Proceedings of the 7th ACM Conference on Computer and Communications Security (CCS'00), ACM Press (2000) 43–52
10. Koved, L., Pistoia, M., Kershenbaum, A.: Access rights analysis for Java. In: Proceedings of the 17th ACM Conference on Object-Oriented Programming, Systems, Languages, and Applications (OOPSLA'02), ACM Press (2002) 359–372
11. Mehta, N.V., Sollins, K.R.: Expanding and extending the security features of Java. In: Proceedings of the 7th USENIX Security Symposium (Security'98), Usenix (1998)
12. Corradi, A., Montanari, R., Lupu, E., Sloman, M., Stefanelli, C.: A flexible access control service for Java mobile code. In: Proceedings of the 16th Annual Computer Security Applications Conference (ACSAC'00), IEE (2000) 356–365
13. Venkatakrishnan, V., Peri, R., Sekar, R.: Empowering mobile code using expressive security policies. In: Proceedings of the New Security Paradigms Workshop (NSPW'02), ACM Press (2002) 61–68
14. Hertzum, M., Jørgensen, N., Nørgaard, M.: Usable security and e-banking: Ease of use vis-à-vis security. In: Proceedings of the Annual Conference of CHISIG (OZCHI'04). (2004)
15. Nilsson, M., Adams, A., Herd, S.: Building security and trust in online banking. In: Proceedings of the Conference on Human Factors in Computing Systems (CHI'05), ACM Press (2005) 1701–1704
16. Furnell, S.M.: Why users cannot use security. Computers & Security 24(4) (2005) 274–279
17. Johnston, J., Eloff, J.H.P., Labuschagne, L.: Security and human computer interfaces. Computers & Security 22(8) (2003) 675–684
18. Wool, A.: The use and usability of direction-based filtering in firewalls. Computers & Security 23(6) (2004) 459–468
19. Sandhu, R.S.: Good-enough security. IEEE Internet Computing 7(1) (2003) 66–68
20. Smetters, D., Grinter, R.E.: Moving from the design of usable security technologies to the design of useful secure applications. In: Proceedings of the New Security Paradigms Workshop (NSPW'02), ACM Press (2002) 82–89
21. Whitten, A., Tygar, J.: Safe staging for computer security. In: Proceedings of the CHI2003 Workshop on Human-Computer Interaction and Security Systems. (2003)
22. DiGioia, P., Dourish, P.: Social navigation as a model for usable security. In: Proceedings of the Symposium on usable privacy and security (SOUPS'05), ACM Press (2005) 101–108
23. Yee, K.P.: Guidelines and strategies for secure interaction design. [26]
24. Leveson, N.: Safeware: System Safety and Computers. Addison Wesley (1995)
25. Garfinkel, S.L.: Design Principles and Patterns for Computer Systems That Are Simultaneously Secure and Usable. PhD thesis, Massachusetts Institute of Technology (2005)
26. Cranor, L.F., Garfinkel, S.L.: Security and Usability. O'Reilly & Associates, Inc (2005)

Considering the Usability of End-User Security Software

Steven Furnell, Adila Jusoh, Dimitris Katsabas, and Paul Dowland

Network Research Group
University of Plymouth, Plymouth, United Kingdom
info@network-research-group.org

Abstract. Security features can now be found in a variety of end-user applications. However, the extent to which such features can actually be understood and used by the target audience is often undermined by poor attention to human-computer interaction factors. This paper considers the problem, and highlights a number of common issues that can compromise the usability of security features in practice. The discussion evidences the problems by means of examples from well-known applications, as well as drawing upon the results from a survey of over 340 end-users, which benchmarks the extent to which some of the observed issues actually affect them. It is concluded that users can currently face real difficulties, but could be relatively easily avoided though better design and implementation of the features concerned.

1   Introduction

In the face of an increasing volume and variety of threats, the use of security safeguards is an important consideration for end-user systems. However, getting users to realise and act upon this is often a challenge, and unless they have already had experience of a troublesome incident, users may need significant persuasion that security is something they need to worry about. Unfortunately, winning the awareness battle is only part of the challenge, and users can still be put off if they cannot understand and use the features that are placed before them. Sadly, this is often the reality of the situation, with security software that makes significant assumptions about users' technical capabilities and presents features in a manner that is more likely to reduce protection rather than encourage its use.

The importance of making systems usable is by no means a new discovery. Indeed, the principles of human-computer interaction (HCI) are now well-established, and a variety of information is now available to inform and guide the design of software to suit its intended user community [1, 2]. In spite of this, it is still possible to identify many examples of poor practice, with the affected software being less easily used and understood as a result. The implementation of security features is an area that appears to fare particularly badly here, and this paper highlights a series of problems that can be commonly observed in relation to security functionality, based upon practical examples from a series of end-user applications.

Please use the following format when citing this chapter:

Author(s) [insert Last name, First-name initial(s)], 2006, in IFIP International Federation for Information Processing, Volume 201, Security and Privacy in Dynamic Environments, eds. Fischer-Hubner, S., Rannenberg, K., Yngstrom, L., Lindskog, S., (Boston: Springer), pp. [insert page numbers].

2   Common Problems in End-User Security Features

This section highlights a number of examples of common failings that are apparent in programs that target end-users. For the purposes of discussion, five key themes are used to group the problem issues. However, it should be noted that several of the points are inter-related, and the practical examples used to illustrate them can certainly be seen to be suffering from more than one of the problems. It should also be noted that none of these issues are specifically related to the implementation of security functionality, and indeed the themes identified here are closely related to usability heuristics proposed by Nielsen for systems in general [3].

In addition to practical examples, the discussion draws upon the results from an online survey of end-users, which was conducted in order to assess understanding of application-level security features amongst the general user population. The survey presented respondents with screenshots relating to the security functionality within a number of popular end-user applications, and attempted to determine whether they were meaningful (e.g. in relation to the terminology used) and correctly interpreted (i.e. whether the intention of the functionality was properly understood). A total of 342 responses were received, and the main characteristics of the respondent group were as follows:
- almost equally split between male and female
- over 80% in the 17-29 age group
- over 80% have university-level education
- over 96% are regularly use a computer at home and/or at work
- almost 90% rated themselves as intermediate or advanced users

These factors suggest that the respondents as a whole were likely to have a high level of IT literacy, making them well-placed to provide relevant comments about the usability of security features within the targeted applications. Some of the significant findings from the survey are therefore used to support the discussion presented here. For readers interested obtaining further information, the full details of the survey and the associated results can be found in [4].

2.1   Reliance upon Technical Terminology

One of the traditional barriers to newcomers into IT is the significant degree of technical terminology that accompanies the domain. Over time, efforts have been made to ease this burden, with increased use of pictures and plain language as a means of expressing concepts to novices. However, security is one area in which the message is still very likely to be unclear, with technical terms often being an intrinsic part of how features are conveyed. An example of this problem is illustrated in Figure 1, which shows the means by which users are able to set the 'security level' for browsing sites within Internet Explorer (IE). Provided as the standard browser within the most popular operating system environments, IE is, of course, the means by which most users come into contact with the Web, and browsing is a context in which appropriate security is most definitely required. However, although the interface initially looks quite straightforward, with the use of a slider control to set the desired security level on a four-point scale (low, medium-low, medium, and high), it becomes somewhat less intuitive if users try to understand the descriptions of the settings. For example, one of the characteristics of the 'medium' setting described in the Figure is that "Unsigned ActiveX controls will not be downloaded". Although this would be unlikely to cause problems for users with a technology background, it has clear potential to confuse the average user (who might nonetheless have an interest in setting up their system securely, and so could certainly find themselves looking at the related options). As a result, while they will appreciate the idea of the low-to-high scale, the descriptions may impede their ability to relate this to their browsing needs.

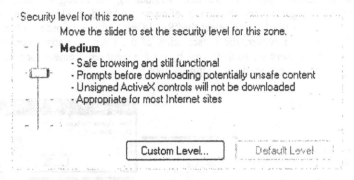

Fig. 1. Setting the 'Security level' within Internet Explorer.

Respondents to the authors' survey were presented with this screenshot, and asked to indicate whether they understood it. The results revealed that 34% did not. Although this is already a sizeable proportion of users to lose, the authors anticipated that some respondents would claim to understand the interface even though they did not actually understand all of the terminology. As such, the questionnaire proceeded to ask whether respondents had heard of ActiveX before, and if so, whether they actually knew what it meant. Although the initial finding here was mostly positive, with 65% claiming to have heard of the term, only 54% of these people (i.e. only 35% of the overall respondent group) knew the meaning. This puts a rather different interpretation upon the proportion of people who would fully understand the setting in Figure 1, with almost two thirds of the overall respondent group unable to comprehend the complete description.

2.2   Unclear and Confusing Functionality

If users are confronted with security features that they do not understand, then it increases the chance that they will make mistakes. In some cases, these mistakes will put their system or data at increased risk, whereas in others they may serve to impede the user's own use of the system. Confusion can often arise from the way in which features are presented, with the result that even the most straightforward and familiar security safeguards can become challenging to use. As an example, we can consider the way in which password protection is used in several Microsoft Office applications. Excel, PowerPoint and Word all allow two levels of password to be applied to user files – to control access to the file (i.e. in order to maintain confidentiality), or to restrict the ability to modify it (i.e. controlling integrity). Such passwords are set via two distinct fields in the 'Security' tab that users can access from the Tools-Options menu (as depicted in the left side of Figure 2). Users who subsequently attempt to open such a password-protected file are then presented with the dialogs on the right-hand side of Figure 2 (the prompts in this case being taken from Microsoft Word). However, whereas the prompt for opening an accessed-controlled file (the upper dialog) is relatively easy to understand (i.e. you need a password and cannot open the document without it), the dialog for files that are merely protected against modification is often misunderstood. Users who wish to simply view or print the file can select the 'Read Only' option, in order to bypass the password request. However, the presentation of the interface causes confusion in practice, and many users are so distracted by the apparent requirement for a password that they believe they cannot do anything without it.

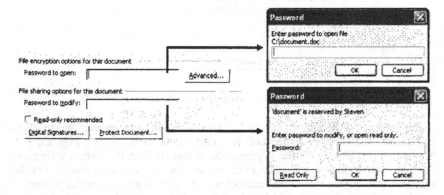

Fig. 2. Password options and the resulting prompts within Microsoft Word.

In the authors' survey, respondents were presented with an example of the lower password dialog, and asked to indicate which of three options they understood it to mean. Although the majority correctly indicated that it meant the document could not be modified without a password, 23% incorrectly believed that the file could not be *opened* without a password, and a further 13% were not sure how to interpret it. As such, more than a third of users would not have been in a position to make the correct decision.

2.3   Lack of Visible Status and Informative Feedback

Users ought to know when security is being applied and what level of protection they are being given. This not only provides a basis for increasing their confidence when using particular services, but can also remind them to configure the system correctly. Without such a reminder, users may proceed to perform sensitive tasks without adequate protection, or may inadvertently leave settings at a level that impedes their legitimate usage. As such, the lack of visible status information is another example of undesirable HCI. As an illustration of how this can cause problems, the screenshots in Figure 3 show two attempts to reach Microsoft's Hotmail service via Internet Explorer, with the browser security level set to 'high'.

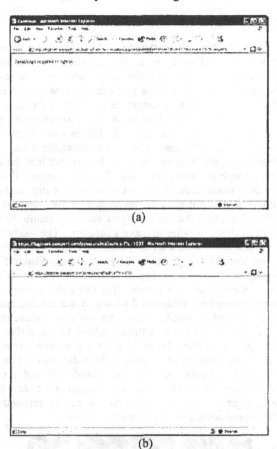

Fig. 3. Attempts to access Hotmail with Internet Explorer security set to 'high' – (a) directly via URL (b) indirectly via MSN Messenger.

Figure 3a shows the effects of attempting to reach the service by typing the 'www.hotmail.com' into the address bar.   The result is a message advising "JavaScript required to sign in" – which would be unlikely to be a sufficiently informative message to alert many users to the fact that their security settings were preventing the site from loading correctly.   Meanwhile, Figure 3b shows an even worse scenario, with the user having attempted to log in via the MSN Messenger service. In this case, the user receives no message at all, and there is no indication of what the problem might be. As such, they may conclude that the site is simply not operational. What the user should receive is a clear message to remind them that their

312   Steven Furnell et al.

browser security is set to 'high', and to indicate that this may cause the site to operate incorrectly.

2.4   Forcing Uninformed Decisions

Even if users do not go looking for security-related options and attempt to change the settings, they may still find themselves confronted with the need to take security-related decisions during the course of their normal activities. In these contexts, it should be all the more important for the information to be conveyed to them in a meaningful fashion, with minimal assumptions of prior knowledge and maximum help available to ease the process. Unfortunately, however, users may again find themselves at a disadvantage in practice, with dialogs often being conveyed in a manner that only advanced participants would be comfortable with. To illustrate the point, Figures 4 and 5 present two examples of dialogs that may be encountered by users during standard web browsing activities. The first example illustrates the type of warning that a user would receive when a website's security certificate has been issued by a provider that is not specified as trusted in their security configuration. This does not, of course, mean that the certifying authority cannot be trusted, but the user is being asked to check in order to make a decision. The likely problem here is that most users will not know what a security certificate is, let alone be able to make a meaningful decision about one. Meanwhile, the example in Figure 5 is warning the user that a web page they are attempting to download contains active content that could potentially be harmful to their system. The difficultly for most users is again likely to be that they would not understand what they were being asked, with terms such as 'active content' and 'ActiveX' being more likely to confuse than explain. Of course, part of the problem in these examples relates to the earlier issue of using technical terminology. However, the problem here goes somewhat deeper, in the sense that both cases are obliging the user to make a decision without the option to seek further help from the system. As such, they would be forced to make a decision in the absence of sufficient information. As an indication of the scale of this problem, the example from Figure 5 was presented to the survey respondents, and 56% indicated that they would not know how to make a decision.

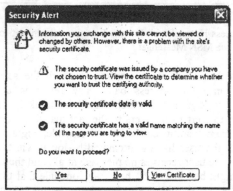

Fig. 4. Website security certificate warning.

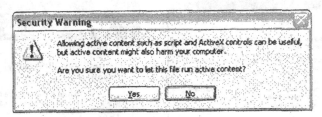

Fig. 5. Active content warning.

2.5   Lack of Integration

Another way in which the presentation of security features may serve to confuse users is if different aspects do not integrate together in a meaningful fashion. Although individual mechanisms are often provided in different software from different vendors, it would not be unreasonable for users to expect security features to work in concert. Unfortunately, it is possible to identify examples in which such integration does not occur, and users receive contradictory messages as a consequence. As an example, Figure 6a shows the security settings for macro functions within Microsoft Word. The significant part of the image is near the very bottom, with the indication that no virus scanner is installed. In actual fact, this screenshot was taken from a machine running McAfee VirusScan Enterprise 7 (the icon for which is visible as the third item in the system tray), and so receiving a message claiming that no virus protection is installed is hardly useful to the user. Meanwhile, Figure 6b presents an example of a pop-up message that appeared on a Dell PC during normal daily usage. Although this could be considered useful as a friendly reminder to general users that they need to be concerned about security, the problem in this case was that the message popped up on a machine running Norton Internet Security – which meant it already had the firewall and anti-virus protection being referred to. Some users will interpret the wording of the message ("you should have a firewall…") to mean that the system is telling them that they are not adequately protected - which could cause obvious confusion and concern for users who considered they already had suitable safeguards. It would be preferable to offer more specific advice, tailored to user's actual circumstances (e.g. "You have a firewall and virus protection, but should also have anti-spyware protection installed"). Failing this (e.g. if it was not possible to determine existing protection status), the wording could still be adjusted to something that would pose a question rather than make an apparent statement (e.g. "Do you have a firewall?"), and therefore allow users who knew they were protected to pass by without concern.

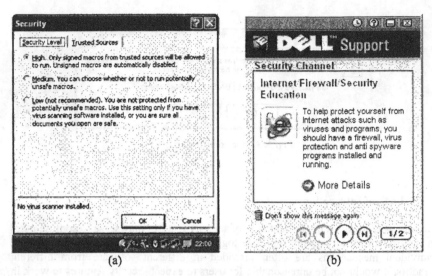

(a)   (b)

Fig. 6. Examples of misinformation due to lack of integration.

Although the messages in both of these examples aimed to be helpful, warning and reminding users that security needs to be considered, it could be argued that if the system is unable to give an accurate message that it would be preferable to say nothing at all.

3   Improving the Situation

Appropriate presentation of security features is unlikely to happen by chance, and software designers should therefore pay specific attention to making sure that their systems are easily understood and used by the target audience. Of course, attempting to reach such a goal ought not to be an ad hoc endeavour, and the aforementioned good practice in domains such as HCI may be used to assist the process. In addition, a number of published works specifically consider guidelines for developing usable security systems [5, 6].

Having identified a series of less desirable examples, it is also relevant to observe that many examples of stronger interface design can be found. As an illustration, Figure 7 presents two screenshots taken from the Norton Internet Security package, which aims to provide an integrated security solution (including firewall, anti-virus, anti-spam, and intrusion detection) for end-user systems. The tool, of course, differs from the earlier examples in the paper, because it represents an example of software that has been specifically designed to fulfil a security role, rather than a wider application within which security is just one of the supporting functions. As such, it can be assumed that the designers and developers would have been in a position to devote more specific attention to the presentation and usability of the protection features. As a result, some of the positive observations arising from this particular interface are that:

– all of the top-level security options are visible and configurable from a single window;
– the status of each option is clearly conveyed, along with the consequent security status of the overall tool;
– brief and clearly-worded explanations are provided to accompany each main option, and further help is easily accessible in each case.

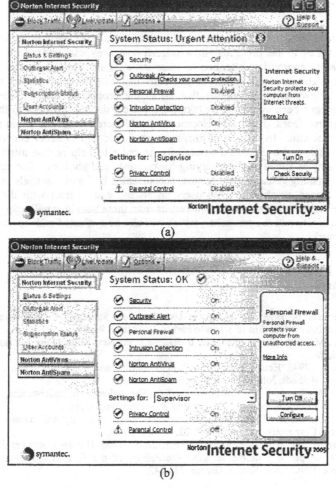

Fig. 7. Examples of stronger interface design

In Figure 7a, the user receives a clear visual indication that things are amiss, with the 'Urgent Attention' banner and the warning icon beside the aspect that is causing the concern (in addition, the background of the information area is shaded red). Meanwhile, the next dialogue (Figure 7b) shows the system to be in the more desirable state of having all the critical elements working correctly (note that although the 'Parental Control' option is disabled, it does not affect the overall security status, and the window is now shaded with a reassuring green background). Comparing the dialogs to the earlier examples, it is apparent that none of the previous problems are immediately on show.

4   Conclusions

If users are to be expected to make use of security, then it is clearly important for the related features to be presented in a manner that they can understand and use. Unfortunately, appropriate attention to these issues is far from guaranteed, and the paper has highlighted a number of problems that can be encountered in current software. However, it is notable that all of the problems indicated here would essentially have been avoidable by taking a more considered approach to the design of the user interfaces. Future developments should therefore seek to avoid repeating the same problems. In support of this, research should aim to better understand the ways in which end-users relate to security, in order to help realise interfaces and interaction styles suited to their varying backgrounds and abilities. The authors are currently pursuing research in this area, accompanied by hands-on trials in order to enable a deeper insight into how users understand and interact with the security features already at their disposal. The results from these activities will help to inform the design of alternative approaches, which will also be evaluated and reported as part of future work.

References

1. Shneiderman, B. 1998. Designing the User Interface: Strategies for Effective Human-Computer Interaction. (3rd ed.). Menlo Park, CA: Addison Wesley.
2. Carroll, J.M. 2001. Human-Computer Interaction in the New Millennium, Addison-Wesley Professional.
3. Nielsen, J. 1994. "Heuristic evaluation", in Nielsen, J. and Mack, R.L. (Eds.), Usability Inspection Methods, John Wiley & Sons, New York.
4. Furnell, S.M., Jusoh, A. and Katsabas, D. 2006. "The challenges of understanding and using security: A survey of end-users", Computers & Security, vol. 25, no.1.
5. Johnston, J., Eloff, J.H.P. and Labuschagne, L. 2003. "Security and human computer interfaces", Computers & Security, vol. 22, no. 8, 675-684.
6. Katsabas, D., Furnell, S.M., Dowland, P.S. 2005. Using Human Computer Interaction principles to promote usable security. Proceedings of the Fifth International Network Conference (INC 2005), Samos, Greece, 235-242.

Utilizing the Common Criteria for Advanced Student Research Projects

Thuy D. Nguyen and Cynthia E. Irvine

Naval Postgraduate School
Monterey, CA 93943, USA
{tdnguyen,irvine}@nps.edu

Abstract. In most computer science graduate programs, students must complete an advanced research project that demonstrates the students technical competence in both the theory and practice of the field. Information security is a specialization area of computer science whose research results have direct benefits to real world problems. The Common Criteria (CC) is an international standard for security evaluation of products. This paper describes the utilization of the CC paradigmatic framework for advanced student research projects focused on security engineering. Three CC-based efforts of varying levels of difficulty are presented and the suitability and benefits of applying the CC in this context are discussed.

1 Introduction

Information security is a specialization area of computer science that is increasingly attracting attention of academic, government, and industry-based communities. This interest is driven by the exploitability of the Internet and the heightened awareness of the lack of assurance in commodity computers. Although work in computer security has been ongoing for several decades, it has not been adopted along with other rapid advances in computer and network technologies. This gap stems from the fact that the commercial sector is under constant pressure to reduce time-to-market and compete with the latest technical gimmicks. Thus, the commercial sector has tended to ignore the principles [1] and fundamentals of information security in product development. Accelerating government and commercial adoption of emerging technologies has created significant financial and national security risks that must be addressed.

While the academic community has been more proactive in addressing the need for better security education to prepare students for the real world workplace [2], typical computer security coursework often tends to focus on static code analysis, cryptography, secure protocols, and intrusion detection and analysis. The security track of the Computer Science (CS) department at our institution incorporates additional disciplines in information assurance and security with an emphasis on high assurance secure systems and security engineering.

The Common Criteria (CC) is an internationally-recognized set of criterions for Information Technology (IT) security evaluation [3]. It is the result of a multinational effort to harmonize different security evaluation criteria independently developed by several North American and European governments [4–6]. As the use of the CC in the

Please use the following format when citing this chapter:

Author(s) [insert Last name, First-name initial(s)], 2006, in IFIP International Federation for Information Processing, Volume 201, Security and Privacy in Dynamic Environments, eds. Fischer-Hubner, S., Rannenberg, K., Yngstrom, L., Lindskog, S., (Boston: Springer), pp. [insert page numbers].

commercial sector becomes more widespread, a natural progression would be to use it in education and research to both prepare students for proficiency in secure system and software engineering techniques and to nurture their appreciation of the value of rigorously-developed secure systems. CC hegemony remains an uncertain prospect, but the pedagogical value of applying the CC to information security education and research is clear. Our premise is that if the CC framework and methodology are used in both instructional courses and student research projects, the students understanding of the fundamental principles of information security will be more effectively strengthened and the quality of student work will improve quantitatively. The central notion is that this holistic approach enables the students to become better practitioners of the fundamental knowledge gained during their academic endeavor.

This paper describes how the CC was utilized as a practical tool for security requirements derivation in advanced student research projects. Background information on CC coursework and information security research projects is presented, followed by the description of three thematic projects guided by the CC framework. A discussion of the experience with the CC-based research approach is included.

2   Background

Our nascent framework on CC education combines both traditional coursework and faculty-supervised student theses that are part of multi-year research efforts.

2.1   Information Assurance Courses

The computer science (CS) coursework portfolio in our department consists of a set of core computer science classes and a number of specialization courses. The information assurance and security track augments the core CS classes with principles and techniques of developing secure systems [7]. The CC concepts and goals covered in some of the security track courses are described in Table 1.

2.2   Information Security Research Projects

Trusted Computing Exemplar (TCX) Project. The TCX project provides an openly disseminated worked example of how high robustness trusted components can be constructed. The CC plays a crucial role, since the project reference implementations, the TCX Separation Kernel and Trusted Path Extension application, are targeted for the CC Evaluation Assurance Levels 7 and 6 (EAL7 and EAL6), respectively [8, 9].

The security requirements (both functional and assurance) for the TCX kernel will be based on the Separation Kernels Protection Profile (SKPP) [10]. Although the TCX team has considerable previous experience in high assurance development, our participation in the authoring of the SKPP provides a different perspective on the process to produce secure software and systems. Specifically, we have found that with its iterative requirements derivation process and structured requirements specification methodology, the CC can also be used to effectively capture requirements for software and systems that are not intended to undergo formal evaluation.

Table 1. CC Coverage in IA Courses.

Course	Common Criteria Coverage
CS3600 Introduction to Information Assurance: Computer Security	This class offers an introductory overview of the CC taxonomy, basic concepts in requirements specification and security evaluation, Evaluation Assurance Levels, and evaluation methodology for government-certified evaluation labs.
CS3670 Information Assurance: Secure Management of Systems	This class teaches secure system administration and management and discusses requirements covered in CS3600 in the context of DoD policies and national standards (e.g., NIST publications).
CS4600 Secure Systems	This class addresses the principles and techniques of high assurance secure system development. It includes a CC-based laboratory project that introduces the students to the CC methodology and assurance requirements. The students learn how to apply in the CC framework in projects such as requirements formulations and security extensions to an existing operating system.
CS4614 Advanced Topics in Computer Security	This class discusses academic papers on advanced topics in computer security, including the CC interpretation process and the notion of high assurance composite evaluation. The students gain exposure to how the CC standard process is driven at the national level and the needs to improve the CC methodology to support high assurance composite evaluations.
CS4680 Introduction to Certification and Accreditation	This class provides an introduction to the Certification and Accreditation (C&A) process as applied to government systems. The CC fundamentals covered in CS3600 are iterated in the context of C&A, with emphasis on hierarchical Evaluation Assurance Level differences.

Monterey Security Architecture (MYSEA) Project. The MYSEA project establishes an overarching framework that facilitates research and experimentation with ergonomic, i.e., user-centric, multilevel security (MLS). MYSEA is a client-server distributed network environment that comprises a federation of high assurance MLS servers and a number of local and remote networks of both security-enhanced and unmodified commercial off-the-shelf clients [11, 12]. The MYSEA server enforces the overall system security policy and its trusted operating base recently completed a CC EAL5 evaluation [13]. The security-enhanced client system consists of a specialized security appliance (named Trusted Path Extension) and commodity PCs executing popular commercial software. The Trusted Path Extension provides user authentication and access control support mechanisms, and the TCX Kernel will be used as its trusted operating base.

Although the provenance of MYSEA can be traced back to the TCSEC, recent and current research activities are based on the CC framework. The CC paradigm of defining secure systems in terms of the desired assurance level and security capability, and against a well-defined threat analysis has been successfully adopted for use in a number of MYSEA-related student projects.

Multilevel Print Server (MPS) Project. The MPS project is part of a network-centric information assurance solution that provides secure sharing of network resources across different security domains. The goal of the MPS project is the design and development of a trusted print server that can securely separate print jobs originating from networks operating at different security levels. Since the MLS print server is targeted for a CC evaluation at EAL4-plus, i.e., EAL4 with augmentation, the initial project goal is to develop a CC protection profile (PP) sketch that defines the necessary set of security requirements at that level for the MLS print server. The PP sketch was originally developed using Version 2.2 of the CC and is now being transitioned to Version 3.0 of the CC [14]. To achieve Version 3.0, the CC underwent a major overhaul and a significant amount of effort is required to fully understand the ramifications of the changes. The lack of requirements regarding hardware assurance, trusted initialization, and the application of the principle of least privilege to both internal functions and external subjects (e.g., programs) is a notable omission.

3   Theses as Case Studies in Common Criteria Application

A number of advanced student research projects have emanated from the above research efforts. Completing a thesis that demonstrates the students mastery in both core and specialized subjects acquired through course work is a curriculum requirement for all students. Three theses are described here to illustrate the effectiveness of applying the CC framework to student research. The CC affords students a systematic means to organize and conduct information security research with different levels of difficulty. It also provides the thesis advisors with quantitative metrics to assess the research result. Qualitative assessment of the students ability to perform independent, graduate level research is subjective. However, the students technical strength can be partially determined based on the students ability to navigate and articulate the large selection of security requirements defined by the CC.

In the sections that follow three theses are examined. These theses were selected based on the extent of their CC utilization, the difficulty level of the research project, and the students research ability. Table 2 summarizes the project characteristics. In all cases, the students were expected to apply analytical reasoning skills and graduate level research techniques to their work.

Table 2. Project Characteristics.

Project	CC Utilization	Difficulty Level	Student Ability
TCX Dissemination System	Informally defined requirements; low robustness	Low	Above average
MYSEA Single Sign-On Framework	Informally defined requirements; medium robustness	Medium	Excellent
MLS Print Server Protection Profile Sketch	Formally defined requirements; medium robustness	High	Above average

3.1 TCX Dissemination System

Open dissemination of project material is one of the core objectives of the TCX project. For TCX, open dissemination does not mean unrestricted dissemination. TCX materials have access control markings that are used as the basis for distribution by the dissemination system [15].

The design of the TCX dissemination system is a worked example of the application of the CC methodology to derive and express security requirements for an informally specified system. The research activities for this effort can be logically separated into three stages: system requirements elicitation, security requirements derivation, and proof-of-concept prototype implementation. The CC plays an important role in the second stage.

Based on the threat properties of the TCX dissemination system, e.g., a web interface that is to be available online to the general public, a threat analysis of the trusted delivery mechanisms required for the TCX kernel was completed first. The result of this analysis helped narrow down the list of high level system requirements for the dissemination system. In contrast with the next stage where the use of the CC is prominent, the requirements elicitation process was conducted informally.

In the second stage, a CC-based requirements derivation process was used to translate, through structured analysis, the high level system requirements into a set of informal security requirements for both the dissemination system and its environment.

The CC requirements expression rules were loosely followed to help organize and represent these security requirements. A number of improperly specified objectives and requirements were discovered and redefined as the result of iteratively applying the CC traceability methodology. The last stage involved the construction of an initial implementation that satisfies a subset of the system requirements.

In the U.S. evaluation scheme, the robustness level of a system is determined by the value of the resources that the system needs to protect and the authorization of external entities that can access the resources [16]. A basic level of robustness was selected for the dissemination system because the project materials that can be disseminated online are low-value data, reducing the likelihood of attacks by external entities (i.e., Internet users). High-value project materials are handled separately, on a case-by-case basis.

Although the CC requirements derivation process was used, the difficulty level of this thesis is rated low because the requirements need not be stated with CC constructs. Furthermore, the design of the dissemination system was from a clean slate, with no backward compatibility burdens. However, due to the students steep learning curve on both the CC and the web technology required to implement the initial prototype, the thesis took longer than expected to complete.

3.2   MYSEA Single Sign-On Framework

To address scalability, the MYSEA design allows the use of more than one MYSEA server in a local operating environment. Support for such a federation of servers is not available in the current MYSEA implementation. To avoid requiring the user to separately authenticate to different servers, a secure single sign-on user authentication mechanism is needed. Hence, the primary objective of this student research project is to define an architectural framework and high level design for a single sign-on (SSO) solution for MYSEA [17].

Central to the SSO design is the MYSEA Authentication Server. One of the MYSEA servers in the federation will assume this role and be responsible for user authentication and session negotiation. The other SSO component is the MYSEA Application Management Server. This component provides application services to authenticated users and can colocate with the authentication server on the same platform. Although the SSO design allows the Authentication Server functionality to be distributed among multiple servers, the thesis focused primarily on the single Authentication Server configuration. The security, usability, and to a lesser extent, performance and reliability requirements of the Authentication Server were within the scope of this thesis.

Similar to the TCX dissemination system project, the decision to use the CC as a guiding tool for security analysis was made early in the thesis process. The CC methodology for defining security requirements based on threats, security assumptions, organizational security policies, and security objectives in the context of a protection profile was applied to develop security requirements for the Authentication Server component. Security analysis of the Application Management Server component and the distributed Authentication Server configuration were identified as future work.

Ideally the robustness level of the Authentication Server should be high since the MYSEA network is an MLS environment. However, medium robustness was chosen for this thesis for three reasons: 1) guidance for high robustness PP development is currently not available, 2) other than the emerging SKPP there were no existing high assurance protection profiles that the student could examine for reference, and 3) the work had to be at an attainable level so that the student could complete within the time allotted for thesis work.

The difficulty level of this thesis was expected to be medium because the SSO design was required to fit into the existing MYSEA architecture. Furthermore, security analysis of a distributed architecture is complex, especially when the use of structured security evaluation criteria is imposed on the analysis. The learning curve on the CC methodology was not as steep as in the case of the TCX dissemination system thesis (discussed earlier) since the dissemination system thesis was available for use as example. Not using the CC constructs and wording to express the security requirements also simplified the work.

3.3 MLS Print Server Protection Profile Sketch

A multilevel print server (MPS) enforces a mandatory access control policy regarding input received from multiple networks at different sensitivity levels, and provides trusted separation pages indicating the sensitivity level of print jobs sent to either a dedicated or networked system high printer. The MPS also enforces supporting policies to include: detection of malicious print jobs, audit generation, audit logging and alarms, a trusted path for administrators, security and audit administrator tools, and operator services. The thesis goal was to develop a necessary set of security requirements, in the context of an EAL4 (with augmentation) protection profile sketch, for an MPS supporting Hewlett Packard Print Command Language (PCL) [18].

In the case of this thesis, the difference between a PP sketch and a complete PP was the omission of the rationale sections. In the CC paradigm, a PP must provide rationale that explains how the security requirements satisfy the stated security objectives, and how the objectives mitigate the threats and implement the organizational policies. Writing a comprehensive rationale is difficult and it was determined a priori that it would be an unachievable goal for the student.

Multiple factors distinguished this student project from the last two. It was our first experiment involving students in structured CC work in the form of a protection profile sketch. The PP sketch was developed to address a real-world security need and had to satisfy specific system requirements established by the intended users. Last, the PP sketch required structured expression of security requirements that conform to the Consistency Instruction Manual for PP development [19]. The thesis difficulty level was high due to these factors.

This thesis is highly technical because it requires a good understanding of the CC, multilevel security, component composition, and PCL printer technology. These prerequisites together with the students steep learning curve necessitated extensive faculty involvement in order to complete the project on time.

4 Discussion

For the theses examined, the CC security analysis methodology was an effective tool for analyzing and deriving security requirements. However, the suitability of the CC for non-instructional education does not stop there. When used as an organizational framework in student research projects, the CC provides a structure for keeping the project goal in focus and making decisions, both technical and logistic. It also affords the thesis advisors a means to encourage students to employ self-governance of their work. Each student met weekly with the faculty advisors. A weekly goal emerged from each meeting. For example, students might be required to produce a certain section of their requirements document in the CC format, e.g., threats, assumptions, etc., prior to the next meeting at which a review of the work would be conducted. These reviews provided the student with feedback which either resulted in another iteration of the section or transition to a new section or phase of the effort.

4.1   Student Readiness

It became apparent that the CC-based approach was challenging and expensive for the faculty advisors since the CC learning curve was steep for the students. The CC coverage in the six core and specialized courses described earlier was not enough to prepare the students for CC-based research work. It has also become evident that classroom instruction on the CC must be reinforced by hands-on experience in order for the information learned from these classes to sink in.

4.2   Commonalities of Theses

The CC defines a system that undergoes evaluation as a Target of Evaluation (TOE) and a set of hardware and software mechanisms of the TOE that enforces the security policy as the TOE Security Functions (TSF) [3]. Although each thesis addressed a different TOE, all required the students to go beyond what they had learned of the CC in their classes.

First, each student had to define the system sufficiently to allow the identification of the TOE and its boundary. The use of the CC paradigm affords the student a systematic way to identify security critical functionality, resulting in a more precise system definition. As it was, each student had to identify elements of the system that were beyond the control of the TOE. They then had to determine the boundary of the TSF. As each system was in its conceptual stage, this process tended to be difficult and required considerable design discussion with the faculty advisors. What added to the challenge was the initial lack of intuition on the part of the students regarding the distinctions among TOE, TSF, and the external components with which the TOE would interoperate.

Creation of the requirements creation was iterative and, for the students, this generally presented a challenge. Some were used to a very linear approach to problem solving that did not require adjustments. The thought of revisiting a stage that had already been addressed (often with the belief that the previous work at that stage was complete) seemed to be viewed as failure rather than an opportunity for improvement. Thus, the students needed to develop a new perspective to problem solving.

The CC-based process used by the students to derive security requirements is depicted in Figure 1. The process consisted of three iterative phases. In Phase I, the system description was prepared, starting with the general description of the thesis topic and followed by a series of refinements. The resulting system description covered different

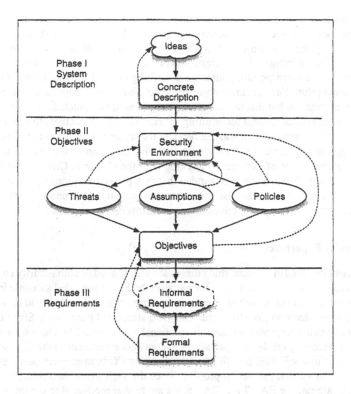

Fig. 1. Feedback cycles in requirements process.

aspects of the target system, including its concept of operation, conceptual architecture and system access policy. Phase II involved the establishment of the security objectives. This was started with the definition of the systems security environment stated in terms of anticipated threats, environmental assumptions, and organizational security policies. The appropriate PP authoring manual [16, 19] was consulted to create the initial set of threats, assumptions, and organizational policies, which were then solidified through an iterative pruning and feedback process. A careful analysis of the security environment resulted in a set of security objectives that satisfied the intended functional goals and purpose of the target system. The articulation of the security requirements took place in Phase III. Depending on the nature of the thesis, the security requirements were specified either informally using an ad hoc format or formally using CC constructs and wording. The development of the requirements was also iterative and often caused subsequent reassessments of the security objectives.

The CC paradigm for requirements derivation is iterative by nature and requires the results of a given activity be traceable to the derived elements of the previous activity. The traceability is demonstrated by the evidential material defined as rationale description. In two theses, the rationale that mapped the threats, assumptions, and organizational policies to security objectives was produced. Each threat and organizational policy was mapped to an objective that addressed it and a rationale was provided for why that objective mitigated the threat. Assumptions were mapped to environmental objectives, with a corresponding rationale describing how the environmental objective met the assumption. Each security objective should have been mapped to one or more security requirements but this last set of mappings was not conducted.

There were several reasons for omitting the rational in the objectives-to-requirements mapping. Primary among them was the fact that the students simply ran out of time due to the steep learning curve they had experienced with the Common Criteria. In addition, we felt that their level of experience working with the Common Criteria was insufficient for that task. Thus, had we demanded that they prepare a rationale, it would have amounted to a mechanical exercise for them and would not have contained the subtle observations that make the objectives-to-requirements rationale useful.

4.3 Faculty Experience

The advisors involved in the case study theses are well trained in both security engineering and security evaluation criteria. Our work on the SKPP provided valuable insights into how the CC works, which triggered the realization that the CC could be adapted for use in areas that traditionally do not require a structured framework. Since the CC is constantly being improved at both international and national levels, we have been concentrating mostly on the interpretations and guidance pertinent to the U.S. scheme. Our approach to keep abreast with the ever-changing CC is to actively participate the development of various protection profiles. Since the TCX kernel and reference applications are targeted for EAL 7 and EAL 6, we are further motivated to continue to stay on top of the latest CC developments.

5 Conclusion

The goal of this paper is to demonstrate that the use of the Common Criteria as a research framework for graduate students is beneficial as it imposes disciplines required for secure systems and software development on the research work. For thesis advisors, these disciplines help establish a trackable process to monitor student performance and progress.

To better prepare the students for CC-based research, we are currently developing a full-quarter course on the application of the Common Criteria for security analysis and engineering of secure systems and software. In addition to its primary objective, we intend for this course to provide an in-depth understanding of how security evaluation criteria can be adapted for use in non-evaluation activities, including academic research. Included in the course work is the examination of existing Protection Profiles and Security Targets which gives students both insight on domain-specific requirements expression and familiarity with the complicated CC-prescribed constructs and rules. It is anticipated that this hands-on approach will smooth out the students learning curve prior to thesis work, making it less demanding for both the student and thesis advisors.

We are continuing our experiment in this area with an in-progress thesis on the development of a high robustness PP sketch for a trusted platform. Since guidance for authors of high robustness protection profiles does not exist and the security issues associated with a high assurance platform that the PP sketch must address are highly complex, it remains to be seen if our approach will be as effective as in the past.

Related future work is to determine if requirements derivation would be easier if one could assume that it is possible to determine when a class of failures could be detected.

Acknowledgements

This work was sponsored in part by the Office of Naval Research, National Reconnaissance Office, and SPAWAR PMW-160. Any opinions, findings, and conclusions or recommendations expressed in this material are those of the authors and do not necessarily reflect the views of the sponsoring organizations.

References

1. Benzel, T. V., Irvine C. E., Levin, T. E., Bhaskara, G., Nguyen, T. D., Clark, P. C., Design Principles for Security, NPS Technical Report NPS-CS-05-010, September 2004.
2. Bishop, M., Frincke, D., Joining the Security Education Community, IEEE Security and Privacy Magazine, V. 2, No. 5, 2004, pp. 61 63.
3. Common Criteria for Information Technology Security Evaluation, Version 2.2, CCIMB-2004-01-[001, 002, 003], Common Criteria Project Sponsoring Organizations, January 2004.
4. Department of Defense Trusted Computer System Evaluation Criteria, DoD 5200.28-STD, National Computer Security Center, December 1985.
5. Canadian Trusted Computer Product Evaluation Criteria, Communications Security Establishment, Government of Canada, Canadian System Security Centre, Ottawa, Canada, January 1993.
6. Information Technology Security Evaluation Criteria, Office for Official Publications of the European Communities, Commission of the European Communities, Luxembourg, 1991.
7. Irvine, C., A Common Criteria-based Project for High Assurance Secure Systems, Proceedings of the IFIP TC 11 WG 11.8, 4th World Conference on Information Security Education, Moscow, Russia, May 2005, pp. 82-93.
8. Irvine, C. E., Levin, T. E., Nguyen, T. D., and Dinolt, G. W., The Trusted Computing Exemplar Project, Proc. IEEE Systems Man and Cybernetics Information Assurance Workshop, West Point, NY, June 2004, pp. 109-115.
9. Nguyen, T. D., Levin, T. E., and Irvine, C. E., TCX Project: High Assurance for Secure Embedded Systems, Proc. 11th IEEE Real-Time and Embedded Technology and Applications Symposium, Work in Progress Session, San Francisco, CA, March 2005, pp. 21-25. (Also appeared in SIGBED Review, Vol. 2, No. 2, April 2005, Special Issue on IEEE RTAS 2005 Work-in-Progress.)
10. U.S. Government Protection Profile for Separation Kernels in Environments Requiring High Robustness, Version 0.621, National Security Agency, 1 July 2004.
11. Irvine, C. E., Levin, T. E., Nguyen, T, D., Shifflett, D., Khosalim, J., Clark, P. C., Wong, A., Afinidad, F., Bibighaus, D., and Sears, J., Overview of a High Assurance Architecture for Distributed Multilevel Security, Proc. IEEE Systems Man and Cybernetics Information Assurance Workshop, West Point, NY, June 2004, pp. 38-45.

12. Nguyen, T. D., Levin, T. E., and Irvine, C. E., MYSEA Testbed, Proc. 6th IEEE Systems, Man and Cybernetics Information Assurance Workshop, West Point, NY, June 2005, pp. 438-439.

13. Common Criteria Evaluation and Validation Scheme Validation Report for BAE System Information Technology LLC XTS-400/STOP 6.1.E, Report Number: CCEVS-VR-05-0094, National Institute of Standards and Technology and National Security Agency, 1 March 2005.

14. Common Criteria for Information Technology Security Evaluation, Version 2.0 Revision 2, CCIMB-2005-07-[001, 002, 003], Common Criteria Project Sponsoring Organizations, June 2005.

15. Kane, D. R., Web-based dissemination system for the Trusted Computing Exemplar Project, Masters Thesis, Naval Postgraduate School, Monterey, CA, June 2005.

16. Consistency Instruction Manual For Development of US Government Protection Profiles For Use in Basic Robustness Environments, Release 3.0, National Security Agency, 1 February 2005.

17. Bui, S., Single Sign-on Solution for MYSEA Services, Masters Thesis, Naval Postgraduate School, Monterey, CA, September 2005.

18. Lysinger III, J. E., Multilevel Print Server Requirements for DoN Application, Masters Thesis, Naval Postgraduate School, Monterey, CA, June 2005.

19. Consistency Instruction Manual For Development of US Government Protection Profiles For Use in Medium Robustness Environments, Release 3.0, National Security Agency, 1 February 2005.

On the Relationship of Privacy and Secure Remote Logging in Dynamic Systems

Rafael Accorsi

Department of Telematics
Albert-Ludwigs-Universität Freiburg, Germany
accorsi@iig.uni-freiburg.de

Abstract. We investigate a mechanism for secure remote logging to improve privacy guarantees in dynamic systems. Using an extended threat model for privacy, we first describe outer and inner privacy: outer privacy denotes the traditional attacker model for privacy where identity management systems control the collection of personal, observable information; inner privacy denotes the threat posed by an attacker who attempts to get hold of private log data by tampering with a device. While privacy-enhancing technologies should take outer and inner privacy into account, there is, to our knowledge, no approach for inner privacy, in particular for dynamic systems. To this end, we develop protocols to address inner privacy based on secure logging. Our approach accounts for the capacity limitations of resource-poor devices in dynamic systems, as it allows for the remote storage of log data, while fulfilling its security guarantees. Furthermore, our approach can be smoothly integrated into identity management systems to combine outer and inner privacy.

1 Introduction

"Logging" refers to a sort of prophylactic process of collecting and storing information about the events in the system. Provided that the collected data is authentic, it gives a sound basis upon which other functionalities can be deployed. Initially, log data was chiefly used by system administrators to investigate the behaviour of a system in case of malfunction. The advent of the Internet and e-commerce brought along the need for accountability and billing mechanisms, which are also deployed using logged data. Subsuming the previous functionalities, dynamic systems also use log data for self-management tasks in autonomous components [9] and, more recently, as "digital witnesses" in forensic disputes [12].

Log mechanisms can be seen as a privacy-endangering technology, as they greedily collect information and prepare it for a proceeding analysis. This becomes a threat when the logged data includes personal attributes. This situation is a result of the underlying attacker model under consideration. Traditionally, the attacker is taken to be the current communication partner or the devices capturing observable attributes of an individual. To minimise the chances of a violation of privacy, identity management and privacy aware systems have been devised [1, 2, 13]. These tools employ several techniques to diminish an individual's observability and give him control over the release of personal

Please use the following format when citing this chapter:

Author(s) [insert Last name, First-name initial(s)], 2006, in IFIP International Federation for Information Processing, Volume 201, Security and Privacy in Dynamic Environments, eds. Fischer-Hubner, S., Rannenberg, K., Yngstrom, L., Lindskog, S., (Boston: Springer), pp. [insert page numbers].

attributes, thus allowing the characterisation and, to some extent the enforcement, of his privacy policies.

However, it is questionable whether such an attacker model for privacy is realistic in dynamic systems. We consider dynamic systems, i.e. systems allowing for the omnipresent availability of computing power, communication and data, as mixed-mode infrastructures: they combine resource-rich and resource-poor components. (We consider this as a result of advances in distinct aspects of computing systems, namely autonomy [9], pervasiveness [15], and reachability [8] of devices.) The underlying computational ubiquity makes it impossible to fully control observability: data will inevitably be collected. Nevertheless, what the next privacy threat in dynamic systems will be remains to be defined.

In this paper, we distinguish between two concepts of privacy: *outer* and *inner* privacy. These are distinguished in terms of the underlying threat model: while outer privacy denotes the customary privacy threats as lack of observability and control over the release of data, inner privacy is defined by an attacker who attempts to obtain private information by tampering with private log data. These concepts are complementary and cannot be considered in isolation: getting hold of private log data indeed invalidates the effort that prevented its release.

Nevertheless, while there is a plethora of mechanisms addressing outer privacy, tools to address inner privacy are lacking. To this end, we present a secure logging approach to tackling inner privacy based on techniques for tamper-evident logging presented in [17]. Due to the underlying mixed-mode setting, capacity limitations should be taken into account. Our approach is tailored to dynamic systems, in particular for resource-poor devices: we equip our secure logging mechanism with features to allow for secure remote storage. This is achieved by an acknowledgement phase in which the data collector proves the possession of log data to the transmitting device. Moreover, selective access control mechanisms for each entry are built in, thereby facilitating the analysis without disclosing the whole logfile. We remark, though, that the applicability is not restricted to resource-poor devices. Resource-rich components could employ similar techniques to secure logging, while omitting the acknowledgement phase.

Overall, our work sheds a light on the relationship between security and privacy in dynamic systems on the one hand, and secure logging mechanisms on the other. Although we focus here on privacy, we see our contribution as a wider one. Dynamic systems are characterised by a high degree of autonomy, which can only take place when the components are able to adapt themselves to the needs of a particular context. This requires an analysis of logged data, which, if inaccurate, leads to an incorrect functioning: *ex falsum quod libet*, i.e., from a falsity everything follows. By providing the necessary authenticity guarantees, we ensure that log data provides a reliable basis for this, as well as similar processes.

We proceed as follows. In §2 we describe outer and inner privacy and describe the requirements the latter puts on secure logging mechanisms. We present our approach to secure remote logging in §3 and discuss its security properties and limitations in §4. In §5, we report on related work and conclude in §6.

Preliminaries. We refer to the components involved in logging services according to their role: the *device* generates a log message; the *relay* receives a log message and forwards it to another service; and the *collector* receives a message and, in one way or another, stores it. To simplify matters, we consider that a device and a collector communicate either without an intermediary relay, or that the relay does not misbehave. (We are currently investigating an approach where we leave out these assumptions; see §6 for details.) We employ the following notation:

- d_i denotes the ith device, r_i the ith relay and c_i the ith collector.
- $\{X\}_K$ denotes the symmetric encryption of message X under the key K. $Sign(X)_K$ stands for the signature of X with K.
- X, X' stands for the concatenation of the messages X and X'.
- K_s stands for the public key of the service s and K_s^{-1} the corresponding private key of s.
- $MAC_K(X)$ denotes the message authentication code of X under K.
- $Hash(X)$ is the one-way hash of X.

We assume that the cryptographic primitives above fulfil the expected properties in that, e.g., it is infeasible for an attacker to induce collisions of hash values. These primitives are described in, e.g., [16].

2 Outer and Inner Privacy

In order to make the discussion on the relationship between privacy and logging mechanisms clear, it is necessary to distinguish between two views of privacy: *outer* and *inner* privacy. Roughly speaking, these standpoints are circumscribed in terms of the underlying attacker model used to characterise an attacker's potential threat. We first illustrate the idea behind the attacker model defining outer privacy by means of an example.

Example 1 (Outer privacy). Suppose an individual goes shopping in the city centre. There are hundreds of other individuals there and everybody can see him entering a shop, choosing a product and paying for it. Now suppose the individual simply asks for the article and receives it packed in the store's carrier bag. Nobody appart from the seller knows what has been bought. However, if the individual leaves the shop, it is possible to infer he was in that shop by the carrier bag in his possession. In turn, if we assume that the carrier bag given by the seller has no name or logo, it can be inferred that something has been bought, however not knowing what. Finally, if the individual packs the carrier bag into his backpack before leaving the shop, it is impossible to infer whether anything has been bought at all.   ⊣

The scenario depicted above can be compared to a dynamic system. Pedestrians in our example are sensors capturing the context, i.e. an individual's actions, in various ways. Individuals are devices that communicate with other devices. Privacy protecting measures, such as bundling the product or packing it into a backpack, involve the communication over secure channels and the use of identity management systems.

In computing systems, privacy-enhancing technologies such as identity management and privacy aware systems attempt to deter an attacker impersonated by the communication partner itself, as it stores attributes of an individual and the surrounding context that can observe this communication. These are represented in our example by the seller and other individuals observing the transaction. To account for privacy, systems offer a knob to control the release of data, and minimise individuals observability. Overall, they control what can be observed, while avoiding the correlation of this information with the individual behind it. Technically, mechanisms like network anonymisers, pseudonyms and partial identities are employed to control individuals' observability and the disclosure of data. They thus protect what we refer to as outer privacy. We now look at Example 1 from a different perspective.

Example 2 (Inner privacy). Take the same situation as in Example 1. Irrespective of the level of privacy the individual aims at, the information "logged" by this individual does include the purchase of a particular product, as well as the preferences leading to this transaction. Assume that a preventive measure, e.g. packing the purchased good into a backpack, is carried out. This expresses the individual's unwillingness to share this information, namely the purchase of a particular product, with individuals other than the seller. Hence, if this action is somehow stored—and there is enough evidence to assume that it will be—, then it must be securely stored, for the release of this information entails loss of privacy.   ⊣

Note that we consider a different attacker in this example. Namely, an attacker who tries to obtain private information by tampering with the individual's device. This unveils a, to our knowledge novel, tight relationship between the preventive measures chosen to protect the individual's privacy during a transaction and the log data associated with this transaction: the preventive measures determine the degree of sensibility ascribed to log data. Inner privacy denotes the confidentiality of private log data.

Unless strong, albeit hypothetical, assumptions regarding tamper resistance are made (or, equivalently, we assume that the underlying attacker model disregards intrusion), outer and inner privacy cannot be considered in isolation: an unbalanced distribution between them harms the overall privacy level. This balance is essential in dynamic systems. Due to an extended attack vector, tamper resistance for resource-poor devices can hardly be achieved, and improvements on tamper resistance usually come at the cost of performance. Nevertheless, research into privacy mechanisms is tailored to address outer privacy. Below, we present an approach to protecting inner privacy based on secure remote logging.

2.1 Inner Privacy by Secure Remote Logging

Three issues arise from the discussion on inner privacy. First, since complete tamper resistance is infeasible, mechanisms should be in place to guarantee that the logged data cannot be tampered with. Second, the usual amount of data logged by a device is enormous. This already causes problems to resource-poor devices and, if additional data ensuring the security of log data is added, log data grows in size and the device is bound to run out of storage. Hence, a secure log service should also allow for the secure remote storage of data. Third, if log data is remotely stored, the logging mechanisms should ensure that a third-party service only gains access to those entries it has permission to. Together, these three characteristics build the setting within which we introduce our approach to protecting inner privacy.

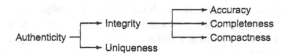

Fig. 1. Authenticity property for secure logging.

In our approach, log data is secured at logging the entry associated to an event and not as a separate process. Each log entry is (symmetrically) encrypted with a unique key. The techniques we employ guarantee forward integrity, i.e. if an attacker succeeds in breaking in at time t, all the log data stored before t cannot be compromised. (We introduce forward integrity in §3.) Forward integrity also helps assessing the circumstances that allowed for and led to an intrusion. Moreover, we ensure that attempts to tamper with logged data do not go undetected.

Further, our logging mechanism supports secure remote storage. By addressing this issue, we consider that the collector can misbehave or, similarly, that it is not tamper resistant enough. Thus, while in our protocol the collector possesses enough information to prove the (integral) possession of log data, it cannot derive the keys necessary to decrypt the log entry. Moreover, even if the collector (or an attacker) succeeds in decrypting one entry by guessing the right key, this does not reveal enough information to derive the keys used to encrypt the previous or next entries. This stems from the secrecy of a piece of information we refer to as A_0, which is not known by the collector.

Finally, we allow the selective disclosure of log data based on techniques introduced in [17]. The permission mask W works as an access control list and indexes the service (or group thereof) that can access an entry. The symmetric key used to encrypt the log entry can be recomputed and given to authorised services when needed. (Protocols to regulate the delegation and access from collector and third-party services are not in the scope of our work.) Note that this is also in line with a common understanding of privacy that postulates that an individual should have the chance to actively determine who learns information about him.

3   An Approach to Secure Remote Logging

Log data can only provide a sound basis for further services when it is authentic. We define authenticity as the simultaneous fulfilment of data *integrity* and *uniqueness*, as illustrated in Fig. 1. *Confidentiality* of log entries is necessary for privacy and is considered as an extra protection goal. A log service is labelled *secure* when integrity, uniqueness and confidentiality properties are fulfilled.

- Integrity states that log data faithfully reflects the state of the devices, i.e., the log data is accurate (entries have not been modified), complete (entries have not been deleted), and compact (entries have not been illegally added to the logfile). Thus, log data is not modified, deleted, or appended during the transmission to, and storage at, the collector.

- Uniqueness states that log data shall not allow for parallel realities. Concretely, it is impossible to intercept log data sent from d_1 to c_1 and to resend it (possibly in modified form and claiming a different device identity) to c_2. Log data must be uniquely tagged.
- Confidentiality states that log entries cannot be read by unauthorised individuals, for this would harm inner privacy. Note that confidentiality is also related to uniqueness, for log data transmitted in clear-text can be easily duplicated.

These properties are realised with cryptographic techniques, which need to ensure *tamper evidence*, i.e., attempts to illicitly manipulate log data must be detectable to a verifier [11], and *forward integrity*, i.e. log data contains sufficient information to confirm or rebuke allegations of log data modification before the moment of the compromise [5].

The goal of the attacker is to gain access to private log data and, thus, to violate its integrity, uniqueness, and confidentiality. The threats posed by an attacker are described using an attacker model. While we are aware of recent ongoing research on formally characterising attacker models for dynamic environments [6], we refrain from sticking to a particular model.

3.1 Overview of our Approach

Our approach to secure remote logging services in dynamic systems is based on and extends the techniques proposed in [17]. The idea is to devise a protocol to securely store log data. The protocol starts at the device: it is in charge of applying cryptographic techniques to ensure tamper evidence and forward integrity. When the device runs out of storage, it contacts the collector to request remote storage. The protocol ends with an irrefutable proof of possession of the collector. In detail:

1. *initialisation and construction of the logfile*: the device is in charge of applying cryptographic techniques to safeguarding the integrity and uniqueness of its logfile. To this end, it computes a secret random value pv_0 and, for each entry, a proof value Z associated with that entry based on pv_0. The Z-values build a chain, so that the integrity of the whole chain can be checked by analysing its last link.
2. *mutual authentication of services*: apart from authentication, the device and the collector also agree on a secret value pv_0 that will be used to ascertain authenticity of log messages.
3. *acknowledgement of receipt from collector*: by receiving the chunk of log data, the collector computes the Z-value associated with each entry and sends the last Z-value signed together with a timestamp and protocol sequence number back to the device. The device then stores this unambiguous piece of information, as it demonstrates that the collector received the chunk of log data correctly and can be thus held accountable for attacks upon this data.

We describe the initialisation, appending, and acknowledgement processes below; the authentication phase and the secure exchange of pv_0 are taken for granted.

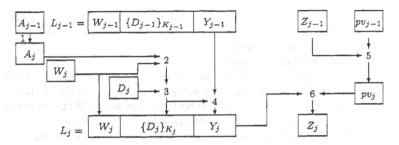

Fig. 2. Adding an entry to the logfile.

3.2   Initializing the Logfile

Assuming that the device d successfully generates a secret value pv_0, d creates the log file by inserting the first entry into it. Entries have the following fields and are initialised as:

- W_0 is a permission mask to regulate the access to the log entry L_0. As in [17], the initialisation value is **LogfileInitializationType**.
- $\{D_0\}_{K_0}$ is the symmetrically encrypted log data for the entry L_0 and K_0 is a random session key. To provide the necessary security guarantees, D contains not only the event to be logged, but also a timestamp and a protocol identifier. (The former states the recentness of the entry, the latter avoids harmful protocol interactions.)
- Y_0 is the first link of a hash chain.(In the simplest form, a hash-chain Y can be inductively defined as $Y_1 = Hash(Y_0)$ and $Y_n = Hash(Y_{n-1})$.)
- A_0 is the authentication key for the first entry. As we discuss in §4, this is the secret upon which the security of the whole protocol rests. In practice, since we do not assume that the device is tamper resistant, we suggest that this secret should be kept off-line.
- $L_0 = W_0, \{D_0\}_{K_0}, Y_0$ stands for the initial log entry.
- Z_0 is the message authentication code of L_0 defined as $MAC_{pv_0}(L_0)$. This piece of information is used to compute the proof value associated with the whole chunk of log entries and can thence be used as a challenge against the collector. For this, it will *not* be send along with L_0 to the collector.

3.3   Appending Log Entries

After creating the logfile, the device starts adding entries to the logfile. This is schematically illustrated in Fig. 2, where the numbers mean:

1. $A_j = Hash(A_{j-1})$ denotes the authentication key of the jth log entry. The confidentiality of this information is essential, as it is used to encrypt log entries. Thus, we assume that the computation of the new value irretrievably overwrites the previous value.

2. $K_j = Hash(W_j, A_j)$ is the cryptographic key with which the jth log entry is encrypted. This key is based on the permission mask W_j, so that only authorised services gain access to the entry.
3. $\{D_j\}_{K_j}$ is the encrypted log entry.
4. $Y_j = Hash(Y_{j-1}, \{D_j\}_{K_j}, W_j)$ is the jth value of the hash chain. Each link of the hash chain is based on the corresponding encrypted value of the log data. This ensures that the chain can be verified without the knowledge of the actual log entry.
5. $pv_j = Hash(Z_{j-1}, pv_{j-1})$ is the proof value associated with entry j.
6. $Z_j = MAC_{pv_j}(Hash(L_j))$ is the authenticator of the jth log entry. We compute the message authentication code for the whole entry instead of a field of it (in the case of [17], the hash-chain value Y).

The log entry L_j generated by the device consists of the permission mask W_j, the encrypted log entry $\{D_j\}_{K_j}$, and the hash-chain value Y_j; it is denoted by $L_j = W_j, \{D_j\}_{K_j}, Y_j$.

3.4 Acknowledgement Phase

The last phase of the protocol aims to provide irrefutable evidence regarding a collector's possession of the chunk of log data sent by the device, as well as the chunk's integrity. For this, the following steps are taken:

- by receiving the chunk L_j–L_k (with $j < k$), the collector computes for each entry L_i the corresponding pv_i and, thus, Z_i values.
- after $k - j$ iterations, the collector obtains $Z_k = MAC_{pv_k}(Hash(L_k))$.
- the signed proof value is sent to the device $Sign(Z_k)_{K_c^{-1}}$. This message includes a timestamp and protocol step identifier.
- the device then checks whether the authenticator Z_k matches with the authenticator computed during the second phase. If it does, the device frees the storage by deleting the chunk.

4   Security Properties and Limitations of our Protocol

Our logging protocol ensures inner privacy by guaranteeing the authenticity of log data, and by fulfilling tamper evidence and forward integrity. We describe the properties achieved and its underlying limitations.

Security Properties. The integrity of log messages is by the message authentication code Z and the hash chain Y. The message authentication code ensures that accuracy, completeness and compactness have not been violated during transmission. Similarly, the hash chain provides long-lasting security guarantees regarding the stored data.

The message authentication code is essential in the acknowledgement phase to ensure the receipt of log data. We use a one-way function to hash the proof value pv and the message authentication code Z of the previous log entry, thereby building a chain of log values. Since the value of the last link depends on the previous values, it suffices to verify the last link of the chain to ensure the integrity of the whole chunk. The hash-chain Y plays a similar role. However, unlike Z, Y is part of the log entry.

We ensure uniqueness by means of timestamps, as well as sequence numbers, and the confidentiality of log data. This combination makes it impossible for an attacker to reuse chunks of log data. Timestamps are used in protocols to prevent replay attacks and their implementation is straightforward. This contrasts with the subtleness associated with the mechanism to ensure confidentiality. The contents of the jth log entry is encrypted using an entry authentication key derived from A and the permission mask, as in [17]. This key is derived using an one-way function and the secrecy of the entry depends on the knowledge of the attacker about A, for if the attacker knows A_{j-1}, he can obtain K_j and, thus, D_j.

Finally, tamper evidence is given by the message authentication code and the hash-chain values: while the former provides tamper evidence in the acknowledgement phase, the latter ensures this property for the time that log data is kept on the collector. Note that the timestamps also play an accessory role, as they help detecting illegal entries. Forward integrity is provided by the secrecy of A. Since the previous values of A are deleted right after their use, an attacker who succeeds in breaking in can only access the current (and the subsequent) entries. We discuss this issue below.

Limits of the Logging Protocol. The logging protocol we present has several limitations, thereby confining the class of its potential applications.

- Timepoint of a successful attack: the integrity of the logfile can only be ensured up to the point in time at which the attacker takes over the collector (or device). Once an attacker succeeds in compromising a machine, he can misuse log information at will.
- Deletion of log entries: tamper evidence allows us to detect the deletion of log data. However, it is always possible for an attacker to completely (and irretrievably) delete the log file or entries thereof, in particular when we assume that no write-only hardware or media is at hand.
- Collector's behaviour: unless it is compromised, the collector is assumed to follow the protocol. However, the device does not acquire any evidence about the correct behaviour of the collector.
- Computational cost: the computational cost associated with running the logging protocol we propose is relatively high and could be an overkill for resource-poor devices. Two alternatives arise: either simplify our approach, or delegate some of the tasks to a (trusted) relay.
- Denial of service (DoS): although we consider the potential for a DoS attack upon the protocol, there is too little we can do in our protocol to prevent a DoS from happening. According to [10], DoS attacks have an inherent practical characteristic, so that outsmarting these attacks requires preventive measures during the implementation.

5 Related Work

Our work lies in the intersection of two research fields: privacy mechanisms and secure logging. While this intersection is not void, it has mainly focussed on outer privacy or ignored the challenges of dynamic systems.

Research into outer privacy includes the development of anonymising proxies such as JAP, identity management systems to control the disclosure of personal data, and privacy aware systems. Here we focus on a few of them closer to our work; see [14] for further approaches. JAP is a sophisticated mechanism to anonymise an individual [3]. Perfect anonymity is usually useless for practical purposes, for electronic transactions cannot be carried out without an adequate level of accountability. For this, identity management systems use anonymising services to implement partial identities and pseudonyms. Examples of such systems are iManager [2] and idemix [1], where the overall goal is to control the release of data and, at the same time, avoid the inference of further personal data; in particular, to deduce the real identity of the individual behind a pseudonym. pawS is a privacy aware system for dynamic systems [13]. In line with our work, Langheinrich assumes that the collection of data will occur anyway, so that perfect protection of personal information will be hardly achievable. To counteract the problem, his system ensures that privacy policies are known to, and to some extent enforced by, individuals.

Regarding privacy and secure logging, Flegel introduces an approach to tackle privacy in unix log files [7]. He extends outer privacy techniques for pseudonymisation of log data generated by the syslog. This addresses only the data collected from an individual, i.e., outer privacy.

Research on secure logging mechanisms is mostly of a practical nature, somehow based on extensions of syslog, and not tailored to dynamic systems. An exception is Schneier und Kelsey [17], who describe an approach to secure log data in marginally trusted collectors. While the approach we propose employs and extends their techniques, we act upon a different assumptions and problem, i.e. provide log services in dynamic systems.

6 Conclusion and Ongoing Work

We distinguish between outer and inner privacy, and present a mechanism to address inner privacy in dynamic systems. Our characterisation of inner privacy is based on an extended threat model where the attacker attempts to access private log data, instead of collecting data about an individual's behaviour. To cope with inner privacy problems, we propose a secure logging mechanism that allows for tamper-evident remote storage of data, being thus in line with dynamic systems and their resource poor-devices.

This work is part of an effort to bring basic security mechanisms into dynamic systems, and several interesting issues remain open. First, although we characterise outer and inner privacy, we do so by means of examples. Defining these terms is essential to clarify our contribution.

Second, to-date outer privacy prevails and there is no mechanism that combines outer and inner privacy. We are adapting the iManager, an identity manager system for outer privacy [2], with our techniques. This provides practical insights into the complexity involved in dealing with inner privacy by testing it in a relatively resource-poor device. Third, secure logging is a demanding process and only selected events should be securely logged. To describe these events, we investigate policy languages and its interplay with our secure logging. Fourth, the collector may misbehave. To make assertions regarding collector's behaviour, we envisage the use of trusted computing and remote attestation techniques. Our goal is not only to assert collectors' behaviour, but, chiefly, to delegate part of the logging protocol to the collector, thereby saving the computing power needed to carry out the protocol. Theoretical comparisons exhibit an extraordinary alleviation of devices' load [4] and current practical work investigates the issue further.

Finally, while our protocol allows for a selective disclosure of log data, we have neither investigated how this could be practically performed, nor the overheads thereby involved. We plan to develop further protocols to address this issue.

References

1. idemix. http://www.zurich.ibm.com/security/idemix/,2005.
2. iManager. http://www.iig.uni-freiburg.de/telematik/atus/idm.html, 2005.
3. JAP anonymity and privacy. http://anon.inf.tu-dresden.de/,2005.
4. R. Accorsi and A. Hohl. Delegating secure logging in pervasive computing systems. To appear in the *3rd Conf. Security in Pervasive Computing*, 2006.
5. M. Bellare and B. Yee. Forward integrity for secure audit logs. Tech. report, Univ. of California at San Diego, Dept. of Computer Science & Engineering, 1997.
6. S. Creese, M. Goldsmith, R. Harrison, B. Roscoe, P. Whittaker, and I. Zakiuddin. Exploiting empirical engagement in authentication protocol design. In *2nd Conf. Security in Pervasive Computing*, vol. 3450 of *LNCS*, pages 119–133, 2005.
7. U. Flegel. Pseudonymizing unix log files. In *Infrastructure Security Conference*, vol. 2437 of *LNCS*, pages 162–179, 2002.
8. G. Forman and J. Zahorjan. The challenges of mobile computing. *IEEE Computer*, 27(4):38–47, 1994.
9. W. Gibbs. Autonomic computing. *Scientific American*, 2002.
10. M. Graff and K. van Wyk. *Secure Coding: Principles & Practices*. O'Reilly, 2003.
11. G. Itkis. Cryptographic tamper evidence. In *Conf. on Computer and Communication Security*, pages 355–364, 2003.
12. E. Kenneally. Evidence enhancing technology. *;login*, 28(6):62–66, 2003.
13. M. Langheinrich. A privacy awareness system for ubiquitous computing environments. In *4th Conf. on UbiComp*, vol. 2498 of *LNCS*, pages 237–245, 2002.
14. G. Müller and S. Wohlgemuth. Study on mobile identity management. Deliverable for Fidis Project, Institute for Computer Science and Social Studies, 2005.
15. M. Satyanarayanan. Pervasive computing: Vision and challenges. *IEEE Personal Communications*, pages 10–17, 2001.
16. B. Schneier. *Applied Cryptography*. John Wiley and Sons, Inc, 1996.
17. B. Schneier and J. Kelsey. Security audit logs to support computer forensics. *ACM Transactions on Information and System Security*, 2(2):159–176, May 1999.

Privacy-Preserving Shared-Additive-Inverse Protocols and Their Applications

Huafei Zhu, Tieyan Li, and Feng Bao

Department of Information Security
Institute for Infocomm Research, A-Star, Singapore 119613
{huafei, litieyan, baofeng}@i2r.a-star.edu.sg

Abstract. Privacy-preserving clustering algorithms group similar databases populated at distributed locations to improve data qualities and enable accurate data analysis and thus provide fundamental security components for distributed data mining with privacy concerns. This paper makes three contributions regarding shared k-means clustering algorithms. First, a new notion called shared-additive-inverse (SAI) protocols – a building block for efficient implementation of shared k-means clustering protocols within the arbitrarily partitioned database model, is introduced and formalized. Second, a generic implementation of SAI protocols from shared-scalar-product (SSP) protocols is proposed which is provably secure in the semi-honest model assuming that any underlying SSP protocol is privacy-preserving. Finally, we propose an immediate application of SAI protocols for privacy-preserving computation of shared cluster means – a crucial step in the shared k-means clustering algorithms. To the best of our knowledge, this is the first implementation of shared k-means clustering algorithms with provable security from SAI protocols which in turn are derived from SSP protocols.

1 Introduction

Privacy-preserving clustering algorithms group similar databases populated at distributed locations to improve data qualities and enable accurate data analysis and thus provide fundamental security components for distributed data mining with privacy concerns. The solutions to privacy-preserving clustering algorithms have been presented with respect to horizontally, vertically and arbitrarily partition databases. For instance, Kantarcioglu and Clifton [12] describe algorithms for mining association rules in horizontally partitioned data and Vaidya and Clifton [16] develop analogous algorithms for vertically partitioned data. Jagannathan and Wright [11] provide the extensions for doing secure clustering protocols in arbitrarily partitioned data using well known k-means clustering algorithms.

k-means clustering algorithms have many applications, such as bio-medical and DNA data analysis, financial data analysis, targeted marketing, forensics (see [11, 12, 16] for further reference). Informally, a k-means clustering algorithm is an iterative algorithm that successively refines potential cluster in an attempt to minimize the k-means objective function. The main idea for k-means clustering algorithms is to define k cluster centers, one for each cluster. The k cluster centers should be placed in a cunning way because of different location causes different result. So, the better choice is

Please use the following format when citing this chapter:

Author(s) [insert Last name, First-name initial(s)], 2006, in IFIP International Federation for Information Processing, Volume 201, Security and Privacy in Dynamic Environments, eds. Fischer-Hubner, S., Rannenberg, K., Yngstrom, L., Lindskog, S., (Boston: Springer), pp. [insert page numbers].

to place them as much as possible far away from each other. There is some research on picking the initial cluster means [2]. The next step is to take each point belonging to a given data set and associate it to the nearest center. These two steps are alternated until a stopping criterion is met, i.e., when there is no further change in the assignment of the data points. In order to create a privacy-preserving version of k-means, we have to devise a privacy-preserving protocol to compute the cluster means (see Section 5 for more details). For instance, Alice has her input (x, a) and Bob has his input (y, b) when we consider a two-party k-means clustering algorithm. Both participants wish to jointly compute the cluster mean $\frac{x+y}{a+b}$, the output of the participants can be the following three cases, where $s_a + s_b = (a + b)^{-1}$ mod m and $s_a \in Z_m$ and $s_b \in Z_m$ are the random shares of Alice and Bob respectively:

Case 1: either Alice or Bob learns the cluster mean $\frac{x+y}{a+b}$ (this is a special situation of the case 3 when $s_a = 0$ or $s_b = 0$);

Case 2: Alice and Bob learn $\frac{x+y}{a+b}$ (this is a special situation of the case 3 when Alice and Bob learn s_a and s_b simultaneously);

Case 3: Alice learns s_a and Bob learns s_b such that $s_a + s_b = \frac{x+y}{a+b}$ (a general case in which we are interested in this paper).

In the next section, we will briefly sketch previous works for k-means clustering algorithms and at the same time we will state the problems regarding these implementations.

1.1 Previous works and problem statement

Jagannathan and Wright [11] first introduced the notion of arbitrarily partitioned data and then proposed a simple solution to shared two-party k-means clustering protocols (with respect to the Case 3). Their solution is to first approximate the function $\frac{x+y}{a+b}$ by a circuit C, and then use the heuristic implementations [1, 6, 7, 17] to construct a privacy-preserving protocol. Although, the architecture for privacy-preserving clustering protocols is attractive, their approach is heuristic. Consequently, a less heuristic approach would be a great step forward. The recent work of Jha, Kruger and McDaniel [10] can be viewed as such a forward step.

At ESORICS 2005, [10], Jha, Kruger and McDaniel presented two solutions to the Case 2 protocols (Alice and Bob learn $\frac{x+y}{a+b}$ simultaneously) – the first one is based on oblivious polynomial evaluation and the second one is based on homomorphic encryption. We would like to provide the following observation on their solutions: oblivious polynomial evaluation first introduced and formalized by Naor and Pinkas [13], is a protocol involving two parties, a sender whose input is a polynomial $f(x) \in F[x]$, and a receiver whose input is a value $a \in F$, where F is a finite field. At the end of the protocol the receiver learns $f(a)$ and the sender learns nothing. Two oblivious polynomial evaluation (OPE) protocols have been proposed by Naor and Pinkas [13] – the first construction is based on a conjecture that given a randomly chosen input to the noisy polynomial interpolation problem, the value of the polynomial P at $x = 0$ is pseudo-random; – the second construction is more efficient one based on a stronger assumption that the value of the polynomial at $x = 0$ is pseudo-random even given some additional hints about the location of the values of the polynomial. The security of the protocols is based on the assumptions that the noisy polynomial interpolation problem[1] was as hard as the polynomial reconstruction problem[2]. Unfortunately, Naor and Pinkas's construction were shown to be weaker than expected by Bleichenbacher and Nguyen [3]. More precisely, Bleichenbacher and Nguyen presented new methods to solve noisy polynomial interpolation problem which do not apply to the polynomial reconstruction problem. In particular they show that the noisy polynomial interpolation problem can be transformed into a lattice shortest vector problem with high probability, provided that the parameters satisfy a certain condition that is explicitly stated in [3]. The method is similar to the well-known lattice-based methods to solve the subset sum problem. They further show that most practical instances of the noisy polynomial interpolation problem with small m can be solved, thus the noisy polynomial interpolation problem is much easier than expected and should be used cautiously as an intractability assumption. It follows that the cryptographic protocols should be based on the polynomial reconstruction problem rather than the noisy polynomial interpolation problem (we refer the reader to [3] for further reference). Since Naor and Pinkas's construction is based on the hardness assumption of the noisy polynomial interpolation problem rather than the polynomial reconstruction problem, it follows that the k-means clustering algorithm protocol proposed by Jha, Kruger and McDaniel inherently suffers from this weakness. Thus any more satisfactory construction of k-means clustering protocols is certainly welcome.

The second approach is based on any semantically secure homomorphic encryption, and thus their second methodology avoids using oblivious polynomial evaluation protocols as building blocks. We stress that there is no secret sharing mechanism deployed within their constructions (both the OPE-based and non-OPE based constructions, i.e., the authors only consider the implementation of the Case 2 in their paper), it follows that their method cannot be extended for the construction of k-means clustering protocols with respect to the general case (the Case 3 where secure computation of shared k-means of clustering protocols is processed within the arbitrarily database model). Since no result is known regarding the construction of general k-means clustering protocols from semantically secure homomorphic encryptions (to the best of our knowledge), we thus provide an interesting research problem below.

Research problem: How to construct shared k-means clustering algorithms from semantically secure homomorphic encryptions in the arbitrarily partitioned database model?

---

[1] The noisy polynomial interpolation problem is the following thing: let P be a k-degree polynomial over a finite field F, given $n > k + 1$ sets $S_1, \cdots, S_n$ and n distinct elements $x_1, \cdots, x_n \in F$ such that each $S_i = \{y_{i,j}\}_{1 \leq j \leq m}$ contains $m - 1$ random elements and $P(x_i)$, recover the polynomial P, provided that the solution is unique.

[2] The polynomial reconstruction problem is the following thing: given as input integers k, t and n points $(x_1, y_1), \cdots, (x_n, y_n) \in F^2$, output all polynomials P of degree at most k such that $y_i = P(x_i)$ for at least t values of i.

1.2   This work

In this paper, a new notion called shared-additive-inverse protocol is introduced and formalized as a building block for k-means of clustering protocols. Informally, a shared-additive-inverse (SAI) protocol is the following thing – there are two participants Alice with her input $inp_A = a$ and Bob with his $inp_B = b$ who wish to compute $s_a + s_b$ $= (a + b)^{-1} \bmod m$, where $s_a \in Z_m$ and $s_b \in Z_m$ are the random shares of Alice and Bob respectively. The output of Alice is $s_a \in Z_m$ while the output of Bob is $s_b \in Z_m$. We then provide a generic construction of SAI protocols from shared-scalar-product (SSP) protocols. Our implementation of SAI protocols is provably secure in the semi-honest model assuming that the underlying SSP is privacy-preserving. Using any privacy-preserving SAI protocol a build block, we can simply compute a shared cluster mean $\mu_x + \mu_y = \frac{x+y}{a+b} = (x + y)(s_a + s_b)$ by means of any secure shared-scalar-product protocol so that Alice learns μ_x and Bob learns μ_y. As a result, a secure k-means clustering algorithm for distributed data mining is derived as an immediate application of our SAI protocol.

In summary, this paper makes three contributions regarding privacy-preserving clustering algorithms. First, a new notion called shared-additive-inverse (SAI) protocols is introduced and formalized. Second, a generic implementation of SAI protocols from shared-scalar-product (SSP) protocols is proposed which is provably secure in the semi-honest model assuming that the underlying SSP protocol is privacy-preserving. Finally, we transform any secure SAI protocol to privacy-preserving computation of shared cluster means protocol in the semi-honest model – a crucial step in the shared k-means clustering algorithms. To the best of our knowledge, this is the first implementation of shared k-means clustering algorithms with provable security from SAI protocols which in turn are derived from SSP protocols.

Road map   The rest of paper is organized as follows: In Section 2, syntax, functionality and security definition for shared-additive-inverse protocols are presented; And we briefly introduce the building block for SAI protocols in Section 3. Our implementation of SAI protocols and the proof of security are presented in Section 4. An application of SAI protocols to k-means clustering protocols is presented in Section 5. We conclude our works in Section 6.

2   Syntax, functionality and security definition

2.1   Syntax

A shared-additive-inverse protocol consists of the following two probabilistic polynomial time (PPT) Turing machines.

- On input a system parameter m (throughout the paper, we assume that Z_m is a finite field. Furthermore, we ignore the trivial case when $a = 0$ or $b = 0$ since the general technique presented in Section 4 can be tailored to solve the trivial case), a PPT Turing machine A (say, Alice), chooses $a \in_r Z_m$ uniformly at random. The initial input of Alice is denoted by $inp_A = a$;

- On input a system parameters m, a PPT Turing machine B (say, Bob), chooses $b \in Z_m$ uniformly at random. The initial input of Bob is denoted by $inp_B = b$;
- On inputs inp_A and inp_B, Alice and Bob jointly compute $s_a + s_b = (a+b)^{-1}$ mod m, where $s_a \in Z_m$ and $s_b \in Z_m$ are random shares of Alice and Bob respectively;
- The output of Alice is $s_a \in Z_m$ while the output of Bob is $s_b \in Z_m$.

2.2 Functionality

The functionality $\mathcal{F}_{SAI}$ of shared-additive-inverse protocols (SAI) can be abstracted as follows:

- A player (say Alice) has her initial input $inp_A = a \in Z_m$; Another player (say Bob) has his initial input $inp_B = b \in Z_m$; Each participant sends the corresponding input to TTP — an imaginary trusted third party in the ideal world via a secure and private channel.
- Upon receiving inp_A and inp_B, TTP tests whether $a \in Z_m$ and $b \in Z_m$.
  - if the conditions are satisfied, then TTP chooses $s_a \in Z_m$ uniformly at random and computes s_b from the equation $s_a + s_b = (a+b)^{-1}$ mod m.
  - if $a \notin Z_m$, then TTP chooses an element $a' \in_r Z_m$ and substitutes a with a'.

  Similarly, if $b \notin Z_m$, then TTP chooses an element $b' \in_r Z_m$ and substitutes b with b'. By $inp_A = a$ (using the same notation of the initial input of Alice), we denote the valid input of Alice which may be modified by TTP; By $inp_B = b$ (again using the same notation of the initial input of Bob), we denote the valid input Bob which may be modified by TTP. Once given valid inputs inp_A and inp_B, TTP chooses $s_a \in Z_m$ uniformly at random and computes s_b from the equation $s_a + s_b = (a+b)^{-1}$ mod m.
- The output of Alice is $s_a \in Z_m$ which is sent by TTP to Alice via the specified secure and private channel between them. The output of Bob is $s_b \in Z_m$ which is sent by TTP to Bob via the specified secure and private channel between them such that $s_a + s_b = (a+b)^{-1}$ mod m.

2.3 The definition of security

Privacy-preserving protocols are designed in order to preserve privacy even in the presence of the adversarial participants that attempt to gather information about the inputs of their inputs. There are however different levels of adversarial behavior — a semi-honest adversarial behavior and a malicious adversarial behavior (see [5] for more details). This paper however, concerns SAI protocols in the semi-honest model (the security definition of k-means clustering algorithms is inherently within the semi-honest model therefore).

Let $f: \{0,1\}^* \mapsto \{0,1\}^* \times \{0,1\}^*$ be probabilistic, polynomial time functionality, where $f_1(x,y)$ (respectively, $f_2(x,y)$) denotes the first (resp., second) element of $f(x,y)$; and let π be two-party protocol for computing f. Let the view of the first (resp., second) party during an execution of the protocol π on input (x,y), denoted $view_1^\pi(x,y)$ (resp., $view_2^\pi(x,y)$), be $(x, r_1, m_1, \cdots, m_t)$ (resp., $(y, r_2, m_1, \cdots, m_t)$).

r_1 represents the outcome of the first (resp., r_2) party's internal coin tosses, and m_i represents the i-th message od it has received. The output of the first (resp., second) party during the an execution of π on (x, y) is denoted $output_1^\pi(x, y)$ (resp., $output_2^\pi(x, y)$) and is implicit in the party's view of the execution.

Definition 1. *Two distribution ensembles $X = \{X_s\}_s \in S$ and $Y = \{Y_s\}_s \in S$ are computationally indistinguishable if for any probabilistic polynomial time distinguisher D and all sufficiently large s, there is a negligible function ν such that $|Pr(D(X_s) = 1) - Pr(D(Y_s) = 1))| \leq \nu$.*

Definition 2. *π privately computes f if there exist probabilistic polynomial time algorithms, denotes S_1 and S_2 such that*

$$\{S_1(x, f_1(x, y), f_2(x, y))\}_{x,y \in \{0,1\}^*} \equiv \{(view_1^\pi(x, y), output_2^\pi(x, y))\}_{x,y \in \{0,1\}^*}.$$

$$\{(f_1(x, y), S_2(x, f_2(x, y)))\}_{x,y \in \{0,1\}^*} \equiv \{output_1^\pi(x, y), (view_2^\Pi(x, y))\}_{x,y \in \{0,1\}^*}.$$

where $\equiv$ denotes computational indistinguishability.

Definition 3. *An oracle-aided protocol is a protocol augmented by a pair of oracle types, per each party, an oracle-call steps defined as follows: Each of the parties may send a special oracle request message, to the other party, after writing a string called the query on its write-only oracle tape. In response, the other party writes a string, its query, on its own oracle tape and respond to the first party with a oracle call message. At this point the oracle is invoked and the result is that a string, not necessary the same, is written by the oracle on the ready-only oracle tape of each party. This pair of strings is called the oracle answer.*

Definition 4. *An oracle-aided protocol is said to privately reduce g to f when using the oracle functionality f. In such a case, we say that g is privately reducible to f.*

Composition theorem for the semi-honest model [5]: Suppose that g is privately reducible to f and that there exists a protocol for privately computing f, then there exists a protocol for privately computing g.

3 Building blocks

Privacy preserving data mining is a new and rapidly emerging research area, where data mining algorithms are analyzed for the side-effects they incur in data privacy. Secure scalar product protocols are the fundamental cryptographic build blocks for building secure data mining protocols [14]. Several private (shared) scalar-product protocols have been proposed in the context of privacy-preserving data ming [4, 8, 9, 16]. Informally, a scalar-protocol is the following things: there are two participants Alice who holds her input vector $(x_1, \cdots, x_l)$ and Bob who holds his input vector $(y_1, \cdots, y_l)$. They wish to compute $\sum_{i=1}^l x_i y_i$ such that at the end of the protocol, Alice holds the value $\sum_{i=1}^l x_i y_i$, while Bob holds nothing. A sibling notion is shared-scalar-product protocols (SSP). An SSP protocol is the following thing: there are two participants Alice who holds her input vector $(x_1, \cdots, x_l)$ and Bob who holds his input vector $(y_1, \cdots, y_l)$. They wish to compute random shares of scalar product s_a and s_b such that $\Sigma_{i=1}^{l} x_i y_i = s_a + s_b$. At the end of the protocol, Alice holds the value s_a while Bob holds s_b. Clearly, a scalar-product protocol is a special case of a shared-scalar-product protocol when s_b=0.

Since the SSP protocol due to [8] will be used as a building block for our construction, we sketch the protocol below:

- Private input of Alice: $inp_A = (x_1, \cdots, x_l)$, $x_i \in Z_m$ for $i = 1, \cdots, l$;
- Private input of Bob: inp_B=$(y_1, \cdots, y_l)$, $y_i \in Z_m$ for $i = 1, \cdots, l$;
- Private output of Alice (resp., Bob) is $s_a \in Z_m$ (resp., $s_b \in Z_m$) such that $s_a + s_b$ $= \Sigma_{i=1}^{l} x_i y_i$.

System setup: Alice generates a public key and private key pair (sk, pk) of Paillier's encryption scheme [15] (i.e., sk=(P, Q), P and Q are large safe primes, pk=(g, N), where N=PQ, $g = (1 + N)$).

Step 1: for i=1 to l, Alice generates a random string r_i and sends c_i=$\text{Enc}_{pk}(x_i, r_i)$ to Bob; Step 2: Bob computes $w = \prod_{i=1}^{l} c_i^{y_i} \text{Enc}_{pk}(-1)^{s_b}$ and sends w to Alice; Step 3: Alice decrypts w and obtains $s_a \in Z_m$.

Lemma 1. *(due to [8]) The protocol is secure in the semi-honest model assuming that the underlying Paillier's encryption scheme is semantically secure and $lm^2 < |N|$.*

4   Implementation and proof of security

We propose an efficient implementation of SAI protocols in this section based on the privacy-preserving shared-scalar-product protocols in the semi-honest model.

4.1   Our implementation

Our implementation of SAI protocols consists of the following steps:

Step 1: on input inp_A =$x \in Z_m$ and $y \in Z_m$, Alice and Bob then choose $r_x \in_r Z_m$ and $r_y \in_r Z_m$ uniformly at random. Two participants then jointly compute the following value $z \in Z_m$:

$$z = (x + y)(r_x + r_y)$$
$$= xr_x + (xr_y + r_x y) + yr_y$$
$$= (xr_x + t_x) + (yr_y + t_y)$$
$$= z_x + z_y,$$

where $z_x := xr_x + t_x$ and $z_y := yr_y + t_y$ and the intermediate shares $t_x \in Z_m$ and $t_y \in Z_m$ satisfying the equation $t_x + t_y$ =$xr_y + r_x y$ are computed from any privacy-preserving shared-scalar-product protocol defined over the finite field Z_m such that Alice learns $t_x \in Z_m$ while Bob learns $t_y \in Z_m$;

Step 2: Alice sends z_x to Bob, and at the same time Bob sends z_y to Alice;

Step 3: once given z_x and z_y, both Alice and Bob can compute the inverse of z individually;

Step 4: the output of Alice is $s_x := r_x z^{-1} \bmod m$ while the output of Bob is $s_y := r_y z^{-1} \bmod m$.

4.2 The proof of security

The correctness of the protocol can be easily verified:

$$
\begin{aligned}
s_x + s_y &= r_x z^{-1} + r_y z^{-1} \\
&= (r_x + r_y) z^{-1} \\
&= (r_x + r_y)(r_x + r_y)^{-1}(x + y)^{-1} \\
&= (x + y)^{-1},
\end{aligned}
$$

Lemma 2. *Our implementation of SAI protocols securely reduce SAI protocols to SSP protocols in the semi-honest model.*

Proof: The fist party Alice, sends her input $inp_A = (x, r_x)$ to the SSP oracle $\mathcal{F}_{SSP}$ while the second party, Bob sends his input $inp_B = (y, r_y)$ to $\mathcal{F}_{SSP}$. $\mathcal{F}_{SSP}$ outputs (t_x, t_y) so that Alice learns t_x while Bob learns t_y. As a result, the distribution $view_1^\pi(x, y)$ can be defined as $\{x, r_x, t_x, z_x, z_y, s_x\}$, where $z_x \leftarrow x r_x + t_x$, $z_y \in_r Z_m$, $s_x \leftarrow r_x(z_x + z_y)^{-1}$. We then define the distribution of $output_2^\pi(inp_A, inp_B)$. By the implementation, we have equations: $z_y = y r_y + t_y$ and $t_x + t_y = x r_y + y r_x$. Consequently, we have the equation $z_y = y r_y + t_x - x r_y - y r_x$. Furthermore, for fixed variables (x, r_x, t_x, z_y) and y, there is a unique solution of r_y such that $r_y = (y - x)^{-1}(y t_x + z_y - t_x)$ if $x \neq y$. Since $s_y = r_y z^{-1} = r_y(z_x + z_y)^{-1}$, it follows that s_y is uniformly distributed over Z_m assuming that y is uniformly distributed over the finite field Z_m. Finally, we need to show that there exists a simulator S_1 for the honest-but-curious party Alice. This can be done as follows: we choose $s_y \in_r Z_m$ uniformly at random and set $f_2(inp_A, inp_B) \leftarrow s_y$. We then define $S_1(inp_A, s_y)$ according to the following steps:

- on input $inp_A = (x, r_x)$, S_1 runs the sub-simulator for the (sub-protocol) SSP protocol. Such a sub-simulator exists since the underlying SSP protocol is secure in the semi-honest model. The distribution of the sub-simulator is denoted by (t_x, t_y);
- S_1 then computes z_x from the equation $z_x = x r_x + t_x$, where S_1 learns t_x from the distribution of the simulator (we stress that S_1 does not learn t_y). And then S_1 chooses $z_y \in_r Z_m$;
- S_1 then computes s_x from the equation $s_x = r_x(z_x + z_y)^{-1}$;
- The distribution of S_1 is $(x, r_x, t_x, z_x, z_y, s_x)$.

Obviously, the following two distributions are computationally indistinguishable:
$$
\{S_1(inp_A, f_1(inp_A, inp_B), f_2(inp_A, inp_B))\}_{inp_A, inp_B \in \{0,1\}^*}
$$
$$
= \{(x, r_x, t_x, z_x, z_y, s_x), s_y\}
$$
$$
= \{(view_1^\pi(inp_A, inp_B), output_2^\pi(inp_A, inp_B))\}_{inp_A, inp_B \in \{0,1\}^*}.
$$
Similarly, we can define a simulator S_2 for the honest-but-curious party Bob satisfying the security definition. It follows that our implementation is securely reduce SAI protocols to SSP protocols in the semi-honest model.

Combining the Lemma 1 and the Lemma 2, we have the main statement below (the composition theorem for the semi-honest model):

Theorem 1. *Our implementation of SAI protocols in secure in the semi-honest model assuming that the Paillier's encryption scheme is semantically secure.*

5   Applications

SAI protocols can be used to compute clustering means in the horizontally partitioned database model, and vertically partitioned database model. We also would like to provide an interesting application of SAI protocols to the general case of the privacy-preserving distributed k-means clustering algorithms for the arbitrarily partitioned database model [11]. Let $D=\{d_1, d_2, \cdots, d_n\}$ be a database set consists of n objects. Each object d_i is described by the value of the l numerical attributes. That is each d_i is partitioned into two disjoint subsets d_i^A and d_i^B. Let μ_j^A (resp. μ_j^B) for $1 \leq j \leq k$ denote Alice's (resp., Bob's) share of the j-th mean. The candidate cluster center are given by $\mu_j^A + \mu_j^B$ for $1 \leq j \leq k$. For each object d_i, Alice and Bob securely compute the distance $\text{dist}(d_i, \mu_j)$ for $1 \leq j \leq k$, between the object and each of the k cluster centers. The result of the distance calculation is learned as random shares between Alice and Bob. Using the random shares, they then securely compute the closest cluster for each object in the database (all computations are performed over a finite filed Z_m). At the end of each iteration, Alice and Bob learns his or her share of the cluster centers. The next iteration requires the recomputing each of the k-cluster centers. Suppose that Alice has objects $d_{i_1}^A, \cdots, d_{i_p}^A$ and Bob has objects $d_{i_1}^B, \cdots, d_{i_q}^B$, for $1 \leq j \leq k$. Each of the d_i^A and d_i^B is an l-tuple, where $d_{i,j}^A$ (resp., $d_{i,j}^B$) denotes the j-th coordinate of the corresponding l-tuple.

Alice (resp., Bob) calculates the shares s_j and n_j (resp. t_j and m_j) for $1 \leq j \leq l$, where $s_j = \Sigma_{r=1}^{p} d_{i_r,j}^A$ (resp., $t_j = \Sigma_{r=1}^{q} d_{i_r,j}^B$), and n_j (resp., m_j) denotes the number of objects in $d_{i_1}^A, \cdots, d_{i_p}^A$ (resp., $d_{i_1}^B, \cdots, d_{i_q}^B$) for which Alice (resp., Bob) has the values for the attribute A_j. If Alice (resp., Bob) does not have the value for the attribute j for some object d_i^A (resp., d_i^B), she (resp., he) treats it as zero. Thus the j-th components of i-th cluster center is given by $\mu_{i,j} = \frac{s_j + t_j}{m_j + n_j}$. For convenience, we simply assume that Alice has her input $inp_A = (a, r_a)$ while Bob has his input $inp_B = (b, r_b)$. They wish to securely compute $s_a + s_b = \frac{a+b}{r_a + r_b}$ over Z_m. We now can provide alternative solution to the problem below[3]:

- Private input of Alice: $inp_A = (a, r_a) \in Z_m \times Z_m$;
- Private input of Bob: $inp_B = (b, r_b) \in Z_m \times Z_m$;
- Private output of Alice (resp., Bob) is $s_a \in Z_m$ (resp., $s_b \in Z_m$) such that $s_a + s_b = \frac{a+b}{r_a + r_b}$.

  Step 1: On inputs $inp_A = r_a$ and $inp_B = b$, Alice and Bob jointly run the SAI protocol to compute t_a and t_b such that $t_a + t_b = (r_a + r_b)^{-1}$, where Alice learns $t_a \in Z_m$ and Bob learns $t_b \in Z_m$;

  Step 2: On inputs $inp_A = (a, t_a) \in Z_m \times Z_m$ and $inp_B = (b, t_b) \in Z_m \times Z_m$, Alice and Bob jointly run any privacy-preserving shared-scalar-product protocol to compute $w_a \in Z_m$ and $w_b \in Z_m$ such that $w_a + w_b = a t_b + b t_a$;

  Step 3: Alice computes $s_a \leftarrow a t_a + w_a$ and Bob computes $s_b \leftarrow b t_b + w_b$;

  Step 4: The output of Alice is $s_a \in Z_m$ and while the output of Bob is $s_b \in Z_m$.

---

[3] There are two solutions suggested in [11]: one is based on Yao's circuit evaluation protocol [17]; another solution is based on Bar-Ilan and Beaver's protocol [1]. Unfortunately, no detailed solution is available in [11] yet.

As an immediate application of the Theorem 1, we have the following corollary:

Corollary 1. *The recomputing k-means protocol is secure assuming that the underlying SAI protocol is secure in the semi-honest model.*

6 Conclusion

In this paper, a notion called shared-additive-inverse (SAI) protocols has been introduced and formalized. We then have proposed a novel construction of SAI protocols from any secure shared-scalar-product (SSP) protocols, and shown that the implementation is secure assuming that the underlying SSP protocol is secure in the semi-honest model. Finally, an immediate application of SAI protocols to the k-means cluster recomputing algorithm has been presented. To the best of our knowledge, our algorithm is the first practical solution to the k-means cluster recomputing algorithm suitable for the arbitrarily partitioned database model.

Acknowledgment

The research of the first author is partially supported by National Natural Science Foundation of CHINA under the Project number 60273058.

References

1. Judit Bar-Ilan, Donald Beaver: Non-Cryptographic Fault-Tolerant Computing in Constant Number of Rounds of Interaction. PODC 1989: 201-209.
2. P.S. Bardley and U.M. Fayyad. Refining initial points for k-means clustering. In Proceedings of 15th International Conference on Machine Learning (ICML), pages 91–99, 1998.
3. Daniel Bleichenbacher1 and Phong Q. Nguyen. Noisy Polynomial Interpolation and Noisy Chinese Remaindering. EUROCRYPT 2000, LNCS 1807, pp. 53–69, 2000.
4. Wenliang Du and Zhijun Zhan, Building decision tree classifier on private data, In Proceedings of the IEEE ICDM Workshop on Privacy, Security and Data Mining (2002).
5. Oded Goldreich. Foundations of Cryptography, Volume 2, Cambridge University Press, 2004.
6. O.Goldreich, S.Micali, and A. Wigderson. How to play any mental game – a completeness theorem for protocols with honest majority. In 19th Symposium on Theory of Computer Science, pages 218–229, 1987.
7. O.Goldreich, S. Micali, and A. Wigderson. Proofs that yield nothing but their validity or all languages in NP have zero-knowledge proof systems. Journal of the ACM, 38(1):691–729, 1991.
8. Bart Goethals, Sven Laur, Helger Lipmaa, Taneli Mielikäinen: On Private Scalar Product Computation for Privacy-Preserving Data Mining. ICISC 2004: 104–120
9. Ioannis Ioannidis, Ananth Grama, and Mikhail Atallah, A secure protocol for computing dot products in clustered and distributed environments, In Proceedings of the International Conference on Parallel Processing (2002). Geetha KDD 2005: 593–599.
10. Somesh Jha, Louis Kruger, Patrick McDaniel: Privacy Preserving Clustering. ESORICS 2005: 397–417

11. Geetha Jagannathan, Rebecca N. Wright: Privacy-preserving distributed k-means clustering over arbitrarily partitioned data. KDD 2005: 593–599.
12. M. Kantarcioglu and C. Clifton. Privacy-preserving distributed mining of association rules on horizontally partitioned data. In The ACM SIGMOD Workshop on Research Issues on Data Mining and Knowledge Discovery (DMKD'02), June 2, 2002.
13. Moni Naor, Benny Pinkas: Oblivious Transfer and Polynomial Evaluation. STOC 1999: 245–254
14. Benny Pinkas, Cryptographic Techniques for Privacy-Preserving Data Mining. Newsletter of the ACM Special Interest Group on Knowledge Discovery and Data Mining, January 2003.
15. Pascal Paillier: Public-Key Cryptosystems Based on Composite Degree Residuosity Classes. Proc. of EUROCRYPT 1999: 223–238, Springer Verlag.
16. Jaideep Vaidya and Chris Clifton, Privacy preserving association rule mining in vertically partitioned data, In the 8th ACM SIGKDD International Conference on Knowledge Discovery and Data Mining (2002), 639–644.
17. Andrew Chi-Chih Yao: How to Generate and Exchange Secrets (Extended Abstract) FOCS 1986: 162–167.

Click Passwords

Darko Kirovski, Nebojša Jojić, and Paul Roberts

Microsoft Research
One Microsoft Way, Redmond, WA 98052, USA
{darkok,jojic,proberts}@microsoft.com

Abstract. We present a set of algorithms and tools that enable entering pass-words on devices with graphical input (touch-pad, stylus, mouse) by clicking on specific pixels of a custom image. As one of the most important features, when entering a password, the user is given limited tolerance for inaccuracy in the selection of pixels. The goal of the proposed click password system is to maximize the password space, while facilitating memorization of entered secrets. Besides enabling personalization of the login procedure through selection of the background image, the proposed system provides superior password space compared to traditional 8-character textual passwords.

1 Introduction

Traditional textual passwords leave a lot to be desired with respect to the two most important characteristics of any password system: security and usability. Whereas a truly random 8-character password potentially may produce a reliable $95^8 > 10^{15}$ password space, memorizing and entering such a password on a keyboard is an uncomfortable task that only very few practice. The fact that many users chose textual passwords that are relatively easy to guess has been analyzed and emphasized in several studies [9], [1], [13], [2]. By analyzing 14,000 UNIX passwords, Klein has concluded that nearly one quarter of them belonged to a relatively small dictionary of $3 \cdot 10^6$ words [9]. Thus, in the past decade hackers have focused on utilizing "the dictionary attack" along with buffer overflow and packet sniffing more than any other type of attack [11]. Textual passwords have been used as a de facto standard login mechanism, primarily because of the dominance of the keyboard as an input device. With the recent proliferation of mobile devices which typically have some form of graphical input (touch-pad, stylus) and graphics display, many routines, so as the login process, require adaptation to point-and-click mediated human-computer interaction.

The idea of using visual content to create password systems is not new. Several other techniques have been developed to date with such a goal: (*i*) icon-based passwords [3], (*ii*) passfaces [10], and (*iii*) draw-a-secret [8]. The first two systems use self-contained icons and facial photos as symbols that the user selects while creating a password. In a sense, such systems mimic a keyboard with letters replaced by distinct self-contained images. Draw-a-secret passwords are a step forward as they are conceived by creating a secret drawing on a grid of rectangles. The motion of the stylus across rectangles is encoded into a password.

Please use the following format when citing this chapter:

Author(s) [insert Last name, First-name initial(s)], 2006, in IFIP International Federation for Information Processing, Volume 201, Security and Privacy in Dynamic Environments, eds. Fischer-Hubner, S., Rannenberg, K., Yngstrom, L., Lindskog, S., (Boston: Springer), pp. [insert page numbers].

The difficulty in adopting visual password systems stems from several facts. First, in case of icon-based systems (*i-ii*), large area of the display is reserved to clearly distinguish the tiled icons. In order to have easily recognizable content, individual icons usually contain entire objects, whereas the granularity of visual detail that can be semantically selected by the user is commonly far smaller. Icon-based systems cannot enable users to select an arbitrary region of an image as a password construct. As a consequence, such systems rarely explore the real potential of visual content to build password systems.

Second, due to the nature of point-and-click user interfaces, in case of both image-based (e.g., *i-ii*) and in particular draw-a-secret (*iii*) systems, users should be given certain tolerance to an input error while entering a password. Tolerance to misaligned input is difficult to achieve because password systems do not memorize password's plain-text but its cryptographically secure hash. Thus, a slight change in the entered password results in a hash value which is at a large distance from the hash of the set up password. As a consequence, graphics-based password systems are typically either not secure due to a small number of symbols just as textual passwords or have a high likelihood of erroneous logins.

Fig. 1. An image and the result of image analysis. The darker regions are estimated to be more likely to be used as symbols in a click password. Cardinality of the password alphabet for this high-resolution image exceeds 500 symbols.

2   Click Passwords

In order to address the main concerns of visual password systems, we introduce *click passwords* – a login mechanism that uses an arbitrary image as a domain for creating a password. The user creates a password by clicking on several arbitrary pixels of the image. At login, the user is required to click in a certain neighborhood of the originally selected pixels in the same order as during the password setup. A desired tolerance to input error can be adjusted by the user before the password is set up. Since the image is not visibly partitioned into regions, the user is free to select and memorize arbitrary visual features of the image. The task of the underlying mechanisms is to maximize system security for a given image while providing robustness to limited erroneous input.

A click password system uses the domain image to build an alphabet of distinct symbols. The alphabet is built by tiling the image with Voronoi polygons where each polygon corresponds to a unique symbol. The tiling is not displayed to the user; it is used within the click password system to convert user clicks into an string of symbols that is hashed and stored during password setup. The user sets a password by selecting an ordered set of pixels. Each selected pixel is translated into a symbol that corresponds to the identifier of the polygon which contains the pixel. For each click password, the system stores three objects: (*a*) the **username**, (*b*) the **hash** value of the arithmetic concatenation of the selected symbols, and (*c*) for each selected pixel, an alignment **offset** of the polygon grid that moves the selected pixel to a random pixel in the neighborhood of the center of the polygon that contains the selected pixel. The offset is stored as plaintext and it guarantees limited tolerance to pixel selection inaccuracy at logon. Radius of the neighborhood central to a polygon equals the maximum tolerance to error that can be adjusted by the user to a desired value. Since the offsets are stored as plain-text, their values reveal information that can reduce the complexity of a brute force attack (e.g., see example in Figure 2). Thus, a click password system is tailored to a given image in two steps: first, a cognitive system extracts a map of pixels likely to be selected as part of a password and then, an optimization system creates a Voronoi polygon tiling of the image that maximizes the entropy of a selected password under the assumption that the adversary conducting a brute force attack may have access to the password offsets.

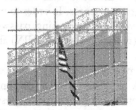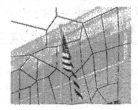

Fig. 2. In this image, one of the pixels likely to be clicked is the top of the flag. In the left subfigure, this pixel is in the upper left corner of a rectangular cell. An offset that moves this pixel to its polygon center is most likely pointing to this cell, as most of the other cells have clickable pixels in other regions. An optimized Voronoi tiling in the right subfigure rectifies this problem by creating a grid in which pixels likely to be clicked are placed near the centers of each polygon.

The click password system has two goals: **improved security** and **usability**. The expectation is that an image with visually diverse content can create a symbol alphabet of significantly higher cardinality than the alphabet that consists of printable characters of a standard US keyboard. Similarly, understanding cross-symbol dependencies in text is commonly attributed to the fact that most passwords have semantic value, whereas clicks on an image, at least intuitively, may not have strong and well-defined interactions. Using images with content tailored for a particular user, click passwords are supposed to be significantly easier to memorize than textual secrets of comparable level of security.

We have developed a set of algorithms that initiate the click password system as follows. During password setup, the user selects an image as a domain for pixel selection. Next, a component of the platform, the *image analyzer*, evaluates for each pixel the likelihood that it can be selected as part of a password. For brevity, in this version of the manuscript we do not overview this component. The image analyzer also quantifies, as feedback to the user, whether the selected image contains sufficient graphical diversity to enable the desired level of security. Finally, based on the information provided by the image analyzer, the *grid designer* builds a grid of enumerated Voronoi polygons that tile the image such that the cardinality of the password space is heuristically maximized. An example of an image that we have used in our user study as well as the corresponding output of our image analyzer is presented in Figure 1.

3   Related Work

Traditional approach to logging onto a system is to type in a password associated with the username. When a password is entered for the first time, the system computes a secure hash of the entered password and stores it into one of the system files (e.g., on UNIX systems /etc/passwd). Upon login, the system computes again the hash of the entered password and compares this value with the stored one. In UNIX, the password hash is computed by encrypting 64 zero bits with the password using 25 rounds of DES. If they match, the user is granted access. In order to prevent one user from identifying another with the same password, before hashing, passwords are usually salted with a user-specific random variable (two characters in UNIX) also stored in the passwd file.

Although such a login mechanism has provable reliability [6], one of the most common related attacks is the dictionary attack [9]. The extent of dictionary attacks can be grasped from hacker web sites which commonly provide 100+ password cracking utilities [11]. The dictionary attack can be launched on- and off-line. The success rate of an on-line attack can be made low by prohibiting access to the system after a certain number of unsuccessful logins. It is difficult to prevent the off-line variant of the dictionary attack, where the adversary obtains the passwd file through a Trojan horse or as a system user.

4   Security of Click Passwords

Initially, the user selects the image $\mathcal{I}$ used as a domain for password selection. Next, the system builds the passwords space by tiling the image using a grid Π of L non-overlapping polygons. The polygons can be of arbitrary sizes. The grid is not displayed to the user. It is constructed with polygons of different size such that each polygon is approximately equally likely to be clicked. Given the map that quantifies the likelihood that a pixel is selected as part of a password, this approach aims at maximizing the password space. Such a map can be constructed empirically or using image processing for feature extraction [5].

Definition 1. Image Grid. *Given an image* $\mathcal{I}$ *of* $m \times n$ *pixels with a weight map* $W = \{\mathbb{R}\}^{m \times n}$, *where each weight* $w(x,y) \in W$ *corresponds*[1] *to pixel* $P(x,y)$ *with* x *and* y *as coordinates, an image grid* $\Pi(\mathcal{I}) = \{\pi_i, i = 1..L\}$ *is defined as tiling of* $\mathcal{I}$ *into* L *non-overlapping polygons.*

The weight $w(x,y)$ associated with pixel $P(x,y)$ equals the probability that this pixel can be selected while setting up a password. Thus, matrix W quantifies the visual effect of the image on the selectivity of certain pixels. The user sets up a p-long click password by selecting an ordered set C_p of p pixels.

Definition 2. Password Setup. *Given an image* $\mathcal{I}$ *of* $m \times n$ *pixels, a click password* C_p *of length* p *is set up as an ordered set* C_p *of* p *user-selected pixels.*

At logon time, the user selects an ordered set D_p of p pixels which are required to be in the ε_2-neighborhood of the pixels selected at password setup time C_p. Pixel P is in the ε_2-neighborhood of pixel Q if the Euclidean distance between them is $\|P - Q\| \leq \varepsilon_2$[2]. We enable such bounded tolerance with a requirement that the pixels in D_p map to the same polygons to which pixels from C_p map.

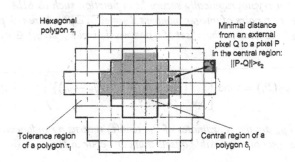

Fig. 3. An example of a hexagonal polygon π_i, its central δ_i (grey pixels) and tolerance τ_i region (white pixels). Minimal distance ε_2 between an external pixel Q and an internal pixel $P \in \delta_i$ must be greater than ε_2.

Definition 3. Central Region of a Polygon. *Given a polygon* π_i, *its central region* δ_i *is defined as a non-empty subset of pixels* $\delta_i \subset \pi_i$ *for which the minimal Euclidean distance with respect to any pixel outside the polygon is greater than a constant real number* ε_2.

Definition 4. Tolerance Region of a Polygon. *Given a polygon* π_i *and its central region* δ_i, *the corresponding tolerance region is defined as:* $\tau_i = \pi_i - \delta_i$.

---

[1] For $P(x,y)$, we denote its weight as $w(x,y)$ or $w(P)$.

[2] $\|P(x_p, y_p) - Q(x_q, y_q)\| \equiv \sqrt{(x_p - x_q)^2 + (y_p - y_q)^2}$.

An example of a hexagonal polygon and its central and tolerance region is presented in Figure 3. For the example polygon in the figure, its central region is defined using $3 \leq \varepsilon_2 < \sqrt{10}$ assuming pixel dimensions are 1×1.

We define the two regions of a polygon because of the following problem. During password setup, the user may select a pixel P which is in the tolerance region of its containing polygon π_i. This means that at logon, the user may click a pixel Q which is at distance $\|P - Q\| \leq \varepsilon_2$ from P but does not belong to π_i. To avoid this situation, at setup time, the system records an offset associated with P which realigns the grid such that P is in the central region of π_i. Thus, the central region of a polygon must contain at least one pixel.

Definition 5. Click Password Storage. *For a click password* $C_p = \{P_i \in \mathcal{I}, i = 1..p\}$, *the data* $\{\psi_0, \psi_1, \psi_2\}$ *is stored on the host computer, where* ψ_0 *is a pointer to a user,* ψ_1 *equals:*

$$\psi_1 = \text{CSH} \left(\sum_{i=1}^{p} L^{i-1} \cdot (j | P_i \in \pi_j \wedge P_i \in C_p) \right) \tag{1}$$

where CSH is a cryptographically secure hash function such as SHA-256, and ψ_2 *is an ordered set of p pairs of integer numbers* $\psi_2 = \{\mathbb{Z}, \mathbb{Z}\}^p$, *where i-th pair* $\psi_2(P_i) = \{a_i, b_i\} \in \psi_2$ *is denoted as the offset of a password pixel* $P_i(x_i, y_i) \in \pi_j$ *and equals:*

$$\psi_2(P_i) = \text{rand} \left[\left(\bigcup_{\forall P_k \in \delta_j} \{(x_k - x_i), (y_k - y_i)\} \right) \cap \Psi \right], \tag{2}$$

where x_k *and* y_k *are the coordinates of* P_k, rand(t) *returns a random element from the set t, and* Ψ *is a set of all possible offsets that can occur in* Π:

$$\Psi = \{0,0\} \cup \left(\bigcup_{\forall \pi_i \in \Pi} \bigcup_{\forall P_j \in \tau_i} \{(x_q - x_j), (y_q - y_j)\} \right), \tag{3}$$

$$Q = (x_q, y_q) = \arg\min_{Q \in \delta_i}(\|P_j - Q\|). \tag{4}$$

For a given ε_2, the set of all possible offsets Ψ in Π is limited to:

$$\Psi \subseteq \{\{a,b\} | a, b \in \mathbb{Z}, |a| \leq \varepsilon_2, |b| \leq \varepsilon_2\}. \tag{5}$$

A password is stored as a 3-tuple of the username, the hash of the encoded selection of polygons, and the grid offsets used to realign the image grid prior to selecting each pixel at logon time. The data hashed in Eqn.1 can be salted and the salt can be stored as a fourth component of the stored password entry. The alignment offsets ψ_2 are randomized to disable analysis which may exclude certain polygons from the password space.

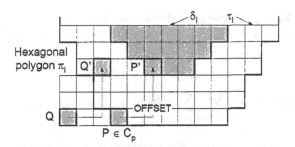

Fig. 4. An example of using an offset to realign a polygon grid such that each selected pixel of a click password is located in the center region of the containing polygon. Pixel P is originally selected in the tolerance region τ_i of π_i. Offset $\psi_2(P) = \{2, 3\}$ realigns P to P' which belongs to δ_i. Pixel Q entered at logon is at a distance of $\|Q - P\| \leq \varepsilon_2$, hence this error should be tolerated. However, Q does not belong to π_i which results in an incorrect selection. Using the offset, the translated pixel $Q' = Q + \psi_2(P)$ results in a correct selection as it belongs to π_i.

An example of how offsets are used to enable correct password entry with ε_2-tolerance is presented in Figure 4.

A pixel (polygon) is correctly selected at logon if it is within a distance smaller or equal to ε_2 from the pixel selected at setup. Logon is granted, iff the ψ_1 function of the entered pixels D_p realigned for ψ_2, equals the stored $\psi_1(C_p)$.

Definition 6. Click Password Logon. *Let C_p be a selected p-long click password and let D_p be an ordered set $D_p = \{Q_i(x_i, y_i), i = 1..p\}$ of p pixels selected at logon time. System access is granted only if:*

$$\psi_1(C_p) \equiv \text{CSH}\left(\sum_{i=1}^{p}[L^{i-1} \cdot (j|(Q_i + \{a_i, b_i\}) \in \pi_j)]\right) \qquad (6)$$

where $\{a_i, b_i\}$ corresponds to the i-th offset pair in ψ_2 and $P(x, y) + \{a, b\}$ equals $P(x + a, y + b)$.

4.1 Security Metrics

Once constructed, the image grid creates a certain password space with respect to the content of the image and the potential offsets. It is important to quantify this metric as it directly impacts the security of the system against brute-force attacks. Naïve computation of the password space would raise the number of polygons to the power of the number of pixels in a password. However, it is not likely that an image can provide sufficient visual diversity, such that each polygon in a grid of regular polygons is selected with equal probability. In addition, the security of the system must be accounted for the fact that the grid structure and grid offsets ψ_2 may be obtained by the adversary. In order to provide better insight on the security of click passwords, we measure the entropy of polygon selection. A grid of L polygons Π which results in maximum entropy, is the objective of the grid designer.

Definition 7. Entropy of Polygon Selection. *Given an image $\mathcal{I}$, its weight map W, and a grid of L polygons $\Pi(\mathcal{I}) = \{\pi_i | i = 1..L\}$, the entropy of selecting a polygon equals:*

$$H(\Pi) = - \sum_{\forall \{a,b\} \in \Psi} \sum_{i=1}^{L} \vartheta(\{a,b\}, \pi_i) \cdot \log_2(\vartheta(\{a,b\}, \pi_i)), \qquad (7)$$

where Ψ is the set of all possible offset combinations in the grid structure (see Eqn.3) and $\vartheta(\{a,b\}, \pi_i)$ denotes the probability that a pixel from polygon π_i is selected with an offset $\{a,b\}$ and equals:

$$\vartheta(\{a,b\}, \pi_i) = \sum_{\forall P_j \in \pi_i | P_j + \{a,b\} \in \delta_i} w(P_j). \qquad (8)$$

Brute Force Attack. The general assumption for any attack on a click password system is that the system file with the corresponding entries $\{\psi_0, \psi_1, \psi_2\}$ is available to the adversary as well as the domain image $\mathcal{I}$, its weight map W, and resulting grid structure Π. In order to find the list of polygons that constitutes a given password C_p, the adversary can launch the following brute force attack:

- In the first step, for each pixel $P_i \in C_p$, the adversary computes the subset of polygons $\Omega(P_i) \subseteq \Pi$ of minimal cardinality such that for the corresponding offset $\psi_2(P_i)$,

$$\sum_{\forall \pi_j \in \Omega(P_i)} \vartheta(\psi_2(P_i), \pi_j) < \varepsilon_3 \cdot \sum_{\forall \pi_j \in \Pi} \vartheta(\psi_2(P_i), \pi_j). \qquad (9)$$

  In this case, ε_3 is a parameter that balances computational complexity and likelihood of success. Typically, $\varepsilon_3 > 0.9$.
- In the second step, the adversary generates the set of attack vectors as all possible p-long combinations of polygons $C_A = \{\pi_{A1}..\pi_{Ap}\}$, where each variable π_{Ai} takes the values of all polygons in the corresponding $\Omega(P_i)$. For each attack vector $C_a \in C_A$, the adversary computes $\psi_1(C_a)$ until it matches $\psi_1(C_p)$ retrieved from the password file. The cardinality of the set of attack vectors C_A equals: $|C_A| = \prod_{\forall P_i \in C_p} |\Omega(P_i)|$. In order to minimize the expected length of the search, the adversary tests test vectors from C_A with decreasing probability of occurrence.

Under the assumption that the weight map W used by the adversary is accurate, the likelihood of success for this attack is strongly governed by the cut-off threshold ε_3 and equals $\Pr[C_p \in C_A] = 1 - \varepsilon_3^p$.

4.2 Grid Designer

In order to maximize the difficulty of a brute force attack, the Voronoi grid Π has to be such that the entropy $H(\Pi)$ of polygon selection is maximized for a given tolerance ε_2 of pixel selection. From Eqn.7, we conclude that maximal entropy is achieved for a set Π of L polygons if the likelihood of selecting a particular offset within a polygon is equivalent across all polygons and for all offsets. This case can occur only if the weight map W is constant across all pixels. It is not likely that any image can provide visual diversity such that human eye can equiprobably select any pixel as a password symbol. Thus, certain variance in the probability that a polygon π has been selected with an offset $\{a, b\}$ must exist with respect to distinct polygons and offset values. For simplicity and brevity, we adopt the following model of the image weight map W. For each pixel P, its weight takes randomly one of the two values:

$$w(P) = \begin{cases} 0, \ \Pr[w(P) = 0] = 1 - \frac{1}{mn\mu} \\ \mu, \ \ \Pr[w(P) = \mu] = \frac{1}{mn\mu} \end{cases} \tag{10}$$

where $0 < \mu \leq 1$ and m and n are image dimensions in pixels. In addition, we denote pixels with $w(P) = \mu$ as "clickable."

We demonstrate the trade-offs related to the size of the Voronoi polygons as well as their central regions using the following two examples. Consider the polygons π_1 and π_2 in Figure 5. Note that only a single pixel represents the central region δ_1 of polygon π_1. Hence, one of 25 distinct offset values $\{a, b\} \in \Psi$ is used to realign every pixel of π_1 to the pixel in δ_1. This means that a single recorded offset points to one pixel in each polygon. One advantage of tiling an image with polygons similar to π_1 is that there are more polygons due to their size. However, this comes at the expense of having a smaller ratio of polygons with a "clickable" pixel for a given offset value.

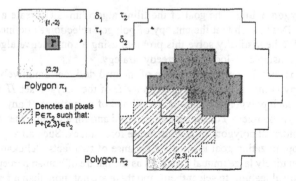

Fig. 5. An example of two polygons with central regions that consist of one and several pixels. An example of how offset is used to realign pixels selected within the tolerance region into pixels in the central region of the corresponding polygon.

Figure 5 also depicts a subset of pixels (shaded region) that belongs to polygon π_2, where each pixel in the subset can be moved for offset $\{2, 3\}$. Roughly, for any offset in Ψ, the cardinality of this subset equals approximately $|\delta_2|$. The likelihood that this subset contains a "clickable" point is substantially greater than in the case of π_1. This characteristic comes at the expense of increased polygon size which results in fewer polygons used in order to tile an image.

Preliminaries. In this subsection, we introduce several entities that facilitate the description of the tiling algorithm. First, we define an offset-$\{a, b\}$ region of a polygon as a subset of pixels within a region π which are translated with the offset $\{a, b\}$ into the central region of the polygon.

Definition 8. Offset-$\{a, b\}$ Region of a Polygon. *For a given polygon π with an associated central region δ, its offset-$\{a, b\}$ region, denoted as $\sigma_\pi(\{a, b\})$, is defined as a subset of pixels in π, such that for each pixel $P \in \sigma_\pi(\{a, b\})$, $P + \{a, b\} \in \delta$.*

Note that in general $|\sigma(\{a, b\})| \leq |\delta|$. For example, we have $|\sigma_2(\{2, 3\})| = |\delta_2| - 1$ in Figure 5. Next, we define how a Voronoi grid is constructed and represented for a digital image.

Definition 9. Pixel-based Voronoi Grid. *For an image $\mathcal{I}$, a Voronoi grid of L polygons, $\Pi(\mathcal{I}) = \{\pi_i, i = 1..L\}$, is defined with a set of L corresponding pixels $\Gamma = \{P_i, i = 1..L\} \subset \mathcal{I}$, $P_i \rightarrow \pi_i$, such that a given pixel $Q \in \mathcal{I}$ belongs to the polygon $\pi_j \in \Pi$, iff polygon's defining pixel, P_j, has the shortest Euclidean distance from Q with respect to all other pixels in Γ. If there are several pixels in Γ that share the same shortest distance from Q, they are sorted in the decreasing order of their x-ordinates and y-abscissas respectively, and the top-sorted pixel is selected.*

According to Def.9, the grid is defined using the subset of pixels Γ. For a given click tolerance ε_2, the central region of each polygon is defined using Def.3.

Voronoi Polygon Tiling The goal of the tiling algorithm is to create a Voronoi grid as defined in Def.9, such that the entropy of polygon selection as defined in Def.7, is maximized. We heuristically solve this problem using a constructive algorithm which tiles the image using an 1-lookahead greedy strategy.

First, we revisit the optimization goal of the grid designer. Intuitively, polygon selection entropy is maximized if the cardinality L of the polygon set Π is maximized while within each polygon the minimal likelihood of occurrence of any offset from Ψ (see Eqns.3,1) is non-zero. For such a polygon grid and for a given offset, the adversary needs to consider all polygons in Π in its brute force attack. Such an approximation of the original optimization goal is effective because of two facts: "clickable" islands of pixels have relatively large mutual distances as the nature of human perception requires isolated graphical features to select them, and there are not more than a few "clickable" pixels per polygon, as we intend to keep the polygon size as small as possible.

This results in relatively small variance in the likelihood that a certain polygon is selected given a certain offset across all polygons in the grid. The quality of the final solution Π can always be verified via the computation of its true security metric, $H(\Pi)$, according to Eqn.7. Finally, the optimization objective can be generalized such that L is maximized under the condition that within each polygon $\varrho \cdot |\Psi|$ of offsets from Ψ have a non-zero likelihood of selection. For brevity and simplicity, we constrain $\varrho = 1$.

Pivotal part of the tiling algorithm are two maps: a binary coverage map $M_C = \{0,1\}^{m \times n}$ where each element $M_C(x,y)$ denotes that pixel $P(x,y) \in \mathcal{I}$ has been covered during polygon tiling, and an integer polygon-size map $M_P = \{\mathbb{Z}\}^{m \times n}$, where each element $M_P(x,y)$ equals the minimal radius of the pixel-rasterized circle centered at $P(x,y)$ which has a non-zero likelihood occurrence of any offset in Ψ. The radius of the circle is at least $\varepsilon_2 + 1$ pixels.

For a given click tolerance ε_2 and a given pixel $P(x,y)$, its value $M_P(x,y)$ is computed in the following way. In the starting iteration, a polygon π of circular shape centered at $P(x,y)$ with radius $\varepsilon_2 + 1$ is created. If for all possible offsets in Ψ, their offset-regions contain at least one "clickable" pixel, then π is accepted as the resulting polygon and $M_P(x,y)$ is set to the value of polygon's radius. In the subsequent iterations, the radius of polygon π is increased until $2\varepsilon_2$. If a polygon with satisfactory characteristics is not found, then $M_P(x,y) = \infty$. Polygons larger than this maximal size are never selected explicitly during tiling, because a polygon with radius $2\varepsilon_2$ and a "clickable" pixel at $P(x,y)$, is guaranteed to contain at least one "clickable" pixel for each possible offset-region. Once all polygons are selected, their borders are recomputed according to Def.9.

The goal of the Voronoi tiling algorithm is to find a max-cardinality subset Γ of pixels in $\mathcal{I}$ such that all polygons defined with Γ have non-zero likelihood of occurrence for any offset in Ψ. This problem is NP-complete as it can be mapped to the SET PACKING problem [7] (problem SP3, pp.221 in [7]) as follows. For each pixel $P(x,y)$, we create a set which encompasses all neighboring pixels covered by the polygon π centered at P and with radius $M_P(P)$. The domain of the problem is the collection of such sets for all pixels P with a finite value of their corresponding polygon-size map $M_P(P) \neq \infty$. The goal is to find the selection of mutually disjoint sets from this collection with maximal cardinality.

Voronoi tiling is performed in a sequence of steps as follows. In the first step, the coverage map M_C is initialized to zero, the polygon-size map M_P is computed as described, and finally the resulting set Γ is initiated to an empty set. The solution is built in a sequence of constructive iterations. In each iteration, we first compute the set Λ of all points which are not covered and with finite polygon-size map values. Per iteration, a single pixel $P(x,y)$ is added to the final solution – the added pixel has the following properties:

– it belongs to the set $\lambda_1 \subset \Lambda$, where each pixel $Q \in \lambda_1$ has a smaller or equal polygon-size value with respect to all other pixels in Λ and
– it has the largest value among all pixels in λ_1 for the following objective:

$$g(P) = \begin{cases} \infty & , M_C(P) = 1 \\ \frac{|\theta_2(P)|}{\eta(P)} - |\theta_1(P)| & , M_C(P) = 0 \end{cases} . \tag{11}$$

Sets $\theta_1(P)$ and $\theta_2(P)$ are created as a collection of "clickable" pixels in the circular polygon centered at P with radius $M_P(P) + \varepsilon_2 + 1$ and a collection of yet uncovered "clickable" pixels in the ring of pixels centered at P and with outer radius $M_P(P) + 2\varepsilon_2$ and inner radius $M_P(P) + \varepsilon_2 + 1$ respectively. More formally, sets $\theta_1(P)$ and $\theta_2(P)$ are defined as follows:

$$\theta_1(P) = \{Q \in \mathcal{I} \mid w(Q) > 0 \ \wedge \tag{12}$$
$$\|Q - P\| \le M_P(P) + \varepsilon_2 + 1\}, \tag{13}$$
$$\theta_2(P) = \{Q \in \mathcal{I} \mid M_C(Q) = 0 \ \wedge w(Q) > 0 \ \wedge \tag{14}$$
$$M_P(P) + \varepsilon_2 + 1 < \|Q - P\| \le M_P(P) + 2\varepsilon_2\}. \tag{15}$$

The scalar ratio $\eta(P)$ quantifies the ratio of covered vs. total pixels in the above mentioned ring of pixels. Function $g(P)$ in Eqn.11 heuristically directs the search by enforcing intermediate solutions that have the following properties:

Least constraining – small number of "clickable" pixels in the circular polygon centered at P with radius $M_P(P) + \varepsilon_2 + 1$. By covering as few as possible "clickable" pixels with the selection of each Voronoi polygon, consequently the part of the image not yet covered with polygons, has as many as possible "clickable" pixels. This improves the likelihood for obtaining a better solution.

1-lookahead most constrained – the neighborhood of each selected polygon, i.e. the ring of pixels Q at distance $M_P(P) + \varepsilon_2 + 1 < \|Q - P\| \le M_P(P) + 2\varepsilon_2$ from P, proportional to its cardinality, should have as many as possible "clickable" pixels. Consequently, the likelihood that we find a better solution in the neighborhood of the current polygon, is improved.

After a pixel $P(x, y)$ is selected, all pixels $Q(x, y) \in \mathcal{I}$ at Euclidean distance $\|Q - P\| \le M_P(P) + M_P(Q)$ are marked as covered $M_C(Q) = 1$. The constructive iteration is repeated until all "clickable" pixels are covered or an additional polygon of minimal area cannot be added to Γ. The aggregated collection of pixels in Γ, defines the resulting Voronoi polygon tiling according to Def.9.

In summary, the problem behind Voronoi polygon tiling for maximized entropy of polygon selection can be modeled as SET PACKING – a task which is NP-complete. In order to generate effective solutions, we have derived a constructive heuristic with complexity linearly proportional to the number of "clickable" pixels in the considered image. In our experiments, the optimization of the Voronoi tiling resulted in an average 20% increase in the system entropy.

References

1. A. Adams et al. Users are not the enemy: Why users compromise computer security mechanisms and how to take remedial measures. *Comm. of the ACM*, Vol.42, no.12, pp.40–46, 1999.
2. W. Belgers. Unix password security.
   http://www.ja.net/CERT/Belgers/UNIX-password-security.html.
3. G. Blonder. Graphical passwords. United States Patent no.5559961, 1996.

4. S. Brostoff et al. Are passfaces more usable than passwords? *HCI*, 2000.
5. CVonline: Geometric Feature Extraction Methods.
    http://homepages.inf.ed.ac.uk/rbf/CVonline/feature.htm
6. D.C. Feldmeier et al. UNIX Password Security - Ten Years Later. *CRYPTO*, pp.44–63, 1989.
7. M.R. Garey and D.S. Johnson. Computers and Intractability. Freeman, 1979.
8. I. Jermyn et al. The design and analysis of graphical passwords. *USENIX Security Symposium*, pp.1–14, 1999.
9. D.V. Klein. Foiling the Cracker: A survey of, and Improvements to Password Security. *USENIX Security Workshop*, pp.5–14, 1990.
10. Passfaces. http://www.realuser.com
11. Password Portal. http://www.passwordportal.net/.
12. E.E. Schultz. Advanced Windows NT security: network security. *Computer Security J.*, Vol.15, no.3, pp.13–22, 1999.
13. J. Yan et al. The Memorability and Security of Passwords – Some Empirical Results. Tech. Report No.500, Computer Lab., University of Cambridge, 2000.

Cryptographically Enforced Personalized Role-Based Access Control

Milan Petković, Claudine Conrado, and Malik Hammoutène

Philips Research, Information & System Security
High Tech Campus 34 (MS 61), 5656 AE Eindhoven, The Netherlands
{milan.petkovic, claudine.conrado}@philips.com

Abstract. The present paper addresses privacy and security enhancements to a basic role-based access control system. The contribution is twofold. First, the paper presents an approach to personalized access control, i.e. a combination of role-based access control and user-managed access control. Second, the proposed access control approach is cryptographically enforced and an efficient key management method for the personalized role-based access control is described. The proposed solutions are discussed in the context of a system architecture for secure management of Electronic Health Records.

1 Introduction

Data security and privacy issues are traditionally important in the medical domain. However, recent developments such as digitization of medical records, the creation of national health record databases, and extramural applications in the personal health care domain, pose new challenges towards the protection of medical data. In contrast to other domains, such as financial, which can absorb the cost of the abuse of the system (e.g. credit card fraud), healthcare cannot. Once sensitive information about an individual's health problems is uncovered and social damage is done, there is no way to revoke the information or to restitute the individual.

In addition to this, the medical field has some other characteristics, such as data can be accessed only by authorized persons that are assigned a certain role (general practitioner, nurse, etc). To support such requirements, the access control system bases the access decisions on the role that a particular user is associated with. Access rights are grouped by roles so that an individual acting in a specific role may perform only particular sets of operations that are assigned to that role. This approach, called Role-Based Access Control (RBAC) [1], is very important in the healthcare domain, because in addition to practice where it is used, it is also addressed by legislation (e.g. the Health Insurance Portability and Accountability Act (HIPAA) [2]).

Another trend in the healthcare sector towards personal, user-focused healthcare demands more patient-involvement at all levels of healthcare. Patients are taking a more active role in their own healthcare management, which includes obtaining disease information, discussing with doctors, tracking symptoms and managing their illnesses. Consequently, patients are also more involved in keeping and managing important medical documents. This also has some backing in the legislation such as

Please use the following format when citing this chapter:

Author(s) [insert Last name, First-name initial(s)], 2006, in IFIP International Federation for Information Processing, Volume 201, Security and Privacy in Dynamic Environments, eds. Fischer-Hubner, S., Rannenberg, K., Yngstrom, L., Lindskog, S., (Boston: Springer), pp. [insert page numbers].

HIPAA [2] which gives patients more rights with respect to Electronic Health Records (EHRs)[1] [3]. For example, patients have the right to have more influence with respect to access control to their health records. Consequently, a patient could request additional restrictions on the disclosure of their records to certain individuals involved in his care that otherwise would be permitted (based on role-based access control governed by the care institution). If the care provider agrees with his request, it is required to comply and enforce the agreement. This poses additional requirements on access control. Namely, in addition to access based on roles, individual restrictions have to be taken into account. Furthermore, a patient should be able to allow his family or friends to access his personal record. Therefore, there is a clear need for a combination of role-based access control and user-managed access control, which is addressed in this paper as *personalized* role-based access control.

While access control mechanisms do play a crucial role in EHR security, they have also some limitations. One of these limitations, which is addressed in this paper, concerns the possibility of anyone bypassing the access control mechanism and having direct access via the file system to the EHR database where data is stored in plain text. A straightforward solution to this problem is to enhance access control with data encryption, providing in this way a "cryptographically-enforced" access control mechanism. This is an important feature since it also supports the secure *off-line* usage of EHR, when the data is no longer protected by the access control mechanism, thus increasing data availability. The problem of key management for access control has already been addressed in the literature. However, most of the approaches focus on hierarchical key management (see for example [4, 5]) and do not dynamically handle role-based access control policies which may include patient-defined policies. Therefore, this paper describes an efficient key management method within the context of a *cryptographically-enforced* personalized RBAC system.

The rest of the paper is organized as follows. The basic concept of personalized role-based access control is described in the next section. Section 3 enhances the security of the proposed access control method by enforcing it cryptographically. Furthermore, this section presents an efficient key management method in the context of the personalized RBAC. Section 4 presents the architecture of a secure EHR management system that deploys the proposed solutions. Finally, Section 5 draws conclusions.

2 Personalized Role-based Access Control

In a classical RBAC model, data access decisions are based on a user's role in the system. In the case of EHR, a user identified as a general practitioner (GP), for instance, may be able to see the data of his patients without restriction, as long as he stays within the scope of a GP's rights. It may occur, however, that a patient uses his rights given by legislation to deny access to a specific GP who has by default rights to

---

[1] According to the Healthcare Information and Management Systems Society, an Electronic Health Record (EHR) is "a secure, real-time, point-of-care, patient-centric information resource for clinicians". The EHR supports the decision-making process by providing access to patient health record information where and when needed.

access his data. A simple solution to this problem is to include this doctor in a "black list". To access the patient's record, the practitioner is checked if he belongs to the black list. However, this approach is not scalable considering the medical system with thousands of users and patients who may want to deny access to many of them. Moreover, some patients might deny access to all doctors except one. Therefore, to deal with this issue, an approach is proposed in this section that uses overriding policies, called personalized policies, and an exception list, where the rights and restrictions are re-defined per user and per concerned data.

The method proposed is based on two main components, namely, the policy repository and the exception list. The policy repository contains all policies in the system. Initially, it contains only *default* policies. A default policy defines default access rights for all existing roles in the system (e.g., general practitioner, emergency doctor, etc.). At this point, there is no patient influence on the definition of policies. When a patient wants to add some change to a default policy, an exception list is created. The exception list is defined as a list of all the users (care providers) that are in conflict with the policy which is applied. Typically, the exception list reflects patient's wishes by restricting or adding rights to any of the patient's pieces of data for each of the listed users. A piece of data is considered here as any subset of the EHR that may have its specific access rules.

When a patient creates an exception list, the system decides whether it is necessary or not to replace the default policy by a personalized policy. The idea is to keep the exception list as light as possible. If the same restrictions specified in the exception list concern the majority of the users, the default policy is overridden by a personalized policy. A personalized policy is a set of rules, an identifier for the rule-combining algorithm and (optionally) a set of obligations [6]. Rules, rule-combining algorithm and obligations are themselves combinations of resources, subject and actions that find their origin in a set of predefined atomic policy blocks. An atomic policy block is a logical unit defined as the smallest element in eXtensible Access Control Markup Language (XACML) [7] that is executed completely or not at all. By combining different atomic policy blocks we obtain complete personalized policies. When created, personalized policies are dominant over default policies. Moreover, the personalized policies themselves could be changed, as new restrictions or grants may be introduced, therefore these policies may be highly dynamic.

An example is given below for a patient P. The default atomic policy block in his case is that all GPs (A, B, C, D and E) can initially have access to the piece of his EHR data concerning sexual diseases (D_1). If patient P now wants to restrict access to D_1 to all GPs, except A, instead of listing B, C, D and E in the black list, the old default policy for data pieces D_1 is replaced by a personalized atomic policy block. This is now the policy which is default, so in order to allow GP A to access data piece D_1, an exception list is then created:

Default Atomic Policy Block: all GPs have access to D_1 of EHR of patient P
Personalized Atomic Policy Block: no GP has access to D_1 of EHR of patient P
Exception List: GP A: +D_1

The symbol "+" above indicates that the user (GP A) has granted rights on the concerned data (D_1). If the patient wants to do the same for data piece D_2, a corresponding personalized atomic policy block will replace the old one and the exception list will be extended with a new entry (+D$_2$).

With the policy repository and the exception list dynamically updated as above, when a user requests data of a given patient, the system must check the policy repository for that patient as well as whether an exception list exists which includes that user/data-object. In this way, patient-defined access policies may be handled more efficiently in the system. Instead of having up to n-1 entries in the list (where n is the total number of doctors), the exception list has now a maximum of n/2 entries.

When there is a change in the subject-role assignment (e.g. a new user is added as a member of a role) related to the patient-defined exception, the patient could be informed about this change. In this case, he must explicitly requests this action from the system.

To further optimize the solution, we can define several ways of grouping the patients. Indeed, most patients could have the same policies (probably the majority of them will not even use personalized policies, but only the default ones). Therefore, they can be joined based on their personalized policies and exception list, or only based on their personalized policies. Figure 1a shows an example where patients have the same personalized policies (that can be NULL), as well as the same exception lists. Figure 1b shows an example where patients have the same personalized policies, but different exception lists.

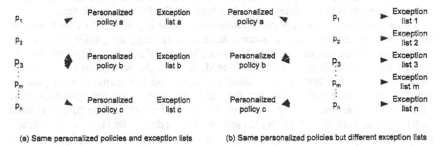

(a) Same personalized policies and exception lists   (b) Same personalized policies but different exception lists

Fig. 1. Different ways of grouping.

3 Cryptographic enforcement and efficient key management for Personalized RBAC

3.1 Cryptographically-protected EHR

In order to enhance the security of the proposed RBAC system and to allow the secure off-line usage of data, access to data is cryptographically enforced. This means that the EHR is encrypted at all times and data access is achieved via access to the decryption keys. More specifically, encryption of EHR is implemented by having a different key to encrypt each data piece. Access control can then be enforced by a key hierarchy scheme where the "data key" (the fixed and unique key that encrypts a piece of data) is encrypted by "access keys". Access keys may be, for instance, the public keys of the parties that are allowed access to the data. In this way, if these parties do change, only the key encrypting the data, and not the data itself, has to be re-encrypted with the new rightful parties' access keys. It is often the case that different pieces of data have the same access policies. In this case, the number of needed keys can be significantly reduced because different data pieces with the same access policy can be grouped and encrypted with the same data key. However, in case the access policy of one or more of these data pieces changes over time, they must be re-encrypted with different data keys.

In the proposed approach, the EHR of a patient is composed not only of the encrypted health data, but also of key material needed to decrypt the health data, i.e. the data keys encrypted with the authorized users' access keys. This is depicted in Figure 2 which shows an EHR record with two fields: a data field including the data encrypted with key *sym* and a key field including the encryptions of *sym* with the access keys *a*, *b*, and *c*. The data field is typically static, whereas the key field may be frequently updated, in accordance with the system access policies.

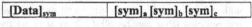

Fig. 2. An EHR record.

Given the structure above, when a user downloads any EHR to a portable device, he also downloads the encrypted data keys. Therefore, he is able to access the data if he has the *access keys* that decrypt the *data keys* that finally decrypt the data.

The access keys for an EHR record together with the key material enforce now the access policies for that record. Access keys may be, e.g., the public keys of the individuals who can access the data. However, because of the scalability problem, the role-based approach is more suitable. Indeed, defining the access keys as *role* keys greatly improves the system's efficiency by facilitating key management (typically there are much more individuals than the number of roles in a given system). On the other hand, the approach using role keys does not efficiently handle patient-defined restrictions, as defined in the previous section. This is due to the fact that individuals, and not only roles, must be addressable in this case. To support this requirement from the legislation as well as its efficient cryptographic enforcement, we propose an efficient key management scheme based on Broadcast Encryption.

3.2 Efficient key management

A Broadcast Encryption (BE) approach can be used to efficiently manage encryption keys in the cryptographically-enforced personalized RBAC (CEPRBAC) system. In brief, a BE scheme allows a dynamic group of entities to establish a common secret by receiving broadcasted messages sent by a central authority without the need for a return communication channel. In common schemes [8, 9], a binary tree is used to represent the entities and the key material. Each entity is assigned a leaf in the tree, and all nodes (and leaves) are associated with unique (secret) symmetric keys. Each entity knows all the symmetric keys on the path between its assigned leaf and the root of the tree, therefore the root key of the tree is known to all entities.

When the central authority wants to create a new group, it encrypts the information to be shared by group members (common secret) with keys in the tree that cover only those new group members. The encrypted value can then be safely broadcasted to the entire world, since only the intended group members will be able to decrypt it. This scheme works best when the selected entities cluster together under a tree's sub-tree. In this case, the common secret only needs to be encrypted under the key at the root of the sub-tree.

In the CEPRBAC system, the encrypted data is *not* broadcasted by a central authority, but it is stored in the EHR database accessible by all users. The central authority is a party in the healthcare organization responsible for applying the access control policies (it is part of the "control unit" discussed in Section 4). Therefore, what is relevant for our scheme from the BE approach is the fact that, while *all* users have access to the encrypted messages, these messages can *only* be decrypted by a (possibly changing) privileged subset of users.

The messages referred to above are simply the encrypted data keys that encrypt the pieces of data. The entities in the BE scheme are the individuals in the system who are able to access patient data (doctors, nurses, etc). According to the defined access policies (default or personalized), the central authority decides which individuals should learn which data keys. Therefore, it encrypts the data key for each data piece with keys in the tree that cover only the individuals with the right to access that piece of data. In this way, the encrypted data keys can be stored in the database to which *all* parties have access: only the parties that have the right to access a given piece of data will have the keys to decrypt the corresponding data key.

Regarding the construction of the broadcast tree, it can be built based on roles, in line with the RBAC approach. As depicted in Figure 3, there is a root node (to which a key K_{root} is associated) and, attached to the root node, all the role sub-trees (with associated node keys K_{R1}, K_{R2}, ..., K_{Rn}). Therefore, the leaf nodes are grouped based on individuals' roles that they represent. In order to address all individuals in a given role, the role key can be used. For instance, K_{Ri} can be used to encrypt a value to be accessible only to individuals in Role i. Note that *at the root* the tree is not necessarily binary. The binary construction is used in the role sub-trees.

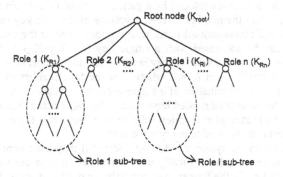

Fig. 3. Grouping nodes based on roles.

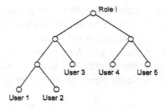

Fig. 4. An example tree for Role i.

Each role sub-tree accommodates in its leaves all the individual users in that particular role. In Figure 4, an example is shown with five users in Role i, so the sub-tree's last level is incomplete.

If there are no patient-defined policies, the system is simply a cryptographically-enforced RBAC in which the data keys are encrypted with the role keys (the keys K_{R1}, K_{R2}, etc). When a patient denies access to his data to a given user (e.g., User 4 in Figure 4), the corresponding data key must be re-encrypted with node keys in the tree that cover only the allowed users (keys K_{123} and K_5 in Figure 5). This is more efficient than having to encrypt the data key with the keys K_1, K_2, K_3 and K_5 of all allowed users.

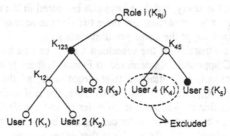

Fig. 5. Excluding a user.

When only a single user is excluded by a patient, there is a clear gain in efficiency in the system regarding the number of re-encryptions of the data key (and therefore the number of *stored* messages): all users who do not belong to the excluded user's largest sub-tree can be addressed with a single key (the key K_{123} in the example above). When more users are excluded, say m users, still the number of re-encryptions of the data key is smaller than $(n-m)$, where n is the total number of users in the system. For instance, the elimination of a single user from a role in a complete binary tree implies that the number of needed keys is of order log_2n rather than n. The worst possible case in the broadcast encryption scheme is in fact when the leaf keys of all non-excluded users must be used to encrypt the data key.

Some of the keys in the system need to be updated if they are compromised. The disclosure of an access key has typically much more serious consequences than the disclosure of a data key. In the former case, not only the disclosed access key needs to be updated, but also all data keys that are encrypted with that access key. This is especially troublesome when the access key is a role key. Then a large number of data keys will probably be involved as pure role-based policies are expected to be more common in the system.

3.3 Adding and deleting users

When a new user enters the system or a user leaves the system, the broadcast tree has to be updated. These two situations are discussed below.

When a new user enters the system, he is positioned in the tree according to his role (or roles) and his similarities concerning access rules with other users in the tree. For instance, if there is already in the tree a (first) user whose access rights are very similar to the right of the new user, a new level is added from the first user: his leaf becomes then an internal node from which two new leaves emerge, one assigned to the first user and the other to the new user. In case there are no users in the tree with any similarity to the new user, a new branch for the user is created from the root node (for a more detailed description see [10]). The new user must now learn his new (leaf) key and all the keys on his path to the root-node. Once the tree is updated, the database itself must be updated to take the new user parameters into account and the affected data keys must be encrypted with new access keys.

When a user leaves the system, his leaf in the tree is deleted and the sibling node must go one level up in the tree. Since the user knows all keys on his path to the root-node, all keys in that path must be renewed to ensure the system's security. To avoid involving a number of users in the node-key update process, the system can use smartcards for storing the access keys in a secure way. Then the user will not be able to learn the keys he possesses while using the system. In the case of leaving the system, the user is required to return the smartcard so that the keys are not compromised. Consequently, the tree could keep some free nodes reserved for new users.

3.4 Discussion: positioning users in the tree

The issue of how to position users in the leaves of the broadcast tree is an important one since an optimal positioning may give significant savings on the number of node keys necessary to address a certain group of users. In other words, key management can be made much more efficient if the keys which are higher in the tree are used as much as possible. Pure RBAC is a straightforward case, with an optimal tree that is simply based on roles.

For the role-based broadcast tree, however, additional regrouping may further optimise the system. It may be possible that the roles themselves are grouped together: if the roles are different but have similar access rights, they can be put under the same sub-tree (and therefore most often addressed with a single node key). This is the case, e.g., of anaesthesiologists and emergency doctors who may need to access very similar types of data. Furthermore, there are also degrees of freedom regarding the positioning of individuals within a role sub-tree. In case, e.g., personalized policies exist which are similar for a number of individuals within a role, these individuals may be also regrouped under the same sub-tree.

Another important issue concerning user positioning in the tree is the fact that some users may have multiple roles within the institution, which they may assume according to a daily-defined schedule (e.g., a user may be a GP one day and an Emergency Doctor (ED) the next day). For such users, as against the *single-role* users, the positioning in the tree requires more thought, as discussed below.

In order to handle multiple roles, a tree can be built still based on roles. After all single-role users have been assigned to leaves on their role sub-tree, multiple-role users can be assigned to leaves with use of extra information (e.g., the statistics of assignment of users to one or another role and users' similarities). Some cases are:

- If the user has *predominantly* a given role (e.g., he works mostly as a GP, but sometimes as an ED), then he is assigned to a leaf under the sub-tree of the predominant role.
- If the user has no predominant role, but normally his role schedule strongly *correlates* with that of a second user (e.g., very often they both work together as EDs), then he may be grouped together with that second user.
- If the user has no predominant role, and there are no role correlations with other users, then he may be assigned to a leaf under the sub-tree of any of the possible roles he may have.

Moreover, the addition of the multiple-role users to a role sub-tree is done preferably by keeping the single-role users (who have been allocated firstly) isolated as much as possible under some sub-tree.

Given above is a set of *guidelines* that can be used to build the broadcast tree when users may have multiple roles in the system. If enough new information is gained with the use of the system in time (e.g., information that help group together users with the same role at the same time), then it can be used to re-build the tree at any time.

4   An EHR Management System

This section places the above-proposed solutions in the architectural context of a system for secure management of EHR. First, the system components are described followed by a description of the general system architecture as well as the system dynamics. The two different usages of the system, on-line in a secure environment as well as off-line in an untrusted environment, are addressed.

4.1 System Components

The CEPRBAC system consists of five main components: the control unit, the EHR database, the trust center, the access device, and the repository of default and personalized policies.

The **control unit** is the core component of the system. It links the architecture components together performing two main tasks. First, it manages access to the data based on roles and personalized polices. Second, it identifies the users and handles their queries.

The **EHR database** is a collection of XML documents (each patient's EHR is considered by the system as an XML document). If the system security is based on data encryption, then the EHR database will actually store encrypted XML documents as well as "data keys" encrypted with "access keys", as defined in section 3.1. In addition, the EHR database will also provide an HL7 interface for data exchange.

The **trust center** is a trusted server that keeps sensitive information. It stores the important keys of the system. For key management the trusted center uses XML Key Management Specification (XKMS) [11], which defines a Web services interface to a public key infrastructure. The role of the Trust Center is twofold. First, it generates a public key pair for each user. The secret key is stored on the user smartcard and is used for identification and to sign data. Second, it stores all the necessary information to retrieve patients' data, including the symmetric keys used to protect the data.

The **access device** is a device that the user will use to view or update the EHR data. It could be an integral part of the system (the server depicted in Figure 6). However, it could be also a client device from which the data is accessed remotely. We assume compliance, especially for off-line scenarios where this device is used in an untrusted environment. With compliance we mean among the rest that device will not export in the clear the data or the keys which are used to decrypt EHR data.

The **repository of policies** stores default and personalized policies as well as exception lists. This component is not needed for the off-line use as the policies are stored together with the data in the form of encrypted data keys.

4.2 General Architecture

Having described the main components of the system, let us look at how they interoperate and support secure management of the EHR. Depending on the security context in which the system is used, the components can be differently combined and deployed. For example, in a secure environment of a hospital it might be decided to rely on traditional security mechanisms and not to encrypt the data. Let us look how the EHR could be managed in this case (Figure 6).

A user logs into the system using the user-name password procedure. Once the user is authenticated, the medical control unit consults the default policies as well as policies specific for this user and keeps them in memory (steps 1.1 to 1.4 in Figure 6).

From this point, the user can make two types of queries: writing or reading. "Writing" is used to add data and "reading" to view data. Deleting and updating data is strictly forbidden by the system. Those two actions have to be considered as particular kinds of writing: if a user wants to update or delete data, he enters new data with a comment explaining that the previous data is deprecated or not to be used any more. For each operation the user performs, the control unit checks first using the policies if the user is allowed to perform the operation based on the data provided in the query (operation, data piece and patient identifier). It checks which personalized policies are applicable (steps 2.2 – 2.3 in Figure 6) and if allowed performs the operation.

A patient can influence the personalized policies if he wishes to add or restrict rights to a specific user. However, the final approval of new policies comes from the administrator who checks if the new policy is compliant with the hospital policies. This is depicted in Figure 6 in steps 3.1 till 3.4.

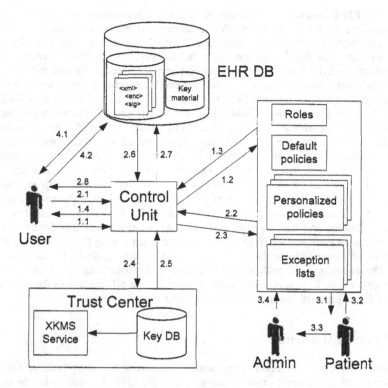

Fig. 6. Architecture of the EHR management system.

The hospital could also decide to enhance the security of a traditional access control mechanism using cryptography. If the data in the EHR database is encrypted that would prevent an attacker bypassing the access control mechanisms of being able to get the data in the clear. However, this will influence the architecture of the system in a way that the control unit will get additional responsibilities and the trusted center will start playing a role. For example, during the add operation, the control unit, in addition to consulting the policies, extracts also the metadata which is later used in the retrieval process. This metadata is stored in the trust center (steps 2.4 – 2.5 in Figure 6). Indeed, because the data is stored encrypted it furnish no information about its content, the system needs this metadata. To encrypt the data, a symmetric key is generated in the trusted center for each data piece. The data is encrypted with this key, signed with the creator's private (secret) key and together with patient ID, data piece ID and the creator ID stored in the database (steps 2.4 – 2.7).

The introduction of encryption and the method proposed in this paper, which actually builds in the data itself the data access policies, allows the off-line use of the portions or complete EHR database. The required parts of the database only have to be copied on a CD or portable device that will be used off-line. In this way an authorized user, such as a doctor visiting a patient or any of a group of emergency doctors in an ambulance car, will be able to access related EHRs offline. This can be accomplished by using a smartcard and a compliant software installed on a portable device without the complete hospital infrastructure (4.1 – 4.2 in Figure 6). This is a first step towards Digital Rights Management (DRM) functionality [12, 13] for the EHR management system.

5 Conclusions

This paper presents and discusses a system for personalized role-based access control that combines traditional role-based access control with user-managed access control. As required by legislation in the healthcare domain (e.g. HIPAA), the system allows a user to define individual access rights restrictions (or grants) on top of the default role-based policies. Furthermore, the proposed methods supports efficient evaluation of this combination in rum-time. This is achieved by means of dynamic revisions of personalized policies and exception lists that always list the minority of the users who are in conflict with the personalized policy.

Furthermore, security is enhanced by cryptographic enforcement of the proposed access control method. This prevents both an authorized insider as well as an attacker from outside to bypass the access control mechanism and have direct access to the EHR database where all data is in the clear[2]. Even more importantly, the proposed approach increases the data availability (the most important requirement in healthcare), supporting a simple offline usage of the data by incorporating access policies within the data. The paper discusses also important issues relating to key management, which appear in this approach, and proposes an efficient solution based on broadcast encryption. It is found that broadcast encryption is highly applicable to the method of personalized role-based access control proposed in this paper, not only in the healthcare domain, but in any domain that needs to cope with role-based access control and individual restrictions.

The work presented in this paper suggests some interesting directions for future research, which are discussed below.

An interesting and important issue already brought up in section 3.4, is how to arrange an optimal distribution of users in the broadcast tree given that similarities (other than role-based) may exist in the access rights of the users. These similarities may reflect patient-defined policies, for instance, but they may be also based on similarities and correlations between users if they have multiple roles.

A related topic to the construction of the tree concerns role hierarchy (role to sub-role relations), which this paper does not address. Therefore, an important question is how to map the role hierarchy on to the broadcast tree.

Furthermore, with the basic framework in place, it would be worthwhile to investigate if the proposed approach could be scaled up. That means, assuming the proposed framework would apply, e.g., to different health institutions within a

---

[2] Note that an insider has access to the EHR database and is authorized to view specific parts of it. However, he can bypass the database access control mechanisms and access all the data through the file system. The same holds for an attacker from outside who has managed to break into the system.

country, issues regarding the integration of such frameworks on a national level could be investigated.

Finally, the secure off-line usage of data requires the integration of functionality into the system which resembles that of DRM. This is an important direction for our future work.

Acknowledgements

We are grateful to our colleagues Joop Talstra, Toine Staring, Paul Koster, and Jordan Chong for fruitful discussions and valuable comments. Furthermore, we would like to thank the anonymous referees for their constructive remarks.

References

1. D.F. Ferraiolo and D.R. Kuhn "Role Based Access Control" 15th National Computer Security Conference, 1992.
2. The Health Insurance Portability and Accountability Act of 1996 (HIPAA), HIPAA Administrative Simplification - Regulations & Standards, http://www.cms.hhs.gov/hipaa/hipaa2/regulations/default.asp.
3. HIMSS Electronic Health Record Definitional Model Version 1.0, HIMSS Electronic Health Record Committee, http://www.himss.org/content/files/EHRAttributes.pdf.
4. Selim G. Akl and Peter D. Taylor, "Cryptographic solution to a problem of access control in a hierarchy", ACM Trans. Computer System, 1(3):239-248, 1983.
5. R. S. Sandhu. On some cryptographic solutions for access control in a tree hierarchy. In ACM '87: Proceedings of the 1987 Fall Joint Computer Conference on Exploring technology: today and tomorrow, IEEE Computer Society Press, pp: 405-410, 1987.
6. Organization for the Advancement of Structured Information Standards, http://www.oasis-open.org/home/index.php.
7. Tim Moses, eXtensible Access Control Markup Language (XACML) Version 2.03, http://docs.oasis-open.org/xacml/2.0/access_control-xacml-2.0-core-spec-os.pdf.
8. Kou, L., G. Markowsky, L.Berman, "A Fast Algorithm for Steiner Trees", Acta Informatica, Springer-Verlag, 1981: vol. 15, pp.141-145.
9. A Survey of Broadcast Encryption, Jeremy Horwitz, Manuscript, 2003, http://math.scu.edu/~jhorwitz/pubs/b5oadcast.pdf.
10. Malik Hammoutene, "Secure Management of Medical Data", EPFL Master Thesis Series, 2005.
11. W3C Recommendation, XML Key Management Specification (XKMS 2.0), http://www.w3.org/TR/xkms2/.
12. M. Petkovic, M. Hammoutène, C. Conrado and W. Jonker, "Securing Electronic Health Records using Digital Rights Management", In Proceedings of the 10th International Symposium for Health Information Management Research (iSHIMIR), Greece 2005.
13. C. Conrado, M. Petkovic, M. vd Veen, W. vd Velde, "Controlled Sharing of Personal Content using Digital Rights Management", In Security in Information Systems, Eduardo Fernandez-Medina, Julio Hernandez, Javier Garcia (Eds), 3rd International Workshop on Security in Information Systems (WOSIS), Miami, USA, 2005, pp. 173-185.

Using VO Concept for Managing Dynamic Security Associations

Yuri Demchenko, Leon Gommans, and Cees de Laat

[1] University of Amsterdam, System and Network Engineering Group
Kruislaan 403, NL-1098 SJ Amsterdam, The Netherlands
{demch, lgommans, delaat}@science.uva.nl

Abstract. This research paper presents results of the analysis how the Virtual Organisation (VO) concept can be used for managing dynamic security associations in collaborative applications and for complex resource provisioning. The paper provides an overview of the current practice in VO management at the organisational level and its support at the security middleware level in Grid based applications. The paper identifies open issues and basic requirements to the VO security functionality and services and suggests possible directions of further research and development, in particular, VO management concept, dynamic interdomain trust management for user-controlled applications, multi-domain policy decision and security context management. Proposed conceptual VO model addresses VO management issues and VO security services operation. The paper is based on experiences gained from the major Grid based and Grid oriented projects in collaborative applications and complex resource provisioning.

1 Introduction

Virtual Organisation (VO) and resource virtualisation are among the key concepts proposed in the Grid. According to the initial definition in one of the Grid foundational papers the "Anatomy of the Grid" [1], "Grid systems and applications aim to integrate, virtualise, and manage resources and services within distributed, heterogeneous, dynamic "virtual organizations".

The more detailed Grid definition includes such main components as distributed infrastructure, dynamics, virtualisation, and user-defined security – the components that provide a framework for coordinated collaborative resource sharing in dynamic, multi-institutional virtual organizations [1, 2].

Resources and services virtualisation together with provisioning are two major concepts in the Open Grid Services Architecture (OGSA) [3]. OGSA Security is built around VO concept and targeted for the security policies enforcement within a VO as an association of users and resources. VO provides a framework for inter-organisational and inter-domain trust managements. VO allows overcoming the problem of accessing by external users the enterprise internal network without affecting integrity of the enterprise security perimeter protected by the firewall. VO may run own security services, e.g. credential validation service, trust service,

Please use the following format when citing this chapter:

Author(s) [insert Last name, First-name initial(s)], 2006, in IFIP International Federation for Information Processing, Volume 201, Security and Privacy in Dynamic Environments, eds. Fischer-Hubner, S., Rannenberg, K., Yngstrom, L., Lindskog, S., (Boston: Springer), pp. [insert page numbers].

authorisation service, and attributes service but still many other services will remain in member domains and their authority needs to be translated into VO domain through established trust relations and shared semantics.

Although presenting a basic approach to understanding security services interaction in virtualised Grid environment, the VO definition in OGSA needs to be extended with more conceptual model and basic operational models required to support such typical use cases like project based collaboration, members' resource sharing or dynamic provisioning of complex multidomain distributed resources in general.

Current VO concept and existing practice lack a common theoretical foundation and as a result cause different understanding of the VO concept and functionality by different groups of potential adopters and users.

This is the goal of this work to contribute to further development of the VO conceptual model and its application to typical collaborative applications and complex resource provisioning in open service oriented environment.

The paper is organized as follows: Section 2 presents typical use cases for collaborative resource sharing and complex resources provisioning and defines required basic VO functionality to provide dynamic security associations for secure resource access and sharing. Section 3 provides an overview and critical analysis of current VO usage practice in major Grid related projects. Section 4 attempts to approach the VO definition and use for managing dynamic security association in collaborative applications and dynamic resource provisioning from the conceptual point of view. It defines basic dynamic security associations of which the VO is currently used for the project oriented resource sharing and collaboration. Different VO operational models are suggested to reflect the specifics of typical use cases.

Section 5 attempts to formalise the conceptual VO model and define basic VO security services. Suggestions are given how the conceptual VO model maps to the related security services in current Grid middleware implementations. This section is actually based on the initial research about the VO functionality and identity management in [4] and intends to contribute to further VO concept development based on the OGSA VO definition [3].

The proposed approach and solutions are being developed to respond to both common and specific requirements in the Collaboratory.nl (CNL)[1] and GigaPort Research on Network (GigaPort-RoN)[2] projects and are based on current experience in the EGEE[3] and LCG2[4] projects. The analysis and proposed conceptual model can also be used for other use cases that require creation of dynamic security association or inter-organisational trust management and may also provide a basis for further development of the VO management services and tools. Implementation suggestions are provided for the Optical Light Path Provisioning (OLPP) [5] and Open Collaborative Environment (OCE) [6] and intended integration with the AAA Authorisation Framework [7, 8].

---

[1] http://www.collaboratory.nl/.
[2] http://ron.gigaport.nl/.
[3] http://public.eu-egee.org/.
[4] http://lcg.web.cern.ch/LCG/.

2   Collaboration and complex resource provisioning and required VO functionality

Basic VO security services and functionality discussed in this section are defined based on two major use cases that benefit from using core Grid middleware services and infrastructure: to access complex experimental equipment in OCE and network facilities in OLPP.

Effective use of advanced and unique experimental equipment for research and for production work requires complex infrastructure and the collaboration of many specialists that may be distributed and span multiple organisations. Computer Grids and Web Services technologies provide a relevant platform for building a virtual collaborative environment.

Typical OCE use cases require that the collaborative environment:
- is dynamic since the environment can potentially change from one experiment to another,
- may span multiple trust domains,
- can handle different user identities and attributes/privileges that must comply with different policies (both experiment and task specific).

Security services are an important component of Grid based collaborative infrastructure to provide a reliable and secure operational environment that is capable of managing customers' and providers' resources. Collaborative applications require a sophisticated, multi-dimensional security infrastructure that manages secure operation of user applications between multiple administrative and trust domains associated with the particular experiment.

Proposed in [6] the Job-centric security model uses the Job description as a semantic document, created on the basis of a signed order (or business agreement). The document contains all the information required to run the analysis, including allocated resources, assigned users and roles, and a trust/security anchor(s) in the form of the resource and additionally the customer's digital signature. In general, such approach allows binding security services and policies to a particular job and/or resource and provides customer-controlled security environment with the job security context defined by a user/subject (i.e., their identity or secure credentials).

Job-centric security model is logically integrated with other stages and components of the collaborative (virtual) organisation managing the experiment stages. These stages include the initial stage of order creation and the main experimental stage that requires secure access to the instrument or resource.

OLPP is another important component of the distributed collaborative environment when dedicated high-speed communication channels are required for the experiment that may last from few hours to few months. OLPP provides an effective business model with current widely deployed optical network and dark optical cables. Further in the paper the OLPP use case will be also referred to as a complex resource provisioning as a more general definition.

OLPP and complex resource provisioning in general require creation of dynamic user-controlled resource allocation that may span multiple administrative and security domains. In comparison to the Job-centric security model where trust relations and consequently security associations are defined by an Agreement shared by all cooperating members, in OLPP user/customer may have agreement and consequently trust relations with only one, usually home, network provider. However, the provisional model must ensure that finally provisioned lightpath is securely associated with the user credentials or identity.

Typically provisioning process comprises of 4 steps: resource lookup, complex resource composition (including options), reservation of individual resources and their association with the reservation ID/ticket, and finally provisioning or delivery. Reservation ID/ticket created at the reservation stage actually defines a security association between user/customer and service provider(s) that will exist for all period when the complex resource is used. It is logically to suggest that the (dynamic) VO model can be used here for creating and managing dynamic security association.

In both cases, the VO model and framework are suggested as a relevant approach to provide the following security functionality for the dynamic collaboration and service provisioning:

1. Dynamic trust management - VO as a security association created dynamically at the reservation/negotiation stage will provide a security context for other security operations such as Authentication (AuthN) and Authorisation (AuthZ) and also for general session management.
2. Attributes and metadata resolution and mapping - correct policy evaluation and combination in multidomain scenario requires either use of common attributes and metadata format and namespace or mapping between used formats. Actual attribute and metadata mapping can be provided by authoritative/trusted Identity Providers (IdP) and/or Attribute services belonging to the VO or VO trust domain.
3. Policy combination and aggregation – VO can provide a framework for the multiple policies combination that may be defined and managed by the VO common or federated/associated policy. This may be especially important when individual policies may have potential conflicts at different levels and in different domains; in this case the VO association policy should defined how these conflicts can be resolved.

3   Virtual Organisations in Grid Applications

3.1   VO Management Practice in EGEE and LCG projects

In Grid applications and projects, VO is used as a framework for establishing project related resource sharing. The Grid Resource Centers (GRC) contribute some of their resources to the VO. Access to these shared distributed resources is provided based on the VO membership and other VO-related attributes like groups and roles.

Current VO management practice in LCG and EGEE projects provides a good example of the instant implementation of the VO concept. They have well-defined VO registration procedure, basic Security Policy, and simple Acceptable Use Policy (that relies on more detailed local VO member policies). Major VO membership management tool is the VO Membership Service (VOMS) that provides VO-defined attributes for authorisation and also supports user registration procedure.

The VO management framework in LCG/EGEE is defined by two main documents the Virtual Organisation Registration Procedure [9] and the LCG/EGEE Virtual Organisation Security Policy [10]. The first document lists the necessary steps and decisions a Virtual Organisation (VO) should take in order to get registered, configured and integrated in the LCG/EGEE infrastructure.

The Virtual Organisation Security Policy document defines a set of responsibilities placed on the members of the VO and the VO as a whole through its managers. It aims to ensure that all Grid participants have sufficient information to properly fulfil their roles with respect to interactions with a VO, including VO Acceptable Use Policy, contact information for responsible people and URL of one or more VO Membership Servers.

3.2 VO support in Grid middleware

Widely used in Grid applications the Virtual Organization Membership Service (VOMS) was initially proposed in the framework of the EU project EDG, and currently it is being developed in the framework of the EGEE project [11, 12]. VOMS goal is to solve the problem of granting users authorization to access the resources at VO level, providing support for group membership, roles and capabilities.

In VOMS design, a VO is represented as a complex, hierarchical structure with groups and subgroups [11] what is required to clearly separate VO users according to their tasks and home institutions. From the administrative point of view, management of each group can be independently delegated to different administrators. In general a user can be a member of any number of groups contained in the VO hierarchy.

Every user in a VO is characterized by the set of attributes defining their group membership, roles and capabilities in the scope of the VO that can be expressed in a form of 3-tuples (group, role, capability). The combination of all 3-tuple values forms a unique attribute, the so-called "Fully Qualified Attribute Name" (FQAN) [12]. This user related FQAN is included into VOMS Attribute Certificate based on X.509 Attribute Certificate for authorisation [13].

The VOMS system supports user requests for attributes with user server and client, and administrative tasks on VO management with administrative server and client [11]: VOMS infrastructure suggests that VO may have few VOMS servers with synchronised membership databases, but one VOMS server can serve multiple VO's. Central membership database maintained by a VO must contain information about all registered VO members.

3.3 GridShib profile for VO attributes management

GridShib is an ongoing project that intends to integrate the Globus Alliance's Globus Toolkit[5] (GT) security infrastructure and widely used among university federations the Shibboleth[6] Attribute Authority service (SAAS) to form a robust attribute infrastructure for campus environments to enable secure verification of user attributes for inter-institutional Grid users and also allow participants in multi-organizational collaborations to control the attribute information that they want to publish, share, and reveal to other parties through the user-controlled attribute release policy [14].

---

[5] Globus Toolkit. - http://www.globus.org/toolkit/.
[6] Shibboleth Project. - http://shibboleth.internet2.edu/.

GridShib will enable Web Services access to Shibboleth services by using GT4 application integration tools. This will allow Shibboleth's use for non-web-based applications. GridShib will support two basic attributes handling models in which attributes are requested by the resource (attribute pull) or obtained by the requestor prior to the request (attribute push) and bound to the real requestor identity. Two additional attribute handling models will allow attribute binding to the requestor's pseudonymous identity or to an anonymous account. In both cases SAAS will provide a mechanism for the privacy enhancement in attribute handling.

4   VO and Dynamic Security Associations

This section attempts to review current VO concept and understand how the VO as an abstract concept and as a practical implementation can be used for federated and/or dynamic trust management. In other words, we will discuss relations between VO and dynamic security associations, i.e. which part of the VO organisation and operation is static (like Certification Authority (CA) or Attribute Authority Service (AAS)) and which can support dynamic associations (and dynamic trust management).

First of all we need to clarify one of widely used misunderstanding between VO as a virtual entity and dynamic processes and associations. To do it consistently we need to look at different types of security associations and their dynamics (or lifetime characteristics). In relation to this we can propose the following classification:

– **Session** – establishes security context in the form of session key that can be a security token or simple UID bound to secure credential or session ticket. Session may associate/federate users, resources and actions/processes.

– **Job/workflow** – this may be more long-lived association and include few sessions. Job or workflow is built around specific task that is defined either by contract to perform some work or deliver product, or business process unit that also deliver some service and provides orchestration of many other processes. They may need to associate more distributed collection of users and resources for longer time required to deliver a final product or service. Job and workflow may contain decision points that switch alternative flows/processes. Security context may change during workflow execution or Job lifetime. Job description, as it is used in the Job-centric security model [6], may contain both user and resource lists, and also provide trust anchor(s) (TA) and specify security policy. Job TA is derived from the requestor and the service trust relations established on the base of the contract to perform a specific job. Workflow TA can be implicitly derived from the parent process.

– **Project or mission oriented cooperation** – this type of association is established for long time cooperation (involving people and resources) to do some research, development or production but it still has well-defined goals and area of activity and often criteria of mission fulfillment. This is actually the area of currently existing VO based associations.

– **Inter-organisational association or federation** – this type of association is built on long-term (often indefinite) cooperation agreements and may have a wide scope of cooperative areas. This is the area of inter-university associations which example is the Shibboleth based InCommon[7] federation.

Proposed above classification allows to assume that all identified types of associations will have its place and use in the future responding to different goals and tasks. Another suggestion that can be made from the above discussion in the context of user controlled service provisioning (UCSP) is that Job-centric/VO-based associations may scale to each other and consequently use each other's technical infrastructure and tools by adopting the dynamics to their specific tasks.

Further analysis intends to identify possible VO operational models depending on major service provisioning use cases that require dynamic security associations.

VO creation is normally initiated by one of organisational or business/project entity and has a specific goal and mission. VO can be created for the project based collaboration, members' resource sharing or dynamic provisioning of complex multidomain distributed resources in general. VO concept can be also used for general purpose user associations.

VO attribute or membership service is used for trusted attributes brokering between (member) organisations when requesting resources or services from the VO members or their associates. However, VO operation will differ depending on what are the VO associated members and how the VO membership service is used in VO related activities or services.

In this context three basic and one additional VO operational models can be defined:

– **User-centric VO (VO-U)** that manages user federation and provides VO related attribute assertions based on user (client) identity/credentials.
– **Resource/Provider centric VO (VO-R)** that supports provider federation and allows SSO/access control decision sharing between resource providers.
– **Agent centric VO (VO-A)** that provides a context for inter-domain agents operation, which process a request on behalf of the user and provide required trust context to interaction with the resource or service.
– **Project centric VO (VO-G)** that combines User centric and Provider centric features what actually corresponds to current VO use in Grid projects.

Although in different applications and use cases VO operations will differ in sense of providing primary association of users, resource providers or services providers the VO management infrastructure will require the same basic set of services. The above classification should help to understand how basic security services will operate in each of the different types of VO.

User-centric VO-U manages user federation and provides attribute assertions on user (client) request. For this purpose, VO-U maintains AAS that receives requests from user clients and provides VO member attribute certificates or other type of attribute assertion. AAS can also validate user credentials on request from services. However, this is the user who presents attribute credentials to the service in order to obtain access control permission. VO AAS is the central service for this type of VO. This can be considered as current operational model for the VOMS in Grid application. GridShib profile will allow decentralisation of attributes management and also user-controlled attributes release.

---

[7] http://www.incommonfederation.org/

Resource/Provider centric VO-R supports provider federation and allows Single-Sign-On (SSO) and access control decision sharing between VO members, i.e. resource providers. In this respect, VO-R may run own VO-wide AuthN and AuthZ services and correspondently VO-wide access control policy. It is logically that all services in the VO-R association can accept the VO AuthZ service decision once issued for the user on their request.

Agent centric VO-A provides a context for inter-domain agent operation. In this VO model the agent acts as a representative and a broker of the trust and other services for the specific domain. Agents are considered more independent in the VO-A than users or providers in other models VO-U and VO-R. Agents may have central attribute or certificate service but, in more specific for the VO-A model case, they will maintain mutual trust relations (which initial establishment for the time being is out of scope for this study).

Project centric VO-G (as originated from Grid projects) can be introduced to reflect typical use case when a VO is established to support user cooperation in the framework of the long-running project and to overcome existing/legacy organisational boundaries. VO-G associates both users and resources and actually combines two identified earlier models VO-U and VO-R. It maintains central VO membership/attribute service and may run also VO-wide security services such as AuthN/IdP/SSO and AuthZ.

There may not be clear difference in real life VO implementations to which operational model they adhere but proposed abstraction will help to more flexibly design supporting middleware security services. For example, it can be suggested that current VOMS based VO in Grid will evolve from currently used VO-U model to more appropriate VO-G model.

The major motivation behind defining basic VO operation models is to define possible profiles for the VO security services as well as suggested gateway services to interact with other infrastructural components.

Benefit of using VO based trust and attribute management/brokering is that VO can be created and used as a dynamic association for wide range of duration given the VO as a concept that can potentially combine virtualisation and dynamic.

5 Conceptual VO model

5.1 VO Management Framework

VO is defined in OGSA as a key concept for operation and managing Grid services [3, 4]. VO supplies a context to associate users, resources, policies and agreements when making and processing requests for services related to a particular VO.

VO management service should provide the following functionality: a) registration and association of users and groups with the VO; b) management of user roles; c) association of services with the VO; d) associating agreements and policies with the VO and its component services. They should support the VO operation during the whole VO lifecycle including creation, operation and termination stages. Depending on implementation the VO management service can be centralized or distributed relying on related services in member organisations.

Implementing and using VO concept requires a mechanism to reference the VO context and associate it with the user request. VO membership service (VOMS*) contains authoritative information about the entities and services associate with the VO, or VO's associated with the particular entity or user. Prior to VO creation there must be a formal agreement established between the VO members. In this way, VO follows the same procedure as real organisation and in case of business oriented VO this stage may require relevant legal basis for establishing and operating such a VO. WS-Agreement [15], WS-Trust [16], WS-Policy [17], and WS-Federation [18] can provide the initial technological platform for dynamic VO creation.

In order to securely process requests that traverse between members of a VO, it is necessary for the member organisations to have established trust relations. These trust relations may be direct or mutual, or established via intermediaries like VO Trust Management Service.

In wider VO and Grid infrastructure there may be a need to establish a VO Registry service that will provide a VO reference/ID registration and resolution and can also keep VOMS public credentials. Current LCG/EGEE VO naming and registration procedure [9] actually allows using DNSSEC [19] for populating VO together with its public key that can be used for initial trusted introduction of the VO and secure session request by the requestor.

5.2 VO Security Services and Operation

VO can be established according to a well-defined procedure and based on common agreement between member organisations to commit their resources to the VO and adhere common policy that may be simple enough but not to contradict to the local security policies at member institution. And opposite, if some specific enforcement is required by a specific VO, it should be also supported by local policies. Otherwise VO should provide direct individual membership for users which home organisation (HO) credentials can not be used or not trusted.

VO establishes own virtual administrative and security domains that may be completely separate or simply bridge VO members' security domains. This is required to enable secure service invocations across VO security domain but also requires coordination with the security policies in member organisations.

The following security services and related functionalities are required for the VO:
1. Identity Management Service, normally provided by the Identity Provider (IdP), provides federated identity assertions for users or resources.
2. Attribute Authority (AAS, e.g. VOMS) that issues attributes bound to user or resource identity that primary can be used for authorization decision when accessing VO resources or services.
3. Authorization service to enforce access control to the resource or service based on entity's attributes/roles and authorisation policies.
4. Policy Authority to provide VO-wide policies related to authorisation, trust management, identity federation, mapping of identities, attributes and policies
5. Trust management service that may include CA and associate PKI management services, and Security Token Services as defined by WS-trust. VO Agreement provides initial base for building trust relation inside VO.

VO can also have other services, which are important for it's functioning such as logging, accounting, auditing/non-repudiation, etc. Physically, all VO services may be provided by member organisations on behalf of the VO and be distributed. In case of distributed VO membership or Attribute service, mapping between user/requestor local identities and attributes can be provided either by IdP or AAS.

Figure 1 illustrates relationship between Virtual Organisation X and two member organisations A and B, which can be either real or virtual. VO X has been created to perform some task or provide some service(s) for designated group of users that constitute VO user community. VO established its own administrative and trust domain. Some of the users of organisations A and B may become the members of the virtual organisation; some of the services provided by member organisations may become VO services. Based on their VO identity or attributes, the VO users and services can interact in the trusted manner using VO security services.

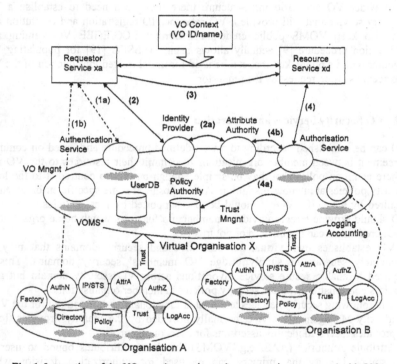

Fig. 1. Interaction of the VO security services when processing a request inside VO.

The picture shows basic services representing VO security infrastructure that provides reliable, secure and accountable VO operation, and illustrates in details how the request from the service xa (that actually represents service Aa from the member organisation A) to the service xd (representing service Bb from the member organisation B) is handled using VO context. To become an active entity in the VO, a service or user must authenticate themselves to the VO AuthN Service (step 1a) or present AuthN assertion from the requestor home organisation A (step 1b). Then, the requestor service requests a security token from the Identity service (step 2), this step may also include obtaining specific attributes for the service xd from the Attribute Authority (step 2a). Now the security token together with the obtained attributes may be presented to the target service xd (step 3). It's suggested that the resource will trust security credentials issued by the VO's Identity service and presented in the request, otherwise it may request their confirmation by the issuer. Before granting or denying access, the resource may request VO Authorisation service to evaluate user request and presented credentials against access control policy that may be obtained from the Policy Authority (steps 4, 4a, 4b).

6   Conclusion and Summary

The results presented in this paper are a part of ongoing research and development of the generic AAA Authorisation framework in application to user controlled resource provisioning and collaborative resource sharing conducted by the System and Network Engineering Group (SNEG) in the framework of different EU and nationally funded projects including EGEE, NextGRID, Collaboratory.nl, and GigaPort Research on Network. All of these projects are dealing with the development, deployment or use of the Grid technologies and middleware.

The particular focus in this research paper is how the Virtual Organisation (VO) concept can be used for managing dynamic security associations in collaborative applications and for complex resource provisioning in general.

The paper provides extended overview of the current practice with the VO management at the organisational level and its support at the Grid security middleware level. It identifies open issues and basic requirements to the VO security functionality and services and discusses possible areas of research and development, in particular, related to the VO management concept, dynamic interdomain trust management for user-controlled applications, user identity and attributes management.

Based on proposed VO definition as a framework for managing dynamic security associations of users and resources in service oriented environment, the paper identifies a few basic VO operations models depending on what is the VO primary goal to associate users, resources, or agents as active business intermediaries.

Proposed conceptual VO model addresses VO management issues and VO security services operation and can be used as a conceptual basis for developing VO management tools to support required creation, management and termination of dynamic security associations.

The authors believe that the proposed approach and ideas will provide a good basis for further wider discussion how the VO concept can be developed to provide a more flexible framework for identity and attributes management in dynamic task oriented virtual associations. There is also an intention to contribute this work to the Global Grid Forum standardisation process as a practical input from such application areas as complex resource provisioning and collaborative resource sharing.

References

1. Foster, I., Kesselman, C. and Tuecke, S. The Anatomy of the Grid: Enabling Scalable Virtual Organizations. International Journal of Supercomputer Applications, 15 (3). 200-222. 2001.
2. Foster, I., Kesselman, C., Nick, J. and Tuecke, S. The Physiology of the Grid: An Open Grid Services Architecture for Distributed Systems Integration. Globus Project, 2002. www.globus.org/research/papers/ogsa.pdf.
3. The Open Grid Services Architecture, Version 1.0 – 29 January 2005. - - http://www.gridforum.org/documents/GFD.30.pdf
4. Demchenko Yu. Virtual Organisations in Computer Grids and Identity Management. – Elsevier Information Security Technical Report - Volume 9, Issue 1, January-March 2004, Pages 59-76.
5. B.Oudenaarde, et al. "Grid Network Services: Lessons and proposed solutions from Super Computing 2004 demonstration", GGF Draft. - https://forge.gridforum.org/projects/ghpn-rg/document/Grid_Network_Services_in_the_SC04_Demonstrator/en/1
6. Job-centric Security model for Open Collaborative Environment, by Yuri Demchenko, Leon Gommans, Cees de Laat, Bas Oudenaarde, Andrew Tokmakoff, Martin Snijders. - Proceedings 2005 International Simposium on Collaborative Technologies and Systems (CTS2005). - May 15-19, 2005, Saint Louis, USA. - IEEE Computer Society, ISBN: 0-7695-2387-0. - Pp. 69-77.
7. RFC 2903, Experimental, "Generic AAA Architecture",. de Laat, G. Gross, L. Gommans, J. Vollbrecht, D. Spence, August 2000 - ftp://ftp.isi.edu/in-notes/rfc2903.txt
8. RFC 2904, Informational, "AAA Authorization Framework" J. Vollbrecht, P. Calhoun, S. Farrell, L. Gommans, G. Gross, B. de Bruijn, C. de Laat, M. Holdrege, D. Spence, August 2000 - ftp://ftp.isi.edu/in-notes/rfc2904.txt
9. Virtual Organisation Registration Procedure. By Maria Dimou, Ian Neilson. - https://edms.cern.ch/document/503245/
10. LCG/EGEE Virtual Organisation Security Policy. Version 1.1, by Ian Neilson - https://edms.cern.ch/document/573348/
11. Virtual Organization Membership Service (VOMS) project homepage - http://infnforge.cnaf.infn.it/voms/
12. VOMS Attribute Certificate for Authorisation. - http://infnforge.cnaf.infn.it/voms/AC-RFC.pdf
13. RFC 3281, Standard Track, "An Internet Attribute Certificate Profile for Authorization" S. Farrell, R. Housley, April 2002 - http://www.ietf.org/rfc/rfc3281.txt
14. GridShib - A Policy Controlled Attribute Framework - http://grid.ncsa.uiuc.edu/GridShib/
15. Andrieux, A. et al, "Web Services Agreement Specification (WS-Agreement)," August 2004, available from https://forge.gridforum.org/projects/graap-wg/document/WS-AgreementSpecification/
16. Web Services Trust Language (WS-Trust) - ftp://www6.software.ibm.com/software/developer/library/ws-trust.pdf
17. Web Services Policy Framework (WS-Policy). Version 1.1. - http://msdn.microsoft.com/ws/2002/12/Policy/
18. Web Services Federation Language (WS-Federation) Version 1.0 - July 8 2003 – http://msdn.microsoft.com/ws/2003/07/ws-federation/
19. R. Arends, R. Austein, M. Larson, D. Massey, S. Rose, "Resource Records for the DNS Security Extensions", RFC4034. - http://www.rfc-archive.org/getrfc.php?rfc=4034

Secure Fast Handover in an Open Broadband Access Network using Kerberos-style Tickets

Martin Gilje Jaatun[1], Inger Anne Tøndel[1], Frédéric Paint[2], Tor Hjalmar Johannessen[2], John Charles Francis[3], and Claire Duranton[4]

[1] SINTEF ICT, Trondheim, Norway
[2] Telenor R&D, Fornebu, Norway
[3] Swisscom Innovations, Bern, Switzerland
[4] France Telecom R&D, Issy-les-Moulineaux, France
Martin.G.Jaatun@sintef.no

Abstract. In an Open Broadband Access Network consisting of multiple Internet Service Providers, delay due to multi-hop processing of authentication credentials is a major obstacle to fast handover between access points, effectively preventing delay-sensitive interactive applications such as Voice over IP. By exploiting existing trust relationships between service providers and access points, it is possible to pre-authenticate a mobile terminal to an access point, creating a Kerberos-style ticket that can be evaluated locally. The terminal can thus perform a handover and be authenticated to the new access point, without incurring communication and processing delays by involving other servers.

1 Introduction

The Open Broadband Access Network (OBAN) [1] seeks to utilise excess capacity available in residential broadband connections, by opening up private wireless access points to passers-by. It is intended as a multi-ISP network, where a roaming OBAN user may consume mobile IP services from residential wireless access points regardless of whether or not he has a contract with the same ISP as the residential user. In addition to serving as a lower-cost, higher-bandwidth alternative to services such as UMTS [2] or WiMAX [3], OBAN also intends to incorporate multi-lateral roaming agreements [4] towards such services, in effect creating a ubiquitous, world-wide network. A more detailed description of the OBAN concept can be found in [5] and [6].

1.1 Problem Definition

The ISP that the OBAN user has a subscription with is known as the OBAN Service Provider (OSP), while the ISP of the residential user (and access point) is known as ISP_{RU}. When the OBAN user wishes to use a residential network connected to an ISP_{RU} that is different from his/her own, the AAA[1] server of ISP_{RU} must act as a proxy toward a AAA server in the OSP's domain, since only the OSP can verify the OBAN user's credentials. However, this creates a problem with respect to executing

---

[1] "Triple-A": Authentication, Authorisation and Accounting - e.g. RADIUS [7].

Please use the following format when citing this chapter:

Author(s) [insert Last name, First-name initial(s)], 2006, in IFIP International Federation for Information Processing, Volume 201, Security and Privacy in Dynamic Environments, eds. Fischer-Hubner, S., Rannenberg, K., Yngstrom, L., Lindskog, S., (Boston: Springer), pp. [insert page numbers].

the handover fast enough for the user to experience a seamless service [4]: Since the authentication protocol requires multiple round trips between several servers that potentially are situated physically far from each other, communication delays alone make it impossible to meet the requirement of a maximum handover latency of 120 ms [2].

1.2 Tickets to the Rescue

While a full authentication at every handover thus is unacceptably slow, the residential users and ISPs are unlikely to be enthusiastic about letting strangers with whom they have no prior trust relationship avail themselves of their networking resources without any form of access control. In order to solve this conundrum, we have to make use of trust relations that are already in place.

In a typical AAA configuration, the AAA server needs to be in possession of a shared secret with the 802.1X [9] authenticator; among other reasons in order to be able to securely communicate the session key that has been established as part of the authentication process between terminal and AAA server. This shared secret can be exploited to create a Kerberos-style ticket [10] that can be used to authenticate a terminal during handover, without on-line involvement of the OSP AAA server. The ticket will in effect represent a dynamic trust relationship between the terminal and the access point. Note that in contrast with the solution suggested in [11], the use of a Kerberos ticket does not require a mobile user to have visited the access point previously, nor does it require a trust relationship between access points.

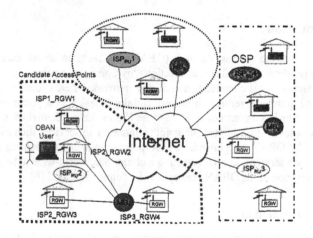

Fig. 1. An OBAN network with 3 Mobility Brokers.

---

[2] 120 ms is chosen as a conservative threshold for interactive applications such as Voice over IP, although computer networking textbooks such as [8] state that delays can be up to 150 ms without being perceived by a human listener.

2   Fundamental Components

Our solution to the fast handover problem requires some components that are briefly described in the following.

2.1   Residential Gateway

The most important hardware component of the OBAN network is the Residential Gateway (RGW), which among other things contains a RADIUS server. This RADIUS server will be responsible for verifying the Kerberos tickets, but will in all other respects act as a proxy toward the Mobility Broker (MB – see below). The RGW is placed as a gateway between the wireless access point and the fixed broadband connection.

The 802.1X authenticator in the wireless access point must be configured in pass-through mode, with the embedded RADIUS server in the RGW as Authenticaton Server.

For simplicity, the term RGW may be in the following be interpreted as "RGW and access point".

2.2   Full Authentication

When a terminal first joins the OBAN network (i.e. when it is switched on), an OBAN user will not find it unreasonable that the connection process takes a fairly substantial amount of time; this is already the case when you turn on a GSM phone upon arriving in a new country.

Due to the desire to enable interoperability between OBAN and existing wireless communication networks, EAP-SIM [12] has been chosen as the full authenticaton method in OBAN. However, any EAP method that conforms to [13] could in theory be used.

2.3   Pre-authentication

A Kerberos ticket can be seen as a sort of letter of recommendation, where the recipient of the ticket doesn't know the sender; but since the recipient trusts the entity that created the ticket, it can also trust the sender. Prior to generating the ticket, the issuer will authenticate the terminal. This can be seen as a form of pre-authentication, where all the tedious work (with associated delays) is performed.

2.4   Mobility Broker

A ticket-based solution for fast handover *could* have been implemented using only existing infrastructure of ISP$_{RUS}$ and OSPs, but to ease information gathering with respect to candidate access points, the Mobility Broker (MB) has been introduced as a new network component with respect to [6]. The MB is a neutral party that has a direct trust relationship with all ISPs in a given geographical area, and also a direct trust relationship with all the corresponding RGWs. For our purposes, the MB has three main functions:

- Serve as AAA proxy toward ISP$_{RU}$ for full authentication
- Provide information about nearby access points via the CARD protocol [14]
- Issue Ticket-Granting Tickets (TGT) and access tickets to OBAN terminals.

Each MB will in effect represent the hub of a geographical "cell", as depicted in Fig. 1. This is analogous to base stations in e.g. GSM networks. A terminal should then be able to get TGTs for all ISPs in a given cell with a single full authentication.

Every RGW in the cell must have the MB configured as (proxy) authentication server. This also means that the MB will need to have a shared secret with each RGW in its cell. The MB must also have a shared secret with every ISP$_{RU}$ in the cell, and will pass all authentication requests on to the relevant ISP$_{RU}$'s (proxy) AAA server. This implies that the MB cannot reside in the administrative domain of a single ISP, if there are other participating ISPs in the relevant cell. All tickets will be issued by the MB, regardless of which ISP$_{RU}$ a given RGW belongs to. Handover between cells (i.e. from one MB to another) will then be a special case that for now requires a new full authentication[3].

Since the MB has complete overview of the terminal's geographical location, and also the location of all RGWs in its cell, the terminal does not need to identify candidate RGWs in order to get tickets for them; the MB already knows.

2.5   Brief Review of the Kerberos Ticket Concept

A Kerberos ticket consists primarily of an access key[4] and timestamp information which are encrypted with a (long-term) key known only to the issuer and to the final recipient. When the ticket is issued to the terminal, it must thus be accompanied by a structure that contains the same access key, but which is encrypted with a key that is in the possession of the client. Thus, what the terminal receives looks approximately like this:

$$E_{K_{terminal}}[AccessKey] + E_{K_{RGW}}[AccessKey, Timestamp]$$

When the client uses the ticket for authentication, it must prove to the recipient (e.g. the RGW) that it possesses the access key within the ticket. It does this by generating an authenticator[5] message; primarily by encrypting a challenge from the RGW (and some other information) with the access key. The recipient verifies this message, and if the timestamp in the ticket indicates that it has not expired, the recipient considers the client authenticated.

The possession of an access key in a TGT thus implicitly grants the OBAN user the right to request tickets for nearby RGWs; the possession of an access key in an RGW ticket grants the OBAN user access to the wireless access network.

The Kerberos tickets will have a limited validity, and we are assuming that it will be in the OBAN users' self interest to keep the access keys secret (i.e. that OBAN use is

---

[3] However, current efforts are looking into options that involve "make-before-break" session establishment using e.g. UMTS networks when transitioning between cells.

[4] In traditional Kerberos notation, the key embedded in the ticket is referred to as the *session key*; however, in an OBAN context, this is too easily confused with the session key for encryption of the wireless traffic; hence the name change.

[5] Not to be confused with the 802.1X authenticator.

Table 1. Mapping from Kerberos to OBAN.

Kerberos actor	OBAN party
AS (Authentication Server)	Mobility Broker (proxy toward OSP via ISP_{RU})
TGS (Ticket Granting Server)	Mobility Broker
C (Client)	OBAN user (terminal)
V (serVice granting server)	RGW

metered). If a flat-rate business model were to be applied to OBAN, however, additional misuse detection mechanisms (akin to the ones used to detect cloned cell phones) must be deployed.

Note that we don't attempt to create a full-blown multi-realm Kerberos authentication system, but in effect multiple disjoint Kerberos realms, based on each Mobility Broker. In the following, we assume that the reader is familiar with the Kerberos protocol (see e.g. [10] or [15]).

In Table 1 we provide a mapping from Kerberos terms to their respective OBAN counterparts. The fact that both the role of AS and TGS is assumed by the MB is no anomaly in Kerberos terms; this occurs so often that the combined AS-TGS pair frequently is referred to as the Key Distribution Centre (KDC).

3 Assumptions

The Kerberos-style ticket solution relies on some fundamental assumptions that will be elaborated below.

Pre-shared Secret: A fundamental assumption is that the access point (i.e., RGW) shares a secret with the AAA server. This is typically the case in a situation where 802.1X [9] is employed in conjunction with RADIUS [7].

Minimum Stay: The terminal needs to exhibit a "minimum stay-time" at each RGW, i.e. it has to stay connected for a certain minimum of time before moving on. The minimum stay is defined as the time required by the terminal to acquire all necessary tickets prior to the handover. Thus this minimum time period will be longer or shorter depending on how many tickets are requested, which in turn depends on how well we can predict which RGW we will hand over to next. Depending on the expiry times of the tickets, a terminal may also already possess tickets for many candidate RGWs for $handover_{n+1}$ when it performs $handover_n$; this will reduce the minimum time between these two handovers.

Loosely Synchronised Clocks: Kerberos assumes that all participants have roughly the same idea of what the current time is, while allowing for a certain (configurable) clock skew. This is used to prevent replay of Kerberos authenticators, which must always be "fresh".

There is currently no automatic mechanism to ensure this loose synchronisation, but future investigations will show whether it will be possible to achieve it as a side-effect of the initial full authentication towards OSP.

4   Informal Description

In this section we provide an informal verbal description of the different phases of authentication in OBAN. The actors involved are depicted in Fig. 2.

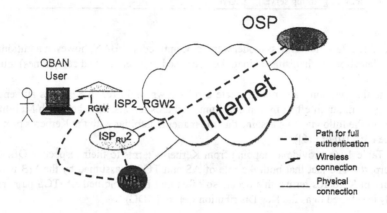

Fig. 2. OBAN actors involved with initial authentication.

4.1   Initial Authentication

1. The RGW will always request authentication with a ticket when a new OBAN user arrives.
2. If the user has no ticket (i.e. this is a new session, not a handover), it will reply with an EAP-NAK.
3. Upon receipt of an EAP-NAK (or an expired ticket), the RGW will initiate a "normal" authentication using the preferred OBAN authentication protocol (e.g. EAP-SIM). This will be proxied by the RGW toward the Mobility Broker, which in turn will act as a proxy towards ISP_{RU}, which finally proxies the messages towards OSP.
4. Upon successful completion of the EAP-SIM authentication, the OSP will issue an EAP-SUCCESS, which is forwarded back to the terminal via ISP_{RU}, MB and RGW.

At this point, the terminal is authenticated, and may communicae towards the MB and the rest of the Internet.

4.2   TGT Acquisition

Once the terminal has authenticated successfully, it needs to get information on nearby RGWs, and get a TGT if it doesn't have one.

1. Upon completion of the normal authentication, the terminal will issue a CARD request, which will be forwarded to the mobility broker.
2. The MB will reply with information on nearby access points, including an URI indicating where the terminal may obtain the required tickets.
3. If the terminal does not possess a TGT for this MB, it will then initiate a new EAP-SIM authentication directly toward the MB, which will roughly assume the role of 802.1X authenticator, using ISP_{RU} as (proxy) authentication server. This EAP-SIM authentication will be encapsulated in HTTP messages[6]. Upon completion of this exchange, the MB and the terminal will have established a shared secret. This shared secret will be used in the following instead of the traditional long-term Kerberos key (i.e. password).
4. Upon successful completion of the second EAP-SIM authentication, the MB will issue a Ticket-Granting-Ticket (TGT) to the OBAN user. The shared secret is used to protect the Kerberos TGT access key that is transmitted back to the user along with the ticket.

The terminal is now in a position to request tickets for candidate RGWs.

4.3 Ticket Acquisition

1. The OBAN user will use the TGT to request a service ticket for the RGW (TicketRGW), using HTTP. From the CARD response above, it already possesses one or more URIs for requesting tickets. This ticket will contain a new access key to be used to encrypt the air interface[7]; the new access key is also transmitted to the OBAN user encrypted with the *TGT access key*. The ticket itself is encrypted with the (permanent) shared secret between RGW and MB.
2. MB returns TicketRGW to the OBAN user.

The terminal is now ready to perform a handover.

4.4 Ticket Usage

After the handover takes place, the OBAN user can now reply to the EAP-Request/Kerberos-OBAN with a ticket. The new RGW will verify the ticket, and admit the OBAN user without needing to communicate with any other parties.

5 Detailed Protocol Description

The following Message Sequence Charts (MSC) describe the EAP-Kerberos-OBAN protocol in detail, using EAP-SIM as full authentication protocol, with RADIUS as AAA-protocol. Note that the new EAP method EAP-Kerberos-OBAN strictly speaking

---

[6] In theory, any suitable encapsulation protocol may be used.
[7] Strictly speaking, the access key will be used to *derive* the key that is used for traffic encryption.

only covers the description in section 5.4, but it is of course not particularily useful without the supporting encapsulated mechanisms for acquiring tickets.

In the following illustrations, protocol elements that are new with respect to commonly available solutions are highlighted using red courier text. In each MSC, actors that do not participate in the message exchanges are identified by rounded corners and grey fill colour.

5.1   Start and Identity

To limit the size of the MSCs, the EAPOL-Start message has been omitted. Since the Kerberos ticket contains a (pseudonym) ID, the EAP-Request/identity and EAP-Response/Identity have generally been removed from the protocol; the identity message is only needed for the "full" authentication, in order to identify the OSP of the terminal.

5.2   First-time Authentication

When a terminal is first switched on, the chosen RGW will request a Kerberos ticket, but the terminal doesn't have one, and replies with an EAP-NAK (Fig. 3). The RGW then initiates a full authentication pretty much as it would have done in the case of common enterprise authentication systems in use today (for brevity, the standard EAP-SIM messages are omitted from Fig. 3, see [16], [12] and [17] for further details).

When the first EAP-SIM authentication is complete, the terminal will request CARD information from the RGW (again, not shown for brevity). The terminal will then realise that it has no TGT for this MB, and initiate a second EAP-SIM authentication encapsulated in HTTP by sending a "TGT start" message. This authentication process results in the establishment of a shared secret between MB and terminal that is used to encrypt the TGT access key (randomly created by MB) that is transmitted along with the TGT in the final message.

5.3   Ticket Request

Once the terminal has a valid TGT, the MB will issue service tickets to RGWs without bothering ISP_{RU} or OSP. In the messages previously received from the CARD server, URIs for requesting tickets for relevant RGWs are listed. Each URI will require the sequence depicted in Fig. 4, but multiple requests may of course be carried out in parallel.

5.4   Ticket Authentication

The message exchange in Fig. 5 illustrates the EAP-Kerberos-OBAN method, as it would be observed immediately after the terminal has associated with a new RGW. The terminal transmits the appropriate ticket along with a Kerberos authenticator (see section 2.5). Note that only the terminal and the RGW are involved in the authentication process.

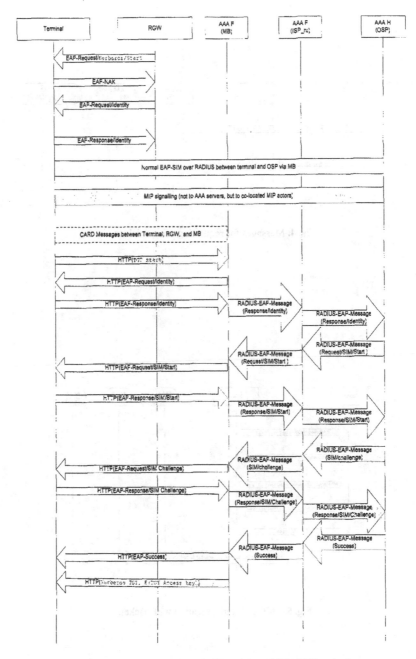

Fig. 3. Messages for initial authentication of OBAN Terminal.

398   Martin Gilje Jaatun et al.

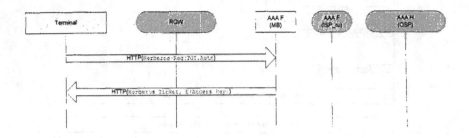

Fig. 4. Messages for requesting access tickets.

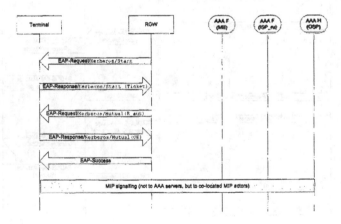

Fig. 5. MSC for Authentication with Ticket.

5.5 Delay Estimation

During handover, only one[8] Round-Trip Time (RTT) is needed between the terminal and the RGW to achieve necessary layer 2 authentication of the terminal to the RGW. According to our preliminary studies, this RTT can be estimated to 5 ms in the best case scenario, and to 20 ms in the worst case scenario. In addition there will be some processing delay (decryption and evaluation of the ticket). Kerberos uses symmetric encryption, and thus Triple-DES can be viewed as a reasonable worst-case scenario with respect to algorithm efficiency. In this case decryption delay will be 108 clock cycles per encrypted byte[15]. Even with a low-end modem processor, this delay should be negligible. If AES is used (something that is preferable), the delay will be even smaller.

The current description of the EAP-Kerberos-OBAN method requires an additional RTT to achieve mutual authentication of terminal and RGW. The delay due to authentication will therefore lie between 10 ms and 40 ms plus a negligible processing delay.

6 Mobility

The alert reader will have noticed that our proposed scheme only covers L2 authentication and encryption issues in connection with a handover. This implies that additional mechanisms must be applied to ensure that e.g. Mobile IP [18] sessions are retained during handover. This is the subject of ongoing research.

7 Conclusion

Kerberos-style tickets offer an opportunity for achieving fast, secure handover in wireless open broadband access networks. This paper has proposed a new EAP method, EAP-Kerberos-OBAN, which can be used to authenticate a roaming user to an access point without requiring communication with external servers, and without requiring a pre-existing trust relationship between the terminal and the access point.

Acknowledgments

This paper is based on joint research in the EU 6th framework programme. The authors would like to thank all the participating OBAN partners for their contribution to the fast handover effort. Special thanks to Frans Panken (Lucent Technologies Netherlands) for first suggesting the use of tickets for fast handover, as well as proposing to separate ticket acquisition from the initial authentication.

References

1. OBAN Consortium. [Online]. Available: http://www.ist-oban.org

---

[8] This excludes the EAPOL/Start message, since it is present for all solutions.

2. J. F. Huber, D. Weiler, and H. Brand, "UMTS, the mobile multimedia vision for IMT 2000: a focus on standardization," *IEEE Communications Magazine*, vol. 38, no. 9, pp. 129–136, 2000.

3. *IEEE Standard for Local and metropolitan area networks Part 16: Air Interface for Fixed Broadband Wireless Access Systems*, IEEE Std. 802.16-2004, 2004.

4. F. Steuer, M. Elkotob, S. Albayrak, H. Bryhni, and T. Lunde, "Seamless Mobility over Broadband Wireless Networks," in *Proceedings of 14th IST Mobile & Wireless Communications Summit*, 2005.

5. E. Edvardsen, T. G. Eskedal, and A. Åmes, "Open Access Networks," in *INTERWORKING*, ser. IFIP Conference Proceedings, C. McDonald, Ed., vol. 247. Kluwer, 2002, pp. 91–107.

6. M. G. Jaatun, I. A. Tøndel, M. B. Dahl, and T. J. Wilke, "A Security Architecture for an Open Broadband Access Network," in *Proceedings of the 10th Nordic Workshop on Secure IT Systems (Nordsec)*, 2005.

7. C. Rigney, S. Willens, A. Rubens, and W. Simpson, "Remote Authentication Dial In User Service (RADIUS)," RFC 2865, June 2000.

8. J. F. Kurose and K. W. Ross, *Computer Networking - A Top-Down Approach Featuring the Internet*. Addison-Wesley, 2001.

9. *Port-Based Network Access Control*, IEEE Std. 802.1X-2001, 2001.

10. C. Neuman, T. Yu, S. Hartman, and K. Raeburn, "The Kerberos Network Authentication Service (V5)," RFC 4120, July 2005.

11. T. Aura and M. Roe, "Reducing Reauthentication Delay in Wireless Networks," in *Proceedings of the First International Conference on Security and Privacy for Emerging Areas in Communication Networks (SecureComm)*, 2005.

12. H. Haverinen and J. Salowey, "Extensible Authentication Protocol Method for Global System for Mobile Subscriber Identity Modules (EAP-SIM)," RFC 4186, January 2006.

13. D. Stanley, J. R. Walker, and B. Aboba, "Extensible Authentication Protocol (EAP) Method Requirements for Wireless LANs," RFC 4017, March 2005.

14. H. Chaskar, D. Funato, M. Liebsch, E. Shim, and A. Singh, "Candidate Access Router Discovery (CARD)," RFC 4066, July 2005.

15. W. Stallings, *Cryptography and Network Security - Principles and Practices*. Prentice Hall, 2003.

16. B. Aboba, L. J. Blunk, J. R. Vollbrecht, J. Carlson, and H. Levkowetz, "Extensible authentication protocol (EAP)," RFC 3748, June 2004.

17. B. Aboba and P. R. Calhoun, "RADIUS (Remote Authentication Dial In User Service) support for Extensible Authentication Protocol (EAP)," RFC 2865, June 2000.

18. C. E. Perkins, "Mobile IP," *IEEE Communications Magazine*, vol. 40, no. 5, pp. 66–82, 2002.

Network Forensics on Packet Fingerprints

Chia Yuan Cho, Sin Yeung Lee, Chung Pheng Tan, and Yong Tai Tan

DSO National Laboratories
20 Science Park Drive, Singapore 118230
{cchiayua, lsinyeun, tchungph, tyongtai}@dso.org.sg
http://www.dso.org.sg

Abstract. We present an approach to network forensics that makes it feasible to trace the content of all traffic that passed through the network via packet content fingerprints. We develop a new data structure called the "Rolling Bloom Filter" (RBF), which is based on a generalization of the Rabin-Karp string-matching algorithm. This merges the two key advantages of space efficiency and an efficient content matching mechanism. This also achieves analytically predictable False Positive Rates that can be controlled by tuning the RBF parameters. Leveraging upon these insights, we have designed and implemented a practical Network Forensic System that gives the ability to reconstruct the sequence of events for post-incident analysis.

1 Introduction

Network forensics is the "capture, recording, and analysis of network events in order to discover the source of security attacks or other problem incidents" [1]. Where the security of an organization is concerned, the role of network forensics is complementary to intrusion detection – where intrusion detection fails, network forensics is useful for obtaining information about the attack, based on which the source of the attack can be identified and the damage can be contained.

Network Forensic Analysis Tools (NFAT) can capture and store all network traffic and provide the analysis engine to the security analyst [2], [3], [4]. Examples of the features provided include trend analysis, content clustering, traffic playback, detection of traffic patterns and anomalous traffic. While many of these features are useful for network monitoring, in many cases, a form of content-based searching would be far more useful. However, this presents two problems – searching through enormous amounts of raw data is extremely time-consuming and inefficient. On top of that, the enormous amount of data imposes huge storage requirements. For an idea of the magnitude this involves, data corresponding to only 4.6 days for 10% usage of a 100-Mbit/s WAN circuit takes up 1TB [5]. Therefore, it is a widespread practice to write over old data, and the forensic data may be gone precisely when it is needed.

Motivated by the above, we believe that a network forensic system should capture the contents of all packets, and store them in compact representations to efficiently support investigative queries. With storage efficiency, it becomes more feasible to keep data for extended periods of time, thus ensuring that attacks can always be traced even if undetected by Intrusion Detection Systems.

Please use the following format when citing this chapter:

Author(s) [insert Last name, First-name initial(s)], 2006, in IFIP International Federation for Information Processing, Volume 201, Security and Privacy in Dynamic Environments, eds. Fischer-Hubner, S., Rannenberg, K., Yngstrom, L., Lindskog, S., (Boston: Springer), pp. [insert page numbers].

Our contribution in this paper is to present an approach to network forensics which ensures that all packets that passed through the network will always leave behind traceable content fingerprints. We present a new data structure, the "Rolling Bloom Filter" (RBF), which allows string matching to be efficiently performed on content fingerprints by generalizing the Rabin-Karl string matching algorithm. This enables analytically predictable False Positive Rates that can be controlled by tuning the RBF parameters. Leveraging upon these insights, we implement a practical network forensic system that gives the ability to reconstruct the sequence of events for post-incident analysis.

The next section presents the background and some related work. We develop the generalized Rabin-Karp algorithm in Section 3, and show how it can be used for the RBF. In Section 4, we present the performance analysis and optimization of the RBF. The RBF is then used to build a Network Forensic System, the architecture of which is shown in Section 5 and the implementation results are presented in Section 6. We then conclude this paper in Section 8 after a discussion on future work in Section 7.

2 Background

2.1 Bloom Filter Preliminaries

The Bloom Filter is a space-efficient randomized data structure for supporting set membership queries [6]. A Bloom Filter is described as an m bits array, initialized by setting all bits to '0' to denote an empty set. To insert an element, the element is hashed with k independent hash functions, for which each hash output gives an index in the bit array to be set to '1'. Thus, a queried element belongs to the set only if all k bits are set to '1'.

The Bloom Filter posses a number of interesting properties: space efficiency, constant $O(k)$ query complexity, zero False Negatives, and controllable False Positive Rates. After n elements are inserted, the False Positive Rate of the Bloom Filter is

$$FP_o = \left(1 - \left(1 - \frac{1}{m}\right)^{kn}\right)^k \approx \left(1 - e^{\frac{-kn}{m}}\right)^k. \qquad (1)$$

The False Positive Rate is minimized when $k = \ln 2 \times m/n$, with optimized $FP_o = (1/2)^k = (0.6185)^{m/n}$. There are other standard Bloom Filter operations which can be useful in practical applications – if too few elements are inserted, a Bloom Filter can be halved in size. This is realized by simply taking an OR between the first half of the Bloom Filter and the second half [7]. In addition, if the Bloom Filter density is less than 1/2, further space efficiency is gained through compression [8].

2.2 Applications of Bloom Filters to Network Forensics

To our best of knowledge, the first application of Bloom Filters to network forensics was the Source Path Isolation Engine (SPIE) [9], where it was proposed that each router stored the digest of all forwarded packets into Bloom Filters. In the event of an attack, each router would be queried to map out the path of the attack, so malicious packets could be traced to their origin. However, packet digests were constructed by hashing the unique fields in the IP packet header together with a predetermined number of bytes from the payload. This means that this scheme supported only the tracing of packets rather than packet contents.

The tracing of packet contents was introduced using Hierarchical Bloom Filters (HBF) in [10]. Content matching was possible because the packet payload was parsed in fixed-size blocks, and the index of each block was appended before insertion into the Bloom Filter. The HBF attempts to reduce False Positives by *aggregating* the results of individual Bloom Filter queries hierarchically. To illustrate this, Fig. 1 shows the insert and query mechanisms for a 3-level HBF with 4-byte unit block size.

Fig. 1 shows that 7 blocks are formed from the 16-byte portion of the content string for the insert operation. What is straightforward is that the same 16-byte substring would match all 7 blocks when used as a query. However, *all* other 16-byte substrings fall into the worst case. For example, consider the substring "BCDE ... NOPQ". Due to difference in block alignment, only 4 out of 7 blocks can be matched even after trying alignment shifts. This effect gives variable effective False Positive Rates for the HBF, with common worst case performance. Also, storage is inefficient because only about 1/2 the number of inserted blocks are used in the worst case.

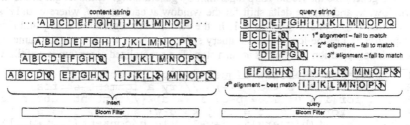

Fig. 1. The HBF with 3 layers of hierarchy, where shaded regions indicate matched portions of the content string for the given query string.

2.3 Rabin-Karp Hash-based String Matching

The Rabin-Karp [11], Boyer-Moore [12], and Knuth-Morris-Pratt [13] string matching algorithms are known to be the most efficient, but we chose the Rabin-Karp because upon generalization, it can be used with Bloom Filters for storage efficiency.

Given a content string of length p and a query string of length q, where $p \geq q$, the Rabin-Karp algorithm slides a window of length q through the content string and compares each hash value against that of the query string. The key to this is the "rolling hash function" [11], where the hash value for each window position can be used to efficiently compute the hash value for (i.e. rolls over to) the next window position. One way to achieve this is via modulo hashing, where a q-byte query string is represented as a number of base b and modulo L, such that b is large and b and L are relatively prime. Since the rolling hash function computes each hash in constant time, the complexity is $O(p)$ and $O(pq)$ for the average and worst case respectively.

3 String Matching on Content Fingerprints

In this section, we develop the Rolling Bloom Filter (RBF), a space-efficient data structure that implicitly performs generalized Rabin-Karp string matching.

3.1 Generalized Rabin-Karp Algorithm

Viewing the ordered series of hash values as fingerprints, our objective is to store the fingerprints of content strings into Bloom Filters so that the efficient Rabin-Karp algorithm can be adapted to use Bloom Filters. This merges the storage space efficiency of Bloom Filters with the string matching efficiency of Rabin-Karp, making it ideal for network forensic applications. More importantly, the Rabin-Karp algorithm inspired us to conceive a technique to aggregate individual Bloom Filter queries *linearly* instead of *hierarchically* (in the HBF). This achieves analytically predictable effective False Positive Rates that can be controlled by tuning the RBF parameters. We show how these advantages can be achieved by first generalizing the Rabin-Karp algorithm.

We generalize the Rabin-Karp algorithm by generalizing: (i) the length of the hash window, w, and (ii) the delta shift for the window at each step, d, where w and d are such that $w \geq d$ and $w \leq q - d + 1$. In the Rabin-Karp algorithm, $w = q$ and $d = 1$ respectively, i.e. the lengths of the query string and hash window are the same, and the window position increments at each step. The generalized algorithm is as follows:

```
1   generalizedRabinKarp(query[0..q-1], content[0..p-1]) {
2     for(s = 0; s < d; s++)   //try alignment shifts
3       for(i = 0; i <= p-q; i += d) {//content substrings
4         for(j = s, t = i; j <= q-w; j += d, t += d)
5           if(h(query[j..j+w-1]) != h(content[t..t+w-1]))
6             return NOT_FOUND;
7         if(query[0..q-1] == content[i..i+q-1])
8           return i;
9         else return NOT_FOUND;
10      }
11 }
```

Fig. 2 illustrates the generalized Rabin-Karp algorithm with $d = 2$ and $w = 4$, so that there are also 7 blocks within the 16-byte portion of the content string as in the HBF example. This example reveals the *first key significance* of our generalization. It is clear from Fig. 2 that *any* 16-byte query which is a substring of the content string will *always* match *at least* 6 out of 7 blocks, an advantage over the highly variable number of matched blocks in the HBF. The comparison of False Positive Rates will be presented in sub-Section 4.2

Note also that the complexity of the generalized algorithm can be shown to be $O(p)$ and $O(pq)$ for the average case and worst case respectively, similar to the original algorithm. The key is that the innermost loop makes only $1/(1 - FP_0)$ iterations on average, where FP_0 is the collision probability.

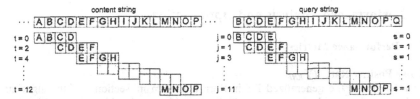

Fig. 2. Illustration of generalized Rabin-Karp with $w = 4$ and $d = 2$. The shaded (unshaded) regions indicate matched (unmatched) regions through hash comparisons.

3.2 RBF Primitives

The Rolling Bloom Filter (RBF) is a space-efficient data structure that stores content string fingerprints into Bloom Filters to support approximate string matching. A RBF is described by a set of defined parameters $\{m, n, k, w, d, N\}$ and is represented by a series of N Bloom Filters, where each ith Bloom Filter of $m_i \leq m$ bits stores the ith overlapping fragment of any content string, content$[di \ldots di + w - 1]$ such that $0 \leq i \leq N - 1$. To accommodate varying string lengths, the number of Bloom Filters, N, grows with the maximum length of any inserted content string according to the relationship $N = 1 + \lfloor (p_{max} - w)/d \rfloor$, where p_{max} is the maximum length of any inserted content string. The RBF is considered "full" after n content strings are inserted.

Initializing the RBF is the same as initializing a Bloom Filter – each ith Bloom Filter initially takes up $m_i = m$ bits and all bits are initialized to zero. The RBF supports three other primitives – Insert, Query and Optimize.

Insert
To insert a string into the RBF, insert each ith overlapping fragment content$[di \ldots di + w - 1]$ into the ith Bloom Filter, $0 \leq i \leq N - 1$. In reference to generalized Rabin-Karp, this facilitates hash value comparisons in Line 5 of the algorithm.

Query
Generalized Rabin-Karp is the underlying algorithm of the Query primitive, with some modifications. Unlike the generalized algorithm, the RBF does not keep the original content strings for exact string matching. Therefore, the RBF supports only *approximate string matching*. In reference to Fig. 2, we note that a query string can have an unmatched length of at most $(d - 1)$ at each end of the matched substring. Thus, an approximately match is a substring of length l such that $q - 2(d - 1) \leq l \leq q$.

Optimize
This optimizes the RBF size just prior to storage. This primitive is used after n strings are inserted into the RBF, i.e. when the RBF is "full". Since content strings can be of any length, each ith Bloom Filter in the RBF may contain too few elements n_i, i.e. $n_i \leq n$, and so $m/n_i \geq m/n$. This means the bits per element ratio m/n_i for the ith Bloom Filter may be higher than desirable for storage efficiency. The Optimize primitive optimizes the size of each ith Bloom Filter m_i by iteratively halving its size while doubling its bits per element ratio till $m/2n \leq m_i/n_i \leq 3m/2n$ so that $E[m_i/n_i] = m/n$.

4 Performance Analysis and Optimization

4.1 Performance Metrics

False Positive Rate, FP_{RBF}

In reference to the generalized Rabin-Karp algorithm in Section 3.1, the algorithm makes a string match attempt at each fixed position (s, i) with False Positive Rate $FP_{s,i}$. We approach the problem by first determining $FP_{s,i}$.

Let us denote the outcome events of each individual Bloom Filter query as {'X': negative result, 'A': positive result due to actual existence of the string within the hash window, and 'F': positive result due to False Positive}. Thus, each string match attempt produces a series of events which terminates with an 'X' if the string is not matched, or a series of any combination of 'A' and 'F' if the string is successfully matched. For example, if a string requires 6 individual queries, "A, X" is unmatched and any one of the following: "A, A, A, A, A, A", "F, F, F, F, F, F" or "F, A, F, F, A, A" indicates a successful match. Combinations of 'A' and 'F' contribute to $FP_{s,i}$ and are undesirable. The probability $P(F) = FP_o$ can be tuned through the Bloom Filter parameters $\{m, n, k\}$. Further, in uniformly distributed content, $P(A) = 1/2^{8w}$ and random occurrences of 'A' vanish as the hash window length w increases. This makes $P(F) \gg P(A)$, and so $FP_{s,i}$ is dominated by the series of 'F' events.

In reference to the generalized Rabin-Karp algorithm, the minimum number of positive events required for a successful string match is $\lfloor (q-w+1)/d \rfloor$. Thus, if $P(F) \gg P(A)$, the False Positive Rate for the string match attempt at each fixed (s, i) is

$$FP_{s,i} = (FP_o)^{\left\lfloor \frac{q-w+1}{d} \right\rfloor}. \tag{1}$$

As (s, i) varies within its entire space of possible values, at most $(p_{max} - q + d)$ string match attempts are made. Thus the probability that the RBF query *does not return a* False Positive is expressed as

$$\left(1 - FP_{RBF}\right) = \left[1 - FP_{s,i}\right]^{p_{max}-q+d} = \left[1 - (FP_o)^{\left\lfloor \frac{q-w+1}{d} \right\rfloor}\right]^{p_{max}-q+d}. \tag{2}$$

Finally, by expanding the right hand side via Binomial Theorem, the effective False Positive Rate of each RBF query is approximately

$$FP_{RBF} \approx (p_{max} - q + d)(FP_o)^{\left\lfloor \frac{q-w+1}{d} \right\rfloor}. \tag{3}$$

Note that any aggregation of Bloom Filter queries may still produce high False Positive Rates if occurrences of event 'A' are not controlled – otherwise, all permutations of 'X' and 'A' events add to False Positives. Indeed, this explains the abnormally high False Positive Rates (beyond worst case) experienced by the HBF on "structured traffic" as reported in the extended version of [10]. Herein lies the *second key significance* of our algorithm. Without requiring extra resources, the hash window length w can be increased (within its constraints) to vanish occurrences of event 'A', so that the aggregation of Bloom Filter queries *must* exponentially reduce False

Positive Rates. This produces analytically predictable False Positive Rates that can be controlled by tuning the RBF parameters.

Data Reduction Factor, D

The Data Reduction Factor quantifies the factor of storage space reduction by the RBF. On average, each content string is stored into $1+\lfloor(\hat{p}-w)/d\rfloor$ Bloom Filters, where $\hat{p}$ is the mean length of the n content strings inserted into the RBF. Since the mean bits per element ratio is m/n after using the Optimize primitive, we have

$$D = \frac{8\hat{p}}{\left(1+\left\lfloor\dfrac{\hat{p}-w}{d}\right\rfloor\right)\left(\dfrac{m}{n}\right)} \geq \frac{8d}{m/n} \text{ since } w \geq d. \tag{4}$$

As a result of the lower bound, we can set $D_{des} = 8d/(m/n)$ as the *desired minimum Data Reduction Factor* to be achieved by the RBF. Note that our Rabin-Karp generalization allows d to be tuned to achieve the desired Data Reduction Factor.

Minimum Query Length, q_{min}

Since the RBF does not rely on the original content strings to resolve hash collisions, the query length will have to be bounded by q_{min} if we wish to achieve a desired False Positive Rate. This will be elaborated upon in the following section.

4.2 Performance Analysis

Given the desired minimum Data Reduction Factor D_{des}, our objective is to study the RBF performance. We first note that the set of RBF parameters $\{m, n, k, w, d, N\}$ can be reduced since it contains many non-independent variables. From Section 2.1, the False Positive Rate for each Bloom Filter, FP_o, is optimized at $k = \ln 2 \times m/n$. Given $D_{des} = 8d/(m/n)$, we can also determine d from m/n. Finally, N need not be predetermined since it grows with the maximum content string length p_{max}. The reduced set of RBF parameters that change independently is thus simply $\{k, w\}$.

We now analyze the performance of the RBF using some numerical examples. Let us first assume that w is sufficiently large and the claim $P(F) \gg P(A)$ in Section 4.1 is true so that the RBF False Positive Rate is given by Eq. (3). Note that otherwise, the False Positive Rate is higher than given in Eq. (3), which then constitutes the lower bound. The relationship between FP_{RBF} and the query length q is shown in Fig. 3 as k and D_{des} vary at $w = 2d$. By drawing a horizontal line at desired $FP_{RBF} = 10^{-5}$ we obtain the minimum query length $q_{min} = 167$ required to achieve $FP_{RBF} = 10^{-5}$. It is also apparent that the lowest FP_{RBF} at any q and D_{des} is at $k = 1$, where the individual Bloom Filter False Positive Rate is $P(F) = FP_o = 1/2$.

In practice, $P(A)$ depends on the nature of the content. It is likely that $P(A) = 1/2^{8w}$ for uniformly distributed content can never be found in natural text. However, even for a 26 – alphabet character set, $P(A) = 1/26^w$ if all characters are independent or $P(A) = 1/26$ if all characters within the window are completely dependent. Since FP_{RBF} is optimized at $k = 1$ giving $P(F) = 1/2$, then $P(F) \gg P(A)$ is satisfied for all cases by choosing $k = 1$. Finally, choosing $w = 2d$ (at least) is required to vanish random occurrences of event 'A' and for Eq. (3) to be valid.

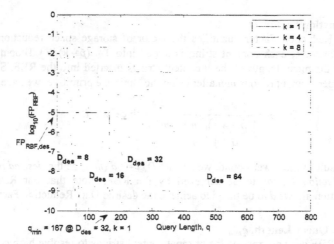

Fig. 3. Log Scale variation of the FP_{RBF} with q, at different D_{des} and m/n.

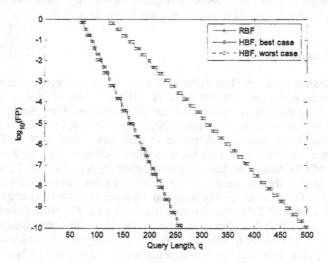

Fig. 4. Comparison of False Positive Rates of the RBF and the HBF.

We now compare the performance of the RBF with the Hierarchical Bloom Filter (HBF). The False Positive Rate of the HBF can be evaluated following the principles presented in this paper. Fig. 4 compares the effective False Positive Rates of the RBF in comparison with the HBF, both using the same parameters to give the same desired Data Reduction Rate $D_{des} = 32$. It is evident that the RBF consistently achieves False Positive Rates same as or near to the *best case* for the HBF.

5 The Network Forensic System

The Network Forensic System supports content-based queries on all traffic that has passed through the network within the monitoring period. Given a file binary or fragment as the query input, the Network Forensic System returns the "information of interest" on all occurrences of that input, or a null reply if the input has not been encountered. This includes the time of occurrence, source and destination IP addresses, MAC addresses, source and destination ports, traffic statistics and of course, if possible, references to more information about the content.

Depending on the desired level of security, the Network Forensic System may be deployed at all hosts throughout the network, or only at the network perimeter, or a hybrid between the two, e.g. on shared segments or subnet gateways. At each monitoring point, data is stored in archive units, each of which consists of three core components – a Meta-Fingerprint Filter, a Micro-Fingerprint Filter database, and a Connection Endpoint Table. These are illustrated in Fig. 5.

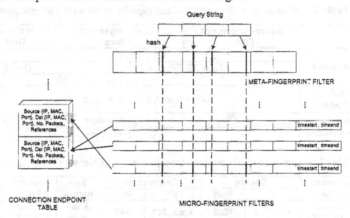

Fig. 5. Core components of an archive unit in the Network Forensics System.

The Meta-Fingerprint Filter is a RBF with predefined parameters $\{m, n, k, w, d\}$. The RBF parameters are chosen such that the performance requirements are satisfied as outlined in Section 4.2. The Meta-Fingerprint Filter is the front-end filter for input queries – it allows null replies to be quickly returned if a string is not found, the most frequent case in practice. A Micro-Fingerprint Filter is a small RBF that stores more precisely the fingerprints of a small group of n_μ packets referencing the same entry in the Connection Endpoint Table, where $1 < n_\mu < 10$.

When a match occurs in the Meta-Fingerprint Filter, a precise match is attempted on the database of Micro-Fingerprint Filters, where a match indexes the information entry on the Connection Endpoint Table. For space efficiency, the Connection Endpoint Table stores aggregated information such as the source and destination IP addresses, MAC addresses, source and destination ports, and traffic statistics; timestamps are appended to the Meta-Fingerprint Filter instead. By doing so, the same entry in the Connection Endpoint Table can be referenced by a large number of Meta-Fingerprint Filters, thereby achieving space efficiency.

If each Micro-Fingerprint Filter uses the same RBF parameters $\{m, n, k, w, d\}$, the mean number of False Positive entries returned by the Micro-Fingerprint database given a matched Meta-Fingerprint can be evaluated as

$$\mu = \frac{n}{n_\mu} (FP_o)^{\left\lceil \frac{q-w+1}{d} \right\rceil}. \tag{5}$$

6 Implementation Results

We implemented a Network Forensic System with parameters as indicated in Table 1. Each archive unit took up about 70MB, compared to near to 1GB from raw packet traces. Since redundancy exists even in the RBF, each archive unit could be further compressed using Lempel-Ziv Markov Chain (LZMC) compression to around 55MB.

Table 1. Performance, RBF parameters and capacity of Network Forensic System.

	Macro-Fingerprint Filter	Micro-Fingerprint Filters	Archive Unit
Performance	$q_{min} = 167$		
	$D_{des} = 32$, $FP_{RBF} = 10^{-5}$		$D \approx 16$
	-	$\mu = 1.3 \times 10^{-3}$	
RBF Parameters	$m/n = 1/\ln 2$, $k = 1$, $w = 12$, $d = 6$		
Capacity (No. packets)	$n = 2^{20}$	$n = 2^{20}$ (all Filters)	$n = 2^{20}$
	-	$n_\mu = 8$ (each Filter)	

Table 2. Summary of results returned from queries to the Network Forensic System.

	Approx. Time	Source		Destination		Sig-nature	Monitor Point	Pkts
		IP	Port	IP	Port			
1	17:08:44 ~ 17:08:44	x.x.x.133	1083	x.x.x.241	445	Shell-code	Machine 1 & 2	11
2	13:39:03 ~ 14:10:08	x.x.x.133	54321	x.x.x.131	1175	Cmd-banner	Machine 1	72
3	13:38:49 ~ 13:50:49	x.x.x.131	1174	x.x.x.133	445	Shell-code		16
4	12:43:20 ~ 12:43:20	x.x.x.131	1118	x.x.x.193	445		Server	1814
5	12:23:56 ~ 12:23:57	x.x.x.194	80	x.x.x.131	1097	Source code	Perimeter	12
6	12:23:41 ~ 12:23:57	x.x.x.194	80	x.x.x.131	1094			13

Machine1: x.x.x.133   Machine2: x.x.x.241   Internal Server: x.x.x.193
External Web Server: x.x.x.194   Attacker: x.x.x.131

We deployed the Network Forensic System in an experimental testbed with monitoring points at the network perimeter, servers, and host machines and simulated an insider attack using a recent publicly available exploit based on MS05-039 [14]. We simulated the scenario where the attack was not detected by IDSs, but anomalies were discovered later at the victim machine. We suppose an exploit binary was recovered at the victim machine, from which its shellcode is used as the signature query string. Starting from this single host and attack signature, all hosts involved in the attack can be identified and more signatures can in turn be extracted from their recovered files, command banners and protocol banners to paint a complete picture of the attack.

The sequence of events is shown in reverse chronological order in Table 2. The attacker browsed the web, downloaded the exploit source code (rows 5 and 6), and launched the exploit on an internal server as first attempt (row 4). The second attempt was launched on the discovered victim machine, Machine1 (row 3) and was successful (row 2). This time the attacker gained shell, and hours later (row 1), Machine1 was used to attack Machine2 in proxy.

We verified the False Positive Rate of the Micro-Fingerprint Filter database by using real samples of varying lengths to query the Network Forensic System. The variation of μ, the mean number of false positive entries returned, with query length q is shown in Fig. 6. The discontinuities in the measured results with increased query length were due to the lack of False Positive matches at the Meta-Fingerprint Filter level. Actual measurements show that the Network Forensic System perform better than the analytical bound, and this is likely to be due to the fact that not all RBFs were filled up, giving variations in the actual density of RBFs within the database.

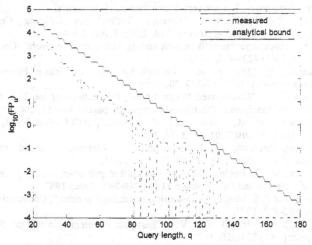

Fig. 6. Log scale variation of μ, the mean number of False Positive entries returned by the Micro-Fingerprint Filter database given a Meta-Fingerprint Filter match.

7 Future Work

At present, False Negatives are possible because a file can be split over multiple packets. This is minimized currently by using multiple different parts of a file as query signature strings. For future work, this can be totally eliminated by extending the RBF Query primitive to take this into account. Also, since network content is sometimes encoded (e.g. MIME for email), a useful improvement would be to iterate queries over multiple encoders in the Network Forensic System.

8 Conclusion

We have presented an approach to network forensics that makes it feasible to trace the content of all traffic that passed through the network via packet content fingerprints. To achieve this, we have developed the Rolling Bloom Filter, which is based on a generalization of the Rabin-Karp string-matching algorithm. This successfully merged the two advantages of space efficiency and an efficient content matching mechanism. Our technique also achieved analytically predictable False Positive Rates that can be controlled by tuning the RBF parameters. Using these results, we have designed and implemented a practical Network Forensic System that gives the ability to reconstruct the sequence of events for post-incident analysis.

References

1. "Network Forenics", searchSecurity.com Definitions, http://searchsecurity.techtarget.com.
2. NIKSUN, NetDetector, http://www.niksun.com.
3. Computer Associates, eTrust Network Forensics, http://www3.ca.com.
4. Sandstorm Enterprises, NetIntercept, http://www.sandstorm.com.
5. T. Nisase, M. ItohNetwork, "Forensic Technologies Utilizing Communication Information", NTT Technical Review, Vol. 2, No. 8, Aug 2004.
6. B. Bloom, "Space/time tradeoffs in hash coding with allowable errors", Communications of the ACM, 13(7):422--426, 1970.
7. A. Broder and M. Mitzenmacher, "Network Applications of Bloom Filters: A Survey", Internet Mathematics, 1(4):485-509, 2004.
8. M. Mitzenmacher, "Compressed bloom filters", Proceedings of the 20th Annual ACM Symposium on Principles of Distributed Computing, pages 144–150, 2001.
9. A. C. Snoeren, et. al., "Hash-based IP traceback", ACM SIGCOMM, San Diego, California, USA, August 2001, pp. 3–14, 2001.
10. K. Shanmugasundaram, H. Brönnimann, N.D. Memon, "Payload attribution via hierarchical bloom filters", ACM CCS 2004, pp 31-41.
11. R. M. Karp, M. O. Rabin, "Efficient randomized pattern-matching algorithms", IBM Journal of Research and Development 31 (2), 249-260, March 1987.
12. R. S. Boyer and J. S. Moore, "A fast string searching algorithm", Communications of the ACM, 20:762-772, 1977.
13. Knuth D.E., Morris (Jr) J.H., Pratt V.R., "Fast pattern matching in strings", SIAM Journal on Computing 6(1):323-350, 1977.
14. House of Dabus, "Microsoft Windows Plug-and-Play remote overflow universal exploit that is related to MS05-039", http://www.packetstormsecurity.org/.

Oscar – File Type Identification of Binary Data in Disk Clusters and RAM Pages

Martin Karresand[1,2] and Nahid Shahmehri[1]

[1] Department of Computer and Information Science
Linköpings universitet,
Linköping, Sweden
[2] Department of Systems Development and IT-security
Swedish Defence Research Agency,
Linköping, Sweden
{g-makar,nahsh}@ida.liu.se

Abstract This paper proposes a method, called Oscar, for determining the probable file type of binary data fragments. The Oscar method is based on building models, called centroids, of the mean and standard deviation of the byte frequency distribution of different file types. A weighted quadratic distance metric is then used to measure the distance between the centroid and sample data fragments. If the distance falls below a threshold, the sample is categorized as probably belonging to the modelled file type. Oscar is tested using JPEG pictures and is shown to give a high categorization accuracy, i.e. high detection rate and low false positives rate. By using a practical example we demonstrate how to use the Oscar method to prove the existence of known pictures based on fragments of them found in RAM and the swap partition of a computer.

1 Introduction

There are many examples of situations within the information security field where the ability to identify the file type of a data fragment is needed. For example, in network based intrusion prevention the structure of the packet payloads can be used to filter out traffic not belonging to a certain service, and in that way defend against new and yet unknown attacks [1].

Another example would be a military network where only encrypted traffic is allowed. By looking at the structure of the payloads of the data it is possible to determine if there are any services sending unencrypted data over the network, without having to rely on packet headers, or checking well-known ports. It is even possible to do so without interpreting the payload, thereby avoiding the potential security compromise associated with an in-transit decryption.

A third example can be found in the computer forensics field where a forensic examiner might have to do a manual search through several hundreds of gigabytes of unrecognisable data. A possible scenario would be a forensic examiner conducting an examination of a computer with several large hard disks, all deliberately corrupted by the owner, who is suspected of trafficking in child pornographic pictures. The examiner uses the available tools and manages to retrieve a lot of JPEG picture headers and

Please use the following format when citing this chapter:

Author(s) [insert Last name, First-name initial(s)], 2006, in IFIP International Federation for Information Processing, Volume 201, Security and Privacy in Dynamic Environments, eds. Fischer-Hubner, S., Rannenberg, K., Yngstrom, L., Lindskog, S., (Boston: Springer), pp. [insert page numbers].

specific markers, but no complete and viewable pictures can be found. In theory the examiner could start brute force matching of every disc cluster against a database of known child pornographic pictures. In reality such a solution would not be feasible since the case would be closed due to time constraints and legal implications long before the matching operation had finished.

As described in the scenario the existing tools (for example PC Inspector [2], Sleuth Kit [3], and The Coroner's Toolkit (TCT) [4], or the commercial Encase [5], File Scavenger [6], and Search and Recover [7]) would not be of much help, because they all need some remnants of a file allocation table or file header to be able to recover lost files, and even if there are headers to be found the data might still be fragmented, making the tools unable to identify more than the header part of the files.

Unfortunately it is not only corrupted hard disks that cause problems for a forensic examiner, the situation has become even more complicated since the introduction of Knoppix and related live CD distributions [8]. These distributions have made it possible to run a full-fledged computer system from a CD, without ever touching the hard disk. All necessary files are loaded into RAM, with a working read/write virtual file system, and hence no traces are left on the hard disk. There are also several methods [9,10,11] for remote execution of code in RAM only on a victim host. Both RAM and swap partitions are fragmented and unstructured by nature, due to the constant changes induced by the CPU's process scheduling. Hence, if one of these techniques is used for illegitimate purposes, finding evidence in the form of complete binary data or executables would be hard considering the limited abilities of the existing tools.

Consequently there is a need for a method making it possible to identify the type of a data fragment by its internal structure only, and to the best of our knowledge there is no tool available that can do that. Our claim is supported by the National Laboratory of Forensic Science (SKL) [12] in Sweden. They have, together with the National Criminal Investigation Department (RKP) [13] in Sweden, expressed an interest in the ability to automatically bring order to a large amount of unsorted binary data. This paper proposes a method for identifying the type of a binary data fragment and subsequently mapping out the contents of various storage media.

The proposed method, called the Oscar method or simply Oscar, has been implemented in a few proof-of-concept pieces of software. Together, these utilities form a toolbox, the Oscar toolbox, consisting of a JPEG data extractor, a byte frequency distribution extractor, a data fragment categorizer, and a search tool for hexadecimal strings. To evaluate the concept we have used the JPEG standard and extracted fragments of a JPEG file from a disk image file. We have also tested the toolbox using the computer forensics scenario mentioned earlier.

2   Proposed solution

Hard disks store data in *sectors*, which are typically 512 bytes long. The operating system then combines several sectors into *clusters*. Depending on the size of the partition on the hard disk clusters can vary in size, but currently the usual cluster size is 4 kB, which often also is the size of *pages* in RAM. Using data blocks that are the same size as clusters and RAM pages, the Oscar method builds vector models, called *centroids* [14,

p. 845], of different file types based on statistics of their byte frequency distribution. The statistics are calculated using data in vector format, and by using the mean and standard deviation for each file type, unknown clusters or pages can be categorized. The similarity of the centroid and the sample vector to be categorized is then measured by calculating the distance between them in vector space. If the distance is less than a threshold, the sample is categorized as being of the same type as the centroid. To increase the detection rate and decrease the false positive rate, other type-specific features may also be used in the categorization process.

In Fig. 1 the histograms of the centroids of four different file types, .exe, JPEG, .ps, and .zip, are shown. As can be seen the histogram of the text-based .ps file is radically different from the binary-based JPEG, .exe, and .zip files. Please observe that the JPEG histogram is based only on the data part of the files used for the centroid. Even though the histograms of the binary files are fairly similar, they still differ, with the most uniform histogram belonging to the .zip type, then the JPEG, and last the .exe. All three binary file centroids also contain a higher number of 0x00 than other byte codes, probably due to padding. For the .exe the significantly higher rates of 0x00 and 0xff is worth noticing. The JPEG histogram shows a decrease in the higher byte codes, which might be a result of the RGB coding in combination with the lossy compression. Probably the cameras we used are tuned to what might be called a "normal" colour palette, and hence extreme values for one or more of the three parts of a RGB triplet is less likely in ordinary pictures. The lossy compression will also decrease the number of extreme values by reducing high frequencies in the pictures, i.e. rapid changes in colour and saturation. Additionally, the marker segment indicator 0xff is not to be used in the data part, apart from in a few special cases, and is therefore less likely to appear in the data.

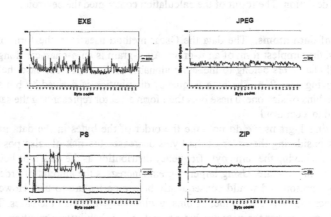

Figure 1. Histograms of the centroids of four different file types, .exe, JPEG, .ps, and .zip. Only the data part of the files was used when creating the JPEG centroid. A logarithmic scale is used for the Y-axis.

As mentioned earlier the JPEG standard has been used to illustrate the method. To further enhance the detection capability of the Oscar method we use the fact that byte

0xff is only allowed in combination with a few other bytes in the data part of a JPEG file. If there is any pair of bytes representing a disallowed combination, the block will not be categorized as JPEG.

In the following subsections we present and discuss some of the main theoretical aspects of the Oscar method, together with some implementation specific features. Oscar is meant to be generalizable, but is at the moment mainly aimed at finding fragmented JPEG picture disk blocks. However, the metric used for categorization is also applicable to other types of data.

2.1 Metrics

There are many ways of measuring similarity between data samples. The approach chosen for Oscar is to measure the distance between a sample vector and a centroid [14, p. 845]. A weighted variant of a quadratic distance metric is used.

Creation of Centroid. The term centroid is defined as the average vector of a set of vectors belonging to a cluster [14, p. 845], i.e. the vectors being categorized as the same type. In our case the centroid consists of two vectors representing the mean and standard deviation of each byte value's frequency distribution.

To create the centroid for the JPEG type we used 255 pictures of normal family life. The pictures came from 5 scanned paper copy photographs and 250 digital photographs from three photographic sessions using two different digital cameras. The pictures' data parts were extracted and concatenated into one file. The resulting file was then used to create a matrix, which was fed to GNU Octave [15] for calculation of the mean and standard deviation. The result of the calculation constituted the centroid.

Length of data atoms. The data the Oscar method uses is in the form of 1-grams, i.e. bytes, the simplest form of an n-gram. An n-gram is an n-character long sequence where all characters belong to the same alphabet of size s, in our case the ASCII alphabet giving $s = 256$. The byte frequency distribution is derived by bin sorting the bytes into bins of size one. These bins then form a vector representing the sample to be compared to a centroid.

By using 1-grams we do not take the order of the bytes in the data into consideration. Considering the order of the bytes decreases the risk of false positives from disk clusters having the same byte frequency distribution as the data type being sought, but a different structure. Using larger n-grams increases the amount of ordering taken into consideration and would consequently be a nice feature to use. However, when using larger n-grams the number of bins, b where $b \leq s^n$, also increases. The size of b depends on whether the n-grams have a uniform probability distribution or not. The maximum value is required when the distribution is uniform, or nearly uniform and the fact that a JPEG file is compressed gives it an almost uniform n-gram probability distribution.

Since the alphabet used has size 256 and we use 4 kB large data fragments, the Oscar method is in practice limited to the use of 1-grams. Using larger n-grams requires $b > 4096$, which in this case gives a mean for the frequency of each n-gram less than one. Every sequence of characters longer than one byte will therefore have too large an impact on the calculations of the distance, and consequently the method becomes unstable and hence not usable.

Measuring Distance. The distance metric is the key to a good categorization of the data. Therefore we chose to use a quadratic distance metric, which we extended by weighting the difference of each individual byte frequency with the same byte's standard deviation. In Equation (1) the standard deviation of byte i is represented as σ_i. A smoothing factor, α, is used to avoid division by zero when $\sigma_i = 0$

$$d\left(\boldsymbol{x}, \boldsymbol{y}\right) = \sum_{i=0}^{n-1} \left(x_i - y_i\right)^2 / \left(\sigma_i + \alpha\right) \ . \tag{1}$$

The advantage of using a more computationally heavy quadratic-based metric over a simpler linear-based metric is the quadratic-based method's ability to strengthen the impact of a few large deviations over many small deviations. Assuming the vector sums, i.e. $\|\boldsymbol{x}\|_1$ and $\|\boldsymbol{y}\|_1$, are constant, Equation (1) gives lower distance values for two vectors separated by many small deviations, than for two vectors separated by a few large deviations. A linear-based method gives the same distance, regardless of the size of the individual deviations, as long as the vector sums remain the same. Since we are using 4 kB blocks of data $\|\boldsymbol{x}\|_1 = \|\boldsymbol{y}\|_1 = 4096$ and we are, in reality, forced to use a quadratic distance metric to achieve decent categorization accuracy.

Some file types generate fairly similar histograms and it is therefore necessary to know which byte codes are more static than others to discern the differences in spectrum between, for example, an .exe file and a JPEG picture. We therefore have to use the more complex method of looking at the mean and standard deviation of individual byte codes, instead of calculating two single values for the whole vector.

2.2 Implementation of Tools

We implemented a toolbox in C containing a number of tools to support testing the Oscar method. The Oscar toolbox consists of a JPEG data extractor, *extr_data*, a byte frequency distribution extractor, *extr_1-gram*, a categorizer, *type_mapper*, and a hexadecimal string search tool, *hexgrep*.

The *extr_data* tool steps through the markers in the header of a JPEG file until the data part starts and then extracts the data part to a file. The *extr_1-gram* tool is used for the creation of the centroid. It mainly sorts and counts the bytes in one 4 kB block at a time. The output of extr_1-gram is fed to GNU Octave [15], which is used to create the mean and standard deviation vectors constituting the centroid.

The *type_mapper* tool is given an image file of a disk, RAM or swap partition. The tool then calculates the distance to the centroid for each 4 kB block of the file. At the same time it counts and filters some JPEG-specific markers, which we use to lower the number of false positives from other file types also having more or less uniformly distributed byte frequencies, for example .zip files and encrypted files.

The marker filters of the type_mapper tool are set to only accept the occurrence of Restart (RST) markers, 0xffdx, the End-Of-Image (EOI) marker, 0xffd9, and the marker

0xff00 in the data. Disk clusters where the RST markers do not loop through $x = \mod 8$ in consecutive order are discarded. Likewise we filter out clusters where there are more than one EOI marker present. There is also a filter for 0xff00 set to require at least one such marker. The threshold is based on tests where we found the mean frequency of that marker to be 2365, with a standard deviation of 1686.1 for a 1 MB block of JPEG data. This corresponds to a mean of 9.2 and a standard deviation of 6.6 for a 4 kB block of data.

The *hexgrep* tool was created because we could not find an easy way to *grep* for hexadecimal data in a file. This would be useful when looking for JPEG Start-Of-Image (SOI) markers or other header related information. The tool could also be used for counting the number of blocks categorized as probable JPEG data in a type_mapper map.

3   Test Cases

Two evaluations of the Oscar method and toolbox were performed using two different setups. The first evaluation was done using a file containing several different types of data. The second evaluation was designed as a more practical experiment where two dump files, representing the RAM and swap partition of a computer, were searched for fragments of two JPEG files.

Although the detection rate of the Oscar method is important, the false positives rate is more important because of the intended use of the method. Therefore the test cases were focused on measuring the number of false positives generated in the different settings.

3.1   Evaluation Using Prepared File

The evaluation file for the first experiment was created by concatenating 53 files of 49 file types (see Table 1) into one. Three JPEG files were included to enable testing of the detection rate. Two of the pictures were taken by different digital cameras and one was produced by a scanner from an ordinary paper photograph. One of the digital camera JPEG files was previously unknown to the type_mapper tool. The scanner JPEG file contained RST markers (see Sect. 2.2) to test the filtering of markers.

Table 1. File types used for the evaluation.

.ACM	.ENU	.NLD	.SVE	.cpl	.html	.sys
.BMP	.INF	.NLS	.TLB	.dll	.jar	.tgz
.COM	.INI	.OCX	.UCE	.doc	.mp3	.tsp
.CPI	.ITA	.OLB	.ax	.dsk	.pdf	.txt
.DAT	.JPG	.RLL	.bin	.exe	.png	.vbs
.DEU	.MSC	.ROM	.bz2	.gif	.ps	.xls
.DRV	.MSI	.SQL	.chm	.gpg	.rpm	.zip

The files to be included in the evaluation were chosen based on their file size and picked subjectively from a laptop running Windows XP, SP 2. We wanted as large files as possible to decrease the impact of the file headers, because a header's structure of often differs significantly from the data part's structure. The total size of the evaluation file was 70.4 MB, giving an average size of the included files of 1,3 MB.

3.2 Evaluation of RAM and Swap Dump

The second experiment was based on the scenario described in Sect. 1, but changed from searching a hard disk to searching RAM and the swap partition of a computer. The evaluation was designed to measure the number of false positives generated when using the Oscar toolbox in a practical setting, and to see whether it was possible to apply the toolbox to such a scenario.

The test was performed by storing and viewing two JPEG pictures in a computer running Knoppix 3.9. Both pictures were taken from the set used to construct the centroid: one was from a digital camera and one was a scanned picture. The two dump files were created and searched for remnants of the two JPEG files. It is worth mentioning is that the swap file Knoppix used was also used by a Gentoo Linux installation on that computer, therefore the file could have contained data fragments from previous sessions.

The tools were applied in the following way:

1. the type_mapper tool was applied to the RAM and swap dump files containing fragments of the pictures,
2. the disk clusters marked as "probably JPEG data" were extracted, and
3. the hexgrep tool was used to find any matches between the extracted fragments and the two JPEG pictures used.

The work-flow described above could be used by a forensic examiner looking for pictures of child pornography. We used pictures portraying a pile of wood and a wedding, not child pornography, but since the algorithms of the Oscar method work on a binary level, the subject of the pictures does not affect the result of the evaluation.

4 Result

In this section the results of the two evaluations are presented. We also discuss whether it is possible to regard a match between a 4 kB data fragment and a complete picture as evidence of the complete picture once having existed on the storage media where the fragment was found.

4.1 Evaluation Using Prepared File

The evaluation file contained 17608 full 4 kB blocks, of which 476 should be categorized as JPEG. The algorithm categorized 466 of them correctly and produced 1 false positive (see Table 2).

Table 2. Result of the evaluation using the prepared file.

	# of 4 kB blocks	% of category
True pos.	466	97.90
True neg.	17131	99.99
False pos.	1	0.01
False neg.	10	2.10

All false negatives were generated by the digital camera picture included in the centroid. The reason for the false negatives was that some parts of the picture lacked 0xff00 codes. We repeated the experiment with the 0xff00 filter disabled and got a 100% detection rate, but 20 false positives.

The false positive was generated by the *win32.sys* binary, which happened to have an almost perfectly symmetrical fragment at one place, giving a distance measure of 764.4. The mean distance of the JPEG data in our tests was approximately 1500. In this case using longer n-grams might have helped, but the current level of 1 false positive out of 17132 possible might be acceptable.

4.2   Evaluation of RAM and Swap Dump

There were 119 disk blocks categorized as possibly containing JPEG data in the RAM dump. When comparing them to the two JPEG files used, all matched. There were no false positives; the reason for this is not completely clear to us because we did not have full control of the contents of the RAM and swap, but we know that there were no other pictures present.

In the swap dump there were 126 fragments categorized as possibly JPEG data. All of them matched the pictures used, and consequently, there were no false positives in this dump either.

The fact that there were no false positives in this test, but a large number of true positives, is encouraging. The results also show that technically the method described in Sect. 3.2 for finding traces of child pornography is working.

There is, however, a legal aspect of the problem: evidence used in a trial must be trustworthy. Thus, if a certain number of fragments belonging to the same known child pornographic picture is found on a hard disk, the disk has probably contained that specific picture. What must be determined, then, is the number of matching fragments necessary to say with certainty that the picture once existed on the disk. While a 100% match cannot be achieved unless the entire image can be retrieved from the disk, it is possible to estimate the possibility that a partial match is equivalent to a complete match.

To find an approximate value for the probability of a partial match we have to start by figuring out the number of pixels stored in a disk cluster sized data fragment, i.e. the compression rate of JPEG. An estimation of the compression rate, c, can be made using the equation $c = \frac{3*x*y}{s}$, where 3 comes from the number of bytes used to encode RGB colour, x and y gives the size of the image in pixels, and s is the size of the data part of the JPEG file in bytes. The compression rate depends on the diversity of the pixel values, but for normal pictures, such as those in Fig. 2, we found the compression rate to be in the range of 8 to 15.

Figure 2. The four pictures that shared the same 12 to 22 first bytes in the data part of the files.

At that compression rate, 4096 bytes of JPEG data approximately correspond to an area of between 10900 (104^2) and 20500 (143^2) pixels. Large areas of the same colour and saturation are compressed more by the JPEG algorithm than highly detailed areas where colour and saturation change rapidly. In other words, the entropy of a group of bytes is almost the same regardless of what part of the picture they represent. Therefore the larger part of the bytes of a fragment is made up of details of the picture. If two fragments are equal, it is likely that their details are equal too, and if so we can in reality draw the conclusion that the fragments came from the same source.

One interesting thing to notice is that of the pictures shown in Fig. 2, skogPICT0049. jpg and skogPICT0063.jpg have the first 22 bytes of the data part in common, and f23.jpg and skogPICT0026.jpg share their first 12 bytes. The file skogPICT0026.jpg also shares its first 14 bytes with skogPICT0049.jpg and skogPICT0063.jpg.

5   Related Work

Wang and Stolfo have written a paper[1] presenting PAYL, an intrusion detection system built on a method related to the Oscar method. Another paper[16] by Li, Wang, Stolfo and Herzog apply the fundamentals of PAYL to create so called *fileprints*, which are used for file type identification. Similarly to our method PAYL and the fileprints use a centroid modelling the mean and standard deviation of individual bytes. To speed up the file type identification Li, Wang, Stolfo and Herzog experiment with truncating the data and only using a certain number of bytes from the beginning of each data block.

To detect anomalies both PAYL and the fileprints make use of what is called a *simplified Mahalanobi distance* to measure the similarity between a sample and a centroid. The simplified Mahalanobi distance is described by Equation (2), where two vectors, called x and y, represent the sample and the centroid respectively:

$$d(x, y) = \sum_{i=0}^{n-1} \left(|x_i - y_i| / (\sigma_i + \alpha) \right) . \tag{2}$$

The standard deviation of byte i is represented as σ_i, the value of α is used as a smoothing factor to avoid division by zero when $\sigma_i = 0$. As can be seen this is similar to a linear-based distance metric between the sample and a model, weighted by the standard deviation of the byte frequency distribution.

In Sect. 2.1 we described the problem of a linear-based method giving the same result regardless of whether there is one large byte frequency deviation, or several small deviations. Since Equation (2) is linear-based its results depend heavily on the standard deviations, σ_i, of the bytes frequencies. If the standard deviation of the σ_i:s is low, the results of the equation will be almost equal, regardless of the distribution of the deviations of the sample vectors and the centroid. Our metric, where each byte frequency difference is squared, can in a better way handle byte frequency distributions where the standard deviation of the σ_i:s is low, because it favours many small differences over a few larger ones.

When Li, Wang, Stolfo and Herzog use truncated data for creating fileprints it makes them dependent on header data to be able to categorize files, which in turn requires the files not to be fragmented and preferably the file system to be intact. The Oscar method uses only the structure of a data fragment to identify its file type and therefore can work regardless of the state of the file system or degree of fragmentation.

Another method related to the Oscar method was presented by McDaniel and Heydari [17] in 2003. They use their method for determining the type of contents of different files, but use complete files or the header and trailer parts of files to create the fingerprints used as models. In order to incorporate byte order, to a certain extent, into the fingerprints the authors use what they call *byte frequency cross-correlation*. Most of the paper describes ways to improve the statistical features of the algorithms, enabling them to better handle discrepancies in the byte frequency of single files during creation of the fingerprints.

The main differences between the Oscar method and the method described in [17] is that the latter depends on the header and footer parts of files to create fingerprints.

Two of the more popular open source tools for forensic file carving are *lazarus* and the *Sorter* tool. The first one is part of the Coroner's Toolkit (TCT) [4] and the second tool is included in the Sleuth Kit [3]. Both of them depend on the Unix *file* [18] utility, which uses header information to categorize different file types. Consequently these two tools depend on header information for file type identification, which the Oscar method does not.

6 Conclusion and Future Work

We propose a method, called Oscar, for categorizing binary data on hard disks, in memory dumps, and on swap partitions. The method is based on creating models of different data types and then comparing unknown samples to the models. The foundation of a model is the mean and standard deviation of each byte, given by the byte frequency distribution of a specific data type.

The proposed method has been shown to work well in some smaller evaluations using JPEG files. The Oscar toolbox has been used to identify fragments of known pictures in RAM and memory dumps. The same methodology for using the tools can be put to immediate use by the police in the hunt for child pornography.

Future work will include further development of the tools, providing better integration between them as well as extended functionality. The number of centroids of different file types will be increased and eventually included in the type_mapper tool. Another example of planned improvements are the possibility to extract fragments directly to file when generating a map of the input data.

The idea of incorporating ordering in the centroid is interesting and thus the use of 2-grams and larger n-grams must be investigated further, as well as other ways of creating the centroid and measure the similarity of samples and centroids. We will also look further into finding a good method to recreate files from fragments found using the Oscar method.

References

1. Wang, K., Stolfo, S.: Anomalous payload-based network intrusion detection. In E. Jonsson el al., ed.: Recent Advances in Intrusion Detection 2004. Volume 3224 of LNCS., Springer-Verlag (2004) 203–222
2. CONVAR Deutschland: Pc inspector. (http://www.pcinspector.de/file_recovery/uk/welcome.htm) accessed 2005-10-31.
3. Carrier, B.: The Sleuth Kit. (http://www.sleuthkit.org/sleuthkit/index.php) accessed 2005-10-25.
4. Farmer, D., Venema, W.: The Coroner's Toolkit (TCT). (http://www.porcupine.org/forensics/tct.html) accessed 2005-10-25.
5. Guidance Software: Encase forensic. (http://www.guidancesoftware.com/products/ef_index.asp) accessed 2005-10-31.
6. QueTek Consulting Corporation: File scavenger. (http://www.quetek.com/prod02.htm) accessed 2005-10-31.
7. iolo technologies: Search and recover. (http://www.iolo.com/sr/3/) accessed 2005-10-31.
8. Brand, N.: Frozentech's livecd list. (http://www.frozentech.com/content/livecd.php) accessed 2005-10-28.
9. grugq: Defeating forensic analysis on unix. Phrack 11(59) (2002) www.phrack.org/show.php?p=59&a=6, last visited 2004-11-19.
10. grugq: Remote exec. Phrack 11(62) (2004) www.phrack.org/show.php?p=62&a=8, last visited 2004-11-19.
11. Pluf, Ripe: Advanced antiforensics : SELF. Phrack 11(63) (2005) http://www.phrack.org/show.php?p=63&a=11, accessed 2005-11-03.

424   Martin Karresand and Nahid Shahmehri

12. Rhodin, S.: Forensic engineer, Swedish National Laboratory of Forensic Science (SKL), IT Group. (several telephone contacts during October and November 2005)
13. Ericson, P.: Detective Sergeant, National Criminal Investigation Department (RKP), IT Crime Squad, IT Forensic Group. (telephone interview 2005-10-31)
14. Damashek, M.: Gauging similarity with n-grams: Language-independent categorization of text. Science **267**(5199) (1995) 843–848
15. Eaton, J.: Octave. (http://www.octave.org/)
16. Li, W.J., Wang, K., Stolfo, S., Herzog, B.: Fileprints: Identifying file types by n-gram analysis. In: Proceedings from the sixth IEEE Sytems, Man and Cybernetics Information Assurance Workshop. (2005) 64–71
17. McDaniel, M., Heydari, M.: Content based file type detection algorithms. In: HICSS '03: Proceedings of the 36th Annual Hawaii International Conference on System Sciences (HICSS'03) - Track 9, Washington, DC, USA, IEEE Computer Society (2003) 332.1
18. Darwin, I.: file(1). (http://www.die.net/doc/linux/man/man1/file.1.html) accessed 2005-10-25.

Organizational Security Culture: More Than Just an End-User Phenomenon

Anthonie B. Ruighaver and Sean B. Maynard

Department of Information Systems
University of Melbourne, Australia
{anthonie, seanbm}@unimelb.edu.au

Abstract. The concept of security culture is relatively new. It is often investigated in a simplistic manner focusing on end-users and on the technical aspects of security. Security, however, is a management problem and as a result the investigation of security culture should also have a management focus. This paper discusses security culture based on an organisational culture framework of eight dimensions. We believe that use of this framework in security culture research will reduce the inherent biases of researchers who tend to focus on only technical aspects of culture from an end users perspective.

1 Introduction

It was not until the start of this century that researchers first began to recognise that an organisation's security culture might be an important factor in maintaining an adequate level of information systems security in that organization [1]. None of these early researchers, however, presented a clear definition of what they meant with "a security culture", nor were there any clear views on how to create this organizational culture to support security.

In the last few years, research in this new area of (information) security culture has been expanding rapidly. Unfortunately, a lot of this research still has a limited focus and often only concentrates on the attitudes and behaviour of end-users as well as on how management can influence these aspects of security culture to improve the end-user's adherence to security policies [2]. Schlienger et al [3] more or less defines security culture as "all socio-cultural measures that support technical security measures", which not only limits its focus to a small sub-dimension of information security but also enforces the old belief that information security is mostly a technical problem. Information security is, in general, a management problem and the security culture reflects how management handles this problem. Subsequently, we argue that technical security measures and security policies will often need to be (re)designed to support an organisation's security culture.

Please use the following format when citing this chapter:

Author(s) [insert Last name, First-name initial(s)], 2006, in IFIP International Federation for Information Processing, Volume 201, Security and Privacy in Dynamic Environments, eds. Fischer-Hubner, S., Rannenberg, K., Yngstrom, L., Lindskog, S., (Boston: Springer), pp. [insert page numbers].

2   Exploring Organizational Security Culture

Our initial research in organisational security culture [4] adopted a framework with eight dimensions from Detert et al [5], who had illustrated their framework by linking it to a set of values and beliefs that represent the 'cultural backbone' of successful Total Quality Management (TQM) adoption. These eight dimensions of organizational culture are briefly identified in Table 1.

Table 1. The Organizational Culture Framework [5].

1.   **The Basis of Truth and Rationality**
2.   **The Nature of Time and Time Horizon**
3.   **Motivation**
4.   **Stability versus Change/Innovation/Personal Growth**
5.   **Orientation to Work, Task, Co-Workers**
6.   **Isolation versus Collaboration/Cooperation**
7.   **Control, Coordination and Responsibility**
8.   **Orientation and Focus – Internal and/or External**

In the remainder of this paper we give our current views of what the important aspects are of security culture in each of these dimensions. While a few of our case studies have been in organisations that have a high-level of security enforced by a strict enforcement of rules and regulations, the majority of our research has been in organisations where decision making about security is distributed and loosely controlled. This may have slightly coloured our views expressed below.

2.1   The Basis of Truth and Rationality

What we initially considered our most important findings in our early research on security culture related to how the importance of security for the organization is seen by the employees and the organization as a whole. Obviously, different organizations need different levels of security. But, although the security requirements for a particular company may not be as high as the security requirements of other companies, achieving optimal security for that organization's particular situation will still be important, as is the need to ensure that their employees believe that security is important.

While the literature on security culture recognizes that the most crucial belief influencing the security in the organization is the belief that security is important [6], not much is mentioned about the importance of other beliefs. We found that the beliefs of the decision makers within the organisation about the quality of security, and about the quality of the different processes used to manage security, are often much more important than the end-users beliefs. Many of the organizations that we investigated do, for instance, believe that their security is good. But most organizations did not make any attempt to evaluate the quality of their security. Similar problems seem to exist with their beliefs about the quality of their risk analysis and security audits.

The quality of a security culture should, however, not only be determined by the beliefs that an organisation has, but more by how the organisation evaluates and manages the basis of truth and rationality in the various beliefs that end-users and managers hold about that organisation's security. Staff being critical about their own beliefs and an organisation having processes in place to challenge the quality of the beliefs of its employees is what distinguishes a good security culture from a bad one.

2.2 Nature of Time and Time Horizon

As literature already indicated [7], we found that all too often the security focus of an organisation is on things demanding immediate attention, not on the things that may prove more important in the long run. If an organisation had any long-term goals, these only covered a time frame of one or two years and were simply aimed at building a security infrastructure in line with International Security Standards.

While we argue that organisations with a high-quality security culture should place an emphasis on long-term commitment and strategic management, we found no good examples in practice. Unfortunately, there is not much discussion in literature on possible long-term strategies either. There seems to be a tendency, however, to completely overhaul security management/governance structures when current security is no longer adequate and/or becomes too expensive to maintain. Once again, we did not find any evidence that those initiating this restructuring have even considered what long-term strategies and plans can or should be developed and by whom.

2.3 Motivation

Organisations with a good security culture need to have appropriate processes in place to ensure employees are motivated in relation to security. While literature suggests that employees need to learn that security controls are necessary and useful to discourage them from attempting to bypass these controls [8], motivation should not only be aimed at ensuring that an employee's behaviour is not compromising IS security. Unfortunately, security is one of the few areas in organisational culture where punishment still plays a large role and where active participation in achieving goals is rarely encouraged.

2.4 Stability versus Change/Innovation/Personal Growth

In organisations that have a high requirement for security, we found a tendency to favour stability over change. Change is often seen as bad, as it can result in the introduction of new risks or in the invalidation or bypass of controls to existing risks.

However, although change should be carefully managed, security is never 100% and organisations need to ensure that their security posture is not static.

While most organisations that have lower requirements for security do not have this "fear" of change, they often fail to realize that an organisation's security procedures and practices need to improve continually, and that the organisation will need to constantly adapt its security to the inevitable changes in the organisation's environment. Organisations that have adopted a security policy lifecycle methodology will have a culture of continuous change in that area of security, but it is not clear whether this will extend to other areas such as security strategy development and security governance processes, or even implementation of security measures.

2.5   Orientation to Work, Task, Co-workers

An important principle in information security is that there is always a trade-off between the use of an organisation's assets and their security. By limiting access to an asset, we can significantly improve its security. However, limiting access can sometimes result in a serious impediment to the daily operations of employees. Finding a balance between security and how constrained employees feel in their work is therefore an important aspect of a security culture. Of course, staff will feel less restricted if they are motivated and feel responsible for security

While it is obvious that employees should be made to feel responsible for security in the organisation, it is just as important that staff responsible for particular security areas have as strong sense of ownership [9]. Both can be negated easily when staff feels that management does not take any suggestions for the improvement of security seriously. Hence, a positive response from management and a continuous adaptation of security practices to at least some of the suggestions may not only help improve security itself directly but also help improve the orientation of staff towards security.

2.6   Isolation versus Collaboration/Cooperation

We have been surprised in how often we encountered that an organisation's security planning and implementation was handled by only a small group of specialists and managers. While organisations often realise that security policies should be created collaboratively using the input of people from various facets of the organisation to ensure its comprehensiveness and acceptance, they tend to ignore that principle in the day to day management of security. As a result, the efforts of the security management team are often negated by other decisions taken by managers in the business units and on the work floor.

Our current research in security governance processes and structures at the middle management level [10] is indicating that this lack of collaboration with the stakeholders in the day to day decision making on security is not only likely to negatively impact motivation and orientation to work, but may often also lead to a dangerously narrow focus of security. As coverage is just as important in information security as the quality of the selected security controls, ignoring particular areas such as personnel security or data security can lead to a significant collapse of an organisation's security posture.

2.7   Control, Coordination and Responsibility

This dimension of an organization's security culture is clearly related to the security governance in that organization and has been the main reason that our security group extended its research from security culture to security governance. The primary feature of security governance in an organization is whether there is a tight control or loose control. An organization with centralized decision making has a tight control, while an organization that has flexible decentralized decision making is likely to have a loose control, although change management processes may still influence how loose the control actually is.

It should be clear that security culture is not independent from organizational culture, so tight control of security in an otherwise loosely controlled organization is not likely to work very well. We believe that this lack of alignment between organizational culture and intended security culture is often one of the major reasons why acceptable use policies fail.

It does not matter whether there is a tight control or a loose control of security, it is still essential that there are clear guidelines on who has decision rights in the different areas of security and when. This aspect is often called responsibility and ensuring that all responsibilities have been assigned is a required feature of any strategic security policy.

With responsibility comes accountability. We believe that an important aspect of the security culture is how the organization handles accountability for decisions in security management. Lack of even the most simple accountability processes, such as simple feedback loops where decisions are discussed with higher levels of management, is a fairly common occurrence in security management.

2.8   Orientation and Focus – Internal and/or external

The orientation and focus of an organization's security clearly depends on the environment in which the organization operates. If the organization is forced to conform to external audit and government requirements, the emphasis of their risk management processes is often only on meeting these requirements, not on improving their security. Other organizations aim to bring their IS security in line with international industry standards and, again, the emphasis is often geared towards passing an audit to prove that they have achieved this goal, rather than on achieving the best security for the organization within the obvious limitations of resources and budget.

As security in an organisation is influenced by both external factors and internal needs, we believe that an ideal security culture has a balance between an internal and external focus. The external focus should at least include an awareness of the organisation's external security environment and how this changes over time. This will allow the organisation to pro-actively meet any new threats. Just as important, however, is that the organisation builds up an awareness of its internal security environment. If the organisation is not trying to identify what security breaches occur and why they occur, it will never know if its security strategies are working and how it can improve the implementation of these strategies.

3 Conclusion

While there has been an abundance of research in the area of organizational security and how it should be improved, the majority focuses only on certain discrete aspects of security and not how these aspects should be assimilated into an organisation's culture. Even our own research in security culture initially had a clear bias to end-user issues. However, the broad framework we adopted from organisational culture research has ensured that we not only recognised this bias in our research, but also provided insight in how to extend our research in new areas such as security governance and risk assessment.

In investigating security cultures in organisations, we have often found that many specific aspects of a security culture, such as attitudes, norms, and shared expectations do not fit nicely within a single dimension of our framework. It is obvious that the concept of a security culture is too complex to be covered by a single framework or model. We do believe, however, that any researcher involved in investigating any aspect of an organisation's security culture will find the use of this framework essential in ensuring that they take a comprehensive view of how the many dimensions of an organisation's security culture relate to that particular aspect they are interested in.

References

1. Von Solms, B.: Information Security - The Third Wave? Computers and Security, Vol. 19. No. 7. (2000) 615-620.
2. Schlienger, T. and Teufel S.: Information Security Culture - The Socio-Cultural Dimension in Information Security Management. IFIP TC11 International Conference on Information Security, Cairo Egypt (2002).
3. Schlienger, T. and Teufel, S.: Analyzing Information Security Culture: Increased Trust by an Appropriate Information Security Culture. 14th International Workshop on Database and Expert Systems Applications (DEXA'03), Prague Czech Republic (2003).
4. Chia, P. Maynard, S., Ruighaver, A.B.: Understanding Organisational Security Culture. In Information Systems: The Challenges of Theory and Practice, Hunter, M. G. and Dhanda, K. K. (eds), Information Institute, Las Vegas, USA. (2003) 335-365.
5. Detert, J., R. Schroeder & J. Mauriel.: A Framework For Linking Culture and Improvement Initiatives in Organisations. The Academy of Management Review, Vol. 25. No. 4. (2000) 850-863.
6. Conolly, P.: Security Starts from Within. InfoWorld, Vol. 22. No. 28. (2000) 39-40
7. Wood, C.: Integrated Approach Includes Information Security. Security, Vol. 37. No. 2. (2000) 43-44.
8. Lau, O.: The Ten Commandments of Security. Computers and Security, Vol. 17. No. 2. (1998) 119-123.
9. Koh, K. Ruighaver, A.B. Maynard, S. Ahmad, A.: Security Governance: Its impact on Security Culture. 3rd Australian Information Security Management Conference, Perth Australia (2005).
10. Tan,T.C.C. Ruighaver, A.B.: Developing a framework for understanding Security Governance. 2nd Australian Information Security Management Conference, Perth Australia (2004).

Cyber Security Training and Awareness Through Game Play

Benjamin D. Cone, Michael F. Thompson, Cynthia E. Irvine, and Thuy D. Nguyen

Naval Postgraduate School
Monterey, CA 93943, USA
{bdcone,mfthomps,irvine,tdnguyen}@nps.edu

Abstract. Although many of the concepts included in staff cyber-security aware-ness training are universal, such training often must be tailored to address the policies and requirements of a particular organization. In addition, many forms of training fail because they are rote and do not require users to think about and apply security concepts. A flexible, highly interactive video game, CyberCIEGE, is described as a security awareness tool that can support organizational security training objectives while engaging typical users in an engaging security adven-ture.

1 Introduction

Effective user security awareness training can greatly enhance the information assur-ance posture of an organization. [1] Yet holding a trainees attention sufficiently long to impart a message is a considerable challenge, particularly when the training is mandated and the topic is viewed by the target audience as potentially mundane. Video games have been proposed as an engaging training vehicle. [2] This paper describes how a video game-like tool called CyberCIEGE was employed to develop security awareness training targeted for the requirements of a specific organization, and how this extensible tool can offer training and education for a range of target audiences.

Our study centers on cyber security training for uniformed and civilian personnel associated with the U.S. Navy. We describe how two CyberCIEGE scenarios, one for general awareness and the other for IT personnel, were created to fulfill organizational information assurance training and awareness requirements.

2 Background

The United States Computer Security Act of 1987 mandated periodic security training for all users of federal information systems. In response, the Department of the Navy placed the burden of responsibility for training and awareness on local Information Systems Security Managers [10], who were, in turn, responsible for developing local training sessions or computer-based training (CBT). To supplement other IA directives [3, 4], in 2004, the U.S. Department of Defense (DOD) issued DOD Directive 8570.1 [5], which mandated initial and annual refresher information assurance training for all DOD information system users. Since then, all users of Navy information systems have

Please use the following format when citing this chapter:

Author(s) [insert Last name, First-name initial(s)], 2006, in IFIP International Federation for Information Processing, Volume 201, Security and Privacy in Dynamic Environments, eds. Fischer-Hubner, S., Rannenberg, K., Yngstrom, L., Lindskog, S., (Boston: Springer), pp. [insert page numbers].

been instructed to complete a DOD IA awareness CBT. The CBT is a web-enabled slide presentation. It is trivial for personnel to click through the training to its successful completion without absorbing any of the material.

Directive 8750.1 has highlighted the importance of fostering a security culture and the need to find training techniques that will actively engage the typical user. A participatory video game requires more user involvement than slide presentations or other standard training and awareness vehicles.

2.1 Common Current Training and Awareness Techniques

Training and awareness is generally accomplished using one of a combination of several techniques described below.

Formal Training Sessions can be instructor-led, brown-bag seminars, or video sessions. Formal training in sessions facilitated by local information security personnel represents the traditional approach to user training and awareness within the Department of the Navy. The success of this approach depends upon the ability of the training facilitator to engage the audience.

Passive computer-based and web-based training represents a centralized approach to the training and awareness problem. CBT offers the user the flexibility of self-paced training, and provides the organization with the ability to train users to an enterprise-wide standard. Its disadvantage is that training and awareness becomes a monotonous slide show that fails to challenge the user and provides no dialogue for further elaboration. Often, users attempt to complete CBT sessions with minimal time or thought. The CBT developer must attempt to provide engaging instruction within the constraints of a passive medium.

Strategic placement of awareness messages seeks to raise the level of consciousness through the delivery of messages in the workplace. Some of the more common delivery methods include organizational newsletters and memos, email messages, posters, screen savers, and security labels.

Interactive computer-based training, such as a video game, generally falls into two broad classes: first-person interaction games or resource management simulations. The majority of games fall into the first category and include first-person shooter games where the player is confronted by an adversary or problem and must take an appropriate action or is penalized, sometimes severely. In contrast, resource management games require the player to manage a virtual environment using limited resources. The player attempts to make choices that improve the environment within the constraints of the available resources. Good choices result in a richer environment and additional resources. SimCity^{TM}, other "sims" games, and RollerCoaster Tycoon (R) are popular examples of resource management games.

2.2 CyberCIEGE

In 2005, the Naval Postgraduate School released a U.S. government version of CyberCIEGE, a video game intended to support education and training in computer and network security. Simultaneously, our collaborators at Rivermind, Inc. made a version available to non-government organizations. The game employs resource management and simulation to illustrate information assurance concepts for education and training. [6, 7] In the CyberCIEGE virtual world, players construct and configure the computer networks necessary to allow virtual users to be productive and achieve goals to further the success of the enterprise. Players operate and defend their networks, and can watch the consequences of their choices, while under attack by hackers, vandals and potentially well-motivated professionals.

CyberCIEGE Components. The building blocks of CyberCIEGE consist of several elements: a unique simulation engine, a domain-specific scenario definition language, a scenario development tool, and a video-enhanced encyclopedia. [8] CyberCIEGE is intended to be extensible in that new CyberCIEGE scenarios tailored to specific audiences and topics are easily created. [9]

The scenario definition language expresses security-related risk management trade-offs for different scenarios. The CyberCIEGE simulation engine interprets this scenario definition language and presents the player with the resulting simulation. What the player experiences and the consequences of the player choices are a function of the scenario as expressed using the scenario definition language.

The game engine and the language that feeds it are rich in information assurance concepts so that it is possible to simulate sophisticated environments subject to a variety of threats and vulnerabilities. They also include substantial support for relatively brief, scripted training and awareness scenarios. This support includes cartoon-like balloon speech by the virtual users, message tickers, pop-up quizzes and conditional play of video sequences, e.g., a computer worm.

3   Requirements Analysis

Training and awareness requirements were developed from the legacy Information Security program of the U.S. Navy and from the current Department of Defense IA training and awareness computer-based training course.

Many of the requirements for the awareness scenario were obtained from the U.S. Navy Information Security Program. Navy requirements for user security training are found in the Navy INFOSEC program guidebooks for local Information System Security Officers [11] and Network Security Officers [12]. These documents offer recommended training curriculum topics and subtopics.

- Value of information, e.g., personnel files, legal records, and trade secrets.
- Communication and Computer vulnerabilities such as malicious software, internet risks, human errors, and internet security risks.
- Basic safe computing practices such as locking computers when unattended.
- Password management including password generation, protection, and change frequency.
- Local security procedures, e.g., cipher locks and violation reports.

The other requirements source was the DOD Information Assurance Awareness CBT. The majority of naval organizations currently use the "DOD Information Assurance Awareness" CBT [13] to fulfill obligations for enterprise-wide annual refresher training. It addresses the following topic areas:

- Importance of IA (overview, evolution, and policy)
- IA Threats (threats, vulnerabilities, social engineering, and internet security)
- Malicious Code (overview, protection, and internet hoaxes)
- User Roles (system security and protecting DOD information)
- Personal and Home security (online transactions and security tips)

These topics provided the requirements for the video game-based training and awareness.

4 Scenarios for Training and Awareness

Two CyberCIEGE scenarios were designed to fulfill the Navy IA training requirements. The first seeks to make the player aware of basic IA problems and principles. The second is intended is for more sophisticated users of computer-based assets. An brief summary of other CyberCIEGE awareness and training scenarios is provided in Section 4.2.

The basic user scenario focuses on computer security fundamentals. The player is placed in the role of a security decision maker aboard a ship, who must complete objectives that raise the security posture of the organization. If objectives are not completed within a specified time, appropriate attacks are triggered by the game engine and the player is penalized. After completing each objective, the player is presented with an awareness message that relates the action taken in the game with real-life circumstances and provides feedback regarding the players choices. The player wins by completing all the objectives without incurring "fatal" penalties.

For each topic identified in the requirements analysis, a scenario element was created that requires the player to do something that will convey the concept to be learned. Some of the topics and activities are described in Table 1. Features that made this scenario Navy-specific included the protection of classified information and cultural aspects of organizational security associated with the hierarchical command structure of the DOD.

4.1 Scenarios for IT Staff

Navy IT training requirements for staff with IT-related jobs are addressed by a second scenario that focuses on network security, and serves to introduce technical users into the roles they must assume. The player assumes the role of acting security manager while the "boss" is away. The player must manage three internal networks, one of which processes classified information. During this scenario, the player must complete technical objectives addressing physical security mechanisms, access control, filtering, antivirus protection, data backups, patching configurations, password policies, and network vulnerability assessment.

Table 1. Basic Awareness Topics and Player Activities.

Topic	Player Activity
Introductory IA briefing	This briefing includes definitions and descriptions of important IA elements and how they interact.
Information value	The user must protect high value information and answer questions about information dissemination.
Access control mechanisms	The player is introduced to both mandatory and discretionary access control, with the latter as a supplement to controls on classified information.
Social engineering	The player is presented with a scenario that will lead to a social engineering attack if proper action is not taken.
Password management	The player must prevent a game character from revealing his password to an outside contractor.
Malicious software and basic safe computing	The player must determine and expend resources to procure three procedural settings that will prevent malicious software propagation.
Safeguarding data	The player is presented with a situation where it appears that a game character is leaving the premises with sensitive information. Actions taken by the player allow the importance of secure storage of backups to be conveyed.
Physical security mechanisms	The player must select cost-effective physical security mechanisms to prevent unauthorized entry into sensitive areas.

4.2 Other Scenarios

The rich and flexible CyberCIEGE scenario definition language supports information assurance training beyond military environments. For example, an identity theft scenario was built to teach users about methods of identity theft prevention in home computing environments. [14] This scenario focuses on a few basic user behaviors that can greatly reduce the risk of identity theft, while highlighting consequences of risky behavior through an engaging story line.

One set of scenarios was developed solely to help train users to reduce the risks of distributing worms and viruses. Here, the player can see the damaging effects of worms and viruses, and learns that a major cause of malicious software proliferation is through user execution of email attachments.

Other CyberCIEGE scenarios illustrate more complex and subtle information assurance concepts. These longer, more sophisticated scenarios are more like traditional simulation and resource management games. For these, the target audience may be advanced computer security students, or information security decision makers.

5 Discussion and Conclusion

This paper demonstrates that information assurance awareness and training can be provided in an engaging format. CyberCIEGE was employed to meet a specific set of Navy

IA training requirements, thus demonstrating that it is sufficiently flexible to illustrate a range of security topics in a variety of environments, both generic and organization-specific. Initial test results for the basic user training scenario are positive and illustrate the utility of CyberCIEGE in supporting awareness programs.

References

1. National Institute of Standards and Technology, People: An Important Asset in Computer Security, NIST-CSL Bulletin, October 1993.
2. Prenski, M., Digital Game-Based Learning. New York: McGraw-Hill, 2001.
3. DoD Directive 8500.1, Information Assurance. October 24, 2002.
4. DoD Instruction 8500.2, Information Assurance (IA) Implementation. February 6, 2003.
5. DoD Directive 8570.1, Information Assurance Training, Certification, and Workforce Management. August 15, 2004.
6. Irvine, C.E., and Thompson, M.F.: Teaching Objectives of a Simulation Game for Computer Security. Proc. Informing Science and Information Technology Joint Conference, Pori, Finland, June 2003, pp. 779-791.
7. Irvine, C.E. and Thompson, M.F.: Expressing an Information Security Policy Within a Security Simulation Game, Proc. of the 6th Workshop on Education in Computer Security, Naval Postgraduate School, Monterey, CA, July 2004, pp. 43-49.
8. Irvine, C.E., Thompson, M.F.: and Allen, K., CyberCIEGE: An Information Assurance Teaching Tool for Training and Awareness.Federal Information Systems Security Educators' Association Conference, North Bethesda, MD, March, 2005.
9. Irvine, C. E., Thompson, M. F.: and Allen, K., CyberCIEGE: An Extensible Tool for Information Assurance Education. Proc. 9th Colloquium for Information Systems Security Education, Atlanta, GA, June 2005, pp. 130-138.
10. Navy Staff Office Pub. 5239-04, Information Systems Security Manager (ISSM) Guidebook. September 1995.
11. Navy Staff Office Pub. 5239-07, Information Systems Security Officer (ISSO) Guidebook. February, 1996.
12. Navy Staff Office Pub. 5239-08, Network Security Officer (NSO) Guidebook. March, 1996.
13. DOD Information Assurance Awareness CBT Version 2.0. December 2004.
14. Ruppar, C., Identity Theft Prevention in CyberCIEGE, Masters Thesis, Naval Postgraduate School, Monterey, CA, December 2005.

Internalisation of Information Security Culture amongst Employees through Basic Security Knowledge

Omar Zakaria[1]

Information Security Group, Royal Holloway
University of London, Egham, Surrey, TW20 0EX, UK
o.b.zakaria@rhul.ac.uk

Abstract. This paper discusses the concept of basic security knowledge. This concept is about organisational members possessing basic security knowledge that can be applied to perform security tasks in their daily work routine. The intention of this paper is not to attempt an exhaustive literature review, but to understand the concept of basic security knowledge that can be used to cultivate a culture of information security in an organisation. The first part highlights some of the basic ideas on knowledge. The second part interprets the concept of basic security knowledge in the case study. Finally, a synthesised perspective of this concept is presented.

1 Introduction

There is often confusion between the terms – "data", "information" and "knowledge". The term *data* is used to refer to a set of discrete and objective facts about events [3]. In an Information Communication Technology (ICT) system, data is stored in structured records such as a spreadsheet, a database, a log and a document. Data must be sorted and logically coordinated to produce crucial information [4]. Whilst, the term *information* means that manipulated data are crucial for a specific use [4]. The term *knowledge* is about experience, beliefs, norms, concepts or information that can be communicated and shared [1]. In short, information is a result from an analysed data. [2] adds that knowledge is reasoning about information to actively guide task execution, problem solving, and decision making in order to perform, learn and teach. [8] states that characteristics of knowledge are about derives from minds at work, which develop over time, supported by rules, an action-oriented, keep constantly changing, which in turn becomes internalised in the minds of knower.

In organisational context, therefore, knowledge is often imbedded not solely in the documents or even repositories but also in organisational processes, practices, routines and norms. Thus, basic security knowledge can be treated as organisational members able to perform, learn and teach security task in terms of inspection, protection, detection, reaction, and reflection procedures on security matters.

---

[1] Omar Zakaria has been awarded a scholarship from the University of Malaya, Kuala Lumpur, Malaysia to pursue his PhD at the Royal Holloway, University of London.

Please use the following format when citing this chapter:
Author(s) [insert Last name, First-name initial(s)], 2006, in IFIP International Federation for Information Processing, Volume 201, Security and Privacy in Dynamic Environments, eds. Fischer-Hubner, S., Rannenberg, K., Yngstrom, L., Lindskog, S., (Boston: Springer), pp. [insert page numbers].

According to [6], there are two types of knowledge – tacit knowledge and explicit knowledge. Tacit knowledge is stored in someone's head, it is not usually internalised and generally lost when the individual resigns or retires. Whilst, explicit knowledge is what that is available to other individuals in whatever form like codified knowledge. Some examples of codified knowledge are reports, best practices, procedures, policies and patents.

[9] elaborate that knowledge is the entire set of insights, procedures and experiences that are considered true, and therefore guide the communications, behaviours and thoughts of people. It sounds ideal, but can we manage knowledge especially security knowledge in practice? According to [5], managing knowledge (i.e., well known as knowledge management) is considered as knowledge creation to an individual process (e.g., tacit knowledge) that can be tranformed into a collective practice (e.g., explicit knowledge). In terms of security context, we can say that managing knowledge can change 'centric responsible', as in operation unit staff to 'collective responsible', such as everyone. This is because through collective practice, everyone in an organisation knows how to perform security tasks, and in turn, creates a collective security responsibility amongst employees. This implies that some security tasks like basic security tasks can be delegated to everyone in the organisation (i.e., this means that we can relate basic security knowledge with basic security tasks).

As already mentioned above, it is essential to change tacit knowledge to explicit knowledge in terms of knowledge creation especially on security knowledge amongst employees in organisations. This is because security knowledge must be externalised in order to share and learn everyone's security practices, which in turn can encourage each employee to perform, learn and teach security tasks effectively and efficiently.

In summary, the combination of everyone's security practices can help the security management people to redesign a better security practice amongst organizational members (see Figure 1).

2 Interpreting Concept of Need to Know Basic Security Knowledge in the Case Study

We use the conceptual idea of basic security knowledge in Figure 1 to interpret the theme of basic security knowledge concept in the ABC company case study. Users in ABC are already concerned with security matters but some of them still do not share their security knowledge in order to overcome current security incidents. Through our analysis in ABC and based on the virus attack in August 2003, some employees managed to perform security tasks based upon the operation unit's instruction and their own experience. However, others did not manage to do it themselves. The reasons were that some subordinates were afraid to teach their superiors how to perform the tasks and others still assume that the security tasks were the operation unit's responsibility.

Research in ABC shows that there were brainstorming sessions, dialogues and discussions conducted in this organisation as a platform to share security knowledge amongst staff. However, not all users came to these sessions to share and learn about security matters. There were the same persons attending almost all these programmes.

Other users assumed that attendance was not compulsory and expected that only technical staff who are ICT-qualified should attend such programmes. It seems that sharing security knowledge is amongst technical staff only and not all users know this knowledge, which might be useful to tackle any security problems during daily work routines. In addition, awareness and training programmes were not solely focusing on ABC's staff participation but the whole Malaysian public sector.

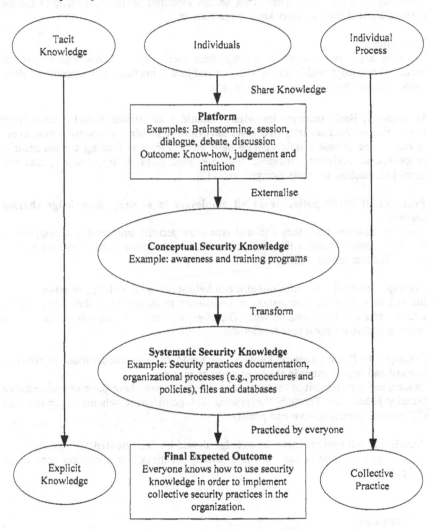

Fig. 1. Externalisation of basic security knowledge in the development of collective security practices in an organisation.

3 A Synthesised Perspective on the Concept of Basic Security Knowledge

It is clear from the discussion so far that organisations also need to develop a strategic vision that ties corporate security plans with the development of basic security knowledge amongst employees. This section identifies some key principles for the manipulation of basic security knowledge concept.

Principles
There is a general lack of knowledge from tacit security knowledge to explicit security knowledge within an organisation and how it interacts with employees' daily work routines. In short, these principles are:

Principle 1: Basic security knowledge should cover fundamental aspects from evaluating current security processes to reviewing incident response procedures.
A basic security task should contain basis aspects from evaluating current security processes to reviewing incident response procedures – inspection, protection, detection, reaction and reflection processes [7].

Principle 2: Participation from all employees in security knowledge sharing sessions.
Through these sessions, they can understand the security problems that everyone in the organisation. Besides this, they can obtain information from others on how to perform certain security tasks.

Principle 3: Good peer relationships can help security knowledge sharing.
Individuals will share information or knowledge to others when they have already established a good relationship with. Therefore, we can relate use this natural way in order to establish a good peer relationship.

Principle 4: Basic security knowledge should include recognition of what is reward and punishment in terms of security matters.
Reward and punishment in terms of security matters are about positive and negative security behaviour. Through the reward and punishment scheme, everyone can differentiate what is honour and penalty.

Principle 5: All basic security knowledge should be documented.
Knowledge should be documented into security practices documentation, procedures and policies.

4 Summary

It seems clear what basic security knowledge means for the development of security culture within an organisation. These proposed principles could also help change security task paradigm from specific individual security processes (i.e., only operation unit are responsible for security) to collective security practices (everyone is responsible on security).

References

1. Allee, V. (1997), The knowledge revolution: expanding organizational intelligence. Boston, Butterworth-Heinemann.
2. Beckman, T. J. (1997) A methodology for knowledge management. International Association of Science and Technology for Development (IASTED) AI and Soft Computing Conference Banff, Canada.
3. Davenport, T. H. and Prusak, L. (1997). Working knowledge: how organizations manage what they know. Boston, MA, Harvard Business School Press.
4. Gatewood, R. D., Taylor, R. R. and Ferrell, O. C. (1995). Management: comprehension, analysis and application. Chicago, Irwin.
5. Lilley, S., Lighfoot, G., and Amaral, P., (2004), Representing organization: knowledge, management, and the information age, Oxford, UK, Oxford University Press.
6. Nonaka, I. and Takeuchi, H., (1995). The knowledge creating company, New York, Oxford University Press.
7. Pipkin, D L (2000). Information security: protecting the global enterprise. Upper Saddle River, New Jersey, Prentice-Hall.
8. Sveiby, K. E., (1997), The new organizational wealth: managing and measuring knowledge-based assets, San Francisco, CA, Berrett-Koehler Publishers.
9. Van der Spek, R. and Spijkervert, A. (1997). Knowledge management: dealing intelligently with knowledge. In Knowledge management and its integrating elements, Ed by Liebowitz and Wilcox, CRC Press.

Bridging the Gap between General Management and Technicians – A Case Study in ICT Security

Jabiri Kuwe Bakari, Charles N. Tarimo, Christer Magnusson, and
Louise Yngström

Department of Computer and System Sciences, Stockholm University/KTH, Forum 100
SE- 164 40 Kista, Sweden
{si-jba, si-cnt, cmagnus, louise}@dsv.su.se

Abstract. The lack of planning, business re-engineering, and coordination in the whole process of computerisation, is the most pronounced problem facing organisations in developing countries. These problems often lead to a discontinuous link between technology and the business processes. As a result, the introduced technology poses some critical risks to the organisations due to the different perceptions of the management and technical staff in viewing the ICT security problem. This paper discusses a practical experience of bridging the gap between the general management and ICT technicians.

1 Introduction

The paper outlines a successful mission of how to bridge the gap between general management and ICT technicians. It is based on practical experiences obtained from an ongoing study which aims at developing guidelines for managing ICT security in developing countries' organisations. The study was guided by using the BRITS framework [1, 2, 3] where ICT risks are viewed as part of the actual business rather than primarily as part of the ICT. The framework also includes a repository of mitigation suggestions, hosted in the EMitL database, which was used together with ITIL, ISO 17799 and COBIT [4, 5, 6, 7]. The findings are organised in a list of ten initial steps or aspects of importance to successfully bridge the gap. The presentation highlights the motivation and practical experiences of each step.

2 The Ten Aspects of Importance in Bridging the Gap between the Management and Technicians

In this section, the 10 steps are outlined and discussed with respect to the experience encountered when executing each. It is a part of the findings of a study conducted at the beginning of 2005, at a government-owned service provider organisation in Tanzania. The organisation is operating in 21 out of 26 regions of the country. It has 900 staff in total and its operations are based on four main core services, where three of them are greatly dependent on ICT to meet their intended objectives. The

Please use the following format when citing this chapter:

Author(s) [insert Last name, First-name initial(s)], 2006, in IFIP International Federation for Information Processing, Volume 201, Security and Privacy in Dynamic Environments, eds. Fischer-Hubner, S., Rannenberg, K., Yngstrom, L., Lindskog, S., (Boston: Springer), pp. [insert page numbers].

organisation has approximately 2 million customers scattered throughout the country, with approximately 25% active customers. The steps included:

(i)   Getting top management's sponsorship (the chief executive officer (CEO) buying into the idea first)

(ii)   Getting technical management sponsorship (the technical department is the custodian of ICT in the organisation)

(iii)   Set up the special ICT security project team (Start by forming a provisional ICT security task force)

(iv)   Quick scan of the ICT related risks and their consequences to the organisation (Risk exposure due to ICT)

(v)   Getting management's attention and sponsorship (The management as a whole needs to buy into the idea as well)

(vi)   Getting the current status of ICT security documented (Take stock of the existing situation)

(vii)   Conduct awareness sessions (To allow staff to recognise ICT security problems and respond accordingly)

(viii) Carry out Risk assessment/analysis

(ix)   Work out the Mitigation plan (Short term plan for issues that need immediate attention and long term plan)

(x)   Develop countermeasures

Step 1: Getting top management's sponsorship (the CEO buying into the idea first)

ICT security appeared to be a new concept to most CEOs in the organisations studied. As confirmed by numerous researches, management sponsorship is important in any effort to improve security in organisations [8]. However, getting an appointment to meet the CEO and talk about ICT security was not easy. In this case, we were directed to see either the IT director or chief security officer or accept a long waiting appointment to see CEO. Eventually, on succeeding, the appointment lasted for about 10 to 15 minutes in which we introduced our agenda on what ICT related risks are and the challenges in managing them. Further, the consequences of not managing such risks to the shareholder value were also discussed emphasising that today's (information age) CEOs will be responsible to their board on the state of ICT security in their organisations. The discussion was based on risk exposures such as business interruption, which can propagate through to the balance sheet with great financial implications and cause embarrassing media coverage, loss of confidence to customers, staff and hence loss of credibility.

Step 2: Getting technical management sponsorship (the technical department is the custodian of ICT in the organisation)

It was relatively hard to talk about ICT related issues in the organisation without the permission of its IT department. From most of those who were asked for an appointment, the reaction was "Have you consulted the IT department?" On the other hand, the technical staff are aware of the ICT security problems, though mostly as a technical concern and not as a business concern. In order to get their support, we had to describe the security problem more holistically, i.e. including both technical and non-technical issues and reasons why we should include and talk to other departments as well. Our observation indicated that the difference in perception between the management and the technical department made it difficult for the technical department to address the problem adequately [1]. Getting technical staff to understand the non-technical components of the problem and how to communicate the problem to the management as risk exposures which needed management attention was yet another important step to take.

Step 3: Address the ICT Security problem as a special project (Forming a provisional ICT security taskforce)

The important question at this stage was how or where do we start? It was at this point that we formed the special ICT security project team. The composition of this team included three technical staff (software, network and hardware), one legal officer, one human resource officer, one internal auditor, one security (physical/traditional) officer, and one from operational departments (where core services of the organisation are processed). Also one more member of staff from the insurance department was in the team purposely for risk management as there was no other department than insurance that was handling/managing risks in the organisation. The main question we faced here was why then only staff from these departments and not others? Our response was based on the facts below:

Technical: Partly the ICT security problem is a technical issue which could be as a result of software, hardware or network problems.

Auditors: Traditionally, auditors are used to auditing the financial transactions or operational processes and compliance to laws and regulations, policies, standards and procedures. Given the nature of their work they can also see the risk exposure of an organisation as part of the big picture. Auditing in ICT is usually considered operational. The prime focus for ICT audit is security—evaluating whether the confidentiality, integrity and availability of data are ensured through the implementation of various controls. It also involves evaluating the realisation of benefits to the business from investment in IT.

Legal: As the dependence on ICT in an organisation grows, legal issues, in particular computer/cyber crime, are becoming an indispensable part of ICT risk management. Involvement of a legal officer in the team facilitates the need to address the ICT security problems from a legal perspective.

Physical Security: Most security departments, particularly in the studied organisations, still value physical assets. So the strategies end up taking more care of tangible assets than intangible ones. The involvement of security staff helps the re-engineering of physical security.

Operations: Operations is where the core services of the organisation are taking place and so is the main source of risk exposure which could prevent the organisation from achieving its mission. In our work we considered having a senior member of staff from the operations department who is fully knowledgeable of operation transactions. His participation in the team would assist in the risk assessment exercise.

Insurance/Risk manager: ICT security management is basically risk management focusing on ICT—mainly how to insure valuable information assets [10].

Step 4: Quick scan of the ICT related risks and their consequences to the organisation (Risk exposure due to ICT)

Before meeting the management as a whole, we needed some kind of justification and this was obtained by first working out some facts on likely consequences of ICT related risks to the organisation. We achieved this by carrying out a quick scan of such risks with the help of the ICT security team. This exercise involved capturing information on how core services are linked to the use of ICT. Face-to-face interviews with the CEO, chief financial officer (CFO), IT managers and the heads of the departments involved in the provision of the core services were conducted. This step was accomplished by using EMitL tool. The tool helped to interpret the consequences of losses in the corporate value based on financial indicators, to technical terminology. This interpretation was based on three groups of damage exposures due to ICT risks, namely liability claims, direct loss of property and business or service interruption [1,2].

Step 5: Getting Management's attention and sponsorship (The management as a whole buy into the idea as well)

The management had to be convinced and understand that their organisation was vulnerable to ICT related risks. Furthermore, we had to educate them on the magnitude of the security problem, and insist that ICT security was more than a technological issue. This means it has something to do with the kind of administration, policies and procedures that were in place; the kind of legal and contractual obligations the organisation had, particularly in delivering services, and also the ethics and culture of the individual staff. This was achieved by presenting to the management the worked out status of their ICT security from step 4 and by discussing their role in managing the identified problems with respect to their positions in the organisation.

Step 6: Getting the current status of ICT security documented (Take stock of the existing situation)

Our next step involved taking stock of what is existing in terms of systems: hardware, software, platforms, networks, applications, users and information assets; Environment: (location and services)—security threats, and countermeasures as well as policies and procedures that are currently in place. This information helped to identify the current status and also highlighted areas that may need immediate attention. In addition, we later, during the awareness sessions, used this information to help staff understand and appreciate the type of problem they have.

Step 7: Conduct awareness sessions among users (with some feedback from steps 1-6)

Our approach was top down, starting with the management, and the topic was "Managing Technology risks, the role of the management, including legal issues in a computerised environment". Along with the presentation notes, we attached the timetable of other training sessions for their departments/staff as well. This helped to get the message across to other staff through their bosses who made sure that their staff attended their respective sessions. More than 90% of the targeted staff during the awareness sessions attended in person. We made some observations during the sessions, for example, if you look at the staff as they were getting into the awareness session room, you could read their faces indicating something like "this session is not for me". However, after some time into the session the situation changed, and you could observe that, staff were getting concerned on the discussed issues. ICT Security awareness efforts were designed to allow staff from various departments to recognise ICT security concerns and respond accordingly as detailed in [9]. Apart from the general awareness session, we also conducted special sessions with individual departments, namely legal, accounts, human resources, internal auditing, physical security and technical. These were meant to address relevant departmental-specific issues in more detail.

Step 8: Carry out Risk assessment and analysis
Using the security team, we started to conduct risk assessment and analysis starting with the operations department followed by the IT department, physical security and later other departments. Information obtained from this step was vital for the discussion we held later with individual managers, e.g. when discussing with CFO on how to financially hedge the identified risks. The obtained information was also used to estimate the security awareness and in proposing countermeasures based on the output of the EMitL tool (the output of step 4) [1].

Step 9: Work out the Mitigation plan (Short term plan for issues that need immediate attention and long term mitigation plan)
This is the step that came in with pressure from the management. Having realised how risky it was to go without proper ICT security management in place, the management was now in the forefront, suggesting to the security team that they should come up with the mitigation plan. From the risk assessment and analysis, step 8, we found that there were issues that needed immediate attention. For example, the issues of licences, patching management, training, and improvement of the infrastructure. Although there was no budget for these, the management saw the reason to re-allocate their budget immediately. A long term plan was then worked out which included among other things disaster recovery and business continuity plans, the development of countermeasures including policies and procedures on ICT security.

Step 10: Developing the countermeasures
The main question here was what set of countermeasures would provide the best protection against the identified risks and the state of ICT security in the organisation. By taking into consideration the suggestion made from the EMitL tool (what should have been in place), ITIL (why), ISO 17799 (what), COBIT (how) and finally the environment in which the organisation is operating, we started deriving the relevant countermeasures to be implemented in order to address the identified ICT risk exposure [4, 5, 6].

3 Discussion and Conclusion

Perception and interpretation of the word ICT security often leads to the misunderstanding of the actual ICT security problem and causes inconsistency in addressing it. To the management it may sound better if we could use Managing technology risks instead of Managing ICT security as detailed in [10]. The ten steps describe above were used to bring a common view to the problem of ICT security among the management and technical staff. Reviewing the steps as described here, one can easily see that they fit well with issues discussed under aspects such as Organisational information security governance and the like such as those presented in [7, 8].

Our objective to bridge the gap between the management and the technical department was achieved through the ten steps. These included, CEO buying into the idea first, recognising that technical department is the custodian of ICT in the organisation, starting it as a special project, showing where the risks and their consequences are, getting the entire management attention, taking stock of the existing situation, conducting awareness sessions to address the ICT security problem with respect to the organisation's specific environment, carrying out detailed risk assessment and working out a short term plan for issues that needed immediate attention and long term plan, and finally developing countermeasures for the identified problems. The study showed that the success of an ICT security management process begins with the management realising the importance of ICT security management.

References

1. Bakari, J. K., Magnusson, C., Tarimo, C. and Yngström, L.: Ensuring ICT Risks Using EMitL Tool: An Empirical Study, IFIP, Springer, USA. (2005) 157-173.
2. Bakari, J.K.: Towards A Holistic Approach for Managing ICT Security in Developing Countries: A Case Study Of Tanzania", Ph.L thesis, SU-KTH, Stockholm. (2005).
3. Magnusson, C. Hedging Shareholders Value in an IT dependent Business Society, THE FRAMEWORK BRITS, Ph.D Thesis, SU-KTH, Stockholm, (1999).
4. ITIL, (April, 2005); http://www.itil.org.uk/.
5. COBIT, (20th October, 2005); http://www.isaca.org/cobit/.
6. ISO 17799 Standards.
7. Solms, B. V. Information Security governance: COBIT or ISO 17799 or both? Computer & Security Vol 24 (2005) 99-104.
8. Solms, B. V. and Solms, R. V. The 10 deadly sins of information security management, Computers & Security, Vol.23 No 5 ISSN 0167–4048, (2004) 371-376.
9. Wilson, M. & Hash, J. 'Building an Information Technology Security Awareness and Training Program' NIST Special publication 800-50, USA, (2003).
10. Blakley, B. McDermott, E. & Geer, D.: Information Security is Information Risk Management, ACM Press New York, NY, USA, (2001).

Value-Focused Assessment of Information Communication and Technology Security Awareness in an Academic Environment

Lynette Drevin, Hennie Kruger, and Tjaart Steyn

North-West University,
Private Bag X6001, Potchefstroom, 2520, South Africa
ldrevin@acm.org, rkwhak@puk.ac.za, rkwts@puk.ac.za

Abstract. The aim of this paper is to introduce the approach of value-focused thinking when identifying information and communications technology (ICT) security awareness aspects. Security awareness is important to reduce human error, theft, fraud, and misuse of computer assets. A strong ICT security culture cannot develop and grow in a company without awareness programmes. How can personnel follow the rules when they don't know what the rules are? [1] This paper focuses on ICT security awareness and how to identify key areas of concern to address in ICT security awareness programmes by making use of the value-focused approach. The result of this approach is a network of objectives where the fundamental objectives are the key areas of concern that can be used in decision making in security planning.

1 Introduction

Employee errors are among the top ten threats to information assets according to Whitman and Mattord [2]. Security education, training and awareness are part of the process to educate staff on information security. Pfleeger and Pfleeger [3] state that people using security controls must be convinced of the need for it. They have to understand why security is important in a given situation. Cribb [1] looks at security from a business point of view and states that a single case of abuse can cause more costs than the establishment of a security system. He feels that the cost of training employees is less than the potential penalties incurred if legislation was not adhered to or the company's systems were attacked. Employees should know the rules otherwise they can't be expected to follow them. Training can prevent staff from accidentally acting inappropriately. Effective use of security controls that are in place can only be achieved when employees are aware of the need for security. BS 7799:1 has a section on user training and the objective is to 'ensure that all users are aware of information security threats and concerns, and are equipped to support organizational security policy in the course of their normal work' [4].

It is necessary to do an assessment to measure the awareness of staff members regarding information communication and technology (ICT) security in general. Focus areas are necessary to measure relevant areas otherwise many aspects can be looked into without getting to the real shortcomings or issues. The value-focused thinking method [5] was used in an university environment as part of a bigger security awareness project.

The aim of this paper is to introduce the approach of value-focused thinking as applied to ICT security awareness. This paper will first discuss the value-focused thinking method of arriving at fundamental objectives to identify important security awareness aspects. Next, the security awareness project will be discussed after which the results obtained will be given. A short discussion of the fundamental objectives will follow and lastly a conclusion and further research possibilities will be given.

2 Methodology: Value-Focused Thinking

Value-focused thinking is a decision technique suggested by Keeney [5]. The approach calls for the identification of the stakeholders that will be impacted by the decision. These persons or groups of persons are then questioned about their values, concerning the specific area under consideration. Their responses are then used to identify objectives. Values are those principles that one strives to and define all that one can care about in a specific situation [5]. Objectives are characterized by three features, namely: a decision context, an object and a direction of preference [6]. Keeney states that one of the greatest benefits of this approach is that better alternatives for a decision problem can be generated once objectives have been established. This is in contrast with the more traditional method, called attribute-focused thinking, where alternatives are first identified after which the objectives are specified. Following the determination of objectives, a process to distinguish between means and fundamental objectives is performed. Fundamental objectives refer to the objectives underlying the essential reasons for the problem being under consideration while means objectives are regarded as those whose attainment will help achieve the fundamental objectives [7]. Finally a means-ends objective network is constructed to show the interrelationships among all objectives. The network is then used to derive cause-effect relationships and to generate potential decision opportunities.

The value-focused thinking approach has already been applied successfully in different areas. Hassan applied it to the environmental selection of wall structures [8] while Nah, Sian and Sheng used the approach to describe the value of mobile applications [7]. Other examples can be found in Dhillon et al [9], [10] where the value-focused thinking approach was used in assessment of IS security in organizations and privacy concerns for Internet commerce. In this study the value-focused approach was applied at a university to identify key areas of concern to ICT security awareness.

3 Application of Value-Focused Thinking

Keeney's value-focused approach was used to conduct interviews and to organize the data into the required network. The primary objective of the interview process was to identify stakeholders' wishes, concerns, problems and values pertaining to ICT security awareness.

A discussion document, rather than a questionnaire, was used to obtain information from the interviewees. The discussion document contained six statements or questions and was compiled according to the techniques for the identification of objectives suggested by Keeney [5]. Examples of issues discussed with interviewees include:
- What would you do or implement to increase the level of security awareness?
- What is important to you regarding ICT security awareness and how would you achieve it?

The same interview process used by Nah et al [7] was followed and interviews were conducted until no new values or objectives could be identified. A total of 7 employees were interviewed, however, no new values were obtained after the fourth interview. The interviews were recorded for future reference. Each interview lasted approximately one and a half hours. Respondents included staff from both management and non-management levels and were selected from the IT department and from users. The immediate result of the interview process was a list of values that apply to ICT security awareness. These values were then converted into objectives by changing statements such as: 'lock doors when out of office or keep laptops out of sight' into a structure consisting of a decision context, and object and a direction of preference, e.g. 'maximize physical access control'. The fundamental and means objectives were then derived from the list of objectives. This was done following Keeney's 'why is it important?' test. If an objective is important because it helps achieve another objective, it is categorized as a means objective, otherwise it is a fundamental objective. Finally the means-ends objective network was constructed graphically by linking means and fundamental objectives to one another to show the interrelationships among them. A more detailed discussion on this network follows in the next section.

4 Results

A network of objectives was constructed from the data obtained during the interviews and is presented in Figure 1. On the left are the means objectives that show the concerns, wishes and values of the interviewees pertaining to ICT security awareness. The right hand side shows the fundamental objectives that are derived from the means objectives or stated by the stakeholders.

The fundamental objectives are in line with the acknowledged goals of ICT security e.g. integrity, confidentiality and availability. Other objectives that emerge from this exercise are more on the social and management side e.g. responsibility for actions and effective use of resources. The results confirm that no new aspects of security awareness could be identified in an academic environment neither could any aspects be ignored. The six fundamental objectives should be addressed when planning, shaping and developing ICT security awareness programmes in order to comply with what management and users identified as crucial.

Means Objectives   **Fundamental Objectives**

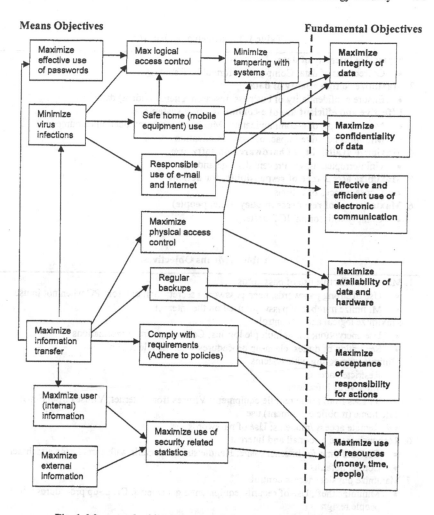

Fig. 1. Means-ends objectives network for ICT security awareness.

Overall objective: Maximize ICT security awareness to assist the university to provide a sustainable service to its staff, students and other stakeholders.

The fundamental and means objectives derived from the network are listed in tables 1 and 2. Table 2 can be used to see what aspects influence the means objectives according to the interviewees while table 1 shows the fundamental objectives and the factors describing them. The value of the results is that the information will be used to develop a measuring instrument that will cover and focus on the identified means objectives in order to address fundamental objectives. It also serves as a framework for management to structure an awareness programme that includes all the appropriate learning areas.

Table 1. Fundamental Objectives.

1. **Maximize integrity of data**
   - Correctness of data; Comply with formal ICT strategy
2. **Maximize confidentiality of data**
   - Ensure confidentiality of business, research, client (student) data
3. **Effective and efficient use of e-communication systems**
   - Minimize cost of e-communication; Maximize e-communication resources
   - Minimize negative impact of e-communication
4. **Maximize availability of hardware and software**
   - Uninterrupted usage; Prevent damage and loss
5. **Maximize acceptance of responsibility for actions**
   - Consequences of actions
6. **Maximize use of resources (money, time, people)**
   - Comply with formal ICT strategy

Table 2. Means Objectives.

1. Maximize effective use of passwords
   - Use of strong passwords, keep passwords secret; Sign off from PC when not in use
   - Minimize number of password used on the Internet
2. Maximize logical access control
   - Use encryption; Limit multiple log-ins; Correct system authorizations
   - Separation of duties, clean-up procedures when people resign
3. Minimize tampering with systems
   - Restricted access
4. Minimize virus infections
   - Viruses from home/mobile equipment; Viruses from Internet; Viruses from e-mail
5. Safe home (mobile equipment) use
   - Remote access /modems; Use of passwords
6. Responsible use of e-mail and Internet
   - Cost and time for Internet usage; Handle strange e-mails with care: Large attachments
   - Correct defaults
7. Maximize physical access control
   - Minimize theft; Use of security equipment e.g. cameras; Clean-up procedures when people resign
8. Make regular backups
   - Minimize loss of data; Criteria on how long to keep data
   - Correct default saves; Criteria for important data; Availability of equipment to make backups
9. Maximize information transfer to employees
   - Maximize IT literacy; Use communication channels (posters, bulletin boards, contracts)
   - Criteria for important data; Illegal use of software
10. Comply with requirements (Adhere to policies)
   - Make risks clear; Make security implications clear
11. Maximize user (internal) information
   - Use user feedback; Use internal audit statistics; Minimize loss of knowledge e.g. when resign

12. Maximize external information :
  - Use external input/reports e.g. external auditors, Gartner
13. Maximize use of security related statistics
  - Use all comparable statistics

5 Conclusion and Further Research

The overall objective that resulted from this phase of the project is the maximization of ICT security awareness to aid the university in providing a sustainable service to its staff, students and other stakeholders. Fundamental objectives to achieve this were identified by constructing a network using the value-focused approach. These objectives can serve as a basis for decision making and to guide the planning, shaping and development ICT security awareness in a company. ICT security awareness programmes can be used to train staff and sensitize them in the security arena to get a more secure environment compliant to standards such as BS 7799 and others.

This work is ongoing and the next step will be the formal definition and description of the objectives followed by the development of a measuring tool. The completed network will be used to develop a measuring instrument to ensure that all areas are appropriately covered. At management level the identified objectives can be used as a guideline to structure security awareness programmes.

References

1. Cribb, B. Lack of policy causes IT risks. In ITWEB. 15 Jul 2005.
2. Whitman, M.E., Mattord, H.J. Principles of Information Security. 2nd edn. Thomson (2005).
3. Pfleeger, C.P., Pfleeger, S.L. Security in Computing. 3rd edn. Prentice Hall (2003).
4. BS 7799. http://www.thewindow.to/bs7799/4.htm. Used on 31 Oct 2005.
5. Keeney, R.L. Creativity in decision making with value-focused thinking. Sloan Management Review, Summer (1994) 33-41.
6. Sheng, H., Nah, F.F., Siau, K. Strategic implications of mobile technology: A case study in using value-focused thinking. Journal of Strategic Information Systems. (2005) 1-22 (Article in press).
7. Nah, F.F., Siau, K. & Sheng, H. The value of mobile applications: A utility company study, Communications of the ACM, 48(2). (2005) 85-90.
8. Hassan, O.A.B. Application of value-focused thinking on the environmental selection of wall structures, Journal of environmental management, 70. (2004) 181-187.
9. Dhillon, G., Torkzadeh, G. Value-focused assessment of information system security in organizations. Proceedings of the twenty second international conference on Information Systems. (2001) 561-566.
10. Dhillon, G., Bardacino, J., Hackney, R. Value focused assessment of individual privacy concerns for Internet commerce. Proceedings of the twenty third international conference on Information Systems. (2002) 705-709.

Using Phishing for User Email Security Awareness

Ronald C. Dodge and Aaron J. Ferguson

Department of Electrical Engineering and Computer Science
United States Military Academy, West Point, NY, USA
{ronald.dodge, aaron.ferguson}@usma.edu

Abstract. User security education and training is one of the most important aspects of an organizations security posture. Using security exercises to reinforce this aspect is frequently done by education and industry alike; however these exercises usually enlist willing participants. We have taken the concept of using an exercise and modified it somewhat to evaluate a users propensity to respond to email phishing attacks.

1 Introduction

The quest for information systems security has a significant, almost self cancelling facet—the user. User information assurance (IA) awareness is a random variable that is very difficult to characterize due to user's individual nature. Users create an open back door into our corporate networks through their internet and third party application use. This vulnerability is increased from mobile systems that join home and other commercial networks. While the application of host and network based security applications can provide some mitigation of this threat, one well timed or lucky random shot can provide a malicious user unauthorized access to the intranet. Security training and awareness programs have done a good job of mitigating this risk – but just how good? What measures exist to verify that users understand and consistently apply the best practices they are exposed to during periodic training?

The use of exercises to reinforce concepts in an educational setting has been written about frequently [1]. Typically, these exercises involve participation by knowing participants and involve a network attack/defense scenario. The United States Military Academy (USMA) took the concept of a hands-on exercise and developed an email phishing exercise with the intent of evaluating the efficacy of our user IA training. The exercise first ran as a prototype in the spring of 2004 and has since been run two additional times. The most recent exercise (at the time of this writing) ended in November 2005.

The phishing exercise at USMA was developed under the name of "Carronade". As described in [3], a Carronade is a Navy cannon used in the early 1770 and seemed an appropriate name.

"The Carronade although possessing limited range, was destructive at close quarters (less than 0.6 miles). It is important to note that in offensive operations

Please use the following format when citing this chapter:

Author(s) [insert Last name, First-name initial(s)], 2006, in IFIP International Federation for Information Processing, Volume 201, Security and Privacy in Dynamic Environments, eds. Fischer-Hubner, S., Rannenberg, K., Yngstrom, L., Lindskog, S., (Boston: Springer), pp. [insert page numbers].

during the 1700s, the objective was not to sink an enemy vessel but rather to avoid damaging the hull so as to capture it as intact as possible, so it would be retained as a 'prize.'

In keeping with this military theme, this exercise was named the Carronade because: (a) while the emails had the potential to be destructive, the intent was to get the attention of cadets, not to cause damage to the Academy network or to penalize the cadets; and (b) the exercise was short range--conducted inside the USMA security perimeter--only cadets with a usma.edu domain name could launch the embedded link."

In this paper, we will present a background discussion on the exercise, describing its origin and planning considerations. We will further describe the evolution of the exercise from a prototype to a multi-email exercise designed to evaluate different forms of phishing and the efficacy of training. We will provide results from each exercise and offer some assessment of our awareness and training program. We then conclude with a look toward future exercises.

2 Background and Previous Work

We begin explaining the exercise by first addressing the specific considerations common to each phishing exercise and then later describe the evolution of implementation.

We first must recognize that USMA is a very "connected" campus. Each student has a computer with a specific suite of software. While they are allowed to install third party applications that are not part of the official suite, they must purchase them on their own and the computer staff at USMA will not support them. Given these limitations virtually all students have the same basic configuration. In addition, email is a very heavily relied upon management and information dissemination tool.

Our first consideration was devising an email that a student would definitely be interested in opening and reading. One of our design decisions was to avoid common phishing email content such as financial or services emails. We decided for our final email prototype that the student would be instructed to visit a website (hyperlink) to validate course grades. The second specific consideration, timing, fit nicely with the email content.   For the prototype we constructed the email near the end of the semester when students would be most concerned about grade correctness. The third specific consideration focused on the target. Prior to the exercise, a target population needs to be identified. For our prototype a very small sample population across all classes was selected. Lastly, our fifth consideration, post event notification and follow-up mechanism, needed to be defined. In the prototype, immediate notification via an automated email was selected.

The prototype (Carronade I) was limited in nature. The emails were sent 512 students at USMA (roughly 12% of the student body). The student body at USMA (called the corps of cadets) is broken down into four regiments, each with eight companies. Each company has approximately 130 cadets. Four cadets were randomly selected from each class (i.e., four freshman, four sophomores, four juniors, and four seniors) for a total of 512 cadets out of a total of approximately 4200 cadets. A detailed analysis of the exercise background can be found in [2].

2.1 Carronade Evolution

We conducted an assessment of the prototype and determined that the exercise could provide useful insights into the efficacy of our awareness and training program. Our focus for Carronade II was to develop a repeatable exercise that over time would serve as a yard stick to measure our programs. To that end, the exercise was conducted in September, 2004. The timing of the exercise was set to ensure the new freshman class had an opportunity to become familiar with their computer and the email system at USMA. The exercise was conducted prior to any regularly scheduled IA training. A detailed discussion of the technical implementation of Carronade II can be found in [3].

To validate that the email content was consistent with current training foci, we decided to seek input using a survey of information technology instructors. The survey asked the instructors to identify the top information assurance-related negative behaviors of their students. Using the survey, we developed the following requirements for Carronade II, incorporating four different styles of emails:

- The system must be able to deliver an email to all students.
- The first email type asks the student to click on an embedded link in an HTML encoded questionable email to fix a problem with a fictitious grade report; clicking on the link records information readily available from the browser.
- The second email type is identical to the first email except that the email asks the student to open the corresponding .html attachment.
- The third email type asks the student to click on a link that takes them to a web form that asks for sensitive information (i.e., their social security number).
- The fourth email type asks the students to click on a link, download an application and run the application. (This was implemented, however due to technical problems, the results were not valid).
- Each of the emails should be questionable enough to raise the suspicions of the end user.
- None of the emails, if opened outside of the USMA domain, would collect, track, or transmit any user data.

As noted, a significant difference in Carronade II was the number of cadets targeted with the emails. This time the scope increased to the entire student body (minus those involved in the planning and execution). Of the total number of 4155 in the student body, 4118 received the emails. The email breakdown by type was: 1010 embedded link emails, 1014 attachment emails, 999 sensitive information emails, and 1095 download emails were sent out. (As stated, in the final results these emails are discounted due to technical problems.)

Carronade III was implemented functionally with very few changes from Carronade II. A similar sample population was used (everyone minus the exercise coordinators), however the timing was changed to more closely follow the required IA training that each student receives. The date was selected to assess whether the recently received training produced lower "violations". The exercise was implemented in November 2005.

We chose a very similar email package – embedded link, attachment, sensitive information, and download emails. Unfortunately, different but similar problems plagued the download email and the results from this set are not included in the final analysis. The total emails sent 4136; were broken down as follows: 1006 embedded link, 1013 attachment emails, 1058 sensitive information emails, and 1059 download emails. (As stated, in the final results these emails are discounted due to technical problems.)

3 Results

We elected to examine the results of the exercises in three facets. First, by overall percentage, by year, of the number of students that succumbed to the phishing email. Second, we look at the distribution of failures by class for each exercise. Then finally, we look at the performance of a specific class over the two years.

3.1 Failure Percentage by Exercise

As seen in Figure 1, the failure rate in the prototype is very high. This is more than likely explained by the very small sample size (512). The results for 2004 and 2005 suggest minimal impact due to the recently conducted training. This however will require further data points to accurately draw this conclusion. It should be noted that in post exercise discussion with the students, the majority that did "fail" said they found the emails odd, however responded anyways.

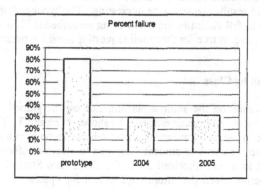

Fig. 1. Percentage of Failure by Exercise.

3.2 Distribution Summary

The breakout of failures by exercise, type of email, and class is interesting and should shed interesting insight as additional data is gathered through future exercises. Figure 2 shows to major groups (left to right), the first full Carronade exercise and the second full exercise. With in each group the data is further broken down by class (freshman, sophomore, junior, and senior), then again, by email type.

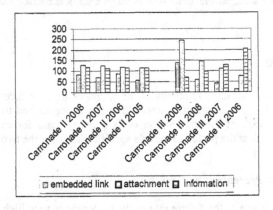

Fig. 2. Failure Breakout.

The primary difference between the two major exercises was the timing in relation to training. In Carronade II, training had not yet been conducted when the exercise was conducted. In Carronade III, training had been conducted within the previous 2 weeks. The first exercise produced results that are not very interesting. The second exercise produced results that are quite interesting. The "younger" the class, the more likely they were to fall victim to the email using an embedded link or an attachment. The opposite however is true for the email requesting sensitive personal information.

3.3 Distribution by Class

The final observation on the student performance can be gained by examining the students who participated in each exercise, as shown in Figure 3. The results show a positive increase in the user awareness across all classes on clicking embedded links and opening attachments. Our students continue to disclose information that should not be disclosed to an unauthorized user. For the United States Military, this is an important distinction given the future requirement for operational security once the students graduate and enter the Army. This information will help us not only modify the IA awareness program, but also provide input to the other areas where operational security is important.

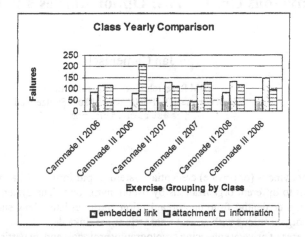

Fig. 3. Comparison of Class Performance over two Exercises.

4 Conclusions and Future Work

The phishing exercises served to provide an insight into the awareness levels of our students and help us better focus our IA and awareness training. The results are still very immature; however they provide an opportunity to look at the effectiveness of our programs. One might look at the assessment of the programs using an exercise as "poisoning the well", given the very fact that the exercises themselves may raise awareness, making it difficult to separate out any increased awareness due solely to the annual training. While this is true, when looking at the exercise from a bottom line – if our user's awareness is increased, providing enhanced network security whatever the cause is a worthwhile cause.

We intend to continue the phishing email exercises, increasing the frequency to once every semester. One exercise will follow closely existing training; the second will be used to assess longer term retention.

References

1 Dodge, R., Hoffman, L., Rosenberg, T., Ragsdale, D., "Exploring a National Cyber Security Exercise for Universities," IEEE Security and Privacy, September/October 2005, pp 52-58.
2 Ferguson, A., "Duty, Honor, Country and Email Attachments: The West Point Carronade" Educause Quarterly, Number 1 2005, pp 54-57.
3 Jackson, J., Ferguson, A., Cobb, M., "Building a University-wide Automated IAAwareness Exercise: The West Point Carronade", Frontiers in Education Conference, 19-22 October 2005, pp T2E7-10.

Anonymous Credentials: Opportunities and Challenges

Jan Camenisch

IBM Research, Zurich Research Lab
Säumerstrasse 4, CH-8803 Rüschlikon, Switzerland
jca@zurich.ibm.com

In an anonymous (or private) credential system as put forth by Chaum in 1985, a user is known to different organizations by pseudonyms only. The system allows the user to obtain a credential from one organization and then later show such credentials to another organizations without that transactions are linkable.

The area of privacy enhancing cryptography protocols and, in particular, anonymous credential systems have recently gained considerable momentum in research and indeed many substantial contributions have been made in last few years. At the same time, the interest in applying such systems in the real world has grown. Despite of this, the area is still relatively young and there are still many open research challenges to overcome.

In this talk, we will review the state of the art in anonymous credential systems. We will then discuss their applications including privacy enhancing identity management (www.prime-project.eu.org) and anonymous attestation. Finally, we will discuss research directions and challenges.

Please use the following format when citing this chapter:

Author(s) [insert Last name, First-name initial(s)], 2006, in IFIP International Federation for Information Processing, Volume 201, Security and Privacy in Dynamic Environments, eds. Fischer-Hubner, S., Rannenberg, K., Yngstrom, L., Lindskog, S., (Boston: Springer), pp. [insert page numbers].

Practical Private Regular Expression Matching

Florian Kerschbaum

SAP Research
Karlsruhe, Germany
Florian.Kerschbaum@sap.com

Abstract. Regular expressions are a frequently used tool to search in large texts. They provide the ability to compare against a structured pattern that can match many text strings and are common to many applications, even programming languages. This paper extends the problem to the private two-party setting where one party has the text string and the other party has the regular expression. The privacy constraint is that neither party should learn about the input of the other party, i.e. the string or the regular expression, except the result of the computation which is wether the string matches the regular expression or not. Secure Multiparty Computation provides general algorithms for any such problem, but it has been recommended to develop special protocols for important cases that provide better performance using the domain knowledge of that problem. This paper presents two protocols: One with perfect secrecy that provides a lower-bound on protocols using circuit construction and a fast one that provides better performance bounds, but the secrecy it provides is limited and tuned for practical applications. The fast protocol presented here uses permutation and commutative encryption as its only building blocks.

1 Introduction

Regular expressions provide a very powerful tool to search in text databases. They can search for structured patterns matching up to an infinite number of strings. Therefore they also have often been used in genome database searches [4, 12]. Especially in genome searches there may be a privacy requirement, since the search pattern may reveal sensitive data, such as the searcher's identity, predisposition for certain health risks, or simply patented material. Also the database may need protection, since the data can be economically valuable and privacy–sensitive, because of person or health–related data. A private regular expression search protects searcher and database equally well.

Regular expressions are also used in programming languages [26]. Regular expressions can be extended with powerful matching techniques using special algorithms. In this paper the capabilities following in table 1 have been considered.

The regular expression $a?(b|c)(b|c)*$ matches any string that is constructed from b and c only, but may begin with an optional a, e.g. c, $bbbccc$, abc and many more. Regular expression matching is to determine whether a given string can be constructed from the regular expression.

Imagine a setting where one party has the regular expression and another party has the string, but they don't want to exchange their information. A common situation

Please use the following format when citing this chapter:
Author(s) [insert Last name, First-name initial(s)], 2006, in IFIP International Federation for Information Processing, Volume 201, Security and Privacy in Dynamic Environments, eds. Fischer-Hubner, S., Rannenberg, K., Yngstrom, L., Lindskog, S., (Boston: Springer), pp. [insert page numbers].

Table 1. Symbols for regular expressions.

Symbol	Description
a	Matches the character exactly: "a"
ab	Matches the character sequence in this order: "a" then "b", so "ab"
$a?$	Matches the character zero or one time: "" or "a"
$a*$	Matches the character zero to infinite times: "", "a", "aa", ...
$a\vert b$	Matches either of both characters: "a" or "b"
(x)	Groups the pattern x, such that it can be used in subsequent operations

would be where one party has a text database and the other party wants to search for the occurrences of a regular expression. The privacy requirement is that neither learns about the input of the other party except what can be inferred by the result. If Alice has the string and Bob the regular expression, Alice should not learn the regular expression, its size or composition and Bob should not learn the string or its characteristics. They should only learn whether the regular expression matches the string or not. Secure Multiparty Computation provides the ability to solve any such problem by constructing a binary circuit and executing it privately, but it is recommended to find specific solutions to important problems. The solutions presented in this paper uses only permutation, randomization and commutative encryption. No circuit emulation techniques or slow, e.g. homomorphic, encryption are being used as building blocks. As the commutative encryption scheme RSA [22] with a common modulus could be used. The very similar Pohlig-Hellman encryption [21] can be used, as well. The common modulus attack [10] is not possible, since public keys are never exchanged during the protocol. Semantically secure (probabilistic) encryption is not needed, since the plain text will be randomized when required. To learn more about RSA and commutative encryption, see [23].

A regular expression can be converted (via a non deterministic finite automaton) into a deterministic finite automaton (DFA). The DFA has a transition matrix M with a row for each state and a column for each symbol in the alphabet Σ. Each field contains the number of the state being transited to. Each state has an attribute attached to it: $accept$ or $non - accept$. Accepting states indicate a successful match, while non-accepting states indicate that the sub-string up to the current position does not match. The result of our computation is whether the automaton is in an accepting state at the last character of the input string. Each automaton has a start state. The start state can already be an accepting state and is the first state of each matching. The protocol presented here can be used to evaluate any DFA in a private manner, where one party has its input and the other party has the automaton. For further information about regular expressions and automatons, the reader is referred to [18].

The next section describes previous work in private computations and secure multiparty computation. The third section describes notation. Then follow the protocols: First the perfect-secret one, then the fast, yet not so secure protocol as the main result of the paper.

2   Related Work

Secure Multi-Party Computation (SMC) was introduced in [27]. SMC computes a function $f(a, b)$ where Alice has input a and Bob has input b, such that Alice learns nothing about b, except what can be inferred from $f(a, b)$ and a, and Bob learns nothing about a, except what can be inferred from $f(a, b)$ and b. Any such problem can be solved using a trusted third party, but the goal of SMC is to replace that third party by a protocol between Alice and Bob. Clever general solution to SMC are described in [3, 8, 16, 17]. In [16] a method to transform any protocol secure in the semi-honest setting into a protocol secure in the malicious setting is provided. This solution emulates a circuit constructed for function $f(\cdot, \cdot)$ and executes that circuit privately. Since circuit emulation is slow, [15] suggests to find faster solutions for important problems. One such problem is Private Information Retrieval (PIR). In PIR Alice has a set of data items v and Bob has an index i. Bob retrieves v_i and learns nothing about the other data items and Alice does not learn i. Several elegant techniques for PIR exist that provide better performance than circuit emulation [6, 9, 14, 20]. There is also a large amount of literature on other specific problems. Recently, protocols for database operations such as join, have been published [1]. These protocols provide perfect-secrecy, and use techniques such as commutative encryption and permutation similarly to the presented protocol. In [24] schemes for searching on encrypted data have been presented. They provide perfect secrecy with cleverly adapted encryption schemes, but allow only for exact searches of entire words in an outsourcing model. Not computationally-secure protocols for mathematical problems have been presented in [5, 11]. These provide solutions for secure dot-product and division. A fast protocol with weak security requirements has been recommended for privacy-preserving data mining in [25]. Similar protocols exist for many algorithmic problems, e.g. binary search [13] or edit distance [2].

3   Notation

Let $E(x)$ denote the encrypted value of x. Encryption by Alice and Bob is denoted as $E_A(\cdot)$ and $E_B(\cdot)$, respectively. All encryption is done using a commutative encryption scheme, i.e. $E_A(E_B(x)) = E_B(E_A(x))$. Similarly decryption is denoted by $D_A(\cdot)$ and $D_B(\cdot)$.

Permutations are denoted as Π. Application of permutation is denoted as $\Pi(\cdot)$. Π^{-1} denotes the inverse permutation that returns the items to their original ordering: $\Pi^{-1}(\Pi(v)) = \Pi(\Pi^{-1}(v)) = v$. Permutation is not commutative, i.e. $\Pi_A(\Pi_B(v)) \neq \Pi_B(\Pi_A(v))$.

Let $M, M^1, M^2, M^3, \ldots$ denote matrices and $m_{i,j}^k$ denote the i-th element of the j-th row of matrix M^k. Let $(v_1, v_2, \ldots, v_n)$ denote vector v of length n with elements v_1 through v_n.

A mapping Ψ is a set of pairs $\{(a, b), \ldots\}$ where $a \mapsto b$. It is not required that a be unique.

Let the variable t range over the states of the automaton.

4   Protocols

4.1   Setup

In the remainder of this paper, it will be assumed that Alice has a string $x = (x_1, x_2, x_3, ..., x_l)$ of length l and Bob has the regular expression R. Bob converts his regular expression R into a deterministic finite automaton represented by transition matrix M and start state s. M has m rows, one for each state in the automaton and n column, one for each symbol in the alphabet Σ. As in any secure multi-party computation (or even encryption) the lengths of the inputs is not hidden. So the parameters l, m, and n are public. The only technique (as in encryption) to hide the length of the inputs is padding, but, as it comes at the expense of runtime, its discussion is not expanded here. The protocols operate in the "Honest-but-Curious" model, i.e. both parties follow the protocol as intended, but are allowed to record information along the way to make inferences about the input of the other party.

4.2   Perfect Secret Protocol

The Perfect Secret Protocol is used as a reference, so the output is defined as all (ending) position where the regular expression matches. In section 4.3 protocols to compute other results, such as does the regular expression match at all, are presented for the fast protocol. Similar techniques could obviously be applied to the Perfect Secret Protocol, but are left out due to space constraints. The main operation the protocol has to provide is the indexing into the automaton iterating the state of the automaton. Let t be the current state of the automaton, then this operation can be written as

$$t := M[t, x[i]]$$

This operation only contains t as a state variable, that needs to be shared between Alice and Bob. In a circuit construction this state (t) would be shared in a XOR-like fashion and the indexing would be done using binary gates in an iterative or recursive algorithm. The obvious lower bound on that is $O(\log m)$ operations for the indexing. The operation would need to be repeated for each symbol x_i and the overall complexity is $O(m \cdot n \cdot l \cdot \log m)$. This can already be optimized by sharing the state not in an XOR-like fashion, but by using the modular operation. Let Alice have t_A and Bob have t_B, then the state would be $t = t_A + t_B \bmod m$. This sharing is perfectly secret, since t can be any value for any given value of t_A or t_B that Alice or Bob, respectively, has. Bob needs to implement two operations: $add(h)$ and $rotate(h)$. In the $add(h)$ operation Bob adds $h \bmod m$ to each value in the transition matrix M. In the $rotate(h)$ operation Bob rotates the rows of the transition matrix M by h rows, i.e. row i becomes row $i + h \bmod m$. The protocol then works as follows:

1. Alice gets start state s and sets $t_A = s(t_B = 0)$.
2. Bob chooses a random number r and applies $add(r)$.
3. Alice and Bob engage in an Oblivious Transfer (OT) protocol for all items in the transition matrix M and Alice retrieves the element corresponding to index t_A, x_i as its new value for t_A. *Note:* A special, unused bit can indicate whether the state is *accept*. Alice communicates this bit back to Bob.

4. Bob applies $rotate(r)$ and they repeat from step 2 for each character in x.

Theorem 1. *The "Perfect Secret Protocol" is secure in the semi-honest model.*

Proof. The composition theorem for secure multi-party computation [7] states, loosely speaking, that a protocol using secure building blocks protocols is secure if it is secure when those are replaced by invocations to ideal trusted third party. In this case the building block protocol is OT and the security of the protocol must be proven if those were done by ideal functionality. It will be shown that the view of each party can be simulated using a probabilistic polynomial time (PPT) algorithm from the inputs and outputs of each party alone. Let o be the output at each party (the bits indicating the state attribute). The view of each is the messages collected (assuming that OT is done using the ideal model). Bob is sent the output by Alice, so the simulator for his view $VIEW_{Bob}$ is simply: $VIEW_{Bob} = o$. Alice's view is the shares t_A and the simulator for view is to uniformly select l random numbers r'_i, $0 \leq r'_i < m$ for $i = 0, \dots, l$. The simulator and Alice's view are computationally indistinguishable, because the probability that a certain number x appears is equal in the view and the simulator and independent of previous events in both cases:

$$Pr[VIEW^i_{Alice} = x] = Pr[x = t - t_B \bmod m]$$
$$= \frac{1}{m}$$
$$= Pr[r'_i = x]$$
$$= Pr[SIMULATOR^i_{Alice} = x] \qquad \square$$

The communication cost is $O(m \cdot n \cdot l)$ and the $\log m$ factor has been replaced by a constant for the encryption system as the protocol works on integer numbers rather than on bits. This protocol also provides a lower bound on circuit construction protocols as they have to implement the indexing in a similar fashion and it already has been combined with the OT protocol in the above protocol. But the communication cost for this protocol can be prohibitively large, especially for large texts where the text length l dominates the cost. This paper therefore presents a second protocol that provides better performance characteristics for large texts, but at the expense of some privacy.

4.3 Fast Protocol

The fast protocol proceeds in the following general steps which will be detailed in later sections:

1. Bob prepares and encrypts the matrix M, such that Alice cannot extract any information about the regular expression. Alice then permutes the matrix, such that Bob cannot relate any column index to an input symbol of Alice. This relies on the fact that undoing a permutation in a graph is a hard problem related to the graph isomorphism problem. This is called the Obfuscation Protocol.
2. Then Alice and Bob engage in the State Transition Protocol for each character in Alice's string and proceed through the states of the automaton.
3. When all characters of Alice have been processed Alice and Bob engage in a short protocol to find the result.

Obfuscation Protocol The entire Obfuscation Protocol is composed of a number of building blocks. Each building block will be presented separately and by itself. The protocol is very complex, because it is a combination of so many parts and the reader be referred to [19] for a detailed, mathematical description of the protocol.

The basic protocol permutes the transition matrix of Bob. The general idea of the protocol is to create a permutation as a mapping of double-encrypted values. The mapping can then be applied to the encrypted values, such the permutation takes place without Alice knowing the original values. The protocol proceeds as follows:

1. Bob encrypts each entry of transition matrix M with $E_B(\cdot)$ and sends them to Alice.
2. Alice (double-)encrypts each entry with $E_A(\cdot)$.
3. Alice permutes the rows of M with a random permutation Π_A.
4. Alice creates a mapping Ψ of $i \mapsto \Pi_A(i)$. She encrypts i with $E_A(\cdot)$ and $\Pi_A(i)$ with $E_{A'}(\cdot)$. She sends the result to Bob.
5. Bob encrypts the first element of each pair with $E_B(\cdot)$ and the second element with $E_{B'}(\cdot)$. He applies a random permutation Π_B to the mapping and sends the result back to Alice.
6. Alice replaces each occurrence of $E_A(E_B(i))$ in M with its mapping $E_{A'}(E_{B'}(\Pi_A(i)))$.
7. She decrypts each value with $D_{A'}(\cdot)$ and sends the result to Bob.
8. Bob decrypts each value with $D_{B'}(\cdot)$.

Bob obtains the permuted transition matrix and could use it in the protocol. The first obvious problem is that this does not generate an isomorphic graph, since each edge has an assigned symbol. Alice needs to permute each row and permute each row differently. Adding such a step into the protocol is not difficult, but the transition matrix cannot be used "as-is" anymore for the evaluation of the regular expression. So Alice needs to maintain a copy of each such permutation (or the random seed that generated it) and undo it during the State Transition protocol.

The second problem is that the graph of the automaton might not be big enough to generate a difficult isomorphism problem. Therefore Alice needs to increase the size of the graph. She can split each node into k nodes where k is a security parameter agreed to by both parties. Of course, edges are not copied, but a target (from the split nodes) is chosen randomly. Details can be found in [19]. This also creates obfuscation in the graph and increases the difficulty of undoing the permutation. Introducing this into the protocol, Alice can simply copy the nodes when they are encrypted. The mapping then needs to be increased to $k \cdot m$ pairs where each i is mapped to k new values. She then randomly picks one of the pairs.

The third problem is that one node may have multiple in-edges, i.e. a number i can appear multiple times in M and the cipher text would reveal that. The in-degrees of all nodes would be revealed, such that one can more easily guess the automaton. This can be prevented by randomizing each entry in the transition matrix, such that its encrypted value is unique. Bob can choose such a randomization before sending the transition matrix to Alice, but then the mapping needs to be adapted. In the mapping process Bob needs to send the unencrypted values (remember they are just randomized versions of $1, \ldots, m$) to Alice. As the mapping needs to hide the in-degrees of each node, the mapping needs to be padded with random values for nodes that are not of the maximum degree. This increases the size of the mapping to $k \cdot m \cdot \delta$ where δ is the maximum in-degree of any node. The proposed protocol in [19] suggests leaking this information, but for perfect secrecy $\delta = m \cdot n$ can be chosen. Now there is an entry in the mapping for each entry in the (split) transition matrix with additional random elements that are discarded.

The final protocol has communication complexity $O(k \cdot n \cdot m^2)$.

State Transition Protocol The State Transition protocol has to compute the function $t := M[t, x[i]]$ where t is the current state of the automaton. Recall that Alice's has applied different permutations to each row, so there is a different permutation to be undone for each distinct t. The general outline of the protocol is as follows:

1. Alice sends an encryption of the inverse permutations to Bob, i.e. she encrypts the original index of each permuted element. This step has communication complexity $O(m \cdot n)$.
2. For each element x_i of the string:
   (a) Bob sends the double-encrypted inverse permutation to Alice. This step has communication complexity $O(n)$.
   (b) Alice selects the index i and returns the decrypted element.
   (c) Bob decrypts and obtains the permuted index to obtain the next element.

A detailed mathematical description can be found in [19]. This protocol has communication complexity $O(l \cdot n)$, if $m < l$, since the steps 2(a) to 2(c) are executed l times.

Combating the Frequency Attack Bob obtains the current state during the State Transition Protocol. (Alice does so via the encrypted permutation, as well, but does not have the original automaton.) This state has been permuted from the original automaton, but Bob can try to deduce information about the permutation by observing the intermediate values. Bob can try to identify certain patterns, such as repeating states, but the split operation and permutation can transform any such pattern into a number of similar ones. But such patterns are not only determined by the automaton, but by the string, as well. Furthermore, Bob does not have complete freedom in choosing the automaton, since he wants to compute the matching of the regular expression. The structure of the automaton is tied to the regular expression, although Bob can influence the structure.

There is another technique Bob can use to relate permuted to initial states. Each state has an a priori probability p of occurring depending on some distribution of the string x. If that distribution is known to Bob, he can use the frequency attack on the State Transition Protocol. In the worst case, imagine Bob searching for the letter e. The automaton has two states and the probability of the state corresponding to an occurrence of e has significantly lower probability than the other, namely the probability of e occurring in the text. This probability can be refined for a second matching depending on what information was leaked by the result of the first (e.g. the number of actual appearing e's). Bob can then rank the permuted states by their occurrence. He adds them up starting at the least frequent state and stops when he has reached probability p. Although, through splitting and permutation he will probably get a number of wrong states in this selection, the probability of these states of belonging to the original low probability state (e.g. e) is probably higher than an uniform distribution, i.e. the protocol leaks some information.

To counter this problem, the following solutions are suggested. Ideally each state would be split into a number of states proportional to p. Bob would transmit a probability of occurrence for each state along with M^1 to Alice, but he might not be trusted with the computation of these probabilities, since he can gain from incorrect information. In another approach, Alice might apply remedial action if she detects derivation from an uniform distribution. Bob sends the current state t along with each double-encrypted inverse permutation v in the State Transition Protocol. Alice monitors the statistical distribution of the states, and if one state deviates from the expected value $\frac{1}{m}$ by a fixed value, she will re-apply the Obfuscation Protocol, but this time split this state into a constant number c states. This will also permute all states again, such that the gathered statistics so far, don't relate to statistics gathered later. If the number of such re-obfuscation is bounded by the security parameter k, the overall cost of obfuscation would rise to $O(k^2 \cdot m^2 \cdot n)$.

Identifying the start state Alice and Bob need to identify the start state of the automaton after the Obfuscation Protocol. Alice therefore sends the encrypted inverse permutation (similar to the State Transition Protocol step 1) to Bob. Bob picks randomly one of the start states and sends it to Alice who decrypts and returns it Bob. This weakens the isomorphism problem for Bob, but since Alice also has split the start state there are still many possibilities for Bob to choose from. The detailed description can again be found in [19].

Obtaining the result There are different computations that a regular expression match (or search) can answer. First we will try to answer the question whether the (entire) text matches the regular expression. Bob has state attributes $accept, non - accept$ for each state in M. The answer to the question above is the state attribute of the last state. Alice and Bob need to track the attributes of the states. Therefore Bob encrypts them randomly: a random number with parity 0 for $accept$, a random number with parity 1 for $non - accept$, each encrypted with $E_B(\cdot)$. He sends them along with M^1 to Alice who tracks them during the "Obfuscation" protocol. She double encrypts with $E_A(\cdot)$ and returns them to Bob. Bob can then decrypt the state attribute of the final state and send it to Alice who announces it after decrypting. Note that the randomization is removed by Alice, and can therefore not be used to track the values. This protocol has communication complexity $O(m)$. For details, the reader is referred to [19] again.

An automaton for detecting a regular expression can be modified in such a way that it can be used for an entire text and each input symbol is processed only once. This provides a speed-up compared reading up to l_{max} symbols for each position in the text, but the results need to be obtained with a different protocol. The idea is to collect all state attributes in encrypted form during the "State Transition" protocol and then run a protocol to obtain the results. First each encrypted state attribute is accompanied by an encrypted index by Bob and both vectors are randomly permuted. Then Alice filters the vectors, such that only the encrypted indices of matches remain. The following questions can then be answered easily. Protocols with detailed steps can again be found in [19].

1. *What are the position of matches?*
   Alice returns the encrypted indices to Bob who decrypts and announces them.
2. *What is the minimum position of a match?*
   Bob splits the indices into two additive shares. He sends one part unencrypted and the other part encrypted using a homomorphic encryption. Alice re-randomizes Bob's shares after filtering, such that he cannot track individual indices. In [2] a protocol is presented to find the minimum of a vector split in this way.
3. *How many matches are there?*
   Alice counts the number of matches and announces the result.
4. *Is there any match at all?*
   Bob generates a number of fake entries. He obtains Alice's encryption by sending the values encrypted under his key first and then after Alice responded with the double-encrypted values, he in the second step sends them encrypted only under Alice's key. Let the number of false matches be r. Then Alice counts the number of matches in the resulting vector and stores it in r'. Alice and Bob compare privately (using double encryption) r and r'. If they match, the regular expression did not match.

5 Conclusion

This paper presented two protocols for evaluating an automaton. One perfect-secret and one adapted to provide better performance at cost of such some privacy. The second protocol has been extended into a protocol for privately searching a text using a regular expression. It uses double-encryption, randomization and permutation as its only building blocks. The communication cost was kept low and only practical building blocks were used. The construction of the protocol shows that the security relies on the computational difficulty of the graph isomorphism problem. Future research would be to extend the regular expression matching algorithm with more powerful matching techniques, e.g. look-ahead. The problem of repeated searches using different regular expressions is subject to further investigation.

References

1. R. Agrawal, A. Evfimievski, and R. Srikant. Information sharing across private databases. *Proceedings of the ACM SIGMOD international conference on Management of data*, 2003.
2. M. Atallah, F. Kerschbaum, and W. Du. Secure and Private Sequence Comparisons. *Proceedings of the 2nd Workshop on Privacy in the Electronic Society*, 2003.
3. M. Ben-Or, and A. Wigderson. Completeness theorems for non-cryptographic fault-tolerant distributed computation. *Proceedings of the 20th ACM symposium on Theory of computing*, 1988.

4. D. Betel, and C. Hogue. Kangaroo – A pattern-matching program for biological sequences. *Bioinformatics 3(20)*, 2002.
5. M. Bykova, M. Atallah, J. Li, K. Frikken, and M. Topkara. Private Collaborative Forecasting and Benchmarking. *Proceedings of the 3rd Workshop on Privacy in the Electronic Society*, 2004.
6. C. Cachin, S. Micali, and M. Stadler. Computationally private information retrieval with poly-logarithmic communication. *Proceedings of EUROCRYPT*, 1999.
7. R. Canetti. Security and composition of multiparty cryptographic protocols. *Journal of Cryptology 13(1)*, 2000.
8. D. Chaum, C. Crepeau, and I. Damgard. Multiparty unconditionally secure protocols. *Proceedings of the 20th ACM symposium on Theory of computing*, 1988.
9. B. Chor, O. Goldreich, E. Kushilevitz, and M. Sudan. Private Information Retrieval. *Proceedings of the 36th Symposium on Foundations of Computer Science*, 1995.
10. J. DeLaurentis. A further weakness in the common modulus protocol for the RSA cryptoalgorithm. *Cryptologia 8(3)*, 1984.
11. W. Du, and M. Atallah. Privacy-Preserving Cooperative Scientific Computations. *Proceedings of the 14th IEEE Computer Security Foundations Workshop*, 2001.
12. B. Eckman, A. Kosky, L. Laroco. Extending traditional query-based integration approaches for functional characterization of post-genomic data. *Bioinformatics 17(7)*, 2001.
13. K. Frikken, and M. Atallah. Privacy Preserving Electronic Surveillance. *Proceedings of the 2nd Workshop on Privacy in the Electronic Society*, 2003.
14. Y. Gertner, Y. Ishai, and E. Kushilevitz. Protecting data privacy in private information retrieval schemes. *Proceedings of the 30th ACM Symposium on Theory of Computing*, 1998.
15. S. Goldwasser. Multi party computations: past and present. *Proceedings of the 16th ACM symposium on Principles of distributed computing*, 1997.
16. O. Goldreich. Secure Multi-party Computation. Available at *http://www.wisdom.weizmann.ac.il/~oded/pp.html*, 2002.
17. O. Goldreich, S. Micali, and A. Wigderson. How to play any mental game. *Proceedings of the 19th ACM conference on Theory of computing*, 1987.
18. J. Hopcroft, R. Motwani, and J. Ullman. Introduction to Automata Theory, Languages, and Computation. *Addison Wesley*, 2000.
19. F. Kerschbaum. Practical Private Regular Expression Matching. *Technical Report, University of Dortmund*, available at *http://www4.cs.uni-dortmund.de/RVS/FK/*, 2005.
20. E. Kushilevitz, and R. Ostrovsky. Replication is not needed: single database, computationally–private information retrieval. *Proceedings of the 38th Symposium on Foundations of Computer Science*, 1997.
21. S. Pohlig, and M. Hellman. An improved algorithm for computing logarithms over GF(p) and its cryptographic significance. *IEEE Transactions on Information Theory 24*, 1978.
22. R. Rivest, A. Shamir, and L. Adleman. A Method for Obtaining Digital Signatures and Public-Key Cryptosystems. *Communications of the ACM 21(2)*, 1978.
23. B. Schneier. Applied Cryptography, 2nd Edition. *John Wiley & Sons*, 1996.
24. D. X. Song, D. Wagner, and A. Perrig. Practical Techniques for Searches on Encrypted Data. *Proceedings of IEEE Symposium on Security and Privacy*, 2000.
25. J. Vaidya, and C. Clifton. Privacy Preserving Association Rule Mining in Vertically Partitioned Data. *Proceedings of the 8th ACM SIGKDD International Conference on Knowledge Discovery and Data Mining*, 2002.
26. L. Wall, T. Christiansen, J. Orwant. Programming Perl, 3rd Edition. *O'Reilly*, 2000.
27. A. Yao. Protocols for Secure Computations. *Proceedings of the IEEE Symposium on Foundations of Computer Science 23*, 1982.

A System for Privacy-Aware Resource Allocation and Data Processing in Dynamic Environments

Siani Pearson and Marco Casassa-Mont

Hewlett-Packard Research Labs, Filton Road, Stoke Gifford, Bristol, BS34 8QZ. UK.
{Siani.Pearson, Marco.Casassa-Mont}@hp.com

Abstract. In this paper we describe a system for allocating computational resources to distributed applications and services (within distributed data centres and utility computing systems) in order to perform operations on personal or confidential data in a way that is compliant with associated privacy policies. Relevant privacy policies are selected on the fly, based on related meta-policies, depending on contextual information (potentially including location) and properties of the resources. One or more Trusted Privacy Services are involved to mediate the access to the data, based on the satisfaction of pertinent policies. Resources might be equipped with trusted computing components (e.g. Trusted Platform Modules [1]) to provide higher assurance and trust about the contextual statements or properties of these resources (such as their location, their status and integrity, etc.).

1 Introduction

Enterprises store large amounts of confidential data about their employees, customers and partners. On the one hand, accessing and managing this data is fundamental for their business: confidential information is retrieved, analysed and exchanged between people (and applications) that have different roles within an organisation (or across organisations) to enable the provision of services and transactions. On the other hand, data protection and privacy laws, including [2, 3, 4], and data subjects' privacy preferences dictate increasingly strict constraints about how these data have to be protected, accessed and managed. Failure to comply with such privacy laws can have serious consequences for the reputation and brand of organisations and have negative financial impacts. There is therefore a need to reveal sensitive data but this must be done in a way that is legally compliant and consistent with data subjects' expectations.

A special case is where privacy management capabilities process confidential data in environments (such as dynamic and distributed enterprises, GRIDs, etc.) where IT resources are dynamically allocated. These environments can be subject to varying geographical, legal and organisational constraints. Because of the specific location of the resource different privacy policies could apply, and privacy management based on static assumptions is no longer valid.

This paper describes HP Labs' approach to addressing the problem above by providing an adaptive privacy management system in which relevant policies

Please use the following format when citing this chapter:

Author(s) [insert Last name, First-name initial(s)], 2006, in IFIP International Federation for Information Processing, Volume 201, Security and Privacy in Dynamic Environments, eds. Fischer-Hubner, S., Rannenberg, K., Yngstrom, L., Lindskog, S., (Boston: Springer), pp. [insert page numbers].

(governing conditions to be satisfied by data requestors in order to access data) are dynamically determined based on the current context. Our solution consists of mechanisms for:

1. Specifying constraints for the dynamic allocation of resources based on privacy policies. This is achieved via Privacy Policy Packages strongly associated to confidential data. A Privacy Policy Package contains "localised" privacy policies (specific for a given context) along with meta-policies specifying the criteria for selection between the localised privacy policies;
2. Dynamically driving the selection of resources based on checking privacy constraints, specified in the above Policy Package, against the properties of available resources, including their localisation;
3. Enforcing the disclosure of confidential data, given a previously selected resource. This is based on a Trusted Privacy Service checking the relevant privacy constraints (specified in the Policy Package) against local credentials and contextual information;
4. (Optionally) providing trusted localisation of resources based on a Trusted Registration Service coupled with Trusted Localisation Providers leveraging trusted platform technologies.

In this paper we describe the main concepts underpinning our work and current results.

2 Addressed Problem

Dynamic, distributed and adaptive enterprises [5], utility data centers and grid systems allocate on-demand IT resources driven by business and computational needs. Resources could run applications and services that, amongst other things, might need to process personal and confidential data. These resources can be physically located in a variety of environments subject to different legislative and organisational rules and policies. Confidential and personal information might need to be transferred across organisational and geographical boundaries. In cases where this is legally allowable, this information might still be subject to different privacy policies or privacy guidelines depending on where it is processed. For example, data might be transferred between different data centres located in EU countries. Despite the fact that the same EU Data Protection Directive would apply, local privacy policies (dictated by the local government or organisation) or other types of constraint might require the data to be accessed and processed in different ways.

In addition, varying contextual information could influence choices for access control and data protection mechanisms relating to dynamic computational resources including personal and mobile resources such as laptops, mobile phones and PDAs. Employees (especially HR people, managers, doctors, etc.) need to process confidential data as part of their daily jobs, and as ubiquitous computing spreads, the resources used to do this need to be taken into account - different policies, settings and rules might apply if different computers, infrastructures, etc. were used at a given time.

Privacy management based on static assumptions is no longer valid as we move from a static processing model to a dynamic one: confidential data has to be processed adaptively depending on the context and the relevant policies and laws. Failure to comply with privacy laws can have serious consequences for the reputation and brand of organisations and service providers and have negative financial impacts.

We address this problem and in particular provide a solution to the following key issues:

1. how to ensure that confidential data is processed only on resources (and in contexts) that satisfy privacy policies relevant for these data
2. how to increase assurance about the trustworthiness of properties of computational resources, including their physical location.

3 Our Solution

Our solution consists of a system to address the above problems. This section discusses some relevant scenarios we aim to address, introduces the model underpinning our privacy management solution and describes technical approaches for its implementation.

3.1 Addressed Scenarios

In this section we briefly describe some dynamic enterprise-based scenarios where our solution adds value.

Dynamic allocation of resources within data centres spread across geographic locations. In this scenario resources (e.g. servers) are dynamically allocated to run applications and services to process data, for example, in dynamic and distributed enterprises. Workloads are spread based on the availability of such resources, to optimise their usage. However, there are privacy issues because computational resources that belong to different geographical locations, organisational boundaries and administration domains, etc. can be subject to different privacy policies. So, the "location" of the resources is an essential input to decisions about resource allocation and privacy management.

Mobile employees. Employees can be dynamic, both in the sense of travelling around and using different mobile resources (devices and enterprise tools including laptops, PDAs, mobile phones, etc.) to process different types of confidential or private data used in daily work activities (such as confidential e-mails and documents, medical data, access private databases, etc). It could be desirable to ensure that such sensitive data would only be processed within well defined locations and potentially well defined types of devices (e.g. a certified laptop but not a cellular/smart phone or PDA). This is increasingly the case as ubiquitous computing spreads. Here, privacy policies could describe constraints not only on location but also type of device or resource.

3.2 Overall Model

The model underpinning our solution consists of mechanisms to:
- model and represent a set of "alternative" privacy policies associated with confidential data: one or more of these policies can be selected and enforced depending on the resource's context and location. Meta-policies describe the selection criteria. We refer to these aggregations of policies as the Policy Package;
- strongly associate a Policy Package to confidential data. Confidential data is obfuscated and can only be put 'in clear' if the constraints defined by the policy package are satisfied;
- constrain the dynamic selection of resources based on the content of the Policy Package;
- check and enforce privacy policies based on the current relevant set of privacy policies and trusted "localisation" information. We refer to this as the Trusted Privacy Service;
- provide trusted information about the "locality" of a computational resource. This mechanism involves a Registration Entity and Trusted Localisation Provider.
Figure 1 shows the high-level architecture of a system implementing our solution.

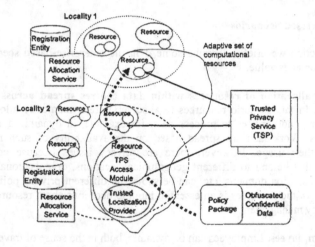

Fig. 1. High level architecture.

A Trusted Localisation Provider (TLP), installed on resources, supplies trusted "location" information: it can be based on Trusted Computing Group (TCG)-compliant trusted components and a trusted software layer [6]. At the very least the TLP can be used, for each resource, to provide and retrieve a "trusted certification" of where the resource is. The resource administrator must be trusted and accountable for keeping these location-based certificates up-to-date. In a more complex scenario the TLP can leverage any "localisation techniques" (such as hardened GPS, GPRS triangulation, etc.) to provide trustworthy localisation information.

When confidential data needs to be moved (or a copy transmitted) from one resource to another, it is obfuscated and strictly associated to a Policy Package (by a resource controller or the resources themselves), by using traditional cryptographic techniques (RSA public key cryptography) or alternative cryptographic schemas [7]. The Policy Package dictates which privacy policies need to be enforced based on a variety of contextual information, including location of the resource. This drives the selection of the computational resource that will process a piece of confidential data.

Specifically, we focus on the concept of "resources" as the entities that require access to data instead of people. Resources need to interact with one or more Trusted Privacy Services (TPSs) (via their interaction module) in order to access the content of the obfuscated confidential data. The TPS is a secure Web Service that checks for policy compliance and audit interactions. Resources can be equipped with trusted computing components to provide higher assurance and trust about the contextual statements. The "third party" component, the TPS, mainly interacts with resources to grant or deny them access to data (via disclosing decryption keys) based on their compliance to policies associated to data. Resources' trusted components can be directly involved in this process.

We envisage two alternative mechanisms to dynamically allocate resources based on their "localisation" and the interpretation of Policy Packages:

1. A Registration Entity (RE) may be used during the resource allocation process – within a Resource Allocation Service – to mediate the provision of localisation information. This is a central (domain-based) mechanism for administering the localisation information associated with the resources it manages.

2. The allocation decision is made on-the-fly, by identifying a potential resource and checking if it is compliant with the policies defined in the Policy Package. The resource has its own "localisation information" that is provided by the TLP (either self-generated or injected by the RE).

This basic model can be extended and adapted to a variety of scenarios including enterprise and inter-enterprise contexts. In particular the TPS can be provided by an organisation for internal consumption or by one or more external trusted third parties, to enable multi-party interactions and at the same time increase the overall trust and accountability. For more details about the role of trusted third parties in such systems see [8].

Localisation is just one of the contextual aspects that we need to take into account during the policy verification and enforcement phase. Our approach to defining localisation of resources is mainly based on certificates (signed declarations) issued by resources, by relying on local trusted computing components; of course, other mechanisms could be used in order to provide contextual information within such a system.

Further details follow about the Policy Package, the TPS and the TLP.

3.3 The Policy Package

The Policy Package describes sets of context-related policies along with meta-policies to enable their selection. It is strongly associated to obfuscated confidential data and dictates terms and conditions under which this data can be disclosed. Figure 2 shows the high level elements of a Policy Package:

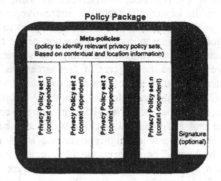

Fig. 2. Policy Package.

Meta-policies and privacy policies can be expressed via logical expressions dictating constraints, which can be based on contextual information such as location, trust domain, type pf device, etc.:

- **Meta-policies**. These enable the selection of relevant privacy policy sets (there might be no policy set that satisfy specific conditions or more than one could be active), based on contextual information. For example a meta-policy could "activate" (select) a specific policy set, based on its relevance for a given location.
- **Privacy Policy sets**. These contain privacy policies dictating the conditions, obligations and requirements to be satisfied in order to allow a resource to access the obfuscated data. Constraints can refer to contextual information too.

The above policies can be represented by using standard formats, such as digitally signed XML. Suitable standards for expressing such rules include Extensible Access Control Markup Language (XACML) [9] and the Enterprise Privacy Authorisation Language (EPAL) [10]. The content of the Policy Package has a double function:

- To drive the selection of the computational resource that will process a piece of confidential data: the policy package can discriminate, via meta-policies, which resources can or cannot process its associated confidential data, for example based on the resource location;
- To designate the right set of privacy policies to be satisfied: given the "location" of a resource, the Policy Package can be used to determinate which privacy policies apply. In order to access confidential data, the resource will have to interact with the TPS that will interpret and enforce relevant policies.

3.4 Trusted Privacy Service (TPS)

Figure 3 describes the high-level architecture of the TPS and the resource's TPS access module. In our approach, resources are configured to host a TPS Access Module and a TLP module. The former can be considered as a locally installed "agent" and the second as a trusted computing component. Once resources receive obfuscated confidential data, they need to interact with one or more TPSs via their

TPS Access Module in order to access the content of these data. The TPS, shown in figure 3, is a secure and trusted web service that checks for policies' compliance and audit interactions. The TPS Access Module exposes its functionalities via well defined APIs: applications/services running on resources can call these APIs either explicitly or via application plug-ins (for example for e-mail browsers or word processors).

Both the TPS and the Access Module have a policy engine to interpret policies. These engines can be implemented by using traditional rule-based systems. As shown in figure 3, the resource, via its TPS access module, sends the Policy Package (1) to the TPS in order to satisfy the relevant privacy policies and access to the associated confidential data.

The TPS contains a module to interact with the resource's TLP. It gathers trusted contextual information from the resource (2) and processes the relevant set of privacy policies, identified by the execution of the package's meta-policies.

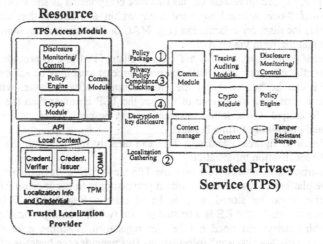

Fig. 3. Architectural detail of Trusted Privacy Service (TPS).

Multiple interactions between the TPS and the resource (3) might be required to check its compliance to the privacy policies (the resource might need to provide additional credentials, etc.). The exchanged information is audited and logged. If the resource satisfied the privacy policies, the TPS uses its cryptographic module to generate the keys to de-obfuscate confidential data (for example based on IBE [7] or traditional cryptography) and sends it to the resource (4).

3.5 Trusted Localisation Provider (TLP)

This subsection provides more details about the TLP and its interaction with the TPS.

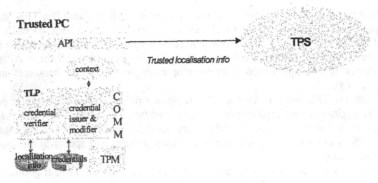

Fig. 4. Trusted Localisation Provider (TLP).

The TLP, located on resources, has two core components as shown in figure 4:

1. *a trusted "localisation" software layer* within a platform that certifies and/or provides localisation information (e.g. MAC or IP address or system information) about that platform via an API. T

2. *a trusted component*, such as a TCG-compliant TPM [1], to provide certified and trustworthy information so that a greater degree of trust may be achieved.

A TLP can be built only of the "localisation" software layer, with no trusted platform: in this case the degree of trust in the TLP is lower than the case where a TPM is leveraged. Localisation information may be certified by one or more TLPs; these could potentially form a hierarchy.

As shown in figures 3 and 4, a TPS can directly interact with the local TLP to gather the localisation information.

An alternative mechanism for how the TPS may receive "localisation" information about the platforms (resources) on which processing is to occur or on which sensitive information is to be stored, etc., is based on the Registration Entity (RE). As described previously, the RE is a trusted service (which could potentially be run by a trusted third party, but need not be) for registering machine information and its association with "localisation" information. This provides the benefits of a centralised service and being able to call upon a combination of further external trusted entities or knowledge and its own domain of expertise (or checks for which it takes responsibility) to provide a degree of trust in the information that it certifies that can be measurable, quotable and is commensurate to the type of checks applied (analogous to security checking).

In the case of a TLP leveraging a trusted platform (TP), normal software will operate in conjunction with the trusted hardware root (TPM) [1] within the TP, as follows. Whenever new localisation information is to be created on the client machine, the TLP instructs the TPM to create a new public key pair based on random sources comprising a new public key and a new private key. For security, the private key is never revealed outside the TPM, and the TLP will request the TPM to form any operations involving it. Depending upon the circumstances, a RE (or other third party with enhanced CA functionality) can:

1. Add an association between the platform ID and localisation information in a database which may be queried by third parties.

2. Create an attribute certificate that certifies that the holder has certain "localisation" attributes. The RE will then need to send the attribute certificate to the TLP.

3. By analogous means to 2. above, use a previously certified identity to create another representation of that identity, possibly with additional attribute values, for use in different circumstances.

The TPM would protect this trusted mechanism; this involves third parties publishing integrity metrics of parts of the trusted mechanism (including the TLP) so that its correct operation could be checked as part of the TP boot integrity checking process, or in response to a challenge.

4 Deployment of Our Solution

We envisage the deployment of our solution in data centres whose IT resources may span across organisational and national boundaries and might be subject to different privacy policies. We assume that each resource will run the TPS Access Module.

To deploy our solution we require that administrators create and store a model of the managed types of data, along with the relevant privacy policies (and meta-policies), This can be done within the Resource Allocation Service. A model of managed applications and services is also required along with the specification of which types of data they will need to access.

The mechanisms provided by our solution can be leveraged directly by the Resource Allocation Service to dynamically allocate IT resources to applications and services. Based on the models mentioned above, the Resource Allocation Service can retrieve the relevant policies and check the suitability of potential IT resources against these policies, via the TPS service.

Personal data is stored in standard data repositories (e.g. relational databases, LDAP servers, etc.), hosted by specific data centres' resources. However, these data can now be stored in an encrypted form, along with the associated privacy policies. Copies of these data repositories can be made on IT resources and data will be protected because of this encryption.

The interaction of applications and services with data repositories still happens via standard protocols (e.g. JDBC, LDAP, etc.). However, we envisage the usage of proxies that are able to intercept attempts to access data and will transparently interact with the TPS service to ensure that privacy policies are enforced. Of course applications and services might need to be modified to be aware that part of the retrieved data is encrypted, along with associated policies. This is particularly true when they need to retrieve data not for local processing but to send it to other applications or services running on remote resources. Further details of such an approach are provided in [16].

5 Comparison with Related Work

To the best of our knowledge, we are not aware of anything closely related to our approach. Most of the known approaches are about specific privacy management systems deployed within static environments i.e. subject to well defined (and static) privacy policies. This in particular applies for IBM's work on Enterprise Privacy Architecture (EPA), IBM Tivoli Manager [11] and EPAL (privacy language) [10] and SUN's user access and distributed identity techniques. Microsoft have carried out work in the area of context-aware policies [12]: polices are evaluated on the fly against the current context but there are not such concepts as adaptive set of privacy policies, dynamic enforcement, trusted localisation and accountability. IBM appears to have researched in the area of location-based, environmental and contextual controls to access resources [13]: the same comments as above apply.

Relevant work has been done in the area of protecting personal data by strongly associating privacy policies and managing the disclosure of this data based on the fulfillment of these policies. Related technical approaches include cryptographic schemas to protect sensitive data and allow its disclosure based on the fulfillment of associated policies: they are based on traditional public-key cryptography or alternative schemas, such as Identifier based Encryption [7]). Frameworks and services have also been implemented to leverages these cryptographic schemas and provide the required interaction mechanisms for a selective and conditional disclosure of data [8,14].

Part of this work can be leveraged to provide some of the basic functionalities necessary to build our solution.

It is important to notice that current systems for dynamic allocation of resources do not explicitly consider privacy requirements as a driver for the selection of computational resources. *Ad hoc* or specific approaches are deployed but these are not automated and the enforcement of privacy policies does not adapt to changing circumstances. Our approach explicitly addresses this issue by providing privacy enforcement mechanisms that are adaptable to different privacy contexts. Specifically, we provide mechanisms that use privacy policies for selecting suitable resources and dictating terms and conditions to be satisfied in order to access confidential data. The underlying infrastructure based on trusted privacy services provides mechanisms to enforce privacy policies in an accountable way. A Trusted Localisation Provider system provides further assurance about the location of resources by leveraging TCG technology coupled with a registration mechanism.

6   Current Status and Next Steps

We are currently taking steps towards the development of an integrated prototype of our solution. We have already implemented key sub-system modules and components that can underpin the construction of our overall solution: feasibility of the TPS and TPS Access Module components and the Policy Package mechanisms is demonstrated by our exploitation of Identifier-based Encryption (IBE) schemas and related interaction models [7,8,14]. In the same context, we have also demonstrated the feasibility of associating "sticky policies" to confidential data and using it to drive disclosure processes. A simple implementation of the TLP can be provided by leveraging HPL/TSL expertise on Trusted Computing and TPM technology: work in this direction is ongoing in the context of the EU PRIME project [15]. We anticipate that implementation of the RE component should be straightforward.

We still need to fully quantify the impact of our solution (including delay when performing typical operations) on the applications and services that need to use and access confidential data and must operate in accordance with privacy policies. This will be done once a first implementation of our prototype is available. In the meanwhile, we are exploring how to achieve this in a transparent way for applications and services by using proxy-based mechanisms that can preserve native application and service interactions with repositories where personal data is stored. In terms of dealing with a privacy-aware selection of computational resources, our solution can be seen as an "add-on" for enterprise middleware software or GRID software: further work has to be done to integrate it with a real system but we cannot see any major conceptual or technical problems in doing this.

7 Conclusions

This paper describes an innovative approach to deal with selection and allocation of computational resources in distributed and dynamic environments in order to process sensitive data in a privacy-compliant way. The discussed solution is based on privacy localisation provision and privacy management services and allows operations to be performed on personal and confidential data in a way that is compliant to associated dynamic privacy policies. Both allocation of computational processes to specific IT resources and data access are subject to the fulfilment of these policies. In the outlined approach relevant policies are dynamically determined based on the current context. In general, a set of (potentially quite different) policies can be associated to personal data along with meta-policies, which define criteria for selecting the relevant policies based on the context and resource properties. This allows the system to cope with heterogeneous and distributed environments that could be subject to different privacy policies based on their localisation and context.

These techniques allow management of the movement of private or confidential data throughout a dynamic grid of computing resources so that it is only moved to servers that are trusted as to their level of control for that sensitive data. The data is encrypted under control of a tightly bound agent that enforces the applicable privacy policy and can dynamically qualify computing resources based on that policy and the other elements of the system that let it know which resources can be trusted. This is of value in distributed enterprise software environments in which sensitive data may be computed out in the dynamic virtual grid including trusted and not-so-trusted resources. It would also be of interest in highly secure entities, such as government, which would like to move to virtual utility models so long as they could be convinced that their security policies can be upheld.

Our research and development is work in progress. Part of this research may be carried out within the context of the PRIME project [15], an international project on identity and privacy management funded by the European Union.

References

1. Trusted Computing Group: TCG TPM Specification v1.2. Available via https://www.trustedcomputinggroup.org/home (2005).
2. Laurant, C.: Privacy International - Privacy and Human Rights 2003: an International Survey of Privacy Laws and Developments. Electronic Privacy Information Center (EPIC). Privacy International. http://www.privacyinternational.org/survey/phr2003/ (2003).
3. OECD: OECD Guidelines on the Protection of Privacy and Transborder Flows of Personal Data http://www1.oecd.org/publications/e-book/9302011E.PDF (2001).
4. Online Privacy Alliance: Guidelines for Online Privacy Policies. Online Privacy Alliance http://www.privacyalliance.org/ (2004).
5. Hewlett-Packard Ltd (HP): Adaptive Enterprise - Overview, Technologies and HP Services http://www.hp.com/products1/promos/adaptive_enterprise/us/adaptive_enterprise.html (2005).
6. Pearson, S. (ed.): Trusted Computing Platforms. Prentice Hall (2002).
7. Cocks, C.: An Identity Based Encryption Scheme based on Quadratic Residues. Communications Electronics Security Group (CESG). UK. http://www.cesg.gov.uk/site/ast/idpkc/media/ciren.pdf (2001).
8. Casassa Mont, M., Pearson, S., Bramhall, P.: Towards Accountable Management of Privacy and Identity Management. Proc. ESORICS (2003).
9. OASIS: eXtensible Access Control Markup Language (XACML). http://www.oasis-open.org (2005).
10 IBM: The Enterprise Privacy Authorisation Language (EPAL). EPAL 1.2 specification http://www.zurich.ibm.com/security/enterprise-privacy/epal/ (2004).
11 IBM Tivoli Privacy Manager: Privacy manager main web page - http://www-306.ibm.com/software/tivoli/products/privacy-mgr-e-bus/.
12 Microsoft Corp.: Methods and systems for context-aware policy determination and enforcement, patent no. EP1220510A2.
13 IBM Corp: Protecting resources in a distributed computer system, patent no. US6658573B1.
14 Casassa Mont, M., Harrison, K., Sadler, M.: The HP Time Vault Service: Exploiting IBE for Timed Release of Confidential Information. WWW2003 (2003).
15 PRIME Project: Privacy and Identity Management for Europe. European RTD Integrated Project under the FP6/IST Programme http://www.prime-project.eu.org/ (2005).
16 Casassa Mont, M, Pearson, S.:An Adaptive Privacy Management System for Data Repositories, Proc, TrustBus 2005 (2005).

The APROB Channel: Adaptive Semi-Real-Time Anonymous Communication

Gergely Tóth and Zoltán Hornák

Budapest University of Technology and Economics
Department of Measurement and Information Systems
H-1117 Budapest, XI., Magyar tudósok krt. 2.
{tgm,hornak}@mit.bme.hu

Abstract. Anonymous communication has become a building block of network services. Besides providing anonymity, speed (and thus *real-time guarantees*) are becoming crucial as well. In this paper we will introduce the *global delaying adversary (GDA)*, an active attacker who is capable of arbitrarily delaying messages, while eavesdropping on all communication channels. This type of foe is particularly relevant for inter-mix relationships, where communication between the partners is secured (by authentication and integrity protection), and delaying remains the only effective external active attacking possibility. To counter GDA, the *adaptive semi-real-time APROB Channel* will be introduced. It will be shown that the APROB Channel can provide a guaranteed level of anonymity under semi-real-time[1] conditions considering that the adversary cannot obtain any additional information by delaying messages, thus this type of attack *will not be reasonable*.

1 Introduction

In this paper we will present and analyze systems for anonymous communication. Sending messages in communication networks anonymously is gaining more and more importance nowadays: this technique is used as the foundation for several privacy enhancing technologies (PETs), and has found adaptations in a wide area ranging from web-browsing to e-payments.

For anonymity we identify two factors as crucial: users want *quality of service* (QoS), i.e. an understandable, modifiable and guaranteed level of anonymity; on the other hand, message delivery times should be limited – in fact *real-time* systems (where a maximal delay is ensured) are required.

The foundation on which this paper is built was presented in [1]: senders used *common QoS parameters while using the MIN/MAX technique* and a *global passive observer* (GPO) was assumed. For this environment the *non-adaptive real-time channel* (PROB Channel) was shown to be effective.

The extension presented in this paper assumes *different QoS parameters for each message*, and takes a stronger adversary – the *global delaying adversary* (GDA) – into

---

[1] Naturally, against an adversary who can arbitrarily delay messages, no hard real-time guarantee can be given. The notion *semi-real-time* refers to the property that enables the channel to deliver the messages with the real-time requirements, if the adversary does not delay them.

Please use the following format when citing this chapter:

Author(s) [insert Last name, First-name initial(s)], 2006, in IFIP International Federation for Information Processing, Volume 201, Security and Privacy in Dynamic Environments, eds. Fischer-Hubner, S., Rannenberg, K., Yngstrom, L., Lindskog, S., (Boston: Springer), pp. [insert page numbers].

account. In order to provide anonymity under these circumstances, the *adaptive semi-real-time channel* (APROB Channel) will be introduced.

With the evolution to the APROB Channel presented here our aim was to continue the work aimed at providing anonymous communication systems metting higher and higher requirements. We made our assumed adversary stronger, gave more freedom to the users and developed an anonymity system that could guarantee quality of service under these circumstances as well.

In this paper we will still consider single, black-box channels. Our reason for this is simple: first the basic building blocks have to be analyzed on their own and only after their properties are well understood can we analyze more complex networks built of them.

2   Anonymity background

In this paper techniques for anonymous communication will be evaluated. In order to establish a common understanding, first the model of an anonymous message transmission system (AMTS) will be introduced. The section closes with a description of the foundations for measuring anonymity.

2.1   Notations for the anonymous communication scenario

For the purpose of anonymous electronic communication, several anonymous message transmission systems have been proposed. Their structures and modes of operation differ in various aspects, but some common properties are true for most of them. This common basic framework will be defined in the following.

The goal of an anonymous message transmission system is to deliver *messages* from *senders* to *recipients* so that it becomes algorithmically hard for an *adversary* to link these messages to senders or recipients. Let us look at the formal model:

- Senders ($s_i \in S$) send encrypted messages ($\alpha_j \in \varepsilon_S$) at times $t_S(\alpha_j)$ through the AMTS. These messages have a fixed size and are encrypted for the AMTS.
- The AMTS receives the sent messages and performs cryptographic operations on them to obtain a different representation. In order to further confuse the adversary, the AMTS delays and reorders messages. How messages are actually encoded and transformed is irrelevant for the purposes of this paper, the main assumption being that the adversary is not able to break the cryptographic functions used.
- After the delay, the AMTS delivers the re-encoded messages ($\beta_k \in \varepsilon_R$) to the recipients ($r_l \in R$) at times $t_R(\beta_k)$. These delivered messages also have a common, fixed size, and are encrypted for the recipient.
- The adversary's aim is to either match the delivered messages to senders ($\beta_k \rightarrow s_i = S(\beta_k)$), or the sent messages to recipients ($\alpha_j \rightarrow r_l = R(\alpha_j)$). In order to do this, adversaries may eavesdrop on communication channels and see when messages are being sent or delivered (*passive* observer), or even influence the network traffic by delaying messages or creating new ones (*active* adversary). Furthermore, it is assumed that each message is independent, so both the channel and the adversary operate on single messages – they do not consider message streams.

Finally, the adversary's aim is to break *sender anonymity* [2] and thus link delivered messages to their senders ($\beta_k \to S(\beta_k)$).

2.2 Measuring anonymity

In order to provide guaranteed anonymity with quality of service parameters, first we have to define how anonymity is measured. For this reason different metrics have been proposed.

In this paper we will use the source-hiding property as defined in [1] for measuring sender anonymity[2]. For its definition we have to consider that the adversary assigns probabilities to each delivered message – sender pair and then chooses accordingly. In order to model this, let the notion $P_{s_i, \beta_k} = P(S(\beta_k) = s_i)$ indicate the probability that shows, according to the knowledge of the adversary, what the chance is that s_i was the sender of β_k, the message delivered. With this the level of anonymity is defined as the maximal probability with which the adversary may back-trace messages to their senders.

Thus – according to the definition in [1] – an AMTS is *source-hiding with parameter* Θ, if the adversary cannot assign a sender to a delivered message with a probability greater than Θ[3]:

$$\forall_{\beta_k} \land \forall_{s_i} : P_{\beta_k, s_i} \leq \Theta \tag{1}$$

3 The non-adaptive, real-time channel for the global passive observer

After having introduced the foundations of anonymous communication, in this section the PROB Channel [1] will be introduced. The main goal of this paper is to present the APROB Channel, an efficient adaptive extension of the PROB Channel.

3.1 The PROB Channel

This paper presents an extension to the PROB Channel. In order to better understand the new features, let us introduce the relevant aspects of the PROB Channel. The PROB Channel is: (1) *non-adaptive* – the delay of an incoming message in the channel does not depend on properties or the actual distribution of incoming messages; (2) for each message the delay is calculated independently; and (3) it is *real-time* – the delay (δ) in the channel has a guaranteed maximum (δ_{max}), i.e. the PROB Channel ensures that every incoming message leaves the channel within δ_{max} time.

---

[2] In [3] a detailed analysis of anonymity metrics is presented. The most popularly used measure currently are the simple entropy-based [4] and the normalized entropy-based [5]. Due to the disadvatnages outlined in [3] ones, we will stick to the source-hiding property anonymity metric as it is well understandable by the end user and can be interpreted as the *local* view, what the user wants from an anonymity system.

[3] Note, this definition is yet the *global* view of anonymity with a general quality of service parameter. The extension for local QoS is given as a refinement of this equation is (3).

3.2 The global passive observer (GPO)

As a first step in the analysis of characteristics of anonymity, a *global passive observer* was evaluated. The main properties of the GPO are the following: (1) she has knowledge of the *environment*, thus she knows of the potential senders and recipients and of the generally known parameters; (2) she *eavesdrops* on all the traffic to and from the AMTS, thus she knows of message dispatches and deliveries and their actors and timings; (3) however, GPO *cannot decrypt* the messages entering or leaving the channel and since messages have a common, fixed size, size-based decisions are ruled out as well; (4) GPO *cannot alter* the traffic in any way; and finally (5) GPO is *external*, meaning that she cannot gain information from within the channel, she sees the system as a black-box.

With the above properties, the aim of GPO is to *break sender anonymity* and thus guess who could have been the sender of a delivered message.

3.3 Anonymity in the PROB Channel

Assuming a GPO, the strong anonymity of the PROB Channel could only be enforced with the introduction of the *MIN/MAX property*. The definition was the following: a system possesses the MIN/MAX property with parameters τ_{min} and τ_{max} ($\tau_{min} < \tau_{max}$), if it holds that no sender sends more than one message within any τ_{min} time interval, and all senders send at least one message within every τ_{max} time interval.

With this strict limitation on the frequency of message sending, a guaranteed level of anonymity could be provided with the PROB Channel, where the source-hiding property could be easily tuned by setting τ_{min} and τ_{max} appropriately (2):

$$\Theta_{PROB} \approx \frac{\tau_{max}}{|S| \cdot \tau_{min}} \tag{2}$$

As the first step, the PROB Channel provided only a *global* quality of service, the anonymity guarantee being the same for all messages. However, despite of being non-adaptive, the channel could ensure a guaranteed level of anonymity assuming a global passive observer, if the senders conformed to the MIN/MAX property.

4 Environment for the APROB Channel

In the previous sections a basic framework for anonymous communication has been introduced together with the relevant previous work. In this section the environment for the APROB Channel will now be defined: a guaranteed level of anonymity has to be provided even if a global delaying adversary is assumed and users may specify different QoS levels for their messages.

4.1 The global delaying adversary

In our earlier paper [1] a global passive observer was assumed as the adversary for the system. In this paper we wanted the take a stronger opponent into consideration, so the opportunities open to a *global delaying adversary (GDA)* will be evaluated.

Since we are analyzing a static scenario, senders and recipients do not leave the system and their number is known to all participants. In this scenario, GDA has the following properties: (1) she is *global*, thus sees all messages sent into the channel and delivered from the channel, however since message are encrypted, she cannot read the contents or the QoS parameters[4]; (2) she may *delay* any number of messages for arbitrary time; but (3) she may *not create* new messages, nor alter existing ones; (4) finally, she is also *external* and sees the channel as a black-box, being unable to gain information from within the channel.

With this attacker model the question may arise, why not consider a fully active attacker, who is capable of creating or altering messages – and anyway, in what situations is such a GDA realistic? GDA was defined as the adversary model for *inter-mix communication*, i.e. to evaluate characteristics for internal nodes of an anonymity network. Since most current anonymity network implementations [6] establish authenticated channels between the nodes (e.g. with the help of TLS), the packet creation/modification opportunities opent to an external attacker are eliminated. The only active intervention possible is to *delay* messages, and so GDA comes into the picture.

To show that GDA is a real upgrade relative to a global passive observer, the following theorem can be formulated:

Theorem 1. *Anonymity provided for a particular sender by any non-adaptive channel can be completely compromised by a global delaying adversary.*

Proof. For the proof let us recapitulate the definition of the non-adaptive channel: its operation is not affected by the properties and distribution of the actual incoming messages. Thus, the simplest way a GDA could compromize a non-adaptive channel would be if the GDA acted as a bottleneck between the senders and the channel. If she buffered sent messages before reaching the channel and let one message at a time through, she could wait till the non-adaptive channel delivered that message to its recipient. By observing this delivery, GDA could match it to the one sent message and thus to the one sender. After one message has been compromised in this way, the adversary could feed the next message from its buffer into the channel and carry out the same procedure. With this simple technique GDA could break the anonymity provided by any non-adaptive channel.   □

From this it follows that in order to cope with a global delaying adversary, an adaptive channel is required which internally monitors the distribution and properties of incoming messages and takes corrective action if necessary.

In this paper we focus on real-time communication, i.e. where message delay in the channel has a guaranteed upper limit. Naturally, if we assume a GDA, this real-time delivery cannot be guaranteed any more, since the adversary may delay the messages in addition to the delay introduced by the channel. Therefore the notion of *semi-real-time* is proposed: a semi-real-time channel guarantees real-time message delivery if the messages are not delayed by the adversary; should the opposite happen, then the channel operates on a best-effort basis (considering message delay) by conforming to the anonymity QoS parameters of the messages. The main requirement is that the channel

---
[4] In this regard she has all the capabilities of the global passive observer.

must not allow the adversary to compromize the anonymity provided – if the messages cannot be delivered in real-time with the necessary anonymity guarantees, then the real-time criterium (but not the anonymity requirements) can be dropped.

4.2 QoS diversity

In [1] quality of service was the same for all the senders: they obeyed the MIN/MAX rules and the PROB Channel guaranteed respective source-hiding property ($\frac{\tau_{max}}{|S| \cdot \tau_{min}}$) and guaranteed maximal message delivery (within δ_{max} time).

First we want to loosen the common parameters so that each sender may ask for different source-hiding properties for their sent messages. This way the source-hiding property has to be reconsidered: it is no longer a global requirement (i.e. for all senders and for all messages), but rather a *local* parameter conforming to the needs of each user.

To formalize the above, let the notation $I(\beta_k)$ (*input*) mean the sent message α_j, which was transformed by the AMTS into β_k. Similarly $O(\alpha_j)$ (*output*) means the delivered message β_k corresponding to α_j. Furthermore, QoS diversity is supported by attaching the requested local source-hiding property to each sent message, which will be denoted by $\theta(\alpha_j)$. With these, the following (3) should be ensured by the AMTS:

$$\forall \beta_k \wedge \forall s_l : P_{\beta_k, s_l} \leq \theta(I(\beta_k)) \tag{3}$$

In other words, in the rest of the paper QoS diversity is understood to mean the following: the sender specifies for each sent message α_j a parameter $\theta(\alpha_j)$, which is the requested local source-hiding property of that particular message. The task of the channel is to service these different requests and ensure real-time delivery with the requested QoS parameters.

5 The adaptive, semi-real-time channel

Having defined the environment of the APROB Channel, it is time for the specification of the channel itself. The approach will be the following: first we will construct the channel to provide guaranteed anonymity, then we will extend it to provide real-time guarantees and handle the different QoS requirements. Finally, we will analyze the chances of the adversary.

5.1 Guaranteed anonymity

Withing the context of the local source-hiding property (3) let us construct the APROB Channel in the following way: first it buffers incoming messages until the QoS requirements of *all* messages in the buffer can be fulfilled, and then it flushes the buffer after the messages have been reordered randomly.

This way its operation is similar to that of a simple mix [7]. To finalize the specification, the probabilities that the adversary may calculate for tracing delivered messages β_k back to their senders s_l have to be determined. The following equation defines the adversary's guess for the different probabilities P_{β_k, s_l}:

$$P_{\beta_k, s_l} = \frac{|\{\alpha_j | (\alpha_j \in X_{\beta_k}) \wedge (S(\alpha_j) = s_l)\}|}{|X_{\beta_k}|} \qquad (4)$$

The above equation (4) defines the probabily as the fraction of the number of messages sent by a particular sender and the total number of messages in the batch. Since the APROB Channel is basically an adaptive mix, this is the best guess the adversary can make. Having the adversary's guess, the condition under which the buffer of the channel can be flushed, can be formulated properly:

$$\forall(\alpha_j \text{ in the buffer}) \wedge \forall(s_l): P_{O(\alpha_j), s_l} \leq \theta(\alpha_j) \qquad (5)$$

With this it is ensured that the buffer is only flushed when the local source-hiding property of *every* message in the buffer is fulfilled, thus the APROB Channel provides *guaranteed anonymity*.

5.2 Getting real-time

The next task of the APROB Channel is to provide *real-time* anonymity. Since the source-hiding property considers the worst case that could happen, we have to formulate the following theorem bearing the results from the PROB Channel [1] in mind:

Theorem 2. *If the senders do not conform to the MAX property, a guaranteed reasonable local source-hiding property (i.e. smaller than $\frac{1}{2}$) cannot be provided with a real-time channel.*

Proof. The MAX property demands that each sender has to send at least one message within each τ_{max} time interval. If senders do not conform to the MAX property, then the channel may have fewer messages with which to form the anonymity set than would be required for the QoS parameters.

Considering the least reasonable $\frac{1}{2}$ local source-hiding property, if within the parameters of the real-time delivery only one sender sends a message into the channel (which without the MAX property may happen), the real-time channel can only choose from the following options: (1) if the channel is non-adaptive, it will deliver the messages regardless of the small anonymity set and thus break the anonymity guarantee; (2) if the channel is adaptive, then it has an alternative: it can drop messages for which the anonymity *and* real-time guarantees cannot be fulfilled at the same time or (3) it can wait until the anonymity requirements can be ensured.

From this it can be seen that without the MAX property, if senders do not send enough messages, the real-time *and* anonymity (i.e. local source-hiding property) guarantees cannot be ensured at the same time. $\qquad \square$

On the other hand, with the MAX property, if every sender asks for a local source-hiding property θ equal or greater to $\frac{1}{|S|}$, and every sender sends periodically with τ_{max}, then after τ_{max} time the buffer can always be flushed. This means a guaranteed $\delta_{max} = \tau_{max}$ delay and thus a real-time guarantee.

Naturally, if the APROB Channel functioned this way (i.e. each sender has to periodically send exactly one message), the system would not provide any flexibility. The aim of this section has been to introduce the real-time property *together* with the already guaranteed anonymity. In the next section we will loosen the restrictions and let the APROB Channel unfold.

5.3   Handling the different QoS requirements

Up until now only the MAX property has been described. With that in mind every sender periodically sent one message and thus the real-time requirement *and* the anonymity guarantee could be maintained.

On the other hand, in order to provide flexibility, we have to enable the senders to send faster.

If a particular sender s_l wants to send $\phi(\alpha_j)$ messages within a τ_{max} interval after having sent α_j, then he has to accept a larger source-hiding property $\theta(\alpha_j)$ for α_j, namely:

$$\theta(\alpha_j) = \frac{\phi(\alpha_j) + 1}{|S| + \phi(\alpha_j)} \tag{6}$$

The above equation (6) illustrates the case when all the other senders send only one message in the relevant time interval and s_l sends $\phi(\alpha_j)$.

However, because the number of messages sent and the achievable level of anonymity are strongly connected, (6) can be rearranged for senders wishing a particular source-hiding property $\theta(\alpha_j)$ for a certain message:

$$\phi(\alpha_j) = \frac{\theta(\alpha_j) \cdot |S| - 1}{1 - \theta(\alpha_j)} \tag{7}$$

Naturally, it is up to the sender to specify, how much anonymity is needed and what value should be assigned to the messages. With the help of the above equations we will now create the notion of *well-timed* and *ill-timed* messages. For their definition we introduce the following: α_j^k ($k \geq 1$) indicates the kth sent message after α_j has been sent, where both α_j and α_j^k have the same sender (i.e. $S(\alpha_j) = S(\alpha_j^k)$) and α_j^k follows α_j in a τ_{max} window (i.e. $(t_S(\alpha_j^k) - t_S(\alpha_j)) \leq \tau_{max}$). With these, the sent messages can be divided as follows:

$$\alpha_j : \begin{cases} \text{ill-timed} & \exists \alpha_i \wedge \exists k : (\alpha_j = \alpha_i^k) \wedge (k > \phi(\alpha_i)) \\ \text{well-timed} & \text{otherwise.} \end{cases} \tag{8}$$

With this categorization of messages the specification of the APROB Channel has to be extended – the condition for flushing the buffer of the channel (5) has to be restricted to only consider well-timed messages:

$$\forall(\text{well-timed } \alpha_j \text{ in the buffer}) \wedge \forall(s_l) : P_{O(\alpha_j), s_l} \leq \theta(\alpha_j) \tag{9}$$

It is essential to note that the APROB Channel can decide – based on the number and distribution of messages sent by each sender and the QoS parameters attached to the messages – whether a message is well-timed or not, so the extension of (5) into (9) is valid.

Thus, senders may send *faster* than τ_{max} if they are willing to accept a greater local source-hiding property θ than $\frac{1}{|S|}$ (i.e. you may send more messages with less anonymity). In this case they have to consider the equations (6) and (7) in order to construct well-timed messages. Since the channel only tries to fulfill the anonymity requirements of well-timed messages, with QoS parameters derived from these equations the previous maximal delay of $\delta_{max} = \tau_{max}$ can be kept, so this extension still guarantees real-time delivery.

5.4 Resililence against GDA

Finally, let us consider the adversary (GDA): she may delay certain messages and thus create a situation where for well-timed messages in the channel's waiting queue after τ_{max} time the QoS requirements cannot be fulfilled. In this case, two solutions can be chosen by the APROB Channel.

- The first approach would be to drop such messages. This way the result of the adversary's actions would be the denial of service for the messages, which she might have also achieved by delaying those messages infinitely.
- The other approach would be to drop the real-time restriction and to let such messages wait until the QoS requirements can be fulfilled. Thus the attacker has succeeded in down-rating the system to a non-real-time one. By simply delaying such messages, the she could have achieved the same.

We have to emphasize that in neither case have the anonymity requirements of messages been broken, the adversary could only either down-rate the system into a non-real-time one or force some to be dropped. GDA could *not gain anything* besides what by definition she had already been capable of. Thus:

Theorem 3. *The APROB Channel (1) provides a guaranteed level of anonymity against a global delaying adversary with a local source-hiding property according to (6) and (7) while delivering messages in a semi-real-time manner, and (2) a GDA cannot compromize the achieved level of anonymity by delaying messages.*

6 Conclusion

In this paper the APROB Channel has been introduced for real-time anonymous communication. It has been proven that the construction could provide guaranteed anonymity while also fulfilling semi-real-time guarantees. The channel even enabled users to ask for different anonymity levels (quality of service). Under these circumstances it has been shown that a global delaying adversary cannot gain any new information by delaying messages, and thus it would not be worth for such an adversary to delay messages.

For future work two main directions present themselves. Should the adversary have *a priori* information about the preferences of senders, i.e. how they choose recipients, then this would introduce a serious breach in the anonymity provided by current anonymity systems. Thus, adaptive channels need to be constructed that maintain information about the users' preferences and shape the traffic in order to confuse the adversary. Up to now we have only considered black-box channels and thus external adversaries. A big step forward will be to organize *networks* of the analyzed channels and evaluate their properties.

References

1. Tóth, G., Hornák, Z.: Measuring anonymity in a non-adaptive, real-time system. In: Proceedings of Privacy Enhancing Technologies (PET2004). Springer-Verlag, LNCS, Forthcoming (2004)
2. Pfitzmann, A., Köhntopp, M.: Anonymity, unobservability, and pseudonymity – a proposal for terminology. In Federrath, H., ed.: Designing Privacy Enhancing Technologies. Volume 2009 of Springer-Verlag, LNCS., Berkeley, CA (2001) 1–9
3. Tóth, G., Hornák, Z., Vajda, F.: Measuring anonymity revisited. In Liimatainen, S., Virtanen, T., eds.: Proceedings of the Ninth Nordic Workshop on Secure IT Systems, Espoo, Finland (2004) 85–90
4. Serjantov, A., Danezis, G.: Towards an information theoretic metric for anonymity. In Syverson, P., Dingledine, R., eds.: Proceedings of Privacy Enhancing Technologies (PET2002). Volume 2482 of Springer-Verlag, LNCS., San Francisco, CA (2002)
5. Díaz, C., Seys, S., Claessens, J., Preneel, B.: Towards measuring anonymity. In Syverson, P., Dingledine, R., eds.: Proceedings of Privacy Enhancing Technologies (PET2002). Volume 2482 of Springer-Verlag, LNCS., San Francisco, CA (2002) 54–68
6. Dingledine, R., Mathewson, N., Syverson, P.: Tor: The second-generation onion router. In: Proceedings of the 13th USENIX Security Symposium. (2004)
7. Chaum, D.: Untraceable electronic mail, return addresses, and digital pseudonyms. Communications of the ACM 4 (1981) 84–88

Author Index

494